THE ENCYCLOPEDIA
OF
JUDAISM

THE ENCYCLOPEDIA OF JUDAISM

VOLUME V
SUPPLEMENT TWO

Edited by

JACOB NEUSNER
ALAN J. AVERY-PECK
WILLIAM SCOTT GREEN

PUBLISHED IN COLLABORATION WITH
THE MUSEUM OF JEWISH HERITAGE
NEW YORK

CONTINUUM • NEW YORK
2004

2003

The Continuum International Publishing Group, Inc.
15 East 26th Street, New York, NY 10010, USA

Distribution in the United States and Canada by The Continuum International
Publishing Group Inc., 15 East 26th Street, New York, NY 10010, USA

Distribution in the rest of the world by Brill Publishers, Plantijnstraat 2, P.O.Box 9000,
2300 PA, Leiden, The Netherlands

This book is printed on acid-free paper.

Printed in The Netherlands

ISBN 0-8264-1580-6 (volume V, Supplement Two)

ISBN 0-8264-1460-5 (volume IV, Supplement One)
ISBN 0-8264-1178-9 (volumes I-II-III)

Library of Congress Cataloging-in-Publication Data

The Encyclopedia of Judaism / editors, Jacob Neusner, Alan J. Avery
-Peck, and William Scott Green.
    p. cm.
    Includes bibliographical references and index.
    Contents: v. 5. Supplement 2.
    ISBN 0-8264-1580-6 (alk. paper)
    1. Judaism—Encyclopedias. I. Neusner, Jacob, 1932- .
II. Avery Peck, Alan J. (Alan Jeffery), 1953-   III. Green, William
Scott. IV. Museum of Jewish Heritage (New York, N.Y.)
BM50.E63   1999
296'.03—dc21   99-34729
                                   CIP

TABLE OF CONTENTS

Astrology in Ancient Judaism 2031
Astronomy in Ancient Judaism 2037
Biblical Interpretation, Medieval French 2045
Biography in Rabbinic Judaism 2061
Conversos 2077
Deuteronomy in Judaism 2091
Exodus in Judaism 2101
Genesis in Judaism 2111
Gospels, Oral Traditions of the Mishnah in 2124
Homosexuality in Judaism 2136
Leviticus in Judaism 2153
Medieval Judaeo-Arabic Literature 2167
Numbers in Judaism 2184
Parents, Honor of in Judaism 2191
Pseudo-Philo, Biblical Characters in 2200
Rabbinic Literature, Logics of 2213
Rashi 2226
Samaritan Judaism 2241
Sermons in Modern Judaism 2265
Torah and Culture 2283
Zionism in Moroccan Judaism 2293

List of Illustrations 2308
Cumulative Index to Volumes I-V 2309
   General Index 2309
   Index of Textual References 2356

A

ASTROLOGY IN ANCIENT JUDAISM: Unlike astronomy, the history of astrology was ignored by the early critical study of Judaism, the Wissenschaft des Judentum. In the nineteenth century, when astrology had already been condemned for centuries, the history of Jewish astrology seemed to be irrelevant, if not worse. In a time of enlightenment, there was a place for the history of the Jews as scientists, philosophers, or doctors, but not as people who dealt with the occult (astrology then being considered a branch of that area). In the twentieth century, Gershom Scholem, the founder of the scientific study of Jewish mysticism, published several thousands of pages on Qabbalah and on all kinds of esoteric doctrines but less than one page on astrology. On the other side, unfortunately, were scholars who, enthusiastic to reveal Jewish astrology, did their work incompetently so that the whole issue still waits to be (re)evaluated.

Astrology, like astronomy, was a science, based on astronomical observations, attributing to the heavenly bodies powers over the earth and men. Ptolemy was not only the great astronomer of antiquity but the great astrologer as well, and this model of a scientist played its role until the sixteenth century with very few exceptions. Astrology was astronomy's counterpart. However, many modern scholars prefer to ignore this and consider astrology, rather, a counterpart of magic. Just as modern historiography is aware that history is not necessarily a report of humankind's achievements only, but of misdeeds and failures as well, historians of science should realize that astrology was a science that was later found to be false, and it therefore should be studied as a science. The philosophy of this science, if any, was basically pre-Socratic (Pythago-

rean, to begin with), and "Natural Philosophy." Astrology claimed it could predict the future of individuals, just as astronomy enables the prediction of the future of heavenly bodies. Moreover, astrology was thought to explain the causes of everything, among them diseases, and naturally to be able to cure the ill. Its medical basis, though uncritically thought to be Hippocratic, is the four humors, a pre-Socratic doctrine. Later the Stoics were fond of astrology, and other philosophies were adapted to astrology.

The relation of Jews to astrology is complex, to say the least, from biblical times until this very day. Many texts await analysis to expose the depth of the relationships between Judaism and astrology throughout the ages.

The Biblical Period: Before the fifth century B.C.E. (in Babylonia) there was no astrology in the sense of what later became known as such. Therefore, though Bilaam's practices (Num. 22-23) seem to be connected to astrology, they are more like propitiatory rituals (*namburbis*) to seven different Aramaic Gods (such as Baal), which may be called pre-astrology. Joel 2:10 might be taken to reflect belief in omens of several types: earthquakes, thunders, solar and lunar eclipses, yet all of these represent God's will. True, Jeremiah (10:2) told Israel not to be dismayed at the signs in the heavens, but apparently they did then and centuries later as well. The prophets were well aware of the role of astrologers in Babylonia (Is. 47:13) and their connection to the royal court (Dan. 2:27; 5:10). However, astrology in biblical times was not yet the developed astrology of the Hellenistic era.

The Post-Biblical Period: In Jub. 12:16, Abraham is depicted as an astrologer who observed the stars on the first day of the seventh month (later known as Rosh Hashanah), to know how rainy the coming year would be. This connection between stars and rain is part of the Mesopotamian omen heritage, as the author of Jubilees (11:8) knew as well. The context is not polemical against astrology but rather a claim, in an apologetic manner, that there is no contradiction between faith in God and astrology. The rabbis in later centuries were aware of the connection between Abraham and astrology, claiming either that Abraham was an astrologer (B. B.B. 16b) or that he stopped practicing astrology (B. Shab. 156a).

A few of the texts found at Qumran disclose that some of the people who lived there were practicing astrologers. Among them is an Aramaic text (4Q318), called a *Brontologion*, that interprets thunder in order to forecast the future. Though the text is short and has some lacuna, its concept is clear. First the writer demonstrates the system of the planets' ruling over the days of the solar year (changes in sequence every 2, 2, 3 days = 2 1/3). The beginning of the text is corrupt but from 7 Elul, under the Archer (Sagittarius), the writer gives, in a very technical way, the names of the ruling planets, ending in "(Adar) 27 and 28 under Fishes (Pisces), 2[9, 30 (31?) under Ram (Aries)]." After listing the ruling planets as an introduction, the writer continues: "If it thunders on [a day under the rule of] the Bull (Taurus), it signifies changes in the world and toil for the cities, and destruction in the royal court. . . . If it thunders on the Twins (Gemini)—fear and distress caused by foreigners and by. . . ." There is no doubt that the text derived from (Royal) Babylonian lunar astrology such as *Enuma Anu Enlil* (the first half of the first millennium B.C.E.). The text is assumed to have been written in the first century B.C.E.

Other Qumran texts of astrological character are 4Q186, 4Q534 and 4Q561. 4Q186 presents a physiognomic-astrological description cryptographically. It is also written there: "And this is the nativity in which he was born: in the foot of the Bull" (= Taurus). This kind of precision has no parallel in any known prediction in regard to the nativity of a man (usually, born under a "whole" zodiac sign). Therefore, it is more likely that the text discusses the nativity of the moon. The "molad" (= nativity) is a terminology well known from later Rabbinic sources, and the text alluded to the new moon if seen in Taurus' lower part, either as an astronomical position or, better, as an omen (e.g., "when the new moon is in Taurus' foot, happiness will come to Israel").

The conjecture that these texts should not be taken as revealing the Qumranites' adherence to astrology since they were "collected for critical argumentation against the 'wisdom of the Chaldeans'" should (like the conjecture that the texts found there had nothing to do with those who lived there) be rejected for several reasons: 1) The rabbis, who were much less stringent than the Qumranites, could not tolerate sectarian books (T. Shab. 13:5; B. San. 100b), so the assumption that the Qumranites, like modern scholars, collected their opponents' books seems to be inappropriate; 2) Depriving the Qumranites of astrology does not do them historical justice. In later generations there were many pious Jews who practiced a "harder" astrology than the one found at Qumran (fearing thunder included); 3) the Qumranites had already shown their deep interest in the calendar, that is, astronomy, a fact that leads automatically to some awareness of astrology, even without any text in hand.

In sum, the Qumranites believed in astrology like many other people in Hellenistic times. Their astrology was Mesopotamian in origin, like their astronomy, even though they did not admit it. This astrology was basically omen-type, according to the development of astrology at the time, and it was related to some others of their beliefs and practices, such as healing and belief in predestination.

Among pseudepigraphic books, there is only one in which astrology plays a (minor) role: the Testament of Solomon. There, especially in chap. 18, there is a combination of Egyptian Astrology—of a low level: zodiac signs and thirty-six decans—and demonology, angelology, magic, and medicine. This book is relatively late and originated among Christians. The Testament of Shem is a book of astrology that was wrongfully attached to modern Pseudepigrapha. This is a Syriac book, composed around the fifth—sixth centuries (of Mesopotamian origin). The book deals with astrology related to the letters of one's name (close to Mandean astrology, on the one side, and to modern numerology, on the other). Later, while copying the text, a scribe added to the headline, thus attributing it to Shem, son of Noah. Modern study has failed to recognize this late addition.

Rabbinic Judaism: Among the Tannaim, it seems there are no traces of astrology. However, a few omens were known among them. Meir said that an eclipse is a bad sign for Israel, while another rabbi had a different view. He said:

> When the sun is afflicted (solar-eclipse), it is a bad omen for the pagans; when the moon is afflicted, it is a bad omen for Israel, since Israel calculates according to the moon and the pagans according to the sun. If the affliction is in the east, it is a bad omen for those who dwell in the east; in the west, it is a bad omen for those who dwell in the west; in the middle of the sky, it is a bad omen for the whole world. If the face (of the moon) looks like blood, war is coming to the world; if it looks like a sack, arrows of famine are coming to the world; if it looks like both, war and arrows of famine are coming to the world. If it was afflicted while rising, tribulation sojourns; while setting, (tribulation) comes fast. Some say the other way around (T. Suk. 2:6).

Doubtless, these omens are Jewish adaptations of old Babylonian omens and lore. This tradition is repeated with a slight difference in another source, with the addition: "R. Joshaia says: 'When the zodiac signs are afflicted in the east, it is a bad omen for those who dwell in the east; in the west, it is a bad omen for those who dwell in the west.' R. Jonathan says: 'All these omens were given to the gentiles'" (Mekhilta deRabbi Ishmael, Bo, Pisha, 1). Thus one can see here a dispute among the Tannaim over the validity of omens.

In another case the Tannaim said: "For four reasons there is a solar-eclipse," and then there is a list of four crimes that cause a solar-eclipse (B. Suk. 29a). A modern critic might claim that in the name of

ethics, omens become truth, but it seems the other way around: omens are divine, telling people how (not) to act. R. Isaac b. Abdimi said that in the days of the Temple, on the last day of Sukkot, people observed the direction of the smoke from the altar, for the omen-significance of the wind from any of the directions (B. Yom. 21b). The absence of a northern wind might be taken as a divine rebuke (B. Yeb. 72a). Pappa ruled that on a misty day or on a day when there was a southern wind, one is not to circumcise or let blood, since the weather condition was considered dangerous (B. Yeb. 72a). One of the Amoraim did not declare a fast day since it was misty out, understanding this to denote a curtain between Israel and God (B. Ber. 32b). An earthquake was taken as a sign of God's displeasure with human behavior (B. Ber. 59a). Because of that, Bar Qappara ruled that, after an earthquake, people should fast and pray (Y. Ber. 9:2, 13c). Nehorai claimed that earthquakes happen when Israel does not observe the commandments of heave-offering and tithes. Aha thought earthquakes happen because of homosexuality, while other sages said they happen because of a controversy among Jews. Samuel stated that an earthquake is a sign that a royal reign will end (Y. Ber. 9:2, 13c). Jeremiah b. Eleazar said that for twenty-five years God sent earthquakes to Sodom warning them to repent (Gen. Rabbah, 49:6). So it seems that omens like a solar-eclipse, a lunar-eclipse, "disappearance" of a zodiac sign, wind, mist, an earthquake, and comets played a role among Rabbinic Jews in antiquity. Some of these omens came directly from Babylonian sources, stated by Babylonian rabbis, but apparently some derived from ancient Jewish sources.

Among the Amoraim, there is much more astrological knowledge than among the Tannaim. At least two contrary attitudes prevailed among the rabbis in the land of Israel. "R. Hanina said: 'One's Mazal (= zodiac sign) is what makes one smart; one's Mazal is what gives wealth; and there is Mazal to Israel.' Yohanan said: 'There is no Mazal to Israel' (B. Shab. 156a). This well-known dispute concludes a Talmudic passage as follows. On the *pinax* of Joshua b. Levi, a famous rabbi in third century land of Israel, there was a whole set of celestial omens. For example: "One who is born on a Monday will be a tartar, on a Tuesday—will be a wealthy man; . . . under Venus, he will be a wealthy man and adulterer; under Mercury, clever and smart," etc. On that R. Hanina said: "It is not the sign of the day but rather the sign of the hour that determines." This concept is called genethlialogy, that is, predicting a person's fate according to the star or zodiac sign that was rising at the time of his birth. According to Simeon, (even) each herb has its own zodiacal sign that strokes it and tells it to grow (Gen. Rabbah 10:6). "Everything depends on a zodiac sign, even a Torah-scroll in the shrine" (a quote of Pesiqta Rabbati in Geonim New Responsa).

Samuel, in third century Babylonia, after offering astronomical calculations (intra), ruled as follows: "There is no Nissan-season (vernal equinox) that falls in Jupiter that does not break the trees. There is no Tebet-season (winter solstice) that falls in Jupiter that does not dry out the seedlings (Aramaic addendum: provided that the [previous] new Moon was born either in Moon or in Jupiter" (B. Erub. 56a). This is a purely astrological omen of a kind that is not attested elsewhere in Rabbinic literature. Samuel also ruled concerning blood-letting, which should be done "only on a Sunday, a Wednesday, and a Friday, not on a Monday and a Thursday . . . and (certainly) not on a Tuesday, since Mars governs that day" (B. Shab. 129b). Other Babylonian Amoraim ruled that one is not allowed to consult Chaldeans (B. Pes. 113b), and this might be explained as either a difference of opinion of the sages, as is common in the Talmud, or as a rule against predictions not based on astrology (such as in T. Shab. 7:14). According to Rava (third-fourth centuries, Babylonia): "Life, children and livelihood (literally: food) depend not on one's merit but on Mazal." This might be taken as either mere luck or dependence on a zodiac sign (ibn Ezra in his long commentary on Exod. 32:32; Ecc. 2:21). According to the rabbis, or already in the Bible (Deut. 33:14), it is assumed that the moon ripens

the fruits (Rashi, ad loc.: squash and pumpkin; Gen. Rabbah 10; addendum 2 to ADRN version A). From post-talmudic texts it is clear that there were Jews who ordered a *Mezuzah* to be written on Monday or Thursday only, resembling the rule of Samuel.

Usually astrologers had bad reputations in Rabbinic sources, and they were not allowed to predict concerning Jews. The rabbis understood that the rules of astrology do not affect Jews who recite the Shema and Eighteen Benedictions (Tanhuma Shoftim 10) or give charity (B. Shab. 156b). According to Rabbinic legends, many astrologers were mistaken, such as those who lived at the time of the flood (Kallah Rabbati 2:7), the astrologers of Pharaoh (B. San. 101b; B. Ber. 4a), and there were other cases in Rabbinic legends to exemplify the mischief of astrology. However, in a (late) midrash Solomon is depicted as an astrologer who, after checking the zodiacal signs, tried to free his daughter from her destined groom, in vain (Tanhuma, Buber ed., preface, p. 136).

Texts: In Rabbinic literature some sermons in which the zodiac signs play a literary role have been preserved. Some of the sermons written in the land of Israel included astrological ideas, such as in a sermon by Hama b. Hanina. Here the evil Haman of the story of Esther is portrayed as an astrologer, who checks the zodiac for the optimum date to achieve his goal of destroying the Jews (Esther Rabbah 7:11; Sifre deAgadeta on Esther, Buber ed.). In another sermon, God is depicted as an astrologer who chooses by means of astrology the right month to give the Torah (Pesiqta Rabbati 20). Solomon was an expert in astrology; he excelled in the wisdom of the East as well as of the Egyptians and Pharaoh (Pesiqta Rabbati 14). Though the extent of the belief in astrology in these sermons is not clear, it seems that the audience, if not the rabbi, knew astrology far better than is explicitly stated.

In the *Book of Secrets* (*Sefer ha-Razim*), from the fourth-fifth centuries land of Palestine, there are all sorts of magic prescriptions of which some 10% are of an unsophisticated astrological nature. The author recommends a certain procedure to be carried out on the seventh day of the month in the seventh hour (Heaven 1 line 52). The author knows that there are angels that rule the zodiac signs of men and women and then recommends a rite to be carried out "on the twenty-ninth of the month when the moon is ending" (2:33-36). This book, written by a non-Rabbinic Jew, attests to a kind of amalgamation of astrology (hemerology) and magic (similar to that found in Egyptian papyri) in a way that became famous centuries later.

Among the Hebrew liturgical poems, piyyutim, composed in the fourth-seventh centuries, there are more than ten piyyutim that mention the signs of the zodiac. The authors of most of these piyyutim are anonymous, but a few were composed by Eleazar Ha-Qalir. An anonymous piyyut that discusses the zodiac is a lamentation recited in Orthodox Judaism until this very day on the eve of the ninth of Ab ("Az beHataenu Harab Miqdash," composed around fourth-fifth centuries). In the Palestinian Aramaic translation to the Bible, several piyyutim (from the fourth-seventh centuries) were incorporated. Among them are (at least) two astrological piyyutim. One mentions the zodiac signs, using them as a literary figure only (like in the Hebrew piyyutim), denoting "soft" astrology. However, another piyyut (to be recited at the beginning of Nissan) reflects "hard" astrology, which involves a much deeper astrological knowledge. As a matter of fact, that piyyut demonstrates a poetic derivation of Mesopotamian omens known as *Summa Sin ina tamaritsu* (if the moon in its appearance).

The *Book of Creation* (*Sefer Yetsira*) is the first book on astrology in Hebrew, written by a multi-talented scholar who was obviously a linguist, a mathematician, and an astronomer as well as having other capabilities. He wrote a small book (some two-thousand words), in which he shows his knowledge, inter alia, of medical astrology. His theories, later characterized as *homo-Zodiacus*, reflect (Neo-)Pythagorean, Hellenistic, and Byzantine concepts. The book was written in the fifth-sixth centuries,

probably in Tiberias. Several centuries later this book became the "trigger" of the Qabbalah, and more than sixty commentaries have been written on it during the ages (without necessarily acknowledging the astrology in it).

Baraita deMazalot (intra) includes unique astrological data, taken from various sources. The author focused on genethlialogy, foretelling the life-span of a person who was born under a specific zodiacal sign. For example, one who is born under Saturn will live fifty-seven years, an idea that resembles Paulus of Alexandria (fourth century). The responsibility of each of the planets is described. Thus: "Saturn governs poverty, wretchedness, sore, desolation, sickness, hidden blow in the body an corn," in accordance with Ptolemy (a concept derived from Mesopotamia). Since some of this tractate's ideas penetrated the Qabbalah, some modern scholars have been surprised to find a similarity between Middle-Ages Qabbalistic concepts and old Mesopotamian texts without knowing the role of this book in the chain of astrological tradition.

In *Pirqe de Rabbi Eliezer* there is no explicit astrology, though the author states: "The zodiac signs 'serve' the birth of the moon as well as the births (or: generations, or: history) of humans, and on these the world stands. And anyone who is smart and clever—he knows the births of the moon and of humans as well." However, when the author states that each of the zodiac signs rules 2 1/3 days (3 in a week), just as the astrological text from Qumran, it seems that either the author knew astrology better than he intended to disclose or that the text was censored in later generations.

In *Baraita deShmuel* there is a unique set of omens for the weather. For example: "When the season begins under Mercury— heat." Rain and dew happen only under specific conjunctions of the signs and the planets, such as Cancer and Sun or Virgin and Venus or Gemini and Mercury, etc. Though the author tries to show that his knowledge is based on the Bible, it is quite clear that he drew his knowledge from other sources as well.

The sages made use of astral omens as a

tool to explain some biblical verses. For example, Exod. 10:10 was understood as referring to a star of bad omen (Rashi, ad loc., Mid. Canticles, Greenhut ed.), or that Moses overcame the Amelekites with his sophisticated knowledge of astrology (Exod. 17:12; Rashi, ad loc., Tanhuma Beshalah 28). The editor of the Second Targum on Ecclesiastes included astrology in his translation quite systematically. However, the infiltration of astrological concepts into the Targum is attested to in other verses in the Aramaic translation of the Bible (e.g., 1 Chron. 12:32). Since in the Second Targum on Song of Songs 7:5 there is an allusion to scribes and those in the Sanhedrin who make intercalations, it may be assumed that the translator had evidence of his own eyes, no doubt, in Tiberias (ibid., Numbers 34:8).

A unique text that combines astrology with metoscopy and chiromancy has been found in the Cairo Geniza. This Hebrew text was probably composed by a rabbi in the land of Israel in the Byzantine era, and it is the earliest piece of its kind. A recent discovery in the Geniza shows the similarities between Hermetic literature and Jewish astrology. A text in Aramaic describes the "character" of each day in a month: what is the name of the ruling angel, what is appropriate or not appropriate to do on that day, with a set of omens without precedent. For example, on the twenty-first of the month: "Whatever is lost will not be found," or "Whoever is born shall fall into the hands of wild animals." On each day the author adds the name of a herb that is appropriate to be picked on that day, no doubt to be used as a medicament. The text has magical characters, and its Aramaic, with Greek names, might indicate its original provenance. Though it is difficult to evaluate the text's origin, since it is part of a chain in a long history of astral omens, with some caution it is assumed that it was composed in the land of Israel between the fifth-eighth centuries.

In a text called "Pishra de-Rabbi Hanina ben Dosa," the influence of Hermetic literature on Jewish matters can be seen. In a long text in Aramaic, assumed to be from around the fifth-eighth century, the author gives instructions to a magician to "solve" (= pishra) all sorts of problems he is asked. Each of the cases should be directed to a different angel, first without being aware of the days of the week. However, later the author directs that his procedures depend strictly on the days of the week, the days of the month, the months under a specific zodiac sign, and the hours under a specific planet. That is to say, magic, angelology, and hemerology combined aim to cure all sorts of ailments.

When the first synagogues with zodiac signs were excavated in the land of Israel in the first half of the twentieth century, some scholars conjectured this was proof of an unorthodox Judaism. Now that we have six synagogues of this kind, together with the many texts ignored until now, it is clear that these synagogues actually reflect the Rabbinic Judaism of their time. Under the roofs of the synagogues, astral signs were depicted and written, astrological sermons were given, and astrological data were chanted in prayer and Targum.

Most of the astrologers remain anonymous; however, we do know the names of a few of them. Mash'allah ibn Athri, a Jew of a Persian origin (ca. 762-815) was active in the 'Abbasid court in Baghdad (and may have converted to Islam). He wrote in Arabic a few books on astrology (based on former astrologers), some of which were later translated into Hebrew by R. Abraham ibn Ezra.

The well-known Jewish blessing "*Mazal tob*" (= good zodiac sign) on family occasions is assumed to have been invented in the eleventh century at the latest.

Conclusion: In late antiquity, Jews, like their contemporaries, lived under starry skies, and the role of astrology was much greater than old Jewish texts tend to admit. It is true, a few people condemned and rejected astrology, but no doubt the adherents of this esteemed science and divination were far more numerous, Jews included. Astrology played its role not only in day to day behavior but reached the mainstream of the Jewish religion, synagogues, liturgy, sermons, piyyut and Targum. For a modern scholar who is not afraid to examine the sources, there is no reason to ignore or deny the importance of astrology in Jewish religion and culture in antiquity.

Bibliography

Albani, M., "Horoscopes in the Qumran Scrolls," in Flint, Peter W., and James C. VanderKam, eds., *The Dead Sea Scrolls after Fifty Years* (Leiden, Boston, and Köln, 1999), pp. 279-330.

Charlesworth, James H., "Jewish Interest in Astrology during the Hellenistic and Roman Periods," in Hasse, W., ed., *Aufstieg und Niedergang der Romischen Welt* II.20.2 (Berlin and New York, 1987), pp. 926-950.

MEIR BAR ILAN

ASTRONOMY IN ANCIENT JUDAISM: In antiquity, astronomy was not only a kind of applied mathematics but rather a way of knowing God, science, and religion. When God is depicted as counting the stars and giving them names (Ps. 147:4; Is. 40:26), it is apparent that any believer in God who practices astronomy works together with God while imitating him, *imitatio Dei*, as the ultimate religious practice.

Astronomy: While the Bible has a fair amount to say about medicine, astronomy is rarely mentioned. The idea that there were "rules of Heaven" (Jer. 33:25; Job 38:33) does not say much about the observation of stars or about the Israelite understanding of astronomy, especially in a text that wholly rejects star-worship. Only God knows the exact number of stars as well as their names (Ps. 147:4), while such a task as numbering the stars is beyond humankind's ability (Gen. 15:5). Still, the prophets and sages were aware of at least seven different stars and constellations (Jer. 44:17-19; Amos 5:8, 5:26; Job 9:9, 38:32). Though what we consider astronomy is missing, its offshoot, in the form of a deep consciousness of a heavenly calendar, exists, even if only to a small degree. The way the luminaries are said to have been created (Gen. 1:14) shows awareness of the role of the luminaries in the calendar. The story of the flood (Gen. 7-8) reveals calendrical thinking in the form of an awareness of the eleven day difference in length between a lunar and a solar year (according to the Massoretic text). The five "stops" in the flood narrative show awareness of a (some say: solar) calendar. The

book of Esther shows another kind of calendrical thinking as well as an awareness of astrology, but astronomy is absent.

Post-Biblical Astronomy: Theophrastos (372-288/7 B.C.E.), a disciple of Aristotle, wrote that the Jews watch the stars at night and pray to God. Since Theophrastos wrote in the period of the sacrificial cult, it is evident that he was writing about priests in the Temple, where the exact date had significance for the ritual, sacrifices, and festivals (= calendar). Though there is no other evidence that priests were engaged in astronomy (Ps. 8:4 is not sufficient), it goes well with the Mesopotamian tradition where there was a connection between astronomers and priests. Moreover, before the destruction of the Temple in 70 C.E., there was a priestly court in Jerusalem at which testimony of the sighting of the new moon was analyzed (M. R.H. 1:7). So there is no reason to doubt Theophrastos' evidence.

Post-biblical writings reveal much more interest in astronomy than in former generations. In 1 Enoch, a Priestly Aramaic book edited out of (at least) five books, is an astronomical work (chaps. 72-82), from the third century B.C.E. This book is based on Mesopotamian astronomy, as seen by its measuring the movements the sun's rising point along the horizon as well as from other aspects. The book shows a unique combination of astronomy and religious mystical cognition, based on a 364 day solar year, beginning on Nissan 1. The advantage of this calendar is its simplicity together with its fixed days of the festivals on the week-days (thus, the first day of the year is always on Wednesday). However, losing a day and (almost) a quarter every year leads to a gross deviation from astronomical ("real") time.

The priest who wrote the book of Jubilees, though deeply interested in rewriting the Bible according to a profound understanding of chronology, based his calculations on a 364 day year similar to 1 Enoch (Jub. 6:32-38). The people in Qumran had (better: tried to have) the "Jubilees" calendar of a solar year, made of 364 days, as in the Temple Scroll. But it is most likely that they used other calendars (though not simultaneously). The day probably began at sunrise, as in Lev. 7:15 and Rabbinic priestly traditions (see T. Zeb. 6:18).

Some twenty texts found at Qumran show a deep consciousness of calendrical issues that, although they do not support a new calendar, exemplify the importance the calendar at Qumran. 2 Enoch (which was not found in Qumran) comes from another priestly milieu, most probably from Jerusalem, where Enoch was a hero. The author writes of a more complex calendar than that found in 1 Enoch, of 365 days a year, with seven years of intercalation in a cycle of nineteen years and a great cycle of (19 × 28 =) 532 years (2 Enoch 6:21-26). The author gives the order of the planets in a non-Hellenistic system: Saturn, Venus, Mars, Sun, Jupiter, Mercury, Moon. It is quite obvious that this calendar shows a better knowledge of astronomy than the one in 1 Enoch, reflecting Hellenistic, combined with Mesopotamian, influence.

The Rabbinic Attitude: Rabbinic astronomy cannot be considered a continuation of earlier priestly concepts. Rabbinic astronomy began rather as a popular and practical occupation, with anti-priestly affinities, and only through generations of tradition did it gain a scientific value. In the days of the Temple, rabbis intercalated the calendar according to natural phenomena (T. San. 2:2-3). At first, rabbis relied on any testimony (such as that of cattle-herders; Y. San. 1:2). But after a few generations they began to intercalate according to astronomical calculations, in a much more professional way (T. San. 2:7). The same process of development occurred in establishing the date of the new moon. In the first and second centuries, the rabbis needed witnesses (and therefore even allowed witnesses to transgress the Sabbath, M. R.H. 1:5-6). Several centuries later the rabbis relied instead on their own calculations, thereby establishing a Jewish calendar. The exact development of the Rabbinic attitude towards astronomy and the calendar is difficult to describe, since the evidence is either blurred or contradictory. But the bottom line is clear. The Rabbi decisions exemplify a long course of deepening

awareness of scientific (that is, Hellenistic and Mesopotamian) astronomy. Notably, the Amoraim themselves already were unaware of this process, believing instead that the knowledge of seasons and intercalations was part of the legacy of the children of Issachar, found already in Scripture (1 Chron. 12:33; Gen. Rabbah 72).

Few sundials have been found in the land of Israel, another proof of astronomers' activity, since in this period keeping time was done by astronomers, not instruments. The rabbis used sundials to a small extent (M. Ed. 3:8; Mekhilta deRashbi 12), leaving no impression on their main interest, the development of the law.

The Earth and Cosmos: The rabbis, needing to accurately establish the calendar and correctly to observe the sacrificial ritual, had some need for astronomy. But to accomplish these purposes, they had no motivation to learn geography. Therefore, while Ptolemy excelled in astronomy and geography as well (based on similar doctrines), the rabbis were interested in astronomy alone. Thus there are Jewish traditions of non-scientific concepts about the cosmos. For example, we find at B. Pes. 94a: "Egypt is 400 over 400 parsah (Persian parsang), and Egypt is 1/60 of Kush, and Kush is 1/60 of the world, and the world is 1/60 of a garden. . . ." etc. The schematic narrative shows that this was a kind of Midrash, not a strictly geographic concept. This understanding should be applied to a tradition that appears on the same page: "From Earth to Heaven—walking distance of five hundred years; and the thickness of Heaven—walking distance of five hundred years; and from one Heaven to another—walking distance of five hundred years." The rabbis thought that the heavens were made of water and fire. According to biblical concepts (Job 26:11), the world rests on columns (B. Hag. 12a). However, the rabbis described the world as a ball (Y. A.Z. 3:1, 42c). Rava (third-fourth centuries in Babylonia) said that the whole world is 6,000 parsah (B. Pes. 94a), which is about 24,872 miles, close to modern estimates.

Observations: In the whole of Rabbinic literature covering the first five centuries of this era, there is no evidence that any of the rabbis read any non-Jewish book on astronomy, though the rabbis did have many relationships with non-Jews. These relationships were face to face, some with philosophers and some with astronomers. Still, it seems the rabbis found their own way in astronomy. The four points of the compass (the cardinal points that divide the horizon) were well known to the rabbis (B. Erub. 56a). The rabbis thought a solar year has 365 days (B. R.H. 6b), while a lunar year has 354 days (T. Naz. 1:3). It took the rabbis some generations to realize that their data was not precise enough for calendrical purposes. The state of the rabbis' knowledge of astronomy was improving over the course of centuries of moon-observation and intercalations.

Those who saw the new moon appeared before a court, first of priests and then of rabbis, who evaluated the witnesses' testimony (M. R.H. 1:7). The different courts had different rules, and it is highly probable that they had different calendars in the same period. Yohanan b. Zakkai (first century), one of the founders of the Rabbinic tradition, was said to know all the Torah, *Tequfot* (seasons), and geometry (B. Suk. 28a), that is, calendrical calculations and astronomy. No evidence is given to support this claim.

The eleven days difference between a solar and lunar year is attested as an astronomical observation. Simeon b. Gamaliel said that it is very simple to observe, with a scratch on the wall, that the solar year is eleven days longer than the lunar year (Gen. Rabbah 33:8). Even earlier, the author of Seder Olam (attributed to Yose) thought that this gap was already attested in Scripture's flood story (Seder Olam 4).

The idea that the length of a lunar month is approximately 29.5 days is implicit in the laws concerning the intercalation of a month (T. Arak. 1:8), in which twelve months yield (365 − 11) = 354 days. However, the Talmud stated that Rabban Gamaliel II (second century C.E.) said, according to his family tradition: "A new moon (does not appear) in less than twenty-nine days and a half, two thirds of an hour and seventy-three parts" (B. R.H. 25a). This length equals Ptolemy's value in sexa-gesimal fractions: $29:31,50,8,20^d$. However, modern scholars largely agree (though without any manuscript support) that this testimony was honed by adding a few words to support greater exactness, for three reasons: 1) in the whole of talmudic literature the idea of dividing an hour into 1080 occurs only here; 2) this kind of exactitude has no parallel in talmudic literature; 3) Since Gamaliel says "in less than" (= a minimum), there is no reason to expect the exactitude that follows. This analysis suggests that Gamaliel's words were either "twenty-nine days and a half," which yields a lunar year of (a minimum of) 354 days, or, less likely, "twenty-nine days and a half, two thirds of an hour," which yields a lunar year of 354 1/3 days.

Rabban Gamaliel had all sorts of images of lunar crescents against which he could check the witnesses (M. R.H. 2:8). While he stated the opinions of the sages of Israel as against the sages of the nations, we are told that the sages of Israel contend that the sphere is fixed while the zodiac signs are cycling, but the sages of the nations say the opposite. Judah the Prince, as the last referee, added an argument to prove the Jewish opinion (B. Pes. 94b). However, in another dispute, stated at the same place, concerning the path of the sun at night, Judah said that the opinion of the sages of the nations seems to be superior. According to Maimonides (Guide 2:8), the rabbis held the Pythagorean opinion while the opposing sages were Aristotelians, and they were victorious.

Samuel, one of the most famous Amoraim in third century Babylonia, was an astronomer and astrologer (and maybe even a physician), as attested in his various sayings. He held that a lunar year is not less than 352 days and not more than 356 days (B. Arak. 9b), that is, mean length of 29:12 days. Except for observations of the sun and of the moon in regard to the calendar, the Amoraim watched a minimum of two stars after sunset as denoting a new day (Y. Ber. 1:1, 2:2), but this observation had no astronomical value. There are very few other astronomical observations among the rabbis. Among them was the observation that when Kima (mentioned in Amos 5:8, Job

9:9, 38:31) sets in Iyyar, the fountains give less water, and that is why the flood began on that day (B. Ber. 59a; B. R.H. 11b). Samuel said that Kima is a cold star compounded of some hundred stars (B. Ber. 58b). Later, Kima was identified with the Pleiades. Samuel said that Kesil is a hot star without which the world would not survive (ibid). Samuel said: "the paths of the sky are known to me like the paths of Nehardea, except for a comet whose nature I do not know" (B. Ber. 58b). After Samuel's statement, the Talmud continued: "we have learned that it (a comet) never passes through Kesil, and if it does, the world will be destroyed" (Kesil is mentioned in Amos 5:8, Job 38:31, and identified by ibn Ezra as "the heart of the Crab"). Samuel was asked: "(Is it true), we see that it passes?!" And he answered: "This is impossible, either the comet goes above it or beneath it" (Y. Ber. 9:2, 13c). The rabbis said that there is a star that rises once in seventy years and deceives sailors (B. Hor. 10a). It is assumed they meant the comet later named after Hailey, a comet that appeared around 140 C.E. (seventy is taken as a round number for a cycle of around seventy-eight years).

In a sermon that Afes (third century) delivered in Antioch (Gen. Rabbah 10:1) appear data concerning the times of the planets' circling the earth in a very scientific way (compare to Vitruvius, *On Architecture*, 9:1). This sermon was given on the occasion of reading the beginning of Genesis, and the whole sermon has a flavor of combining Torah and science (as in modern times).

Bar Kappara (second-third centuries C.E.) said: "One who knows how to calculate the seasons and zodiac signs (in calendrical issues), but he does not do so—of him Scripture says: 'But they regard not the work of the Lord, neither have they considered the work of his hands' (Is. 5:12)." Yohanan said that there is a religious commandment to calculate the seasons and the zodiac signs (= months, B. Shab. 75a). These opinions are a continuation of a long tradition that sees the study of astronomy as a religious practice.

Calendar: The Jewish calendar is lunisolar, as in Mesopotamia. It has no preten-

sion to be exact every day, from an astronomical perspective, but, in the long run, it shows adaptations to both solar and lunar cycles. Almost every year is slightly different in length than the former year. Every year has either twelve or thirteen lunar months. Months begin in the evening when the lunar crescent is first visible after conjunction. The calendar played a religious role in determining the days on which festivals occur.

Because of its role in determining festival observances, the calendar was, in talmudic times, a sectarian document. The calendar one followed marked him as either a Rabbinic or a sectarian Jew (M. R.H. 2:9; B. Ber. 63a-b). According to the rabbis, non-Rabbinic Jews did their best to distort the authoritative Rabbinic calendar (M. R.H. 1:1-2; T. R.H. 1:15). Thus Hizqia, a third century Amora in the land of Israel explained that the villains who do not understand the deeds of God in Ps. 28:5 are those who do not know the *Tequfot* (Shoher Tob 28); they are heretics. This early division of Jews according to the calendar they follow became crucial again in the ninth-tenth centuries with the Karaite movement. Samaritans have their own calendar until this very day.

The bud of a calendar can be seen in the third-fourth centuries C.E., when a rabbi initiated rules concerning the "postponing" of Rosh Hashanah so that it would not occur on either a Wednesday or Friday, which meant that Yom Kippur would not fall either before or after the Sabbath (B. R.H. 20a). Simeon ruled that those who calculated the calendar should make sure that the Day of Willow (Tishre 21) does not occur on the Sabbath, which would prevent observance of the commandment of beating the willow (Y. Suk. 4:1, 54b). The meaning of this rule is that Rosh Hashanah should not fall on a Sunday. Thus we see already in the Amoraic period a rule that "Rosh Hashanah never falls on Sunday, Wednesday, or Friday" (in initials: "*lo ADU Rosh*"). In later generations the calendar included more such rules. For example, Elul must have twenty-nine days, a rule that was stated as a (false) historical fact (B. R.H. 19b). The accumulation of rules from about the third-tenth centuries C.E. changed the calendar from a system that accurately determined dates only de facto into one by which millennia could be calculated in advance. But looking back, we cannot today calculate any exact date prior to the tenth century C.E.

Samuel is the first rabbi to give the duration of the solar year more precisely than the Tannaim. Samuel said: "In between every 'season' there are ninety-one days and seven hours" (B. Erub. 56a); that is an average that yields a solar year of 365 days, in accordance with the Julian year. He showed his astronomical knowledge by sending to the land of Israel a calendar with intercalations for sixty years in advance, a calculation that was not enough however to impress Yohanan (B. Hul. 95b). Samuel was also sure he could make calculations of the calendar (without the need for witnesses) for the whole diaspora, but he was shown that he was not aware of some of the rules of the calendar (B. R.H. 20b), or else this rule had no Babylonian origin. A certain Amora in the land of Israel, Yohanan b. Media, said he calculated a date (the twenty-fourth day of the seventh month) mentioned on the Bible (Neh. 9:1), saying that it did not fall on the Sabbath (Y. A.Z. 1:1, 39b). Though it is not clear on what this calculation was based, it does not necessarily mean that Yohanan b. Media was an expert in intercalations. The idea that Ada b. Ahaba (third century, Babylonia) was an expert in the calendar (with more precise data than that of Samuel, such as the length of the *tequfa*: 91:7:28), was known only to medieval rabbis and it is not rooted in the Talmud. The dispute over the authenticity of calculations attributed to Ada has not been settled yet, but it should be noted that in the Talmud there is no mention of his capabilities.

Intercalations: Intercalation, that is, adding a lunar month to the year, is based on the idea of observing the month of Abib, in the spring (B. R.H. 7a; B. San. 13b), while the Mesopotamians had the same idea (without having the Bible), based on astronomical observations. The Rabbinic calendar continues the Mesopotamian tradition in that only Adar is intercalated, that

is, the last month of the year, perhaps because agricultural observation is meaningful only during that month. The Mesopotamians intercalated Elul as well, and though the rabbis were aware of the possibility of adding another Elul, it was understood that it was done under pressure only (T. San. 2:7). The month of Ab may have once been intercalated (B. San. 12a). To enable keeping the laws of the Sabbatical year and because of natural phenomena, the rabbis had no systematic order of intercalation (T. Sheb. 2:9, 2:12). According one of the basic calculations of the Tannaim (T. San. 2:7), a cycle of nineteen years of intercalations might occur, but a set of seven years intercalated in a cyclic of nineteen years is not attested to in the Rabbinic sources before the seventh century C.E. This system was practiced in Babylonia from around the fourth century B.C.E., and it reasonable from several perspectives. Medieval Rabbis claimed that once there had been a Tannaitic rule on intercalations in a cycle of nineteen years, but it was lost. However, authentic Rabbinic sources contradict such a claim (though not all contemporary Rabbinic authorities agreed on this). At the beginning of this era, intercalations were made for non-astronomical reasons, such as the state of livestock and fruits (T. San. 2:6; B. San. 11b). That is to say that from its very beginning the Jewish calendar was more an agricultural calendar (as well as a religious one) than a precise astronomical calendar.

Date of Foundation: According to medieval authorities (Abraham b. Hiyya and Nahmanides quoting Hai Gaon), the Jewish calendar, based on calculations, began with Hillel (the 2nd), son of Judah, in 359. However, not only is this fact not attested in Talmudic sources, but even later authorities (ibn Ezra, Maimonides) failed to mention this Hillel, so that there is doubt concerning his role in the development of the calendar. It has been claimed that a certain piece of paper with an old text was found in the ruins of Tiberias, attributing to Hillel some share in calendar issues, but it is not clear whether this paper is authentic. It should be noted that in the Middle-Ages there were other opinions concerning the beginnings of the calendar. Hai b. Nahshon said that the calendar had been established by Isaac Nafha, but no Talmudic tradition attests that. An Arab writer wrote that a certain Eliezer b. Paroah (elsewhere unknown) initiated the Jewish calendar, once again without any confirmation. Saadya Gaon claimed that the calendar was "a rule to Moses on Sinai," thus giving the calendar absolute authority. It seems that all these explanations (as well as other medieval concepts attributed to the sages of the Talmud) were given against the background of various disputations over the "correct" calendar.

Later scholars and Rabbinic authorities were sure that their own understanding was the same as their ancestors', and speculation became facts of history. Theology went hand in hand with astronomy, and since astronomy required an epoch, that is, a beginning of the calendar based on astronomical observations by deduction, naturally the creation of the luminaries was taken as such an epoch, that is the beginning of the calendar. Jews began to calculate their dates according to *Annus Mundi* not earlier than the seventh century.

Texts: In the talmudic literature are only sporadic statements concerning the stars. However, the observation of the new moon in regard to the Jewish calendar as well as discussing intercalations is one of the main issues of tractate Rosh Hashanah. That is, there was full awareness of the daily calendar while its scientific background was ignored.

In the lost *Midrash of 49 Middot*, from the land of Israel, probably from the fourth-fifth centuries, occurs a sermon that has fortunately been preserved (Yalkut Shimoni, Shemot 418). A rabbi found a correspondence between the zodiac signs in the heavens and the way the tribes of Israel dwelled in the desert. He stated: "Tribe of Judah in the East, Isachar and Zebulun with him. Against them in heavens are Aries, Taurus, and Gemini. With the sun, together they serve five parts out of eight." He probably meant that out of the 180° in the Eastern horizon, the sun on the longest day rises at azimuth of 67.5°. However his words are understood, it is evident that the rabbi (and

his audience) knew something about astronomy, which played a role in the synagogue.

Baraita deMazalot is a unique astronomical and astrological tractate. It gives astronomical data in unprecedentedly scientific ways. The author describes two systems, an Egyptian and a Babylonian one, regarding the position of the stars in the zodiac at the moment of creation. The author gives the exact distances from Earth to the moon, from the moon to Mercury and so forth, in a manner resembling the Mesopotamian *beru ina same*, x heavenly units equal to y earthly units. The author quotes not only Rabbinic sources but states the opinions of "the sages of the gentiles," "the sages of Egypt, Chaldeans, and the Babylonians." There is no doubt that the writer drew some of his data from Ptolemy (not necessarily directly), but his other sources remain to be analyzed. The author used Greek terminology, such as *trigon* (triangle), *Stirigamos* (standing), and *diametron* (diameter). The writer was probably a rabbi who lived in the land of Israel in fifth-sixth centuries, and one of his sermons shows his competence very well.

Eleazar Ha-Qalir, in the sixth-seventh centuries, was a master of the Hebrew language, a sage who knew all Rabbinic traditions, and a prolific poet who wrote hundreds, if not more, Piyyutim, many of them still in use today. In a famous piyyut ("*az raita ve-Safarta*," to parashat Sheqalim), his abilities as a mathematician and geographer are clear. However, in a piyyut only recently discovered ("*Or Hama u-Lebana*"), it becomes apparent that he was an astronomer as well. Ha-Qalir gives data of astronomical value: a solar year is 365 days (like Samuel), and a lunar year is 354 1/3 days (without explicit precedent). His intercalation cycle was nineteen years ("*Ehad beEhad Gashu*"), but he knew another solar cycle of twenty-eight years. Notably, more data in his piyyutim has not yet been evaluated (e.g. in: "*Abi Kol Hoze*"). It is assumed he was the head of the Jewish academy in Tiberias and played a role in the process of intercalations.

Pirqe de Rabbi Eliezer is a midrash from the land of Israel, from the seventh or the beginning of the eighth century (though it claims to be older). Chapters 5-7 discuss the calendar in prosaic Hebrew in a way similar to Ha-Qalir's poetics. The author's solar year is 365 days, and his lunar month is 29:12:793 (assumed to be a Talmudic tradition). The author continues by stating that the length of a lunar year (as precisely multiplied by twelve) is 354:8:876, exactly like in *Midrash Aggadah*, Buber ed., Gen. 1:14, *Midrash Sod Ha-'Ibur*, and in our "modern" data (though slightly bigger than the "real" time). This precision makes the author of this midrash a good candidate for the founder of the Jewish calendar. The author's astronomy is combined with angels, and he uses the terminology of "large hour," that is, two hours, and giving the heavenly windows names, unknown earlier. The author teaches that a human eye can see the new moon sixteen hours after the lunar conjunction. The author gives his calculations in regard to ecliptical limits: A solar eclipse will occur if the moon's latitude at conjunction is at most sixty "ma'alot" (units), and a lunar eclipse at most forty "ma'alot" (units). The moon's great cycle is of twenty-one years while the sun cycles every twenty-eight years, and this leads to a great cycle of eighty-four years (21 × 4 = 28 × 3), that is, (approximately) one hour of God (based on Ps. 90:4), though this cycle is not easy to explain. However, his system of intercalation is based on a nineteen year-cycle, like the "modern" Jewish calendar, while adding one lunar month in years 3, 6, 8, 11, 14, 17, 19. From the way the author portrays biblical heroes as having secret knowledge of intercalation, and from his own description of the process of making decisions on this issue, it is evident that he played an active role in calendar decisions. That is to say, the author, rabbi and astronomer, was one of the heads of the Yeshiva in Tiberias where they met at least once in two or three years to consider whether to intercalate the year or not. The author's data, together with Talmudic halakhah, reveal that the author's calendar could have been as exact as ours.

The "editor" of the Aramaic Targum attributed to Jonathan b. Uziel in his translation of Gen. 1:16 made an addition that places him among the most knowledgeable scholars of the calendar. The translator says: "both (luminaries) were equal in their foundation: 21 hours minus 672 parts of an hour." That is: every month has 29:12:793 days, so the "difference" in the new moon from one year to another (an "ordinary" year) is 4:8:876 (so far like Ravina, according to Rashi in B. Arak. 9b). Now, Adam was created on the New Year (according to Rabbinic tradition), and it was on a Friday, that is 6:14 (considered by Jews of Babylonia to be the beginning of the calendar). From this it is clear that the new moon in the previous year was at 2:5:204 (considered by Jews of Palestine to be the beginning of the calendar). However, since it is written that the luminaries were created on Wednesday, on the very same day, it must have been in the year before (6:14-4:8:876-4:8:876), that is 4:20:408. In other words, both luminaries were created on 4:(21 hours − 672 parts). In short, the calculation of the translator is based on two virtual years before Adam was created, showing the type and level of the astronomy of the translator, and it seems that the translator used the same system as Eleazar HaQalir.

Baraita deShmuel is an astronomical and astrological tractate based on biblical knowledge combined with Greek science, as is clear from its inclusion of a few Greek words, such as *ametron* (without measure). The author uses some of his own terminology. Some of his Hebrew words are mere translations. A degree is called "*hail*," that is, an army-corps (following B. Ber. 32b). The author uses "large hour" as does Pirqe de Rabbi Eliezer. The author shows his ability to use a "reed," *Qane* (a precursor of the theodolite, already known in Egyptian astronomy), which makes him the first Jewish author to do so. The author gives the values of the noon-shadow during the year (Cancer 0; Leo and Gemini 2; Virgo and Taurus 4 . . . Capricorn 12). The author gives the oblique ascension of the zodiac signs such as "Aries 20°, Libra (the cane of Libra) 40°, from Aries to the cane (of Libra) one should add 4° for each sign" (= Taurus 24°; Gemini 28°; Cancer 32°; Leo 36°; Virgo 40°; Libra 40°; Scorpio 36°; etc.). This is precisely a scheme of the Babylonian System A. Some biblical verses are quoted in a midrashic manner. However, the text is full of astronomical data, such as the time it takes each of the planets to circle the Earth, and the apogee and nadir of the zodiac signs. There is a special treatment of the *Teli*, that is Draco (mentioned no less than seventeen times), and other stars are mentioned as well. The author mentions the year 4536 Anno Mundi (= 776 C.E.), and this is used to conclude that the text was composed that year, though there are doubts concerning its authenticity. The author gives the limit of 12° 21' for both solar and lunar eclipses. The tractate was attributed to Samuel the Babylonian (sharing a solar year of 365 days), though its dependence on Baraita deMazalot is very clear. This derivation leads to the probability that the text was composed in the land of Israel with dependence on Babylonian-type arithmetical methods in Hellenistic culture.

It seems that the last adjustment to the Jewish calendar of talmudic times was made by Saadya Gaon. He was a philosopher, poet, translator (into Arabic), well versed in the whole of Jewish literature, and he was an astronomer as well. In 922, there was a dispute between him (before he came to Babylonia) and the head of the Yeshiva in the land of Israel, Aaron b. Meir, over a minor issue (whether the conjunction of the moon after mid-day and 642 parts enables visibility of the new moon in the coming night = conjunction + less than around eighteen hours). This astronomical debate led to two different calendars for the Jews in the land of Israel (Rosh Hashanah of 4683 on Tuesday) and the Jews of Babylonia (Rosh Hashanah on Thursday). At least for a year Rabbinic Jews in Babylonia and in the land of Israel had different calendars, but in the end Saadya won the case. Thus, the Jews in Israel accepted the superiority of their brethren in Babylonia, contrary to the priority of Judea and the land of Israel in calendrical issues until that day

(T. San. 2:13; Y. San. 1:2, 19:1). This case marks the end of the developing process of the Jewish calendar, and all the rules of the calendar known then have prevailed until this very day.

The complexity of the Jewish calendar, relative to the Gregorian, is due to two factors: 1) the Jewish calendar is based on a synchronization of two different systems (luni-solar), while the Gregorian is based on one system only; and 2) the rules of the Jewish calendar were not formulated at one time but rather accumulated over the ages. But despite this, the Jewish calendar became scientific and cosmopolitan, such that observation of the moon in the land of Israel no longer plays a role. The Jewish calendar is based on several assumptions and rules, influenced by different cultures in several generations. Still, since this calendar only adds approximately one day every 216 years (as opposed to the Gregorian calendar, which adds a day every 3,700 years), it is actually quite accurate. Even so, this deviation suggests that some minute changes are to be expected in the future, not without religious controversies.

Bibliography

Feldman, W.M., *Rabbinical Mathematics and Astronomy* (London, 1931; third corrected edition, 1978).
Gandz, S., *Studies in Hebrew Astronomy and Mathematics* (New York, 1970).
Glessmer U., "Calendars in the Qumran Scrolls," in Flint, Peter W., and James C. VanderKam, eds., *The Dead Sea Scrolls after Fifty Years* (Leiden, Boston, and Köln, 1999), pp. 213-278.
Herr, M.D., "The Calendar," in S. Safrai and M. Stern, eds., *The Jewish People in the First Century* (Assen and Amsterdam, 1976), vol. II, pp. 834-864.
Stern, S., *Calendar and Community*, Oxford: Oxford University Press, 2001.
VanderKam, James C., *Calendars in the Dead Sea Scrolls: Measuring Time* (London and New York, 1998).

MEIR BAR ILAN

B

BIBLICAL INTERPRETATION, MED-IEVAL FRENCH: Between the middle of the eleventh century and the end of the twelfth century, a veritable revolution took place in biblical exegesis among the Rabbinic masters of northern France. During that time, a group of Rabbinic scholars began to formulate a new and innovative approach to reading and interpreting biblical texts according to a methodology that came to be called *peshat*, or "contextual exegesis." This revolution paralleled, contributed to, and was influenced by a similar advance made in *ad literam*, or literal, reading methodology by contemporary Christian scholars, most of whom were associated with the cathedral school of St. Victor. Moreover, Jewish and Christian masters were themselves influenced by earlier and contemporary Moslem, Jewish, and Christian scholarship carried out in the Islamic world.[1] The French Rabbinic group included such illustrious figures as Rabbi Solomon ben Isaac, or Rashi (1040-1105); his younger contemporary, Rabbi Joseph Qara (1050-1130); Rashi's grandson, Rabbi Samuel ben Meir, or Rashbam (1080-1160); Rashbam's student, Rabbi Eliezer of Beaugency (mid-twelfth century); and Rabbi Joseph ben Isaac Bekhor Shor (mid- to late-twelfth century), a disciple of Rashbam and Rashbam's younger brother, Rabbi Jacob Tam. Among the Christian scholars who flourished in the twelfth century were Hugh of St. Victor; his disciple, Andrew; and Herbert of Bosham.[2] While this article is concerned with Rabbinic exegesis, a brief detour to one of the fruits of Christian scholarship during the "Renaissance of the Twelfth Century" will serve well to highlight the achievements of Jewish scholarship in that same period.

One of the most significant publications in Christian European scholarship of the twelfth century was the *Didascalicon* of Hugh of St. Victor.[3] In this work, Hugh sought to provide an integrated presentation of all human knowledge; included in it was a guided curriculum of biblical studies. A recent examination of the *Didascalicon* highlights the significance of that book with regard to the history of reading in Western Civilization. Calling the *Didascalicon* "the first book written on the art of reading," the study claims that, due to its impact, "after centuries of Christian reading, the page was suddenly transformed from a score for pious mumblers into an optically organized text for logical thinkers."[4] While Hugh's work may not have been the most innovative piece of Christian scholarship, its pervasive influence makes it a useful fulcrum around which to view the advances in the culture of learning.

Writing in approximately the same generation and living in virtually the same vicinity as Hugh and the other Victorine scholars, the Rabbinic exegetes of northern France reached similar plateaus in transforming the reading process in the Jewish community. While they apparently did not compose works such as Hugh's, nor did they write treatises on rhetoric and poetics as did their Sephardic Jewish brethren, their surviving works of biblical exegesis have much to say on the subject of how to read a text. Though many of the biblical commentaries they composed were subsequently lost, either to the vicissitudes of time or, more specifically, to the Christian purges of Rabbinic texts that occurred throughout the thirteenth century, enough of their exegetical *oeuvre* has survived to enable its evaluation and analysis.

While what we may call "the Bible project" of the northern French school was not encyclopaedic, the Talmud commentary of Rashi (and Rashbam), together with their literary (and often genealogical) descendants, the Tosafists, represent a rather comprehensive study and critical reading of the Babylonian Talmud. Through their presentation and exegesis of the Talmud, the northern French exegetes in a sense established it as the foundational text of medieval French Jewry; their unique methodology ultimately influenced Spanish Jewry as well. Rashi's commentary is to this day essential, and the Tosafists' comments are often semi-encyclopaedic, as they cover Bible as well as Rabbinic literature. In addition, many of these exegetes, particularly Joseph Qara, also glossed the allusive, virtually impenetrable *piyyutim*, or Rabbinic liturgical poetry and made its language accessible to its readership. These poetic texts are themselves rich in biblical exegesis. While these other commentaries are not the focus of this article, it is important to keep in mind that the northern French exegetes applied their contextual reading methodology to the entire range of Jewish literature at their disposal. This article will consider the contribution of the northern French Rabbinic masters to the advances in biblical studies made during the "Renaissance of the Twelfth Century."

From *Derash* to *Peshat*: Learning to Read a New Way: In the development of contextual reading, perhaps no single aspect of late eleventh and early twelfth century exegesis factors more prominently than the abandonment of the authoritative midrashic readings of the ancient rabbis in favor of one that is rooted in what the commentator senses to be the "actual" meaning of a text. The pioneer in this effort was the great Rashi (an abbreviation comprised of the initial Hebrew letters of his name, Rabbi Shelomo Yitzhaki). He lived in Troyes, in Champagne country of northern France, and as a young man spent some years of study in the Jewish academies of the Rhineland. It is clear that there were important precedents to Rashi's quest to develop contextual reading. These are mainly to be found in the work of the anonymous *poterim*, who glossed difficult words in the Hebrew Bible and translated them into the vernacular Old French; and in the exegesis of Menahem bar Helbo, an eleventh century Provencal Rabbinic master whose commentaries were brought north by his nephew, Joseph Qara, later one of Rashi's disciples.[5] However, it is Rashi's work that became the most influential in orienting Jewish Bible study away from ancient Rabbinic midrash and towards truly contextual reading.

Rashi began developing a methodology for reading on the basis of one's own intuitive sense of a given passage. In his celebrated comment on Gen. 3:8, he describes his approach to interpreting Scripture:

> There are many homiletical midrashim (on these verses), and the rabbis have long ago arranged them in their proper place in Genesis Rabbah and the other midrashim. Whereas I have only come to explain Scripture according to its contextual [*peshuto*] understanding, and according to the *aggadah* that reconciles the words of Scripture, each word understood according to its character.

Rashi's ability to discern between contextual and midrashic exegesis is likewise clear in his comment on Gen. 12:5, a gloss that is typical of his Pentateuchal commentary as a whole. The verse relates that, in setting out for Canaan, Abram and his family took "the persons that they had made in Haran." The question animating Rashi is: in what way are persons "made"? In glossing the verse, Rashi first relates the midrashic tradition (Gen. Rabbah 39:14) that Abram and Sarai "made," that is, converted, gentiles in Haran to the faith in one God (Theodor-Albeck, 1965):

> *That they made in Haran*: In other words, whom they caused to enter under the wings of God's Presence. Abraham converted the men, and Sarah converted the women. Moreover, the verse considers them as though they actually had made them.

However, Rashi immediately supplements this reading with one that he considers to reflect the contextual, historical meaning of the words:

> However, the sense of the passage refers to male and female slaves whom they had acquired, as in the case of Jacob, of whom Scripture reports that *he has made all this wealth* (Gen. 31:1); and as in the case of the Israelites in the desert, of whom Scripture reports that *Israel has gained wealth* (Num. 24:18). These examples contain the language of "acquiring" and "gathering in."

Here Rashi is not correcting or rejecting the midrash. Rather, he provides both a midrashic and a contextual reading, in attempting to offer as best he can the fullest possible accounting of biblical language.[6] In this case, Rashi would consider that adapting the midrashic tradition did not reflect the conventional meaning of the verb "to make" in Biblical Hebrew. So he added the contextual reading to provide the circumstances through which Abram and Sarai had an opportunity to convert gentiles to the worship of God. Alternatively, he might have thought that the "purely contextual" reading—that is, that Abram and Sarai had acquired a retinue of servants—did not fully represent the religious dimensions of their characters. He therefore included the midrashic tradition as well. In either case, Rashi drew upon his tremendous sensitivity to the nuance of language, as well as upon his mastery of the talmudic-midrashic tradition, in order to make sense of the text for his readers. While the problems associated with Rashi's "dual readings" should not be oversimplified, it is best to understand his exegetical efforts as an early stage in the developing *peshat* methodology.[7]

Midrash is, however, explicitly rejected as a reading methodology by Rashi's disciple, Joseph Qara. His commentaries are replete with diatribes against the excesses of *derash*: "It is not the way of a prophet in any of the twenty-four books of Scripture to make his language so obscure that one needs to learn what he had to say through resorting to aggadic literature" (at Judges 5:4); "In aggadic literature, Scripture is expounded with different intent, but it cannot be reconciled with the heart; therefore I will hold back my hand and refrain (from even reacting to it) so that ink will not be spilled nor quills be broken" (at 2 Sam. 12:30). In what is, perhaps, the fullest extant description of the methodology of *peshat*, Qara advocates contextual reading not only on the basis of its efficacy as a coherent approach to understanding a text, but also as fulfilling a divine command (comment on 1 Sam. 1:17-18):

> ... but know this, that when Scripture (lit. "the prophecy") was written, it was written as a complete document, together with its explanation and every need, so that generations subsequent (to its composition) would not stumble in it, and from its context it lacks nothing. Moreover, one does not need to bring proofs from outside of its context, and certainly not midrash, for as for Torah—perfectly was it given (see Ps. 19:8), perfectly was it written, and there is nothing lacking in it. Whereas the midrash of

> our sages—(it was written) for the purpose of magnifying Torah and exalting it. But anyone who does not know the contextual understanding of Scripture (*peshuto shel miqra*), and prefers the midrash on some matter, is like one whom the current of a river has washed away and whom the depths of water have inundated, and who grasps at anything he can to save himself. Whereas if he had set his heart on the word of the Lord, he would have searched after the meaning of the matter and its contextual explanation—and in doing so would have fulfilled that which is taught by Scripture: *If you seek it as you do silver, and as for treasures search for it, then you will understand the reverence of the Lord, And the knowledge of God will you find* (Prov. 2:4-5).

The significance of the last part of Qara's comment should not be overlooked: the search for contextual exegesis did not represent a turning-away from religious values for these commentators. They fully appreciated "the religious significance of the *peshat*," even if they did not always articulate it.[8] While elsewhere in his commentaries, Qara expresses an appreciation for the value of midrash as a source of religious wisdom, in general he steers clear of it as a reading strategy, and relies almost exclusively on the methodology of *peshat*.

Among the northern French Rabbinic exegetes, it is in the writings of Rashbam (Samuel ben Meir, Rashi's grandson), that we find the clearest articulation of the need to distinguish between the worlds of *peshat* and *derash*. Indeed, in his strict adherence to the *peshat* methodology, Rashbam contrasts his approach to Scripture with that of everyone (!) who has come before him (see, e.g., his commentary on Exod. 3:11-12). His commentary on Gen. 37:2 contains the most extensive presentation of his understanding of the relative places of *peshat* and *derash* in Rabbinic Judaism:

> May lovers of reason understand it well that, as our rabbis tell us, no Scriptural verse ever loses its contextual meaning. Although it is also true that the main aim of the Torah is to teach us laws, doctrines and rules of conduct which are derived by hint or by the use in Scriptural verses of superfluous words or by means of the thirty-two rules of R. Eliezer b. R. Yosi the Galilean or the thirteen rules of R. Ishmael. In their piety the early scholars devoted all their time to the midrashic explanations,

which contain, indeed, the main teachings of the Torah. But, as a result, they became unfamiliar with the deeper aspects of the text's contextual meaning. Furthermore, the sages say (B. Ber. 28b): "Do not allow your children to meditate too much on the Bible." And the sages also say (B. B.M. 33a): "It is of value when one studies the Bible, but there is no greater value than when one studies Talmud." As a result of all this they were not so familiar with the contextual meaning of Scripture. As it is said in the Talmud (B. Shab. 63a): "I had reached the age of eighteen and by that time I was intimately acquainted with the whole of the Talmud, yet I had not realized that no Scriptural verse ever loses its contextual meaning." Our Master, Rabbi Solomon, my mother's father (i.e., Rashi), who illumined the eyes of all those in exile, and who wrote commentaries on the Torah, Prophets, and the Writings, also set himself the task of elucidating the contextual meaning of Scripture. And I, Samuel, son of his son-in-law Meir, may the memory of the righteous be for a blessing, argued it out with him (Rashi) and in his presence. He admitted to me that if he had the time he would have written new commentaries in accordance with the contextual interpretations being innovated every day. . . .

It is highly likely that Rashbam is not spouting pious platitudes in designating the *derash* as the most essential element in Torah study. He was a famous rabbi who wrote an important Talmud commentary, and he was known for his great piety and meticulous observance of Rabbinic norms. However, he is, as it were, making a distinction between searching (*derash*) Scripture as a source of religious edification and halakhic observance, on the one hand, and reading Scripture as an exercise of pure textual study, on the other. In his elevation of the Talmudic dictum, "no Scriptural verse ever loses its contextual meaning" (lit. "no verse ever escapes the clutches of its context;" B. Shab. 63a), Rashbam turns what is a most infrequent and unused observation in the ancient sources into the linchpin of the kind of reading he advocates.

Moreover, Rashbam goes out of his way to announce his absolute adherence to *peshat* as a reading strategy even when dealing with legal matters. In pausing before beginning to comment on the Torah's first extended section of law (Exod. 21-23), he offers a recapitulation of his purpose:

Let knowers of wisdom know and understand that I have not come to explain halakhot, even though these are the essence of Torah, as I have explained in my Genesis commentary (e.g., at Gen. 1:1; 37:2). For it is from the apparent superfluousness of Scriptural language that aggadot and halakhot are derived. Some of these can be found in the commentary of our Rabbi Solomon, my mother's father, may the memory of the righteous be for a blessing. But I have come to explain the contextual meaning of Scripture. And I will explain the laws and halakhot according to realia (lit. "the way of the world"). And (I will do this) even though (the Rabbinic understanding of) the halakhot is the essence, as the rabbis taught: "halakhah uproots Scripture" (B. Sot.16a, with emendation).

Rashbam's willingness to expound Torah against the ancient Rabbinic interpretation, even when touching on matters of law and Jewish observance, may be seen throughout his commentary. For example, he interprets what the ancient rabbis had understood as the Torah's first reference to tefillin ("It shall be for you as a sign on your hand and as a reminder between your eyes;" Exod. 13:9) as simply metaphoric language. Additionally, he comments on Gen. 1:5 ("There was setting, there was dawning: one day") that the language of Scripture clearly states that a day begins at sunrise, in contradiction to Rabbinic teaching that, for Jewish ritual purposes, a day begins the preceding evening. Indeed, this willingness to read against Rabbinic tradition occasionally served as cause for religious attacks on him by Jewish scholars who claimed that his interpretations would undermine religious observance (cf., e.g., Abraham Ibn Ezra's *Iggeret Hashabbat*; Joseph Bekhor Shor's comment on Num. 12:6).[9]

It is true that the origins of *peshat* should be sought in the heritage of Sephardic Judaism and the Islamic world, and in the complex historical processes that led to the twelfth century Renaissance in Christian Europe.[10] Other factors are bound up in the often polemical relationships among Judaism and Christianity. Faced with an ever more compelling Christian environment, both in the sense of its being culturally enriching as well as theologically challenging, the northern Rabbinic exegetes developed interpretative strategies that would meet the needs of the Jewish community. At least in part, the adoption of *peshat* by the rabbis (and of *ad litteram* by the churchmen) afforded both Jew and Christian a kind of common ground in which to engage their interfaith polemics.

However, in addition to these factors, the *peshat* methodology espoused by the northern French Rabbinic exegetes was born at least in part out of dissatisfaction with the type of reading engaged in by the ancient sages of Talmud and Midrash. In the movement away from *derash* and towards *peshat*, these medieval masters essentially expressed their independence in determining the meaning of Scripture and their unwillingness to accept the authority of the ancients when it came to the reading process.

Context as the Primary Determinant in Exegesis: In the course of commenting on a biblical text, the northern French Rabbinic exegetes occasionally find opportunities to directly address their audience and point out rhetorical features found in biblical composition. Below, we will examine several of these types of comments. In general, however, literary and rhetorical observations were for these rabbis secondary to their primary purpose, which was to explicate the *meaning* of the biblical text. Our question is: what was the principle that enabled them to determine the meaning? While there were, of course, many factors in this—knowledge of biblical Hebrew and an uncanny ability to apply other biblical texts that shed meaning on the one under review are but two of the prominent elements—the factor that towers above the rest is their developing sense of what the immediate *context* indicates the meaning to be.

In attempting to arrive at the meaning of a biblical word, verse, or longer text, the northern French Rabbinic exegetes relied on a wide variety of exegetical strategies. However, their overall approach to the explanation of a passage is determined by their sense of its contextual meaning, which they often indicate through the term *ʿinyan*. There is a long and widespread history of its use in ancient and medieval Rabbinic literature. It is often found with a meaning of "subject" or "matter" in Talmudic and Midrashic texts.[11] However, it is its appearance in sources such as the introduction to Sifra, in the "Thirteen Rules of Rabbi Ishmael," that the word becomes more directly related to our topic. There, the twelfth principle of Rabbinic exegesis formulated is: "a matter learned from its context." Sifra itself gives several examples of legal rulings derived from Scriptural context, and the ancient sages also relied on the rule in homiletical or exegetical midrashim. However, it was never systematically applied in the way that it was during the medieval period.

In his dictionary of biblical Hebrew, the *Mahberet*, the tenth century Sephardic-Jewish grammarian Menahem ibn Saruq expanded the use of *ʿinyan* into terminology more closely approximating what we would call "context" and employed a variety of formulations using the term. Since Menahem composed the *Mahberet* in Hebrew, unlike all of the other Sephardic-Jewish grammarians who wrote in Arabic, the Rabbinic exegetes of northern France had access to and made great use of this work: all of Menahem's terms and formulaic expressions for context were later used by the northern French commentators. For example, like Menahem, they all use the expression *pitrono lefi ʿinyano*, "its explanation is according to its context," and other, virtually identical formulas. As with his other exegetical and grammatical technical terminology, Menahem either developed his terminology directly from Saadia and/or from Rabbinic, Qaraite, Masoretic, and other sources that preceded him, or innovated and invented them himself.[12] While it is not our purpose to analyze the function of these and of all the other technical terminology in the *Mahberet*, it is important to see the critical nature of this source for the developing hermeneutic of the northern French exegetes. Whether as innovator or synthesizer, Menahem seems to have been a major catalyst for northern French exegesis, both in terms of the contents of the *Mahberet* and the technical language he employed.

It is in the commentaries of Rashi that we first find evidence of consistent use of the *ʿinyan* terminology. Rashi regularly turns to the twelfth rule of the *Baraita de Rabbi Ishmael* (discussed above) as an exegetical tool: in claiming that the commandment "you shall not steal" in the Decalogue (Exod. 20:13) refers to kidnapping and not material theft, he invokes the rule to demonstrate that this is so: "you must say that it is a matter learned from its context: just as *you shall not murder* (and) *you shall not commit adultery* speak of matter(s) that require a judicially imposed death penalty, so does *you shall not steal* (speak of) a matter that requires a judicially imposed death penalty." Lest there be some question of whether Rashi in fact understands the term *ʿinyan* specifically to mean "context," we may refer to the definition of the rule that he offers in his commentary to the Talmud (B. Hul. 115b): "*a matter learned from its context*: an obscure matter, in which it is not made explicit what the subject is (lit. 'what is being spoken about')—learn it from the context, the passage where what the context is referring to is written" (see also at B. Hul. 140a). The term for Rashi, therefore, clearly denotes "a frame of reference, a context."

Rashi, however, not only borrows exegetical phrases directly from Talmudic literature; he employs the formulas developed by Menahem. For example, in his comment on Dan. 6:15, when explaining an Aramaic word of whose meaning he is uncertain, he comments: "I don't know any cognate for it, but its context indicates its meaning" (see also at 2 Sam. 17:20; 2 Kgs. 17:9; Ezek. 21:20; Micah 1:10). Thus we find Rashi, like Menahem ibn Saruk before him, using the terminology of *ʿinyan* to explain difficult words.

Presumably under Rashi's impact, use of the *ʿinyan* formulas spread to, and was further applied by, the rest of the northern French school. Joseph Qara employs this terminology throughout his commentaries. One example will suffice to demonstrate a typical usage. In his commentary on Is. 13:2, Qara makes the precise meaning of an elusive phrase (which NJPS translates as "upon a bare hill"), the focus of his concern:

Many explanations have I seen for this word: There are those who interpret this as "on a hill which is situated high up, in (the sense of) in security"—which is the kingdom of Babylonia. And we have reviewed all of Scripture and we have not found that the kingdom of Babylonia is (ever depicted as) dwelling on a mountain, but rather in a valley. My uncle Rabbi Menaham (bar Helbo) interpreted (the phrase) as "on a dark hill—these are the hills of Babylonia, which are dark on account of their great height." Even according to (the principle of) a matter learned from its context I say (the phrase means) on a high mountain; anything high is called steep, as in "the steepness of a hat" (see B. Hul. 19a), whose meaning is: the height of a hat. . . .

Thus, Qara is essentially giving the same interpretation as his Uncle Menaham; both say the sense is "high."

Rashbam also relies on the formulaic expressions to articulate interpretations based on context. A typical example would be his commentary on Num. 18:19. This verse includes one of the promises of God to the hereditary Aaronide priesthood: "(All of the sacred offerings) . . . shall be an everlasting covenant of salt before the Lord. . . ." Rashbam feels intuitively that this verse is not actually referring to "real" salt:

A *covenant of salt*: it seems to me to be the language of endurance (i.e., salt preserves). And so is: (the Lord God of Israel has given the kingship) to David . . . to him and to his sons a covenant of salt (see 2 Chron. 13:5)—because their explanation is according to their context. But *you shall not omit (from your meal offering) the salt of your covenant with God* . . . (Leviticus 2:13) speaks about real salt. A *covenant of salt* (is) an enduring covenant, lasting for generations.

Similarly, in attempting to precisely explain the term for "breastpiece" in Exod. 28:4, he virtually identifies "context" with "*peshat:*" "*breastpiece*: according to the context and the *peshat*, (this is) a type of pouch or pocket." While Rashbam does not extensively employ this technical language, he is, of course, firmly rooted in the contextual exegetical approach and does on occasion rely on the "inherited" terminology (see, e.g., his commentary at Gen. 30:20; 41:23; 50:2; Lev. 19:26; Num. 7:3; 18:19; Deut. 32:24).

Eliezer of Beaugency was a mid-twelfth century exegete. Next to nothing is known of his life, although it is likely that he was a student of Rashbam. In his commentary on Ezek. 42:3, he urges his readers not to turn to any outside source for an explanation of an elusive term, in cases in which the context permits one to make a deduction about the word's meaning. With regard to a difficult phrase (NJPS: *ledge by ledge in three tiers*), he thus offers the following contextual interpretation:

> . . . with regard to the "edges"—their construction and function—their context will explain them below (see his commentary to Ezek. 42:5) as much as the mind can discern. For with regard to a word that has no cognate and which you can understand from its function in context, why cast your eyes to the ends of the earth!? Its context indicates its meaning. Behold, the verse has informed you. . . .

The formulation of his comment is reminiscent in its approach to the definition of *peshat* methodology by Joseph Qara (cited above); Eliezer uses almost the exact wording in his explanation of the Psalms passage he uses to illuminate Ezek. 20:23.

In his commentary to a famous *crux interpretum* in Amos 3:12, Eliezer makes the claim that "the most important principle in biblical exegesis is 'a matter learned from its context'" (see also his comment at Zech. 4:14). In this instance the meaning of the difficult phrase generally translated along the lines of "with the leg of a bed or the head of a couch" has eluded the commentator's precise grasp. Thus, he has to rely on his sense of the entire couplet in order to offer his interpretation:

> And similarly with regard to *or the head of a couch*, since both *a bed* and *a couch* are types of beds, and in view of the fact that they (i.e., the bed and couch) are constructed of component parts, what is called the "crown" (or "edge") of the bed is called the ("head," or "foot") of the couch.

Relying on his understanding of the entire passage (and on his sense of the parallelism in the verse), Eliezer produces a contextual interpretation of this elusive term.

He makes a similar claim in his commentary to Ezek. 1:4. While lamenting the fact that because of our (relative) lack of knowledge of biblical Hebrew, the precise force of the term *hashmal* eludes us, he does feel that the context allows him to make at least some general assumption about the word's meaning:

> We are compelled (to understand) that to a thing that is visible to us does the prophet make an analogy: *(The wheels . . . gleamed) like beryl* (Ezek. 1:16); *like the appearance of torches* (v. 13); *like a terrible frost* (v. 22); *like the appearance of lightning* (v. 14); *like burnished bronze* (v. 7); *like the appearance of the rainbow* (v. 28): all of these are visible to the world. So, too: *like the appearance of hashmal* (v. 4), this is a thing in the world, but we are not expert in the language of Scripture in so many areas, and we only have the context; but its context indicates its meaning. . . .

What is important is Eliezer's reliance on literary context to determine the meaning of a difficult word. He applies this approach to explain difficult terms in many other biblical texts (see, e.g., his commentary on Is. 9:4, 18; 65:11; Hos. 13:7; Joel 1:17).

In conclusion, all of the various formulas featuring the term *'inyan* used by the medieval grammarians and exegetes seem to have a similar function. There does not appear to be a specific type of exegetical comment in which a commentator would use any one of the variations in particular: all of the formulas seem interchangeable. However, it is important to remember that the contextual approach practiced by the school of Rashi is not only expressed when the technical terminology is employed. It should be apparent that the attempt in the overwhelming majority of comments is to offer an explanation of the passage under consideration that is contextual in nature. However, it is mainly when coming to a difficult word or phrase that the formulaic expressions are applied.

The Redaction of the Biblical Book: In engaging in contextual reading, the twelfth century northern French Rabbinic exegetes also turned their attention to more global compositional issues: the literary arrangement and redaction of the Biblical books. Accordingly, they deduced that the books of the Bible underwent a process of redaction before achieving their final status in the canon of Jewish Scriptures. While they differ slightly in the terminology they employ to describe the figure of the redactor, these exegetes each share the view of the human, non-prophetic redactor who did more than simply serve as the receptacle of divine writ. Rather, the redactor of each biblical book gathered up the words and speeches of the various prophets, edited, and, indeed, composed the books that constitute the Hebrew Bible. These redactors approached the text they had received as holy writ, but that did not prevent them from arranging the material according to the various literary principles and/or criteria for editing that they had adopted. Moreover, the northern French exegetes understood that the biblical redactors operated in what modern scholarship generally construes as two central but distinct areas. The first of these is biblical poetics, in which the commentators included such concerns as the order and arrangement of verses and chapters, certain aesthetic and/or rhetorical devices concerned with the composition of the text, and other literary issues. The second of these central concerns is connected with issues more commonly associated under the rubric "redaction," such as editing an already finished work and adding supplementary material to a completed text at a later date. While contemporary Christian exegetes occasionally employ two separate terms to indicate these editorial and compositional concerns, namely *scriptor* and *auctor*, we will see that the Rabbinic exegetes do not readily distinguish between these activities. On the contrary, they specifically attributed to the biblical redactors both rhetorical and compositional roles, as well as those more strictly associated with editing.

Apparently Rashi was the first of the northern French Rabbinic exegetes to point to an explicit occasion of the redaction of a biblical text. In his commentary to Judges 5:31, Rashi felt that the final four Hebrew words of the chapter, which are presented in the Masoretic text as integral to the Song of Deborah, are not really part of the Song. He glosses:

> *And the land was quiet*: these are not the words of Deborah; rather they are from the redactor [lit. "writer"] of the book [*kotev hassefer*].

Rashi thus makes a distinction for his readers between the author of a composi-

tion (in this case, Deborah) and the redactor responsible for the placement of the song into its literary surroundings. And who is the redactor? Let us observe that Rashi does not explicitly adopt here the position of the Babylonian Talmud that the prophet Samuel was the author of Judges (B. B.B. 14b-15a). Instead, he relates the composition of the book to an anonymous "writer" or "redactor."

While Rashi distinguishes between the author of at least part of a book (the Song of Deborah) and that book's redactor, it appears that his grandson, Rashbam was the first among the northern French Rabbinic exegetes who explicitly articulated the process of redaction of an entire book of the Bible: Ecclesiastes. This is clear from his commentary on the *incipit* of the book, "the words of Koheleth: Vanity of vanities . . ." Rashbam comments: "(the verses), *the words of Koheleth* (i.e., 1:1) and *vanity of vanities* (1:2), were not said by Koheleth, but by the one who redacted [lit.: 'arranged;' Heb.: *sidder*] the words as they are (presently found in the book)." Similarly, at Ecc. 12:8, Rashbam writes: "now the book is completed. And those who redacted it [Heb.: *sidderuhu*] speak from here on." Thus Rashbam presents Ecclesiastes as a composition presented within a framework of two introductory verses and six concluding verses.[13]

For Eliezer of Beaugency, as for his teacher Rashbam, the redactor is not identical with the prophet whose speeches are included in the book that bears his name. Rather, Eliezer envisions a two-tiered compositional process: the prophet speaks the word of God and may even participate in the process of composing his speeches into written form. Following this, a redactor gathers the speeches of the prophet together, and arranges them in book form.

In his commentary on Ezekiel 1:1, Eliezer specifically refers to the responsibility of a redactor for the present composition of the Biblical text:

> *And I saw visions of God . . . I looked, and lo, a stormy wind . . .* (Ezek. 1:1,4): Ezekiel's words did not continue from the beginning, and even his name he did not make explicit, since the context of the book will make it clear below, as in *and Ezekiel shall become a*

portent for you (Ezek. 24:24). And, relying on this, he allowed himself to abbreviate, as I have told you with regard to *(in the) thirtieth year*, that (there) the content of the book provides the proof for its (meaning, i.e., of the "thirtieth year"). But the redactor [Heb.: *hassofer*] who wrote all of his words together added to what (Ezekiel) had left unclear and abbreviated, in these two verses.

This comment is important on several grounds. First, whereas Rashi had assigned the third-person narration in vv. 2-3 to the Holy Spirit, Eliezer attributes them to a redactor. Thus, the comment demonstrates Eliezer's exegetical boldness in contradicting Rashi's authority.[14] But more significantly, the comment makes clear how Eliezer has related to the role of the redactor in the process of composition of the Biblical text. Eliezer has depicted a redactor taking prophetic material in some sort of prior stage, adding to it and compiling a finished literary product. This prior stage was not necessarily "raw" material. Rather, the redactor had at his disposal oracular material and background information, arranged in some way that is no longer possible for us to retrieve. It may have been "finished" as discrete, short pieces, but it was not in *book* form. But the excerpt is important for another reason. According to Eliezer, the one who does this work is separate from the prophet, or, to put it another way, the prophet is not the author of the text. To be sure, the Talmudic rabbis had explicitly stated that "Ezekiel didn't write the book called by his name" (B. B.B. 14b-15a). However, Eliezer does not deem it sufficient to attribute the book to "the men of the Great Assembly," or some other "traditional" type of designation. Instead, perhaps with the example of Baruch, Jeremiah's secretary, in mind (Jer. 36:26), he explicitly employs the term "redactor" to denote the human writer responsible for the production of the biblical book.

In at least one case, one of the northern French exegetes explicitly contradicts the Talmudic tradition on the authorship of a biblical book. In his comment on 1 Sam. 9:9, Joseph Qara sees the anachronism in the biblical narrator's disclosure that "formerly in Israel, when a man went to inquire of God, he would say, 'come, let us go to the seer,' for the prophet of today was formerly called a seer." He comments:

> When Scripture says "for the prophet of today was formerly called a seer" . . . you can deduce that when this book was written, they had already reverted to calling a "seer" a prophet. It follows that this book was not written in the days of Samuel. For when you review the entire Bible you will not find that a prophet is called a "seer," except here . . . you can deduce that it is the generation of Samuel that is called "formerly in Israel," or the generation following Samuel, and it is about that generation that Scripture says "for the prophet of today was formerly called a seer." Our rabbis, may their memory be a blessing, said that Samuel wrote his book (B. B.B. 14b-15a)—may God who gives light to the earth turn darkness into light and rough places into level ground (see Is. 42:16)!

Thus Joseph Qara implies that some person other than the biblical prophet authored the book of Samuel.

We saw that in his commentary on Ecclesiastes, Rashbam cast the work of the author ("Koheleth") within the framework established by the redactor(s). In his Torah commentary, he often casts Moses in the role of the redactor of God's Torah. In his comment on Gen. 19:37, Rashbam explains the phrase "until this day" as referring to the time of the one who set the text in writing—i.e., to the time of Moses: "Until this day: (i.e.), in the days of Moses. And so (should we understand) every (occurrence of) *until this day*—(it means) until the days of the redactor [Heb.: *hassofer*] who wrote down the passage." Thus we may say that for Rashbam, while God is undoubtedly the divine "source" of the Torah, Moses functions as God's redactor, as it were; Moses composes God's divine, "oral Torah," into the human, "written Torah."

This is particularly evident in Rashbam's commentary on the opening passage of Genesis. In discussing his view of the arrangement of the biblical text, Rashbam often explains that it is composed by Moses according to the principle of narrative prolepsis, that is, "any narrative maneuver that consists of narrating or evoking in advance an event that will take place later."[15] Rashbam explicitly states that Moses placed the entire Creation narrative at the beginning of the Torah for the sake of the Israelites at Mount Sinai, who when hearing the fourth pronouncement of the Decalogue, would have been otherwise astonished that God had created the world in such an ordered fashion:[16]

> The following is the true contextual meaning of the passage, which follows the Scriptural pattern of regularly anticipating and explaining some matter which, though unnecessary to the immediate context, serves the purpose of elucidating some matter to be mentioned further on, in another passage. For example, when the text writes (Gen. 9:18), "Shem, Ham and Japheth," why does it then proceed to write, "Ham being the father of Canaan"? It is because it is written later (Gen. 9:25), "Cursed be Canaan." Had we not known beforehand who Canaan was, we would not have understood why Noah cursed him. . . . Similarly, this type of anticipatory style can be found in many places. Moreover, this entire section, concerning the six days of creation, was also written by Moses for anticipatory purposes, so as to explain to the reader what God said when he gave the Torah (Exod. 20:8-11), "Remember the Sabbath day and keep it holy . . . for in six days did YHWH make heaven and earth and sea, and all that is in them, and he rested on the seventh day." For this reason it is written (Gen. 1:31), "there was evening and there was morning, *the* sixth day," a reference to that same sixth day, the end of the creation process, of which God spoke when he gave the Torah. That is why Moses related this entire chapter about creation—in order to inform them that what God said was true. In other words, Moses said, "Do you think that this world has forever existed in the way that you now see it, filled with all good things? That is not the case. Rather, *bereshit bara elohim*—i.e., at the beginning of the creation of the heaven and the earth, when the uppermost heavens and the earth had already been created for some undetermined length of time—then, "the earth" which already existed, "was unformed and void"—i.e., there was nothing in it.

This is by no means the only text on which Rashbam assigns to Moses the status of redactor (see also, e.g., his commentary on Gen. 31:33; 37:2).[17] In other words, it is Rashbam's view that Moses, in his capacity as redactor, has determined the order of presentation of material in the Torah of which the author—ultimately—is God.

There are even cases when the Rabbinic exegetes of northern France are willing to consider certain, specifically anachronistic verses as having been written after the time of Moses. A prime example of this is seen in Rashbam's commentary on Num. 22:1: "The Israelites then marched on and encamped in the steppes of Moab, across the Jordan from Jericho." The phrase "across the Jordan from Jericho" only makes sense to a writer who is already living in the land of Israel, whereas Moses, of course, never makes it that far. Rashbam, apparently detecting the anachronistic nature of the verse, comments: "It makes sense to understand the phrase 'across the Jordan' to have been written only after they had crossed the Jordan, for only to them are the steppes of Moab called 'across the Jordan'" (ignoring the emendation in Rosin's edition).[18] This audacious comment shows how far Rashbam was willing to go in search of a truly contextual reading.

This type of audacity is shared by Joseph of Orleans, known by the nickname of Bekhor Shor (after Deut. 33:17). He was a younger contemporary of Eliezer of Beaugency (see Bekhor Shor's commentary on Lev. 22:25). Reportedly a student of Rabbenu Tam, the younger brother of Rashbam, he was also likely to have been a disciple of Rashbam himself. He employs terminology similar to that of Rashbam and Eliezer to indicate the redactor. An instance in which we can see this is found in Bekhor Shor's commentary on Gen. 32:21. In that passage, Jacob is sending tribute to Esau his brother, upon his return home from twenty years of labor for his father-in-law, Laban, in Aram. Jacob has instructed messengers to inform Esau that the gifts are from his brother Jacob: "thus shall you say: 'indeed, your servant Jacob is right behind us,' for he said if I propitiate him with presents in advance, and then face him, perhaps he will show me favor." The question, of course, concerns the latter phrase, following the words "for he said:" who said them? Are these words a continuation of Jacob's instructions to the messengers (Ramban), or are they perhaps better understood as Jacob's own internal dialogue (Rashbam, Ibn Ezra)? Bekhor Shor has another idea:

> *For he said*: The redactor [Heb.: *ba'al hasse-fer*] has made this explicit. For this is the reason that Jacob had done all of this, to cause to pass away from Esau's face a countenance of anger, if he had intended evil towards Jacob. But the shepherds didn't say this to Esau, for if they had it would have reminded him of his prior enmity and hatred.

From other comments of Bekhor Shor, it seems clear that he, like Rashbam, considers Moses to be the redactor (see also Bekhor Shor's comment on Gen. 35:20, and the gloss in his commentary at Gen. 19:37). This is seen clearly in his comment on Deut. 1:1, where Bekhor Shor indicates just such a role for Moses:

> *These are the words that Moses spoke to all Israel*: Around the time of his death, he redacted [*sidder*] the Torah for them, so that the commandments would not be forgotten. . . . Therefore he enumerated the places wherein Torah that he wanted to redact [*le-sadder*] had been given, for the Torah was given in many places.

Likewise, in his commentary on Num. 20:8, Bekhor Shor claims that the narrative about the Waters of Meribah in Num. 20:1-13 is an alternative version of the *Massa* and *Meribah* narrative in Exod. 17:1-7.

> As I understand it, this is the same incident as in *Beshallah*, in which it is written: *strike the rock, that water may come out.* However, there it relates how the Holy One, Blessed be God, sustains Israel with the manna, the quail, and water in the desert; afterwards he wrote [*katav*] each one in its place. But know that it is one, this incident and that one . . . And thus it is in many portions, that he obscures his words in one place and makes them explicit in another place.

In drawing the conclusion that the two incidents are one, Bekhor Shor reveals his understanding of biblical discourse as being determined by a compositional technique: the Numbers text presents the incident in its sequential position in the wilderness narrative, whereas Exodus joins that episode to thematically related ones.[19] Although he does not employ in this comment one of the

technical designations for redaction, in light of what we have already seen in the writings of the northern French exegetes it seems reasonable to conclude that Bekhor Shor considers Moses as the party responsible for that arrangement.

Thus, the northern French Rabbinic exegetes all held that the biblical text underwent a process of redaction. Their comments are expressive of their understanding that, with regard to the Prophets and Writings at least, a human redactor, with whom God did not "speak," was responsible for the creation of the books of the Bible and for the inclusion in the Biblical texts of additional verses of his own volition. With regard to the Torah, it seems that they uniformly held to the position that Moses functioned as the redactor of God's own Divine instruction.

Compositional Techniques: We have already seen that the Rabbinic exegetes of twelfth century northern France attributed the arrangement of the biblical text to a human redactor who composed his work according to a variety of principles. Moreover, these exegetes were quite innovative in describing many compositional techniques employed by the redactors, and they employed consistent technical terminology to describe them.

In addition to Rashbam's observation of the technique of including anticipatory information in biblical narrative (cited above), the exegetes were aware of different types of narrative and chronological disorder.[20] Occasionally, a medieval commentator is faced with blatant temporal disorder. This is often produced by the redactor of the Biblical text, who will sometimes provide detailed chronological information relative to when a narrative event or a prophetic speech actually "happened." That narratives do not always relate their events in chronological order is of course not an insight that originates in medieval times. But the old Rabbinic rule "there is no early or late in the Torah," which had been infrequently invoked in the ancient sources, had already been expanded by Rashi, who used it over fifteen times in his biblical commentaries to explain apparent disruption in the narrative order (see, e.g., at Exod. 19:11; 31:18; Num. 9:1). Rashbam, too, used the phrase at least once (see at Lev. 10:1-3). With these two influential predecessors having already paved the way, it is not surprising that the technique of presenting events out of chronological sequence was also noticed by later commentators such as Eliezer of Beaugency.

Let us first consider Eliezer's comment on Ezek. 29:1, which he immediately identifies as being out of chronological order. Eliezer notes that the heading of 26:1 (i.e., an earlier chapter) states that the prophecy against Tyre took place "in the eleventh year," whereas this one against Egypt took place "in the tenth year." He writes:

> In the tenth year: (i.e.,) before the prophecy against Tyre (Ezek. 26:1-28:19). But on account of the punishment (inflicted against) the rest of the nations that reviled and opened wide their mouths against Jerusalem (after Psalms 44:17 and 35:26), the redactor placed the prophecy against Tyre with them as well; since she (Tyre), too, reviled (Jerusalem) and rejoiced in her downfall, she was punished like them.

Ezek. 25 contains oracles against many of the nations surrounding Israel, which likewise rejoiced in Jerusalem's destruction; these oracles are similar in style and tone to the one against Tyre beginning in Ezek. 26. According to Eliezer, this similarity warrants a disruption in the chronological order. Thus, he establishes that for reasons of thematic congruity, the redactor has placed this prophecy against Egypt out of chronological order, after the oracle against Tyre. In other words, according to Eliezer's understanding of Biblical poetics, historical verisimilitude (in this case, chronological sequence) takes a back seat to rhetorical concerns.

Like his teacher Rashbam, Eliezer is aware of the compositional technique of prolepsis. Eliezer will apply this principle not only to *events*, but also to elements of a prophetic *speech* which seem out of sequence. Moreover, Eliezer uses the technical language developed by Rashbam in making observations about narrative pro-

lepsis. An example of this is found in his comment on Is. 37:38:

> . . . and his son Esarhaddon reigned after him: and nevertheless, powerful Assyrians ceased coming into the Land, because the fear of the God of Israel had fallen upon them. And that is what it says below: and from the hand of the King of Assyria I will save you (Isaiah 38:6). And if (Scripture) had not anticipated to say and his son Esarhaddon reigned after him, you would have wondered from whom Hezekiah was in fear, that God would need to strengthen his heart.

In other words, Eliezer understands the phrase *and in those days . . .* (38:1ff.) *sequentially*; the prophecy in 38:6 only refers to Sennacherib's *son*. Thus, the reassurance of 38:6 makes no sense after Sennacherib has left the scene; therefore, the text anticipates by relating that Esarhaddon continued the dynasty and policies of Sennacherib. The implication is that if it weren't for God's providential care over Judah, Esarhaddon, who was his father's son, would have done the same as Sennacherib. Thus, Eliezer reads the reference of Esarhaddon's succession of his father in Isaiah 37:38 as *proleptic* in regard to the prophecy in 38:6 about protecting Hezekiah from the king of Assyria. This, according to Eliezer, enables the reader to know in advance about which king the prophet is speaking.

Another compositional technique of which the exegetes were aware was the "summary-elaboration" pattern. Gen. 28:10 may be considered an example of this literary feature. The verse, which begins the narrative about Jacob's travels to Aram, states that "Jacob left Beer Sheba and went towards Haran." Following this verse, the narrative proceeds to give the details of Jacob's journey (Gen. 28:11-29:1). Bekhor Shor's comment on Gen. 28:10 reflects a sensitivity to the pattern: "*Jacob left Beer Sheba and went towards Haran*: and afterwards (the text) goes on to render in detail how he went and what happened to him on the journey." Virtually the identical literary observation and the language for expressing it are found in Rashbam's commentary on Job 3:3. There, in considering the relationship of the poem's first verse to the entire passage, Rashbam explains that the verse there gives a summary of Job's curse of the day on which he was born and the night during which he was conceived, and that the verses that follow elaborate on this curse and make it more explicit both with regard to the day and to the night: "*And the night which said*: in abbreviated fashion he curses here the day of his birth and the night of his conception, and afterwards he recapitulates and elaborates his curse with regard to each one separately."

This type of reading seems to show the influence of the ancient Rabbinic rule of interpretation, which states that Scripture may be interpreted by means of "a general statement, and a specific statement" (see the Tannaitic "Thirteen Rules of Rabbi Ishmael" in the introduction to Sifra; and the Gaonic "Thirty-Two Rules for Aggadic Exegesis"). This rule states: "(the narrative portions of Scripture may be interpreted according to) an overview that is followed by a story, and which (story) is itself only a detailed accounting of the first (verse, i.e., the overview) . . . the listener might think that (the second) is a new story, but it is none other than a detailed account of the first." According to this particular rule, then, Eliezer of Beaugency's comment on Is. 7:2 is a parade example. The previous verse (7:1) relates that the forces of the Aram-Israelite alliance "marched upon Jerusalem to attack it, but they were not able to attack it." This is formulated in standard Biblical Hebrew prose, intended to narrate a completed action sequence. However, in the subsequent verse (7:2), it is related that "when it had been related to the House of David that Aram had allied itself with Ephraim (Israel)," the people and the royal house became terrified. Thus, the second verse relates events which occurred prior to the narration of 7:1. According to Eliezer, the redactor gives a summary of the events in the first verse. Then, beginning in the second verse, he relates the events that precede the focus of the summary:

> *Aram had allied*: "The kingdom of Aram has allied and joined with Ephraim, and they have made an alliance against you." Now they had not yet attacked him, but the narrator's way is to relate at the beginning of his words the main topic of the matter in

abbreviated form . . . and then later make the matter explicit. First he said that Rezin and Pekah had attacked, and only later does he elaborate the matter: for when they joined forces to attack the House of David in war, it was told to (the House of) David, causing his (Ahaz's) heart to tremble; then he (Isaiah) told him not to fear. . . .

This, then, is an example in which Eliezer seems to adapt one of the "Thirty-Two Rules" as an aid in determining the meaning and structure of Biblical literature.

Eliezer is often of the opinion that the *presentation* of material is a matter of *discursive style*, performed by the redactor. The "theoretical statement," for expressing what we may regard as Eliezer's position on the redactional process leading to the formation of biblical composition, is found in his comment on Is. 20:2. The specific feature he addresses, narrative analepsis (or "flashback"), is actually the opposite of the anticipatory principle, discussed above. In this chapter, it is related that "in the year that the Tartan came to Ashdod" (v. 1), God had told Isaiah to "untie the sackcloth from your loins." The question for the commentator arises from the lack of any previous command of God to the prophet to put on sackcloth, or of any narrative statement that he had in fact done so. This gap gives Eliezer the opportunity to generalize about Biblical discourse:

> And if you should say: where did the text relate to us that he had put on sackcloth? There are many statements in Scripture which the text doesn't relate at first, and only informs you about them in its (own) way. And the reason for this, is that it did not want to interrupt its narrative sequence on this account, and no other place for it presented itself. And the sackcloth of Jehoram will prove (the point): Where did the text inform you that he was wearing sackcloth? When it said: *(as he walked on the wall), the people could see he was wearing sackcloth underneath* (2 Kings 6:30).

In this comment, Eliezer is able to extract from the passage an important deduction about biblical narrative poetics. With regard to Jehoram, explains Eliezer, the text doesn't inform the reader towards the *beginning* of that section of the narrative (2 Kings 6:26) that the king was wearing sackcloth; the reader only learns this fact when the people do, in verse 30, as they watch the king from beneath the city wall. Likewise in the case of Isaiah: the reader only learns that Isaiah had been wearing sackcloth through God's command to him to remove it. Literary "facts" such as these enable Eliezer to make the observation that for some reason (he doesn't articulate one), Scripture doesn't choose to "interrupt" its own narration in order to provide all of the necessary details, but will choose to do so at a moment which it deems opportune. In fact, Eliezer understands that Scripture occasionally orders its narrative in such a way that the reader only becomes aware of information as that information becomes available to characters in the narrative (see also his comment on Jonah 1:10).

Additionally, the northern French exegetes exhibit awareness of the principle of resumptive repetition, a device often employed by the redactor to express synchroneity and simultaneity in biblical narrative.[21] An example of this may be found in Rashi's commentary on Exod. 6:29-30 (although it is likely that at least part of this comment has been interpolated into Rashi's commentary by a later hand, perhaps from Rashbam's commentary). The two verses seem like an inverse recapitulation of Exod. 6:11-12; an archival genealogical list intervenes. Rashi notes the connection between the two sections, and understands them to be in fact the same Divine speech:

> *And YHWH spoke* (v. 29): This is the very same statement made above: *come speak to Pharaoh, King of Egypt . . .* (v. 11). But since it had interrupted the matter, so as to present the lineage of Moses and Aaron, it repeated the same matter so as to begin with it (again). *And Moses said to YHWH* (v. 30): This is the same statement that he said above: *Now, the Israelites have not listened to me . . .* (v. 12). But Scripture repeated it here, since it had interrupted the matter. This is the *modus* of Scripture. It is like a person who says, "let us go back over the initial points" (i.e., "let's recapitulate").

Thus, Rashi understands a resumptive repetition has taken place, on account of the genealogy that interrupted the narrative sequence. Scripture "repeats" the two speeches to indicate their simultaneity, that had been interrupted by the archival list.

Eliezer of Beaugency likewise understands the principal of resumptive repetition. For example, in the opening chapter of Ezekiel, Eliezer notices that elements of Ezekiel's inaugural vision which are narrated at the beginning of the prophecy are mentioned again at its end. Thus, in v. 4, Ezekiel mentions the *hashmal* that he places at the center of his vision: "and from its midst, like the color of amber, from the midst of the fire." In v. 27, at the end of the opening narration, the prophet returns to this element: "And I saw (something) like amber, like the appearance of fire surrounding it . . ." In his comment on 1:27, Eliezer writes: "he returns to the beginning of the vision to complete it, and to make explicit things which he had heard from it." Likewise, in his comment on 1:4, he makes a similar comment about the "radiance" in v. 4 being mentioned again and explained in 1:27-28: "and the appearance of radiance is made explicit at the end of the narration (as being) like the appearance of the rainbow." Again in his comment on v. 4, when he discusses the fire that Ezekiel sees towards the center of his vision, Eliezer notes that this, too, is made more explicit at the end of the chapter: "and this is what he says below *like the appearance of fire encased around it* (1:27)." Thus, what Eliezer is in fact concluding is that Ezekiel, having observed the divine vision and the flashing fire at its core (1:4), begins to describe the phenomenal sight; when he is ready to relate the message which God has transmitted to him (beginning in chapter two), he resumes describing that part of the vision with which he began (1:27), i.e., the center, for it was from that center that he heard the divine voice (1:28 end). In other words, Eliezer is saying that the narration of 1:4 is resumed in 1:27; it is the *repetition of the language* that is used to signal the fact of that resumption. Thus, the bulk of the description of the divine "chariot" and of the animal figures associated with it (vv. 5-26) is in Eliezer's estimation an "interruption" (not to say interpolation) of the main narrative, which is to describe the divine *locus* from which he receives his prophetic charge.

Eliezer also finds resumptive repetition

in Ezek. 10:4. However, to understand the force of his comment, we have to consider first Ezekiel's vision of Jerusalem's destruction at God's hands in the preceding chapter. In 9:1-2, God had begun the command to the six "men" to destroy the city and its inhabitants, which command is continued and completed in 9:3b-7. In the midst of this portion of the narrative (9:3a), the prophet had paused, as it were, to observe the movement of the "physical presence" of God from its prior position: "now the presence of the God of Israel had alighted from the cherub on which it had rested, to the platform of the Temple." However, no further description of the consequences of God's motion is offered at this stage of the narration. In chapter 10, when Ezekiel more directly concerns himself with the physical manifestation of God's presence in his vision, he returns to this (previous) moment in time, in order to "fill in" that which was left undescribed earlier:

> And when the presence of YHWH rose from the cherub to the platform of the Temple, the Temple was filled with the cloud and the court filled up with the radiant presence of YHWH. And the sound of the cherubs' wings was heard as far as the outer court, like the voice of El Shaddai when He speaks.

Eliezer is aware of the potential to misunderstand the narrative as chronologically disordered, but prefers to understand the passage as a resumed narrative from the same moment in time:

> And it's impossible to say that *at this point* the presence of the Lord rose from off the cherub to the platform of the Temple, since (Scripture) had already said (9:3): *now the presence of the God of Israel had alighted from the cherub on which it had rested, to the platform of the Temple.* Moreover, we have not seen that (the presence) had returned to the cherub subsequently, that (Scripture) should now say "and it rose from off the cherub." Additionally: why should it (now) alight (on) to the platform of the Temple? It's getting ready to leave! The entire sequence is confused with this (kind of reading). But this is the solution: *when (the presence of the Lord) rose* (10:4)—(should be understood) as I have explained. And since (Scripture) has said that when (God's presence) was getting ready to leave, the courtyard filled up with

the cloud, it tells you what had happened in the beginning (9:3), when it lifted off from the platform.

To summarize the preceding, then, this is how Eliezer presents the resumptive repetition: the events of 10:6ff. resume or express simultaneity with those of 9:4ff., with 9:3 and 10:4 providing the "fulcrum" around which the resumed or simultaneous narrative is centered. In other words, the event described in 9:3 *is identical to* that which is described in 10:4. Through a deft juxtaposition of words, earlier in his commentary, Eliezer had explained that the occurrence of the verb "to go up" in 10:4 should be understood as identical to the verb "to arise" in 9:3: "then the presence of the Lord *rose and alighted*—beforehand—from off the cherub, to the platform of the Temple. . . ." It is this identification in Eliezer's mind between the two semantically-linked Hebrew words that enable him to consider this a resumed narration. Although we do not find him using the technical language here that we have seen him occasionally use elsewhere to describe resumptive repetition, that does not rule out his reading of this as a resumed narration. More significantly, the expression he employs makes it clear that he reads this as one single narrative, which includes within it two simultaneous "sub-narratives."

Another compositional device of which Eliezer is aware is the inclusio pattern. Simply put, inclusio occurs when a word or words found in the beginning of a literary unit, are repeated at the end of the unit. To understand how Eliezer relates to and describes inclusio, let us look at an example found in Ezek. 32. The chapter opens (v. 2) with God's command to the prophet to "intone a dirge over Pharaoh king of Egypt." At the conclusion of the lament, the word "dirge" returns: "this is a dirge, and they shall intone it" (32:16). Alone among the northern French commentators, Eliezer remarks on the closure created by this repetition: "*this is a dirge*: that with which he begins (the composition), he (also) concludes." While one might have hoped for a lengthier discursive analysis of the functions of the device, his observation is an undeniable acknowledgment that a literary device is at play. The fact that the following verse

(32:17) features a (presumably new) dated prophecy only strengthens the force of Eliezer's observation.

Another example of inclusio of which Eliezer is aware is contained in Ezek. 36:22-32. Here, the prophet both begins and ends a speech with an announcement that God acts not on Israel's but on God's own behalf: "not for your sake will I act, O House of Israel." Eliezer's comment on Ezek. 36:32 at once explains the function of the repeated phrase and demonstrates that he considers vv. 22-32 to be a discrete unit of discourse: "that with which it began, it concludes, and in this way has the prophet expressed himself in many places." The second half of Eliezer's comment indicates that he is aware that this is a recurrent technique in Ezekiel. Thus we have seen that while Eliezer seems to have no difficulty recognizing inclusio as a compositional technique in both poetic and prose contexts, and repeatedly calls the reader's attention to this device, he does not seem to be inclined to derive any semantic conclusions from his observations. In other words, on the question of the explicit relationship between structure and meaning (at least in reference to this particular device), Eliezer is silent. However, we may consider there to be an *implied* exegetical conclusion. Through use of what we may regard as his technical vocabulary for relating to the phenomenon of inclusio, Eliezer indicates to the reader that the repetition is a way of closing a unit. Thus, while his comments may not have *semantic* import, they do have *rhetorical, discursive* import.

Conclusions: The components of *peshat* exegesis examined here do not by any means exhaust the subject. For example, the understanding of the northern French exegetes of the principle of parallelism in poetic compositions and their awareness of rhetorical dimensions in biblical discourse themselves merit further consideration. However, enough has been demonstrated here to illustrate the exegetes' sensitivity to rhetorical factors. In their identification of context as the most important determinant in meaning; in their understanding that the biblical canon had undergone a process of redaction; and in their attention to compo-

sitional technique in biblical literature, the northern French Rabbinic exegetes transformed the concept of what reading a text meant. Given this achievement, it is surprising that the *peshat* school declined almost as quickly as it arose. Moreover, the reasons for this are not altogether clear. Some attribute it to the shift in Christian society from twelfth century humanism to scholasticism, mysticism and allegory in the thirteenth century. Others have theorized that while *peshat* held sway with the intellectual elite, the masses found it dry, and so ultimately the course was abandoned.[22] A major factor undoubtedly was the Christian destruction of European Jewry, with attendant communal dislocation and book burnings on a large scale (not even to speak of pogroms); these all took their toll on *peshat* scholarship, as countless unique manuscripts were likely destroyed. But whatever the causes, the results are clear: other than the occasional *peshat* reading found in compilatory exegetical works such as Hizkuni, or in multivalent and "four fold" commentaries such as Nahmanides and Bahya ben Asher, the thirteenth century saw Jewish biblical learning turn to tosafistic exegesis, gematriot and other types of numerology, and mysticism.

And what of the "common ground" achieved between Jews and Christians in their attention to contextual reading? Through their participation in Jewish-Christian dialogue, the northern French Rabbinic exegetes reviewed here indirectly contributed to the immense changes in European intellectual life that occurred in succeeding centuries. While the tragic fact that Christians destroyed Jewish society—and, quite possibly, Jewish *peshat* scholarship—in Western Europe from the thirteenth to the fifteenth centuries should not be overlooked, the fact remains that for about one-hundred years, there was much productive intellectual contact between the two communities. During this period, when the leading intellectual voices in the Jewish community of northern France engaged the Bible and other sources of Jewish tradition, they eschewed the traditional, midrashic approach, and instead practiced *peshat*, contextual reading.

Bibliography

Abulafia, Anna Sapir, *Christians and Jews in the Twelfth-Century Renaissance* (London and New York, 1995).

Chazan, Robert, *Medieval Jewry in Northern France* (Baltimore and London, 1973).

Gelles, Benjamin, *Peshat and Derash in the Exegesis of Rashi* (Leiden, 1981).

Lazarus-Yafeh, Hava, *Intertwined Worlds: Medieval Islam and Bible Criticism* (Princeton, 1992).

Simon, Uriel, "The Religious Significance of the Peshat," in *Tradition* 23, no. 2 (1988), pp. 41-63.

Notes

[1] See Avraham Grossman, "The School of Literal Exegesis in Northern France," in Magne Saebo, ed., *Hebrew Bible/Old Testament: The History of Its Interpretation. Volume I: From the Beginnings to the Middle Ages (until 1300). Part 2: The Middle Ages* (Gottingen, 2000), pp. 321-71; Hava Lazarus-Yafeh, *Intertwined Worlds: Medieval Islam and Bible Criticism* (Princeton, 1992); Theodore Pulcini, *Exegesis as Polemical Discourse: Ibn Hazm on Jewish and Christian Scriptures* (Atlanta, 1998).

[2] See Beryl Smalley, *The Study of the Bible in the Middle Ages* (Oxford, 1952).

[3] Jerome Taylor, ed. and trans., *The Didascalicon of Hugh of St. Victor* (New York and London, 1961).

[4] Ivan Illich, *In the Vineyard of the Text: A Commentary to Hugh's Didascalicon* (Chicago and London, 1993).

[5] See Grossman, op. cit.

[6] Edward L. Greenstein, "Sensitivity to Language in Rashi's Commentary on the Torah," in Mayer I. Gruber, ed., *The Solomon Goldman Lectures VI* (Chicago, 1993), pp. 51-71.

[7] See Sarah Kamin, "Rashi's Exegetical Categorization with Respect to the Distinction between Peshat and Derash," in *Immanuel* 11 (1980), pp. 16-32; Benjamin Gelles, *Peshat and Derash in the Exegesis of Rashi* (Leiden, 1981).

[8] See Uriel Simon, "The Religious Significance of the Peshat," in *Tradition* 23, no. 2 (1988), pp. 41-63.

[9] Uriel Simon, "The Exegetical Method of Abraham Ibn Ezra, as Revealed in Three Interpretations of a Biblical Passage," in *Bar Ilan* 3 (1965), pp. 92-138 [Hebrew]; Sarah Kamin, "The Polemic against Allegory in the Commentary of Rabbi Joseph Bekhor Shor," in Yair Zakovitch, ed., *Jews and Christians Interpret the Bible* (Jerusalem, 1991), pp. 73-98 [Hebrew].

[10] See Grossman, op. cit.

[11] Benjamin Zeev Bacher, *Midrashic Terminology. Volume I: Tannaitic Terms; Volume II: Amoraitic Terms* (Jerusalem, 1970), 2 vols. [Hebrew].

[12] See Angel Saenz-Badillos, ed., *Menahem Ben Saruq: Mahberet* (Granada, 1986).

[13] Sara Japhet and Robert Salters, eds., *The Commentary of R. Samuel Ben Meir (Rashbam) on Qoheleth* (Jerusalem and Leiden, 1985).

[14] Edward L. Greenstein, "Medieval Bible Commentaries," in Barry Holtz, ed., *Back to the Sources* (New York, 1984), pp. 212-59.

[15] Gerard Genette, *Narrative Discourse: An Essay in Method* (Ithaca, 1980); Nahum Sarna, "The Anticipatory Use of Information as a Literary Feature of the Genesis Narrative," in R.E. Friedman, ed., *The Creation of Sacred Literature* (Los Angeles, 1981), pp. 76-82.

[16] See Kamin, "Rashi's Exegetical Categorization."

[17] Martin I. Lockshin, ed., *Rabbi Samuel Ben Meir's Commentary on Genesis: An Annotated Translation* (Lewiston, Lamperer, and Queenston, 1989), Vol. 5.

[18] Martin I. Lockshin, *Rashbam's Commentary on Leviticus and Numbers: An Annotated Translation* (Providence, 2001), p. 260, n. 60.

[19] See Greenstein, "Medieval Bible Commentaries."

[20] David A. Glatt, *Chronological Displacement in Biblical and Related Literatures* (Atlanta, 1993).

[21] Shemaryahu Talmon, "The Presentation of Synchroneity and Simultaneity in Biblical Narrative," in Joseph Heinemann and Shmuel Werses, eds., *Studies in Hebrew Narrative Art Throughout the Ages* (Jerusalem, 1978), pp. 9-26.

[22] See Grossman, op. cit.

ROBERT A. HARRIS

BIOGRAPHY IN RABBINIC JUDAISM: About not a single Rabbinic sage of late antiquity, the first six centuries C.E., do we have the materials that sustain anything like a serviceable biography.[1] That is not merely because the sources do not serve for critical history in the conventional sense, but because they intend a different kind of treatment of lives of persons. Paradigmatic episodes in place of distinctive and individual biography yield the model of the life framed by the Torah: a life lived within the rules of nature, but facing outward toward supernature, a life transcending the natural world, measured by moments of transcendence. Hence "lives" are not recounted, but paradigmatic events of Rabbinic Judaism are. These comprise only four topics: [1] advent into the Torah, [2] the active and complex realm of negotiation within the Torah, [3] virtue measured by the Torah and responding to the special vices that the Torah can nurture, and [4] death in the supernatural setting that overcomes nature: not dirt to dirt, but soul to Heaven, along with the Torah.

Linear and sustained narrative of the

events of the social entity ("nation," in general, "Israel" in particular) corresponds to biography, in the present context, lives of sages.[2] Just as the historical mode of thought generates the composition of sustained narratives, so practitioners of history also write lives of persons, e.g., Moses, or at least continuous tales of a biographical character, with some sort of connected narrative, real or contrived, to give the impression of personal history. Not only so, but practitioners of the historical sciences—Josephus for instance—give us not only biography but autobiography, just as much as philosophers or theologians of history, Augustine being the best example, supply a biographical counterpart to a history. It obviously follows that where history leads, biography follows close behind.

But among the sages, who engaged in not historical but paradigmatic thinking, what place can we define for the counterpart to biography? The answer is, exemplary anecdotes, the counterpart to singular events, but no "lives" or biographies, the counterpart to sustained historical narrative. That answer is obvious. The real question is the character of those exemplary, one-time anecdotes, for knowing that they are going to exemplify paradigmatic concerns or realize the model through the medium of persons, rather than public events does not guide us to a theory of the particular character of the personal anecdotes that the model generates. Paradigmatic thinking about the social order yields not only anecdotes instead of continuous history. It also attends to the representation of persons, but solely for paradigmatic purposes and in a manner calculated to yield not continuous narrative but that which is here deemed of definitive consequence: a restatement, in individual terms, of the paradigm. And that is to be expected. For once time loses its quality of continuity and sequentiality, marking time calls upon other indicators of order and division than those demanded by the interplay of nature's telling time and humanity's interposing its rhythms. Lives of persons, beginning to end, need not be told; indeed, cannot be told, for the same reason that sequential, continuous narrative also cannot be constructed.

The paradigm, formed out of the congruence of humanity's and nature's time, rather than their incongruity, will identify, out of the moments presented by a human life, those that gain importance by appeal to the paradigm itself; the natural course of a human life, from death to birth, bears no more meaning in the amplification of the paradigm than the passage of empires, viewed as singular, or the story of a reign or a dynasty, viewed in its own terms. These matter, for paradigmatic thinking, when the pattern or model determines; otherwise, they do not register at all. Of the many empires of antiquity, four counted to the paradigm of Rabbinic Judaism, Babylonia, Media, Greece, and Rome. What of Parthians, what of Sasanians, certainly weighty as Greece and Rome and for long centuries quite able to hold their own (with their huge Jewish populations) against Greece and Rome? They did not count, so were not counted.

We know, of course, why they did not matter: they never intersected with the natural life of the holy people, Israel, in the holy land, the Land of Israel; they never threatened Jerusalem, in the way in which Babylonia, Greece (in Seleucid times), and Rome did. That principal part of the paradigm points to one main principle of selection in the range of events. Working back from events to the principle of selection that operates within the model governing Rabbinic Judaism's disposition of time (past, present, future), we are able to define out of what is selected the operative criterion: the congruence of the selected model to nature's time, not its contrast in conjunction therewith. Then what is to be said about the paradigm's points of interest in human lives? Since, we must anticipate, the paradigm will not elicit interest in a continuous life and so will not produce biography let alone autobiography, at what points will the model encompass episodes in human lives? To state the question more simply: where, when, and why, will individual persons make a difference, so as to warrant the writing down of details of personal lives?

Asked in this way, the question produces a ready answer, in three parts, two of which take but a moment for their exposition.

First, does the paradigm before us take an interest in the lives of persons? It does. Second, if it does, then at what point in a human life will anecdotes preserve the model for exemplary conduct, defining, then, the principle of selection, out of a human life as much as out of the happenings of the social world, of what counts? The principle of selection, at each point, somehow relates to the Torah. And, third, how does the paradigm emerge, having received a richer and more nuanced definition, out of the encounter with individual lives?

The answer is that the model that governs the formation of the Rabbinic writings examined here certainly does narrate episodes in personal lives, not only events in the social order. Second, the points of special interest are [1] how an individual studies the Torah; [2] remarkable deeds of virtue in the individual's life; [3] how the individual dies. Learning, virtue, and a dignified death—these form the paradigmatic points of interest. Only after reviewing a few instances of the way in which the writings set forth their paradigms of Torah-study, on the one side, and virtue, on the other, shall we address the third question. This review will yield questions of a still deeper order than has yet been suggested here, questions that concern the interplay of nature, the Torah, and truth. The stakes grow higher.

The Paradigmatic Person: The function of—not biography but—exemplary *episodes* in named individual's lives is to show the union of the nature and the social order through the person of the sage. That union takes place within the medium of the Torah, which corresponds to nature and lays out the governing rules thereof, but also encompasses the social order and defines its laws as well. Anecdotes about the master of the Torah then serve to convey principles of the Torah, with the clear proviso that anecdotes about events may equally set forth precisely those same principles. So the paradigm describes regularities without regard to considerations of scale, whether social or private, any more than matters of earlier or later, past or present or future, make any difference at all.

That fact, by the way, also explains why the paradigm in play really excludes not only biography but personality in any form. Individuals make a difference, so as to warrant the writing down of components of personal lives, at that point at which they lose all individuality and serve in some way or other to embody and exemplify a detail of the paradigm best set forth in the dimensions of private life. We then identify no difference between the social entity and the private person, because the paradigm works out indifferent to matters of scale or context; says what it says wherever it says it. How does the paradigm emerge out of the encounter with individual lives? The answer is now clear. A paradigm that proposes to present a single, coherent, and cogent picture of the life of Israel under the aspect of the timeless Torah has to make its statement about not only the social order viewed whole, but the individuals who comprise that order. The paradigm requires the counterpart to biography, as much as the counterpart to history, for its own reasons; it cares about individuals for the same reason that it cares about the social entity, Israel.

Biography does for history what personal anecdotes do for the paradigm at hand. Just as the one renders the large conclusions of its companion manageable and in human scale, so the other expresses the statements of the paradigm in a form accessible of human imitation and identification. But anecdotes about people also deepen our perception of the paradigm. For the issue of time is recast, now, as the span of a human life enters consideration. Paradigm in place of history yielded the narrative of the cult and the story of the Temple, not the history of the people and the life of the sage.[3]

If Paradigm, Why not Biography? Having set forth a positive proposition, let me now turn to the negative. First, why no gospels[4] in Rabbinic Judaism? The answer *cannot* be, because there were no data. On the contrary there were ample data, as the work of Rabbinic biography with which scholarship occupied itself for a century demonstrates. Indeed, the final organizers of the Talmud of Babylonia, who, it is commonly alleged, flourished circa 500-600 C.E., had in hand a tripartite corpus of inherited materials awaiting composition into a final, closed document.[5]

The first type of material, in various states and stages of completion, addressed the Mishnah or took up the principles of laws that the Mishnah had originally brought to articulation. These the framers of the Bavli organized in accord with the order of those Mishnah-tractates that they selected for sustained attention.

Second, they had in hand received materials, again in various conditions, pertinent to Scripture, both as Scripture related to the Mishnah and also as Scripture laid forth its own narratives. These they set forth as Scripture-commentary. In this way, the penultimate and ultimate redactors of the Bavli laid out a systematic presentation of the two Torahs, the oral, represented by the Mishnah, and the written, represented by Scripture.

And, third, the framers of the Bavli also had in hand materials focused on sages. These in the received form, attested in the Bavli's pages, were framed around twin biographical principles, either as strings of stories about great sages of the past or as collections of sayings and comments drawn together solely because the same name stands behind all the collected sayings. These can easily have been composed into biographies. In the context of Christianity and of Judaism, it is appropriate to call the biography of a holy man or woman, meant to convey the divine message, a gospel.

Hence the question raised here: why no gospels in Judaism? The question is an appropriate one, because there could have been. The final step—assembling available stories into a coherent narrative, with a beginning, middle, and end, for example— is what was not taken. No document was devoted to the life of a given sage and his teachings, and none to lives of sages and their teachings individually grouped.

Take the Talmud of Babylonia for example. The Bavli as a whole lays itself out as a commentary to the Mishnah. So the framers wished us to think that whatever they wanted to tell us would take the form of Mishnah commentary. But a second glance indicates that the Bavli is made up of enormous composites, themselves completed prior to inclusion in the Bavli. Some of these composites—around 35% to 40% of them, if my sample is indicative—were selected and arranged along lines dictated by a logic other than that deriving from the requirements of Mishnah-commentary. The components of the canon of the Judaism of the dual Torah prior to the Bavli had encompassed amplifications of the Mishnah, in the Tosefta and in the Yerushalmi, as well as the same for Scripture, in such documents as Sifra to Leviticus, Sifre to Numbers, another Sifre, to Deuteronomy, Genesis Rabbah, Leviticus Rabbah, and the like.

But there was no entire document, now extant, organized around the life and teachings of a particular sage. Even the Fathers according to Rabbi Nathan, which contains a good sample of stories about sages, is not so organized as to yield a life of a sage, or even a systematic biography of any kind. Where events in the lives of sages do occur, they are thematic and not biographical in organization, e.g., stories about the origins, as to Torah-study, of diverse sages; death-scenes of various sages. The sage as such, whether Aqiba or Yohanan ben Zakkai or Eliezer b. Hyrcanus, never in that document defines the appropriate organizing principle for sequences of stories or sayings. And there is no other in which the sage forms an organizing category for any material purpose.

Accordingly, the decision that the framers of the Bavli reached was to adopt the two redactional principles inherited from the antecedent century or so and to reject the one already rejected by their predecessors, even while honoring it. They organized the Bavli around the Mishnah. But they adapted and included vast tracts of antecedent materials organized as scriptural commentary. These they inserted whole and complete, not at all in response to the Mishnah's program.

And, finally, while making provision for small-scale compositions built upon biographical principles, preserving both strings of sayings from a given master (and often a given tradent of a given master) as well as tales about authorities of the preceding half millennium, they never created redactional compositions, of a sizable order, that focused upon given authorities. But sufficient materials certainly lay at hand to allow doing so. In the three decisions, two of what to do and one of what not to do, the final compositors of the Bavli indicated what they proposed to accomplish: to give final form and fixed expression, through their categories of the organization of all knowledge, to the Torah as it had been known, sifted, searched, approved, and handed down, even from the remote past to their own day. So in our literary categories the compositors of the Bavli were encyclopaedists. Their creation turned out to be the encyclopaedia of Judaism, its summa, its point of final reference, its court of last appeal, its definition, it conclusion, its closure—so they thought, and so say those that followed, to this very day.

Shall we then draw so grand a conclusion from so modest a fact as how people sorted out available redactional categories? Indeed so, if we realize that the modes by which thinkers organize knowledge leads us deep into the theses by which useful knowledge rises to the surface while what is irrelevant or unimportant or trivial sinks to the bottom. If we want to know what people thought and how they thought it, we can do worse than begin by asking about how they organized what they knew, on the one side, and about the choices they made in laying out the main lines of the structure of knowledge, on the other.

The Compositions No One Made— Collections of Wise Sayings and Biographies: The Yerushalmi and the collections of scriptural exegeses comprise compositions made up of already-worked-out units of discourse focused upon the Mishnah and Scripture, respectively. Other completed units of thought, such as we might call paragraphs or even short chapters, deal with individual sages. Midrash-compilations and Mishnah-commentaries, both the Yerushalmi and the Bavli, contain a sizable quantity of sage units of discourse. These can surely have coalesced in yet a third type of book. Specifically, sayings and stories about sages could have been organized into collections of wise sayings attributed to various authorities (like Avot), on the one side, or sequences of tales, e.g., brief snippets of biographies or lives of the saints, on the other. Let me spell out what we do find, which will underline the noteworthy character of the fact at hand: materials not used for their obvious purpose, in the way in which materials of a parallel character were used for their purpose.

Let me define more fully the character of the discourse that focuses upon the sage. In this type of composition, e.g., a paragraph of thought, a story, things that a given authority said are strung together or tales about a given authority are told at some length. Whoever composed and preserved units of discourse on the Mishnah and on Scripture ultimately preserved in the two Talmuds did the same for the sage. What that fact means is simple. In the circles responsible for making up and writing down completed units of discourse, three distinct categories of interest defined the task: (1) exegesis of the Mishnah, (2) exegesis of Scripture, and (3) preservation and exegesis, in exactly the same reverential spirit, of the words and deeds of sages. Not only so, but the kind of analysis to which Mishnah- and Scripture-exegesis were subjected also applied to the exegesis of sage-stories.

That fact may be shown in three ways. First, just as Scripture supplied proof texts, so deeds or statements of sages provided proof texts. Second, just as a verse of Scripture or an explicit statement of the Mishnah resolved a disputed point, so what a sage said or did might be introduced into discourse as ample proof for settling a dispute. And third, it follows that just as Scripture or the Mishnah laid down Torah, so what a sage did or said laid down Torah. In the dimensions of the applied and practical reason by which the law unfolded, the sage found a comfortable place in precisely the taxonomic categories defined, to begin with, by both the Mishnah and Scripture. Let us examine a few substantial examples of the sorts of sustained discourse in biographical materials turned out by circles of sages. What we shall see is an important fact. Just as these circles composed units of discourse about the meaning of a Mishnah passage, a larger theoretical problem of law, the sense of scriptural verse, and the sayings and doings of scriptural heroes seen as sages, so they did the same for living sages themselves.

In the simplest example we see that two discrete sayings of a sage are joined together. The principle of conglomeration, therefore, is solely the name of the sage at hand. One saying has to do with overcoming the impulse to do evil, and the other has to do with the classifications of sages' program of learning. What the two subjects have in common is slight. But to the framer of the passage, that fact meant nothing. For he thought that compositions joined by the same tradent and authority—Levi and Simeon—should be made up (B. Ber. 4b.XXIII):

> A. Said R. Levi bar Hama said R. Simeon b. Laqish, "A person should always provoke his impulse to do good against his impulse to do evil,
> B. "as it is said, 'Provoke and do not sin' (Ps. 4:5).
> C. "If [the good impulse] wins, well and good. If not, let him take up Torah study,
> D. "as it is said, 'Commune with your own heart' (Ps. 4:5).
> E. "If [the good impulse] wins, well and good. If not, let him recite the Shema,
> F. "as it is said, 'upon your bed' (Ps. 4:5).
> G. "If [the good impulse] wins, well and good. If not, let him remember the day of death,
> H. "as it is said, 'And keep silent. Sela' (Ps. 4:5)."
> I. And R. Levi bar Hama said R. Simeon b. Laqish said, "What is the meaning of the verse of Scripture, 'And I will give you the tables of stone, the law and the commandment, which I have written, that you may teach them' (Exod. 24:12).
> J. "'The tables' [here] refers to the Ten Commandments.
> K. "'Torah' refers to Scripture.
> L. "'Commandment' refers to Mishnah.
> M. "'Which I have written' refers to the Prophets and the Writings.
> N. "'That you may teach them' refers to the Gemara.
> O. "This teaches that all of them were given to Moses from Sinai."

The frame of the story at hand links A-H and I-O in a way unfamiliar to those ac-

customed to the principles of conglomeration in legal and biblical-exegetical compositions. In the former, a given problem or principle of law will tell us why one item is joined to some other. In the latter, a single verse of Scripture will account for the joining of two or more otherwise discrete units of thought. Here one passage, A-H, takes up Ps. 4:5; the other, I-O, Exod. 24:12. The point of the one statement hardly goes over the ground of the other. So the sole principle by which one item has joined the other is biographical: a record of what a sage said about topics that are, at best, contiguous, if related at all.

A second way of stringing together materials illustrative of the lives and teachings of sages is to join incidents involving a given authority or (as in the following case) two authorities believed to have stood in close relationship with one another, disciple and master, for instance. Often these stories go over the same ground in the same way. In the following, the two farewell stories make essentially the same point but in quite different language. What joins the stories is not only the shared theme but the fact that Eliezer is supposed to have studied with Yohanan b. Zakkai (B. San. 68A.II):

> A. Our rabbis have taught on Tannaite authority:
> B. When R. Eliezer fell ill, his disciples came in to pay a call on him. They said to him, "Our master, teach us the ways of life, so that through them we may merit the world to come."
> C. He said to them, "Be attentive to the honor owing to your fellows, keep your children from excessive reflection, and set them among the knees of disciples of sages, and when you pray, know before whom you stand, and on that account you will merit the life of the world to come."
> D. And when R. Yohanan b. Zakkai fell ill, his disciples came in to pay a call on him. When he saw them, he began to cry. His disciples said to him, "Light of Israel! Pillar at the right hand! Mighty hammer! On what account are you crying?"
> E. He said to them, "If I were going to be brought before a mortal king, who is here today and tomorrow gone to the grave, who, should he be angry with me, will not be angry forever, and, if he should imprison me, will not im-

prison me forever, and if he should put me to death, whose sentence of death is not for eternity, and whom I can appease with the right words or bribe with money, even so, I should weep.

F. "But now that I am being brought before the King of kings of kings, the Holy One, blessed be he, who endures forever and ever, who, should he be angry with me, will be angry forever, and if he should imprison me, will imprison me forever, and if he should put me to death, whose sentence of death is for eternity, and whom I cannot appease with the right words or bribe with money,

G. "and not only so, but before me are two paths, one to the Garden of Eden and the other to Gehenna, and I do not know by which path I shall be brought,

H. "and should I not weep?"

I. They said to him, "Our master, bless us."

J. He said to them, "May it be God's will that the fear of Heaven be upon you as much as the fear of mortal man."

K. His disciples said, "Just so much?"

L. He said to them, "Would that it were that much. You should know that, when a person commits a transgression, he says, 'I hope no man sees me.'"

M. When he was dying, he said to them, "Clear out utensils from the house, because of the uncleanness [of the corpse, which I am about to impart when I die], and prepare a throne for Hezekiah king of Judah, who is coming."

The links between B-C and D-M are clear. First, we have stories about sages' farewells. Second, people took for granted, because of the lists of M. Abot 2:2ff., that Eliezer was disciple of Yohanan b. Zakkai. Otherwise, it is difficult to explain the joining of the stories, since they scarcely make the same point, go over the same matters, or even share a common literary or rhetorical form or preference. But a framer of a composition of lives of saints, who is writing a tractate on how saints die, will have found this passage a powerful one indeed.

Yet another approach to the utilization of tales about sages was to join together stories on a given theme but told about different sages. A tractate or a chapter of a tractate on a given theme, for example, suffering and its reward, can have emerged

from the sort of collection that follows. The importance of the next item is that the same kinds of stories about different sages are strung together to make a single point (B. Ber. 5B.XXXI-XXXIII):

XXXI.

A. R. Hiyya bar Abba got sick. R. Yohanan came to him. He said to him, "Are these sufferings precious to you?"

B. He said to him, "I don't want them, I don't want their reward."

C. He said to him, "Give me your hand."

D. He gave him his hand, and [Yohanan] raised him up [out of his sickness].

E. R. Yohanan got sick. R. Hanina came to him. He said to him, "Are these sufferings precious to you?"

F. He said to him, "I don't want them. I don't want their reward."

G. He said to him, "Give me your hand."

H. He gave him his hand and [Hanina] raised him up [out of his sickness].

I. Why so? R. Yohanan should have raised himself up?

J. They say, "A prisoner cannot get himself out of jail."

XXXII.

A. R. Eliezer got sick. R. Yohanan came to see him and found him lying in a dark room. [The dying man] uncovered his arm, and light fell [through the room]. [Yohanan] saw that R. Eliezer was weeping. He said to him, "Why are you crying? Is it because of the Torah that you did not learn sufficiently? We have learned: 'All the same are the ones who do much and do little, so long as each person will do it for the sake of heaven.'

B. "Is it because of insufficient income? Not everyone has the merit of seeing two tables [Torah and riches, as you have. You have been a master of Torah and also have enjoyed wealth].

C. "Is it because of children? Here is the bone of my tenth son [whom I buried, so it was no great loss not to have children, since you might have had to bury them]."

D. He said to him, "I am crying because of this beauty of mine which will be rotting in the ground."

E. He said to him, "For that it certainly is worth crying," and the two of them wept together.

F. He said to him, "Are these sufferings precious to you?"

G. He said to him, "I don't want them, I don't want their reward."

H. He said to him, "Give me your hand."

I. He gave him his hand, and [Yohanan] raised him up [out of his sickness].

XXXIII.

A. Four hundred barrels of wine turned sour on R. Huna. R. Judah, brother of R. Sala the Pious, and rabbis came to see him (and some say it was R. Ada bar Ahba and rabbis). They said to him, "The master should take a good look at his deeds."

B. He said to them, "And am I suspect in your eyes?"

C. They said to him, "And is the Holy One, blessed be he, suspect of inflicting a penalty without justice?"

D. He said to them, "Has anybody heard anything bad about me? Let him say it."

E. They said to him, "This is what we have heard: the master does not give to his hired hand [the latter's share of] vine twigs [which are his right]."

F. He said to them, "Does he leave me any! He steals all of them to begin with."

G. They said to him, "This is in line with what people say: 'Go steal from a thief but taste theft too!'" [Simon: If you steal from a thief, you also have a taste of it.]

H. He said to them, "I pledge that I'll give them to him."

I. Some say that the vinegar turned back into wine, and some say that the price of vinegar went up so he sold it off at the price of wine.

The foregoing composite makes the same point several times: "Not them, not their reward." Sufferings are precious, but sages are prepared to forego the benefits. The formally climactic entry at XXXIII makes the point that, if bad things happen, the victim has deserved punishment. In joining these several stories about sages—two involving Yohanan, the third entirely separate—the compositor of the passage made his point by juxtaposing two like biographical snippets to a distinct one. Collections of stories about saints can have served quite naturally when formed into tractates on pious virtues, expressing these virtues through strong and pictorial language such as is before us.

The foregoing sources have shown two important facts. First, a principle of composition in the sages' circles was derived from interest in the teachings associated with a given sage, as well as in tales and stories told about a sage or groups of sages. The first of the passages shows us the simplest

composition of sayings, the latter, an equivalent conglomeration of related stories. Up to this point, therefore, the reader will readily concede that biographical materials on sages, as much as Mishnah-exegesis and Scripture-exegesis, came forth out of circles of sages. But I have yet to show that such materials attained sufficient volume and cogency from large-scale compilations—conglomerates so substantial as to sustain entire books.

Chapters and Tractates on Lives of Sages—What Might Have Been: Had the framers of large-scale Rabbinic compositions wished, they could readily have made up tractates devoted to diverse sayings of a given authority (or, tradent-and-authority, that is, "Rabbi X says Rabbi Y says"). What follows to demonstrate the possibility are two enormous compositions, which together can have made up as much as half of a Talmud chapter in volume. If anyone had wanted to compose a chapter around Rabbinic authorities' names, he is thus shown to have had the opportunity.

The first shows us a string of sayings not only in a single set of names but also on discrete subjects. We also see how such a string of sayings could form the focus of exactly the kind of critical analysis and secondary amplification to which any other Talmudic passage would be subjected. So there can have been not only a Talmud based on the Mishnah and a Midrash composition based on the Scripture but also a life of a saint (a gospel?) based on a set of rabbis' sayings. Here is the Talmud that can have served a collection of sayings of Yohanan-in-the-name-of-Simeon b. Yohai (B. Ber. 7B-8A.LIX-LXV):

LIX.

A. [7B] Said R. Yohanan in the name of R. Simeon b. Yohai, "From the day on which the Holy One, blessed be he, created the world, there was no man who called the Holy One, blessed be he, 'Lord,' until Abraham came along and called him Lord.

B. "For it is said, 'And he said, O Lord, God, whereby shall I know that I shall inherit it' (Gen. 15:8)."

C. Said Rab, "Daniel too was answered only on account of Abraham.

D. "For it is said, 'Now therefore, O our

God, hearken to the prayer of your servant and to his supplications and cause your face to shine upon your sanctuary that is desolate, for the Lord's sake' (Dan. 9:17).

E. "'For your sake' is what he should have said, but the sense is, 'For the sake of Abraham, who called you Lord.'"

LX.

A. And R. Yohanan said in the name of R. Simeon b. Yohai, "How do we know that people should not seek to appease someone when he is mad?

B. "As it is said, 'My face will go and then I will give you rest' (Exod. 33:14)."

LXI.

A. And R. Yohanan said in the name of R. Simeon b. Yohai, "From the day on which the Holy One, blessed be he, created his world, there was no one who praised the Holy One, blessed be he, until Leah came along and praised him.

B. "For it is said, 'This time I will praise the Lord' (Gen. 29:35)."

C. As to Reuben, said R. Eleazar, "Leah said, 'See what is the difference [the name of Reuben yielding reu (see) and ben (between)] between my son and the son of my father-in-law.

D. "The son of my father-in-law, even knowingly, sold off his birthright, for it is written, 'And he sold his birthright to Jacob' (Gen. 25:33).

E. "See what is written concerning him: 'And Esau hated Jacob' (Gen. 27:41), and it is written, 'And he said, is he not rightly named Jacob? for he has supplanted me these two times' (Gen. 27:36).

F. "My son, by contrast, even though Joseph forcibly took away his birthright, as it is written, 'But for as much as he defiled his father's couch, his birthright was given to the sons of Joseph' (1 Chron. 5:1), did not become jealous of him, for it is written, 'And Reuben heard it and delivered him out of their hand' (Gen. 37:21)."

G. As to the meaning of the name of Ruth, said R. Yohanan, "It was because she had the merit that David would come forth from her, who saturated (RWH) the Holy One, blessed be he, with songs and praises."

H. How do we know that a person's name affects [his life]?

I. Said R. Eleazar, "It is in line with the verse of Scripture: 'Come, behold the works of the Lord, who has made desolations in the earth' (Ps. 46:9).

J. "Do not read 'desolations' but 'names' [which the same root yields]."

LXII.

A. And R. Yohanan said in the name of R. Simeon b. Yohai, "Bringing a child up badly is worse in a person's house than the war of Gog and Magog.

B. "For it is said, 'A Psalm of David, when he fled from Absalom, his son' (Ps. 3:1), after which it is written, 'Lord how many are my adversaries become, many are they that rise up against me' (Ps. 3:2).

C. "By contrast, in regard to the war of Gog and Magog it is written, 'Why are the nations in an uproar? And why do the peoples mutter in vain?' (Ps. 2:1).

D. "But it is not written in that connection, 'How many are my adversaries become.'"

E. "A Psalm of David, when he fled from Absalom, his son (Ps. 3:1):

F. "'A Psalm of David'? It should be, 'A lamentation of David'!

G. Said R. Simeon b. Abishalom, "The matter may be compared to the case of a man against whom an outstanding bond was issued. Before he had paid it, he was sad. After he had paid it, he was glad.

H. "So too with David, when he the Holy One had said to him, 'Behold, I will raise up evil against you out of your own house,' (2 Sam. 2:11), he was sad.

I. "He thought to himself, 'Perhaps it will be a slave or a bastard child, who will not have pity on me.'

J. "When he saw that it was Absalom, he was happy. On that account, he said a psalm."

LXIII.

A. And R. Yohanan said in the name of R. Simeon b. Yohai, "It is permitted to contend with the wicked in this world,

B. "for it is said, 'Those who forsake the Torah praise the wicked, but those who keep the Torah contend with them' (Prov. 28:4).

C. It has been taught on Tannaite authority along these same lines:

D. R. Dosetai bar Matun says, "It is permitted to contend with the wicked in this world, for it is said, 'Those who forsake the Torah praise the wicked, but those who keep the Torah contend with them' (Prov. 28:4)."

E. And if someone should whisper to you, "But is it not written, 'Do not contend with evildoers, nor be envious against those who work unrighteousness' (Ps. 37:1)," say to him, "Someone whose conscience bothers him thinks so.

F. "In fact, 'Do not contend with evildoers' means, do not be like them, 'nor be envious against those who work unrighteousness,' means, do not be like them.

G. "And so it is said, 'Let your heart not envy sinners, but fear the Lord all day' (Prov. 23:17)."

H. Is this the case? And lo, R. Isaac has said, "If you see a wicked person for whom the hour seems to shine, do not contend with him, for it is said, 'His ways prosper at all times' (Ps. 10:5).

I. "Not only so, but he wins in court, as it is said, 'Your judgments are far above, out of his sight' (Ps. 10:5).

J. "Not only so, but he overcomes his enemies, for it is said, 'As for all his enemies, he farts at them' (Ps. 10:5)."

K. There is no contradiction. The one [Isaac] addresses one's own private matters [in which case one should not contend with the wicked], but the other speaks of matters having to do with Heaven [in which case one should contend with them].

L. And if you wish, I shall propose that both parties speak of matters having to do with Heaven. There is, nonetheless, no contradiction. The one [Isaac] speaks of a wicked person on whom the hour shines, the other of a wicked person on whom the hour does not shine.

M. And if you wish, I shall propose that both parties speak of a wicked person on whom the hour shines, and there still is no contradiction.

N. The one [Yohanan, who says the righteous may contend with the wicked] speaks of a completely righteous person, the other [Isaac] speaks of someone who is not completely righteous.

O. For R. Huna said, "What is the meaning of this verse of Scripture: 'Why do you look, when they deal treacherously, and hold your peace, when the wicked swallows up the man that is more righteous than he' (Hab. 1:13)?

P. "Now can a wicked person swallow up a righteous one?

Q. "And lo, it is written, 'The Lord will not leave him in his hand' (Ps. 37:33). And it is further written, 'No mischief shall befall the righteous' (Prov. 12:21).

R. "The fact therefore is that he may swallow up someone who is more righteous than he, but he cannot swallow up a completely righteous man."

S. And if you wish, I shall propose that, when the hour shines for him, the situation is different.

LXIV.

A. And R. Yohanan said in the name of R. Simeon b. Yohai, "Beneath anyone who establishes a regular place for praying do that person's enemies fall.

B. "For it is said, 'And I will appoint a place for my people Israel, and I will plant them, that they may dwell in their own place and be disquieted no more, neither shall the children of wickedness afflict them any more as at the first' (2 Sam. 7:10)."

C. R. Huna pointed to a contradiction between two verses of Scripture: "It is written, 'To afflict them,' and elsewhere, 'To exterminate them' (1 Chron. 17:9).

D. "To begin with, merely to afflict them, but, at the end, to exterminate them."

LXV.

A. And R. Yohanan said in the name of R. Simeon b. Yohai, "Greater is personal service to Torah than learning in Torah [so doing favors for a sage is of greater value than studying with him].

B. "For it is said, 'Here is Elisha, the son of Shaphat, who poured water on the hands of Elijah' (2 Kings 3:11).

C. "It is not said, 'who learned' but 'who poured water.'

D. "This teaches that greater is service to Torah than learning in Torah."

It is not difficult to pick up the main beams of the foregoing construction, since they are signified by Yohanan-Simeon sayings, LIX.A, LX.A, LXI.A, LXII.A, LXIII.A, LXIV.A, LXV.A—seven entries in line. The common theme is not prayer; no other topic is treated in a cogent way either. The sort of inner coherence to which any student of the Bavli is accustomed does not pass before us. Rather we have a collection of wise thoughts on diverse topics, more in the manner of Proverbs than in the style of the great intellects behind the sustained reasoning in passages of the Bavli and much of the Yerushalmi as well.

What is interesting is that, at a later stage, other pertinent materials have been inserted, for example, Rab's at LIX.C-E, and so on down. There is no reason to imagine that these sayings were made up in response to Yohanan-Simeon's statement. Quite to the contrary, framed in their own terms, the sayings were presumably tacked on at a point at which the large-scale construction of Yohanan-Simeon was worked over for a purpose beyond the one intended by the original compositor. For what he wanted to do he did, which is, compose a collection of Yohanan-Simeon sayings. If he hoped that his original collection would form part of a larger composition on Yohanan, he surely was disappointed. But even if he imagined that he would make up material for compositions of lives and sayings of saints, he cannot have expected his little collection to end up where and how it did, as part of a quite different corpus of writing from one in which a given authority had his say or in which stories were told in some sort of sensible sequence about a particular sage. The type of large-scale composition, for which our imagined compositor did his work, in the end never came into being in the Rabbinic canon.

In the following, still longer example I begin with the passage to which the entire composition, organized in the name of a tradent and a sage, is attached. At B. Ber. 6B/1:1 XLI, we have a statement that a synagogue should have a regular quorum. Then the next passage, 1:1 XLII, makes the secondary point that a person should pray in a regular place—a reasonable amplification of the foregoing. That is, just as there should be a quorum routinely organized in a given location, so should an individual routinely attach himself to a given quorum. This statement is given by Helbo in Huna's name. What follows is a sizable set of sayings by Helbo in Huna's name, all of them on the general theme of prayer but none of them on the specific point at hand. Still more interesting, just as in the foregoing, the passage as a whole was composed so that the Helbo-Huna materials themselves are expanded and enriched with secondary accretions. For instance, at XLIII the base materials are given glosses of a variety of types. All in all, we see what we may call a little tractate in the making. But, as we shall hardly have to repeat, no one in the end created a genre of Rabbinic literature to accommodate the vast collections of available compositions on sages' sayings and doings (B. Ber. 6B.XLI-XLVIII):

XLI.
A. Said R. Yohanan, "When the Holy One, blessed be he, comes to a synagogue and does not find ten present, he forthwith becomes angry.

B. "For it is said, 'Why when I came was there no one there? When I called, there was no answer' (Is. 50:2)."
XLII.
A. Said R. Helbo said R. Huna, "For whoever arranges a regular place for praying, the God of Abraham is a help, and when he dies, they say for him, 'Woe for the humble man, woe for the pious man, one of the disciples of Abraham, our father.'

B. "And how do we know in the case of Abraham, our father, that he arranged a regular place for praying?

C. "For it is written, 'And Abraham got up early in the morning on the place where he had stood' (Gen. 19:27).

D. "'Standing' refers only to praying, for it is said, 'Then Phinehas stood up and prayed' (Ps. 106:30)."

E. Said R. Helbo to R. Huna, "He who leaves the synagogue should not take large steps."

F. Said Abbayye, "That statement applies only when one leaves, but when he enters, it is a religious duty to run [to the synagogue].

G. "For it is said, 'Let us run to know the Lord' (Hos. 6:3)."

H. Said R. Zira, "When in the beginning I saw rabbis running to the lesson on the Sabbath, I thought that the rabbis were profaning the Sabbath. But now that I have heard what R. Tanhum said R. Joshua b. Levi said,

I. "namely, 'A person should always run to take up a matter of law, and even on the Sabbath, as it is said, "They shall walk after the Lord who shall roar like a lion [for he shall roar, and the children shall come hurrying]" (Hos. 11:10),'

J. "I too run."
XLIII.
A. Said R. Zira, "The reward for attending the lesson is on account of running [to hear the lesson, not necessarily on account of what one has learned.]"

B. Said Abbayye, "The reward for attending the periodic public assembly [of rabbis] is on account of the crowding together."

C. Said Raba [to the contrary], "The reward for repeating what one has heard is in reasoning about it."

D. Said R. Papa, "The reward for attending a house of mourning is on account of one's preserving silence there."

E. Said Mar Zutra, "The reward for observing a fast day lies in the acts of charity one performs on that day."

F. Said R. Sheshet, "The reward for delivering a eulogy lies in raising the voice."

G. Said R. Ashi, "The reward for attending a wedding lies in the words [of compliment paid to the bride and groom].”

XLIV.

A. Said R. Huna, “Whoever prays behind the synagogue is called wicked,

B. “as it is said, ‘The wicked walk round about’ (Ps. 12:9).”

C. Said Abbayye, “That statement applies only in the case of one who does not turn his face toward the synagogue, but if he turns his face toward the synagogue, we have no objection.”

D. There was a certain man who would say his prayers behind the synagogue and did not turn his face toward the synagogue. Elijah came by and saw him. He appeared to him in the guise of a Tai Arab.

E. He said to him, “Are you now standing with your back toward your master?” He drew his sword and killed him.

F. One of the rabbis asked R. Bibi bar Abbayye, and some say, R. Bibi asked R. Nahman bar Isaac, “What is the meaning of the verse, ‘When vileness is exalted among the sons of men’ (Ps. 12:9)?”

G. He said to him, “This refers to matters that are exalted, which people treat with contempt.”

H. R. Yohanan and R. Eleazar both say, “When a person falls into need of the help of other people, his face changes color like the kerum, for it is said, ‘As the kerum is to be reviled among the sons of men’ (Ps. 12:9).”

I. What is the meaning of kerum?

J. When R. Dimi came, he said, “There is a certain bird among the coast towns, called the kerum. When the sun shines, it turns many colors.”

K. R. Ammi and R. Assi both say, “[When a person turns to others for support], it is as if he is judged to suffer the penalties of both fire and water.

L. “For it is said, ‘When you caused men to ride over our heads, we went through fire and through water’ (Ps. 66:12).”

XLV.

A. And R. Helbo said R. Huna said, “A person should always be attentive at the afternoon prayer.

B. “For lo, Elijah was answered only at the afternoon prayer.

C. “For it is said, ‘And it came to pass at the time of the offering of the late afternoon offering, that Elijah the prophet came near and said, “Hear me, O Lord, hear me”’ (1 Kings 18:36-37).”

D. “Hear me” so fire will come down from heaven.

E. “Hear me” that people not say it is merely witchcraft.

F. R. Yohanan said, “[A person should also be attentive about] the evening prayer.

G. “For it is said, ‘Let my prayer be set forth as incense before you, the lifting up of my hands as the evening sacrifice’ (Ps. 141:2).”

H. R. Nahman bar Isaac said, “[A person should also be attentive about] the morning prayer.

I. “For it is said, ‘O Lord, in the morning you shall hear my voice, in the morning I shall order my prayer to you, and will look forward’ (Ps. 5:4).”

XLVI.

A. And R. Helbo said R. Huna said, “Whoever enjoys a marriage banquet and does not felicitate the bridal couple violates five ‘voices.’

B. “For it is said, ‘The voice of joy and the voice of gladness, the voice of the bridegroom and the voice of the bride, the voice of those who say, “Give thanks to the Lord of hosts”’ (Jer. 33:11).”

C. And if he does felicitate the couple, what reward does he get?

D. Said R. Joshua b. Levi, “He acquires the merit of the Torah, which was handed down with five voices.

E. “For it is said, ‘And it came to pass on the third day, when it was morning, that there were voices [thus two], and lightnings, and a thick cloud upon the mount, and the voice of a horn, and when the voice of the horn waxed louder, ‘Moses spoke and God answered him by a voice’ (Exod. 19:16, 19), [thus five voices in all].”

F. Is it so [that there were only five voices]?

G. And lo, it is written, “And all the people saw the voices” (Exod. 20:15). [So this would make seven voices.]

H. These voices came before the giving of the Torah [and do not count].

I. R. Abbahu said, “It is as if the one [who felicitated the bridal couple] offered a thanksgiving offering.

J. “For it is said, ‘Even of them that bring thanksgiving offerings into the house of the Lord’ (Jer. 33:11).”

K. R. Nahman bar Isaac said, “It is as if he rebuilt one of the ruins of Jerusalem.

L. “For it is said, ‘For I will cause the captivity of the land to return as at the first, says the Lord’ (Jer. 33:11).”

XLVII.

A. And R. Helbo said R. Huna said, “The words of any person in whom is fear of Heaven are heard.

B. “For it is said, ‘The end of the matter, all having been heard: fear God and keep his commandments, for this is the whole man’ (Ecc. 12:13).”

C. What is the meaning of the phrase, "For this is the whole man" (Ecc. 12:13)?

D. Said R. Eleazar, "Said the Holy One, blessed be he, 'The entire world has been created only on account of this one.'"

E. R. Abba bar Kahana said, "This one is worth the whole world."

F. Simeon b. Zoma says, "The entire world was created only to accompany this one."

XLVIII.

A. And R. Helbo said R. Huna said, "Whoever knows that his fellow regularly greets him should greet the other first.

B. "For it is said, 'Seek peace and pursue it' (Ps. 34:15).

C. "If he greeted him and the other did not reply, the latter is called a thief.

D. "For it is said, 'It is you who have eaten up the vineyard, the spoil of the poor is in your houses' (Is. 3:14)."

What we noted in connection with the Yohanan-Simeon collection needs no restatement here. The scope and dimensions of the passage prove impressive. Again we must wonder for what sort of composition the framer of the Helbo-Huna collection planned his writing. Whatever it was, it hardly fit the ultimate destination of his work.

Now let us turn to the situation of biographies in the counterpart-foundation writings of Christianity. The comparison with the literary situation of Rabbinic Judaism affords perspective on the facts just now surveyed. For the difference is documentary: the very character of the writing-down of the religious systems and structures contains within itself a theological statement.

Comparison and Contrast—The Gospels and the Mishnah, The Church Fathers and the Talmud: If Christianity were written down in the way in which Judaism is, what should we know about Christianity, and how should we know it? In order for New Testament scholars to find out what they need to know about the Rabbinic literature in order to use it for New Testament studies, they require a clear picture of the character of the Rabbinic literature. What better way to provide such a picture than to translate "Judaic" into "Christian"? As a kind of bilingual interpreter, I mean to give a picture of the kind of evidence scholars of earliest Christianity would face, if the New Testament and Patristic writings were truly comparable to the Mishnah and Rabbinic literature.

What I wish to do is to paint a picture of our problem in studying early Christianity, if the sources of early Christianity had reached us in the way, and in the condition, in which those of early Rabbinic Judaism come down to us. That is to say, what should we know, and how should we know it, if the records of early Christianity were like the Rabbinic literature of late antiquity?

(1) What could we know, if all the literature of early Christianity had reached us in a fully homogenized and intellectually seamless form? Not only the New Testament, but all the works of the church fathers, from Justin to Augustine, now would be represented as expressions of one communal mind, dismembered and built into a single harmonious logical structure on various themes. True, they would be shown constantly to disagree with one another. But the range of permissible disagreement would define a vast area of consensus on all basic matters, so that a superficial contentiousness would convey something quite different: one mind on most things, beginning to end. The names of the fathers would be attached to some of their utterances. But all would have gone through a second medium of tradents and redactors—the editors of the compendium (the Patristic Talmud, so to speak, and these editors picked and chose what they wanted of Justin, and what of Origen, what of Tertullian, and what of Augustine, in line with what the editors themselves found interesting. In the end, the picture of the first six centuries of early Christianity would be the creation of people of the sixth century, out of the shards and remnants of people of the first five. Our work then would be to uncover what happened before the end through studying a document which portrays a timeless world.

Not only would the document be so

framed as implicitly to deny historical development of ideas, but the framers also would gloss over diverse and contradictory sources of thought. I do not mean only that Justin, Irenaeus, and Tertullian would be presented as individual authors in a single, timeless continuum. I mean that all Gnostic and Catholic sources would be broken up into sense-units and their fragments rearranged in a structure presented as representative of a single Christianity, with a single, unitary theology. This synthesized ecumenical body of Christian thought would be constructed so as to set out judgments on the principal theological topics of the day, and these judgments would have been accepted as normative from that day to this. So the first thing we must try to imagine is a Christianity which reaches us fully harmonized and whole—a Christianity of Nicaea and Chalcedon, but not of Arians, Nestorians, monophysites and the rest, so there is no distinctive Justin nor Augustine, no Irenaeus and no Gnostics, and surely no Nag Hammadi, but all are one "in Christ Jesus," so to speak.

(2) Let me emphasize that this would be not merely a matter of early Christian literature's reaching us without the names of the authors of its individual documents. The thing we must try to imagine is that there would be no individual documents at all. Everything would have gone through a process of formation and redaction which obliterated the marks of individuality. Just as the theology would be one, so would the form and style of the documents which preserved it. Indeed, what would be striking about this picture of Christianity would be not that the tractate of Mark lacks the name of Mark, but that all of the tractates of the Gospels would be written in precisely the same style and resort to exactly the same rhetorical and redactional devices. Stylistic unity so pervasive as to eliminate all traces of individual authorship, even of most preserved sayings, would now characterize the writings of the first Christians. The sarcasm of Irenaeus, the majesty of Augustine, and the exegetical ingenuity of Origen, the lucid historicism of Aphrahat—all are homogenized. Everyone talks in the same way about the same things—one uni-

form rhetoric, a single topical agendum serves nearly everybody.

(3) And now to come to a principal task of the study of early Christianity: what should we know about Jesus, and how should we know it, if sayings assigned to Jesus in one book were given to Paul in a second, to John in a third, and to "They said," or, "He said to them," in a fourth. Can we imagine trying to discover the historical Jesus on this turf? If even the provenance of a saying could not be established on the basis of all those to whom it is attributed, if, often, even a single *Vorlage* and *Urtext* could not be postulated? Then what sort of work on the biography and thought of any of the early figures of Christianity would be credible?

(4) This brings me to the most difficult act of imagination which I must ask readers to perform: a supererogatory work of social imagination. Can we imagine a corner of the modern world in which this state of interpretation—of total confusion, of harmonies, homologies, homogenies, is not found confusing but reassuring? Can we mentally conjure up a social setting for learning in which differentiation is avoided and credulity rewarded? in which analysis is heresy, dismissed as worthless or attacked as "full of mistakes"? Can we conceive of a world in which repetition, in one's own words, of what the sources say is labeled scholarship, and anthologizing is labeled learning? In New Testament scholarship, we must imagine, the principal task now is to write harmonies of the Gospels, and, in Patristic studies, to align the Catholic with the Gnostic, the second century with the fifth, the Arian and the Athanasian, monophysite and Nestorian.[6] In a word, we speak of a world in which the Diatesseron is the last word in scholarship, and in which contentiousness about trivial things masks a firm and iron consensus. In this imagined world, scholars further hold that all the sources are historical, and merely alluding to them suffices to establish facts of history.

If readers can envision such a state of affairs, then we have entered the world of sources and scholarly orthodoxies confronted by us who study the ancient Judaism emergent from the Rabbinic literature. And, it follows, scholars of New Testament history and exegesis will grasp the fact that Rabbinic literature is simply not homologous to the writings on which they work and cannot be used in anything like the same way. Not only so, but that literature deals with different types of problems and answers altogether different questions, with the result that we cannot present to Rabbinic literature questions deemed appropriate for address to another kind of writing altogether. A life of Jesus or of Augustine is plausible; a life of Aqiba or Hillel is not. An account of the intellectual biography of Paul and his theology is entirely a propos, the sources answering precisely the questions that are asked. A counterpart picture of Judah the Patriarch, who wrote up the Mishnah, or of Rabbah, Abbaye or Raba, the greatest geniuses of the Talmud, is not. Then to use one type of writing to address questions appropriate to another type of writing is surely a dubious operation. Or—it would be, if it were not entirely routine, as the entries on sages in the *Jewish Encyclopaedia* show.

(1) I can spell out matters now very simply and very rapidly. First, as to the axioms of scholarship, all the Rabbinic sources are treated as representatives of a single, seamless world view and as expressions of a single, essentially united group, either the views as a whole, or, among the enlightened, *the* rabbis as a group. While some more critical souls concede there may have been distinctions between the first century rabbis' thought and that of the fourth, the distinctions make no material difference in accounts of "the rabbis" and their thought. Whether anthologies or anthological essays (Moore, Montefiore and Loewe, Bonsirven, Urbach), *the* rabbis are represented in their views on God, world, and redemption, as though all rabbis for seven hundred ears had the same thing to say as all others.

Now this representation of *the* rabbis is subject to an important, commonplace qualification. Everyone knows that the Talmuds abound in the recognition of differences between the teachings of different rabbis in different periods on different points in discussions of which traditions or source was followed by the proponent of this or that opinion. But the recorded differences are about particular, trivial points. The Talmudic discussion, moreover, is directed normally towards reconciling them. What is particularly lacking in available accounts of "the Rabbinic mind" is, first, recognition and delineation of different general positions or basic attitudes, of the characteristic make-up, and backgrounds of different schools; second, what is lacking is anything like adequate reporting of the change of teachings over the course of time and in relation to historical changes. Obviously, there is plenty of speculation on how an individual or group reacted to a particular historical situation or event. But these random speculations are unsystematic and appear to be made up for the occasion. So these apparent exceptions to what I say have to be recognized—because they prove the accuracy of my description of the prevailing consensus that governed until the final quarter of the twentieth century.

(2) Second, as to the sources, the documents of earlier Rabbinic Judaism exhibit an internally uniform quality of style. So the scholars who represent a seamless world accurately replicate the literary traits of the sources of the portrait. It is exceedingly difficult to differentiate on formal or stylistic grounds among the layers of the Mishnah, which is the document of Rabbinic Judaism first brought to redaction. The two Talmuds then so lay matters out as to represent themselves as the logical continuity from the Mishnah. They do so by breaking up the Mishnah into minute units and then commenting on those discrete units of thought. Consequently, the Mishnah as a document, a document which presents its own world view and its own social system, is not preserved and confronted. Nor do the Talmuds present themselves as successive layers, built upon, but essentially distinct from the Mishnah. Rather, the Talmuds aim at completely harmonizing their own materials both with the Mishnah and among themselves, despite the self-evidently contradictory character of the materials. Once more we observe, there are limits to disagreement. The continuing contentiousness of the documents, their preservation of diverse viewpoints on single issues,

underline the rigidly protected limits of permissible disagreement. Intense disagreement about trivialities powerfully reinforces basic unities and harmonies. The fact that, out there, were Jews who decorated synagogues in ways the Talmuds cannot have led us to anticipate, is mentioned only in passing, as if it is of no weight or concern. What matters to this literature is not how the Jews lived, nor even how they worshipped, but only the discussions of the Rabbinic schools and courts. What the documents say is what we are supposed to think, within the range of allowed difference. Consequently, the intellectually unitary character of the sources is powerfully reinforced by the total success of the framers and redactors of the sources in securing stylistic unity within documents and in some measure even among them.

(3) These facts have not prevented scholars from writing about history and biography, upon the basis of the unanalyzed and unchallenged allegations of the Rabbinic sources. Just as people had arguments about what Jesus really said and did before the rise of form-criticism, so the rage and secure contentiousness of scholars in this field mask the uncertainty of their entire structure. It is as if, as in the Talmuds themselves, by arguing on essentially minor points, the colleagues may avoid paying attention to the epistemological abyss beneath them all. Instead of analysis and argument, dogma took over. There were two: [1] "believe unless you have to doubt," and, by way of settling all doubts, [2] "Would our holy rabbis lie?"—there being no substantive difference between the two theological dogmas). The one was promulgated at the Hebrew University of Jerusalem, the other at Bar Ilan University, the one under secular, the other under Orthodox, auspices. There is no difference between them.

So there are agreed-upon solutions to the problems of diverse authorities behind the same saying and amplification and variation of details in a single story. These commonly lead to very felicitous conclusions. If the same saying is in three mouths, it is because they agreed to say it. True, "we cannot be sure that they were not talking simultaneously in different places (thanks to the holy spirit)." Or, if there are three versions of essentially the same story, like the Sermon on the Mount and the Sermon on the Plain, it is because, in the wonderful ways of Providence, it happened two times. Every time the text says, "One time," that was, indeed, one event.

(4) Finally, as I have already hinted, these serendipitous facts, these happy agreements, these assured and unquestioned results of a hundred years of critical scholarship following upon fifteen hundred years of uncritical scholarship that produced the same results, enjoy the powerful support of the three great communities which read the Rabbinic literature at all. I mean, Orthodox Jews in Yeshivas, scholarly Jews in Rabbinic seminaries and Israeli universities, and the generality of Christian scholars of the New Testament. To the Orthodox, the Rabbinic sources are part of the whole Torah of Moses our rabbi, the revealed word of God. For them, "our holy rabbis" cannot deceive. To the scholars in American and European Rabbinic schools and Institutes of Judaic Studies and Israeli universities, the critical program of scholarship on early Christianity is perceived from a distance. In their books and articles they settle complex questions of literary analysis and historical epistemology with an array of two assumptions, three logical arguments, and four "probative" examples. They do not perceive the immense, detailed work which stands, for example, behind debates on Q and the Synoptic problem. Indeed, the work of analysis of sources bores them. Whether work is original or dull, the bulk of it simply dismisses as settled, questions that would be deemed urgent in biblical and patristic literature and in the history of early Christianity. As to the New Testament scholars, their view is that things go better when we read Rabbinic literature as a set of facts that speak for themselves rather than as complex problems requiring solutions. For them, the Rabbinic literature as it stands, unanalyzed and uncriticized, tells us all about Jerusalem and Galilee in the time of Jesus. Or, to put matters in a more theological way, in Gospels' research, salvation is of the Jews.

Notes

[1] I originally addressed the problem of Rabbinic biography in these works, after which I dismissed the possibility of a critical-historical "life" of any Rabbinic sage of antiquity: *A Life of Yohanan ben Zakkai* (Leiden, 1962; awarded the Abraham Berliner Prize in Jewish History, Jewish Theological Seminary of America. Second edition, completely revised, 1970 (translated into French, Italian, and Japanese); *Development of a Legend. Studies on the Traditions Concerning Yohanan ben Zakkai* (Leiden, 1970); *The Rabbinic Traditions about the Pharisees before 70* (Leiden, 1971, second printing: Atlanta, 1999), 3 vols.; *Eliezer ben Hyrcanus. The Tradition and the Man* (Leiden, 1973), 2 vols. After my *Eliezer ben Hyrcanus*, so far as I know, not a single biography of a rabbi was written in any Western language or—more significantly—accepted for a dissertation in any Western university. The Israeli academic journals—*Tarbiz, Zion, Sinai*, for example—have continued to publish articles on Rabbinic personalities and characters, their philosophy and legal theory and the like, but, significantly, none of this is now translated into English. I should claim responsibility, therefore, for ending research in Rabbinic biography, which, in the conventional framework, I showed to be uncritical. Monographs that argue in favor of the authenticity of attributions of sayings to particular rabbis have not been succeeded by "lives" of those same rabbis, which confirms the utter collapse of biography as a significant episteme for Rabbinic Judaism.

[2] In this context, see my *Why No Gospels in Talmudic Judaism?* (Atlanta, 1988).

[3] I amplify these matters in *The Presence of the Past, the Pastness of the Present. History, Time, and Paradigm in Rabbinic Judaism* (Bethesda, 1996).

[4] I use the word "gospel" with a small G as equivalent to "didactic life of a holy man, portraying the faith." Obviously, the Christian usage, with a capital G, must maintain that there can be a Gospel only about Jesus Christ. Claims of uniqueness are, of course, not subject to public discourse. In the present context, I could as well have referred to lives of saints, since Judaism of the dual Torah produced neither a gospel about a central figure nor lives of saints. Given the centrality of Moses "our rabbi," for example, we should have anticipated a "Gospel of Moses" parallel to the Gospels of Jesus Christ, and, lacking that, at least a "life of Aqiba," scholar, saint, martyr, parallel to the lives of various saints. We also have no autobiographies of any kind, beyond some "I"-stories, which themselves seem to me uncommon.

[5] I compared Bavli and Yerushalmi tractates Sukkah, Sanhedrin, and Sotah, showing the proportion of what I call Scripture-units of thought to Mishnah-units of thought. See my *Judaism. The Classic Statement. The Evidence of the Bavli* (Chicago, 1986).

[6] I wrote this in 1979 and could not foresee that E.P. Sanders would present precisely such a picture of a single, homogeneous Judaism, joining the Judaic counterpart of monophysites and Nestorians into a single conflation. Sanders exhibits an infirm grasp of the entire critical agenda in the study of the Judaic sources, as an examination of his presentation of them in his *Judaism* and in his *Jewish Law from Jesus to the Mishnah* shows. My reply to him is in *Judaic Law from Jesus to the Mishnah. A Systematic Reply to Professor E.P. Sanders* (Atlanta, 1993). To my knowledge Sanders did not respond in public to my reply.

JACOB NEUSNER

C

CONVERSOS: The term "conversos"—"converts" in Spanish—refers generally to those Sephardic Jews who accepted baptism, whether voluntarily or under duress, mostly from the great persecutions of 1391, and into the fifteenth century. There were, however, numerous other conversions, whether volitional or otherwise, individual or *en masse*, from at least the seventh century C.E., under the Visigothic monarchies, through the expulsion from Spain in 1492, and from Portugal in 1497, and even into succeeding centuries in Iberia and the Iberian world. A parallel expression is "confeso," which also means "one who confessed" or "I confess," depending on the placement of the accent mark. From the Jewish perspective, the Hebrew term "*anusim*" (meaning "forced ones") is frequently used. A centuries-long debate concerning the nature of this "conversion" would continue among the Sephardic population of Iberia, and even among their exiled descendants. For many, the converts were little more than "*meshumadim*;" willing and determined apostates undeserving of anything but opprobrium from those who had remained steadfast in their beliefs and practices.

From the Christian side, the term "marranos" often occurs. The origin of this word is still widely debated. It may come from an Arabic expression "*machram*" (or vulgarly "*machran*"), meaning "something forbidden," though other etymologies, of greater or lesser plausibility, are also possible. Another proposal argues that "marrano" comes from the Aramaic "*maran atha*," meaning "the Lord is come" or from the Hebrew "*mara'e ain*," Hebrew for "appearance of the eye," which could accurately depict an unwilling convert, given to secret practice of the previous cult. At any rate, "marrano" would come to mean "swine," a metonymy referring disparagingly to people of Semitic origin and their (or their ancestors') dietary proscriptions. This usage occurs at least as early as the fourteenth century, when a royal proclamation would forbid labeling anyone as a "marrano." This proscription was specifically directed against those Jews who apparently attacked their apostate former brethren, terming them "marranos" and "tornadizos" (traitors or turncoats).

The Jewish "conversos" and their descendants were also labeled "New Christians," as opposed to the Old Christians who were purportedly of ancient Christian lineage. Roman Catholic canon law explicitly forbade such prejudicial distinctions between Christians, going so far as to implement excommunication against those who remained obdurate in teaching or otherwise promulgating such heresy. Indeed, such distinctions effectively would make one baptism more valid than another, while making of God a respecter of persons. This thinking follows in line with the teachings of Jesus of Nazareth, Paul, and other apostles in the infant Church, down to pronouncements by popes and other prelates of various sorts and generations. Nonetheless, the distinction was made and ratified on a variety of levels, both in the popular sphere as well as at more official heights. Thereby, one had to certify the non-Semitic nature of one's genealogy in order to hold civil or ecclesiastic office, to emigrate to the New World, or even live in certain areas. It should be noted here that it was not just the actual converts themselves, but also their descendants for all generations of time, who were made to bear the same stigma. There were many voices of toleration and mercy raised in the "conversos" defense, though these were generally drowned out by a cacophony of infinitely less-gracious tones.

Other distinctive terminology used to separate the Christian flock and distinguish the converts and their descendants from those not of Jewish stock included "*cristiano limpio*" (clean Christian) and "*cristiano lindo*" (beautiful Christian). The former usage perhaps has ironic reference to the Mosaic dietary code, making the "conversos," like the beasts that their predecessors had rejected, permanently unclean, to a degree that no baptism would ever wash away the "stain" of their ancestry. The notion of "*limpieza de sangre*" (cleanness of blood), as explained below, also probably figures into this convoluted equation. In turn, the notion that certain Christians bore the mark of blessedness and divine favor in their very countenances, whereas others did not (and apparently could not) exhibit such beatitude, further separates the "conversos" from the rest of the fold. Additionally, certain regional usages also can be cited, including "*chueta*," used even into the twentieth century to designate those of convert stock on the island of Majorca.

Certainly, conversion to Christianity from Judaism was not unknown throughout the middle ages, though the mass conversions of Iberian Jewry would begin with the murderous riots of 1391 and continue throughout the fifteenth century. There were other forced conversions, starting as early as 613 C.E., when the Visigothic King Sisebut issued an edict mandating the conversion of all Jews on the Peninsula. During these centuries, the Christian monarchs would issue various anti-Judaic decrees, running the gamut from a mandate of baptism to a decree that all contracts between individuals of any persuasion must begin with recitation of the Lord's Prayer and end with consumption of a dish of pork. Moreover, under the rule of Islam, life as a Jew could also become perilous, if not impossible, as tolerance waxed and waned according to the pleasure of the rulers in power. In the twelfth century c.e., Moses Maimonides, the greatest of the medieval Jewish philosophers, and his family fled Iberia because of the persecution of the Almohades faction of Islam. In the wake of his experiences, Maimonides would write—with considerable mercy and understanding—concerning what should be done with those who under duress had failed to sanctify the Name, converting, however nominally, to another faith.

Early on in the fifteenth century, the fervent preaching of Vicente Ferrer and his missionary companions would convert many Sepharadim, though the threat of violence and death at the hands of the mobs stirred to righteous indignation by his exhortations would also convince many to accept baptism. These ministers of the gospel often gained legal (and enforced) access to synagogues, the better to exhort a captive audience concerning their version of the truths of Christianity. Additionally, there were organized "disputations" or "debates" convened periodically by kings and popes to "convince" the Jews of the error of their ways. Of course, the "winning" argument was never in doubt. Under such peril, often physical as well as psychological, many Jews relented and received baptism. On occasion the disputants on both sides were of Jewish background; in other words, their Christian adversaries were sometimes Jewish converts, schooled in the Talmud and thereby supposedly able to reason with their former fellows and show them their folly. Names such as Petrus Alfonsi, Pablo of Burgos, Juan of Valladolid, and Jerónimo de Santa Fe, among numerous others, recall that the adversaries of the Jews—at whatever juncture—were frequently former brethren, now militantly converted to what they perceived to be the Christian cause and even holding high ecclesiastical office. With such forces arrayed against them, Jews, both small and great, did become Christian, at least according to outward ordinances.

It remains a polemical issue whether the majority of the "conversos" of this period were, in fact, good Christians or whether they were archdeceivers, holding to their former beliefs and practices and thereby corrupting the new faith. The concern in various ecclesiastic and political spheres (sometimes the distinction would be artificial, at best) was that the "conversos" were backsliding, often at the behest of those Jews who had not accepted baptism, with whom the newly-baptized and their descendants still actively associated. The belief was rampant that, essentially, once a Jew, always a Jew. This debate continues even today in scholarly circles, as the "Jewishness" of the "conversos" continues in question. Certainly, there were "judaizantes" (Judaizers): sometimes this amounted to little more than a relatively innocuous social observance or dietary preference. Or the "converso" could secretly (at times, even openly) flaunt his Jewish convictions. But most scholars tend to agree that the problem of the Judaizers was probably much less severe than contended by the Catholic monarchs, Ferdinand, King of Aragón (who was, incidentally, of Jewish extraction on his mother's side) and Isabella, Queen of Castile, and the Inquisition (which they petitioned Pope Sixtus IV to organize in their combined domains in 1478). It cannot be denied that many of the "conversos" practiced Roman Catholicism in good faith, to the best of their knowledge and ability, from the very outset of their association with the Church. Indeed, some of those condemned as Judaizers by the Inquisition (those executed were referred to as being "relaxed") even went to their death praying the rosary, while invoking Jesus, Mary, and the saints. Incidentally, there would even be a few converts from Christianity to Judaism, valiant souls willing to sacrifice their lives, while following in the footsteps of the Jewish exemplars.

Much of the vigor directed against the "conversos," as now is generally agreed, was less concerned with their religiosity and even with their "race" and more with their economic and socio-political status. The generations of "conversos" in the first decades of the fifteenth century, whether they secretly practiced aspects of the old faith or not, at least outwardly became good, as well as very upwardly-mobile,

Christians. As a group, they were eminently successful in society, accumulating considerable wealth and power. Many rose to a social and political prominence that quickly generated considerable envy at various levels of the social order. The first manifestation of that envy would arise in Toledo, known since medieval times as a center of "convivencia," the more or less cooperative (if not convivial) coexistence of Christians, Moors, and Jews. In 1449, the first Statutes of Purity of Blood were enacted, decreeing that no one of "converso" origin would hold any significant post in government. Thereafter, another designation for the "conversos" would be "*sangre infecta*" (infected blood) or "*maculada*" (stained). The debate over this blatant discrimination raged long and hard, disuniting still further an already scattered Christian flock.

Popes and other prelates of diverse ecclesiastical station would vociferously denounce the Statutes, enumerating their explicit and implied evils. But eventually these documents and those who espoused them gained sufficient support in ecclesiastical, governmental, and popular circles to spread their poisonous influence into all corners of society for centuries thereafter, in Iberia, as well as across the oceans to all the far-flung colonies of Spain and Portugal. One theoretical justification for the Statutes was that the Jews and their descendants (whether these people had accepted Christian baptism or not) were affected by an "hereditary disease" against which individual volition offered no recourse. Thereafter, no facet of life was unaffected. The need to procure an "*ejecutoria*" (certificate of purity of blood) became rampant and all-consuming, in order to demonstrate one's genealogical purity, so as to secure membership in religious orders, governmental bodies, military orders, and even to receive university degrees. The services of genealogists who could produce such pedigrees—real or imagined—became extremely valuable and costly.

Individuals either of demonstrated or of suspected "converso" lineage, who could not somehow produce such guarantees, were thereby precluded from membership (even *ex post facto* in some cases) in certain religious orders or other organizations, or from holding religious benefices. A noteworthy exception is the Jesuit order, founded in the sixteenth century by Ignatius of Loyola; the Society of Jesus and its founder were generally much more open and tolerant than many of their counterparts. In this context, there are the efforts of the Portuguese Jesuit Antônio Vieira, arguably the greatest preacher of his generation and called the "Apostle of Brazil." Father Vieira challenged the Inquisition and its injustices to "conversos" of his and other nations. For his trouble he was incarcerated for some three years, from 1665-1667. But he would not keep silent and continued to press for reform and righteousness, even in Rome herself.

On the other hand, the Dominican Order would often figure to the converse, that is, as an icon of intolerance: certainly there were decent Dominicans who believed in and practiced the doctrines of their faith, with regard to all comers. But as an order, they came to be known in popular parlance as the "domini canes," a play on words making them out to be the "dogs of the Lord." In such guise, they would hound the Judaizers, worrying and finally driving what they took to be insincere "conversos" to the dungeons of the Inquisitions and even beyond, they hoped, to the fires of hell. In this context, it is an irony at least to be recognized, if not savored, that other epithets applied to the "conversos," from the fifteenth century into the twentieth, were "*perro*" (dog) and "*perro judío*" (Jew dog). Ironically, the term "*gato*" (cat) also could find application to "conversos" or to those accused of such being, in part because, as Sanford Shepard shows, numerous "conversos" would take animal names of one sort or another as a surname, once they separated from Judaism and entered the fold of Christ via baptism (see *Lost Lexicon*).

In turn, certain military orders also prevented "conversos" from membership or from holding offices of significant rank, while various governmental offices, from the local to the national, were forbidden to those of Jewish ancestry, however remote in time and space. The universities also would preclude admission or deny degrees to "conversos," as occurred in the case of the novelist Mateo Alemán (1547-1614?), denied a medical degree by the University of Alcalá de Henares. Fair-minded individuals and organizations defended the "conversos," but the forces arrayed against them and their descendants—once a "converso" always a "converso"—were overwhelming. The "conversos," as a class and as individuals, suffered what Stephen Gilman and others have termed a "fall of fortune:" as the wheel of fortune (a pervasive image in medieval culture) kept turning, they who had been at the pinnacle of prosperity could plunge to the depths of poverty, ignominy, and despair. The slightest slander by a neighbor recollecting details many-decades old, the merest slip in demeanor in an unguarded moment, or the subterfuge and/or the sanctimony of an envious enemy could cast one and one's family into the Inquisitorial dungeons (with automatic confiscation of all worldly wealth and revocation of all earthy honors) and even into their all-consuming fires.

Granted, there were those individuals or small pockets of people that would practice some aspect(s) of Jewish ritual even into the late twentieth century, but, typically, most of the so-called "crypto-Jews" were a function the Inquisitorial imagination. Enjoying nothing like the plentitude, organization, and vigor envisioned by the Inquisitors and their adherents, significant populations of Judaizers probably did not exist much beyond the first years or at most a generation or two after baptism. This was more true of the "conversos" in Spain than in Portugal, where the conversions of 1497, enforced primarily on Jews who had fled the new Spanish kingdom of Ferdinand and Isabella in 1492, involved a less-willing population. Indeed, in Castilian culture for some centuries to come, "portugués" would constitute a synonym for the "Judaizer" unwilling to be assimilated. The Catholic Monarchs' Edict of Expulsion, issued in March, 1492, a document that would give rise to so much grief among Jews who converted and those who chose exile or an early grave, was formulated, ostensibly, to aid the new converts. The Church considered prolonged associations with former brethren to be deleterious to the "conversos'" precarious spiritual well-being; to prevent them from backsliding at the behest of the remaining Jews in Spain, the Edict of Expulsion exhorted the Jews to conversion, granting them until 31 July to do so.

Those who remained recalcitrant would be forced to go into exile, which many did, whether in Portugal (where the Catholic Monarchs' machinations with the new King Manoel cut short their stay, at least in an unbaptized state) or to Italy or to various parts of Arab North Africa, the Middle East, and southeastern Europe. Once again, many others, for a variety of reasons, joined the ranks of the "conversos." Others, after a time abroad, would return to the promise of their former economic and social standing, once they had undergone Christian baptism. However, these new converts would typically face the same strictures as the current "conversos." This is not to say that the "conversos," both individually and collectively, would not rise to great heights. King Ferdinand himself, particularly after his wife's death in 1504, was surrounded by a coterie of "converso" advisors who became incredibly powerful and influential. Indeed, various writers on the subject have suggested that a clear majority of the urban bourgeoisie in fifteenth- and sixteenth-century Spain were "conversos." The immense material success of these people, as a class and as individuals, their often conspicuous display wealth and honors, would continue to provoke a considerable backlash throughout the population.

The political, social, and economic ferment would boil over in a variety of venues: from the Statutes of Purity of Blood to a violent revolt, termed the "Guerra de las Comunidades" (war of the communities) and erupting in 1521, which was a reaction against royal restrictions on the local control and the "conversos" in the various levels of government (though many "conversos" were at least associated with, if not actual ringleaders, in the civil unrest). This movement was finally crushed when the grandson of Ferdinand and Isabella, Charles V, the first Habsburg monarch of

Spain, was able to assert his autocracy. The debate continues concerning the "converso" participation in the "comunero" conflict. It is a story of multiple and shifting allegiances, of divided and divisive loyalties, but when the movement was finally put down, the "conversos" as a class were clearly the losers, particularly in popular opinion. Whether or not the vast heaps of "comunero" dead did lack foreskins, as one wag asserted, the new and now-absolute monarch would continue to exercise a heavy hand against his enemies, real and perceived, as he expanded the scope of his imperial sway. As so often would be the case, the "conversos" became a scapegoat for the Crown and for the populace overall.

Some of the places that the exiled Jews and "conversos" took refuge would become even more dangerous, or at least less hospitable than Spain. Certainly there were many decent, honorable, tolerant individuals and organizations that received, sheltered, or advocated on behalf of the "conversos" already in their midst or those desiring acceptance. Persecution of the refugees often only intensified as they took refuge in foreign lands. Portugal, for instance, would receive many Jews, though by 1497 they were expelled or baptized involuntarily and *en masse*. Later, many of this group of "conversos" (or their descendants) would return to Spain, particularly when Portugal was annexed by that country in 1580. Their adherence (or at least the popular perception thereof) to Christianity was considerably less than that of most of the Spanish "conversos," to the degree that in the Spanish domains during the sixteenth and into the seventeenth centuries, "portugués" (Portuguese) became synonymous with Jew or "converso." The Inquisition would establish deep roots in Portugal, as well as in various parts of Latin America, particularly in Mexico, in Peru, and in parts of Brazil. Even some of the *conquistadores* would be tried and executed for Judaizing. At this point it should be noted that there was a "converso" presence in the New World from the very beginning, as several Jews and "conversos" sailed with Columbus, who was himself, as various writers on the subject would have it, quite possibly of converted Jewish ancestry, as were various of his backers and benefactors, who would make the voyages of discovery (and conquest) possible.

Many exiled Jews and "conversos" also would take refuge in Holland or in others of the "Low Countries," which originally constituted part of the empire established by Charles V, over which, during the next centuries, his successors attempted to maintain hegemony, at an immense material and human cost. Many "conversos" would settle in disputed territory, theoretically far away from the persecutions of the Spanish Crown and its Inquisitorial minions. Numerous individuals, once in this relative safety, would revert to the Judaism of their fathers. The cultural and commercial activities of the "conversos" and the Jews coincided with the first great age of Dutch prosperity. One of the earliest congregations, finally meeting as Jews once more, was initially arrested. Unable to communicate in other that an Iberian language, they were finally released when one of their number, fluent in Latin, made their affiliation clear. Once the authorities realized that it was not a question of papist infiltration, the newcomers were welcomed for what they were and would be, an economic boon (see Cecil Roth, *A History of the Marranos*). This Dutch-"converso" connection would continue even into the Americas, from Manhattan to the Dutch possessions in Brazil. However, for other refugees or their descendants the persecutions were not necessarily at an end, though not necessarily from gentiles. For instance, the synagogue and its elders in Amsterdam would condemn the writings and excommunicate Baruch (Benito) Spinoza, who made his living as a lens grinder, but one day would be recognized internationally as a philosopher. Spinoza's unwillingness to recant his freethinking philosophy was simply not in accord with their more conservative persuasion. His internal exile would last the rest of his life, paralleling that suffered by so many "conversos" in Iberia or in the Iberian New World.

Some of the repercussions for Spinoza and the Jewish community of the Netherlands (with their close cultural and commercial connections all over Europe and the Near East) came about as a result of the centuries-old controversy, stirred up by Maimonides and his successors. Young Jews were on more than one occasion barred by their elders from studying philosophy. Spinoza's defiance to the death was no more than other youth had practiced (or as some would say, perpetrated) in generations before his own. Moreover, Jews or "conversos" in exile in other parts of the world, for instance in the eastern Mediterranean, in places like Salonika, would endure censure or some measure of ostracization, culminating in excommunication, at the hands of their fellows. Indeed, at home or abroad, it was not unusual for the most virulent persecutors of the Jews or of the "conversos" to be themselves "conversos" or Jews: zealots and bigots of various persuasions but all in possession of the exclusive truth, abounded, making life difficult, if not impossible, for many of those who should have been brethren. An example frequently cited is Tomás de Torquemada, the Inquisitor General, a principal force in engineering the expulsion of 1492, who was also apparently of "converso" lineage. It was he who, reputedly, as Ferdinand vacillated (when confronted by an enormous bribe to annul the decree), threw a crucifix down before the King, querying how much Jesus would be sold for this time.

In this regard, Américo Castro, the great pioneer of "converso" studies, has gone so far as to posit that certain ones of the techniques and tactics of the Inquisition, and especially the institutional and individual intolerance, were actually a function of previous Jewish institutions and ideology. Other scholars, such as Benzion Netanyahu, vociferously contradict this line of reasoning point for point, though even the term "malsín" (one who denounced others to the authorities) comes certainly from the Hebrew "malshín" (a slanderer). The Jewish authorities dealt with such evil-spoken individuals long before they would accuse their brethren (or former brethren) to the Christian tribunals. Likewise, the title "don," so coveted by "converso" and Old Christian alike, in an age obsessed with the appearance of nobility, may well derive from the Hebrew "adonai" rather than the Latin "dominus" (Lord). Castro and Netanyahu, among others, have contended concerning the question of whether the Iberian fixation on "limpieza de sangre" and "hidalguía" (noble status) had its origin and impetus in Jewish culture.

This is by no means to make the victim over into a villain but only to assert that more souls could have been won, for whatever faith was in the offing, had its adherents practiced more kindness and tolerance. When a society or a government chooses to make war on its own people, especially when some of the best and brightest are included in that number, all parties are dragged toward the abyss of general suicide. Thus, so many "conversos," who, despite being good Christians, or their defenders, could, at a moment's notice, without anything resembling due process, come under assault from the Inquisitors, their familiars, or other agents of totalitarian religious and political policy. Various ecclesiastical and secular writers would argue for openness in the proceedings, though secrecy, as well as cruelty in the name of truth, became the hallmark of the Inquisition at work. An individual could be imprisoned, often for long periods of time, with no "speedy trial" and no confrontation of the accusers or witnesses or even any official statement of charges. The infraction, real or imagined, could be almost nonexistent, but, nonetheless, sufficient to fan the fires of intolerance. Such "crimes" as insufficient consumption of bacon or other pork products, changing one's linen on Friday, or lack of diligence at work on Saturday, even if such misdeeds occurred many years earlier, were grounds for Inquisitorial zeal. Neighbors were encouraged to denounce neighbors, family members to betray each other, all this somehow to ameliorate their own impiety or other sins or to otherwise curry favor with the Inquisitors. These less-than-impartial judges, centuries before the notion of Papal Infallibility, stood as the supreme arbiters in matters of faith and morals. Until the Spanish Inquisition was finally abolished in 1834 (the last gasp of the Portuguese Inquisition had come in 1778), the Inquisitorial courts stood in lieu of the

Deity, decreeing without appeal in matters of life and death.

Effectively, the "conversos" were caught between the former faith and the new one, which they had accepted to one degree or another, but which to a greater or lesser extent would not accept them; the distinction between Old and New Christian was not abrogated in Portugal until 1773 and continued in Spain well into the nineteenth century. In turn, the old religion was often reluctant to receive them back, counting them as gentiles, apostates, or at least as proselytes, and once the expulsion was carried out, often could not receive them at all. In this vein, then, "Conversos" were sometimes called "*alboraicos*" or "*alboraiques*," names derived from the name of Mohammed's fabulous mount, Al-Borak. This was a composite beast which carried him from Mecca to Jerusalem and then up to heaven. The "conversos" were thus labeled as neither Jew nor Christian, neither one species nor another. In this implosive environment, there were those "conversos" who continued, against all odds, to practice some facets of the faith of their fathers, though generally without benefit of anything resembling a rabbinate or Talmudic traditions or even scriptures themselves. The risk was always there of the eternal "*sambenito*," from "*saco bendito*," the robe worn by the penitents before the Inquisition and often hung in the local church from generation to generation, to remind the repentant heretics, as well as those yet unborn, of the ancestral ignominy in which they had part. Such displays had little or nothing to do with Christian humility and everything to do with humiliation.

Out of the "conversos'" experience, and that of their persecutors, grew a culture of codes, words or phrases that would mean different things to different individuals on different levels. Sanford Shephard has studied and catalogued this "lost lexicon" in a monograph, identifying the "secret meanings in the vocabulary of Spanish literature during the Inquisition." For instance, certain terms used to characterize the "conversos," while originally directed against them by their enemies, sometimes were adopted and adapted, as such pejorative expressions often are by the persecuted or otherwise denigrated. Such incorporation may involve different levels of self-hatred, however feigned or genuine, or of profound irony, or some admixture of both with other possible sentiments (in this regard, the reader could consult Sander Gilman's *Jewish Self-Hatred*). Numerous other terms would communicate, whether among or concerning the "conversos," always indicating their difference, their separateness, making them a breed apart from the Old Christians surrounding them. Another expression that probably was borrowed by "conversos" from their enemies was "*ex illis*" (Latin for "from or of them"), marking the person(s) so designated as irredeemably "other." Additional terms designating Old Christians that eventually were applied by the "conversos" to themselves, signaling their separateness rather than any sort of common Hispanic humanity, included: "*godos*" (Goths), the supposed archetype of Old Christianity and therefore everything the "conversos" were not and could never be; "*gallegos*" (Gallicians), as associated geographically and linguistically with the Portuguese, another type of the crypto-Jews; "*montañés*" (one from the mountainous north of Spain, in Asturias and Cantabria, regions never conquered by the Moors and supposedly never otherwise infected by Semitic peoples of any sort); "*vizcaíno*" (Biscayan), a Basque of impeccable Old Christianity, never tainted by anything Semitic. These and similar terms came to denote their opposite, ironizing both the persecutors and the persecuted, in a nexus of associations that figured difference, rather than commonality.

Another sign of Jewishness in the "conversos," at least according to their enemies, was the pursuit of wealth. In Iberia and the New World colonies thereof, it was by no means a bad thing to be wealthy. But the manner of acquisition or how recently that wealth was acquired could cast a long shadow over individuals and families. Anything even vaguely commercial or the least bit progressive suggested the Semitic and therefore was by definition ignoble. Moreover, the Inquisition always lurked nearby, ready to confiscate entire fortunes from those it processed. There is, first of all, good evidence that King Ferdinand petitioned to have the Inquisition established in Spain for financial reasons, hoping thereby to fund his political and military ambitions. In its own right, the Inquisition would become a self-propelled engine of persecution, supporting itself by confiscated revenues. Certainly, there were Jewish or "converso" bankers who stood to make incredible profits, though almost always at considerable risk to self and capital. Their loans and general fiscal expertise made the empires and their scattered enterprises possible, from the ambitions of monarchs and the nobility to the vast bureaucracies generated on multiple continents to govern, at home and abroad. But their fiscal ministrations were often rejected in favor of "noble" poverty. Indeed, at all levels of society, from the king to the clerk to the day-laborer or even to the beggar, honor universally became a primary (even an exclusive) concern. This was not to be so much the pursuit of virtue as it was to project the appearance of Old Christianity.

Américo Castro (in *De la edad conflictiva*, "Concerning the Conflictive Age") has suggested in this regard an illuminating distinction between two Spanish words that both are rendered as "honor" in English. He suggests, drawing on evidence from a myriad of sources from Iberian culture of the sixteenth and seventeenth centuries and even thereafter, that "honor" is essentially something internal that the world cannot touch or otherwise destroy, whereas "honra" is only perceived in the eyes of those around any particular individual. It is strictly a function of social image and therefore can be defiled or destroyed in an instant. Iberian society, then, would become preoccupied more than anything else with the vain (and certainly impossible) task of controlling what other people might think of their neighbors. The theme of "*qué dirá la gente*" ("what will people say?") pervades all facets of life. This was not just to fool the Inquisitors, but also to deceive all those around and even oneself. In the fever to create this appearance, all activity associated in the popular mind with Jewishness and the "conversos" would come to a

screeching halt, or at least would funnel itself through convoluted patterns, to throw the curious off the trail.

There were certainly those who were morbidly inquisitive, as the pastime of "*saber vidas ajenas*" ("knowing one's neighbor's business") would also become a central theme for hundreds of years in the Iberian kingdoms and their colonies. The converse, attempting to prevent one's neighbors from knowing one's own affairs would become an equally-prevalent pursuit; thus, the guarded life would figure as the order of the day, though one thoughtless act could bring down any and all charades. Certain occupations, whether banking or other money-handling, professional civil service, business of any sort, various trades, particularly that of merchant, were associated with the Jews and the "conversos." For instance, the "*indiano*," a Spaniard who went to the colonies with the express purpose of making money by some commercial enterprise, would stand as a type of the "converso," even if the individual in question were one hundred percent gentile and without a Semitic "blemish" on his ancestry for innumerable generations. Engaging in any of these sorts of practices, especially with success, would mark a person as a "converso," sending up a red flag for the neighbors and soon for the invidious Inquisitors.

The "*hidalgo*" (coming, literally, from "*hijo de algo*," "son of something or someone") class, the lowest rung of the aristocracy, was considered to be riddled with "conversos." Eventually, the only secure class was that of the "*labradores*," actual manual agricultural laborers. As indicated by the notorious *Libro Verde de Aragón* (Green Book of Aragón), written by Juan de Anchias, a secretary to the Inquisitorial tribunal, there existed few noble families without a taint of Semitic blood. So, paradoxically, the only people who could claim outright Old Christian "nobility" were those who had not a drop of noble blood, but were as "common" as dirt. The most visible example of this is Cervantes' Sancho Panza, as opposed to his master, the *hidalgo* Don Quijote. Various writers have suggested that the knight errant may well be New Christian, while his squire is assured of his Old Christian lineage and consequent "nobility." Essentially everyone during the so-called Golden Age of Spanish culture (roughly from 1500-1650 or even to 1700) ceaselessly pursued what could never be had: a spotless public image. This same epoch would mark, though an Age of Gold in the arts, a time of great ruin at the national, the regional, the familial, and the individual levels. Gainful enterprise would sully one's "honra." To such a fate, even idle indigence, though with the appearance of something more, was always preferable.

The archetype of this attitude is encountered in the squire in the picaresque novel *Lazarillo de Tormes*, published anonymously in 1554. Most readers agree that not only the title character but also the author, whoever he might have been, were probably of "converso" background. At age eight, Lazarillo is "apprenticed" by his widowed mother to a blind man. Narrating his life in the first person, the boy passes through the service of many masters, including a priest, the squire in question, a seller of indulgences, and so forth, always revealing the underside of society and ironizing all of its institutions. The squire who the lad serves for a time lives a life focused only on "honra," creating an empty appearance for the world to see, behind which there is only pretense and abject poverty. He is, in fact, so destitute that his servant must support them both by begging: the older man's only concern is that no one learn of this relationship, though only for the sake of his "honor." Numerous other picaresque works would be written, including the *Guzmán de Alfarache* (1599, 1604), by Mateo Alemán. His condition as a "converso" did not preclude his work from achieving extraordinary popularity; nor did it save him from the clutches of the Inquisition. Had he not been rescued by a friend high on the ecclesiastical ladder, Alemán's temerity—signing his name to his bitterly satirical work— would certainly have cost him his life.

Another picaresque work that achieved great literary (if not commercial) success was the *Vida del Buscón* (Life of the Scoundrel), published in 1626, by Francisco de Quevedo, an Old Christian who despised the "conversos" and everything associated with them. Pablos of Segovia, the protagonist of this novel, is the child of a witch and a thief who are processed by the Inquisition. The son passes through a variety of ignoble situations, generally just one step ahead of the Holy Office (as the Inquisition was called). He is portrayed as a scoundrel by nature, one who could never be otherwise. Quevedo's sardonic mockery of the "conversos" also extends to poetry such "A una nariz" (To a nose), describing a surrealistically Semitic proboscis. Other picaresque works, whose characters, if not their authors, are generally considered (or at least suspected) to be of "converso" background, include: Vicente Espinel's *La vida del escudero Marcos de Obregón* (1618), Francisco Delicado's *La lozana andaluza* (1528), and Francisco López de Ubeda's *La pícara Justina* (1605). The *pícaros*, or their female variant, the *pícaras*, spend their lives in the vain pursuit of the "honra" categorically denied them at all junctures. A physical hunger for bread becomes a primary motif in essentially all of the picaresque works, though a more metaphysical hunger, unfulfilled and unfulfillable, for "honra" dominates their marginal existences, as it would in all of the "conversos" in society at large. To this effect, it is after his eye-opening experiences with the squire and other masters that Lazarillo describes so graphically "*la negra que llaman honra*" (the bitch they call honor).

Other literary modalities also originate or receive a major impetus from "converso" authors: for instance, it is quite likely that Lope de Rueda (1510?-1565), an actor, director, and author of some forty short comedic works, the *pasos*, was of "converso" background. He would turn the nascent Spanish theater from its aristocratic leanings in a more popular and realistic direction: the result would be the incredible flowering of the Spanish Golden Age *Comedia*, a corpus eventually to include tens of thousands of plays, many of which rival anything in any other national tradition of the world. Another theatrical, or at least dramatic, work is Francisco de Rojas' *Tragicomedia de Calisto y Melibea* (Tragicomedy of Calisto and Melibea), first published in 1499, although more acts were added in subsequent editions. The actual literary genre of this "play in novel form" (or dramatic novel, or philosophical dialogue) continues to be controversial. At any rate, the work is commonly called the *Celestina*, after the bawd the star-crossed young man, Calisto, employs to secure the favors of Melibea; it figures as one of the principal works of Spanish literature in any age.

Rojas was a "converso" who managed to avoid the clutches of the Inquisition, whether during his time as a student in Salamanca (when he wrote the first draft of the *Celestina*), or during his practice as an attorney in Puebla de Montalbán, near Toledo. Nonetheless, certain members of his immediate family were processed by the Holy Office, so the threat remained very real. In turn, most readers of his work would agree that Celestina herself must surely be a "conversa," though it has also variously been posited that Melibea is of that same ethnicity: therefore the Old Christian Calisto does not approach her father, Pleberio, to legitimize his passion. Likewise, other writers suggest that it is Calisto who is the New Christian, while Melibea is completely "*limpia*" in her antecedents; thus, the love-smitten young suitor cannot seek her hand but will have her body, hiring the *alcahueta* (go-between) who sets up their trysts. Calisto will die falling from the ladder he uses to gain access to Melibea, once Celestina's ministrations have softened her resolve.

This is literally the "fall of fortune" as experienced by so many "conversos" during the fifteenth and sixteenth centuries. They might for a time figure at the top of the "wheel of Dame Fortune," though, soon enough, she, their envious Old Christian neighbors, or even New Christian ones, could plunge them to abjection, economically and emotionally. Thus, once she learns of Calisto's death, Melibea also takes a fall, casting herself down from a tower. Indeed, the motif of the fall of fortune pervades the *Celestina*: the title character is cut down by two of Calisto's servants, Sempronio and Pármeno, who kill her when she refuses to share her profits with them. In turn, as these men flee from the law that is hot on their trail, they must jump from an upper window of her house; their mangled bodies are quickly and sternly dealt with, as their heads fall to the ground in summary execution. One of the primary themes, from the prologue to the final act of the *Celestina*, is the universal animosity and voraciousness of all creation: nature is arrayed against itself, and no being will find an altruistic friend or helper, as even children turn against parents and God seems to be against all. This is an attitude that numerous writers would suggest as corollary to "converso" status: often it must have seemed that everything around them was lying in wait, eager to militate their harm. Even the diety seemed to be distant, as the New Christians (or their ancestors) had abandoned one law and one God for another faith and its God, which, seemingly, refused to receive them.

Another pioneering humanist, who some later writers have suggested was "converso," was Antonio de Nebrija, or sometimes, Lebrija (1441-1522). Nebrija wrote the first Latin grammar in Spanish (1481), as well as the *Gramatica sobre la lengua castellana* (Grammar of the Castilian Language), which was published in 1492 and constitutes the first Spanish grammar, a tome that would help solidify Castilian as the primary language of the new Spanish nation. Additionally, Nebrija worked on the multi-volume *Biblia Poliglota Complutense* (Universal or Polyglot Bible), assembled between 1514 and 1517, at the behest of Cardinal Francisco Jiménez de Cisneros (himself quite likely to have been of "converso" origin). This project, the first critical edition of the Bible, stretched to six volumes and offered the text in Hebrew, Aramaic, Greek, Latin, and Chaldean. Another literary style that would be developed and take shape in "converso" hands is the pastoral novel. Jorge de Montemayor (1520?-1561), generally considered of "converso" antecedents, around 1559 would publish the best and most influential of all these works, *Los siete libros de la Diana* (The Seven Books of Diana). Some writers have gone so far as to call this novel a "converso text," a work written in a sort of "code" by "conversos" to be understood, at least on one level, only by their compatriots (see, for instance, Colbert Nepaulsingh's *Apples of Gold in Filigrees of Silver*, subtitled *Jewish Writing in the Eye of the Inquisition*).

Also considered a pioneer was Juan Luis Vives (1492-1540), called the "father of associationist psychology." This Valencian scholar was a "converso" who for matters of corporeal, as well as intellectual, health, would take refuge in Oxford and had various family members processed by the Inquisition after his exodus. His father was condemned and burned; his mother's bones were disinterred and burned (as was not uncommon practice for the Holy Office); his sisters were left destitute, devoid of support, whether material or religious. Vives turned from medieval Scholasticism, becoming a Renaissance figure of the first magnitude. Among the many works he wrote are: *Introducción a la sabiduria* (Introduction to Wisdom), published in 1524; *De la instrucción de la mujer cristiana* (Concerning the Instruction of the Christian Woman), published in 1528; *Del alma y de la vida* (On the Soul and on Life), published in 1538. Vives was one of many "conversos" who would become devotés of Erasmus of Rotterdam; this universal man of letters, an icon of tolerance and learning who happened to be Dutch by birth, would impact nearly every facet of Spanish civilization in the Renaissance. A statue of Vives stands on the steps of the National Library in Madrid, as a nation recalls with reverence what at another time it rejected.

Additionally, the school of mystical letters counts numerous "conversos" as its pioneers and prime movers. Among these individuals figure some of the most brilliant literary luminaries of the Spanish Golden Age, who also happen to be saints of the Roman Catholic Church, including Saint John of the Cross and Saint Theresa of Avila (or of Jesus). This latter figure is one of only two female Doctors of the Church, meaning her texts are authoritative in matters of doctrine and that from them the faithful can learn without hesitation. Saint John (born Juan de Yepes in 1542) was a religious reformer who pioneered the rededication and purification of the Carmelite Order, to become the Descalced Carmelites (who wore only sandals as a symbol of their spiritual commitment). This order, and particularly Saint John himself, moved away from worldliness toward asceticism, prayerful contemplation, and personal sanctification. His poetry also evidences this pattern, documenting through allegory the passage of the soul from the *vía purgativa* (the way of purgation), wherein the imperfections and disordered passions are purged. Next would come the *vía iluminativa* (the way of illumination), wherein the now-purified soul begins to glimpse spiritual realities and know God. Finally, there is the *vía unitiva* (the way of unity), wherein the soul, free of earthly ties and impurities, flies to God to experience the mystical union. This joining is depicted as a marriage, according to the extended metaphor of the Bible's Song of Songs, where the soul is the Bride, or female lover (it should be recalled that "alma," the word for "soul" in Spanish, is a feminine noun), while God is the male lover, or Bridegroom. Scholars have documented numerous Semitic influences— Jewish as well as Arabic—in Saint John's works, though their pristine Christianity is unquestionable.

It has been suggested by various writers that one of the appeals of mysticism to the "conversos," as individuals and as a class, came as a result of their material existence. The physical bodies of a New Christians, according to the Statutes of Purity of Blood, could never be wholly cleansed by the baptism they had received. Therefore the appeal of a spirituality that moved far beyond the confines of the physical, irredeemably vile body, offering a purified soul and an experience of the Christian God otherwise denied to them by the political and ecclesiastical powers of their time. Nonetheless, Saint Theresa, born in 1515, the daughter of a prosperous New Christian family, would live very much in the real world. Throughout her life (she died in 1582), Saint Theresa worked to reform the female arm of the Carmelites, bringing discipline and spiritual order to lax units as well as founding some thirty new convents. She was a major figure of the Spanish Counter Reformation, initiated in part as a response to Luther, Erasmus, and others, to cleanse the Church from within.

Saint Theresa's narrative of her life, entitled *Su vida* (Her Life), is considered to be one of the best pieces of "confessional" or autobiographical literature written in Spanish. She wrote this volume only at the behest of her confessor; *Su vida* was finally published in 1588, several years after Theresa's death. It is a detailed and intimate analysis of her mystical experiences, written in a colloquial, even conversational style. Another of her works, *Libro de las fundaciones* (Book of Foundations), published in 1573, describes her work as a superior in a religious order, as she goes about aiding individuals and institutions to reform, all the while manifesting a practical, "this-worldly" spirituality. Others of her mystical "how-to" manuals include: *Camino de perfección* (The Road of Perfection) and *El castillo interior* (The Interior Castle) or sometimes *Las moradas* (The Dwelling Places), published after her death, respectively, in 1585 and in 1588. In this latter book she studies the path of the soul as it moves along its prayerful, contemplative inner way to the Divine. *Camino* is also indicative of her practical spirituality, explicating her ideas on the training of nuns.

Another giant of Spanish spirituality, whose poetry is among the best in the language at any age of its history, is Fray Luis de León (1527-1591). Also of "converso" stock, his career as a religious was not officially crowned with the same sanctity as were those of Saint John and Saint Theresa, even though his version of mysticism is no less revealing of a truly noble man, making (and documenting) his inner way through troubled waters. Fray Luis was a member of the Augustinian Order and a professor of theology at the University of Salamanca. His quarrels with colleagues, as well as with members of the rival Dominican Order, particularly with regard to the final authority of the Vulgate Bible (he preferred to refer directly to the texts in Greek and Hebrew, the latter always a suspect language), landed him in a dungeon of the Inquisition for more than four years. During this time he wrote studies of the Book of Job, the Song of Songs, and of the names used throughout Scripture to categorize Jesus Christ. One of his most endur-

ingly popular works is *La perfecta casada* (The Perfect Wife).

Fray Luis was cleared of all charges, though later he would undergo another trial. Stories are told of how, returning to his lectern after the enforced absence, he addressed his students with these words: "Como decíamos ayer . . ." (As we were saying yesterday . . .). He was a good Christian who refused to give an inch to his enemies' innuendo. He chose as an emblem for his post-imprisonment work a tree, newly and severely pruned by a sharp axe still propped up against its trunk. Like the tree, Fray Luis had been trimmed back, but already was beginning to flourish once more. Incidentally, despite his virulent antagonism for the New Christians as a class and for the most part as individuals, Quevedo published an edition of Fray Luis' poetry; he could recognize talent, in spite of otherwise pervasive prejudice.

The single most emblematic and illuminating work, perhaps the truest of fictions with regard to the problems as well as the possibilities of the human spirit in perilous times, is Cervantes' *Don Quijote* (published in two parts, 1605 and 1615). From the very first paragraph of the novel that has become the archetype of Spain, and its protagonist, the archetype of all Spaniards, the author makes clear his radical intentions. First of all, there is good reason to believe that Cervantes himself may have had "converso" antecedents, along with those of his chivalric creation. In an age obsessed with genealogy, we never learn exactly from where the Manchegan *hidalgo* hails or even what his real name is (at least not until part two, when "Alonso Quijano el Bueno" is posited as the best possibility). This impoverished petty landholder, driven mad apparently by his reading of chivalric romances, recreates himself according to his own specifications. He refuses to list his lineage but, rather, starts his story with himself. Blood is less important than character and the deeds it begets. He will be a product not of his ancestors but of his own labors.

He even chooses a new name for himself, Don Quijote, as well as for his mount, his adversaries, his lady-love, and so forth. Like Adam in the Garden of Eden, naming the animals, his words generate a new creation; the word becomes the thing, and vice versa. This new order of things effectively encompasses the dream of the "conversos:" freedom from the crippling burden of the past in order to create a future of their own choice. Of course, the knight errant is continually bumping up against reality, but that does not diminish his resolve, dismissed as madness by so many of his contemporaries and successors. Indeed, such will to change oneself and one's circumstances, in Don Quijote's case, as in that of so many other "conversos," may have construed as a form of lunacy. His efforts might meet with ostensible failure, as did theirs in the "real" world, but the knight's fiction ultimately rings truer than the reality in which he and the other "conversos" were forced to exist. Even if the giants turn into windmills, the armies into sheep, the noble ladies into strumpets, and the knight back into a country gentleman (though his return to "sanity" is never definitive), Don Quijote's quest affirms the self he would be, in spite of all obstacles to the contrary.

There are numerous other important cultural figures in Spain, Portugal, and their colonies who were confirmed, or at least probably, "converso" in extraction: the individuals and their achievements fill the spectrum, of both visible and invisible light, with an array of creative colors. This gamut of literary and cultural luminaries ran from Luis de Góngora (Quevedo talked of annointing his poetry with bacon), Fray Luis de Granada, Bartolomé de las Casas, Juan Álvarez Gato, Antônio José da Silva (called "o Judeu" to this day), João Pinto Delgado, Baltasar Gracián, Andrés de Laguna, Antonio de Guevara, the brothers Valdés (Juan and Alfonso), Juan Alfonso de Baena, Abraham Miguel Cardozo, and many others. There even flourished a tradition of comedy, where court fools and public jesters, such as Alfonso Álvarez de Villasandino, Francesillo de Zúñiga, and Dr. Francisco López de Villalobos, balanced on the razor's edge, lampooning social injustices and pillorying pious hypocrisies, all the while mocking each other, powerful political and even ecclesiastic figures, and even themselves. Needless to say, such laughter could be liberating, but also perilous in the extreme.

In turn, medicine was effectively dominated by "conversos" who continued to treat royalty and commoners, though their own lives sometimes became nearly unlivable. Figures such as Juan Rodrigo (called Amatus Lusitanus), Manoel Álvares, Felipe Rodrígues, Rodrigo de Castro, Joseph and Ephriam Bueno, to name but a few, are included in this panoply of medical luminaries. Equally, finance and business, statecraft and diplomacy were also conducted by a population whose blood would perhaps not bear too close of scrutiny by the omnipresent Inquisition. It was, as Castro states, an age divided against itself, in all facets "conflictive." Estimates reach even into the hundreds thousands of Iberia's native-born offspring, people whose descendants centuries thereafter still talk of home in Spain or Portugal in dialects closely recalling fifteenth-century Castilian, who were forcibly exiled from their homeland. Many thousands more were persecuted, even to the death or subjected to a lifetime of internal exile, for being who they were. Despite such terrible tensions, the Jewish and "converso" presence would continue to make itself felt throughout the generations, at home and abroad. Their experiences, sufferings, and contributions remain a vital area of scholarly investigation.

Besides Américo Castro, then, names of some of the others who have written extensively on a diverse array of "converso" questions include: J. Amador de los Ríos; M. Menéndez y Pelayo; J. Lucio d'Azevedo; J. Mendes dos Remedios; H. Lea; A. Herculano; M. Kayserling, A. Domínguez Ortiz; F. Márquez Villanueva; I. Révah; S. Gilman; E. Glaser; J. Caro Baroja; Y. Baer; C. Roth; C. Nepaulsingh; D. Gitlitz; Y. Yerushalmi; B. Netanyahu; H. Beinart; A. Sicroff; M. Bataillon; E. Sánchez Ruano; S. Shepard; H. Kamen; N. Roth; J. Schraibman; M. Bernardete; S. Armistead; J. Silverman; E. Gutwirth; E. Benbassa; P. Díaz-Mas; J. Solà-Solé; Á. Alcalá; J. Faur; K. Scholberg; A. Paulo; E. Lipiner; Y. Kaplan; E. Cunha de Azevedo Mea; R. Pike. Even an otherwise brilliant historian such as Claudio Sánchez

Albornoz ends up actually highlighting the roles of Semitic peoples, and particularly of the "conversos," in Iberia as he systematically overlooks, minimizes, or otherwise omits them from his texts. This omission creates a blind spot that distorts the rest of the images to be brought into focus.

KEVIN S. LARSEN

D

DEUTERONOMY IN JUDAISM: The book of Deuteronomy reaches Judaism through Sifre to Deuteronomy, attributed to Tannaite authors, a commentary to Deuteronomy completed ca. 300 C.E. Out of cases and examples, sages seek generalizations and governing principles. Since in the book of Deuteronomy, Moses explicitly sets forth a vision of Israel's future history, sages in Sifre to Deuteronomy examined that vision to uncover the rules that explain what happens to Israel. That issue drew attention from cases to rules, with the result that, in the book of Deuteronomy, they set forth an account of Israel's future history, the key to Israel's recovery of command of its destiny. Like Sifra (on Leviticus), Sifre to Deuteronomy pursues a diverse topical program in order to demonstrate a few fundamental propositions. The survey of the topical and propositional program of Sifre to Deuteronomy dictates what is truly particular to its authorship. It is its systematic mode of methodical analysis, in which it does two things. First, the document's compilers take the details of cases and carefully re-frame them into rules pertaining to all cases. The authorship therefore asks those questions of susceptibility to generalization ("generalizability") that first-class philosophical minds raise. And it answers those questions by showing what details restrict the prevailing law to the conditions of the case, and what details exemplify the encompassing traits of the law overall. These are, after all, the two possibilities. The law is either limited to the case and to all cases that replicate this one. Or the law derives from the principles exemplified, in detail, in the case at hand. Essentially, as a matter of both logic and topical program, our author-

ship has reread the legal portions of the book of Deuteronomy and turned Scripture into what we now know is the orderly and encompassing code supplied by the Mishnah. To state matters simply, this authorship "mishnaizes" Scripture. We find in Sifre to Numbers no parallel to this dominant and systematic program of Sifre to Deuteronomy.

But in other aspects, the document presents no surprises. In the two Sifres and Sifra we find a recurrent motif, intense here, episodic there, of how the written component of the Torah, that is, revelation in written form, serves as the sole source of final truth. Logic or reason untested against Scripture produces flawed or unreliable results. Reason on its own is subordinate. For their search for the social rules of Israel's society, the priority of the covenant as a reliable account of the workings of reality, and the prevailing laws of Israel's history decreed by the terms of the covenant, their fundamental claim is the same. There are rules and regularities, but reason alone will not show us what they are. A systematic and reasoned reading of the Torah—the written Torah—joined to a sifting of the cases of the Torah in search of the regularities and points of law and order—these are what will tell the prevailing rule. A rule of the Mishnah and its account of the here and now of everyday life rests upon the Torah, not upon (mere) logic. A rule of Israel's history, past, present, and future, likewise derives from a search for regularities and points of order identified not by logic alone, but by logic addressed to the Torah. So there are these modes of gaining truth that apply equally to Mishnah and Scripture. There is logic, applied reason and practical wisdom, such as sages exhibit; there is the corpus of facts supplied by Scripture, read as sages read it. These two together form God's statement upon the world today.

The topical program of the document intersects at its fundamental propositions with programs of other authorships—beginning, after all, with those of Scripture itself. The writers and compilers and compositors of Deuteronomy itself will have found entirely familiar such notions as the conditional character of Israel's possession of the land of Israel, the centrality of the covenant in Israel's relationship with God and with the other nations of the world, and the decisive role of the covenant in determining its own destiny, and the covenantal responsibilities and standing of Israel's leadership—surely a considerable motif in the very structure of the book of Deuteronomy itself, beginning and end in particular. The reader may well wonder how we may treat as a distinctive authorship a group of writers who simply go over ground familiar in the received literature. In some important ways the authorship of Sifre to Deuteronomy makes a statement that is very much its own. That fact becomes clear when we consider the document's rhetorical, logical, and topical characteristics.

Four principal topics encompass the document's propositions, of which the first three correspond to the three relationships into which Israel entered: with heaven, on earth, and within. These yield systematic statements that concern the relationships between Israel and God, with special reference to the covenant, the Torah, and the land; Israel and the nations, with interest in Israel's history, past, present, and future, and how that cyclic is to be known; Israel on its own terms, with focus upon Israel's distinctive leadership. The fourth rubric encompasses not specific *ad hoc* propositions, that form aggregates of proofs of large truths, but rather, prevailing modes of thought, demonstrating the inner structure of intellect, in our document yielding the formation, out of the cases of Scripture, of encompassing rules.

Israel and God: The Implications of the Covenant: The basic proposition, spelled out in detail, is that Israel stands in a special relationship with God, and that relationship is defined by the contract, or covenant, that God made with Israel. The covenant comes to particular expression, in our document, in two matters, first, the land, second, the Torah. Each marks Israel as different from all other nations, on the one side, and as selected by God, on the other. In these propositions, sages situate Israel in the realm of heaven, finding on earth the stigmata of covenanted election and concomitant requirement of loyalty and obedience to the covenant.

First comes the definition of those traits of God that our authorship finds pertinent. God sits in judgment upon the world, and his judgment is true and righteous. God punishes faithlessness. But God's fundamental and definitive trait is mercy. The way of God is to be merciful and gracious. The basic relationship of Israel to God is one of God's grace for Israel. God's loyalty to Israel endures, even when Israel sins. When Israel forgets God, God is pained. Israel's leaders, whatever their excellence, plead with God only for grace, not for their own merit. Correct attitudes in prayer derive from the need for grace, Israel having slight merit on its own account. Israel should follow only God, carrying out religious deeds as the covenant requires, in accord with the instructions of prophets. Israel should show mercy to others, in the model of God's merciful character.

Second, the contract, or covenant, produces the result that God has acquired Israel, which God created. The reason is that only Israel accepted the Torah, among all the nations, and that is why God made the covenant with Israel in particular. Why is the covenant made only with Israel? The gentiles did not accept the Torah, Israel did, and that has made all the difference. Israel recognized God forthwith; the very peace of the world and of nature depends upon God's giving the Torah to Israel. That is why Israel is the sole nation worthy of dwelling in the palace of God and that is the basis for the covenant too. The covenant secures for Israel an enduring relationship of grace with God. The covenant cannot be revoked and endures forever.

The covenant, terms of which are specified in the Torah, has duplicate terms: if you do well, you will bear a blessing, and if not, you will bear a curse.

That is the singular mark of the covenant between God and Israel. A mark of the covenant is the liberation from Egypt, and that sufficed to impose upon Israel God's claim for their obedience. An important sign of the covenant is the possession of the land. Part of the covenant is the recognition of merit of the ancestors. In judging the descendants of the patriarchs and matriarchs, God promised, in making the covenant, recognition of the meritorious deeds of the ancestors. The conquest of the land and inheriting it are marks of the covenant, which Israel will find easy because of God's favor. The inheritance of the land is a mark of merit, inherited from the ancestors. The land is higher than all others and more choice. All religious duties are important, those that seem trivial as much as those held to be weightier.

God always loves the people Israel. That is why Israel should carry out the religious duties of the Torah with full assent. All religious duties are equally precious. Israel must be whole-hearted in its relationship with God. If it is, then its share is with God, and if not, then not. But Israel may hate God. The right attitude toward God is love, and Israel should love God with a whole heart. The reason that Israel rebels against God is prosperity. Then people become arrogant and believe that their prosperity derives from their own efforts. But that is not so, and God punishes people who rebel to show them that they depend upon God. When Israel practices idolatry, God punishes them, e.g., through exile, through famine, through drought, and the like. Whether or not Israel knows or likes the fact, it is the fact that Israel therefore has no choice but to accept God's will and fulfill the covenant.

The heaven and the earth respond to the condition of Israel and therefore carry out the stipulations of the covenant. If Israel does not carry out religious duties concerning heaven, then heaven bears witness against them. That centers on the land of Israel in particular. Possession of the land is conditional, not absolute. It begins with grace, not merit. It is defined by the stipulation that Israel observe the covenant, in which case Israel will retain the land. If Israel violates the covenant, Israel will lose the land. When Israel inherits the land, in obedience to the covenant and as an act of grace bestowed by God, it will build the Temple, where Israel's sins will find atonement. The conquest of the land itself is subject to stipulations, just as possession of the land, as an act of God's grace, is marked by religious obligations. If Israel rebels or rejects the Torah, it will lose the land, just as the Canaanites did for their idolatry.

The land is not the only, or the most important, mark of the covenant. It is the fact that Israel has the Torah which shows that Israel stands in a special relationship to God. The Torah is the source of life for Israel. It belongs to everyone, not only the aristocracy. Children should start studying the Torah at the earliest age possible. The study of the Torah is part of the fulfillment of the covenant. Even the most arid details of the Torah contain lessons, and if one studies the Torah, the reward comes both in this world and in the world to come.

The possession of the Torah imposes a particular requirement, involving an action. The most important task of every male Israelite is to study the Torah, which involves memorizing, and not forgetting, each lesson. This must go on every day and all the time. Study of the Torah should be one's main obligation, prior to all others. The correct motive is not for the sake of gain, but for the love of God and the desire for knowledge of God's will. People must direct heart, eyes, ears, to teachings of the Torah. Study of the Torah transforms human relationships, so that strangers become the children of the master of the Torah whom they serve as disciples. However unimportant the teaching or the teacher, all is as if on the authority of Moses at Sinai. When a person departs from the Torah, that person becomes an idolator. Study of the Torah prevents idolatry.

Israel and the Nations: The Meaning of History: The covenant, through the Torah of Sinai, governs not only the ongoing life of Israel but also the state of human affairs universally. The history of Israel forms a single, continuous, cycle, in that what happened in the beginning prefigures what will happen at the end of time. Events of Genesis are reenacted both in middle-history, between the beginning and the end, and also at the end of times. So the traits of the tribal founders dictated the history of their families to both the here and now and also the eschatological age. Moses was shown the whole of Israel's history, past, present, future. The times of the patriarchs are reenacted in the messianic day. That shows how Israel's history runs in cycles, so that events of ancient times prefigure events now. The prophets, beginning with Moses, describe those cycles. What happens bears close ties to what is going to happen. The prophetic promises too were realized in Temple times, and will be realized at the end of time.

The periods in the history of Israel, marked by the exodus and wandering, the inheritance of the land and the building of the Temple, the destruction, are all part of a divine plan. In this age Rome rules, but in the age to come, marked by the study of the Torah and the offering of sacrifices in the Temple cult, Israel will be in charge. That is the fundamental pattern and meaning of history. The Holy Spirit makes possible actions that bear consequences only much later in time. The prefiguring of history forms the dominant motif in Israel's contemporary life, and the reenacting of what has already been forms a constant. Israel therefore should believe, if not in what is coming, then in what has already been. The very names of places in the land attest to the continuity of Israel's history, which follows rules that do not change. The main point is that while Israel will be punished in the worst possible way, Israel will not be wiped out.

But the cyclical character of Israel's history should not mislead. Events follow a pattern, but knowledge of that pattern, which is provided by the Torah, permits Israel both to understand and also to affect its own destiny. Specifically, Israel controls its own destiny through its conduct with God. Israel's history is the working out of the effects of Israel's conduct, moderated by the merit of the ancestors. Abraham effected a change in God's relationship to the world. But merit, which makes history, is attained by one's own deeds as well. The effect of merit, in the nation's standing among the other nations, is simple. When Israel enjoys merit, it gives testimony against itself, but when not, then the most despised nation testifies against it.

But God is with Israel in time of trouble. When Israel sins, it suffers. When it repents and is forgiven, it is redeemed. For example, Israel's wandering in the wilderness took place because of the failure of Israel to attain merit. Sin is what causes the wandering in the wilderness. People rebel because they are prosperous. The merit of the ancestors works in history to Israel's benefit. What Israel does not merit on its own, at a given time, the merit of the ancestors may secure in any event. The best way to deal with Israel's powerlessness is through Torah-study; the vigor of engagement with Torah-study compensates for weakness.

It goes without saying that Israel's history follows a set time, e.g., at the fulfillment of a set period of time, an awaited event will take place. The prophets prophesy concerning the coming of the day of the Lord. Accordingly, nothing is haphazard, and all things happen in accord with a plan. That plan encompasses this world, the time of the messiah, and the world to come, in that order. God will personally exact vengeance at the end of time. God also will raise the dead. Israel has overcome difficult times and can continue to do so. The task ahead is easier than the tasks already accomplished. Israel's punishment is only once, while the punishment coming upon the nations is unremitting. Peace is worthwhile and everyone needs it. Israel's history ends in the world to come or in the days of the Messiah. The righteous inherit the Garden of Eden. The righteous in the age to come will be joyful.

God acts in history and does so publicly, in full light of day. That is to show the nations who is in charge. The Torah is what distinguishes Israel from the nations. All the nations had every opportunity to understand and accept the Torah, and all declined it; that is why Israel was selected. And that demonstrates the importance of both covenant and the Torah, the medium of the covenant. The nations even had a prophet, comparable to Moses, who was Balaam. The nations have no important role in history, except as God assigns them a role in relationship to Israel's conduct. The nations are estranged from God by idolatry. That is what prevents goodness from coming into the world. The name of God rests upon Israel in greatest measure. Idolators do not control heaven. The greatest sin an Israelite can commit is idolatry, and those who entice Israel to idolatry are deprived of the ordinary protections of the law. God is violently angry at the nations because of idolatry. As to the nations' relationships with Israel, they are guided by Israel's condition. When Israel is weak, the nations take advantage, when strong, they are sycophantic. God did not apportion love to the nations of the world as he did to Israel.

Israel at Home: The Community and its Governance: A mark of God's favor is that Israel has (or, has had and will again have) a government of its own. Part of the covenantal relationship requires Israel to follow leaders whom God has chosen and instructed, such as Moses and the prophets. Accordingly, Israel is to establish a government and follow sound public policy. Its leaders are chosen by God. Israel's leaders, e.g., prophets, are God's servants, and that is a mark of the praise that is owing to them. They are to be in the model of Moses, humble, choice, select, well-known. Moses was the right one to bestow a blessing, Israel were the right ones to receive the blessing.

Yet all leaders are mortal, even Moses died. The saints are leaders ready to give their lives for Israel. The greatest of them enjoy exceptionally long life. But the sins of the people are blamed on their leaders. The leaders depend on the people to keep the Torah, and Moses thanked them in advance for keeping the Torah after he died. The leaders were to be patient, honest, give a full hearing to all sides, make just decisions, in a broad range of matters. To stand before the judge is to stand before God. God makes sure that Israel does not lack for leadership. The basic task of the leader is both to rebuke and also to console the people.

The rulers of Israel are servants of God. The prophets exemplify these leaders, in the model of Moses, and Israel's rulers act only on the instruction of prophets. Their authority rests solely on God's favor and grace. At the instance of God, the leaders of Israel speak, in particular, words of admonition. These are delivered before death, when the whole picture is clear, so that people can draw the necessary conclusions. These words, when Moses spoke them, covered the entire history of the community of Israel. The leaders of Israel address admonition to the entire community at once. No one is excepted. But the Israelites can deal with the admonition. They draw the correct conclusions. Repentance overcomes sin, as at the sin of the golden calf. The Israelites were contentious, nitpickers, litigious, and, in general, gave Moses a difficult time. Their descendants should learn not to do so. Israel should remain united and obedient to its leaders. The task of the community is to remain united. When the Israelites are of one opinion below, God's name is glorified above.

The Laws and Law. The Structure of Intellect: The explicit propositional program of our document is joined by a set of implicit ones. These comprise repeated demonstrations of a point never fully stated. The implicit propositions have to do with the modes of correct analysis and inquiry that pertain to the Torah. Two implicit propositions predominate. The first, familiar from other compilations, is that pure reason does not suffice to produce reliable results. Only through linking our conclusions to verses of Scripture may we come to final and fixed conclusions. The implicit proposition, demonstrated many times, may therefore be stated very simply. The Torah (written) is the sole source of reliable information. Reason undisciplined by the Torah yields unreliable results. These items may occur, also, within the rubrics of the specific propositions that they contain. Some of them moreover overlap with the later catalogue, but, if so, are not listed twice.

The second of the two recurrent modes of thought is the more important. Indeed, we shall presently note that it constitutes the one substantial, distinctive statement made by our authorship. It is the demonstration that many things conform to a single structure and pattern. We can show this uniformity of the law by addressing the same questions to disparate cases and, in so doing, composing general laws that transcend cases and form a cogent system. What is striking, then, is the power of a single set of questions to reshape and reorganize diverse data into a single cogent set of questions and answers, all things fitting together into a single, remarkably well-composed structure. Not only so, but when we review the numerous passages at which we find what, in the logical repertoire I called methodical-analytical logic, we find a single program. It is an effort to ask whether a case of Scripture imposes a rule that limits or imparts a rule that augments the application of the law at hand.

A systematic reading of Scripture permits us to restrict or to extend the applicability of the detail of a case into a rule that governs many cases. A standard repertoire of questions may be addressed to a variety of topics, to yield the picture of how a great many things make essentially a single statement. This seems to me the single most common topical inquiry in our document. It covers most of the laws of Deut. 12-26. I have not catalogued the laws of history, which generalize from a case and tell us how things always must be; the list of explicit statements of the proposition that the case at hand is subject to either restriction or augmentation, that the law prevailing throughout is limited to the facts at hand or exemplified by those facts, would considerably add to this list. The size, the repetitious quality, the obsessive interest in augmentation and restriction, generalization and limitation—these traits of logic and their concomitant propositional results form the centerpiece of the whole.

In a few units of thought I discern no distinctive message, one that correlates with others to form a proposition of broad implications. Perhaps others can see points that transcend the cases at hand. These items

would correspond to ones we should expect from an authorship that remained wholly within Scripture's range of discourse, proposing only to expand and clarify what it found within Scripture. Were our document to comprise only a commentary, then the messages of Scripture, delivered within the documentary limits of Scripture—that is, verse by verse, in a sustained statement solely of what Scripture says restated in paraphrase—would constitute the whole of the catalogue of this chapter. We now see that that is far from the fact. Relative to the size of the document as a whole, these items do not seem to me to comprise an important component of the whole. They show that had our authorship wished only to amplify and restate the given, without presenting their own thought through the medium of Scripture (as through other media), they had every occasion and means of doing so. But they did so only in a limited measure. Here is a sample passage.

> SIFRE TO DEUTERONOMY PISQA I:I
> 1.A. "These are the words that Moses spoke to all Israel in Transjordan, in the wilderness, that is to say in the Arabah, opposite Suph, between Paran on the one side and Tophel, Laban, Hazeroth, and Dizahab, on the other" (Deut. 1:1):
> B. ["These are the words that Moses spoke":] Did Moses prophesy only these alone? Did he not write the entire Torah?
> C. For it is said, "And Moses wrote this Torah" (Deut. 31:9).
> D. Why then does Scripture say, "These are the words that Moses spoke"?
> E. It teaches that [when Scripture speaks of the words that one spoke, it refers in particular to] the words of admonition.
> F. So it is said [by Moses], "But Jeshurun waxed fat and kicked" (Deut. 32:15).
> 2.A. So too you may point to the following:
> B. "The words of Amos, who was among the herdsmen of Tekoa, which he saw concerning Israel in the days of Uzziah, king of Judah, and in the days of Jeroboam, son of Joash, king of Israel, two years before the earthquake" (Amos 1:1):
> C. Did Amos prophesy only concerning these [kings] alone? Did he not prophesy concerning a greater number [of kings] than any other?

D. Why then does Scripture say, "These are the words of Amos, [who was among the herdsmen of Tekoa, which he saw concerning Israel in the days of Uzziah, king of Judah, and in the days of Jeroboam, son of Joash, king of Israel, two years before the earthquake]"?

E. It teaches that [when Scripture speaks of the words that one spoke, it refers in particular to] the words of admonition.

F. And how do we know that they were words of admonition?

G. As it is said, "Hear this word, you cows of Bashan, who are in the mountain of Samaria, who oppress the poor, crush the needy, and say to their husbands, 'Bring, that we may feast'" (Amos 4:1).

H. ["And say to their husbands, 'Bring, that we may feast'"] speaks of their courts [of justice].

3.A. So too you may point to the following:

B. "And also these are the words that the Lord spoke concerning Israel and Judah" (Jer. 30:4).

C. Did Jeremiah prophesy only these words of prophecy alone? Did he not write two [complete] scrolls?

D. For it is said, "Thus far are the words of Jeremiah" (Jer. 51:64)

E. Why then does Scripture say, "And these are the words [that the Lord spoke concerning Israel and Judah]"?

F. It teaches that [when the verse says, "And these are the words that the Lord spoke concerning Israel and Judah"], it speaks in particular of the words of admonition.

G. And how do we know that they were words of admonition?

H. In accord with this verse: "For thus says the Lord, 'We have heard a voice of trembling, of fear and not of peace. Ask you now and see whether a man does labor with a child? Why do I see every man with his hands on his loins, as a woman in labor? and all faces turn pale? Alas, for the day is great, there is none like it, and it is a time of trouble for Jacob, but out of it he shall be saved'" (Jer. 30:5-7).

4.A. So too you may point to the following:

B. "And these are the last words of David" (2 Sam. 23:1).

C. And did David prophesy only these alone? And has it furthermore not been said, "The spirit of the Lord spoke through me, and his word was on my tongue" (2 Sam. 23:2)?

D. Why then does it say, "And these are the last words of David"?

E. It teaches that, [when the verse says, "And these are the last words of

David"], it refers to words of admonition.

F. And how do we know that they were words of admonition?

G. In accord with this verse: "But the ungodly are as thorns thrust away, all of them, for they cannot be taken with the hand" (2 Sam. 23:6).

5.A. So too you may point to the following:

B. "The words of Qohelet, son of David, king in Jerusalem" (Ecc. 1:1).

C. Now did Solomon prophesy only these words? Did he not write three and a half scrolls of his wisdom in proverbs?

D. Why then does it say, "The words of Qohelet, son of David, king in Jerusalem"?

E. It teaches that [when the verse says, "The words of Qohelet, son of David, king in Jerusalem," it refers to words of admonition.

F. And how do we know that they were words of admonition?

G. In accord with this verse: "The sun also rises, and the sun goes down . . . the wind goes toward the south and turns around to the north, it turns round continually in its circuit, and the wind returns again—that is, east and west [to its circuits. All the rivers run into the sea]" (Ecc. 1:5-7).

H. [Solomon] calls sun, moon, and sea "the wicked" for [the wicked] have no reward [coming back to them].

The focus is upon the exegesis of the opening word of Deuteronomy, "words. . . ." The problem is carefully stated. And yet, without the arrangement within what is going to be a commentary on Deuteronomy, we should have no reason to regard the composition as exegetical at all. In fact, it is a syllogism, aiming at proving a particular proposition concerning word-usages. Standing by itself, what we have is simply a very carefully formalized syllogism that makes a philological point, which is that the word "words of . . .," bears the sense of "admonition" or "rebuke." Five proofs are offered. We know that we reach the end of the exposition when, at 5.H, there is a minor gloss, breaking the perfect form. That is a common mode of signaling the conclusion of discourse on a given point.

SIFRE TO DEUTERONOMY PISQA I:II

1.A. ". . . to all Israel:"

B. [Moses spoke to the entire community all at once, for] had he admonished only part of them, those who were out at the market would have said, "Is this what you heard from the son of Amram? And did you not give him such-and-such an answer? If we had been there, we should have answered him four or five times for every word he said!"

2.A. Another matter concerning ". . . to all Israel:"

B. This teaches that Moses collected all of them together, from the greatest to the least of them, and he said to them, "Lo, I shall admonish you. Whoever has an answer—let him come and say it."

We proceed to the next word in the base verse, but now our comment is particular to the verse. The explanation of why Moses spoke to everyone is then clear. On the one hand, it was to make certain that there was no one left out, so No. 1. On the other, it was to make certain that everyone had a say, so No. 2. These two points then complement one another.

Sifre to Deuteronomy Pisqa I:III

1.A. Another matter concerning ". . . to all Israel:"

B. This teaches that all of them were subject to admonition but quite able to deal with the admonition.

2.A. Said R. Tarfon, "By the Temple service! [I do not believe] that there is anyone in this generation who can administer an admonition."

B. Said R. Eleazar b. Azariah, "'By the Temple service! [I do not believe] that there is anyone in this generation who can accept admonition."

C. Said R. Aqiba, "'By the Temple service! [I do not believe] that there is anyone in this generation who knows how to give an admonition."

D. Said R. Yohanan b. Nuri, "I call to give testimony against me heaven and earth [if it is not the case that] more than five times was R. Aqiba criticized before Rabban Gamaliel in Yavneh, for I would lay complaints against him, and [Gamaliel therefore] criticized him. Nonetheless, I know that [each such criticism] added to [Aqiba's] love for me.

E. "This carries out the verse, 'Do not criticize a scorner, lest he hate you, but reprove a wise person, and he will love you' (Prov. 9:8)."

Nos. 1 and 2 are quite separate units of thought, each making its own point. Shall we say that all we have, at I:I-III, is a sequence of three quite disparate proposi-

tions? In that case, the authorship before us has presented nothing more than a scrapbook of relevant comments on discrete clauses. I think otherwise. It seems to me that in I:I-III as the distinct and complete units of thought unfold we have a proposition, fully exposed, composed by the setting forth of two distinct facts, which serve as established propositions to yield the syllogism of No. 3. But the syllogism is not made explicitly, rather it is placed on display by the (mere) juxtaposition of fact 1 and fact 2 and then the final proposition, I:III.1, followed by a story making the same point as the proposition. The exegesis now joins the (established) facts [1] that Moses rebuked Israel and [2] that all Israel was involved. The point is [3] that Israel was able to deal with the admonition and did not reject it. No. 2 then contains a story that makes explicit and underlines the virtue spun out of the verse. Aqiba embodies that virtue, the capacity—the wisdom—to accept rebuke. The upshot, then, is that the authorship wished to make a single point in assembling into a single carefully ordered sequence I:I-III, and it did so by presenting two distinct propositions, at I:I, I:II, and then, at I:III, recast the whole by making a point drawing upon the two original, autonomous proofs. Joining I:I, and I:II, then led directly to the proposition at which the authorship was aiming. We have much more than an assembly of information on diverse traits or points of verses, read word by word. It is, rather, a purposeful composition, made up of what clearly are already-available materials.

Sifre to Deuteronomy Pisqa I:IV

1.A. "On the other side of the Jordan" (Deut. 1:1):

B. This teaches that he admonished them concerning things that they had done on the other side of the Jordan.

Sifre to Deuteronomy Pisqa I:V

1.A. "In the wilderness" (Deut. 1:1):

B. This teaches that he admonished them concerning things that they had done in the wilderness.

2.A. Another matter concerning "In the wilderness:"

B. This teaches that they would take their little sons and daughters and toss them into Moses's bosom and say to him, "Son of Amram, 'what ration have you prepared for these? What living have you prepared for these?'"

C. R. Judah says, "Lo, Scripture says [to make this same point], 'And the children of Israel said to them, "Would that we had died by the hand of the Lord in the land of Egypt [when we sat by the fleshpots, when we ate bread . . . for you have brought us forth to this wilderness to kill the whole assembly with hunger]" (Exod. 16:3).'"

3.A. Another matter concerning "In the wilderness" (Deut. 1:1):

B. This encompasses everything that they had done in the wilderness.

SIFRE TO DEUTERONOMY PISQA I:VI

1.A. "In the Plain" (Deut. 1:1):

B. This teaches that he admonished them concerning things that they had done in the Plains of Moab.

C. So Scripture says, "And Israel dwelt in Shittim [and the people began to commit harlotry with the daughters of Moab" (Num. 25:1).

SIFRE TO DEUTERONOMY PISQA I:VII

1.A. "Over against Suph [the sea]" (Deut. 1:1):

B. This teaches that he admonished them concerning things that they had done at the sea.

C. For they rebelled at the sea and turned their back on Moses days.

2.A. R. Judah says, "They rebelled at the sea, and they rebelled within the sea.

B. "And so Scripture says, 'They rebelled at the sea, even in the sea itself' (Ps. 106:7)."

3.A. Is it possible to suppose that he admonished them only at the outset of a journey? How do we know that he did so between one journey and the next?

B. Scripture says, "Between Paran and Tophel" (Deut. 1:1).

4.A. "Between Paran and Tophel" (Deut. 1:1):

B. [The word Tophel bears the sense of] disparaging words with which they disparaged the manna.

C. And so does Scripture say, "And our soul loathed this light bread" (Num. 21:5).

D. [God] said to them, "Fools! Even royalty choose for themselves only light bread, so that none of them should suffer from vomiting or diarrhea. For your part, against that very act of kindness that I have done for you, you bring complaints before me.

E. "It is only that you continue to walk

in the foolishness of your father, for I said, 'I will make a help meet for him' (Gen. 2:18), while he said, 'The woman whom you gave to be with me gave me of the tree and I ate' (Gen. 3:12)."

The words of admonition, now fully exposed, apply to a variety of actions of the people. That is the main point of I:IV-VII. The matter is stated in a simple way at I:IV, V.1 (with an illustration at I:V.2), I:V.3, I:VI, I:VII. After the five illustrations of the proposition that the admonition covered the entire past, we proceed to a secondary expansion, I:VII.2, 3, which itself is amplified at I:VII.4. The main structure is clear, and the proposition is continuous with the one with which we began: Moses admonished Israel, all Israel, which could take the criticism, and covered the entire list of areas where they had sinned, which then accounts for the specification of the various locations mentioned by Deut. 1:1. When we realize what is to come, we understand the full power of the proposition, which is syllogistic though in exegetical form. It is to indicate the character and encompassing program of the book of Deuteronomy—nothing less.

SIFRE TO DEUTERONOMY PISQA I:VIII

1.A. "And Hazeroth" (Deut. 1:1):

B. [God] said to them, "Ought you not to have learned from what I did to Miriam in Hazeroth?

C. "If to that righteous woman, Miriam, I did not show favor in judgment, all the more so to other people!"

2.A. Another matter: now if Miriam, who gossiped only against her brother, who was younger than herself, was punished in this way, one who gossips against someone greater than himself all the more so!"

3.A. Another matter: Now if Miriam, whom when she spoke, no person heard, but only the Omnipresent alone, in line with this verse, "And the Lord heard . . .," (Num. 12:2), was punished, one who speaks ill of his fellow in public all the more so!"

The basic point is made at the outset and the case is then amplified. The sin concerning which Moses now admonished the people was that of gossiping, and the connection to Miriam is explicit. The argument that each place-name concerns a particular sin thus is carried forward. The entire discourse exhibits remarkable cogency.

SIFRE TO DEUTERONOMY PISQA I:IX

1.A. "And Dizahab (Deut. 1:1):

B. [Since the place name means, "of gold," what he was] saying to them [was this:] "Lo, [following Finkelstein] everything you did is forgiven. But the deed concerning the [golden] calf is worst of them all." [Hammer: "I would have overlooked everything that you have done, but the incident of the golden calf is to me worse than all the rest put together."]

2.A. R. Judah would say, "'There is a parable. To what may the case be compared? To one who made a lot of trouble for his fellow. In the end he added yet another. He said to him, 'Lo, everything you did is forgiven. But this is the worst of them all.'

B. "So said the Omnipresent to Israel, 'Lo, everything you did is forgiven. But the deed concerning the [golden] calf is worst of them all.'"

The place-name calls to mind the sin of the golden calf. This is made explicit as a generalization at No. 1, and then, No. 2, Judah restates the matter as a story.

SIFRE TO DEUTERONOMY PISQA I:X

1.A. R. Simeon says, "There is a parable. To what may the case [of Israel's making the calf of gold] be compared? To one who extended hospitality to sages and their disciples, and everyone praised him.

B. "Gentiles came, and he extended hospitality to them. Thieves came and he extended hospitality to them.

C. "People said, 'That is so-and-so's nature—to extend hospitality [indiscriminately] to anyone at all.'

D. "So did Moses say to Israel, '[Di zahab, meaning, enough gold, yields the sense] There is enough gold for the tabernacle, enough gold also for the calf!'"

2.A. R. Benaiah says, "The Israelites have worshipped idolatry. Lo, they are liable to extermination. Let the gold of the tabernacle come and effect atonement for the gold of the calf."

3.A. R. Yose b. Haninah says, "'And you shall make an ark cover of pure gold' (Exod. 25:17).

B. "Let the gold of the ark cover come and effect atonement for the gold of the calf."

4.A. R. Judah says, "Lo, Scripture states, 'In the wilderness, in the plain.'

B. "These are the ten trials that our fathers inflicted upon the Omnipresent in the wilderness.

C. "And these are they: two at the sea, two involving water, two involving manna, two involving quails, one involving the calf, and one involving the spies in the wilderness."

D. Said to him R. Yose b. Dormasqit, "Judah, my honored friend, why do you distort verses of Scripture for us? I call to testify against me heaven and earth that we have made the circuit of all of these places, and each of the places is called only on account of an event that took place there [and not, as you say, to call to mind Israel's sin].

E. "And so Scripture says, And the herdsmen of Gerar strove with the herdsmen of Isaac, saying, 'The water is ours.' And he called the name of the well Esek, because they contended with him' (Gen. 26:29). 'And he called it Shibah' (Gen. 26:33)."

I:X.1-3 carries forward the matter of DiZahab and amplifies upon the theme, not the proposition at hand. No. 4 then presents a striking restatement of the basic proposition, which has been spelled out and restated in so many ways. It turns out that Judah takes the position implicit throughout and made explicit at I:X.4. There is then a contrary position, at D. We see, therefore, how the framers have drawn upon diverse materials to present a single, cogent syllogism, the one then stated in most succinct form by Judah. The contrary syllogism, that of Yose, is not spelled out, since amplification is hardly possible. Once we maintain that each place has meaning only for what happened in that particular spot, the verse no longer bears the deeper meaning announced at the outset—admonition or rebuke, specifically for actions that took place in various settings and that are called to mind by the list of words (no longer place-names) of Deut. 1:1.

SIFRE TO DEUTERONOMY PISQA I:XI

1.A. Along these same lines [of dispute between Judah and Yose:]

B. R. Judah expounded, "'The burden of the word of the Lord. In the land of Hadrach, and in Damascus, shall be his resting-place, for the Lord's is the eye of man and all the tribes of Israel" (Zech. 9:1):

C. "[Hadrach] refers to the Messiah,

who is sharp [*had*] toward the nations, but soft [*rakh*] toward Israel."

D. Said to him R. Yose b. Dormasqit, "Judah, my honored friend, why do you distort verses of Scripture for us? I call to testify against me heaven and earth that I come from Damascus, and there is a place there that is called Hadrach."

E. He said to him, "How do you interpret the clause, 'and in Damascus, shall be his resting-place'?"

F. [Yose] said to him, "How do we know that Jerusalem is destined to touch the city-limits of Damascus? As it is said, 'and in Damascus, shall be his resting-place. And 'resting place' refers only to Jerusalem, as it is said, 'This is my resting place forever' (Ps. 132:14)."

G. [Judah] said to him, "How then do you interpret the verse, And the city shall be built upon its own mound' (Jer. 30:18)?"

H. [Yose] said to him, "That it is not destined to be moved from its place."

I. [Yose continued,] saying to him, "How do I interpret the verse, 'And the side chambers were broader as they wound about higher and higher; for the winding about of the house went higher and higher round about the house, therefore the breadth of the house continued upward' (Ezek. 41:7)? It is that the land of Israel is destined to expand outward on all sides like a fig tree that is narrow below and broad above. So the gates of Jerusalem are destined to reach Damascus.

J. "And so too Scripture says, 'Your nose is like the tower of Lebanon, which looks toward Damascus' (Song 7:5).

K. "And the exiles will come and encamp in it, as it is said, 'And in Damascus shall be his resting place' (Zech. 9:1).

L. "'And it shall come to pass in the end of days that the mountain of the Lord's house shall be established at the top of the mountains and shall be exalted above the hills, and all nations shall flow into it, and many peoples shall go and say . . .' (Is. 2:2-3)."

SIFRE TO DEUTERONOMY PISQA I:XII

1.A. Along these same lines [of dispute between Judah and Yose:]

B. R. Judah expounded, "'And he made him to ride in the second chariot which he had, and they cried before him, "Abrech"' (Gen. 41:43):

C. "[Abrech] refers to Joseph, who is a father [*ab*] in wisdom, but soft [*rakh*] in years."

D. Said to him R. Yose b. Dormasqit, "Judah, my honored friend, why do you distort verses of Scripture for us? I call to testify against me heaven and earth that the meaning of Abrech pertains to knees and is simply, 'I shall cause them to bend their knees' [appealing to the causative applied to the root for knee].

E. "For everyone came and went under his authority, as Scripture says, 'And they set him over all of Egypt' (Gen. 41:43)."

I:XI-XII simply lay out further instances of the same hermeneutical dispute between Judah and Yose. All three items—I:X-XII—form a single cogent dispute on its own terms. Then the composite establishes a distinct statement, which concerns figurative, as against literal, interpretation. Once worked out, the whole found an appropriate place here, at I:X.4.

JACOB NEUSNER

E

EXODUS IN JUDAISM: The book of Exodus is mediated to Rabbinic Judaism by the midrashic compilation Mekhilta Attributed to R. Ishmael. That is a miscellany, not a coherent and systematic reading of the biblical book.

The document, seen in the aggregate, presents a composite of three kinds of materials concerning the book of Exodus. The first is a set of *ad hoc* and episodic exegeses of some passages of Scripture. The second is a group of propositional and argumentative essays in exegetical form, in which theological principles are set forth and demonstrated. The third consists of topical compositions—what we might call articles—some of them sustained, many of them well crafted, about important subjects of the Judaism of the dual Torah. The document forms a sustained address to the book of Exodus, covering Exod. 12:1-23:19, Exod. 31:12-13, and Exod. 35:1-3. It comprises nine tractates, Pisha (Exod. 12:1-13:16), Beshallah (Exod. 13-17, 14-31), Shirata (Exod. 15:1-21), Vayassa (Exod. 22-17:7), Amalek (Exod. 17:8-18:27), Bahodesh (Exod. 19:1-20:26), Neziqin (Exod. 21:1-22:23), Kaspa (Exod. 22:24-23:19), and Shabbata (Exod. 31:12-17 and 35:1-3). There are eighty-two sections, subdivided into paragraphs. The division of the book of Exodus has no bearing on the lections read in the synagogue as we now know them. While the date of the document is subject to debate, the consensus of scholarship tends to favor ca. 250-300 C.E. That guess is, though, rejected with sound reason by others, who place the document square in medieval times.

Mekhilta Attributed to R. Ishmael comprises the first scriptural encyclopedia of Judaism. A scriptural encyclopedia joins together expositions of topics, disquisitions on propositions, in general precipitated by the themes of scriptural narrative or the dictates of biblical law and collects and arranges in accord with Scripture's order and program the exegeses—paraphrases or brief explanations—of clauses of biblical verses. The nine authorships of Mekhilta Attributed to R. Ishmael treat as a given, that is to say, a corpus of facts or, more aptly, a body of tradition, what the other authorships or compilers of Midrash-compositions set forth as components of a system that requires defense and demands apologetic exposition. For our authorship, the facts comprise a corpus of information, to which people require ready access. By setting forth an important component of information, that is, the data of revealed truths of the Judaism of the dual Torah, that authorship provides such access. What is needed, then, is an encyclopaedia of things one should know on themes Scripture dictates, and the sequence of topics and propositions, in the order demanded by Scripture, results.

A model for long centuries to come—but for no one in the formative age—Mekhilta Attributed to R. Ishmael in medieval and modern times has attracted imitators and continuators. The conception of collecting information and holding it together upon the frame of Scripture attracted many, so that a vast literature of Midrash-compilation much like this compilation came into being in succeeding periods. Not one but dozens, ultimately hundreds, of Midrash-compilations, interesting, traditional, and, of course, pointless and merely informative, would fill the shelves of the library that emerged from the canon of the Judaism of the dual Torah. Accordingly, Mekhilta Attributed to R. Ishmael stood at the beginning of centuries of work carried on in the pattern set by that authorship. There would be only one Bavli, but many, many Midrash-compilations: Mekhiltas, Yalquts, Midrash-this and Midrash-that, and, in due course, a secondary development would call into being commentaries to Scripture (as to the Bavli) as well. So Mekhilta Attributed to R. Ishmael formed not only a scriptural encyclopedia of Judaism, but, as it turned out, the first of many, many such compilations of revealed, received truth, set forth in the framework of the written Torah.

The sincerest compliment is imitation. We have only one Mishnah, no other writing of its kind; only one Sifra; only one Leviticus Rabbah (with a document that uses some of its materials and copies its style, Pesiqta deRab Kahana, to be sure); only one Talmud of the Land of Israel; and the Talmud of Babylonia is utterly unique. But we have through time dozens of collections and arrangements of information on various scriptural books, and for the long centuries from the closure of the Talmud of Babylonia in the early seventh century to the nineteenth century, people reverently collected and arranged information in that essentially haphazard way, held together only by the book of Scripture at hand, that characterized this document. Whatever people wanted to say for themselves—and even the most unimaginative collector and arranger thinks to make a point, if only one of emphasis and reiteration—they said in the way the framers of Mekhilta Attributed to R. Ishmael did.

Lacking all interest in cogent and sustained argumentation and demonstration of propositions set forth for argument, the authorship of Mekhilta Attributed to R. Ishmael scarcely aspires to make a full and important, well-composed and proportioned statement of its own. The nine tractates of Mekhilta Attributed to R. Ishmael, moreover, prove discrete. We have to take account of a document behind which, even at the end product, stand nine authorships, not one single authorship whose hand is evident through. For in formal and logical traits, all the more so in topical program, the nine tractates are scarcely cogent when seen whole and complete. They make no one point over and over again. They undertake no sustained, methodical analysis that joins bits and pieces of exegesis into a large-scale composition, bearing meaning. They do not pursue a single range of problems in such a way as through discrete results to demonstrate in many ways a single cogent position.

Keenly interested in setting forth what there is to know about a variety of topics, the sages who stand behind Mekhilta. Attributed to R. Ishmael preserve and transmit information necessary for the reader to participate in an ongoing tradition, that is to say, a system well beyond the nascent and formative stage. For framers such as these, important questions have been settled or prove null. For it is a system that is perceived to be whole, complete, fully in place, that the information collected and set forth by our authorship attests. When people present writing in which Scripture supplies information and propositions, but not grammar and syntax of thought, Scripture plays a dominant role at the surface, but none in the substrate of the writing. That is shown here. For when facts serve not for arguing in favor of a proposition but principally for informing a readership of things it must know, then we confront not a systemic exercise expressed through sustained writing by the medium of Scripture but a traditional rite in which Scripture plays a formal role. That is to say, we find merely the repeating of the received facts so as to restate and reinforce the structure served by said facts. That accounts for our characterizing the document, assuming a provenance in late antiquity, as the first encyclopaedia of Judaism. and our seeing the document as a prime example, for late antiquity, of how people did not write with Scripture but used Scripture in other ways altogether.

It follows that, while the authorship of Mekhilta Attributed to R. Ishmael sets forth propositions, these overall do not serve to organize or impose cogency upon the document as a whole. That is why it is an encyclopedia, cogent in the pieces, but not overall. Only one tractate, Neziqin, clearly does exhibit fundamental cogency, since, in the main, it follows a single program of exegesis, aimed at establishing a set of uniform conceptual results. These, briefly stated, point to the conclusions that [1] cases may be generalized into rules; [2] Scripture does not repeat itself even when it covers the same legal subjects more than once; [3] the categories that make sense of reality derive from Scripture's classification of things, not from the traits of things viewed independently of Scripture. The other eight tractates into which the document is divided present a variety of conclusions.

That miscellaneous character of the whole should not obscure the fact that the parts really do form coherent statements, each on its own. Indeed, what makes the document interesting is the laconic and uncontroversial character of its discourse. Its framers clearly take for granted that what they are telling us are the established, accepted truths of the faith. That is why they can find it appropriate just to collect and present information, certain of the knowledge that everyone knows what they say is so. The main points that this Midrash-compilation makes in its several parts may be conveniently divided into three classifications: [1] generalizations about the character of Scripture, [2] rules for correct conduct, and [3] theological teachings, with special reference to the relationship between Israel and God and the implications of that relationship for the fate of Israel among the nations. The first two are in volume and intellectual dimensions not imposing, the third is enormous and important, bearing the weight of the burden of our document.

Traits of Scripture: The order in which Scripture sets forth two or more propositions does not necessarily indicate the priority assigned to those items. Scripture itself will dictate priority. Scripture uses euphemistic language. Scripture is not bound by temporal considerations, e.g., of sequence.

The moral life in Israel: When one party pays respect to another, they speak in harmony. With the measure with which one metes out to others is one's own reward meted out. Whoever welcomes a fellow is as if one welcomed the face of the Presence of God. Do not favor either rich or poor in judging a case.

Theological Convictions: These add up to a great collection of the basic theses of the theology of the Judaism of the dual Torah. Let me simply state the items as they come.

Through doing religious duties Israel was redeemed, and preparation of the rite well in advance was the religious duty to which redemption for Israel would serve as reward. What God says he will do, he does. Wherever Scripture indicates that God has said something, we can find in some other passage precisely where and what he had said. The upshot, of course, is that by carefully reading Scripture, we are able to identify the rules that govern history and salvation. The vindication of Moses's demands turns the demands into prophecies of precisely what would come about. This further is underlined by the careful delineation of the degradation and humiliation of Pharaoh, portrayed as running about. And then comes the striking contrast between the reverence in which Israelites hold the rule of God and the humiliation of the Egyptian ruler. People get what is coming to them. Divine punishment is inexorable, so too divine reward. When God exacts punishment of the nations, his name is made great in the world. Merit is what saved Israel at the sea. The issue to be pursued is, what sort of merit, e.g., deriving from what actions or persons? The acts of healing of the Holy One, blessed be he, are not like the acts of healing of mortals. The redemption at the sea prefigures the redemption at the end of time. Faith in God is what saves Israel.

God punishes the arrogant person by exacting a penalty precisely from that about which such a person takes pride. With that in which the nations of the world take pride before him he exacts punishment from them. Numerous cases on a long line of instances, based upon historical facts provided by Scripture, serve to demonstrate that proposition. Israel is unique among the nations. Mortals have the power to praise and glorify God. God takes many forms. The Lord is master of all media of war. The Lord needs none of those media. The Lord is a man of war, but the Lord is in no way comparable to a man of war, making war in a supernatural way, specifically by retaining, even while making war, the attributes of mercy and humanity. God is just, and God's justice insures that the worthy are rewarded and the unworthy are penalized. God responds to human actions and attitudes. Those who oppose Israel are as though they opposed God. God is unique and God's salvation at the sea will be repeated at the end of time.

Israel gained great merit because it alone was willing to accept the ten commandments. The Israelites deserve praise for accepting the Torah. The "other gods" are not really gods at all. They are called "other" for various theological reasons. Suffering is precious and will not be rejected. One must not act in regard to God the way the outsiders treat their gods. They honor their gods in good times, not in bad, but Israel, exemplified by Job, honors God in bad time as much as in good. These fundamental principles of faith hardly exhaust the allusions to, or representations of, theological and normative statements in Mekhilta Attributed to R. Ishmael. They represent only those convictions that are spelled out in massive detail and argued with great force, the points of emphasis within a vast fabric of faith.

While familiar, these propositions form a miscellany. The characterization of the propositional message of our authorship(s) strongly suggests that we are dealing with a repertoire of standard and established, normative dogmas of the Judaism of the dual Torah. Nothing in the representation just now set forth points toward controversy or can be shown to contradict convictions contained within other documents. In Mekhilta Attributed to R. Ishmael we deal with a compilation of teachings, not a sustained argument: a systematic presentation of conventions, not a focused argument in behalf of distinct and urgent propositions. Here is a sample passage.

MEKHILTA. THE SECTION CALLED SHIRATA [SONGS]
CHAPTER ONE
XXVI:I.

1.A. "Then [Moses and the people of Israel sang this song to the Lord, saying, 'I will sing to the Lord, for he has triumphed gloriously; the horse and its rider he has thrown into the sea]:"

B. There are cases in which the word "then" refers to times past, and some in which the word "then" refers to times future:

C. "Then men began to call upon the name of the Lord" (Gen. 4:26); "Then she said, A bridegroom of blood" (Exod. 4:26); "Then sang Moses" (Exod. 15:1); "Then David said" (1 Chr. 15:2); "Then Solomon spoke" (1 Kgs. 8:12)—these are cases in which the word "then" refers to times past.

D. And there are cases in which the word "then" refers to times future:

E. "Then you shall see and be radiant" (Is. 60:5); "Then shall your light break forth as the morning" (Is. 58:8); "Then shall the lame man leap as a hart" (Is. 35:6); "Then the eyes of the blind shall be opened" (Is. 35:5); "Then shall the virgin rejoice in the dance" (Jer. 31:12); "Then our mouth will be filled with laughter . . . then they will say among the nations, The Lord has done great things with these" (Ps. 126:2)—these are cases in which the word "then" refers to times future.

2.A. Rabbi says, "What is written is not, 'Then Moses sang,' but, 'Then Moses will sing.'

B. "We turn out to derive from this passage proof on the strength of the Torah for the resurrection of the dead."

3.A. "Moses and the children of Israel:"

B. Moses was equal in weight to Israel,

C. and Israel was equal in weight to Moses,

D. at the moment at which they sang the song.

4.A. Another interpretation of the clause, "Moses and the children of Israel:"

B. This indicates that Moses sang the song before all Israel.

5.A. ". . . this song:"

B. But is it a single song? Are there not ten in all?

C. The first was recited in Egypt: "You shall have a song, as in the night when a feast is sanctified" (Is. 30:29);

D. the second at the sea: "Then sang Moses;"

E. the third at the well: "Then sang Israel" (Num. 21:17);

F. the fourth, said by Moses: "And it came to pass, when Moses had finished writing . . . Moses spoke in the ears of all the assembly of Israel the words of this song, until they were finished" (Deut. 31:24-30);

G. the fifth, said by Joshua: "Then spoke Joshua to the Lord" (Josh. 10:12);

H. the sixth, said by Deborah and Barak the son of Abinoam: "Then sang Deborah and Barak son of Abinoam" (Jud. 5:1);

I. the seventh said by David: "And David spoke to the Lord the words of this song" (2 Sam. 22:1);

J. the eighth, said by Solomon: "A Psalm, a song at the dedication of the house of David" (Ps. 30:1). [The catalogue is now interrupted for an exposition of this matter. It resumes below, No. 10.]

6.A. Now did David build it? Did not Solomon build it, as it is said, "And Solomon built the house and finished it" (1 Kgs. 6:14).

B. So why does Scripture say, " 'A Psalm, a song at the dedication of the house of David" (Ps. 30:1)?

C. Since David was prepared to give his life for the project to build it, it was named for him, and so Scripture says, "Lord, remember for David all his affliction, how he swore to the Lord and vowed to the Mighty One of Jacob, Surely I will not come into the tent of my house . . . until I find out a place for the Lord. . . . Lo, we heard of it as being in Ephrath" (Ps. 132:1-6).

D. And elsewhere: "Now, see to your own house, David" (1 Kgs. 12:16).

E. Accordingly, since David was prepared to give his life for the project to build it, it was named for him.

7.A. And so you find that any matter for which a person is prepared to give his life is named for him.

B. There are three things for which Moses was prepared to give his life, and all are named for him:

C. He was prepared to give his life for the Torah, and it is named for him: "Remember the Torah of Moses, my servant" (Mal. 3:22).

D. But is it not the Torah of God? "The Torah of the Lord is perfect, restoring the soul" (Ps. 19:8)?

E. Why then is it called "the Torah of Moses, my servant"?

F. It is because he was prepared to give his life for it, so it was named for him.

G. And where do we find that he was prepared to give his life for the Torah?

H. "And he was there with the Lord" (Exod. 34:28); "Then I stayed on the mountain forty days and forty nights" (Deut. 9:9).

I. So, since he was prepared to give his life for the Torah, it was named for him.

8.A. He was prepared to give his life for Israel, and it is named for him:

B. "Go, get down, for your people have dealt corruptly" (Exod. 32:7).

C. But were they not the people of the Lord?

D. For it is said, "Yet they are your people and your inheritance" (Deut. 9:29); "in that men said of them, 'These are the people of the Lord'" (Ezek. 36:20).

E. How come Scripture says, "Go, get down, for your people have dealt corruptly" (Exod. 32:7)?

F. Since he was ready to give his life for Israel, they were named for him.

G. And where do we find that he was prepared to give his life for Israel?

H. As it is said, "And it came to pass, at that time, when Moses had grown up, that he went out to his brothers and looked at their burdens . . . and he looked this way and that way . . ." (Exod. 2:11,12).

I. So, since he was ready to give his life for Israel, they were named for him.

9.A. "And he was prepared to give his life for laws, and judges therefore were named for him: 'Judges and officers you shall appoint for yourself'" (Deut. 16:18).

B. But is it not the fact that justice belongs to God, for it is said, "For judgment is God's" (Deut. 1:17)?

C. How come Scripture says, "Judges and officers you shall appoint for yourself" (Deut. 16:18)?

D. Since he was prepared to give his life for laws, and judges therefore were named for him.

E. And where do we find that he was prepared to give his life for laws?

F. "He went out the second day . . . and he said, 'who made you a ruler and a judge over us. . . . Now when Pharaoh heard this thing. . . . Now the priest of Midian had seven daughters . . . and the shepherds came and drove them away'" (Exod. 2:13-17).

G. It was from judges that he had fled, and to judging he returned: "He executed the righteousness of the Lord and his judgments with Israel" (Deut. 33:21).

H. Lo, since he was prepared to give his life for laws, and judges therefore were named for him.

10.A. [Resuming the catalogue,] the ninth, said by Jehoshaphat: "And when he had taken counsel with the people he appointed those who were to sing to the Lord and praise in the beauty of holiness, as they went out before the army, saying, 'Give thanks to the Lord for his mercy endures for ever'" (2 Chr. 20:21).

B. Why is this mode of song of thanksgiving differentiated from all other songs of thanksgiving that are in the Torah,

C. in that in the case of all other songs of thanksgiving that are in the Torah it is said, "Give thanks to the Lord for he is good, for his mercy endures for ever," while here we have, "Give thanks to the Lord, for his mercy endures for ever"?

D. But it is as though there were no rejoicing before him in the heights on account of the annihilation of the wicked.

E. If there is no rejoicing before him in the heights on account of the annihilation of the wicked, all the more so in the case of the righteous,

F. one of whom weighs in the balance against the whole world,

G. as it is said, "But the righteous is the foundation of the world" (Prov. 10:25).

H. The tenth, said in the age to come: "Sing to the Lord a new song, and his praise from the end of the earth" (Is. 42:10); "Sing to the Lord a new song and his praise in the assembly of the saints" (Ps. 149:1).

11.A. All the songs that in times past were represented in the feminine form.

B. Just as a woman gives birth, so the acts of salvation in times past were followed by subjugation.

C. But as to the salvation that is destined to come in the future, after it there will be no further subjugation.

D. Therefore in the case just now given, it is represented in the masculine form.

E. For it is said, "Ask now and see whether a man goes into labor with a child" (Jer. 30:6).

F. Just as a male does not give birth, so as to the salvation that is destined to come in the future, after it there will be no further subjugation:

G. "O Israel, saved by the Lord with an everlasting salvation" (Is. 45:17).

12.A. "[Then Moses and the people of Israel sang this song] to the Lord:"

B. "To the Lord" they said it, and they did not say it to mortals:

C. "That the women came out of all the cities of Israel singing and dancing, to meet King Saul" (1 Sam. 18:6); "And the women sang to one another in their play" (1 Sam. 18:7).

D. But here, "To the Lord" they said it, and they did not say it to mortals.

13.A. "[Then Moses and the people of Israel sang this song] to the Lord, saying:"

B. R. Nehemiah says, "The Holy Spirit lighted on Israel, so they recited the song the way people recite the Shema."

C. R. Aqiba says, "The Holy Spirit lighted on Israel, so they recited the song the way people recite the Hallel-Psalms."

D. R. Eliezer b. Taddai says, "Moses would recite the opening words, then the Israelites would repeat them after him and complete the verse.

E. "Moses would begin, saying, 'I will sing to the Lord, for he has triumphed gloriously,'

F. "and the people would repeat that and conclude: 'I will sing to the Lord, for he has triumphed gloriously; the horse and its rider he has thrown into the sea.'

G. "Moses would begin, saying, 'The Lord is my strength and my song,'

H. "and the people would repeat that and conclude: 'The Lord is my strength and my song, and he has become my salvation.'

I. "Moses would begin, saying, 'The Lord is a man of war.'

J. "and the people would repeat that and conclude: 'The Lord is a man of war; the Lord is his name'" [T. Sot. 6:2-3].

14.A. "I will sing to the Lord, for he has triumphed gloriously:"

B. "Greatness is fitting for the Lord, might is fitting for the Lord, glory and victory and majesty are fitting for the Lord."

C. So David says, "To the Lord are greatness, might, glory and victory and majesty" (1 Chr. 29:11).

15.A. "I will sing to the Lord, for he has triumphed gloriously:"

B. When a mortal king comes into a town, everybody gives praise before him, saying that he is mighty, even though he is weak; rich, even though he is poor; wise, even though he is an idiot; merciful, even though he is a sadist; that he is a judge, that he is faithful, even though none of these traits applies to him.

C. Everybody just flatters him.

D. But as to the One who spoke and brought the world into being, that is not how things are.

E. Rather, "I will sing to the Lord," who is mighty: "The Lord, mighty and awful" (Deut. 10:17); "The Lord strong and mighty, the Lord mighty in battle" (Ps. 24:8); "The Lord will go forth as a mighty man" (Is. 42:13); "There is none like you, O Lord, you are great and your name is great in might" (Jer. 10:6).

F. "I will sing to the Lord," who is rich: "Behold the Lord your God owns the heaven" (Deut. 10:14); "The earth is the Lord's and the fullness thereof" (Ps. 24:12); "The sea is his" (Ps. 95:5); "Mine is the silver and mine is the gold" (Hag. 2:8); "Behold, all souls are mine" (Ezek. 18:4).

G. "I will sing to the Lord," who is wise: "The Lord by wisdom founded the earth" (Prov. 3:19); "With him are wisdom and might" (Job 12:13); "For the Lord gives wisdom" (Prov. 2:6); "He gives wisdom to the wise" (Dan. 2:21); "Who would not fear you, O King of the nations? For it befits you, since among all the wise men of the nations and in all their royalty there is none like you" (Jer. 10:7).

H. "I will sing to the Lord," who is merciful: "The Lord, the Lord, God, merciful and gracious" (Exod. 34:6); "For the Lord your God is a merciful God" (Deut. 4:31); "The Lord is good to all, and his tender mercies are over all his works" (Ps. 145:9); "To the Lord our God belong compassion and forgiveness" (Dan. 9:9).

I. "I will sing to the Lord," who is a judge: "For judgment is the Lord's" (Deut. 1:17); "God stands in the congregation of the mighty, in the midst of the judges he judges" (Ps. 82:1); "The rock, his work is perfect" (Deut. 32:4).

J. "I will sing to the Lord," who is faithful: "The faithful God" (Deut. 7:9); "A God of faithfulness" (Deut. 32:4).

K. "Greatness is fitting for the Lord, might is fitting for the Lord, glory and victory and majesty are fitting for the Lord."

16.A. "I will sing to the Lord:"

B. for he is excellent, praiseworthy, and none is like him: "For who in the skies can be compared to the Lord . . . a God dread in the great council of the holy ones" (Ps. 89:7-8); "O Lord, God of hosts, who is a mighty one like you" (Ps. 89:9).

C. What is the sense of "hosts"?

D. He is [Lauterbach:] the ensign among his host.

E. So too: "And he came from the myriads holy" (Deut. 33:3), meaning, [Lauterbach:] he is the ensign among his holy myriads.

F. And so David says, "There is none like you, among the gods, O Lord" (Ps. 86:8), "My beloved is white and ruddy . . . his head is as the most fine gold . . . his eyes are like doves . . . his cheeks are as a bed of spices . . . his hands are as rods of gold . . . his legs are as pillars of marble" (Song 5:10-15).

17.A. R. Yose the Galilean says, "Lo, Scripture says, 'Out of the mouth of babies and sucklings you have founded strength' (Ps. 8:3).

B. "'. . . babies' refers to those yet in their mothers' womb: 'or as a hidden untimely birth I had not been; as infants that never saw light' (Job 3:16).

C. "'. . . sucklings' refers to those who feed at their mothers' breasts: 'Gather the children and those that suck the breasts' (Joel 2:16)."

D. Rabbi says, "'. . . babies' refers to those old enough to be outside: 'To cut off the babies from the street' (Jer. 9:20), 'The babies ask for bread' (Lam. 4:4).

E. "'. . . sucklings' refers to those who feed at their mothers' breasts: 'Gather the children and those that suck the breasts' (Joel 2:16)."

F. R. Meir says, "Even embryos in their mothers' wombs opened up their mouths and recited a song before the Omnipresent: 'Bless God in full assemblies, even the Lord, you who are from the fountain of Israel' (Ps. 68:27).

G. "And it was not Israel alone that recited the song before the Omnipresent.

H. "Even the ministering angels did so: 'O Lord, our Lord, how glorious is your name in all the earth, whose majesty is rehearsed above the heavens' (Ps. 8:2)."

No. 1 is a general proposition, to which our base-verse contributes an example. Nos. 2, 3 both are singletons. The enormous composite, Nos. 5-10, bears a massive interpolation, and, once more, the whole had to have been completed prior to insertion here, since so much of the composite—Nos. 6-9—has no bearing upon the argument that is begun at 5.B. The inclusion of No. 13 seems to me more justified than Nos. 5-10, since

the set of discrete sayings bear a clear relationship to our base-verse. The only composition that I find genuinely well-realized is No. 15, which systematically illustrates its parable with proof texts showing how God differs from a mortal king. This proves how the authors of a single essay could realize a simple aesthetic program and do so with enormous effect. No. 16 is included because of Meir's statement, 16.F-H. Clearly, the composition, focused on Ps. 8:1-2, was assembled before the whole was inserted here, since the rest of the materials have no bearing upon our base verse.

SHIRATA CHAPTER TWO
XXVII:I.

1A. "[I will sing to the Lord,] for he is highly exalted [RSV: has triumphed gloriously]; [the horse and its rider he has thrown into the sea]:"

B. [The use of the verb, "exalt," two times, translated "highly exalted, yields this meaning:] "He has exalted me and I have exalted him."

C. "He has exalted me:" in Egypt, thus: "And you shall say to Pharaoh, 'Thus says the Lord, Israel is my son, my firstborn'" (Exod. 4:22).

D. "and I have exalted him:" in Egypt, thus: "You shall have a song as in the night when a feast is sanctified" (Is. 30:29).

2.A. Another teaching concerning "for he is highly exalted:"

B. "He has exalted me and I have exalted him."

C. "He has exalted me:" at the sea, thus: "And the angel of God . . . removed" (Exod. 14:19).

D. "and I have exalted him:" at the sea when I sang a song before him, "I will sing to the Lord, for he is highly exalted."

3.A. Another teaching concerning "for he is highly exalted:"

B. "He is exalted and is going to be exalted,"

C. as it is said, "For the Lord of hosts has a day upon all that is proud . . . and upon all the cedars of Lebanon . . . and upon all the high mountains . . . and upon every lofty tower . . . and upon all the ships of Tarshish . . . and the loftiness of man shall be bowed down . . . and the idols shall utterly pass away" (Is. 2:12-18).

4.A. Another teaching concerning "for he is highly exalted:"

B. "He is exalted above all who take pride in themselves."

C. For with that in which the nations of the world take pride before him he exacts punishment from them.

D. For so Scripture says in connection with the men of the generation of the flood, "Their bull genders . . . they send forth their little ones . . . they sing to the timbrel and harp and rejoice" (Job 21:10-12).

E. And what is then stated? "Depart form us, we do not desire knowledge of your ways. What is the almighty that we should serve him" (Job 21:14-15).

D. They said, "Not even for a drop of rain do we need him, for 'There goes up a mist from the earth' (Gen. 2:6)."

E. Said to them the Holy One, blessed be he, "Total idiots! In the very act of goodness which I have done for you do you take pride before me? Through that same act I shall exact a penalty from you."

F. "And the rain was upon the earth forty days and forty nights" (Gen. 7:12).

5.A. R. Yose of Damascus says, "Since they set their eyes both above and below to express their lust. So the Holy One, blessed be he, opened up against them the springs above and below so as to destroy them.

B. "For so it is said, 'All the fountains of the great deep were broken up and the windows of heaven were opened' (Gen. 7:11)."

6.A. And along these same lines, you found in connection with the men of the tower [of Babel], that with that in which they took pride before him he exacts punishment from them.

B. "Come let us build us a city" (Gen. 11:4).

C. What is said in their regard? "So the Lord scattered them abroad from thence upon the face of all the earth" (Gen. 11:8).

7.A. And along these same lines, you found in connection with the men of Sodom, that with that in which they took pride before him he exacts punishment from them.

B. "As for the earth out of it comes bread . . . the stones of it are the place of sapphires . . . that path no bird of prey knows . . . the proud beasts have not trodden it" (Job 28:5-8).

C. The men of Sodom said, "We have no need for travelers to come our way. Lo, we have food near at hand, lo, we have silver and gold. precious stones and pearls, near at hand. [Let us go and] wipe out the law of [protecting] the wayfarer [so as to remove the wayfarer] from our land."

D. Said to them the Holy One, blessed be he, "Total idiots! On account of the act of goodness that I did for you, you take pride and you want to wipe out the law of [protecting] the wayfarer from among you. I shall wipe out the memory of you yourselves from the world."

E. "He breaks open a shaft away from where men sojourn" (Job 28:4).

F. "A contemptible brand . . . the tents of robbers prosper, and they that provoke God are secure" (Job 12:5).

G. That is what made them rebel, namely, "Whatsoever God brings into their hand" (Job 12:6).

H. And so Scripture says, "And they were haughty and committed abominations before me" (Ezek. 16:48-50).

I. And what did it cause for them? "'As I live,' says the Lord God, 'Sodom your sister has not done . . . as you have done. . . . Behold, this was the iniquity of your sister Sodom . . . neither did she strengthen the hand of the poor and needy, and they were haughty'" (Ezek. 16:48-50).

8.A. "Before the Lord destroyed Sodom and Gomorrah they were like a garden of the Lord in the land of Egypt" (Gen. 13:10).

B. Afterward: "And they made their father drink wine" (Gen. 19:33)."

C. Where did they get wine in the cave?

D. The Holy One, blessed be he, made wine available for them: "And it shall come to pass on that day that the mountains shall drip sweet wine" (Joel 4:18).

E. If that is how he provides for those who anger him, all the more so for those who carry out his will."

9.A. So you find in the case of the Egyptians that with that in which they took pride before him he exacts punishment from them.

B. "And he took six hundred chariots" (Exod. 14:7).

C. Then: "Pharaoh's chariots and his host he cast into the sea, and his picked officers are sunk in the Red Sea."

10.A. So you find in the case of Sisera that with that in which he took pride before him he exacts punishment from him.

B. "And Sisera collected all his chariots, nine hundred chariots of iron" (Jud. 4:13).

C. Then: "They fought from heaven, the stars in their courses fought against Sisera" (Jud. 5:20).

11.A. So you find in the case of Samson

that with that in which he took pride before him he exacts punishment from him.

B. "And Samson said to his father, 'Get her for me, for she is pleasing in my eyes'" (Jud. 14:3).

C. Then: "And the Philistines took hold of him and put out his eyes and brought him down to Gaza" (Jud. 16:32).

D. R. Judah says, "The beginning of his corruption was in Gaza, therefore his punishment was inflicted only in Gaza."

12.A. So you find in the case of Absalom that with that in which he took pride before him he exacts punishment from him.

B. "Now in all Israel there was none so admired as Absalom for his beauty . . . and when he cut his hair . . ." (2 Sam. 145:25-26).

C. R. Judah says, "He had taken the oath of a perpetual Nazirite and would cut his hair once every twelve months: 'Now it was at the end of forty years that Absalom said' (2 Sam. 15:7)."

D. R. Yose says, "He was a Nazirite for a specified number of days and would cut his hair every thirty days: 'Now it was after a period of days according to the days after which he cut it' (2 Sam. 14:26)."

E. Rabbi says, "He cut his hair every Friday, for it is the way of princes to cut their hair once a week on Friday."

F. Now what is written thereafter? "And Absalom happened to meet the servants of David, and Absalom was riding upon his mule, and his hair got caught in the terebinth" (2 Sam. 18:9).

13.A. So you find in the case of Sennacherib that with that in which he took pride before him he exacts punishment from him.

B. "By your messengers you have taunted the Lord. . . . I have dug and drunk strange water" (2 Kgs. 19:23-24).

C. Then: "And it happened that night that the angel of the Lord went out and killed in the camp of the Assyrians a hundred eighty-five thousand" (2 Kgs. 19:25).

D. They say that the greatest of them was commander over a hundred eighty-five thousand, and the least was in charge of no fewer than two thousand: "How then can you turn away the face of one captain, even of the least of my master's servants" (2 Kgs. 18:24).

E. "This is the word that the Lord has spoken concerning him, The virgin daughter of Zion has despised you . . . whom you have taunted . . ." (2 Kgs. 19:21-22).

F. "This day he shall halt at Nob" (Is. 10:32).

14.A. So you find in the case of Nebuchadnezzar that with that in which he took pride before him he exacts punishment from him.

B. "And you said in your heart, 'I will ascend to heaven . . . I will ascend above the heights of the clouds'" (Is. 14:13-14).

C. Then: "You shall be brought down to the netherworld" (Is. 27:3).

15.A. So you find in the case of Tyre that with that in which they took pride before him he exacts punishment from them.

B. "You, Tyre, have said, 'I am of perfect beauty'" (Ezek. 27:3).

C. "Behold, I am against you, Tyre, and will cause many nations to come up against you" (Ezek. 26:3).

16.A. So you find in the case of the prince of Tyre that with that in which he took pride before him he exacts punishment from him.

B. "Son of man, say to the prince of Tyre, 'Thus says the Lord God, because your heart is lifted up and you have said, I am a god'" (Ezek. 28:2).

C. Then: "You shall die the death of the uncircumcised by the hand of strangers" (Ezek. 28:10).

17.A. Lo, with that in which the nations of the world take pride before him he exacts punishment from them:

B. "for he is highly exalted."

The use of the duplicated verb, Nos. 1-3, allows a systematic study of the reciprocal acts of exaltation, in Egypt, at the sea, then in the time to come—surely a single, protracted and well-composed demonstration. Then we proceed to a different proposition concerning the same notion of exaltation, namely, self-aggrandizement. This yields the enormous discussion of the proposition, with that in which the nations of the world take pride before him he exacts punishment from them. Numerous cases on a long line of instances, based upon historical facts provided by Scripture, serve to demonstrate that proposition. Once more we have a sustained essay on a single proposition, which is demonstrated through a long sequence of probative cases. The proposition, God exacts punishment through the very thing in which one takes pride, could not be more effectively demonstrated. The fact that, at Sifre Deut. 43, the opening sequence of cases proves a different proposition, has no bearing on the matter before us. It only tells us that the same cases may serve more than a single proposition, and for social science, such as is practiced here, that is hardly surprising.

JACOB NEUSNER

G

GENESIS IN JUDAISM: Classical Judaism reads the book of Genesis through the interpretative construction set forth in Genesis Rabbah, a systematic, verse-by-verse, analysis of the book of Genesis produced in the Land of Israel at ca. 450 C.E. Genesis Rabbah transforms the book of Genesis from a genealogy and family history of Abraham, Isaac, Jacob, then Joseph, into a book of the laws of history and rules of the salvation of Israel: the deeds of the founders become omens and signs for the final generations.

In Genesis Rabbah the entire narrative of Genesis is so formed as to point toward the sacred history of Israel, the Jewish people: its slavery and redemption; its coming Temple in Jerusalem; its exile and salvation at the end of time—the whole a paradigm of exile and return. In the rereading by the authorship of Genesis Rabbah, Genesis proclaims the prophetic message that the world's creation commenced a single, straight line of significant events, that is to say, history, leading in the end to the salvation of Israel and, through Israel, of all humanity. The single most important proposition of Genesis Rabbah is that, in the story of the beginnings of creation, humanity, and Israel, we find the message of the meaning and end of the life of the Jewish people in the here and now of the fifth century. The deeds of the founders supply signals for the children about what is going to come in the future. So the biography of Abraham, Isaac, and Jacob also constitutes a protracted account of the history of Israel later on.

Genesis Rabbah is a composite document. As with the Talmud that it accompanies, so in Genesis Rabbah, some of the material in the compilation can be shown to have been put together before that material was used for the purposes of the compilers. Many times a comment entirely apposite to a verse of Genesis has been joined to a set of comments in no way pertinent to the verse at hand. Proof for a given syllogism, furthermore, will derive from a verse of Genesis as well as from numerous verses of other books of the Bible. Such an argument therefore has not been written for exegetical purposes particular to the verse at hand. On the contrary, the particular verse subject to attention serves that other, propositional plan; it is not the focus of discourse; it has not generated the comment but merely provided a proof for a syllogism. That is what it means to say that a proposition yields an exegesis. That fundamental proposition, displayed throughout Genesis Rabbah, which yields the specific exegeses of many of the verses of the book of Genesis and even whole stories, is that the beginnings point toward the endings, and the meaning of Israel's past points toward the message that lies in Israel's future. The things that happened to the fathers and mothers of the family, Israel, provide a sign for the things that will happen to the children later on.

What is at stake is the discovery, among the facts provided by the written Torah, of the social rules that govern Israel's history. At stake is the search for the order yielded by the chaos of uninterpreted data. It follows that, as with the Mishnah, the governing mode of thought is that of natural philosophy. It involves the classification of data by shared traits, yielding descriptive rules, the testing of propositions against the facts of data, the whole aimed at the discovery of underlying rules out of a multiplicity of details, in all, the proposing and testing, against the facts provided by Scripture, of the theses of Israel's salvation that demanded attention just then. But the issues were not so much philosophical as religious, in the sense that while philosophy addressed questions of nature and rules of enduring existence, religion asked about issues of history and God's intervention in time. Within that rough and ready distinction between nature, supernature, and sanctification, typified by the Mishnah and the Tosefta and the legal enterprise in general, on the one side, and society, history, and salvation, typified by Genesis Rabbah, Leviticus Rabbah, Pesiqta deRab Kahana, and the theological inquiry into teleology, on the other, we may distinguish our documents.

Specifically, we may classify this document and its successors and companions as works of profound theological inquiry into God's rules for history and society in the here and now and for salvation at the end of historical time. That fundamental proposition concerning the search, in the account of the beginnings, of the ending and meaning of Israel's society and history—hence the rules that govern and permit knowledge of what is to come—constitutes the generative proposition that yielded the specific exegesis of the book of Genesis in Genesis Rabbah.

Genesis Rabbah in its final form emerges from that momentous century in which the Rome Empire passed from pagan to Christian rule, and, in which, in the aftermath of the Julian's abortive reversion to paganism, in ca. 360, which endangered the Christian character of the Roman empire, Christianity adopted that politics of repression of paganism that rapidly engulfed Judaism as well. The issue confronting Israel in the land of Israel therefore proved immediate: the meaning of the new and ominous turn of history, the implications of Christ's worldly triumph for the other-worldly and supernatural people, Israel, whom God chooses and loves. The message of the exegete-compositors ad-dressed the circumstance of historical crisis and generated remarkable renewal, a rebirth of intellect in the encounter with Scripture, now in quest of the rules not of sanctification—these had already been found—but of salvation. So the book of Genesis, which portrays how all things had begun, would testify to the message and the method of the end: the coming salvation of patient, hopeful, enduring Israel.

That is why in the categories of philosophy, including science and society, and religion, including a prophetic interpretation of history and teleology, Genesis Rabbah presents a deeply *religious* view of Israel's historical and salvific life, in much the same way that the Mishnah provides a profoundly *philosophical* view of Israel's everyday and sanctified existence. Just as the main themes of the Mishnah evoke the consideration of issues of being and becoming, the potential and the actual, mixtures and blends and other problems of physics, all in the interest of philosophical analysis, so Genesis Rabbah presents its cogent and coherent agendum as well. That program of inquiry concerns the way in which, in the book of Genesis, God set forth to Moses the entire scope and meaning of Israel's history among the nations and salvation at the end of days. The mode of thought by which the framers of Genesis Rabbah work out their propositions dictates the character of their exegesis, as to rhetoric, logical principle of cogent and intelligible discourse, and, as is clear, even as to topic.

In the view of the framers of the compilation, the entire narrative of Genesis is so formed as to point toward the sacred history of Israel, the Jewish people: its slavery and redemption; its coming Temple in Jerusalem; its exile and salvation at the end of time. In the reading of the authors at hand, therefore, the powerful message of Genesis proclaims that the world's creation commenced a single, straight line of events, leading in the end to the salvation of Israel and through Israel of all humanity. That message—that history heads toward Israel's salvation—the sages derived from the book of Genesis and contributed to their own day. Therefore in their reading of Scripture a given story will bear a deeper truth about what it means to be Israel, on the one side, and what in the end of days will happen to Israel, on the other. True, their reading makes no explicit reference to what, if anything, had changed in the age of Constantine. But we do find repeated references to the four kingdoms, Babylonia, Media, Greece, Rome—and beyond the fourth will come Israel, fifth and last. So sages' message, in their theology of history, was that the present anguish prefigured the coming vindication, of God's people.

It follows that sages read Genesis as the history of the world with emphasis on Israel. So the lives portrayed, the domestic quarrels and petty conflicts with the neighbors, all serve to yield insight into what was to be. Why so? Because the deeds of the patriarchs taught lessons on how the children were to act, and, it further followed, the lives of the patriarchs signaled the history of Israel. Israel constituted one extended family, and the metaphor of the family, serving the nation as it did, imparted to the stories of Genesis the character of a family record. History become genealogy conveyed the message of salvation. These propositions really laid down the same judgment, one for the individual and the family, the other for the community and the nation, since there was no differentiating one from the other. Every detail of the narrative therefore served to prefigure what was to be, and Israel found itself, time and again, in the revealed facts of the history of the creation of the world, the decline of humanity down to the time of Noah, and, finally, its ascent to Abraham, Isaac, and Israel.

Genesis Rabbah is made up of one hundred *parashiyyot*, or chapters, and each *parashah* is comprised of from as few as five to as many as fifteen subdivisions. Genesis Rabbah is a huge document, probably five times larger than the book of Genesis itself. The hundred chapters' subdivisions in the main formed cogent statements. That is to say, words joined together to form autonomous statements, sentences. Sentences then coalesced into cogent propositions, paragraphs. Paragraphs then served a larger purpose, forming a cogent proposition of some sort. All together, therefore,

discrete words turned into sentences, and sentences into whole thoughts, that we can discern and understand. The smallest whole units of thought of Genesis Rabbah contain cogent thought. We can discern the ideas presented in the composition at hand. The use of the word "composition" is justified: there is thought, in logical sequence, in proportion, in order, with a beginning, a middle, and an end. Genesis Rabbah then is composed of a long sequence of these smallest whole units of thought, strung together for some purpose or other.

What differentiates this document from its predecessors, as noted at the outset, is that these smallest whole units of discourse or thought join together for a larger purpose. The document intellectually is more than an anthology of discrete passages. How so? Among all the diverse smaller units of discourse, sayings, stories, exegeses of verses of Scripture, protracted proofs of a single proposition, and the like, ordinarily served a purpose cogent to the whole subdivision of a *parashah*. That is to say, whatever finished materials are present have been made by the compositors—the authorities who selected the smallest completed units of thought and arranged them as we now have them—to serve their goals, that is, purposes of the compositors of the larger unit of thought of which the several smallest units of thought now form a part. That is why form-analysis worked its way from the largest components of the document, the *parashiyyot*, to the next largest, and so on down.

The analysis of the logic of coherent discourse shows a kind of writing not apparent in Rabbinic literature in prior documents. The coherence of the document derives from the program of the document as a whole, rather than from the joining of the smaller into the larger units of discourse and thought. True, we find compositions of that present in syllogistic arguments; we find passages joined by the teleological logic of narrative; and the compilation has its share of passages that hold together only through the logic of fixed association. But, overall, the document holds together through what we may call the governing purpose of the entire compilation, not only the sewing together of its components. What accomplishes the ultimate unification of the writing is that the framers of Genesis Rabbah wished to do two things:

First, they proposed to read the book of Genesis in light of other books of the Hebrew Scriptures, so underlining the unity of the Scriptures.

Second, they planned to read the book of Genesis phrase by phrase, so emphasizing the historical progression of the tale at hand, from verse to verse, from event to event.

So the book of Genesis now presents more than a single dimension. It tells the story of things that happened. The exegetes explain the meaning of these events, adding details and making explicit the implicit, unfolding message. Read from beginning to end, time in the beginning moved in an orderly progression. The book of Genesis also tells the laws that govern Israel's history. These laws apply at all times and under all circumstances. Facts of history, emerging at diverse times and under various circumstances, attest to uniform and simple laws of society and of history. That is why verses of Scripture originating here, there, everywhere, all serve equally well to demonstrate the underlying rules that govern. Read out of all historical sequence but rather as a set of exemplifications of recurrent laws, the stories of Genesis do not follow a given order, a single sequence of timely events. Time now moves in deep, not shallow, courses; time is cyclical, or, more really, time matters not at all. The long stretches of timeless rules take over. Sequential exegeses, citing and commenting on verses, classified as Form II, express the former of the two dimensions, and exercises in the clarification of a verse of Genesis through the message of a verse in another book of the Scriptures altogether, on the one side, and propositional or syllogistic compositions, on the other, Forms I and III, express the latter. The book of Genesis is made greater than its first reading would suggest. Hence, Genesis Rabbah, meaning (from a later angle of vision only) a greater conception of the book of Genesis, vastly expands the dimensions of the story of the creation of the world, humanity, and Israel.

The document finds its coherence in the vast conception that it wishes to put forth.

In Genesis Rabbah the entire narrative of Genesis is so formed as to point toward the sacred history of Israel, the Jewish people: its slavery and redemption; its coming Temple in Jerusalem; its exile and salvation at the end of time. The powerful message of Genesis in Genesis Rabbah proclaims that the world's creation commenced a single, straight line of events, leading in the end to the salvation of Israel and through Israel all humanity. Israel's history constitutes the counterpart of creation, and the laws of Israel's salvation form the foundation of creation. Therefore a given story out of Genesis, about creation, events from Adam to Noah and Noah to Abraham, the domestic affairs of the patriarchs, or Joseph, will bear a deeper message about what it means to be Israel, on the one side, and what in the end of days will happen to Israel, on the other. So the persistent theological program requires sages' to search in Scripture for meaning for their own circumstance and for the condition of their people. The single most important proposition of Genesis Rabbah is that, in the story of the beginnings of creation, humanity, and Israel, we find the message of the meaning and end of the life of the Jewish people. The deeds of the founders supply signals for the children about what is going to come in the future. So the biography of Abraham, Isaac, and Jacob also constitutes a protracted account of the history of Israel later on. If the sages could announce a single syllogism and argue it systematically, that is the proposition upon which they would insist.

As a corollary to the view that the biography of the fathers prefigures the history of the descendants, sages maintained that the deeds of the children—the holy way of life of Israel—follow the model established by the founders long ago. So they looked in Genesis for the basis for the things they held to be God's will for Israel. And they found ample proof. Sages invariably searched the stories of Genesis for evidence of the origins not only of creation and of Israel, but also of Israel's cosmic way of life, its understanding of how, in the passage of nature and the seasons, humanity worked out its relationship with God. The holy way of life that Israel lived through the seasons of nature therefore would make its mark upon the stories of the creation of the world and the beginning of Israel

Part of the reason sages pursued the interest at hand derived from polemic. From the first Christian century theologians of Christianity maintained that salvation did not depend upon keeping the laws of the Torah. Abraham, after all, had been justified and he did not keep the Torah, which, in his day, had not yet been given. So sages time and again would maintain that Abraham indeed kept the entire Torah even before it had been revealed. They further attributed to Abraham, Isaac, and Jacob rules of the Torah enunciated only later on, for example, the institution of prayer three times a day. But the passage before us bears a different charge. It is to Israel to see how deeply embedded in the rules of reality were the patterns governing God's relationship to Israel. That relationship, one of human sin and atonement, divine punishment and forgiveness, expresses the most fundamental laws of human existence.

The world was created for Israel, and not for the nations of the world. At the end of days everyone will see what only Israel now knows. Since sages read Genesis as the history of the world with emphasis on Israel, the lives portrayed, the domestic quarrels and petty conflicts with the neighbors, as much as the story of creation itself, all serve to yield insight into what was to be. We now turn to a detailed examination of how sages spelled out the historical law at hand. The lives of the patriarchs signaled the history of Israel. Every detail of the narrative therefore served to prefigure what was to be, and Israel found itself, time and again, in the revealed facts of the history of the creation of the world, the decline of humanity down to the time of Noah, and, finally, its ascent to Abraham, Isaac, and Israel. In order to illustrate the single approach to diverse stories, whether concerning Creation, Adam, and Noah, or concerning Abraham, Isaac, and Jacob, we focus on two matters: Abraham, on the one side, and Rome, on the other. In the former we see that Abraham serves as well as Adam to prove the point of it all. In the latter we observe how, in reading Genesis, the sages who compiled Genesis Rabbah discovered the meaning of the events of their own day.

One rule of Israel's history is yielded by the facts at hand. Israel is never left without an appropriate hero or heroine. The relevance of the long discourse becomes clear at the end. Each story in Genesis may forecast the stages in Israel's history later on, beginning to end. A matter of deep concern focused sages' attention on the sequence of world-empires to which, among other nations, Israel was subjugated: Babylonia, Media, Greece, and Rome—Rome above all. What will follow? Sages maintained that beyond the rule of Rome lay the salvation of Israel:

> XLII:IV.
> 1.A. "And it came to pass in the days of Amraphael" (Gen. 14:1):
> 4.A. Another matter: "And it came to pass in the days of Amraphael, king of Shinar" (Gen. 14:1) refers to Babylonia.
> B. "Arioch, king of Ellasar" (Gen. 14:1) refers to Greece.
> C. "Chedorlaomer, king of Elam" (Gen. 14:1) refers to Media.
> D. "And Tidal, king of Goiim [nations]" (Gen. 14:1) refers to the wicked government [Rome], which conscripts troops from all the nations of the world.
> E. Said R. Eleazar bar Abina, "If you see that the nations contend with one another, look for the footsteps of the king-messiah. You may know that that is the case, for, lo, in the time of Abraham, because the kings struggled with one another, a position of greatness came to Abraham."

Obviously, this presents a most important reading of Gen. 14:1, since it links the events of the life of Abraham to the history of Israel and even ties the whole to the messianic expectation. I suppose that any list of four kings will provoke inquiry into the relationship of the entries of that list to the four kingdoms among which history, in Israel's experience, is divided. The process of history flows in both directions. Just as what Abraham did prefigured the future

GENESIS IN JUDAISM

history of Israel, so what the Israelites later on were to do imposed limitations on Abraham. Time and again events in the lives of the patriarchs prefigure the four monarchies, among which, the fourth, last, and most intolerable was Rome.

Genesis is read as if it portrayed the history of Israel and Rome. For that is the single obsession binding sages of the document at hand to common discourse with the text before them. Why Rome in the form it takes in Genesis Rabbah? And how come the obsessive character of the sages' disposition of the theme of Rome? Were their picture merely of Rome as tyrant and destroyer of the Temple, we should have no reason to link the text to the problems of the age of redaction and closure. But now it is Rome as Israel's brother, counterpart, and nemesis, Rome as the one thing standing in the way of Israel's, and the world's, ultimate salvation. So the stakes are different, and much higher. It is not a political Rome but a Christian and messianic Rome that is at issue: Rome as surrogate for Israel, Rome as obstacle to Israel. Why? It is because Rome now confronts Israel with a crisis, and, I argue, the program of Genesis Rabbah constitutes a response to that crisis. Rome in the fourth century became Christian. Sages respond by facing that fact quite squarely and saying, "Indeed, it is as you say, a kind of Israel, an heir of Abraham as your texts explicitly claim. But we remain the sole legitimate Israel, the bearer of the birthright—we and not you. So you are our brother: Esau, Ishmael, Edom." And the rest follows.

By rereading the story of the beginnings, sages discovered the answer and the secret of the end. Rome claimed to be Israel, and, indeed, sages conceded, Rome shared the patrimony of Israel. That claim took the form of the Christians' appropriate of the Torah as "the Old Testament," so sages acknowledged a simple fact in acceding to the notion that, in some way, Rome too formed part of Israel. But it was the rejected part, the Ishmael, the Esau, not the Isaac, not the Jacob. The advent of Christian Rome precipitated the sustained, polemical, and, I think, rigorous and well-argued rereading of beginnings in light of

the end. Rome then marked the conclusion of human history as Israel had known it. Beyond? The coming of the true messiah, the redemption of Israel, the salvation of the world, the end of time. So the issues were not inconsiderable, and when the sages spoke of Esau/Rome, as they did so often, they confronted the life-or-death decision of the day. Here is a sample passage.

GENESIS RABBAH *PARASHAH* SEVENTY TO GENESIS 28:20-29:30
LXX:I.
1.A. "Then Jacob made a vow, saying, 'If God will be with me and will keep me in this way that I go and will give me bread to eat and clothing to wear, so that I come again to my father's house in peace, then the Lord shall be my God. And this stone, which I have set up for a pillar, shall be God's house; and of all that you give me, I will give the tenth to you'" (Gen. 28:20-22):
   B. "I will perform for you my vows, which my lips have uttered and my mouth has spoken when I was in distress" (Ps. 66:13-14).
   C. Said R. Isaac the Babylonian, "One who take a vow carries out a religious duty [if he does so in time of stress]."
   D. What is the meaning of the statement, "Then Jacob made a vow, saying"? "Saying" to the future generations, so that they too will take vows in a time of stress.

Here we see the working of the base verse/intersecting verse construction, and we can immediately explain the choice of the intersecting verse. What attracts the exegete's attention in Gen. 28:20 is the simple fact that Jacob has taken a vow, and the intersecting verse, Ps. 66:13-14, then underlines that fact. R. Isaac evaluates vow-taking, subjected to criticism, by saying that it can represent a meritorious action. Paragraph D repeats the basic syllogism of Genesis Rabbah: what the founders do, the children carry on, and what happens to the founders tells what will happen to the children, and, finally, the merit accumulated by the founders serves the children later on as their inheritance and source of protection. The amplification of the opening encounter of base verse and intersecting verse follows. This order—base verse, then intersecting verse—will be reversed in the later compilations, which will begin in the distant reaches of Scripture and only slowly and unpredictably recover the point articulated in what becomes the base verse.

> 2.A. Jacob was the first to take a vow, therefore whoever takes a vow should make it depend only upon him.
>   B. Said R. Abbahu, "It is written, '*How he swore to the Lord and vowed to the mighty one of Jacob*' (Ps. 132:2).
>   C. "What is written is not, 'how he [David] swore to the Lord and vowed to the mighty one of Abraham' or 'of Isaac,' but 'of Jacob.'
>   D. "He made the vow depend upon the first person ever to take a vow."

The theme of the passage, taking vows, produces two important points. First is that of No. 1, that, while vowing in general does not meet sages' approval, in times of stress it does, and Jacob is the example of that fact. Then, No. 2, Jacob is the one who started the practice of vowing, so Jacob is the one to whom vows are referred as in the cited passage. These two intersecting verses do not receive detailed exegesis on their own; they contribute themes and propositions. So the passage is not like those in which a long sequence of comments either brings the intersecting verse back to the base verse or reads the intersecting verse as an expression of the views of the principle of the base verse. Later on Jacob's failure to keep his vow in a prompt way elicits comment.

> LXX:II.
> 1.A. R. Yudan in the name of R. Idi: "It is written. 'Then the people rejoiced, for they offered willingly. Wherefore David blessed the Lord before all the congregation, and David said, "Blessed be you, O Lord, the God of Israel our father'" (1 Chr. 29:9-10).
>   B. "It was because they were engaged in carrying out religious duties that were acts of free will and that matters were successful that they rejoiced.
>   C. "What is the meaning of the statement, 'Wherefore David blessed the Lord before all the congregation, and David said, "Blessed be you, O Lord, the God of Israel our father"'? Specifically, we note that what is written is not, 'the God of Abraham, Isaac, and Israel,' but only 'God of Israel'?
>   D. "He made the vow depend upon the first person ever to take a vow."
>   E. Said R. Yudan, "From the document

at hand [the Torah, not merely the Writings] we do not lack further proof of that same fact. For example, 'And Israel vowed' (Num. 21:2), meaning, our father, Israel.

> F. "'Then Jacob made a vow.'"

The same point now recurs, with a different set of proof texts. The rhetorically noteworthy point is at F: we revert to the base verse, and this will form a bridge to the systematic exposition of that base verse, which now begins.

> LXX:III.
> 1.A. "Then Jacob made a vow:"
>   B. Four made a vow, two vowed and lost out, and two vowed and benefited.
>   C. Israel took a vow and Hannah took a vow, and they benefited.
>   D. Jephthah took a vow and lost out, Jacob took a vow and lost out. [Freedman, *Genesis Rabbah*, p. 637, n. 2: His (Jacob's) vow was superfluous, since he had already received God's promise and therefore he lost thereby.]

The fragmentary comment serves the purpose of removing the impression that the text of Scripture goes over the same ground twice and contradicts itself. This same problem will be solved in a different way in what follows. Since, as we know, the Pentateuchal books, including Genesis, are composed of a number of prior strands, some of which go over the same ground two or more times, the text itself, read by sages as single, linear, and unitary, presents its own problems for sages' attention.

> LXX:IV.
> 1.A. R. Aibu and R. Jonathan:
>   B. One of them said, "The passage states matters out of the proper order."
>   C. The other said, "The passage is entirely in the proper order."
>   D. The one who has said, "The passage states matters out of the proper order" points to the following: "And lo, I am with you" (Gen. 28:15) contrasts to the statement, "Then Jacob made a vow, saying, 'If God will be with me.'"
>   E. The other who has said, "The passage is entirely in the proper order" has then to explain the statement, "If God will be with me" in light of the statement already at hand.
>   F. His point is this: "If he will be with me" means "if all of the conditions that

he has stipulated with me will be carried out," [then I will keep my vow].

2.A. R. Abbahu and rabbis:

B. R. Abbahu said, "'If God will be with me and will keep me in '*this way*' refers to protection from gossip, in line with this usage: 'And they turn their tongue in the way of slander [Freedman, p. 637, n. 4], their bow of falsehood' (Jer. 9:2).

C. "'. . . will give me bread to eat' refers to protection from fornication, in line with this usage: 'Neither has he kept back any thing from me, except the bread which he ate' (Gen. 39:9), a euphemism for sexual relations with his wife.

D. "'. . . so that I come again to my father's house in peace' refers to bloodshed.

E. "'. . . then the Lord shall be my God' so that I shall be protected from idolatry.'"

F. Rabbis interpreted the statement "this way" to speak of all of these.

G. [The rabbis' statement now follows:] "Specifically: 'If God will be with me and will keep me in this way that I go' [by referring only to 'way'] contains an allusion to idolatry, fornication, murder, and slander.

H. "'Way' refers to idolatry: 'They who swear by the sin of Samaria and say, As your god, O Dan, lives, and as the way of Beer Sheba lives' (Amos 8:14).

I. "'Way' refers to adultery: 'So is the way of an adulterous woman' (Prov. 30:20).

J. "'Way' refers to murder: 'My son, do not walk in the way of them, restrain your foot from their path, for their feet run to evil and they make haste to shed blood' (Prov. 1:15-16).

K. "'Way' refers to slander: 'And he heard the words of Laban's sons, saying, "Jacob has taken away [everything that belonged to our father]"' (Gen. 31:1)."

No. 1 goes over the problem of the preceding and makes it explicit. No. 2 then subjects the verse to a close exegesis, with the standard repertoire of mortal sins—murder, fornication, slander—now read into the verse. Jacob asks God's protection to keep himself from sinning. That interpretation rehabilitates Jacob, since the picture in Scripture portrays a rather self-centered person, and now Jacob exhibits virtue.

LXX:V.

1.A. ". . . will give me bread to eat and clothing to wear:"

B. Aqilas the proselyte came to R. Eliezer and said to him, "Is all the gain that is coming to the proselyte going to be contained in this verse: '. . . and loves the proselyte, giving him food and clothing' (Deut. 10:18)?"

C. He said to him, "And is something for which the old man [Jacob] beseeched going to be such a small thing in your view namely, '. . . will give me bread to eat and clothing to wear'? [God] comes and hands it over to [a proselyte] on a reed [and the proselyte does not have to beg for it.]"

D. He came to R. Joshua, who commenced by saying words to appease him: "'Bread' refers to Torah, as it is said, 'Come, eat of my bread' (Prov. 9:5). 'Clothing' refers to the cloak of a disciple of sages.

E. "When a person has the merit of studying the Torah, he has the merit of carrying out a religious duty. [So the proselyte receives a great deal when he gets bread and clothing, namely, entry into the estate of disciples].

F. "And not only so, but his daughters may be chosen for marriage into the priesthood, so that their sons' sons will offer burnt-offerings on the altar. [So the proselyte may also look forward to entry into the priests' caste. That statement will now be spelled out.]

G. "'Bread' refers to the show-bread.

H. "'Clothing' refers to the garments of the priesthood.

I. "So lo, we deal with the sanctuary.

J. "How do we know that the same sort of blessing applies in the provinces? 'Bread' speaks of the dough-offering [that is separated in the provinces], while 'clothing' refers to the first fleece [handed over to the priest]."

The interpretation of "bread" and "clothing" yields its own message, intersecting only at one point with the passage at hand. So at issue in this composition is not the exegesis of our base verse but the meaning of "bread" and "clothing" as applied to the proselyte. We now see how the components of the base verse are reread in terms of the base-values of sages themselves: Torah and cult. Sages regard study of Torah as equivalent to a sacrifice, and the sage as equivalent to the priest. This typological reading of Israel's existence then will guide sages' interpretation of such specific passages as the one before us.

LXX:VI.

1.A. ". . . so that I come again to my father's house in peace, then the Lord shall be my God" (Gen. 28:20-22):

B. R. Joshua of Sikhnin in the name of R. Levi: "The Holy One, blessed be he, took the language used by the patriarchs and turned it into a key to the redemption of their descendants.

Now comes the main event in our passage: the reading, in the light of Israel's future history, that is, the story of Israel's salvation, of the deeds of the matriarchs and patriarchs and of God's love for them

C. "Said the Holy One, blessed be he, to Jacob, 'You have said, *"Then the Lord shall be my God."* By your life, all of the acts of goodness, blessing, and consolation which I am going to carry out for your descendants I shall bestow only by using the same language:

D. "'"Then in that day, living waters shall go out from Jerusalem" (Zech. 14:8). "Then in that day a man shall rear a young cow and two sheep" (Is. 7:21). "Then, in that day, the Lord will set his hand again the second time to recover the remnant of his people" (Is. 11:11). "Then, in that day, the mountains shall drop down sweet wine" (Joel 4:18). "Then, in that day, a great horn shall be blown and they shall come who were lost in the land of Assyria" (Is. 27:13).'"

The union of Jacob's biography and Israel's history yields the passage at hand. The explicit details, rather conventional in character, are less interesting than the basic syllogism, which is implicit and ubiquitous.

Another approach to the interpretation of Scripture in which this document's framers pioneered is the imputation to a single verse of a wide variety of coherent, alternative readings. Later on this exegetical mode would be given its own form, introduced by Hebrew words meaning, another matter, and a long sequence of "other matters" would be strung together. In fact, all of the "other matters" turn out to say the same thing, only in different ways, or to convey a single, coherent attitude, emotion, sentiment, or conception. But in the following, we find the substance of the hermeneutics, but not the form it would ultimately be given.

LXX:VIII.

1.A. "Then Jacob lifted up his feet" (Gen. 29:1):

B. Said R. Aha, "'A tranquil heart is the life of the flesh' (Prov. 14:30).

C. "Since he had been given this good news, his heart carried his feet.

D. "So people say: 'The stomach carries the feet.'"

What captures attention is the happiness that is expressed in the description of Jacob's on-ward journey. The good news carried him forward. But I do not see at this point what this good news ("gospel") represents. However, what follows more than fills the gap. It is the gospel of Israel: its salvation, worked out in the principal components of its holy way of life of sanctification. So the base and intersecting verses prepare the way for a powerful and sustained statement. In the following protracted, six-part interpretation of the simple verse about seeing a well in the field, we see the full power of Midrash as proposition yielding exegesis. Elements of both sanctification and salvation are joined in a remarkable message.

2.A. "As he looked, he saw a well in the field:"

B. R. Hama bar Hanina interpreted the verse in six ways [that is, he divides the verse into six clauses and systematically reads each of the clauses in light of the others and in line with an overriding theme]:

C. "'As he looked, he saw a well in the field:' this refers to the well [of water in the wilderness, Num. 21:17].

D. "'. . . and lo, three flocks of sheep lying beside it:' specifically, Moses, Aaron, and Miriam.

E. "'. . . for out of that well the flocks were watered:' from there each one drew water for his standard, tribe, and family."

F. "And the stone upon the well's mouth was great:"

G. Said R. Hanina, "It was only the size of a little sieve."

H. [Reverting to Hama's statement:] "'. . . and put the stone back in its place upon the mouth of the well:' for the coming journeys.

Thus the first interpretation applies the passage at hand to the life of Israel in the wilderness. The premise is the prevailing syllogism: Israel's future history is lived out, the first time around, in the lives of the patriarchs and matriarchs.

3.A. "'As he looked, he saw a well in the field:' refers to Zion.

B. "'. . . and lo, three flocks of sheep lying beside it:' refers to the three festivals.

C. "'. . . . for out of that well the flocks were watered:' from there they drank of the holy spirit.

D. "'. . . The stone on the well's mouth was large:' this refers to the rejoicing of the house of the water-drawing."

E. Said R. Hoshaiah, "Why is it called 'the house of the water drawing'? Because from there they drink of the Holy Spirit."

F. [Resuming Hama b. Hanina's discourse:] "'. . . and when all the flocks were gathered there:' coming from 'the entrance of Hamath to the brook of Egypt' (1 Kgs. 8:66).

G. "'. . . the shepherds would roll the stone from the mouth of the well and water the sheep:' for from there they would drink of the Holy Spirit.

H. "'. . . and put the stone back in its place upon the mouth of the well:' leaving it in place until the coming festival.

Thus the second interpretation reads the verse in light of the Temple celebration of the Festival of Tabernacles.

4.A. "'. . . As he looked, he saw a well in the field:' this refers to Zion.

B. "'. . . and lo, three flocks of sheep lying beside it:' this refers to the three courts, concerning which we have learned in the Mishnah: There were three courts there, one at the gateway of the Temple mount, one at the gateway of the courtyard, and one in the chamber of the hewn stones [M. San. 11:2].

C. "'. . . for out of that well the flocks were watered:' for from there they would hear the ruling.

D. "The stone on the well's mouth was large:' this refers to the high court that was in the chamber of the hewn stones.

E. "'. . . and when all the flocks were gathered there:' this refers to the courts in session in the Land of Israel.

F. "'. . . the shepherds would roll the stone from the mouth of the well and water the sheep:' for from there they would hear the ruling.

G. "'. . . and put the stone back in its place upon the mouth of the well:' for they would give and take until they had produced the ruling in all the required clarity."

The third interpretation reads the verse in light of the Israelite institution of justice and administration. The intrusion of the cited passage of the Mishnah alerts us to the striking difference between our document and Sifra and Sifre to Numbers. The Mishnah-passage serves as mere illustration. It does not generate the question to be answered, nor does it come under detailed amplification itself. It is in no way a focus of interest.

5.A. "'As he looked, he saw a well in the field:' this refers to Zion.

B. "'. . . and lo, three flocks of sheep lying beside it:' this refers to the first three kingdoms [Babylonia, Media, Greece].

C. "'. . . for out of that well the flocks were watered:' for they enriched the treasures that were laid up in the chambers of the Temple.

D. "'. . . The stone on the well's mouth was large:' this refers to the merit attained by the patriarchs.

E. "'. . . and when all the flocks were gathered there:' this refers to the wicked kingdom, which collects troops through levies from all the nations of the world.

F. "'. . . the shepherds would roll the stone from the mouth of the well and water the sheep:' for they enriched the treasures that were laid up in the chambers of the Temple.

G. "'. . . and put the stone back in its place upon the mouth of the well:' in the age to come the merit attained by the patriarchs will stand [in defense of Israel].'

So the fourth interpretation interweaves the themes of the Temple cult and the domination of the four monarchies.

6.A. "'As he looked, he saw a well in the field:' this refers to the Sanhedrin.

B. "'. . . and lo, three flocks of sheep lying beside it:' this alludes to the three rows of disciples of sages that would go into session in their presence.

C. "for out of that well the flocks were watered:' for from there they would listen to the ruling of the law.

D. "'. . . The stone on the well's mouth was large:' this refers to the most distinguished member of the court, who determines the law-decision.

E. "'. . . and when all the flocks were gathered there:' this refers to disciples of the sages in the Land of Israel.

F. "'... the shepherds would roll the stone from the mouth of the well and water the sheep:' for from there they would listen to the ruling of the law.

G. "'... and put the stone back in its place upon the mouth of the well:' for they would give and take until they had produced the ruling in all the required clarity."

The fifth interpretation again reads the verse in light of the Israelite institution of legal education and justice.

7.A. "'As he looked, he saw a well in the field:' this refers to the synagogue.

B. "'... and lo, three flocks of sheep lying beside it:' this refers to the three who are called to the reading of the Torah on weekdays.

C. "'... for out of that well the flocks were watered:' for from there they hear the reading of the Torah.

D. "'... The stone on the well's mouth was large:' this refers to the impulse to do evil.

E. "'... and when all the flocks were gathered there:' this refers to the congregation.

F. "'... the shepherds would roll the stone from the mouth of the well and water the sheep:' for from there they hear the reading of the Torah.

G. "'... and put the stone back in its place upon the mouth of the well:' for once they go forth [from the hearing of the reading of the torah] the impulse to do evil reverts to its place."

The sixth and last interpretation turns to the twin themes of the reading of the Torah in the synagogue and the evil impulse, temporarily driven off through the hearing of the Torah. The six themes read in response to the verse cover (1) Israel in the wilderness, (2) the Temple cult on festivals with special reference to Tabernacles, (3) the judiciary and government, (4) the history of Israel under the four kingdoms, (5) the life of sages, and (6) the ordinary folk and the synagogue. The whole is an astonishing repertoire of fundamental themes of the life of the nation, Israel: at its origins in the wilderness, in its cult, in its institutions based on the cult, in the history of the nations, and, finally, in the twin social estates of sages and ordinary folk, matched by the institutions of the master-disciple circle and the synagogue. The vision of Jacob at the well thus encompassed the whole of the social reality of Jacob's people, Israel. The labor of interpreting this same passage in the profound, typological context already established now goes forward.

LXX:IX.

1.A. R. Yohanan interpreted the statement in terms of Sinai:

B. "'As he looked, he saw a well in the field:' this refers to Sinai.

C. "'... and lo, three flocks of sheep lying beside it:' these stand for the priests, Levites, and Israelites.

D. "'... for out of that well the flocks were watered:' for from there they heard the Ten Commandments.

E. "'... The stone on the well's mouth was large:' this refers to the Presence of God."

F. "'... and when all the flocks were gathered there:"

G. R. Simeon b. Judah of Kefar Akum in the name of R. Simeon: "All of the flocks of Israel had to be present, for if any one of them had been lacking, they would not have been worthy of receiving the Torah."

H. [Returning to Yohanan's exposition:] "'... the shepherds would roll the stone from the mouth of the well and water the sheep:' for from there they heard the Ten Commandments.

I. "'... and put the stone back in its place upon the mouth of the well:' 'You yourselves have seen that I have talked with you from heaven' (Exod. 20:19)."

Yohanan's exposition adds what was left out, namely, reference to the revelation of the Torah at Sinai. As though the demonstration of the ubiquitous syllogism that Israel's history is the story of the lives of the founders, we now go over the same proposition again, with utterly fresh materials. That shows that the proposed syllogism states the deep structure of reality, the syntax that permits words to make diverse, yet intelligible statements. Once we have taken up the challenge of the foregoing, a still greater task requires us to make the same basic point in utterly different cases, and that allows us definitively to demonstrate that syllogism as it is tested against diverse cases presented by Scripture's facts.

LXX:X.

1.A. "Jacob said to them, 'My brothers, where do you come from?' They said, 'We are from Haran'" (Gen. 29:40):

B. R. Yose bar Haninah interpreted the verse at hand with reference to the Exile.

C. "'Jacob said to them, "My brothers, where do you come from"' They said, "We are from Haran:" that is, 'We are flying from the wrath of the Holy One, blessed be he.' [Here there is a play on the words for "Haran" and "wrath," which share the same consonants.]

D. "'He said to them, "Do you know Laban the son of Nahor?"' The sense is this, 'Do you know him who is destined to bleach your sins as white as snow?' [Here there is a play on the words for "Laban" and "bleach," which share the same consonants.]

E. "'They said, "We know him." He said to them, "Is it well with him?" They said, "It is well."' On account of what sort of merit?

F. [Yose continues his interpretation:] "'[The brothers go on,] ". . . and see, Rachel his daughter is coming with the sheep"' (Gen. 29:6-7).

G. "That is in line with this verse: 'Thus says the Lord, "A voice is heard in Ramah, lamentation and bitter weeping, Rachel weeping for her children. She refuses to be comforted." Thus says the Lord, "Refrain your voice from weeping . . . and there is hope for your future," says the Lord, and your children shall return to their own border"' (Jer. 31:15-16)."

Now the history of the redemption of Israel is located in the colloquy between Jacob and Laban's sons. The themes pour forth in profusion, forming propositions of a subordinate character.

LXX:XI.

1.A. ["He said to them, 'Is it well with him?' They said, 'It is well; and see, Rachel his daughter is coming with the sheep'" (Lev. 29:6-7)]: "He said to them, 'Is it well with him?'" "Is there peace between him and you?"

B. "They said, 'It is well.' And if it is gossip that you want, 'see, Rachel his daughter is coming with the sheep.'"'"

C. That is in line with this saying: "Women like gossip."

2.A. "He said, 'Behold, it is still [high day, it is not time for the animals to be gathered together; water the sheep and go, pasture them.' But they said, 'We cannot until all the flocks are gathered together, and the stone is rolled from the mouth of the well; then we water the sheep']" (Gen. 29:7-8):

B. He said to them, "If you are hired hands, 'it is still high day.' [You have no right to water the flock so early in the day.]

C. "If you are shepherding your own flock: 'It is not time for the animals to be gathered together.' [It is not in your interest to do so.]"

3.A. "They said, 'We cannot. . . .' While he was still speaking with them, Rachel came" (Gen. 29:9):

B. Said Rabban Simeon b. Gamaliel, "Come and note the difference between one neighborhood and the next.

C. "Elsewhere [in Midian, when the daughters of Jethro came to water their flocks,] there were seven women, and the shepherds wanted to give them a hard time, as it is said, 'And the shepherds came and drove them away' (Exod. 2:17).

D. "Here, by contrast, there was only one woman, and yet not one of them laid a hand on her, because 'The angel of the Lord encamps around about those who fear him and delivers them' (Ps. 34:8).

E. "This refers to those who live in a neighborhood of those who fear him."

Nos. 1, 2 articulate the conversation between Jacob and the shepherds. No. 3 draws a more general conclusion, using the verse at hand to demonstrate the contrast necessary for the syllogism. It is safer to live in a Jewish neighborhood.

LXX:XII.

1.A. "Now when Jacob saw Rachel, the daughter of Laban his mother's brother, and the sheep of Laban, his mother's brother, Jacob went up and rolled the stone [from the well's mouth and watered the flock of Laban his mother's brother. Then Jacob kissed Rachel and wept aloud. And Jacob told Rachel that he was Rebecca's son, and she ran and told her father]" (Gen. 29:10-12):

B. Said R. Yohanan, "He did it without effort, like someone who takes a stopper out of a flask."

2.A. "Then Jacob kissed Rachel:"

What follows is yet another mode of inquiry, namely, the laying out of a proposition by means of a list. The list collects the relevant data, and the proposition sorts out among the data the classifications that render the facts intelligible. In this pursuit of natural philosophy or science accomplished through list-making and classification of data on lists, sages turn to Scripture, rather than to nature, but the mode of mode of inquiry is the same. In this composition the cited verse plays no important role. It is tacked on, simply a fact, which joins the prepared list to the larger context of the document at hand.

B. Every form of kissing is obscene except for three purposes, the kiss upon accepting high office, the kiss upon seeing someone at an interval after an absence, and the kiss of departure.

C. The kiss upon accepting high office: "Then Samuel took the vial of oil and poured it upon his head and kissed him" (1 Sam. 10:1).

D. The kiss upon seeing someone at an interval [after an absence]: "And he went and met him in the mountain of God and kissed him" (Exod. 4:27).

E. The kiss of departure: "And Orpah kissed her mother-in-law" (Ruth 1:4).

F. Said R. Tanhuma, "Also the kiss exchanged among kin: 'Then Jacob kissed Rachel.'"

3.A. "And he wept aloud:"

B. Why did Jacob weep?

C. [Jacob thus] said, "Concerning Eliezer [Abraham's major domo, who went to find a wife for Abraham's son, Isaac] when he went to bring Rebecca [to Isaac as Isaac's wife], it is written in his regard: 'and the servant took ten camels' (Gen. 24:10). But I do not have even a ring or a bracelet." [That is why he wept.]

4.A. Another matter:

B. Why did Jacob weep?

C. Because he foresaw that she would not be buried with him.

D. That is in line with this statement that Rachel made to Leah: "Therefore he shall lie with you tonight" (Gen. 30:15).

E. "With you he will sleep, and not with me."

5.A. Another matter:

B. Why did Jacob weep?

C. Because he saw that men were whispering with one another, saying, "Has this one now come to create an innovation in sexual licentiousness among us? [That is something we cannot permit.]"

D. For from the moment that the world had been smitten on account of the generation of the flood, the nations of the world had gone and fenced themselves away from fornication.

E. That is in line with what people say: "People of the east are meticulous about sexual purity."

No. 1 supplies a minor gloss. No. 2 uses the base verse as part of a syllogistic statement. No. 3 answers an obvious question. Nos. 4, 5 answer the same question.

LXX:XIX.

1.A. "So Laban gathered together all the men of the place and made a feast" (Gen. 29:22):

B. He brought together all of the men of the place. He said to them, "You know that we were in need of water. But once this righteous man came, the water has been blessed. [So let's keep him around here.]"

C. They said to him, "What is good for you is what you should do."

D. He said to them, "Do you want me to deceive him and give him Leah, and, since he loves Rachel more, he will stay and work here with you for another seven years."

E. They said to him, "What is good for you is what you should do."

F. He said to them, "Give me your pledge that none of you will inform him."

G. They gave him their pledge. Then he went and with the pledges the neighbors had given got them wine, oil and meat.

H. What follows is that he was called Laban the deceiver, since he deceived even the people who lived in his own town.

I. All that day the people were praising him. When the evening came, he said to them, "Why are you doing this?"

J. They said to him, "On your account benefits have been coming to us," and they sang praises before him, saying, "Hey, Leah, Hey, Leah."

K. In the evening they came to bring her in and they put out the lamps. He said to them, "Why so?"

L. They said to him, "Do you want us to be indecent the way you are? [Here we do not have sexual relations in the light.]"

M. All that night he would use the name of Rachel and she answered him. In the morning: "And in the morning, behold, it was Leah" (Gen. 29:24-25)!

N. He said, "How could you have deceived me, you daughter of a deceiver?"

O. She said to him, "And is there a book without faithful readers? [I know your story and so I followed your example.] Did not your father call you 'Esau,' and you answered him accordingly? So you called me by a name other than my own, and I answered you accordingly."

2.A. "And Jacob said to Laban, 'What is that this that you have done to me? Did I not serve with you for Rachel? Why then have you deceived me?' And Laban said, 'It is not so done in our country, to give the younger before the first-born . . . Complete the week of this one and we will give you the other also in return for serving me another seven years' " (Gen. 29?25-27):

B. Said R. Jacob bar Aha, "On the basis of this statement we learn the rule that people may not confuse one occasion for rejoicing with some other."

No. 1 presents a sustained amplification of details of the story, ending with a stunning and apt observation about the appropriate conduct of Leah with Jacob. No. 2, by contrast, just draws a moral. The reference to the deeds of the patriarchs and matriarchs does not always yield complimentary judgments. Quite to the contrary, Jacob's conduct with Isaac accounts for Leah's conduct with Jacob. We look in vain for traces of sentimentality in the intellect of the exegetes at hand, who were engaged in a solemn search for the rules of life, not in a systematic apologetic for a merely-sacred text.

In Genesis Rabbah, the sages show in detail the profound depths of the story of the creation of the world and Israel's founding family. Bringing their generative proposition about the character of the Scripture to the stories at hand, they systematically found in the details of the tales the history of the people Israel portrayed in the lives and deeds of the founders, the fathers and the mothers of this book of the Torah. It is no accident that the exegetes of the book of Genesis invoke large-scale constructions of history to make fundamental judgments about society—Israel's society. Nor is it merely happenstance that the exegetes bring into juxtaposition distinct facts—passages—of scriptural history or appeal to a typological reading of the humble details of the scriptural tale, the simple statement that the shepherds had brought their flocks to the well, for example. A large proposition has governed the details of exegesis, and the individual verses commonly, though not always, address their facts in the proof of an encompassing hypothesis, a theorem concerning Israel's fate and faith.

JACOB NEUSNER

GOSPELS, ORAL TRADITIONS OF THE MISHNAH IN: Oral traditions always accompany a written text. This has always happened and happens today in every culture. Texts, even after having been written down, are alive through the attached notes and commentaries. Such a live tradition is noticeable in the edited Rabbinic Bibles, where the biblical text is framed by masoretic notes, Aramaic targums, and great classical Jewish commentaries. The Bible has been always handed down with an oral tradition. "Tradition—*massoret*—is a fence to the Torah," Aqiba said (M. Ab. 3:13), following the Great Assembly's advice (M. Ab. 1:1).

The Mishnah—"repetition"—is by definition oral tradition. In Aqiba's representation, the Oral Torah is deduced from the Written Torah. In the more popular representation, the Oral Torah came from Moses at Sinai. In any case, it deals with the legitimation of the Oral Torah, i.e., the efforts of every generation to update the immutable written text. So it is understandable that different opinions about the halakhah, even those not accepted by the sages, keep their weight and deserve to be recorded (cf., M. Ed. 2:4-6).

The Gospel literature arose in the first century C.E. from a Jewish movement that accepted the Bible as its reference: for Christians, the Bible is also the Word of God. At that moment the Mishnah was not yet written down, but many of its traditions were alive, as is shown by Qumranic writings (4QMMT), Flavius Josephus, and the New Testament literature. Many halakhic and theological discussions collected in the Gospels could be understood in a similar way to the Rabbinic interpretations in the framework of the Oral Law. Therefore it is not surprising that oral traditions of the Mishnah appear in the Gospels, without necessarily presuming literary dependence in any direction.

The aim of this article is to show some examples of common traditions in these writings. Stories (haggadah), normative rules (halakhah), and theological views are handed down through oral traditions. We also find in oral traditions information about *realia* (objects, facts and customs) and linguistic devices (vocabulary, idioms, images, Semitisms), which we will deal with first. The parallel readings of the traditions in both *corpora* increase our understanding of the texts in their own contexts. I focus on the texts of the Mishnah, leaving out the Tosefta, Midrashim, and the Talmuds, which will be used only as secondary support or in order to show a development.

Realia: *Flutes and wailer women at a funeral:* Mark 5:38-39 (= Matt. 9:23, Luke 8:52) mentions people weeping and wailing loudly at a funeral; Matthew mentions the flute players; Luke says in a general way that "they were all weeping and wailing." In different parts of the Mishnah we are told that weepers and flutes play an important role at funerals. This is a custom felt to be so necessary that Judah says: "Even the poorest in Israel must not furnish less than two flutes and one woman wailer" (M. Ket. 4:4). It is presumed that flute players and wailer women are to be contracted: "If a non-Jew brought flutes on the Sabbath, a Jew may not play on them dirges unless they came from a near-by place" (M. Shab. 23:4); "If one hired an ass-driver or a car-man to bring litter-bearers or pipers for a bride or for a dead person . . ." (M. B.M. 6:1). It also specifies how to do the lamentations and their different types: "During the Intermediate Days women may lament but they may not beat their hands . . ." (M. M.Q. 3:8); ". . . What is a lamentation? When all of them lament together. Wailing? When one speaks up and all respond after her" (M. M.Q. 3:9).

The tax collector: Jesus is presented in the Gospels as "friend of tax collectors and sinners." This association of the tax collectors with sinners reveals their bad reputation: Matt. 5:46; 9:10-13; 18:14-17; Luke 15:1. Tax collectors have the same reputation in the Mishnah.[1] They are hard, without compassion when they require to be paid: "The collectors regularly go their round every day and exact payment from man with his consent or without his consent" (M. Ab. 3:16); they are considered as the gentiles and Samaritans: "If collectors comes into a house, the house becomes unclean" (M. Toh. 7:2). T. Dem. 3:4 tells us that if a fellow (*haber*) becomes a tax collector, he must be expelled from the community.

The Samaritans: The scene in John 4—the meeting of Jesus with a Samaritan woman and the neighbors' conversion—undoubtedly has a historical background. In the first Christian circles there was participation by the Samaritans (Acts 8:25), and some scholars give this Samaritan minority responsibility for the anti-Jewish tone of the Fourth Gospel. The Gospels show the current bad relations between Jews and Samaritans: "The Samaritan woman said to him, How is it that you, a Jew, ask a drink of me, a woman of Samaria? Jews do not share things in common with Samaritans" (John 4:9); "And he sent messengers ahead of him. On their way they entered a village of the Samaritans to make ready for him; but they did not receive him, because his face was set toward Jerusalem" (Luke 9:52-53). In Matt. 10:5, the association of the Samaritans with the gentile can be seen: "These twelve Jesus sent out with the following instructions: Go nowhere among the gentiles, and enter no town of the Samaritans, but go rather to the lost sheep of the house of Israel." Therefore the prominence of the Samaritan in Jesus' parables and miracles is presumed to be deliberate and provocative: Luke 10:25-37; 17:11-19.

The same social background is found in the Mishnah, where Samaria is never considered "the land of Israel," which only includes "Judea, and beyond the Jordan, and Galilee" (M. Sheb. 9:2; M. Ket. 13:10; M. B.B. 3:2). Samaritans and gentiles are put on the same level: "In the case of a non-Jew or a Samaritan, priestly due they set aside is valid" (M. Ter. 3:9); "If a non-Jew or a Samaritan gives the half-shekel, they may not accept it from them" (M. Sheq. 1:5). The Samaritan's image is indeed negative: "R. Eliezer used to say: He that eats of the bread of Samaritans is as one who eats the flesh of swine" (M. Sheb. 8:10); "Any legal document that has a Samaritan as witness to it is invalid, save writs of divorce and writs of manumission of bondmen" (M. Git. 1:5); "And these are they of the uncertain origin: he who knows who his mother, but not his father, the foundling, and the Samaritan" (M. Qid.

4:3); "If there were in a town a mentally defective woman or a gentile woman or a Samaritan woman, all spittle found in the town is unclean" (M. Toh. 5:8; cf., M. Toh. 4:5); "The daughters of the Samaritans are considered unclean as menstruants from their cradle . . ." (M. Nid. 4:1); "This is the general principle: in any matter regarding which they (the Samaritans) are suspect they are not to be believed" (M. Nid. 7:5). Also understandable is, on the one hand, the provocation included in the scene of John 4, and, on the other hand, the contempt included in the answer of the Jews: "The Jews answered him, Are we not right in saying that you are a Samaritan and have a demon?" (John 8:48)

Grinding women: In the so-called "eschatological sermon" Jesus says that at the coming of the Son of Man "two women will be grinding meal together; one will be taken and one will be left" (Matt. 24:41). The image represents two women pushing round the millstone for oil or corn. According to the Mishnaic halakhah, milling is women's work: "These are the tasks that a wife must carry out for her husband: she must grind corn, and bake . . ." (M. Ket. 5:5); this work may be carried out by two women: "A woman may lend to her neighbor, who is suspect regarding the Sabbatical Year, a fine sieve, a coarse sieve, grindstones, and an oven; but she will not sift the grain nor grind the corn with her" (M. Sheb. 5:9); "If the wife of a fellow (*haber*) left the wife of an '*am ha-arets* milling in her house, and the mill ceased from grinding, the house became unclean . . . If there were two wives (of '*amei ha-arets*), the house became unclean in both cases, for while one was grinding the other could wander around touching things" (M. Toh. 7:4).

On the roof: In the eschatological sermon Jesus warns that at the time of the desolation sacrilege "the one on the housetop must not go down or enter the house to take anything away" (Mark 13:15, Matt. 24:18). By the context ("not go down or enter the house") this must be understood as the roof or an upper open terrace. At that time the country houses used to have an upper terrace to dry fruits, vegetables, and other products of the country (M. Mak.

3:6 [olives] and M. Mak. 6:1-2 [figs and garlic]). M. Meg 3:3 prohibits people from spreading out nets in the synagogues "or spreading out produce upon its roof." According to M. Ma. 3:6, "Roofs are exempt (from tithes);" there is no doubt that it is referring to the products spread out there. We are told that "on the top of a roof" one might be reading a scroll (M. Erub. 10:3), and there is a halakhah considering the case of a husband throwing a letter of divorce to his wife while she is "on the top of the roof" (M. Git. 8:3).

Linguistics: It is obvious that in the Gospels, written by Jews or in any case using Hebrew or Aramaic sources, typical Jewish sentences and idioms can be found, which are generally classified as Semitisms. I point out some outstanding examples:

During Jesus' trial, Peter is recognized by a maidservant as a fellow of Jesus the Galilean, but he denied it before all of them, saying, "I do not know what you are talking about" (Matt. 26:69-70). This is the legal form to refuse a charge, as is shown in M. Sheb. 8:3.6: "If [an owner] says, where is my ox?, and [the guardian] says, *I don't know what you are speaking about*" (M. Smith).

"Did not Moses give you the law? *Yet none of you does the law*" (John 7:19). The expression "to do the Law" is strange to our ears, but Paul also uses it three times: "*the doers of the law*" (Rom. 2:13); "*the Gentiles . . . do the Law*" (Rom. 2:14); "every man who lets himself be circumcised that he is obliged *to do the entire law*" (Gal. 5:3). The expression is not found in the Bible; the New Testament writers borrow it from the rabbis: "We find that Abraham, our father, *did the whole Torah* before it was given" (M. Qid. 4:14). It is specially abundant in the halakhic midrashim Sifra and Sifre to Deuteronomy: "R. Jeremiah says: How do I know that even a gentile *who does the Torah*, lo, he is like the High Priest?" (Sifra *Ahare* Pereq 13:12 to Lev. 18:6); ". . . so also the land of Israel cannot contain all its fruits so long as Israel *is doing the Torah*" (Sifre Deut. 37 to 7:12); 'If *you do the Torah*, here is a loaf to eat'" (Sifre Deut. 40 to Deut. 11:12); ". . . God that made you vulnerable to any nation in the world *when you do not do the Torah*" (Sifre Deut. 319 end, to Deut. 32:18); "If these, who brought themselves near, were brought still closer by the Omnipresent, Israelites *who do the Torah* all the more so! (Sifre Num. 78:1); cf., T. B.M. 6:6.

"Give glory to God! We know that this man is a sinner" (John 9:24). "Give Glory to God" is a formula for urging the confession of sins. It is found in the Bible: "Then Joshua said to Achan, My son, give glory to the Lord God of Israel and make confession to him. Tell me now what you have done; do not hide it from me" (Jos. 7:19). This text is quoted by M. San. 6:2 when a person, sentenced to death, is said to make confession of his guilt: the imperative *htwdh* (root *ydh*, "praise, thank, confess") implies that the confession of sins is praise to God (midrashic and targumic traditions about the confession of Judah in the affair with Tamar play with this double meaning of the verb). The formula used by John 9:24 requires that the person cured of blindness confesses his sin or the healer's guilt.

"Go into all the world and proclaim the good news to the whole creation" (Mark 16:15). The Greek term *ktisis* keeps the semantic content of *beriyyah* in Rabbinic Hebrew: "men, people, mankind:" "Hillel said: Be thou of the disciples of Aaron, loving peace, and pursuing peace, loving fellow-creatures (*ha-beriyyot*) and drawing them to the Torah" (M. Ab. 1:12); "R. Joshua said: The evil eye, the evil inclination, and hatred of fellow-creatures put a man out of the world" (M. Ab. 2:11); "R. Yose said: He who honors the Torah will himself be honored by his fellow-men, but whosoever dishonors the Torah will himself be dishonored by mankind" (M. Ab. 4:6); see also M. Ab. 3:10; 4:1.

Jesus' expression, "The harvest is plentiful, but the laborers are few" (Matt. 9:37-38 and Luke 10:2), uses terms and contrasts found also in M. Ab. 2:15: "The day is short, and the task is great, and the laborers are sluggish, and the recompense is ample, and the Master of the house is urgent." Both expressions seem to have been written under the pressure of the eschatological urgency.

The same eschatological atmosphere is perceptible in the Aqiba's words: "The judgment is a judgment of truth, and all is pre-

pared for the banquet" (M. Ab. 3:16). This is an autonomous sentence in a collection of *logoi* whose theme is urgency. The reference to the banquet is easily understood as the eschatological banquet. The same reference is used by Jesus in one of his parables: "Tell those who have been invited: Look, I have prepared my dinner, my oxen and my fat calves have been slaughtered, and everything is ready; come to the wedding banquet" (Matt. 22:4); "Come; for everything is ready now" (Luke 14:17).

"The measure you give will be the measure you get" (Mark 4:24; Matt. 7:2; Luke 6:38). This is a wisdom proverb used by both New Testament and Mishnah traditions in an eschatological context: men will be measured by God with the same measure they use for their neighbors. So in M. Sot. 1:7: "With the kind of measure that a man measures *they shall mete to him*: she adorned herself for transgression, the Almighty reduced her to shame; she exposed herself for transgression, the Almighty laid her bare; with her thigh did she first begin transgression, and then with the belly, therefore shall the thigh be stricken first and afterwards the belly; and the rest of all the body shall not escape." The plural participle *modedin lo* ("they shall mete to him") is an impersonal device to avoid the name of God. The proverb recurs again and again in the Tannaitic literature: Mekhilta to Exod. 13:19; 14:25; 15:4,8; 17:14; Sifre Deut. 296; T. Sot. 3:1ff.; 4:1ff.; also in the Targumim: Targum Neophiti Gen. 38:25; Targum Is. 27:8; etc.

"Just so, I tell you, there will be more joy in heaven over one sinner who repents than over ninety-nine righteous persons who need no repentance" (Luke 15:7) is a sentence whose contrast (heaven—earth) is also to be found in M. Ab. 4:17: "Better is one hour of repentance and good actions in this world than the whole life of the world to come."

M. Qid 1:10: "Whosoever performs even a single commandment it shall go well with him, and his days shall be prolonged, and he shall inherit the Land; and whosoever does not perform a single commandment it shall not be well with him, and he shall not enjoy length of days, and he shall not inherit the Land." There is here a contrasting parallelism in structure and content: opposition and disparity between the *minimum* done and the *maximum* achieved, which is also found in Matt. 5:19: "whoever breaks one of the least of these commandments, and teaches others to do the same, will be called least in the kingdom of heaven; but whoever does them and teaches them will be called great in the kingdom of heaven." The same theme is found in Targum Neophiti Num. 12:16: "Although Miriam the prophetess was responsible for becoming leprous, there is much teaching in this for the sages and for those who keep the Law, *that for a small precept which a man does, he receives for it a great reward.*" Also at M. Hul. 12:5: "And if of so light a command that is merely an issar's value the Law has said 'that it may be well with thee, and that thou mayest prolong thy days' (Deut. 22:7), it follows how much more shall be given for the weighty commandments of the Law." By the way, let me say how absurd it is to oppose Judaism and Christianity as religions of Merit vs. Grace.

We can appreciate a similar contrast in M. Dem. 2:2: "If he is not reliable regarding himself, how can he be relied upon to conserve what belongs to others!" By contrast, Jesus ironically pointed out (M. Smith): "And if you have not been faithful with what belongs to another, who will give you what is your own?" (Luke 16:12)

Haggadah: The Mishnah is not a haggadic work but includes some stories and references to stories supposedly known. Many of these stories are gathered in the Gospels:

The generation of the flood and the men of Sodom. These two groups are excluded from the world to come by Mishnaic tradition: "The generation of the flood has no portion in the world to come, neither shall it stand in the judgment, as it is said, 'My spirit shall not abide in man for ever' (Gen. 6:3). . . . "The men of Sodom have no portion in the world to come, as it is said, 'Now the men of Sodom were wicked and sinners against the Eternal exceedingly' (Gen. 13:13). Wicked means 'in this world', sinners means 'in the world to come'" (M. San. 10:3). The haggadah about both

groups is well known in New Testament times; Jesus himself says: "Truly I tell you, *it will be more tolerable for the land of Sodom and Gomorrah on the day of judgment* than for that town [that did not receive the messengers of Jesus]" (Matt. 10:15); "Just as it was *in the days of Noah,* so too it will be in the days of the Son of Man. They were eating and drinking, and marrying and being given in marriage, until the day Noah entered the ark, *and the flood came and destroyed all of them*" (Luke 17:26-27; cf. Matt. 24:37-39).

The troubles of the Messianic Era. M. Sot. 9:15 describes the horrifying events that will precede the coming of the messiah: heresies, devastation, corruption, insolence. A significant aspect of this situation is the breaking of family relationship: "The young shall put the elders to shame, and the elders shall rise up before little ones, 'the son dishonored the father, the daughter raised up against her mother, the daughter-in-law against her mother-in-law, a man's enemies are the men of his own house' (M. Miq. 7:6). The face of the generation is like the face of a dog" (M. Sot. 9:15). A similar description is found in the Gospel for the return of Christ (*Parousia*): wars, earthquakes, accusations before the tribunals, tortures, and also the conversion of family relations into hate and death: "Brother will betray brother to death, and a father his child, and children will rise against parents and have them put to death" (Mark 13:12). The same cliché is shared by New Testament literature and the Mishnah: the pains of the messianic age.

The parable of the wine and wineskins. A discussion is recorded in the Mishnah about what is better, to learn in childhood or in adulthood. Three rabbis use different images to support their views (M. Ab. 4:20):

> Elisha b. Abuyah says, "If one learns as a child, what is it like? Like ink written on new paper. He that learns as an old man, what is it like? To ink written on blotted paper."
> R. Yose b. R. Judah of Kefar ha-Bavli said, "If one learns from the young, to what is he like? To one that eats unripe grapes, or drinks wine from his winepress. And one who learns from the aged, to what is he like? To one that eats ripe grapes and drinks old wine."

Rabbi said, "Look not at the flask but at what is therein; there may be a new flask full of old wine, and an old flask wherein is not even new wine."

For the first, learning as a child is preferable: it is similar to writing on new paper. For the second learning in adulthood is preferable, similar to tasting ripe grapes and old wine. For the third, what matters is not the container (child or adult) but the content. This kind of parable must have been very popular. Jesus, referring to his own teaching, uses the parable of the wine and the wineskins (although with opposite values of the "new" and the "old," as we shall see later): "And no one puts new wine into old wineskins; otherwise, the wine will burst the skins, and the wine is lost, and so are the skins; but one puts new wine into fresh wineskins" (Mark 2:22, Matthew 9:17, Luke 5:37-39)

Divine providence. Matt. 6:24-34 is a piece of exquisite beauty and great spirituality, based on the contemplation of nature: "Look at the birds of the air; they neither sow nor reap nor gather into barns, and yet your heavenly Father feeds them. Are you not of more value than they?" (v. 26). The same image recurs in Matt. 10:29-31 in a context of persecution: "Are not two sparrows sold for a penny? Yet not one of them will fall to the ground apart from your Father. And even the hairs of your head are all counted. So do not be afraid; you are of more value than many sparrows." And this beautiful lesson from nature is also taught by the Mishnah: "R. Simeon b. Eliezer says: Hast thou ever beheld a wild beast or bird that possesses a craft? And none the less they sustain themselves without care, and were they not created but to serve me? But I was created to serve my Maker. Does it not follow that I should receive my maintenance without care? But I have performed my actions in evil and have foregone my support" (M. Qid. 4:14). Jesus' teaching is boundless trust in the Father in Heaven; Simeon puts a condition: man must serve his Creator. But both of them are sharing the same haggadic tradition.

Halakhot: Especially in the Gospel of Matthew, Jesus appears as a "Master of the Law." The famous sermon of the mount (Matt. 5-7) is set by the Evangelist as a formal and solemn session in the *bet ha-midrash*: the master is session, the disciples and people around at his feet, all attentively listening. The words of the master remind us of the proclamation on Mount Sinai: Jesus is remembering and interpreting the commandments of Moses. Jesus' teaching could be interpreted like the Oral Torah that so many masters—before and after him—have handed down explaining the Written Torah. The critical question—which Jacob Neusner has asked (see his, *A Rabbi talks with Jesus*)—is whether Jesus' teaching could be understood as Torah. Apparently yes, because Jesus starts: "Do not think that I have come to abolish the Law or the Prophets; I have come not to abolish but to fulfill. For truly I tell you, until heaven and earth pass away, not one letter, not one stroke of a letter, will pass from the Law until all is accomplished" (Matt. 5:17-18). For the moment I shall propose some examples of halakhot shared by Jesus and the Mishnaic tradition. In the next section—theology—the most significant differences will be pointed out.

Fraternal warning: "If another member of the church sins against you, go and point out the fault when the two of you are alone. If the member listens to you, you have regained that one. But if you are not listened to, take one or two others along with you, so that every word may be confirmed by the evidence of two or three witnesses. If the member refuses to listen to them, tell it to the church; and if the offender refuses to listen even to the church, let such a one be to you as a Gentile and a tax collector" (Matt. 18:15-17); "If another disciple sins, you must rebuke the offender" (Luke 17:3). The fraternal warning before a punishment is a normative rule observed by the Rabbis. Even one who has been banned is addressed with these words: "May He that dwelleth in this House put it into thy heart *to hearken to the words of thy fellows that they may bring thee nigh again*" (M. Mid. 2:2). The strict law in cases of jealousy (*sotah*) and the serving of the writ of divorce require prior warning by the witnesses (Sifre Numbers 7, to Num. 5:12); see Sifre Num. 19 (to Num. 5:28): "We know that that is the rule *only when there are witnesses who have admonished the couple* that their intended action is punishable by the death-penalty." This rule has a precedent: the man who was surprised gathering wood on the Sabbath (Num 15:32): When the Israelites were in the wilderness, they found a man gathering sticks on the Sabbath day. Those who found him gathering sticks brought him to Moses"). This text is explained by the midrash in this way: "This informs us that *they gave him ample warning* as to the character of the act of labor, forbidden on the Sabbath, that he was carrying out. On the basis of that fact, we learn the rule that *all the generative forms of forbidden labor* listed in the Torah as forbidden on the Sabbath *have to be spelled out in admonition* to those who perform them" (Sifre Num. 113; cf., T. San. 11:1). The fraternal correction has an explicit support in the Torah: "you shall reprove your neighbor, or you will incur guilt yourself" (Lev. 19:17); its interpretation by the Qumran Community also requires "reproach before witnesses" (CD 9:2-8).

Conversion, forgiveness, reconciliation: These are correlative terms in the New Testament and Rabbinic halakhah. Jesus says that conversion is a condition for forgiveness: "Be on your guard! If another disciple sins, you must rebuke the offender, and *if there is repentance, you must forgive*" (Luke 17:3); the reconciliation is before the atonement by sacrifices: "So when you are offering your gift at the altar, if you remember that your brother or sister has something against you, leave your gift there before the altar and go; *first be reconciled to your brother or sister, and then come and offer your gift*" (Matt. 5:23-24). The same correlation can be seen in M. Yom. 8:9: "If one says, 'I will sin and repent, I will sin and repent,' he will not be given [from on high] an opportunity to repent. 'I will sin and the Day of Atonement will effect atonement,' then the Day of Atonement does not effect atonement. For transgressions from man towards God the Day of Atonement effects atonement; *but for transgressions between a man and his fellow man the Day of Atonement does not effect atonement until he shall have first appeased his fellow man.* Thus did R. Eleazar b. Azariah expound,

'From all your sins before the Eternal shall be ye clean' (Lev. 16:30)—for transgressions from man towards God the Day of Atonement effects atonement, *but for transgressions between a man and his fellow man the Day of Atonement does not effect atonement until he shall have first placated his fellow man.*"

Greeting the Gentiles: In the context of the Sermon of the Mount, Jesus is developing the golden rule, "you shall love your neighbor as yourself" (Lev. 19:18), and he adds: "And if you greet only your brothers and sisters, what more are you doing than others? Do not even the gentiles do the same? Be perfect, therefore, as your heavenly father is perfect" (Matt. 5:47). Mishnaic halakhah emphasizes the importance of interpersonal greetings, even considering the interruption of the Shema' for the sake of greeting people and responding to them (M. Ber. 2:1); according to M. Ber. 9:5, "one should greet his fellows by mentioning the name of God." And for the sake of peace gentiles are to be greeted: "And further, they may offer them (gentiles) greetings for the sake of peace" (M. Sheb. 4:3; M. Git. 5:9).

To pluck ears on the Sabbath, Mark 2:23-28; Matt. 12:1-8; Luke 6:1-5: Ears plucked on the Sabbath by Jesus' disciples provoked a discussion between Jesus and the Pharisees. Mark says that the disciples "plucked ears;" Matt: "they began to pluck ears and to eat;" Luke: "his disciples plucked some ears, rubbed them in their hands, and ate them." It is difficult to decide exactly what was done by the disciples. In any case, in the Rabbinic literature we can appreciate the authenticity of the scene and the following discussion. Husking ears is not included in the list of works forbidden on the Sabbath (M. Shab. 7:2, M. Bes. 4:2), but plucking or pulling up could be included. Philo, *De Vita Moses* 2:22, writes: "Pulling up a rice plant, a branch or a leaf, or any kind of fruit is not allowed." In M. Ed. 2:6 it is reported that Ishmael and Aqiba were discussing permission for "crushing-and-chopping . . . ears of corn while it was yet day [before the beginning of the Sabbath]." The possibility of husking barley, wheat by wheat, is posed in M. Ma. 4:5: "If one husks barley, he may husk them singly and eat, but if he husked and put them in his hand, he is liable." Whatever the action of the disciples, it was certainly one discussed in the halakhah.

The Sabbath and the Temple: In the polemic just reported, Jesus argues this way: "Or have you not read in the Law that on the Sabbath the priests in the temple break the Sabbath and yet are guiltless?" (Matt. 12:5). This argument does not fit into the discussion about the ears plucked on the Sabbath. It seems to be a sentence brought here by the Evangelist from another context. In any case, this same argument could be used by the rabbis: M. Erub. 10:11-15 lists a series of activities allowed on the Sabbath in the Temple but not allowed outside; M. R.H. 1:4 reminds us that "when the Temple still stood, they [the witnesses] could profane the Sabbath indeed for all of them [the twelve months] for the correct regulation of the offering." It is especially significant that Hillel was arguing with the same argument used by Jesus in order to prove that the commandment of Passover derogates the commandment of the Sabbath when both of them fall on the same date: "'Now do we have only a single Passover-sacrifice in the course of the year which overrides the Sabbath? We have many more than three hundred Passover-sacrifices in the year, and they all override the Sabbath.' All the people in the courtyard ganged up on him. He said to them, 'The daily whole-offering is a public offering. Just as the daily whole-offering is a public offering and overrides the Sabbath, so the Passover-sacrifice is a public offering and overrides the Sabbath'" (T. Pis. 4:13).

Circumcision on the Sabbath: In one of the many Sabbath polemics reported by the Gospels, Jesus argues: "Moses gave you circumcision—it is, of course, not from Moses, but from the patriarchs—and you circumcise a man on the Sabbath" (John 7:22). Circumcision on the Sabbath is explicitly allowed by the Mishnah, and, as the text of the Gospel demonstrates, it was an ancient praxis: "All things necessary for circumcision may be performed on the Sabbath" (M. Shab. 18:3; 19:2.3.5); "R. Yose says: Great is circumcision since it overrides the stringent Sabbath" (M. Ned 3:11). Jesus goes on with a typical *a minori ad majus* argu-

ment: "If a man receives circumcision on the Sabbath in order that the law of Moses may not be broken, are you angry with me because I healed a man's whole body on the Sabbath?" (John 7:23). In the same way, the rabbis unanimously say that the danger of death overrides the Sabbath: "A case of risk of loss of life supersedes the Sabbath" (M. Yom. 8:6). The same type of argument used by Jesus is found in the Midrash Mekhilta of R. Ishmael: R. Eleazar b. Azariah says: "If in performing the ceremony of circumcision, which affects only one member of the body, one is to disregard the Sabbath law, how much more should one do so for the whole body when it is in danger!" (Mekhilta to Exod. 31:13; see also T. Shab. 15:16).

Theology: The core of Jesus' message is the announcement of the coming Kingdom of God and the call for conversion: "the time is fulfilled, and the kingdom of God has come near; repent, and believe in the good news" (Mark 1:14). This message can be accepted by the Jews, and it is expressed in different ways by the Rabbinic literature: M. Ber. 2:2 and Mekhilta to Exod. 20:3, like other texts, explicitly associate the Kingdom of God and the observance of the Law; also conversion—and not a merely formal observance of the commandments—is an absolute requirement of the Jewish tradition, as we have shown (M. Yom 8:9; M. Ta. 2:1). Jacob Neusner, speaking as would a rabbi who heard to the words of Jesus, comments: "When I accept the yoke of the commandments of the Torah and do them, I accept God's rule. I live in the kingdom of God, which is to say, in the dominion of heaven, here on earth. That is what it means to live a holy life: to live by the will of God in the here and now."[2]

Still, through the Gospels, and especially in the polemics, Jesus' teaching progressively confronts the Jewish tradition. There are of course many details to be discussed by scholars, but deep down one can detect in Jesus an attitude towards the Law very different from that of the rabbis: Jesus seems not to teach the Torah of Moses but a *new torah*. The difficulty of the Jews in accepting Jesus' message is neither the announcement of the Kingdom of God nor the call for conversion. The difficulty lies in the role Jesus plays in that Kingdom and indeed in replacing Moses' Torah with his own torah. That has been underlined by Neusner and was clearly perceived by Klausner: "*Ex nihilo nihil fit*: had not Jesus' teaching contained a kernel of opposition to Judaism, Paul could never *in the name of Jesus* have set aside the ceremonial laws and broken through the barriers of national Judaism. There can be no doubt that in Jesus Paul found justifying support."[3] I am now focusing on the understanding of the Torah that is perceptible through the words of Jesus.

Matt. 7:24-27: "Everyone then who hears these words of mine and acts on them will be like a wise man who built his house on rock. The rain fell, the floods came, and the winds blew and beat on that house, but it did not fall, because it had been founded on rock. And everyone who hears these words of mine and does not act on them will be like a foolish man who built his house on sand. The rain fell, and the floods came, and the winds blew and beat against that house, and it fell—and great was its fall!" These words have a strict parallel in the Mishnah: "He whose wisdom exceeds his deeds, to what is he like? To a tree whose branches are many but whose roots are few, and the wind comes and uproots it and overturns it upon its face. But he whose works exceed his wisdom, to what is he like? To a tree whose branches are few, but whose roots are many, so that even though all the winds in the world come and blow against it, it can not be stirred fro its place" (M. Ab. 3:17).[4] Nevertheless, there is a significant difference between the two texts: Jesus is referring to those who practice his words, while M. Abot refers to the practice of the words of the Torah. Jesus' words are put on the same level as the Torah.

Luke 9:59-62: "To another he [Jesus] said, 'Follow me.' But he said, 'Lord, first let me go and bury my father.' But Jesus said to him, 'Let the dead bury their own dead; but as for you, go and proclaim the kingdom of God.' Another said, 'I will follow you, Lord; but let me first say farewell to those at my home.' Jesus said to him, 'No one who puts a hand to the plow and looks back is fit for the kingdom of God.'" This scene is consciously inspired by 1 Kings, the discipleship of Elisha following Elijah: "He [Elisha] left the oxen, ran after Elijah, and said, 'Let me kiss my father and my mother, and then I will follow you.' Then Elijah said to him, 'Go back again; for what have I done to you?' He returned from following him, took the yoke of oxen, and slaughtered them; using the equipment from the oxen, he boiled their flesh, and gave it to the people, and they ate. Then he set out and followed Elijah, and became his servant" (1 Kgs. 19:19-20). Unlike Elijah, Jesus requires from his disciples such a radical and inhuman following that it shocks Jewish ears: Jesus' demands imply overriding the commandment of honoring parents, even renouncing one of the most appreciated acts of loving kindness in the Jewish piety: burying the dead. The demands Jesus makes of his followers to be in the Kingdom of God greatly exceeds what the Written Torah and the Oral Torah require. This is not an exceptional and isolated *logion* of Jesus; see also: "Whoever comes to me and does not hate father and mother, wife and children, brothers and sisters, yes, and even life itself, cannot be my disciple. Whoever does not carry the cross and follow me cannot be my disciple" (Luke 14:26-27; Matt. 10:37-38).

Jesus puts himself above the Torah in such a way that it is not possible to understand his words as a liberal interpretation. Yes, even Jesus dares to correct Moses: "It was because you were so hard-hearted that Moses allowed you to divorce your wives, but from the beginning it was not so" (Matt. 19:8); "the Son of Man is lord even of the Sabbath" (Mark 2:28). So the famous antithesis of the Sermon of the Mount, "You have heard that it was said. . . . But I say to you" (Matt. 5); although some of them could be taken as a deeper interpretation of the Written Torah, they have the flavor of substitution.

Jesus presents himself with expressions which, according to the Jews, only fit the Torah. The following sentence, "For where two or three are gathered in my name, I am there among them" (Matt. 18:20) is parallel and contrasting to this sentence of the

Mishnah: "But if two sit together and the Words of the Law are between them, the Shekhinah abides between them" (M. Ab. 3:3, 6; see Mekhilta to Exod. 20:24). "My yoke is easy" (Matt. 11:29-30) is Jesus' expression to compare his message and his person with those of the Torah, qualified by Judaism as the "yoke," *'ol torah* (M. Ab. 3:5).

Then we—and Jesus' audience as well—easily perceive that the changes made in the popular metaphor *of the wine and wineskins* found in M. Ab. 4:20 (see *supra*) is neither fortuitous nor a mistake in transmission. Jesus consciously rejects the old wine for the new; he prefers new wine and new wineskins: "And no one puts new wine into old wineskins; otherwise, the wine will burst the skins, and the wine is lost, and so are the skins; but one puts new wine into fresh wineskins" (Mark 2:22, Matt. 9:17, Luke 5:37-39). The reference to the Old and the New Torah is evident. Klausner comments on this text: "John the Baptist, like the Pharisees, thought it possible to keep the old 'bottle' in its old form and even fill it with new wine, repentance and good works, and so hasten the coming of the Messiah. But this is not possible" (p. 248); "A new content requires a new garb: Pharisaic Judaism must be transformed from the root" (p. 275).

"Jesus' arrogance" reaches such a point that he uses expressions reserved by the rabbis only for God. So Jesus says: "Whoever welcomes you welcomes me, and whoever welcomes me welcomes the one who sent me" (Matt. 10:40) or "Whoever welcomes one such child in my name welcomes me, and whoever welcomes me welcomes not me but the one who sent me" (Mark 9:37; Matt. 18:5; Luke 9:48), which has an equivalent in Mekhilta: "When one welcomes his fellow man, it is considered as if he had welcomed the Shekhinah" (Mekhilta to Exod. 18:12). In Matthew 25:35, 40 Jesus says: ". . . for I was hungry and you gave me food, I was thirsty and you gave me something to drink . . .," what is said about God himself in the Midrash Tannaim to Deut. 15:9: "And so the Holy One, blessed be He, said to Israel, 'My children, whenever you feed the poor I count it up for you as if you fed me.'"

Therefore it is not a surprise that a Jew reading the Gospels could admire the ethical message of Jesus and recognize in it the Oral Law of the Rabbis, but at the same time feels disconcerted by Jesus' personal claims: "how deeply personal is the focus of Jesus' teaching: it is on himself, not on his message," and then notices that what is really at stake is "Torah as against Christ," and asks of Jesus' disciples: "And is your master God? For, I now realize, only God can demand of me what Jesus is asking" (Neusner).

This surprise turns to scandal on reading the Gospel of John. In this Gospel there is a varied repertoire of self identifications along the lines of "I am:" "I am the bread of Life," "I am the light of the world," "I am from above," "I am the good shepherd," "I am the resurrection and the life," "I am the way, and the truth, and the life," "I am in the Father and the Father is in me," "I am a king," etc. (John 6:35, 41, 48, 51; 8:12, 18, 23, 24, 28, 58; 10:7, 9, 11, 14; 13:19; 11:25; 14:6, 10, 11; 15:1.5; 18:37). So high Christology is in many aspects a mere transformation of the theology of the Torah. What Klausner said referring to the Pauline Christology (see *supra*) must be said about John's Christology: assuming developments by the evangelist and new linguistic dressing, the roots must be found in Jesus himself. To point out some texts in which the Christological transformation of the theology of the Torah is evident, let me use Rabbinic sources besides the Mishnah.

Torah is the Creating Word/Jesus is the Creating Word: John 1:1-3 starts the Gospel with a song to the Word become flesh in Jesus (John 1:14): "In the beginning was the Word. . . ." This hymn is a prologue in which the pre-existence of Jesus is announced ("and the Word was with God . . . He was in the beginning with God"), also his role in the Creation of the World ("All things came into being through him, and without him not one thing came into being"), and his divinity too ("and the Word was God). The Jewish background is evident: First of all, in the first chapter of Genesis, the world came into being only through God's Word; this creating and powerful Word is sung in the Bible: Ps. 29;

148:5; Is. 55:10-11; etc.; consequently the Rabbinic literature (especially in Mekhilta and both Sifres) God is designed as "He-who-spoke-and-the-world-came-into-being." In the Wisdom literature, the word of God is personalized as Wisdom, partner of God since before the creation, with whom the creation was fulfilled ("then I was beside him, like a master worker;" Prov. 8:23-31), who finally dwelt in Israel as in his holy place ("Thus in the beloved city he gave me a resting place, and in Jerusalem was my domain;" Ben Sira 24:1-17). In the targumic literature, the Word, *memra*', is not only the instrument for the creation, but a Name for God.[5] Let me quote two Tannaitic texts:

M. Ab. 3:14: "Beloved of God are Israel, for to them was given the desirable instrument; still greater was the love known to them, that to them was given the desirable instrument wherewith the universe was created, as it is said, 'for I give you good doctrine; forsake ye not my Law' (Prov. 4:2)"

Sifre Deut. 48, to Deut. 11:22: "If Belshazzar, who used Temple vessels after they had been profaned, was uprooted from this world and the world to come, how much more so will one who uses improperly *the vessel with which the world was created* be uprooted from this world and the world to come."

Torah is the Word of Life/Jesus is Life: The prologue of the Fourth Gospel already announces that "in him was life" (John 1:4), an expression that reminds readers of many Wisdom literature sentences: "Keep hold of instruction; do not let go; guard her, for she is your life. . . . For they are life to those who find them, and healing to all their flesh" (Prov. 4:13.22). Throughout the Gospel, Jesus is presented as the giver of life: "For God so loved the world that he gave his only Son, so that everyone who believes in him may not perish but may have eternal life" (John 3:16). The life Jesus gives is associated with the image of water: "Jesus said to her, 'Everyone who drinks of this water will be thirsty again, but those who drink of the water that I will give them will never be thirsty. The water that I will give will become in them a spring of water gushing up to eternal life'" (John 4:13-14);

"Let anyone who is thirsty come to me, and let the one who believes in me drink. As the scripture has said, 'Out of the believer's heart shall flow rivers of living water'" (John 7:37-38). Jesus repeats with solemnity: "the words that I have spoken to you are spirit and life" (John 6:63). Then the reader concludes: Jesus has taken the role of the Torah: as Torah is Life and gives Life, so Jesus is the same. Let us look at the role of the Torah for the Tannaim:

M. Ab. 2:7; 3:11: ["Hillel] used to say: ". . . *the more Torah, the more life*; the more schooling, the more wisdom. . . . One who has acquired for himself *words of the Torah* has gained for himself *life in the world to come*."

Mekhilta to Exod. 13:3: "R. Ishmael used to say, '. . . If a meal, which is only for ephemeral life, requires a benediction before and after it, it is but logical to assume that the reading from *the Torah, which is for life eternal*, should require a benediction before and after it."

Mekhilta to Exod. 15:26: "And why does Scripture say, 'For I am the Lord that healeth thee' (Exod. 15:26)? God said to Moses, Say to Israel: *The words of the Torah* which I have given you *are life* unto you, as it is said 'For they are life unto those that find them' (Prov. 4:22)"

Sifre Deut. 343, to Deut. 33:2: "This shows that the words of Torah are likened to fire. . . . Just as fire lives forever, so do *the words of Torah live forever*. Just as fire scorches him who draws near it, while he who is far away from it is chilled, so is it with words of Torah: if one occupies himself with them, *they give him life*, but if he departs from them, they cause him death."

Sifre Deut. 48, a Deut. 11,22: "Words of Torah are likened to water: just as water endures forever, so do words of Torah live forever, as it is said, 'For they are life unto those that find them' (Prov. 4:22). Just as water cleanses the unclean of their uncleannesses, so do words of Torah cleanse the unclean from their uncleannesses. . . . Just as water restores a man's soul, as it is said, 'As cold waters to a faint soul' (Prov. 25:25), so do words of Torah restore a man's soul, as it is said: 'The Law of the Lord is perfect, restoring the soul' (Ps. 19:8). . . ."

Mekhilta to Exod. 15:22: "'And found no water' . . . The allegorists say: They did not find words of Torah which are likened to water. And whence do we know that the words of the Torah are likened to water? I is said, 'Ho, every one that thirsteth, come ye for water' (Is. 55:1)." Is. 55:1 is the text evoked by the claim of Jesus: "Let anyone who is thirsty come to me, and let the one who believes in me drink" (John 7:37-38). In Targum Is. 55:1 thirst is interpreted as the desire to listen to and learn the Torah: "Ho, every one who *wishes to learn, let him* come *and learn*, and he who has no money, come, *hear and learn*! Come, *hear and learn*, without *price* and *not with mammon, teaching which is better* than wine and milk" (English translation by B.D. Chilton).[6]

Torah is the Manna/Jesus is the bread come down from heaven: In John 6, Jesus presents himself as the bread from heaven, the bread of life, in opposition to the manna eaten in the desert by the Jews; all of them, nevertheless, died: "For the bread of God is that which comes down from heaven and gives life to the world" (v. 33), "I am the bread of life. Whoever comes to me will never be hungry" (v. 35), "I am the bread of life. Your ancestors ate the manna in the wilderness, and they died. This is the bread that comes down from heaven, so that one may eat of it and not die. I am the living bread that came down from heaven. Whoever eats of this bread will live forever; and the bread that I will give for the life of the world is my flesh" (vv. 48-51).

The Rabbinic literature also associates manna with Torah, the Word of God, and the source for the life of Israel. One of the most significant texts is Exod. 16:32-33, which states: "Let an *omer* of it be kept throughout your generations, in order that they may see the food with which I fed you in the wilderness, when I brought you out of the land of Egypt. And Moses said to Aaron, 'Take a jar, and put an *omer* of manna in it, and place it before the Lord, to be kept throughout your generations." The commentary by Midrash Mekhilta associates the content of the jar with the observance of the Torah:

Mekhilta to Exod.16:33: "'Let an *omer* of it be kept throughout your generations.' R. Joshua says: 'For the generation of the forefathers themselves.' R. Eleazar of Modiim says: 'For subsequent generations.' R. Eliezer says: 'For the time of the Prophet Jeremiah. For when the Prophet Jeremiah said to the Israelites: Why do you not busy yourselves with the Torah? They said to him: If we be kept busy with the words of the Torah, how will we get our sustenance? Then Jeremiah brought forth to them the jar containing the manna, and said to them:

'O generation, see ye the thing (*dabar*)[7] of the Lord' (Jer. 2:31). See with what your forefathers, who busied themselves with the words of the Torah, were provided. You, too, if you will busy yourselves with the words of Torah, God will provide you with sustenance of this sort. And this is one of the three things which Elijah will, in the future, restore to Israel: The jar of manna, the jar of sprinkling water, and the bottle of anointing oil.'"

Mekhilta to Exod. 13:17 explains that the long time spent by Israel in the desert was a strategy planned by God in order to gain enough time for the mixture and assimilation of the manna and the water of the well in their bodies: "But I will make them go round about through the desert forty years, so that, having the manna to eat and the water of the well to drink, they will absorb the Torah. On the basis of this interpretation R. Simon b. Yohai said: Only to those who eat manna is it given really to study the Torah." See in Sifre Numbers 88 (to Num 11:6) a very realistic description of the assimilation of the manna.

In order to complete this overview on the Rabbinic background of John 6, it is necessary to mention the "complaints" in John 6:41, 43, 61 ("the Jews began to complain about him because he said, 'I am the bread that came down from heaven'), a reflection of the complaints of Israel in the desert (Num. 11:4ff.; 21:5), which are especially emphasized by the Rabbinic literature (Sifre Num. 88, to Num. 11:6; Sifre Deut. 1, to Deut. 1:1). The targumic versions are significant because of the similar terminology in the Gospel of John:

Targum Pseudo-Jonathan Num. 11:7: "Woe to the people whose *food is bread from Heaven and who murmured. . . .*!"

Targum Neophiti Num. 21:6 writes this beautiful piece: "The divine voice (*bat qol*, Aramaic: *brt ql*) came forth from Heaven and its voice was heard on high: Come, see all you creatures; and come, give ear, all you sons of the flesh; the serpent was cursed from the beginning, and I said to it: Dust shall be your food. I brought my people up from the land of Egypt and *I had manna come down for them from Heaven*, and I made a well come up from the abyss, and I carried quail from the sea for them, *and my people has turned to murmur before me concerning the manna, that its nourishment is little. Let the serpent which does not murmur concerning its food come and rule over the people which has murmured concerning their food*" (cf., Targum Pseudo-Jonathan Num. 21:6).

It is worth noting that in the Christology of the Fourth Gospel not only is the parallelism with the Torah clear but also the contrast. Jesus overrides the Torah and puts himself in its place. We can say that John, using the Rabbinic symbols for the Torah, took to its farthest conclusion the image of Jesus presented by the Synoptic Gospels. Whether this image fits the historical Jesus is a secondary question for the Jewish reader of the Gospel. In my opinion, the Gospels' image of Jesus is rooted in his own self-presentation.

Bibliography

Hebrew Bible and New Testament quotations are from the *New Revised Standard Version of the Bible*; Mishnah: Ph. Blackman; Mekhilta de R. Ishmael: J.Z. Lauterbach; Sifra and Sifre Numbers: J. Neusner; Sifre Deuteronomy: R. Hammer; Targums: M. McNamara and B.C. Chilton. Only in a few cases is the translation adapted slightly.

Fitzmyer, J.A., *The Semitic Background of the New Testament* (Grand Rapids, 1997).
Malina, B.J., *The Palestinian Manna Tradition* (Leiden, 1968).
Neusner, J., *A Rabbi Talks with Jesus* (Montreal, 2000).
Smith, M., *Tannaitic Parallels to the Gospels* (Philadelphia, 1951).
Urbach, E.E., *The Sages. Their Concepts and Beliefs* (Jerusalem, 1979).

Notes

[1] Cf., J. Klausner, *Jesus of Nazareth. His Life, Times and Teaching* (New York, 1989), pp. 187f.

[2] Jacob Neusner, *A Rabbi Talks with Jesus* (Montreal, 2000), p. 36.

[3] Klausner, op. cit., p. 369.

[4] This is the text according to the Kaufmann manuscript. The *textus receptus* adds a quotation from Jer. 17:6-8, whose exegesis is on the basis of both texts, the Mishnah and the New Testament.

[5] Cf., H.L. Strack and P. Billerbeck, *Kommentar zum Neun Testament aus Talmud und Midrasch* (Munich, 1994), vol. II, pp. 303-333; Ephraim Urbach, *The Sages. Their Concepts and Beliefs* (Jerusalem, 1979), pp. 198ff.; M. Smith, *Tannaitic Parallels to the Gospels* (Philadelphia, 1951), pp. 156-157.

[6] The quotation alluded to by John 7:38 ("and let the one who believes in me drink. As the scripture has said, Out of the believer's heart shall flow rivers of living water"), could be a targum not yet identified (so R. Brown). Many texts have been proposed: Deut. 8:15; Is. 43:20; 44:3; 48:21; 55:1; 58:11; Ezek. 47:12; Zak. 14:8.11; Ps. 78:15-16; 105:40-41; 114:8; etc.); in any case, John 7:38 has in its background a very wide symbolic understanding of Torah as water (cf., Smith, op. cit., p. 157), as can be seen in Targum Pseudo-Jonathan to Exod. 15:22; Abot de R. Nathan A 41; CD VI:4ff.; etc.

[7] *Dabar* means "thing" and "word." The Midrash plays with this ambivalence: the thing people see (jar and manna) is really the Word of God.

MIGUEL PÉREZ FERNÁNDEZ

H

HOMOSEXUALITY IN JUDAISM: What does Judaism, speaking out of its classical sources, have to say about the phenomenon of homosexuality?

To answer this question, we must first view homosexuality against the background of the general changes in moral attitudes in the course of time and, as well, in the context of contemporary life in the Western world. While a full answer would require a volume or several volumes, we will need to make do with a brief summary before we proceed to explore a Jewish response.

First, the complaint that moral restraints are crumbling has a two or three thousand year history in Jewish tradition and in the continuous history of Western civilization. Second, there has been a decided and increasing laxity in our own times at least in the area of sexual attitudes, speech, and expectations, if not in practice. Third, such social and psychological phenomena must sooner or later beget further changes in mores and conduct. And, finally, it is indisputable that most current attitudes are profoundly at variance with the traditional Jewish views on sex and sexual morality.

Of all the current sexual fashions, the one most notable for its militancy, and which most conspicuously requires illumination from the sources of Jewish tradition, is that of sexual deviancy. This refers primarily to homosexuality, male or female, along with a host of other phenomena such as transvestism and transsexualism. They all form part of the newly approved theory of the idiosyncratic character of sexuality. Homosexuals have demanded acceptance in society, and this demand has taken various forms—from a plea that they should not be liable to criminal prosecution, to a demand that they should not be subjected to social sanctions, and thereafter to a strident assertion that they represent an "alternative life-style" no less legitimate than "straight" heterosexuality. The various forms of homosexual apologetics appear largely in contemporary literature and theater, as well as in the daily press. In the United States, "gay" activists have become increasingly and progressively more vocal and militant.

Legal Position: Homosexuals have, indeed, often been suppressed cruelly by the law. For instance, the Emperor Valentinian, in 390 C.E., decreed that pederasty be punished by burning at the stake. The sixth-century Code of Justinian ordained that homosexuals be tortured, mutilated, paraded in public, and executed. A thousand years later, Gibbon said of the penalty decreed by the Code that "pederasty became the crime of those to whom no crime could be imputed." In more modern times, however, the Napoleonic Code declared consensual homosexuality legal in France. Over a century ago, anti-homosexual laws were repealed in Belgium and Holland. In the twentieth century, Denmark, Sweden, and Switzerland followed suit and, more recently, Czechoslovakia and England. The most severe laws in the West are found in the United States, where they come under the jurisdiction of the various states and are known by a variety of names, usually as "sodomy laws." Punishment may range from light fines to five or more years in prison (in some cases even life imprisonment), indeterminate detention in a mental hospital, and even to compulsory sterilization. Moreover, homosexuals are, in various states, barred from the licensed professions, many professional societies, teaching, and

the civil service—to mention only a few of the sanctions encountered by the known homosexual.

More recently, many of these strictures have been evaporating, and a new leniency has been developing in the United States and elsewhere with regard to homosexuals. Thus, in 1969, the National Institute of Mental Health issued a majority report advocating that adult consensual homosexuality be declared legal. The American Civil Liberties Union concurred. Earlier, Illinois had done so in 1962, and in 1971 the state of Connecticut revised its laws accordingly. Yet despite the increasing legal and social tolerance of deviance, basic feelings toward homosexuals have not really changed. The most obvious example is France, where, although legal restraints were abandoned over 150 years ago, the homosexual of today continues to live in shame and secrecy.

But the most draconian punishment for homosexuality is not that legislated by law or imposed by social sanction, but that which homosexuals bring upon themselves by exposing themselves to AIDS and HVD infection. A report in the N.Y. Times of July 3, 2002, offers these awesome statistics: AIDS, which is the fourth-leading cause of death in the world, will claim an additional sixty-five million lives by 2020, according to the United Nations' first long-range forecast of the epidemic. That is more than triple the number who died in the first twenty years of the epidemic and will rival the number of people killed in all the wars in the twentieth century.

Simply dismissing such reporting as "homophobic" will not change the specter of early and miserable death that hangs over the homosexual life-style as a noxious miasma. Derogatory epithets will not cause that poisonous effluvium to evaporate.

Statistics: Statistically, the proportion of homosexuals in society does not seem to have changed much since Professor Kinsey's day (his book, *Sexual Behavior in the Human Male*, was published in 1948, and his volume on the human female in 1953). Kinsey's studies revealed that hard-core male homosexuals constituted about 4-6% of the population: 10% experienced "problem" behavior during a part of their lives. One man out of three indulges in some form of homosexual behavior from puberty until his early twenties. The dimensions of the problem become quite overwhelming when it is realized that, according to these figures, of 200 million people in the United States some ten million will become or are predominant or exclusive homosexuals, and over twenty-five million will have at least a few years of significant homosexual experience. Even though the Kinsey methodology and statistics have been challenged more recently, the problem remains staggering.

The New Permissiveness: The most dramatic change in our attitudes to homosexuality has taken place in the new mass adolescent subculture—the first such in history—where it is part of the whole new outlook on sexual restraint in general. It is here that the fashionable Sexual Left has had its greatest success on a wide scale, appealing especially to the rejection of Western traditions of sex roles and sex typing. A number of different streams feed into this ideological reservoir from which the new sympathy for homosexuality flows. Freud and his disciples began the modern protest against traditional restraints and blamed the guilt that follows transgression for the neuroses that plague humankind. Many psychoanalysts began to overemphasize the importance of sexuality in human life, and this ultimately gave birth to a kind of sexual messianism. Thus, in our own days, Wilhelm Reich and his followers, for whom the sexual revolution is a *machina ultima* for the whole Leninist liberation movement, see rebellion against restrictive moral codes as not merely a way to hedonism but a form of sexual mysticism. Orgasm is seen not only as the pleasurable climactic release of internal sexual pressure but as a means to individual creativity and insight as well as to the Marxist reconstruction of society. Finally, the emphasis on freedom and sexual autonomy derives from the Sartrean version of Kant's view of human autonomy.

Significantly, religious groups have joined the sociologists and ideologists of deviance to affirm what has been called, "man's birthright of unbounded ambisexuality." A number of Protestant churches in America, and an occasional Catholic clergyman, have pleaded for more sympathetic attitudes towards homosexuals. A homosexual relationship is, they implied, no different from a heterosexual marriage; both must be judged by one criterion—"whether it is intended to foster a permanent relation of love." Jewish apologists for deviationism have been prominent in the Gay Liberation movement and have not hesitated to advocate their position in American journals and in the press. Christian groups began to emerge that catered to a homosexual clientele, and Jews were not too far behind. This latest Jewish example of the principle of *wie es sich christelt, so juedelt es sich* will be discussed later in this essay.

Homosexual militants are satisfied neither with a "mental health" approach nor with demanding civil rights. They are clear in insisting upon society's recognition of sexual deviance as an "alternative lifestyle," morally legitimate and socially acceptable. And in the summer of 2002, the N.Y. Times adopted a new policy: opening its Society pages to announcements of same-sex "marriages" in the same manner as traditional marriages—only the latest manifestation of the proactive defense of homosexual conduct by "the newspaper of record."

Gay Marriages: Following the permissive attitudes expressed first in the politically liberal press and then in the many liberal Christian religious groups, elements in the Jewish community were not to be excluded from this chorus of approval for clergymen to officiate at homosexual "commitment ceremonies." Stating eight times that "we, unlike our ancestors, are aware of the possibility of committed, stable, monogamous and loving relationships between members of the same gender," the Central Conference of American Rabbis (Reform) Responsa Committee statement on homosexual marriage, for example, maintains that "gay marriages," of which it nevertheless does not approve "might help end homosexual promiscuity (Dr. Nathaniel S. Lehrman, "Gay Marriages," in *Tradition*, Vol. 34 No. 1, Spring 2001).

The momentum favoring a permissive approach pulled along, albeit reluctantly, the Conservative movement. The Gay Synagogues, about which more towards the end of this article, are occasionally serviced by rabbis ordained by and belonging to the Conservative seminary and Rabbinic group. An article in *The Jewish Week* (July 26, 2002) reports that in 1992 the Rabbinical Assembly officially permitted its members to serve gay and lesbian synagogues, but it does prohibit its members from officiating at their "marriage" ceremonies. Yet "many Conservative rabbis officiate at same-sex ceremonies." The ambivalence is painfully evident. "For the Conservative movement the homosexuality issue has been particularly difficult to resolve. For Orthodox interpreters of Jewish law, it is a closed issue. For Reform and Reconstructionst, it is a non-issue." (Yeshiva University has been forced to refrain from interfering with gay-lesbian support groups meeting in its professional schools and from limiting its residency halls to students and their spouses. But at no time did the university make any concession, direct or indirect, to the gay quest for moral legitimacy or to same-sex unions as constituting "marriage.")

While Orthodox groups are solidly against the current submissiveness in the face of the aggressive gay movement, certain Orthodox individuals have begun to speak up on behalf of a more permissive attitude. One such effort resulted in the film, "Trembling Before God," produced in 2000, artfully portraying the deep pathos of those mired in this terrible conflict. But there is more than a bit of propaganda in identifying the opposition to acceptance of gays with a small group of alien sounding and strangely dressed Hasidim who indulge in superstitious rituals and spout intolerance without any grace at all. Moreover, there does not appear to be any concern for the negative consequences of the special treatment the producers of the film seek. Instead, there is much self-pity—which is acceptable from the vantage of those most intimately concerned with the problem, but is not appropriate for those who must formulate public policy and who must consider the moral welfare of the entire community. Compassion and sympathy are not

out of place for those caught in the web of homosexuality. But it must be understood (and this is where the film fails) that if the law were full of exceptions at all times, law would lose its value for the public good. Maimonides (following Plato) already wrote, over eight centuries ago, that all law must cover the majority of the population, even if inevitably a small number of people will be disadvantaged. The homosexuality issue should thus be seen in the context of other "moral" challenges to the Halakhah.

It is most unfortunate that the film refuses even to allow for the possibility that men and women with homosexual predilections might—with great effort, to be sure—achieve successful and happy marriages to members of the opposite sex. It assumes that same-sex attraction is irreversible, and therefore cannot be morally proscribed. Yet Dr. Robert L. Spitzer, Professor of Psychiatry and Chief of Biometrics at Columbia University, the very psychiatrist who led the team that expunged homosexuality from the diagnostic manual in 1973, avers (in 2001) that sometimes homosexuality may be changeable. "I now believe that's untrue—some people can and do change," he writes. This goes against the psychiatric orthodoxy he himself originally proposed.

Such change is more common than most people realize. An organization—JONAH (Jews Offering New Alternatives to Homosexuality)—has been helping Jews, both Orthodox and others, who wish to overcome homosexual orientations and has met with considerable success. Yet this and other Jewish support groups that help people deal with and overcome homosexuality are not even mentioned in "Trembling" and are conspicuously absent from the resources listed in the film's credits and at the film's promotional web site.

Such are the basic facts and theories of the current advocacy of sexual deviance. What is the classical Jewish attitude to sodomy, and what suggestions may be made to develop a Jewish approach to the complex problem of the homosexual in contemporary society?

Biblical View: The Bible prohibits homosexual intercourse and labels it an abomination: "Thou shall not lie with a man as one lies with a woman: it is an abomination" (Lev. 18:22). Capital punishment is ordained for both transgressors (Lev. 20:13). At Lev. 18:22, sodomy is linked with buggery, and at Lev. 20:13, with incest and buggery. (There is considerable terminological confusion with regard to these words. We shall here use "sodomy" as a synonym for homosexuality, and "buggery" or "bestiality" for sexual relations with animals.) The city of Sodom had the questionable honor of lending its name to homosexuality because of the notorious attempt at homosexual rape, when the entire population—"both young and old, all the people from every quarter"—surrounded the home of Lot, the nephew of Abraham, and demanded that he surrender his guests to them "that we may know them" (Gen. 19:5). The decimation of the tribe of Benjamin resulted from the notorious incident, recorded in Judges 19, of a group of Benjaminites who sought to commit homosexual rape.

Scholars have identified the *kadesh* proscribed by the Torah (Deut. 23:18) as a ritual male homosexual prostitute. This form of heathen cult penetrated Judea from the Canaanite surroundings in the period of the early monarchy. So Rehoboam, probably under the influence of his Ammonite mother, tolerated this cultic sodomy during his reign (1 Kgs. 14:24). His grandson Asa tried to cleanse the Temple in Jerusalem of the practice (1 Kgs. 15:12), as did his great-grandson Jehoshaphat. But it was not until the days of Josiah and the vigorous reforms he introduced that the *kadesh* was finally removed from the Temple and the land (2 Kgs. 23:7). The Talmud too (B. San. 24b) holds that the *kadesh* was a homosexual functionary. (However, it is possible that the term also alludes to a heterosexual male prostitute. Thus, in 2 Kgs. 23:7, women are described as weaving garments for the idols in the *batei ha-kedeshim* [houses of the *kadesh*]; the presence of women may imply that the *kadesh* was not necessarily homosexual. The Talmudic opinion identifying the *kadesh* as a homosexual prostitute may be only an exegetical assertion. Moreover, there are other opinions in Talmudic

literature as to the meaning of the verse; see Onkelos [Lev. 23:18], and Nahmanides and *Torah Temimah*, ad loc.)

Talmudic Approach: At the outset, an important contribution by Rabbi Barry Freundel (*The Journal of Halacha and Contemporary Society* 11, Spring 1986 = Pesach 5746, pp. 70-87) followed by Rabbi Eliezer Finkelman (*J. of the Society of Rabbis in Academia*, June 1991, Vol. 1, Nos. 1-2) should be noted, namely, that there is a very real difference between homosexual *orientation* and homosexual *behavior*. In the words of Finkelman, "A celibate homosexual is fully complying with Jewish law. A man whose sexual orientation is towards members of the same sex, but who does not indulge in prohibited activities, is completely righteous, and should be treated as such. A celibate homosexual who is acceptable on all other accounts ought to be an acceptable candidate for conversion to Judaism."

Beyond the passages discussed above, Rabbinic exegesis of the Bible finds several other homosexual references in the Scriptural narratives. The generation of Noah was condemned to eradication by the Flood because they had sunk so low morally that, according to Midrashic teaching, they wrote out formal marriage contracts for sodomy and buggery—a possible cryptic reference to such practices in the Rome of Nero and Hadrian (Lev. Rabbah 18:13) and hauntingly reminiscent of current attempts to legitimize homosexual conduct by means of "commitment ceremonies."

Of Ham, the son of Noah, we are told that "he saw the nakedness of his father" and told his two brothers (Gen. 9:22). Why should this act have warranted the harsh imprecation hurled at Ham by his father? The Rabbis offered two answers: one, that the text implies that Ham castrated Noah; second, that the biblical expression is an idiom for homosexual intercourse (see Rashi, ad loc.). On the scriptural story of Potiphar's purchase of Joseph as a slave (Gen. 39:1), the Talmud comments that he acquired him for homosexual purposes, but that a miracle occurred and God sent the angel Gabriel to castrate Potiphar (B. Sot. 13b).

Post-biblical literature records remarkably few incidents of homosexuality. Herod's son Alexander, according to Josephus (*Wars*, 1. 2-1:7), had homosexual contact with a young eunuch. Very few reports of homosexuality have come to us from the Talmudic era (Y. San. 6:6, 23c; Jos. *Ant.*, 15:25-30).

The incidence of sodomy among Jews is interestingly reflected in the halakhah on *mishkav zakhur* (the talmudic term for homosexuality: the Bible uses various terms— thus the same term in Num. 31:17 and 35 refers to heterosexual intercourse by a woman, whereas the expression for male homosexual intercourse in Lev. 18:22 and 20:13 is *mishkevei ishah*). The Mishnah teaches that R. Judah forbade two bachelors from sleeping under the same blanket, for fear that this would lead to homosexual temptation (M. Qid. 4:14). However, the sages permitted it (ibid.) because homosexuality was so rare among Jews that such preventive legislation was considered unnecessary (B. Qid. 82a). This latter view is codified as halakhah by Maimonides (*Yad, Issurei Bi'ah* 22:2). Some four hundred years later, Joseph Caro, who did not codify the law against sodomy proper, nevertheless cautioned against being alone with another male because of the lewdness prevalent "in our times" (*Even ha-Ezer* 24). About a hundred years later, Joel Sirkes reverted to the original ruling and suspended the prohibition because such obscene acts were unheard of among Polish Jewry (*Bayit Hadash* to Tur, *Even ha-Ezer* 24). Indeed, a distinguished contemporary of Caro, Solomon Luria, went even further and declared homosexuality so very rare that, if one refrains from sharing a blanket with another male as a special act of piety, one is guilty of self-righteous pride or religious snobbism (for the above and additional authorities, see *Otzar ha-Posekim* IX, 236-238).

Responsa: As is to be expected, the responsa literature is also very scant in discussions of homosexuality. One of the few such responsa is that of the late Abraham Isaac Ha-Kohen Kook, when he was still the rabbi of Jaffa. In 1912 he was asked about a ritual slaughterer who had come under suspicion of homosexuality. After weighing all aspects of the case, Kook dismissed the charges against the accused, considering them unsupported hearsay. Furthermore, he maintained the man might have repented and therefore could not be subject to sanctions at the present time.

The very scarcity of halakhic deliberations on homosexuality, and the quite explicit insistence of various halakhic authorities, provide sufficient evidence of the relative absence of this practice among Jews from ancient times down to the present. Indeed, Kinsey found that, while religion was usually an influence of secondary importance on the number of homosexual as well as heterosexual acts by males, Orthodox Jews proved an exception, and homosexuality was phenomenally rare among them.

Jewish law treated the female homosexual more leniently than the male. It considered lesbianism as *issur*, an ordinary religious violation, rather than a case of *arayot*, a specifically sexual infraction, regarded much more severely than *issur*, such that one must submit to martyrdom rather than violate the law. R. Huna held that lesbianism is the equivalent of harlotry and disqualified the lesbian from marrying a *kohen* (priest). The halakhah is, however, more lenient, and decides that while the act is prohibited, the lesbian is not punished and is permitted to marry a priest (Sifra 9:8; B. Shab. 65a; B. Yeb. 76a). However, the transgression does warrant disciplinary flagellation (Maimonides, *Yad, Issurei Bi'ah* 21:8). The less punitive attitude of the halakhah to the female homosexual than to the male does not reflect any intrinsic judgment on one as opposed to the other, but is rather the result of a halakhic technicality: there is no explicit biblical proscription of lesbianism, and the act does not entail genital intercourse (Maimonides, loc. cit.).

The halakhah holds that the ban on homosexuality applies universally, to non-Jew as well as to Jews (B. San. 58a; Maimonides, *Melakhim* 9:5,6). It is one of the six instances of *arayot* (sexual transgressions) forbidden to the Noahide, i.e., gentile (Maimonides, ibid.).

Most halakhic authorities—such as Rashba and Ritba—agree with Maimonides.

A minority opinion holds that pederasty and buggery are "ordinary" prohibitions rather than *arayot*—specifically sexual infractions that demand martyrdom rather than transgression. But the Jerusalem Talmud supports the majority opinion. (See D.M. Krozer, *Devar Ha-melekh*, I, 22, 23 [1962], who also suggests that Maimonides may support a distinction whereby the "male" or active homosexual partner is held in violation of *arayot*, while the passive or "female" partner transgresses an *issur*, or ordinary prohibition.)

Reasons for Prohibition: Why does the Torah forbid homosexuality? Bearing in mind that reasons proffered for the various commandments are not accepted as determinative, but as human efforts to explain immutable divine law, the rabbis of the Talmud and later Talmudists did offer a number of illuminating rationales for the law.

As stated, the Torah condemns homosexuality as *to'evah*, an abomination. The Talmud records the interpretation of Bar Kapparah who, in a play on words, defined *to'evah* as *to'eh attah bah*, "You are going astray because of it" (B. Ned. 51a). The exact meaning of this passage is unclear, and various explanations have been put forward.

The Pesikta (*Zutarta*) explains the statement of Bar Kapparah as referring to the impossibility of such a sexual act resulting in procreation. One of the major functions (if not the major purpose) of sexual congress is reproduction, and this reason for man's sexual endowment is frustrated by *mishkav zakhur* (so too *Sefer ha-Hinnukh*, no. 209).

Another interpretation is that of the Tosafot and Asher ben Jehiel (in their commentaries to B. Ned. 51a), which applies the "going astray" or wandering to the homosexual's abandoning his wife. In other words, the abomination consists of the danger that a married man with homosexual tendencies may disrupt his family life in order to indulge his perversions. Saadiah Gaon holds the rational basis of most of the Bible's moral legislation is the preservation of the family structure (*Emunot ve-De'ot* 3:1; cf., B. Yom. 9a). (This argument assumes contemporary cogency in the light of the avowed aim of some gay militants to destroy the family, which they consider an "oppressive institution.")

A third explanation is given by a more recent scholar, Rabbi Baruch Ha-Levi Epstein (*Torah Temimah* to Lev. 18:22), who emphasizes the unnaturalness of the homosexual liaison: "You are going astray from the foundations of the creation." *Mishkav zakhur* defies the very structure of the anatomy of the sexes, which quite obviously was designed for heterosexual relationships.

It may be, however, that the very variety of interpretations of *to'evah* points to a far more fundamental meaning, namely, that an act characterized as an "abomination" is *prima facie* disgusting and need not be further defined or explained. Certain acts are considered *to'evah* by the Torah, and there the matter rests. It is, as it were, a visceral reaction, an intuitive disqualification of the act, and we run the risk of distorting the biblical judgment if we rationalize it. *To'evah* constitutes a category of objectionableness *sui generis*; it is a primary phenomenon. (This lends additional force to Rabbi David Z. Hoffmann's contention that *to'evah* is used by the Torah to indicate the repulsiveness of a proscribed act, no matter how much it may be in vogue among advanced and sophisticated cultures; see his *Sefer Va'yikra*. II, p. 54.)

Jewish Attitudes: It is on the basis of the above that an effort must be made to formulate a Jewish response to the problems of homosexuality in the conditions under which most Jews live today, namely, those of free and democratic societies and, with the exception of Israel, non-Jewish lands and traditions.

Four general approaches may be adopted:

1) REPRESSIVE. No leniency toward the homosexual lest the moral fiber of the rest of society be weakened.
2) PRACTICAL. Dispense with imprisonment and all forms of social harassment, for eminently practical and prudent reasons.
3) PERMISSIVE. The same as the above, but for ideological reasons, viz., the acceptance of homosexuality as a legitimate "alternative life-style."
4) PSYCHOLOGICAL. Homosexuality, in at least some forms, should be recognized as a disease, and this recognition must determine the halakhic attitude to the homosexual.

Let us now consider each of these critically.

Repressive Attitude: Exponents of the most stringent approach hold that pederasts are the vanguard of moral malaise, especially in our society. For one thing, they are dangerous to children. According to a recent work, one third of the homosexuals in the study were seduced in their adolescence by adults. It is best for society that they be imprisoned, and if our present penal institutions are faulty, let them be improved. Homosexuals should certainly not he permitted to function as teachers, group leaders, rabbis, or in any other capacity in which they might be models for, and come into close contact with, young people. Homosexuality must not be excused as a sickness. A sane society assumes that its members have free choice and are therefore responsible for their conduct. Sex offenders, including homosexuals, according to another recent study, operate "at a primate level with the philosophy that necessity is the mother of improvisation." As Jews who believe that the Torah legislated certain moral laws for all humankind, it is incumbent upon us to encourage all societies, including non-Jewish ones, to implement the Noahide laws. And since, according to the halakhah, homosexuality is prohibited to Noahides as well as to Jews, we must seek to strengthen the moral quality of society by encouraging more restrictive laws against homosexuals. Moreover, if we are loyal to the teachings of Judaism, we cannot distinguish between "victimless" crimes and crimes of violence. Hence, if our concern for the moral life of the community impels us to speak out against murder, racial oppression, or robbery, we must do no less with regard to sodomy.

This argument is weak on a number of grounds. Practically, it fails to take into consideration the number of homosexuals of all categories, which, as we have pointed out, is vast. We cannot possibly imprison all offenders, and it is a manifest miscarriage of justice to vent our spleen only on the few unfortunates who are caught by the police. It is inconsistent, because there has been no comparable outcry for harsh sentencing of other transgressors of sexual morality, such

as those who indulge in adultery or incest. To take consistency to its logical conclusion, this hard line on homosexuality should not stop with imprisonment but demand the death sentence, as is biblically prescribed. And why not the same death sentence for blasphemy, eating a limb torn from a live animal, idolatry, robbery—all of which are Noahide commandments? And why not capital punishment for Sabbath transgressors in the State of Israel? Why should the pederast be singled out for opprobrium and be made an object lesson while all others escape?

Those who might seriously consider such logically consistent but socially destructive strategies had best think back to the fate of that Dominican reformer, the monk Girolamo Savunarola, who in fifteenth-century Florence undertook a fanatical campaign against vice and all suspected of venal sin, with emphasis on pederasty. The society of that time and place, much like ours, could stand vast improvement. But too much medicine in too strong doses was the monk's prescription, whereupon the population rioted and the zealot was hanged.

Finally, there is indeed some halakhic warrant for distinguishing between violent and victimless (or consensual and non-consensual) crimes. Thus, the Talmud permits a passer-by to kill a man in pursuit of another man or woman when the pursuer is attempting rape. But this is not permitted in the case of a transgressor pursuing an animal to commit buggery or on his way to worship an idol or to violate the Sabbath (M. San. 8:7, and v. Rashi to B. San. 73a, s.v. *al ha-behemah*).

Practical Attitude: The practical approach is completely pragmatic and attempts to steer clear of any ideology in its judgments and recommendations. It is, according to its advocates, eminently reasonable. Criminal laws requiring punishment for homosexuals are simply unenforceable in society at the present day. We have previously cited the statistics on the extremely high incidence of pederasty in our society. Kinsey once said of the many sexual acts outlawed by the various states that were they all enforced, some 95% of men in the United States would be in jail; even assuming exaggeration, the assertion is quite significant. Furthermore, the special prejudice of law enforcement authorities against homosexuals—rarely does one hear of police entrapment of or jail sentences for non-violent heterosexuals—breeds a grave injustice: namely, it is an invitation to blackmail. The law concerning sodomy has been called "the blackmailer's charter." It is universally agreed that prison does little to help the homosexual rid himself of his peculiarity. Certainly, the failure of rehabilitation ought to be of concern to civilized people. But even if it is not and the crime be considered so serious that incarceration is deemed advisable even in the absence of any real chances of rehabilitation, the casual pederast almost always leaves prison as a confirmed criminal. He has been denied the company of women and forced into the society of those whose sexual expression is almost always channeled to pederasty. The casual pederast has thus become a habitual one: his homosexuality has now been ingrained in him. Is society any safer for having taken an errant man and, in the course of a few years, having taught him to transform his deviancy into a hard and fast perversion, then turning him loose on the community? Finally, from a Jewish point of view, since it is obviously impossible for us to impose the death penalty for sodomy, we may as well act on purely practical grounds and do away with all legislation and punishment in this area of personal conduct.

This reasoning is tempting precisely because it focuses directly on the problem and is free of any ideological commitment. But the problem with it is that it is too easy. By the same reasoning one might, in a *reductio ad absurdum*, do away with all laws on income tax evasion, or forgive and dispense with all punishment of Nazi murders. Furthermore, the last element leaves us with a novel view of the halakhah; if it cannot be implemented in its entirety, it ought to be abandoned completely. Surely the Noahide laws, perhaps above all others, place us under clear moral imperatives, over and above purely penological instructions. The very practicality of this position leaves it open to the charge of evading the very real moral issues and halakhic principles entailed in any discussion of homosexuality.

Permissive Attitude: The ideological advocacy of a completely permissive attitude toward consensual homosexuality and the acceptance of its moral legitimacy is, of course, the "in" fashion in sophisticated liberal circles. Legally, it holds that deviancy is none of the law's business: the homosexuals' civil rights are as sacred as those of any other "minority group." From the psychological angle, sexuality must be emancipated from the fetters of guilt induced by religion and code-morality, and its idiosyncratic nature must be confirmed.

Gay Liberationists aver that the usual "straight" attitude toward homosexuality is based on three fallacies or myths: that homosexuality is an illness; that it is unnatural; and that it is immoral. They argue that it cannot be considered an illness, because so many people have been shown to practice it. It is not unnatural, because its alleged unnaturalness derives from the impossibility of sodomy leading to reproduction, whereas our overpopulated society no longer needs to breed workers, soldiers, farmers, or hunters. And it is not immoral, first, because morality is relative, and second, because moral behavior is that which is characterized by "selfless, loving concern."

Now, we are here concerned with the sexual problem as such, and not with homosexuality as a symbol of the whole contemporary ideological polemic against restraint and tradition. Homosexuality is too important—and too agonizing—a human problem to allow it to be exploited for political aims or entertainment or shock value or even ideological polemics.

The bland assumption that homosexuality cannot be considered an illness because of the large number of people who have or express homosexual tendencies cannot stand up under criticism. No less an authority than Freud taught that a whole civilization can be neurotic. Erich Fromm appeals for the establishment of (as his book is entitled) *The Sane Society*—because ours is not. If the majority of a nation is struck down by typhoid fever, does this condition, by so curious a calculus of semantics, become healthy? Whether or not homosexuality can be considered an illness is a serious question, and it does depend on one's definition of health and illness. But mere statistics are certainly not the *coup de grace* to the psychological argument, which will be discussed shortly.

The validation of gay life as "normal" or "natural" on the basis of changing social and economic conditions is an act of verbal obfuscation. Even if we were to concur with the widely held feeling that the world's population is dangerously large and that Zero Population Growth is now a desideratum, the anatomical fact remains unchanged: the generative organs are structured for generation. If the words "natural" and "unnatural" have any meaning at all, they must be rooted in the unchanging reality of humans' sexual apparatus rather than in their ephemeral social-cultural configurations.

Militant feminists along with gay activists react vigorously against the implication that natural structure implies the naturalness or unnaturalness of certain acts, but this very view has recently been confirmed by one of the most informed writers on the subject. "It is already pretty safe to infer from laboratory research and ethnological parallels that male and female are wired in ways that relate to our traditional sex roles. . . . Freud dramatically said that anatomy is destiny. Scientists who shudder at the dramatic, no matter how accurate, could rephrase this: anatomy is functional, body functions have profound psychological meanings to people, and anatomy and function are often socially elaborated" (Arno Karlen, *Sexuality and Homosexuality*, p. 501).

The moral issues lead us into the quagmire of perennial philosophical disquisitions of a fundamental nature. In a way, this facilitates the problem for one seeking a Jewish view. Judaism does not accept the kind of thoroughgoing relativism used to justify the gay life as merely an alternate life-style. And while the question of human autonomy is certainly worthy of consideration in the area of sexuality, one must beware of the consequences of taking the argument to its logical extreme. Judaism clearly cherishes holiness as a greater value

than either freedom or health. Furthermore, if every individual's autonomy leads us to lend moral legitimacy to any form of sexual expression he may desire, we must be ready to pull the blanket of this moral validity over almost the whole catalogue of perversions described by Krafft-Ebing and then, by the legerdemain of granting civil rights to the morally non-objectionable, permit the advocates of buggery, fetishism, incest, or whatever to proselytize in public. In that case, why not in the school system? And if consent is obtained before the death of one partner, why not necrophilia or cannibalism? Surely, if we declare homosexuality to be merely idiosyncratic and not an "abomination," what right have we to condemn sexually motivated cannibalism— merely because most people would react with revulsion and disgust?

"Loving, selfless concern" and "meaningful personal relationships"—the great slogans of the New Morality and the exponents of situational ethics—have become the litany of sodomy since the latter decades of the twentieth century. Simple logic should permit us to use the same criteria for excusing adultery or any other act heretofore held to be immoral; and, indeed, that is just what has been done, and it has received the sanction not only of liberals and humanists but of certain religionists as well. "Love," "fulfillment," "exploitative," "meaningful"—the list itself sounds like a lexicon of emotionally charged terms drawn at random from the disparate sources of both religiously liberal and psychologically oriented agnostic circles. Logically, we must ask the next question: what moral depravities can *not* be excused by the sole criterion of "warm, meaningful human relations" or "fulfillment," the newest semantic heirs to "love"?

Love, fulfillment, and happiness can also be attained in incestuous contacts—and certainly in polygamous relationships. Is there nothing at all left that is "sinful," unnatural or "immoral" if it is practiced "between two consenting adults"? For religious groups to aver that a homosexual relationship should be judged by the same criteria as a heterosexual one—i.e., "whether it is intended to foster a permanent relationship of love"—is to abandon the last claim of representing the "Judeo-Christian tradition."

I have elsewhere essayed a criticism of the situationalists, their use of the term "love," and their objections to traditional morality as exemplified by the halakhah as "mere legalism" (*Faith and Doubt*, chapter IX, p. 249ff.). Situationalists, such as Joseph Fletcher, have especially attacked "pilpulistic Rabbis" for remaining entangled in the coils of statutory and legalistic hairsplitting. Among the other things this typically Christian polemic reveals is an ignorance of the nature of halakhah and its place in Judaism, which never held that the law was the totality of life, pleaded again and again for supererogatory conduct, recognized that individuals may be disadvantaged by the law, and strove to rectify what could be rectified without abandoning the large majority to legal and moral chaos simply because of the discomfiture of the few.

Clearly, while Judaism needs no defense or apology in regard to its esteem for neighborly love and compassion for the individual sufferer, it cannot possibly abide a wholesale dismissal of its most basic moral principles on the grounds that those subject to its judgments find them repressive. All laws are repressive to some extent—they repress illegal activities—and all morality is concerned with changing humans and improving them and their society. Civilization itself imposes restrictions that some find confining and objectionable. Homosexuality imposes on one an intolerable burden of differentness, absurdity, and loneliness, but the biblical commandment outlawing homosexuality cannot be put aside solely on the basis of sympathy for the victim of these feelings. Morality, too, is an element that each of us, given his sensuality, his own idiosyncrasies, and his immoral proclivities, must take into serious consideration before acting out our impulses.

From the context of the biblical prohibition of homosexuality it is apparent that it is associated with other sexual deviancies that civilized society in the Western world has, at least heretofore, regarded as abominable. There is good reason to believe, therefore, that with the lifting of social and religious sanctions against homosexuality there will follow, almost inevitably, a similar permissiveness regarding such things as bestiality and incest.

Thus, in a N.Y. Times article on June 9, 2001, reporter Sara Boxer informs us that in a review entitled "Heavy Petting," Peter Singer, a prophet of the new dispensation, noted that almost all of the taboos on nonprocreative sex (taboos against homosexuality, oral sex, contraception and masturbation) have vanished. But one notable exception still stands: the taboo on sex with animals.

Mr. Singer said the fuss over his review was largely "hysterical" and a big waste of time. "This country is in the grip of a Puritan world view," he added. When it comes to bestiality, the stakes are relatively small: while factory farming kills billions of animals a year, he said, human-animal sexual interactions involve only hundreds or thousands.

"The main effect of Mr. Singer's review . . . will be the one that he intended: A subject which for centuries was taboo will now be out in the open. But something else has changed. Now when it comes to bestiality, the debate is not so much about what God wants as what animals want. . . ." And thus is buggery exposed as humbuggery.

Psychological Attitudes: A number of years ago I recommended that Jews regard homosexual deviance as a pathology, thus reconciling the insights of Jewish tradition with the exigencies of contemporary life and scientific information, such as it is, on the nature of homosexuality (*Jewish Life*, Jan.-Feb. 1968). The remarks that follow are an expansion and modification of that position, together with some new data and notions.

The proposal that homosexuality be viewed as an illness will immediately be denied by three groups of people. Gay militants object to this view as an instance of heterosexual condescension. Evelyn Hooker and her group of psychologists maintain that homosexuals are no more pathological in their personality structures than heterosexuals. And psychiatrists Thomas Szaz in the U.S. and Ronald Laing in England reject all traditional ideas of mental sickness and health as tools of social repressiveness or, at best, narrow conventionalism. While granting that there are indeed unfortunate instances in which the category of mental disease is exploited for social or political reasons, we part company with all three groups and assume that there is a significant number of pederasts and lesbians who, by the criteria accepted by most psychologists and psychiatrists, can indeed be termed pathological. Thus, for instance, Dr. Albert Ellis, an ardent advocate of the right to deviancy, denies there is such a thing as a well-adjusted homosexual. In an interview, he has stated that whereas he used to believe that most homosexuals were neurotic, he is now convinced that about 50% are borderline psychotics, that the usual fixed male homosexual is a severe phobic, and that lesbians are even more disturbed than male homosexuals (see Karlen, *Sexuality and Homosexuality*, p. 223ff.).

No single cause of homosexuality has been established. In all probability, it is based on a conglomeration of a number of factors. There is overwhelming evidence that the condition is developmental, not constitutional. Despite all efforts to discover something genetic in homosexuality, no proof has been adduced, and researchers incline more and more to reject the Freudian concept of fundamental human biological bisexuality and its corollary of homosexual latency. It is now widely believed that homosexuality is the result of a whole family constellation. The passive, dependent, phobic male homosexual is usually the product of an aggressive, covertly seductive mother who is overly rigid and puritanical with her son—thus forcing him into a bond where he is sexually aroused, yet forbidden to express himself in any heterosexual way—and of a father who is absent, remote, emotionally detached, or hostile (I. Bieber, et al., *Homosexuality*, 1962).

More recently, the pro-homosexual advocates have latched upon the "discovery" of a "homosexual gene" to bolster their case that homosexuality is determined biologically and that the homosexual life-style should therefore be accepted as inevitable and hence "normal" for those who possess this gene. On July 15, 1993, a dramatic announcement flashed across the country: a team of scientists at the National Institutes of Health was on the trail of a gene that causes homosexuality. The report was published the next day in *Science*, and the public was convinced that science was on the verge of proving what many had long argued: that homosexuality is genetic and innate and therefore unchangeable—a normal variant of human nature. Having thus attained enlightenment, only the hopelessly bigoted could condemn it in any way.

Shortly afterwards, there followed a watershed legal battle over "Proposition 2" in Colorado, legislation that precluded granting sexual orientation "privileged class" minority status, a status conferred previously only on the basis of immutable factors such as race.

Dr. Jeffrey Satinover, a respected psychiatrist with long experience in dealing with homosexuality, writes that,

> Among the many crucial issues raised by the Colorado legislation was the question as to whether homosexuality was indeed normal, innate and unchangeable. One prominent researcher testified to the court, "I am 99.5% certain that homosexuality is genetic." But this personal opinion was widely misunderstood as "homosexuality is 99.5% genetic," implying that research had demonstrated this. . . . In a few weeks, *Newsweek* would emblazon across its cover the phrase that would stick in the public mind as the final truth about homosexuality: "Gay Gene?" . . . The vast majority of [readers] would think that homosexuality had been all but conclusively proven to be "genetic." But the real question is whether or not there is such a "gay gene." In fact, there is not, and the research being promoted as proving that there is provides no supporting evidence ("The Gay Gene?," in *The Journal of Human Sexuality*).

Wise words indeed, and by the time of the writing of this essay the entire brouhaha of the "gay gene" has receded from almost all the polemics on the subject.

All but lost in this discussion was a commonsensical, reasonable caveat that genetics is not absolute, that if having a specific gene implies total lack of control by the owner of that gene, then consider the consequences: if, for instance, it is known that most heterosexual males are genetically "wired" to impregnate as many females as he can, does that exonerate the polygamist, the rapist, the adulterer, the sex addicts of all kinds? Genetic predispositions are the lot of every human. Some are admirable, some detestable, some harmless. Some are overpowering, some are fleeting. If every genetic predisposition is assumed to deny freedom to resist and control negative impulses, what happens to civilization?

Can the homosexual be cured? There is a tradition of therapeutic pessimism that goes back to Freud, but a number of psychoanalysts, including Freud's daughter, Anna, have reported successes in treating homosexuals as any other phobics (in this case, fear of the female genitals).

The very use of the term "cure" in this context evokes howls of protest by the sexual Left and the politically correct, and the ghost of "homophobia" is conjured up signifying the end of all rational discourse. But that must not be allowed to deter us from unbiased and reasonable discussion. And the fact is that a number of reliable therapists believe that gays can change their orientation, albeit not without much effort and struggle, and not all can succeed. It is generally accepted that about a third of all homosexuals can be completely cured; behavioral therapists report an even larger number of cures.

Dr. Charles W. Socarides, clinical professor of psychiatry at the Albert Einstein College of Medicine/Montefiore Medical Center in New York, who has treated patients psychoanalytically for over twenty years, feels like a member of an embattled minority for insisting, against popular opinion, that "gays aren't born that way." His and his colleagues' homosexual patients who were "caught up in it, were suffering, which is why we called it a pathology. We had patients, early in their therapy, who would seek out one sex partner after another—total strangers—on a single night, then come limping into our offices the next day to tell us how they were hurting themselves. Since we were in the business of helping people learn how not to keep hurting themselves, many of us thought we were quietly doing God's work" ("How America Went Gay," *America*, November 18, 1955).

Of course, one cannot say categorically that all homosexuals are sick—any more than one can casually define all thieves as kleptomaniac. In order to develop a reasonable Jewish approach to the problem and to seek in the concept of illness some mitigating factor, it is necessary first to establish the main types of homosexuals. Dr. Judd Marmor speaks of four categories. "Genuine homosexuality" is based on strong preferential erotic feelings for members of the same sex. "Transitory homosexual behavior" occurs among adolescents who would prefer heterosexual experiences but are denied such opportunities because of social, cultural, or psychological reasons. "Situational homosexual exchanges" are characteristic of prisoners, soldiers, and others who are heterosexual but are denied access to women for long periods of time. "Transitory and opportunistic homosexuality" is that of delinquent young men who permit themselves to be used by pederasts in order to make money or win other favors, although their primary erotic interests are exclusive heterosexual. To these may be added, for purposes of our analysis, two other types. The first category, that of genuine homosexuals, may be said to comprehend two sub-categories: those who experience their condition as one of duress or uncontrollable passion that they would rid themselves of if they could, and those who transform their idiosyncrasy into an ideology, i.e., the gay militants who assert the legitimacy and validity of homosexuality as an alternative way to heterosexuality. The sixth category is based on what Dr. Rollo May has called "the New Puritanism," the peculiarly modern notion that one must experience all sexual pleasures, whether or not one feels inclined to them, as if the failure to taste every cup passed at the sumptuous banquet of carnal life means that one has not truly lived. Thus, we have transitory homosexual behavior not of adolescents, but of *adults* who feel that they must "try everything" at least once or more than once in the course of their lives.

A Possible Halakhic Solution: This rubric will now permit us to apply the notion of disease (and, from the halakhic point of view, of its opposite, moral culpability) to the various types of sodomy. Clearly, genuine homosexuality experienced under duress (Hebrew: *ones*, pronounced oh-ness) most obviously lends itself to being termed pathological, especially where dysfunction appears in other aspects of the personality. Opportunistic homosexuality, ideological homosexuality, and transitory adult homosexuality are at the other end of the spectrum, and appear most reprehensible. As for the intermediate categories, while they cannot be called illnesses, they do have a greater claim on our sympathy than the three types mentioned above.

In formulating the notion of homosexuality as a disease, we are not asserting the formal halakhic definition of mental illness as mental incompetence, as described in B. Hag. 3b, 4a, and elsewhere. Furthermore, the categorization of a prohibited sex act as *ones* (duress) because of uncontrolled passions is valid, in a technical halakhic sense, only for a married woman who was ravished and who, in the course of the act, became a willing participant. The halakhah decides with Rava, against the father of Samuel, that her consent is considered coerced because of the passions aroused in her (B. Ket. 51b). However, this holds true only if the act was initially entered into under physical compulsion (*Kesef Mishneh* to Yad, *San.* 20:3). Moreover, the claim of compulsion by one's erotic passions is not valid for a male, for any erection is considered a token of his willingness (B. Yev. 53b: Maimonides, Yad, *San.* 20:3). In the case of a male who was forced to cohabit with a woman forbidden to him, some authorities consider him guilty and punishable, while others hold him guilty but not subject to punishment by the courts (B. Yeb. 53b; *Hinnukh*, 556; *Kesef Mishneh*, loc. cit.; *Maggid Mishneh* to *Issurei Bi'ah*, 1:9). Where a male is sexually aroused in a permissible manner, as to begin coitus with his wife, and is then forced to conclude the act with another woman, most authorities exonerate him (Rabad and *Maggid Mishneh*, to *Issurei Bi'ah*, in loc.). If, now, the warped family background of the genuine homosexual is considered *ones*, the homosexual act may possibly lay claim to some mitigation by the halakhah. (However, see *Minhat Hinnukh*, 556, end, and Rabbi M. Feinstein, *Iggerot Mosheh* [1973] on YD, No. 59, who holds, in a different context, that any pleasure derived from a forbidden act performed under duress increases the level of prohibition. This was anticipated by R. Joseph Engel, *Atvan de-Oraita*, 24). These latter sources indicate the difficulty of exonerating sexual transgressors because of psychopathological reasons under the technical rules of the halakhah.

However, in the absence of a Sanhedrin and since it is impossible to implement the whole halakhic penal system, including capital punishment, such strict applications are unnecessary. What we are attempting is to develop guidelines, based on the halakhah, which will allow contemporary Jews to orient themselves to the current problems of homosexuality in a manner articulating with the most fundamental insights of the halakhah in a general sense, and consistent with the broadest world-view that the halakhic commitment instills in its followers. Thus, the aggadic statement that "no man sins unless he is overcome by a spirit of madness" (B. Sot. 3a) is not an operative halakhic rule but does offer guidance on public policy and individual pastoral compassion. So in the present case, the formal halakhic strictures do not in any case apply nowadays, and it is our contention that the aggadic principle must lead us to seek out the mitigating halakhic elements so as to guide us in our orientation to those homosexuals who, by the standards of modern psychology, may be regarded as acting under compulsion.

To apply the halakhah strictly in this case is obviously impossible; to ignore it entirely is undesirable, and tantamount to regarding halakhah as a purely abstract, legalistic system that can safely be dismissed where its norms and prescriptions do not allow full formal implementation. Admittedly, the method is not rigorous and leaves room for varying interpretations as well as exegetical abuse, but it is the best we can do.

Hence there are types of homosexuality that do not warrant any special consideration, because the notion of *ones* or duress (i.e., disease) in no way applies. Where the category of mental illness does apply, the act itself remains *to'evah* (an abomination), but the fact of illness lays upon us the obligation of pastoral compassion, psychological understanding, and social sympathy. In this sense, homosexuality is no different from any other anti-social or anti-halakhic act, where it is legitimate to distinguish between the objective act itself, including its social and moral consequences, and the mentality and inner life of the person who perpetrates the act. For instance, if a man murders in a cold and calculating fashion for reasons of profit, the act is criminal and the transgressor is criminal. If, however, a psychotic murders, the transgressor is diseased rather than criminal, but the objective act itself remains criminal. The courts may therefore treat the perpetrator of the crime as they would a patient, with all the concomitant compassion and concern for therapy, without condoning the act as being morally neutral. To use halakhic terminology, the objective crime remains a *ma'aseh averah*, whereas the person who transgresses is considered innocent on the grounds of *ones*. In such cases, the transgressor is spared the full legal consequences of his culpable act, although the degree to which he may he held responsible varies from case to case.

An example of a criminal act that is treated with compassion by the halakhah, which in practice considers the act pathological rather than criminal, is suicide. Technically, the suicide or attempted suicide is in violation of the law. The halakhah denies to the suicide the honor of a eulogy, the rending of the garments by relatives or witnesses to the death, and (according to Maimonides) insists that the relatives are not to observe the usual mourning period for the suicide. Yet, in the course of time, the tendency has been to remove the stigma from the suicide on the basis of mental disease. Thus, halakhic scholars do not apply the technical category of intentional (*la-da'at*) suicide to one who did not clearly demonstrate, before performing the act, that he knew what he was doing and was of sound mind, to the extent that there was no hiatus between the act of self-destruction and actual death. If these conditions are not present, we assume that it was an insane act or that between the act and death he experienced pains of contrition and is therefore repentant, hence excused before the law. There is even one opinion that exonerates the suicide unless he received adequate warning (*hatra'ah*) before performing the act and responded in a manner indicating that he was fully aware of what he was doing and that he was lucid (J.M. Tykocinski, *Gesher ha-Hayyim*, I., ch. 25, and *Encyclopaedia Judaica*, vol. 15, p. 490).

Admittedly, there are differences between the two cases: homosexuality is clearly a severe violation of biblical law, whereas the stricture against suicide is derived exegetically from a verse in Genesis. Nevertheless, the principle operative in the one is applicable to the other: where one can attribute an act to mental illness, it is done out of simple humanitarian considerations.

The suicide analogy should not, of course, lead one to conclude that there are grounds for a blanket exculpation of homosexuality as mental illness. Not all forms of homosexuality can be so termed, as indicated above, and the act itself remains an "abomination." With few exceptions, most people do not ordinarily propose that suicide be considered an acceptable and legitimate alternative to the rigors of daily life. No sane and moral person sits passively and watches a fellow man attempt suicide because he "understands" him and because it has been decided that suicide is a "morally neutral" act. By the same token, in orienting us to certain types of homosexuals as patients rather than criminals. we do not condone the act but attempt to help the homosexual. Under no circumstances can Judaism suffer homosexuality to become respectable. Were society to give its open or even tacit approval to homosexuality, it would invite more aggressiveness on the part of adult pederasts toward young people. Indeed, in the currently permissive atmosphere, the Jewish view would summon us to the semantic courage of referring to homosexuality not as "deviance," with the implication of moral neutrality and nonjudgmental idiosyncrasy, but as "perversion," a less clinical and more old-fashioned word perhaps, but one that is more in keeping with the biblical *to'evah*.

Yet, having passed this moral judgment, we cannot in the name of Judaism necessarily demand that we strive for the harshest possible punishment. Even where it was halakhically feasible to execute capital punishment, we have a tradition of leniency. Thus, R. Aqiba and R. Tarfon declared that had they lived during the time of the Sanhedrin, they never would have executed a man. Although the halakhah does not decide in their favor (B. Mak. end of chap. 1), it was rare indeed that the death penalty was actually imposed. Usually, the biblically mandated penalty was regarded as an index of the severity of the transgression, and the actual execution was avoided by strict insistence upon all technical requirements—such as *hatra'ah* (forewarning the potential criminal) and rigorous cross-examination of witnesses, etc. In the same spirit, we are not bound to press for the most punitive policy toward contemporary lawbreakers. We are required to lead them to rehabilitation (*teshuvah*). The halakhah sees no contradiction between condemning a man to death and exercising compassion, even love, toward him (B. San. 52a). Even a man on the way to his execution was encouraged to repent (M. San. 6:2). In the absence of a death penalty, the tradition of *teshuvah* and pastoral compassion to the sinner continues.

We do not find any warrant in the Jewish tradition for insisting on prison sentences for homosexuals. First, singling-out homosexuals as the victims of society's righteous indignation is patently unfair. In Western history, anti-homosexual crusades have too often been marked by cruelty, destruction, and bigotry. Imprisonment in modern times has proven to be extremely haphazard. The number of homosexuals unfortunate enough to be apprehended is infinitesimal as compared to the number of known homosexuals: estimates vary from one in 300,000 to one in 6,000,000! For homosexuals to be singled out for special punishment while all the rest of society indulges itself in every other form of sexual malfeasance (using the definitions of halakhah, not contemporary sexual liberalism) is a species of double-standard morality that the spirit

of halakhah cannot abide. Thus, the Mishah declares that the "scroll of the suspected adulteress" (*Megillat Sotah*), whereby a wife suspected of adultery was forced to undergo the test of "bitter waters" was cancelled when the sages became aware of the ever-larger number of adulterers in general (M. Sot. 9:9). The Talmud bases this decision on an aversion to the double standard: if the husband is himself an adulterer, the "bitter waters" will have no effect on his wife, even though she too is guilty of the offense (B. Sot. 47b). By the same token, a society in which heterosexual immorality is not conspicuously absent has no moral right to sit in stern judgment and mete out harsh penalties to homosexuals.

Second, sending a homosexual to prison is counterproductive if punishment is to contain any element of rehabilitation or *teshuvah*. It has rightly been compared to sending an alcoholic to a distillery. The Talmud records that the Sanhedrin was unwilling to apply the full force of the law where punishment had lost its quality of deterrence: thus, forty (or four) years before the destruction of the Temple, the Sanhedrin voluntarily left the precincts of the Temple so as not to be able, technically, to impose the death sentence, because it had noticed the increasing rate of homicide (B. San. 41a and elsewhere).

There is thus nothing in the Jewish law's letter or spirit that should incline us toward advocacy of imprisonment for homosexuals. The halakhah did not encourage the denial of freedom as a recommended form of punishment. Flogging is, from a certain perspective, far less cruel and far more enlightened. Since capital punishment is out of the question, and since incarceration is not an advisable substitute, we are left with one absolute minimum: strong disapproval of the proscribed act. But we are not bound to any specific penological instrument that has no basis in Jewish law or tradition.

How shall this disapproval be expressed? It has been suggested that, since homosexuality will never attain acceptance anyway, society can afford to be humane. As long as violence and the seduction of children are not involved, it would be best to abandon all laws on homosexuality and leave it to the inevitable social sanctions to control, informally, what can be controlled.

However, this approach is not consonant with Jewish tradition. The repeal of anti-homosexual laws implies the removal of the stigma from homosexuality, and this diminution of social censure weakens society in its training of the young toward acceptable patterns of conduct. The absence of adequate social reproach may well encourage the expression of homosexual tendencies by those in whom they might otherwise be suppressed. Law itself has an educative function, and the repeal of laws, no matter how justifiable the repeal may be from one point of view, does have the effect of signaling the acceptability of greater permissiveness.

Critics of this position—that certain types of homosexual behavior be treated as *ones*—have appeared in the recent literature. Rabbis Barry Freundel and Eliezer Finkelman have argued against this thesis and have preferred to categorize this sort of homosexual conduct as *mumar*, a heretic who violates the law out of "appetite" rather than to flaunt his violation (this latter would be *mumar le'hakhis*—"a heretic who sins in order to anger" God). Thus, Finkelman maintains that whereas the current author sees the homosexual as an *anuss* (an individual forced by heredity or environment into acts that the Bible forbids), Freundel sees him as a *mumar*. Whereas I effectively remove culpability from him, so Freundel charges, he insists that creating a sense of culpability is an integral part of the approach that Judaism should take in confronting the individual involved in homosexual activity.

This introduction of the *mumar* concept has merit, but it should not be accepted merely because Judaism demands a sense of culpability. What "Judaism says" should be determined by the halakhah, not the other way around.

Now the difference between the two approaches, that of *mumar le'teiavon* and that of *ones*, emerges in only one of the several categories of homosexual enumerated above—that of the "genuine homosexual." The opportunistic or situational or "New Puritan" or other types are clearly deserv-

ing of a harsher judgment, namely that of *mumar le'hakhis*. The same is true of the *ones* approach. I suggest that which category is to apply will depend on the sate of mind of the individual "genuine homosexual." If he entertains some residual heterosexual feelings such that his sexual yearning could be at least minimally satisfied, but he prefers by far the homosexual option, he should be classified as a *mumar le'teiavon*. But if he is thoroughly homosexual, has no heterosexual stirrings at all, feels overwhelmed by desire, and recognizes that what he is doing is unlawful, harmful, and against the sacred teachings of the Torah, he is essentially an *anuss* and should be considered as one coerced by the constitution of his own personality much against his religious commitments, thus—an *anuss*, so that while the act is halakhically reprehensible, the violator is exculpated.

Some New Proposals: Perhaps all that has been said above can best be expressed in the proposals that follow.

First, society and government must recognize the distinctions between the various categories enumerated in this essay. It must offer its medical and psychological assistance to those whose homosexuality is an expression of pathology, who recognize it as such, and who are willing to seek help. We must be no less generous to the homosexual than to the drug addict, to whom the government extends various forms of therapy upon request.

Second, jail sentences must he abolished for all homosexuals, save those who are guilty of violence, seduction of the young, or public solicitation.

Third, the laws must remain on the books, but by mutual consent of judiciary and police, must not be enforced. This approximates to what lawyers call "the chilling effect" and is the nearest one can come to the category so well known in the halakhah whereby strong disapproval is expressed by affirming a halakhic prohibition yet no punishment is mandated. It is a category that bridges the gap between morality and law. In a society in which homosexuality is so rampant, and in which incarceration is counterproductive, this hortatory approach may well be a way of formalizing society's revulsion while avoiding the pitfalls in our accepted penology.

For the Jewish community as such, the same principles, derived from the tradition, may serve as guidelines. Judaism allows for no compromise in its abhorrence of sodomy but encourages both compassion and efforts at rehabilitation. Certainly, there must be no acceptance of separate Jewish homosexual societies, such as or especially synagogues set aside as homosexual congregations. The first such "gay synagogue," apparently, was the "Beth Chayim Chadashim" in Los Angeles. Spawned by that city's Metropolitan Community Church in March 1972, the founding group constituted itself as a Reform congregation with the help of the Pacific Southwest Council of the Union of American Hebrew Congregations some time in early 1973. Thereafter, similar groups surfaced in New York City (see illustration) and elsewhere. The membership sees itself as justified by "the Philosophy of Reform Judaism." The Temple president declared that God is "more concerned in our finding a sense of peace in which to make a better world, than He is in whom someone sleeps with" (cited in "Judaism and Homosexuality," *CCAR. Journal*, Summer 1973, p. 38; five articles in this issue of the Reform group's Rabbinic journal are devoted to the same theme, and most of them approve of the Gay Synagogue). As of the writing of this article, numerous other "gay synagogues" have emerged, most in non-Orthodox but one in Orthodox circles.

It has not, to understate the case, received approbation from any acceptable Orthodox authority.

But reasoning proffered by the advocates of such congregations is specious. Regular congregations and other Jewish groups should not hesitate to accord hospitality and membership, on an individual basis, to those "visible" homosexuals who qualify for the category of the ill. Homosexuals are no less in violation of Jewish norms than Sabbath-desecrators or those who disregard the laws of kashrut. But to assent to the organization of separate "gay" groups under Jewish auspices makes no more sense, Jewishly, than to suffer the formation of synagogues that cater exclusively to idol worshipers, adulterers, gossips, tax evaders, or Sabbath-violators. Indeed, it makes less sense, because it provides, under religious cover, a ready-made clientele from which the homosexual can more easily choose his partners.

In remaining true to the sources of Jewish tradition, Jews are commanded to avoid the madness that seizes society at various times and in many forms, while yet retaining a moral composure and psychological equilibrium sufficient to exercise that combination of discipline and charity that is the hallmark of Judaism. Neither the charge of homophobia nor that of buckling under to gay pressure should deter us from seeking out a genuine and unbiased solution to one of the most perplexing and painful dilemmas of our time.

NORMAN LAMM

L

LEVITICUS IN JUDAISM: SCRIPTURE AND HALAKHAH IN LEVITICUS: The book of Leviticus is mediated to Judaism by two Rabbinic readings of Scripture. The first, Sifra, ca. 300 C.E., asks about the relationship of the laws of the Mishnah and the Tosefta to the teachings of Scripture. The second, Leviticus Rabbah, ca. 450-500 C.E., forms of selected passages of Leviticus, read

in light of other passages of Scripture altogether, large propositional expositions. Here we consider only the relationship of Scripture and Halakhah in Leviticus.

Sifra, a compilation of Midrash-exegeses on the book of Leviticus, forms a massive and systematic statement concerning the definition of the Mishnah in relationship to Scripture. The authorship of Sifra produced a document that coheres not only in its main formal and logical traits but also in its few governing demonstrations. Sifra is unitary, coherent, and purposive, start to finish, and in no way a random sample of we know not what. The authorship of Sifra composed the one document to accomplish the union of the two Torahs, Scripture, or the written Torah, and the Mishnah, or the oral Torah. This was achieved not merely formally by provision of proof texts from Scripture for statements of the Mishnah—as in the two Talmuds—but through a profound analysis of the interior structure of thought. It was by means of the critique of practical logic and the rehabilitation of the probative logic of hierarchical classification (accomplished through the form of *Listenwissenschaft*) in particular that the authorship of Sifra accomplished this remarkable feat of intellect. That authorship achieved the (re-)union of the two Torahs into a single cogent statement within the framework of the written Torah by penetrating into the deep composition of logic that underlay the creation of the world in its correct components, rightly classified, and in its right order, as portrayed by the Torah.

This was done in two ways. Specifically, it involved, first of all, systematically demolishing the logic that sustains an autonomous Mishnah, which appeals to the intrinsic traits of things to accomplish classification and hierarchization. Second, it was done by demonstrating the dependency, for the identification of the correct classification of things, not upon the traits of things viewed in the abstract but upon the classification of things by Scripture in particular. The framers of Sifra recast the two parts of the Torah into a single coherent statement through unitary and cogent discourse. So in choosing, as to structure, a book of the Pentateuch, and, as to form, the exegetical form involving paraphrase and amplification of a phrase of a base-text of Scripture, the authorship of Sifra made its entire statement *in nuce*. Then by composing a document that for very long stretches simply cannot have been put together without the Mishnah and at the same time subjecting the generative logical principles of the Mishnah to devastating critique, that same

authorship took up its position. The destruction of the Mishnah as an autonomous and freestanding statement, based upon its own logic, is followed by the reconstruction of (large tracts of the Mishnah) as a statement wholly within, and in accord with, the logic and program of the written Torah in Leviticus. That is what defines Sifra, the one genuinely cogent and sustained statement among the four Midrash-compilations that present exegetical discourse on the Pentateuch.

The dominant approach to uniting the two Torahs, oral and written, into a single cogent statement, involved reading the written Torah into the oral. In form, this was done through inserting into the Mishnah (that is, the oral Torah) a long sequence of proof texts. The other solution required reading the oral Torah into the written one, by inserting into the written Torah citations and allusions to the oral one, and, as a matter of fact, also by demonstrating, on both philosophical and theological grounds, the utter subordination and dependency of the oral Torah, the Mishnah, to the written Torah—while at the same time defending and vindicating that same oral Torah. Sifra, followed unsystematically to be sure by the two Sifres, did just that. Sifra's authorship attempted to set forth the dual Torah as a single, cogent statement, doing so by reading the Mishnah into Scripture not merely for proposition but for expression of proposition. On the surface that decision represented a literary, not merely a theological, judgment. But within the deep structure of thought, it was far more than a mere matter of how to select and organize propositions.

That judgment upon the Mishnah forms part of the polemic of Sifra's authorship—but only part of it. Sifra's authorship conducts a sustained polemic against the failure of the Mishnah to cite Scripture very much or systematically to link its ideas to Scripture through the medium of formal demonstration by exegesis. Sifra's rhetorical exegesis follows a standard redactional form. Scripture will be cited. Then a statement will be made about its meaning, or a statement of law correlative to that Scripture will be given. That statement sometimes cites the Mishnah, often verbatim. Finally, the author of Sifra invariably states, "Now is that not (merely) logical?" And the point of that statement will be, Can this position not be gained through the working of mere logic, based upon facts supplied (to be sure) by Scripture?

The polemical power of Sifra lies in its repetitive demonstration that the stated position, citation of a Mishnah-pericope, is not only not the product of logic, but is, and only can be, the product of exegesis of Scripture. That is only part of the matter, as I shall explain, but that component of the larger judgment of Sifra's authorship does make the point that the Mishnah is subordinated to Scripture and validated only through Scripture. In that regard, the authorship of Sifra stands at one with the position of the authorships of the other successor-writings, even though Sifra's writers carried to a much more profound level of thought the critique of the Mishnah. They did so by rethinking the logical foundations of the entire Torah.

The framers of the Mishnah effect their taxonomy through the traits of things. The authorship of Sifra insists that the source of classification is Scripture. Sifra's authorship time and again demonstrates that classification without Scripture's data cannot be carried out without Scripture's taxonomic givens, and, it must follow, hierarchical arguments based on extra-scriptural taxa always fail. In the Mishnah we seek connection between fact and fact, sentence and sentence, by comparing and contrasting two things that are like and not alike. At the logical level the Mishnah falls into the category of familiar philosophical thought. Once we seek regularities, we propose rules. What is like another thing falls under its rule, and what is not like the other falls under the opposite rule. Accordingly, as to the species of the genus, so far as they are alike, they share the same rule. So far as they are not alike, each follows a rule contrary to that governing the other.

So the work of analysis is what produces connection, and therefore the drawing of conclusions derives from comparison and contrast in the syllogism, $1 + 1 = 2$—the *and*, the *equal*. The proposition then that

forms the conclusion concerns the essential likeness of the two offices, except where they are different, but the subterranean premise is that we can explain both likeness and difference by appeal to a principle of fundamental order and unity. To make these observations concrete, we shall examine numerous examples of how Sifra's authorship rejects the principles of the logic of hierarchical classification *as these are worked out by the framers of the Mishnah.* It is a critique of designating classifications of things without Scriptural warrant. The critique applies to the way in which a shared logic is worked out by the other authorship. For it is not the principle that like things follow the same rule, unlike things, the opposite rule, that is at stake. Nor is the principle of hierarchical classification embodied in the argument *a fortiori* at issue. What our authorship disputes is that we can classify things on our own by appeal to the traits or indicative characteristics, that is, utterly without reference to Scripture. The argument is simple. On our own, we cannot classify species into genera. Everything is different from everything else in some way. But Scripture tells us what things are like what other things for what purposes, hence Scripture imposes on things the definitive classifications, that and not traits we discern in the things themselves. When we see the nature of the critique, we shall have a clear picture of what is at stake when we examine, in some detail, precisely how the Mishnah's logic does its work.

In Sifra no one denies the principle of hierarchical classification. That is an established fact, a self-evident trait of mind. The argument of Sifra's authorship is that, by themselves, things do not possess traits that permit us finally to classify species into a common genus. There always are traits distinctive to a classification. Accordingly, it is the argument of Sifra's authorship that without the revelation of the Torah, we are not able to effect any classification at all, are left, that is to say, only with species, no genus, only with cases, no rules. The thrust of Sifra's authorship's attack on the Mishnah's taxonomic logic is readily discerned. Time and again, we can easily demonstrate, things have so many and such diverse and contradictory indicative traits that, comparing one thing to something else, we can always distinguish one species from another. Even though we find something in common, we also can discern some other trait characteristic of one thing but not the other. Consequently, we also can show that the hierarchical logic on which we rely, the argument *a fortiori* or *qol vehomer*, will not serve. For if on the basis of one set of traits that yield a given classification, we place into hierarchical order two or more items, on the basis of a different set of traits, we have either a different classification altogether, or, much more commonly, simply a different hierarchy. So the attack on the way in which the Mishnah's authorship has done its work appeals not merely to the limitations of classification solely on the basis of traits of things. The more telling argument addresses what is, to *Listenwissenschaft*, the source of power and compelling proof: hierarchization. That is why, throughout, we must designate the Mishnah's mode of *Listenwissenschaft* a logic of hierarchical classification. Things are not merely like or unlike, therefore following one rule or its opposite. Things also are weightier or less weighty, and that particular point of likeness of difference generates the logical force of *Listenwissenschaft*.

Sifra's authorship repeatedly demonstrates that the formation of classifications based on monothetic taxonomy. What that means is this: traits that are not only common to both items but that are shared throughout both of the items subject to comparison and contrast, simply will not serve. These shared traits are supposed to prove that the items that are compared are alike, and therefore should be subjected to the same rule. But the allegation of comparability proves flawed. The proposition maintains that the two items are alike, because they share one trait in common (thus: "monothetic taxonomy"). But I shall show you that they also exhibit traits that are different for the respective items. Then we have both likeness and difference.

Then, the argument proceeds, at every point at which someone alleges uniform, that is to say, monothetic likeness, Sifra's authorship will demonstrate difference.

Then how to proceed? Appeal to some shared traits as a basis for classification: this is not like that, and that is not like this, but the indicative trait that both exhibit is such and so, that is to say, polythetic taxonomy. The self-evident problem in accepting differences among things and insisting, nonetheless, on their monomorphic character for purposes of comparison and contrast, cannot be set aside: who says? That is, if I can adduce in evidence for a shared classification of things only a few traits among many characteristic of each thing, then what stops me from treating all things alike? Polythetic taxonomy opens the way to an unlimited exercise in finding what diverse things have in common and imposing, for that reason, one rule on everything. Then the very working of *Listenwissenschaft* as a tool of analysis, differentiation, comparison, contrast, and the descriptive determination of rules yields the opposite of what is desired. Chaos, not order, a mass of exceptions, no rules, a world of examples, each subject to its own regulation, instead of a world of order and proportion, composition and stability, will result. Sifra's authorship affirms taxonomic logic when applied to the right categories. It systematically demonstrates the affirmative case, that *Listenwissenschaft* is a self-evidently valid mode of demonstrating the truth of propositions. But *the* source of the correct classification of things is Scripture and only Scripture. Without Scripture's intervention into the taxonomy of the world, we should have no knowledge at all of which things fall into which classifications and therefore are governed by which rules.

While setting forth its critique of the Mishnah's utilization of the logic of comparison and contrast in hierarchical classification, the authorship of Sifra is careful not to criticize the Mishnah. Its position favors restating the Mishnah within the context of Scripture, not rejecting the conclusions of the Mishnah, let alone its authority. Consequently, when we find a critique of applied reason divorced from Scripture, we rarely uncover an explicit critique of the Mishnah, and when we find a citation of the Mishnah, we rarely uncover linkage to the ubiquitous principle that

Scripture forms the source of all classification and hierarchy. When the Mishnah is cited by our authorship, it will be presented as part of the factual substrate of the Torah. When the logic operative throughout the Mishnah is subjected to criticism, the language of the Mishnah will rarely, if ever, be cited in context. The operative language in dealing with the critique of the applied logic of *Listenwissenschaft* as represented by the framers of the Mishnah ordinarily is, "is it not a matter of logic?" Then the sorts of arguments against taxonomy pursued outside of the framework of Scripture's classifications will follow. When, by contrast, the authorship of Sifra wishes to introduce into the context it has already established a verbatim passage of the Mishnah, it will ordinarily, though not always, use, *mikan amru*, which, in context, means, "in this connection [sages] have said." It is a simple fact that when the intent is to demolish improper reasoning, the Mishnah's rules in the Mishnah's language rarely, if ever, occur. When the authorship of Sifra wishes to incorporate paragraphs of the Mishnah into their re-presentation of the Torah, they do so either without fanfare, as in the passage at hand, or by the neutral joining-language "in this connection [sages] have said."

The authorship of Sifra never called into question the self-evident validity of taxonomic logic. Its critique is addressed only to how the Mishnah's framers identify the origins of, and delineate, taxa. But that critique proves fundamental to the case that that authorship proposed to make. For, intending to demonstrate that *The Torah* was a proper noun, and that everything that was valid came to expression in the single, cogent statement of The Torah, the authorship at hand identified the fundamental issue. It is the debate over the way we know things. In insisting, in agreement with the framers of the Mishnah, that there are not only cases but also rules, not only species but also genera, the authorship of Sifra also made its case in behalf of the case for The Torah as a proper noun. This carries us to the theological foundation for Sifra's authorship's sustained critique of applied reason.

At stake is the character of The Torah. I may phrase the question in this way: exactly what do we want to learn from, or discern within The Torah? And the answer to that question requires theological, not merely literary and philosophical, reflection on our part. For in their delineation of correct hierarchical logic, our authorship uncovered within The Torah (hence by definition, written and oral components of The Torah alike) an adumbration of the working of the mind of God. That is because the premise of all discourse is that The Torah was written by God and dictated by God to Moses at Sinai. And that will in the end explain why our authorship for its part has entered into The Torah long passages of not merely clarification but active intrusion, making itself a component of the interlocutorial process. To what end we know: it was to unite the dual Torah. The authorship of Sifra proposed to regain access to the modes of thought that guided the formation of the Torah, oral and written alike: comparison and contrast in this way, not in that, identification of categories in one manner, not in another. Since those were the modes of thought that, in our authorship's conception, dictated the structure of intellect upon which the Torah, the united Torah, rested, a simple conclusion is the sole possible one.

In their analysis of the deepest structures of intellect of the Torah, the authorship of Sifra presumed to enter into the mind of God, showing how God's mind worked when God formed the Torah, written and oral alike. And there, in the intellect of God, in their judgment humanity gained access to the only means of uniting the Torah, because that is where the Torah originated. But in discerning how God's mind worked, the intellectuals who created Sifra claimed for themselves a place in that very process of thought that had given birth to The Torah. Our authorship could rewrite the Torah because, knowing how The Torah originally was written, they too could write (though not reveal) The Torah.

Three forms dictate the entire rhetorical repertoire of this document. The first, the dialectical, is the demonstration that if we wish to classify things, we must follow the taxa dictated by Scripture rather than relying solely upon the traits of the things we wish to classify. The second, the citation-form, invokes the citation of passages of the Mishnah or the Tosefta in the setting of Scripture. The third is commentary form, in which a phrase of Scripture is followed by an amplificatory clause of some sort. The forms of the document admirably expressed the polemical purpose of the authorship at hand. What they wished to prove was that a taxonomy resting on the traits of things without reference to Scripture's classifications cannot serve. They further wished to restate the oral Torah in the setting of the written Torah. And, finally, they wished to accomplish the whole by rewriting the written Torah. The dialectical form accomplishes the first purpose, the citation-form the second, and the commentary form the third.

In the simple commentary form a verse, or an element of a verse, is cited, and then a very few words explain the meaning of that verse. Second come the complex forms, in which a simple exegesis is augmented in some important way, commonly by questions and answers, so that we have more than simply a verse and a brief exposition of its elements or of its meaning as a whole. The authorship of the Sifra time and again wishes to show that prior documents, the Mishnah or Tosefta, cited verbatim (here given in italics), require the support of exegesis of Scripture for important propositions, presented in the Mishnah and the Tosefta not on the foundation of exegetical proof at all. In the main, moreover, the authorship of Sifra tends not to attribute its materials to specific authorities, and most of the pericopae containing attributions are shared with Mishnah and Tosefta. As we should expect, just as in Mekhilta Attributed to R. Ishmael, Sifra contains a fair sample of pericopae which do not make use of the forms common in the exegesis of specific Scriptural verses and, mostly do not pretend to explain the meaning of verses, but rather resort to forms typical of Mishnah and Tosefta. When Sifra uses forms other than those in which its exegeses are routinely phrased, it commonly, though not always, draws upon materials also found in Mishnah and Tosefta. It is uncommon for Sifra to make use of non-exegetical forms for materials peculiar to its compilation. To state matters simply, Sifra quotes Mishnah or Tosefta, but its own materials follow its distinctive, exegetical forms.

Topical Program: As we realize, for its topical program the authorship of Sifra takes the book of Leviticus. For propositions Sifra's authorship presents episodic and ad hoc sentences. If we ask how these sentences form propositions other than amplifications of points made in the book of Leviticus itself, and how we may restate those propositions in a coherent way, nothing sustained and coherent emerges. Sifra does not constitute a propositional document transcending its precipitating text. But, as we have now seen in detail, that in no way bears the implication that the document's authorship merely collected and arranged this and that about the book of Leviticus. For three reasons, we must conclude that Sifra does not set forth propositions in the way in which the Rabbah-compilations and Sifre to Deuteronomy do.

First, in general there is no topical program distinct from that of Scripture. Sifra remains wholly within Scripture's orbit and range of discourse, proposing only to expand and clarify what it found within Scripture. Where the authorship moves beyond Scripture, it is not toward fresh theological or philosophical thought, but rather to a quite different set of issues altogether, concerning Mishnah and Tosefta. When we describe the topical program of the document, the blatant and definitive trait of Sifra is simple: the topical program and order derive from Scripture. Just as the Mishnah defines the topical program and order for Tosefta, the Yerushalmi, and the Bavli, so Scripture does so for Sifra. It follows that Sifra takes as its structure the plan and program of the written Torah, by contrast to the decision of the framers or compilers of Tosefta and the two Talmuds.

Second, for sizable passages, the sole point of coherence for the discrete sentences or paragraphs of Sifra's authorship derives from the base-verse of Scripture that is subject to commentary. That fact corresponds to the results of form-analysis and the description of the logics of cogent discourse. While, as we have noted, the Mishnah holds thought together through propositions of various kinds, with special interest in demonstrating propositions through a well-crafted program of logic of a certain kind, Sifra's authorship appeals to a different logic altogether. It is one that I have set forth as fixed-associative discourse. That is not a propositional logic—by definition.

The third fundamental observation draws attention to the paramount position, within this restatement of the written Torah, of the oral Torah. We may say very simply that, in a purely formal and superficial sense, a sizable proportion of Sifra consists in the association of completed statements of the oral Torah with the exposition of the written Torah, the whole *re*-presenting as one whole Torah the dual Torah received by Moses at Sinai (speaking within the Torah-myth). Even at the very surface we observe a simple fact. Without the Mishnah or the Tosefta, our authorship will have had virtually nothing to say about one passage after another of the written Torah. Far more often than citing the Mishnah or the Tosefta verbatim, our authorship cites principles of law or theology fundamental to the Mishnah's treatment of a given topic, even when the particular passage of the Mishnah or the Tosefta that sets forth those principles is not cited verbatim.

It follows that the three basic and definitive topical traits of Sifra, are, first, its total adherence to the topical program of the written Torah for order and plan; second, its very common reliance upon the phrases or verses of the written Torah for the joining into coherent discourse of discrete thoughts, e.g., comments on, or amplifications of, words or phrases; and third, its equally profound dependence upon the oral Torah for its program of thought: the problematic that defines the issues the authorship wishes to explore and resolve.

That brings us to the positive side of the picture. While Sifra in detail presents no paramount propositions, it demonstrates a highly-distinctive and vigorously-demon-

strated proposition. We should drastically misunderstand the document if the miscellaneous character of the parts obscured the powerful statement made by the whole. For while in detail we cannot reconstruct a topical program other than that of Scripture, viewed in its indicative and definitive traits of rhetoric, logic, and implicit proposition, Sifra does take up a well-composed position on a fundamental issue, namely, the relationship between the written Torah, represented by the book of Leviticus, and the oral Torah, represented by the passages of the Mishnah deemed by the authorship of Sifra to be pertinent to the book of Leviticus. Sifra joins the two Torahs into a single statement, accomplishing a re-presentation of the written Torah in topic and in program and in the logic of cogent discourse, and within that rewriting of the written Torah, a re-presentation of the oral Torah in its paramount problematic and in many of its substantive propositions. What we now wish to find out is what parts of the document bear that burden, and in what proportion; and what the other parts of the document, besides those particular to the document itself, propose to contribute.

Sifra's authorship affirms taxonomic logic when applied to the right categories. It systematically demonstrates the affirmative case, that *Listenwissenschaft* is a self-evidently valid mode of demonstrating the truth of propositions. But *the* source of the correct classification of things is Scripture and only Scripture. Without Scripture's intervention into the taxonomy of the world, we should have no knowledge at all of which things fall into which classifications and therefore are governed by which rules. How then do we appeal to Scripture to designate the operative classifications? Here is a simple example of the alternative mode of classification, one that does not appeal to the traits of things but to the utilization of names by Scripture. What we see is how by naming things in one way, rather than in another, Scripture orders all things, classifying and, in the nature of things, also hierarchizing them. Here is one example among many of how our authorship conceives the right way of logical thought to proceed:

7. Parashat Vayyiqra Dibura Denedabah Parashah 4

VII:V.

1.A. ". . . and Aaron's sons the priests shall
present the blood and throw the blood
[round about against the altar that is
at the door of the tent of meeting]:"

B. Why does Scripture make use of the
word "blood" twice [instead of using a
pronoun]?

C. [It is for the following purpose:] How
on the basis of Scripture do you know
that if blood deriving from one burnt
offering was confused with blood
deriving from another burnt offering,
blood deriving from one burnt
offering with blood deriving from a
beast that has been substituted there-
for, blood deriving from a burnt
offering with blood deriving from an
unconsecrated beast, the mixture
should nonetheless be presented?

D. It is because Scripture makes use of
the word "blood" twice [instead of
using a pronoun].

2.A. Is it possible to suppose that while
if blood deriving from beasts in the
specified classifications, [the blood of
the sacrifice] is to be presented [on the
altar, as a valid offering], for the simple reason that if the several beasts
while alive had been confused with
one another, they might be offered up,

B. but how do we know that even if the
blood of a burnt offering were confused with that of a beast killed as a
guilt offering [it is to be offered up]?

C. I shall concede the case of the mixture
of the blood of a burnt offering confused with that of a beast killed as a
guilt offering; it is to be presented, for
both this one and that one fall into the
classification of Most Holy Things.

D. But how do I know that if the blood
of a burnt offering were confused with
the blood of a beast slaughtered in the
classification of peace-offerings or of
a thanksgiving offering [the mixture is
to be presented]?

E. I shall concede the case of the mixture
of the blood of a burnt offering confused with that of a beast slaughtered
in the classification of peace-offerings
or of a thanksgiving offering [it is to
be presented], because the beasts in
both classifications produce blood that
has to be sprinkled four times.

F. But how do I know that if the blood
of a burnt offering were confused with
the blood of a beast slaughtered in the
classification of a firstling or a beast
that was counted as the tenth [that is,
it is to serve as the tithe of that herd
or flock] or of a beast designated as a
passover [it is to be presented]?

G. I shall concede the case of the mixture
of the blood of a burnt offering confused with that of a beast slaughtered
in the classification of firstling or a
beast that was counted as a tenth or
of a beast designated as a passover [it
is to be presented], because Scripture
uses the word "blood" two times.

H. Then while I may make that concession, might I also suppose that if the
blood of a burnt offering was confused
with the blood of beasts that had
suffered an invalidation, it also may be
offered up?

I. Scripture says, ". . . its blood" [thus
excluding such a case].

J. Then I shall concede the case of a
mixture of the blood of a valid burnt
offering with the blood of beasts that
had suffered an invalidation, which
blood is not valid to be presented at
all.

K. But how do I know that if such blood
were mixed with the blood deriving
from beasts set aside as sin-offerings to
be offered on the inner altar [it is not
to be offered up]?

L. I can concede that the blood of a
burnt offering that has been mixed
with the blood deriving from beasts
set aside as sin-offerings to be offered
on the inner altar is not to be offered
up, for the one is offered on the inner
altar, and the other on the outer altar
[the burnt offering brought as a free
will offering, under discussion here, is
slaughtered at the altar ". . . that is at
the door of the tent of meeting," not
at the inner altar].

M. But how do I know that even if the
blood of a burnt offering was confused
with the blood of sin-offerings that are
to be slaughtered at the outer altar, it
is not to be offered up?

N. Scripture says, ". . . its blood" [thus
excluding such a case].

In place of the rejecting of arguments resting on classifying species into a common
genus, we now demonstrate how classification really is to be carried on. It is through
the imposition upon data of the categories
dictated by Scripture: Scripture's use of language. That is the force of this powerful
exercise. No. 1 sets the stage, simply pointing out that the use of the word "blood"
twice encompasses a case in which blood in
two distinct classifications is somehow confused in the process of the conduct of the
cult. In such a case it is quite proper to pour
out the mixture of blood deriving from distinct sources, e.g., beasts that have served

different, but comparable purposes. We then systemically work out the limits of that rule, showing how comparability works, then pointing to cases in which comparability is set aside. Throughout the exposition, at the crucial point we invoke the formulation of Scripture, subordinating logic or in our instance the process of classification of like species to the dictation of Scripture. I cannot imagine a more successful demonstration of what the framers wish to say.

The reason for Scripture's unique power of classification is the possibility of polythetic classification that only Scripture makes possible. Because of Scripture's provision of taxa, we are able to undertake the science of *Listenwissenschaft*, including hierarchical classification, in the right way. What can we do because we appeal to Scripture, which we cannot do if we do not rely on Scripture? It is to establish the possibility of polythetic classification. We can appeal to shared traits of otherwise distinct taxa and so transform species into a common genus for a given purpose. Only Scripture makes that initiative feasible, so our authorship maintains. What is at stake? It is the possibility of doing precisely what the framers of the Mishnah wish to do. That is to join together masses of diverse data into a single, encompassing statement, to show the rule that inheres in diverse cases. In what follows, we shall see an enormous, coherent, and beautifully articulated exercise in the comparison and contrast of many things of a single genus. The whole holds together, because Scripture makes possible the statement of all things within a single rule. That is, as we have noted, precisely what the framers of the Mishnah proposed to accomplish. Our authorship maintains that only by appeal to The Torah is this fete of learning possible. If, then, we wish to understand all things all together and all at once under a single encompassing rule, we had best revert to The Torah, with its account of the rightful names, positions, and order, imputed to all things.

22. Parashat Vayyiqra Dibura Denedabah Parashah 11
XXII:I.
1.A. [With reference to M. Men. 5:5:] There are those [offerings that require

bringing near but do not require waving, waving but not bringing near, waving and bringing near, neither waving nor bringing near: These are offering that require bringing near but do not require waving: the meal offering of fine flour and the meal offering prepared in the baking pan and the meal offering prepared in the frying pan, and the meal offering of cakes and the meal offering of wafers, and the meal offering of priests, and the meal offering of an anointed priest, and the meal offering of gentiles, and the meal offering of women, and the meal offering of a sinner. R. Simeon says, "The meal offering of priests and of the anointed priest—bringing near does not apply to them, because the taking of a handful does not apply to them. And whatever is not subject to the taking of a handful is not subject to bringing near,"] [Scripture] says, "When you present to the Lord a meal offering that is made in any of these ways, it shall be brought [to the priest who shall take it up to the altar]:"

B. What requires bringing near is only the handful. How do I know that I should encompass under the rule of bringing near the meal offering?

C. Scripture says explicitly, "meal offering."

D. How do I know that I should encompass all meal offerings?

E. Scripture says, using the accusative particle, "the meal offering."

2.A. I might propose that what requires bringing near is solely the meal offering brought as a free will offering.

B. How do I know that the rule encompasses an obligatory meal offering?

C. It is a matter of logic.

D. Bringing a meal offering as a free will offering and bringing a meal offering as a matter of obligation form a single classification. Just as a meal offering presented as a free will offering requires bringing near, so the same rule applies to a meal offering of a sinner [brought as a matter of obligation], which should likewise require bringing near.

E. No, if you have stated that rule governing bringing near in the case of a free will offering, on which oil and frankincense have to be added. will you say the same of the meal offering of a sinner [Lev. 5:11], which does not require oil and frankincense?

F. The meal offering brought by a wife accused of adultery will prove to the contrary, for it does not require oil and frankincense, but it does require bringing near [as is stated explicitly at Num. 5:15].

G. No, if you have applied the requirement of bringing near to the meal offering brought by a wife accused of adultery, which also requires waving, will you say the same of the meal offering of a sinner, which do not have to be waved?

H. Lo, you must therefore reason by appeal to a polythetic analogy [in which not all traits pertain to all components of the category, but some traits apply to them all in common]:

I. the meal offering brought as a free will offering, which requires oil and frankincense, does not in all respects conform to the traits of the meal offering of a wife accused of adultery, which does not require oil and frankincense, and the meal offering of the wife accused of adultery, which requires waving, does not in all respects conform to the traits of a meal offering brought as a free will offering, which does not require waving.

J. But what they have in common is that they are alike in requiring the taking up of a handful and they are also alike in that they require bringing near.

K. I shall then introduce into the same classification the meal offering of a sinner, which is equivalent to them as to the matter of the taking up of a handful, and also should be equivalent to them as to the requirement of being drawn near.

L. But might one not argue that the trait that all have in common is that all of them may be brought equally by a rich and a poor person and require drawing near, which then excludes from the common classification the meal offering of a sinner, which does not conform to the rule that it may be brought equally by a rich and a poor person [but may be brought only by a poor person,] and such an offering also should not require being brought near.

M. [The fact that the polythetic classification yields indeterminate results means failure once more, and, accordingly,] Scripture states, "meal offering,"

N. with this meaning: all the same are the meal offering brought as a free will offering and the meal offering of a sinner, both this and that require being brought near.

The elegant exercise draws together the various types of meal offerings and shows that they cannot form a classification of either a monothetic or a polythetic charac-

ter. Consequently, Scripture must be invoked to supply the proof for the classification of the discrete items. The important language is at H-J: these differ from those, and those from these, but what they have in common is. . . . Then we demonstrate, with our appeal to Scripture, the sole valid source of polythetic classification, M. And this is constant throughout Sifra.

Sifra Parashat Behuqotai Parashah 1 CCLX:I

1.A. ["If you walk in my statutes and observe my commandments and do them, then I will give you your rains in their season, and the land shall yield its increase, and the trees of the field shall yield their fruit. And your threshing shall last to the time of vintage, and the vintage shall last to the time for sowing; and you shall eat your bread to the full and dwell in your land securely. And I will give peace in the land, and you shall lie down and none shall make you afraid; and I will remove evil beasts from the land, and the sword shall not go through your land. And you shall chase your enemies, and they shall fall before you by the sword. Five of you shall chase a hundred, and a hundred of you shall chase ten thousand; and your enemies shall fall before you by the sword. And I will have regard for your and make you fruitful and multiply you, and will confirm my covenant with you. And you shall eat old store long kept, and you shall clear out the old to make way for the new. And I will make my abode among you, and my soul shall not abhor you. And I will walk among you and will be your God and you shall be my people. I am the Lord your God, who brought you forth out of the land of Egypt, that you should not be their slaves; and I have broken the bars of your yoke and made you walk erect" (Lev. 26:3-13).]

B. "If you walk in my statutes":

C. This teaches that the Omnipresent desires the Israelites to work in the Torah.

D. And so Scripture says, "O that my people would listen to me, that Israel would walk in my ways! I would soon subdue their enemies and turn my hand against their foes" (Ps. 81:13-14).

E. O that you had hearkened to my commandments! Then your peace would have been like a river, and your righteousness like the waves of the sea; your offspring would have been like the sand, and your descendants like its grains; their name would never be cut off or destroyed from before me" (Is. 48:18).

F. And so Scripture says, "Oh that they had such a mind as this always, to fear me and to keep all my commandments, that it might go well with them and with their children forever" (Deut. 5:29).

G. This teaches that the Omnipresent desires the Israelites to work in the Torah.

2.A. "If you walk in my statutes":

B. Might this refer to the religious duties?

C. When Scripture says, "and observe my commandments and do them,"

D. lo, the religious duties are covered. Then how shall I interpret, "If you walk in my statutes"?

E. It is that they should work in the Torah.

F. And so it is said, "But if you will not hearken to me."

G. Might that refer to the religious duties?

H. When Scripture says, "and will not do all these commandments,"

I. lo, the religious duties are covered.

J. If so, why is it said, "But if you will not hearken to me"?

K. It is that they should be working in the Torah.

3.A. And so Scripture says, "Remember the Sabbath day to keep it holy" (Exod. 20:8).

B. Might one suppose that what is involved is only to do so in your heart?

C. When Scripture says, "Observe [the Sabbath day]" (Deut. 5:12), lo, keeping it in the heart is covered.

D. How then am I to interpret "remember"?

E. It means that you should repeat with your mouth [the teachings concerning the Sabbath day].

F. And so Scripture says, "Remember and do not forget how you provoked the Lord your God to wrath in the wilderness, from the day you came out of the land of Egypt until you came to this place" (Deut. 9:7).

G. Might one suppose that what is involved is only to do so in your heart?

H. Scripture says, "and do not forget."

I. Lo, forgetting in the heart is covered.

J. How then am I to interpret "remember"?

K. It means that you should repeat with your mouth [the record of your behavior in the wilderness].

L. And so Scripture says, "[Take heed, in an attack of leprosy, to be very careful to do according to all that the Levitical priests shall direct you; as I

commanded them, so you shall be careful to do.] Remember what the Lord your God did to Miriam on the way as you came forth out of Egypt" (Deut. 24:9).

M. Might one suppose that what is involved is only to do so in your heart?

N. When Scripture says, "Take heed, in an attack of leprosy, to be very careful to do,"

O. lo, forgetting in the heart is covered.

P. How then am I to interpret "remember"?

Q. It means that you should repeat with your mouth [the lessons to be learned in respect to Miriam].

R. And so Scripture says, "Remember what Amalek did to you on the way as you came out of Egypt... [you shall blot out the remembrance of Amalek from under heaven; you shall not forget]" (Deut. 25:17, 19).

S. Might one suppose that what is involved is only to do so in your heart?

T. When Scripture says, "you shall not forget,"

U. lo, forgetting in the heart is covered.

V. How then am I to interpret "remember"?

W. It means that you should repeat with your mouth [the record of Amalek].

4.A. And so Scripture says, "And I will lay your cities waste."

B. Might one suppose that that is of human settlement?

C. When Scripture says, "And I will devastate the land,"

D. lo, that covers human settlement.

E. Then how am I to interpret, "And I will lay your cities waste"?

F. It means there will be no wayfarers.

5.A. And so Scripture says, "and will make your sanctuaries desolate."

B. Might one suppose that that is desolate of offerings?

C. When Scripture says, "and I will not smell your pleasing odors,"

D. lo, that covers the offerings.

E. Then how am I to interpret, "and will make your sanctuaries desolate"?

F. They will be laid waste even of pilgrims.

6.A. "If you walk in my statutes and observe my commandments and do them":

B. One who studies in order to do, not one who studies not in order to do.

C. For one who studies not in order to do—it would have been better for him had he not been created.

The proposition, No. 1, that the reference is to study of Torah is demonstrated at

No. 2. The rhetoric, "might this refer . . . when Scripture says . . .," and so on, then generates a series of compositions that use the same rhetorical pattern. The pattern goes forward at Nos. 4, 5, and only at No. 6 do we revert to the point that No. 1 wished to introduce: study in order to observe.

PARASHAT BEHUQOTAI PEREQ 3
CCLXIII:I

1.A. "And you shall eat old store long kept, [and you shall clear out the old to make way for the new. And I will make my abode among you, and my soul shall not abhor you. And I will walk among you and I will be your God and you shall be my people. I am the Lord your God, who brought you forth out of the land of Egypt, that you should not be their slaves; and I have broken the bars of your yoke and made you walk erect:]"

B. This teaches that whatever is better aged tastes better than its fellow.

C. ". . . old":

D. I know only that the rule applies to wine, which customarily is kept for aging. How do I know that the same rule applies to everything that is allowed to age?

E. Scripture says, "Old store long kept."

2.A. ". . . and you shall clear out the old to make way for the new":

B. The granaries will be full of new grain, and the storage bins will be full of the old,

C. so you will wonder how we shall take out the old on account of the new harvest.

3.A. "And I will make my abode among you":

B. this refers to the house of the sanctuary.

4.A. ". . . and my soul shall not abhor you":

B. Once I shall redeem you, I shall never again reject you.

5.A. "And I will walk among you":

B. The matter may be compared to the case of a king who went out to stroll with his sharecropper in an orchard.

C. But the sharecropper hid from him.

D. Said the king to that sharecropper, "How come you're hiding from me? Lo, I am just like you."

E. So the Holy One, blessed be He, said to the righteous, "Why are you trembling before me?"

F. So the Holy One, blessed be He, is destined to walk with the righteous in the Garden of Eden in the coming future, and the righteous will see him and tremble before him,

G. [and he will say to them,] "[How come you're trembling before me?] Lo, I am just like you."

6.A. Might one suppose that my fear will not be upon you?

B. Scripture says, "and I will be your God and you shall be my people."

C. "If you do not believe in me through all these things, nonetheless 'I am the Lord your God, who brought you forth out of the land of Egypt.'

D. "I am the one who did wonders for you in Egypt. I am the one who is going to do for you all these wonders."

7.A. ". . . that you should not be their slaves":

B. What is the point of Scripture here?

C. Since it is said, "And he redeemed you from the house of slavery" (Deut. 7:8), might one suppose that they were slaves to slaves?

D. ". . . their slaves":

E. they were slaves to kings, not slaves to slaves.

8.A. ". . . and I have broken the bars of your yoke":

B. The matter may be compared to the case of a householder who had a cow for plowing, and he lent it to someone else to plough with it.

C. That man had ten sons. This one came and ploughed with it and went his way, and that one came and ploughed with it and went his way, so that the cow got tired and crouched down.

D. All the other cows came back, but that cow did not enter the fold.

E. The owner hardly agreed to accept consolation from that man, but he went and broke the yoke and cut off the carved ends of the yoke.

F. So is Israel in this world.

G. One ruler comes along and subjugates them and then goes his way, then another ruler comes along and subjugates them and goes his way, so that the furrow is very long.

H. So it is said, "Plowmen plowed across my back; they made long furrows. [The Lord, the righteous one, has snapped the cords of the wicked]" (Ps. 129:3-4).

I. Tomorrow, when the end comes, the Holy One, blessed be He, will not say to the nations, "Thus and so have you done to my children!"

J. Rather, he will immediately come and break the yoke and cut off the ends of the yoke.

K. For it is said, "and I have broken the bars of your yoke."

L. And further, "The Lord has snapped the cords of the wicked."

9.A. ". . . and made you walk erect":

B. R. Simeon says, "Two hundred cubits in height."

C. R. Judah says, "A hundred, like the first Adam."

D. I know that that statement applies only to men. How do I know that it applies to women too?

E. Scripture says, "[For our sons are like saplings, well tended in their youth;] our daughters are like cornerstones, trimmed to give shape to a palace" (Ps. 144:12).

F. And how high was the cornerstone of the temple? A hundred cubits.

10.A. Another teaching concerning the clause, "and made you walk erect":

B. Upright, not fearful of anyone.

The eschatological focus is made sharp at No. 4. The polemic throughout is now uniform: Israel is destined to be redeemed in the future, and when that happens, it will be for all time. Then the return to Zion and rebuilding of the temple did not fulfill the prophecies of redemption; Israel will have a future redemption, of which the prophets, including Moses, spoke. The text of No. 5 is somewhat flawed, but the sense is readily recovered. No. 6 reworks the materials at hand for the same purpose. No. 8 once more is explicit, with its parable of how God's redemption of Israel will take place: with impatience, when it comes.

PARASHAT BEHUQOTAI PEREQ 8
CCLXIX:I

1.A. "And you shall perish among the nations, [and the land of your enemies shall eat you up. And those of you that are left shall pine away in your enemies' lands because of their iniquity; and also because of the iniquities of their fathers they shall pine away like them]":

B. R. Aqiba says, "This refers to the ten tribes who went into exile in Media."

C. Others say, "'And you shall perish among the nations': The reference to 'perishing' speaks only of going into exile.

D. "Might one suppose that the sense is literal [that Israel really will perish among the nations]?

E. "When Scripture says, 'and the land of your enemies shall eat you up,' lo, we find a reference to literally perishing.

F. "Then how am I to interpret 'And you shall perish among the nations'?

G. "The reference to 'perishing' speaks only of going into exile."

2.A. "And those of you that are left shall pine away in your enemies' lands because of their iniquity":

B. The sense of "pining away" is on account of their iniquity.

3.A. ". . . and also because of the iniquities of their fathers they shall pine away like them":

B. Now has not the Omnipresent already assured Israel that he will not judge the fathers on account of the sons or the sons on account of the fathers?

C. For it is said, "The fathers shall not be put to death for the children, nor shall the children be put to death for the fathers; every man shall be put to death for his own sin" (Deut. 24:16).

D. If so, why is it said, "and also because of the iniquities of their fathers they shall pine away like them"?

E. When for generation after generation they are enthralled in the deeds of their fathers, then they are judged on their account.

"Exile" is taken to fulfill the curse of "perishing," and then comes the religious duty of "pining away." The important clarification comes at Nos. 2-3, which draws into alignment a variety of pertinent verses.

CCLXIX:II

1.A. "But if they confess their iniquity and the iniquity of their fathers [in their treachery which they committed against me, and also in walking contrary to me, so that I walked contrary to them and brought them into the land of their enemies; if then their uncircumcised heart is humbled and they make amends for their iniquity; then I will remember my covenant with Jacob, and I will remember my covenant also with Isaac and my covenant also with Abraham, and I will remember the land. But the land shall be left by them and enjoy its sabbaths while it lies desolate without them; and they shall make amends for their iniquity, because they spurned my ordinances, and their soul abhorred my statutes. Yet for all that, when they are in the land of their enemies, I will not spurn them, neither will I abhor them so as to destroy them utterly and break my covenant with them; for I am the Lord their God; but I will for their sake remember the covenant with their forefathers whom I brought forth out of the land of Egypt in the sight of the nations, that I might be their God: I am the Lord. These are the statutes and ordinances and laws which the Lord made between him and the people of Israel on Mount Sinai by Moses]" (Lev. 26:40-46):

B. This is how things are as to repentance,

C. for as soon as they confess their sins, I forthwith revert and have mercy on them,

D. as it is said, "But if they confess their iniquity and the iniquity of their fathers in their treachery which they committed against me."

2.A. ". . . and also in walking contrary to me, so that I walked contrary to them":

B. In this world they treated my laws in a casual way, so I shall treat them in a casual way in this world."

3.A. ". . . and brought them into the land of their enemies":

B. This is a good deal for Israel.

C. For the Israelites are not to say, "Since we have gone into exile among the gentiles, let us act like them."

D. [God speaks:] "I shall not let them, but I shall call forth prophets against them, who will bring them back to the right way under my wings."

E. And how do we know?

F. "What is in your mind shall never happen, the thought, 'Let us be like the nations, like the tribes of the countries, and worship wood and stone.' 'As I live,' says the Lord God, 'surely with a might hand and an outstretched arm and with wrath poured out, I will be king over you. [I will bring you out from the peoples and gather you out of the countries where you are scattered, with a mighty hand and an outstretched arm and with wrath poured out'" (Ezek. 20:33-3).

G. "Whether you like it or not, with or without your consent, I shall establish my dominion over you."

4.A. ". . . if then their uncircumcised heart is humbled and they make amends for their iniquity":

B. This is how things are as to repentance,

C. for as soon as they humble their heart in repentance, I forthwith revert and have mercy on them,

D. as it is said, "if then their uncircumcised heart is humbled and they make amends for their iniquity."

5.A. ". . . then I will remember my covenant with Jacob, [and I will remember my covenant also with Isaac and my covenant also with Abraham]":

B. Why are the patriarchs listed in reverse order?

C. It is to indicate, if the deeds of Abraham are not sufficient, then the deeds of Isaac, and if the deeds of Isaac are not worthy, then the deeds of Jacob.

D. Each one of them is worthy that the world should depend upon his intervention.

6.A. And why with reference to Abraham and Jacob are remembrance mentioned, but not with respect to Isaac?

B. His ashes are regarded as though he were scooped up on the altar.

C. And why with respect to Abraham and Isaac, but not with respect to Jacob, is there mention of "also"?

D. This teaches that the bier of Jacob our father was without flaw [since he did not produce an evil son, unlike Abraham with Ishmael and Isaac with Esau].

7.A. I know only that the patriarchs are covered. How about the matriarchs?

B. Scripture uses the accusative particle, and the accusative particle encompasses only the matriarchs,

C. as it is said, "There they buried Abraham and [the accusative particle] Sarah his wife" (Gen. 49:31).

8.A. And how do we know that the covenant is made with the land?

B. Scripture says, "and I will remember the land."

9.A. "But the land shall be left by them and enjoy its sabbaths [while it lies desolate without them]":

B. "I said to them to sow for me for six years and release the year for me for one year, so that they might know that the land is mine.

C. "But that is not what they did, get up and go into exile from it, so that it may enjoy release on its own for all the years of release that it owes to me."

D. For it is said, "But the land shall be left by them and enjoy its sabbaths while it lies desolate without them, and they shall make amends for their iniquity."

10.A. ". . . because [Hebrew: because] and because, [that is, for this item and for that item, exactly] [they spurned my ordinances, and their soul abhorred my statutes]":

B. "Now did I collect item by item from Israel? And did I not exact punishment for them only for one out of a hundred sins that they committed before me?

C. "Why then is it said, 'because' [as though the penalty were exact]?

D. "It is because 'they spurned my ordinances'—this refers to the laws,

E. "and because 'their soul abhorred my statutes,'—this refers to the exegeses of Scripture.

11.A. "[Yet for all] that"—this refers to the sin committed in the Wilderness.

B. "...yet for"—this refers to the sin of Baal Peor.

C. "...yet for all that"—this refers to the sin involving the kings of the Amorites.

12.A. "[Yet for all that, when they are in the land of their enemies,] I will not spurn them, neither will I abhor them so as to destroy them utterly":

B. Now what is left for them, but that they not be spurned nor abhorred? For is it not the fact that all the good gifts that had been given to them were now taken away from them?

C. And were it not for the Scroll of the Torah that was left for them, they were in no way be different from the nations of the world!

D. But "I will not spurn them": in the time of Vespasian.

E. "...neither will I abhor them": in the time of Greece.

F. "...so as to destroy them utterly and break my covenant with them": in the time of Haman.

G. "...for I am the Lord their God": in the time of Gog.

13.A. And how do we know that the covenant is made with the tribal fathers?

B. As it is said, "but I will for their sake remember the covenant with their forefathers whom I brought forth out of the land of Egypt":

B. This teaches that the covenant is made with the tribal fathers.

14.A. "These are the statutes and ordinances and Torahs":

B. "...the statutes": this refers to the exegeses of Scripture.

C. "...and ordinances": this refers to the laws.

D. "...and Torahs": this teaches that two Torahs were given to Israel, one in writing, the other oral.

E. Said R. Aqiba, "Now did Israel have only two Torahs? And did they not have many Torahs given to them? 'This is the Torah of burnt-offering' (Lev. 6:2), 'This is the Torah of the meal-offering' (Lev. 6:27), 'This is the Torah of the guilt-offering' (Lev. 7:1), 'This is the Torah of the sacrifice of peace-offerings' (Lev. 7:11), 'This is the Torah: when a man dies in a tent' (Num. 19:1)."

15.A. "...which the Lord made between him and the people of Israel [on Mount Sinai by Moses]":

B. Moses had the merit of being made the intermediary between Israel and their father in heaven.

C. "...on Mount Sinai by Moses":

D. This teaches that the Torah was given, encompassing all its laws, all its details, and all their amplifications, through Moses at Sinai.

Some of the items begin to reveal a protocol or pattern, e.g., Nos. 2, 3, 4, 9, 14. But overall, the impression I gain is one of a miscellany, since I see no polemical and well-focused proposition. The exegesis of the verse involving the patriarchs is full and rich, Nos. 5, 6, 7. The *heilsgeschichtliche* exercises, e.g., Nos. 11, 12, are not sustained and lack conviction; the order is wrong, and no point is drawn from them. The upshot is that the methodical and rigorous discourse established with reference to the legal passages finds no counterpart here.

JACOB NEUSNER

M

MEDIEVAL JUDAEO-ARABIC LITERATURE: Judaeo-Arabic literature designates the rich *oeuvre*, literary and scientific, created by the Jews of Muslim lands in the Judaeo-Arabic language during the medieval and modern periods. Essentially, this language is a form of medieval (also termed middle) Arabic that deviates from classical Arabic in that it reflects some neo-Arabic dialectic features and pseudo-corrective elements. It is also distinguished by two other features that demonstrate its Jewish origin: the use of Hebrew rather than Arabic script and the occurrence of Hebrew and Aramaic words, usually of religious orientation.

Judaeo-Arabic literature is gradually receiving recognition as an independent field within the Jewish and Arabic studies. This process corresponds to a certain extent to the wider legitimization of the cultural heritage of the Jews from Arab lands during the last two decades, as the result of the changing historical consciousness of Israeli Jews (and to a lesser degree, Jews in the diaspora). Several reasons explain the earlier marginalization and relative neglect of Judeao-Arabic culture and the recent revival of academic and popular interest in it.

From a popular and sociological perspective, the Ashkenazi-centric (Eastern-European) orientation that characterized modern Zionism and the State of Israel in its first decades has given way, particularly since the 1980s, to a pluralistic conception of its cultural heritage. This is partly the result of the successful struggle of Jews originating from Arab lands, who make up more than 50% of Israel's Jewish population, to receive greater recognition and access to positions of political and economic power. The growing prospect of peaceful coexistence with the Arabs, as experienced throughout the 1990s, also contributed to the maturing of Israeli society and to the loosening of its ideological constraints in identifying the "Arab" with the enemy. A new openness towards Arabic music and literature naturally converges with a revival of interest in Judaeo-Arabic culture and in the long individual history of the major Jewish oriental communities (North-African, Iraqi, Persian, Syrian).[1]

In academic circles, the medieval (secular) Hebrew poetry of the Jews of Muslim Spain (Andalucia) had always been regarded as one of the pinnacles of Jewish creativity, studied and taught as an expression of "the Sephardi Golden Era." In this conception were included some philosophical and poetic works written originally in Judaeo-Arabic, which had entered the Hebrew canon through medieval translations, such as ʿArugat ha-Bosem by Moses Ibn Ezra (c. 1055-c. 1138).[2] Nevertheless, the rich and varied Judaeo-Arabic literature written in Spain and outside it, in the fields of science, poetics, philosophy and exegesis, which was not channeled into the Hebrew corpus by the medieval translators (mainly of the Tibon family), was generally left outside the sphere of scholarly interest. Though the extent and importance of this

literature was already known in the nineteenth century, it was neglected partly as the result of the purist tendency of early Jewish studies to concentrate on classical Hebrew sources.

Another reason for this relative neglect was the historical demise of Judaeo-Arabic literature among its native communities: Most of it did not reach print and survived only in manuscript sources. Some of it was lost altogether due to the adoption of spoken Arabic dialects or spoken Spanish (Ladino) in many of the oriental communities that had previously mastered classical Arabic (the most consistent exception to this rule being the Yemenite community, which kept a live tradition of classical Arabic education). This process began in the wake of the disintegration of the Muslim Empire and the great expulsions from Spain during the fourteenth and fifteenth centuries, when waves of Ladino speaking Jews settled in Arab lands and changed the linguistic fabric of their Jewish communities. This process deepened once the colonial powers, generally welcomed by the Jews and favorable to their social mobility, had encouraged accomplishment in European tongues.[3]

Scholarly interest in Judaeo-Arabic literature was revitalized in the 1960s, largely due to Shelomo Dov Goitein's seminal works, most notably his *A Mediterranean Society*, which drew a detailed and vibrant socio-historical portrait of the Jews of the Orient during the tenth-thirteenth centuries, largely based on Judaeo-Arabic sources from the Cairo Genizah.

The renewed availability of Judaeo-Arabic manuscripts housed in the former Soviet Union since the 1990s, especially those known as the Firkovitch Collections, has partly contributed to the intensification of research into this literature.[4] The more salient factors behind this recent development, however, are in my view the theoretical shifts that have occurred, mainly during the past two decades, in Jewish studies as a whole, the maturation of its disciplines, and its entering into what has astutely been called a "post-ideological" era.[5]

The history of the Jews during the Middle Ages, particularly under Christendom, is not as bound as it was to the

Zionist ethos, nor is it studied necessarily as an inevitable precursor to the horrific ending of the age-old Jewish entity in Europe. Although Islam has always enjoyed a more positive image in this respect, the study of the Jews under medieval Islam has to a certain extent been subdued under the effects of the modern Arab-Israeli conflict and by the dominance of European Jewry in defining the cultural agenda of Israeli establishment. As both these factors are gradually being transformed, they have relaxed the former reserve in recognizing the Arabic literary output of the Jews of Islam as a phenomenon worthy of independent research. They have also effected the renewed interest in Jewish-Muslim interaction during the Middle Ages, of which our main documentary source, from the Jewish perspective, is Judaeo-Arabic literature.

Throughout this entry the term "Judaeo-Arabic literature" is used to designate all fields of Arabic writing, whether fiction or non-fiction (literary or scientific), in which the Jews of Arab and Muslim lands gave expression to their interests and creativity. The linguistic characteristics and definitions of "Judaeo-Arabic" are elaborated, followed by a survey of the academic study of Judaeo-Arabic literature. The main part of this entry includes a classification of the Judaeo-Arabic corpus, as reflected in the Cairo Genizah, into major types and genres. These are surveyed from a novel perspective that takes into account the complexity of the Judaeo-Arabic genre system, with more extensive sections devoted to the particular (and interrelated) fields of translation, exegesis and grammar. Due to the vastness of this corpus, which stretches from medieval to modern times, the outline has been delimited to the medieval period, particularly to the "golden" or "classical" era of Judaeo-Arabic literature (tenth-thirteenth centuries), in which it knew a great flowering in all genres and sub-genres. We end with an analysis of the possible functions of these genres.

Linguistic definitions of Judaeo-Arabic: The Judaeo-Arabic language is most simply defined as a form of classical Arabic written in Hebrew script that contains vernacular features unique to the spoken Arabic of medieval (and modern) Jews. In the history of research, Judaeo-Arabic writings have mainly been analyzed from a linguistic perspective, with less attention to their value as expressions of an authentic and vibrant literary culture. This is mostly due to the fact that the foundations in this field were laid by linguists who studied Judaeo-Arabic as an aspect of the development of Arabic language in general.

Joshua Blau provided the first systematic linguistic description of Judaeo-Arabic as a branch of what he termed "middle Arabic."[6] In his view, Jewish and Christian writers of the Middle Ages, who had not internalized the ideal of pure (classical) Arabic expression ('arabiyya), lapsed more easily to substandard forms of writing than did their Muslim contemporaries. They nevertheless did strive to write in classical Arabic, and this caused them to over-hit the mark by using ungrammatical constructions ("pseudo-corrections"), which became a hallmark of their writings. Blau applied the term "middle Arabic" both in a chronological and in a stylistic sense. Chronologically it refers to the medieval stage of Arabic, as a link between old and new Arabic. Stylistically it designates the mixed language of medieval Arabic texts, which are essentially written in classical Arabic yet betray vernacular elements akin to modern Arabic dialects, as well as pseudo-classical features. Christian Arabic and Judaeo-Arabic were thus conceived as two distinctive branches of this mixed medieval form of written Arabic.

This double-fold (problematic) terminology led Blau to re-define middle Arabic and restrict it to the latter stylistic sense, as a mixed language[7] while applying the term neo-Arabic in describing the vernacular elements of middle Arabic. Texts that contain few neo-Arabic elements are defined by him as Middle Arabic Standard, while others in which this element is salient are defined as Substandard. In Blau's current definition, Judaeo-Arabic, as a representative of middle Arabic, is characterized by two additional features: the use of Hebrew script and the use of proper Hebrew and Aramaic words or their Arabicized forms (as loan-words).[8]

This revised definition has also been challenged, mainly from the perspective of socio-linguistics, which provides an alternative model for the linguistic description of Judaeo-Arabic. Kees Versteegh, for instance, considers Jewish and Christian Arabic as creolized dialects, which due to the isolation of these ethnic groups did not reach the stage of decreolization.[9] Another socio-linguistic model is applied by Benjamin Hary, who defines Judaeo-Arabic as an "ethnolect," meaning, a language used by a specific ethnic community, which gives expression, in this case, to specific Jewish themes that constitute the cultural discourse of a Jewish writer and a primarily Jewish audience.[10] Accordingly: "Judaeo-Arabic is not just a language, it is a Jewish language, typical of Jewish communities in the Diaspora which adopted a local language and wrote in Hebrew script with Hebrew and Aramaic elements penetrating the lexicon and the grammar. The language was used by Jews for Jewish readers and speakers and treated mainly Jewish themes in its literature. This, by itself, justifies granting Judeo-Arabic the status of a separate language or at least a separate ethnolect."[11]

Most scholars agree, nonetheless, in tracing the historical development of Judaeo-Arabic to three main periods, according to its orthography, syntax and lexicon: Firstly, the pre-classical stage which is marked by a phonetical form of spelling Arabic in Hebrew letters, attested in manuscript sources dating from the eighth and ninth centuries. Secondly, the classical stage (tenth-thirteenth centuries). During this period Judaeo-Arabic spelling stabilized, emulating, in the main, classical Arabic orthography with regard to the graphic representation of Arabic *matres lectionis* and other features. This stage is closely identified with the relatively stylized Judaeo-Arabic works of Saadiah Gaon (882-942), whose numerous copies in the Cairo Genizah reflect this form of spelling. Thirdly, the post-classical stage (fourteenth century to the modern era), which is characterized by some return to phonetic forms of spelling, vernacular features in writing and the development of new literary types.[12]

Judaeo-Arabic literature and its history of academic study: The stages identified in the linguistic development of Judaeo-Arabic often serve in describing its literary development, without the proper distinction being drawn between linguistic and literary functions. Judaeo-Arabic Bible translations, for instance, are usually divided into three periods: pre-Saadianic, Saadianic and post-Saadianic, mainly according to their orthography.[13]

Recent years have witnessed a renewed interest in Judaeo-Arabic literature and a variety of detailed studies have been devoted to individual Judaeo-Arabic works. These have served to emphasize the growing need for an integrative study of the literary culture of the Jews of Arab lands, whether in the medieval, pre-modern or modern periods. As to the medieval period, which concerns us here, an overall view, encompassing the multifarious documentary, fictional and non-fictional sources of Judaeo-Arabic as an unbroken textual entity remains a major *desideratum* for future research.

Medieval Judaeo-Arabic literature has rarely been regarded as a *sui generis* phenomenon, which requires independent tools of research. In reality, it still suffers from the effects of its nineteenth century portrayal as a "mixed" literature, dressing Jewish themes an Arabic tongue or Arabic themes in a Jewish tongue, "impure" in its forms of expression and writing. The title of Moriz Steinschneider's key work, *Die arabische Literartur der Juden* (Berlin, 1902), reflects something of this standpoint. Its importance lies, nevertheless, in presenting the first systematic attempt to provide a taxonomy of names, writers and branches of Judaeo-Arabic literature, according to the manuscript sources available at the time, dating mainly from the thirteenth-fourteenth centuries. In his the preface to the English adaptation of his work ("Introduction to the Arabic Literature of the Jews," in *JQR* (Old Series) vols. 9-13), Steinschneider describes his arduous search for manuscripts throughout Europe since 1845. He also expresses his personal esteem for the unique phenomenon of Judaeo-Arabic, yet continues to relate to it as a "derived," secondary literary culture:

Arabic and German are the only languages and nationalities which have been of essential and continuing influence on Judaism. A statement of the extent and duration of the usage of the Arabic language by the Jews would, indeed, exceed the limits of what is here our principle subject, viz. The Arabic literature; but here I only give some hints of the life, customs, institutions, and their designations.[14]

Since Steinschneider's seminal work the only overall surveys to have appeared are encyclopedic entries on "Judaeo-Arabic literature." In the *Encyclopaedia Judaica*, Abraham Halkin defined this literature as "writings by Jews in Arabic, generally with Jewish coloring."[15] George Vajda's definition in the *Encyclopaedia of Islam* is no less reflective of the reserved stance which dominated twentieth century scholarship:

> Judaeo-Arabic dialectal literature is essentially "popular," even in the case of a version based on a mediaeval Hebrew translation of a "classical" work originally written in Arabic such as "Duties of the Heart" by Bahya Ibn Pakuda [. . .] The whole spectrum of Judaeo-Arabic writing of the earlier period, however, though of greater cultural range, but most of the time lacking in aesthetic preoccupations, cannot be classified as literature in the strict sense of "belles letters." Given these conditions it is difficult to speak of "the history" of Judaeo-Arabic literature.[16]

S.D. Goitein, on the other hand, appears to have recognized the insufficiency of classicist categories in describing the Judaeo-Arabic *oeuvre*. After devoting an important volume to the education system in the Genizah period, in which he traced the main literary types which served in the higher-education syllabus, on the basis of Cairo Genizah sources, Goitein turned to the socio-historical study of the Jews of Islam.[17] His colossal six-volume achievement in describing their *Mediterranean Society*, which contains significant discussions of cultural, educational and literary manifestations of this society was less concerned, however, with offering a novel classification or analysis of Judaeo-Arabic literature *per se*.[18]

Towards a redefinition of "genre" in Judaeo-Arabic literature: The branches of Judaeo-Arabic literature origi-

nally surveyed by Steinschneider include poetry, grammatical thought, philosophy, polemics, homiletics, translation, exegesis, medicine and astronomy, as well as distinctive literary types such as special commentaries on the Ten Commandments. Considering the difficulties that faced him in obtaining manuscript sources, and the fact that he had no occasion to avail himself to the Arabic and Judaeo-Arabic material in the Cairo Genizah, the fruits of Steinschneider's labor are impressive, both in scope and in detail.

The new manuscript sources uncovered in the Genizah of the Ben Ezra Synagogue in Cairo (known as the "Cairo Genizah"), as well as in "genizot" of Karaite synagogues in the city (contained in the Firkovitch Collections) have mostly become available to scholars throughout the second half of the past century.[19] In themselves these necessitate a comprehensive re-evaluation of Judaeo-Arabic literature. In addition, the modern breakthroughs in anthropological, linguistic and literary thought, inspired by formalist and structuralist trends that took hold throughout the twentieth century, render Steinschneider's evaluative categories insufficient in describing the idiosyncrasies of Judaeo-Arabic literature and explaining its dynamics.

A revision is required on the descriptive level, in which the taxonomy of types and genres may be updated according to new manuscript sources. It is also needed on the theoretical level, in which the application of socio- literary models may yield more productive explanations concerning the functions fulfilled by these types and genres.

Modern discourse analysis has largely abandoned the rigid approach to genre boundaries, which derived from classical and classicist divisions and sub-divisions of epos, lyric and drama. "Genre" is generally more loosely defined, as, for instance, "a distinctive category of discourse of any type, spoken or written, with or without literary aspirations."[20] Structural critics, such as Roland Barth, conceive of genre as "a set of constitutive conventions and codes, altering from age to age, but shared by a kind of implicit contract between writer and reader."[21]

The habitual division between documentary, scientific and literary sources, which still prevails in the description of Judaeo-Arabic literature, seems outdated in the light of conceptions which highlight the communicative function of a text or discourse. The flowery formulas for beginnings and endings of Judaeo-Arabic private and business letters, for instance, function as literary genres no less than rhymed prose. They too are composed of "a set of constitutive conventions [. . .] shared by a kind of implicit contract between writer and reader."[22] Their re-appraisal requires a change in focus, which allows for the study of such documents not only as historical sources, but also as literary sources of creative writing.

A theoretical model that may be fruitfully applied to Judaeo-Arabic literature was developed by the formalist literary critic Tzvetan Todorov, who describes a genre, literary or otherwise, as the outcome of the process of social codification, wherein "the recurrence of certain discursive properties is institutionalized." The norms established by this codification require a measure of transgression so that they retain their visibility and vitality. Thus, "a new genre is always the transformation of one or several old genres: by inversion, by displacement, by combination."[23]

This process of "genre generation" suggests an inherent dependency between old and new literary forms, and controverts attempts to evaluate them in terms of "primary" and "secondary" creations. It suggests a continuing dynamic, both on the synchronic level in which genres are transgressed and restructured in daily forms of discourse, possibly over a range of languages, and on the diachronic level, in which fresh genres rise out of the shells of old transmitted forms and revitalize them. Both levels are essential for the understanding of Judaeo-Arabic literature, whose generative system defies classification for classification's sake and requires clarification of its socio-rhetorical functions, in view of the discourse communities which it served through various periods and regions.[24] This attempt will not be undertaken here, however, since it requires an extensive assimilation of new materials, many of which are still in unedited manuscripts, as well as a long-term perspective on the material which has not yet come into fruition.

The following outlines the main genres of Judaeo-Arabic literature in the light of an extensive research project undertaken recently in the classification of Judaeo-Arabic sources from the Cairo Genizah. The survey still echoes, in part, the conventional grouping into disciplinary fields (philosophy, exegesis, grammar, etc.), which is typical to the above-mentioned encyclopedic entries. It also addresses, nevertheless, the unique contribution of the Cairo Genizah to our understanding of the generation process of Judaeo-Arabic genres and sub-genres and the question of their functions.

Classification of Judaeo-Arabic literature as reflected in the Cairo Genizah sources: The Hebrew term *genizah* (derived from the Persian root *ganaz*) designates the Jewish practice of assigning discarded or worn-out Hebrew writings to special storage or interment. This is for fear they may contain the name of the Lord (the tetragrammaton), which is forbidden to be "taken in vein" (Exod. 20:7, Deut. 5:11). The loft of the main Rabbanite Synagogue, Ben-Ezra, in Old Cairo (Fusṭāṭ) served for this purpose mainly throughout the tenth-fourteenth centuries. Due to its unique climatic and physical conditions some 200,000 fragments, mostly pertaining to this period, were preserved. They were largely recovered by Solomon Schechter in 1897, and two-thirds of them (an estimated total of 140,000 fragments) are now housed in the Cambridge University Library.[25] It is roughly estimated that the language of over a half of the manuscripts found in the Genizah is Judaeo-Arabic.[26] These contain documentary and literary sources of a religious and non-religious nature. They were miraculously preserved, since Hebrew script was an essential feature in the consignment of writings to the Genizah.

The first descriptive volume on Judaeo-Arabic material in the Cairo Genizah Cambridge Collections, containing a detailed survey of the subject matter of around 8,000 fragments, has recently been published.[27] The volume represents an initial attempt to fully identify and system-atically describe a concentrated primary source of classical Judaeo-Arabic literature.[28]

The Genizah's unique contribution lies in the copies of non-canonical and popu-lar Judaeo-Arabic works it has preserved, alongside *ad hoc* personal compositions which also found their way into its corpus. With regard to canonical Judaeo-Arabic writings (such as Maimonides' *Commentary on the Mishnah*) it has preserved additional (and often unattested) textual traditions. In gen-eral, however, copies of such works have also reached us through other manuscript collections, sometimes in a better state of preservation, as in the case of complete codices. In comparison to these collections (including those recovered from Karaite synagogues and burial grounds in Cairo, known as the Firkovitch collections, which contain full or partial codices of Judaeo-Arabic and Hebrew works),[29] the material found in the Ben Ezra Genizah is still unri-valled. This is precisely due to the un-guarded fashion in which it absorbed material of popular nature. In this it sheds light not only on the guest-room of Judaeo-Arabic culture, but also on its kitchen and bedroom, as well as what was hidden under its carpets.

Around 2,500 out of the 8,000 fragments in the above-mentioned classified corpus are defined as documentary, including per-sonal, commercial and official letters, lists and inventories of goods, books and names, financial accounts, legal and administrative documents, pen trials, and writing exercises. The difficulty of separating the documen-tary category from the strictly literary category sharpens our awareness of the lim-itations of any system of classification. The remaining 5,500 fragments are defined as literary in the widest sense, including fiction and non-fiction.

These literary fragments have been ranked below into basic classes of texts, i.e. wide genre groupings, largely based on a thematic outline of their subject matter and some stylistic categorization typical of Judaeo-Arabic literature as a whole. Within this listing, more extensive discussion has

been devoted to the fields of translation, exegesis and grammar.

As mentioned above, the thematic clas-sification essentially follows the known branches of Judaeo-Arabic literature (phi-losophy, *halakhah*, etc.), by expanding them in scope and detail. It is recognized that this process is a continuation of the taxonomic enterprise established by Steinschnedier. The novelty lies in the understanding that archival tagging, however minute, serves as a means of exploring the functions of these literary kinds (see following) and not as an end in itself. A further difference lies in the sub-division of the thematic branches according to stylistic criteria as well as the-matic criteria, which consciously attempt to steer away from charged evaluations of "pure" and "mixed" forms.[30]

Bible translations and commen-taries constitute a major genre of Judaeo-Arabic literature.[31] Although it is possible to categorize them as two separate genres, Judaeo-Arabic translations and commen-taries essentially formed part of the same genre, in that they fulfilled complementary functions in the study and elucidation of the biblical text. Unlike some of the Aramaic *Targumim*, particularly Onkelos, whose func-tion in Synagogue worship influenced their self-contained nature as biblical versions, with an independent transmission tradition, the Judaeo-Arabic versions were cast from the start as biblical study-aids, in a threefold structure, which is reflected in most of the manuscript sources. First, the Hebrew verse or a cluster of Hebrew verses is quoted in Hebrew, usually in the form of an *incipit* (the first word or phrase of the given verse), sometimes in full. Second, a Judaeo-Arabic translation is provided of the full Hebrew verse. Third, the verse is commented upon in Judaeo-Arabic, including explication of matters of language, style and content.

This threefold literary structure appears to have entered Jewish writing on the Bible only from the Muslim period, and to have been influenced by parallel models of Qur'anic exegesis. It is already attested in anonymous Genizah fragments from the ninth century, yet became consolidated in the works of tenth and eleventh century exegetes, whether Rabbanites, such as

Saadiah Gaon and Samuel ben Hofni, or Karaites, such as Salmon ben Yeroham and Yefet ben Eli. Numerous copies of their commentaries have been preserved in the Cairo Genizah, almost all of which attest this threefold structure.

Of Saadiah Gaon's many Arabic translations and commentaries of biblical books preserved in the Genizah, only his translation of the Pentateuch (known as the *Tafsîr*) is sometimes found copied independently from his longer commentary (known as the *Sharḥ*). This is primarily due to the interpretive nature of his translation rather than any oral function it may have fulfilled in synagogue. While some Yemenite communities to this very day are known to read the *Tafsîr* out aloud after *Targum Onkelos* as part of the Sabbath synagogue ritual, this was not the initial function of its separation from the *Sharḥ*. As Saadiah himself attests in his Introduction to the *Tafsîr*, the differentiation was meant for a didactic rather than liturgical purpose. He wished to provide readers and worshipers who could not accommodate his long and complex commentary on the Torah with a succinct self-contained Arabic version of the Torah, which contained the end result of his interpretive deliberations. It is therefore likely that Saadiah himself prepared two editions of his work on the Pentateuch, one containing his translation and commentary and the other the translation alone.[32]

Karaite exegetes, particularly Yefet ben Eli, who during the second half of the tenth century translated and commented on all of the Hebrew Bible, consistently kept to this threefold structure, which served as a primary means of instructing their readers in the biblical text. Their translations are clearly integrative with the commentaries that follow them, so that if the reader wishes to understand the reasoning behind the translation of a particular verse he must attend to the commentary. For the Karaites, translation remained a major medium in clarifying the literal meaning of the biblical text. The establishment of primary meaning was also the object of their grammatical commentaries on the Bible (see below). Grammar and translation were linked in their system of interpretation.

These served as the building blocks of their biblical commentaries, whose third layer, the explicatory section, was usually devoted to forms of "higher criticism," namely, the discussion of structural, literary and theological aspects of the biblical text, with additional references, at times, to their symbolic or messianic implications.

The Karaite tradition of Arabic Bible translation preserved and continued literal modes, typical of early, pre-Saadianic, Judaeo-Arabic renderings of the Hebrew Bible. These did not result from a simple or conservative imitative impulse, but were adapted to the Karaites' ethos of biblical study, reflecting their wish to arrive at an accurate presentation of the language of the biblical text, and hence at a correct understanding of its meaning.[33]

With regard to the Genizah sources, an artificial separation of the Judaeo-Arabic versions from the commentaries that immediately follow them may, nevertheless, be applied for the purpose of isolating the actual translation traditions which were in existence in the Judaeo-Arabic milieu. Five sub-categories emerge as the result of the linguistic analysis of these versions, and in consideration of their social and educational functions:[34]

1. Early (ninth century) anonymous translations written in pre-classical Judaeo-Arabic.
2. Saadiah's translations or those that closely follow his works (Saadianic), written in classical Judaeo-Arabic.
3. Karaite translations, also written in classical Judaeo-Arabic.
4. Late translations (known as *shurûḥ*), post Saadianic, dating from the thirteenth-sixteenth centuries, reflecting post-classical Judaeo-Arabic features.
5. Early and late translation glossaries, which selectively follow a biblical passage, chapter or book, and sometimes contain lists of difficult biblical words or *hapax legomena* from one or several biblical books.[35]

No systematic study has yet been conducted concerning the sub-types of biblical commentaries attested in the Genizah sources. Many recent works, however, have been devoted to aspects of Karaite and Rabbanite Judaeo-Arabic exegesis, and the reader is advised to consult them for further detail.[36]

Grammar and massorah were clearly linked to the larger field of translation and exegesis, as an adjacent genre, more restricted in its scope. Its study and generation were mainly the work of professional circles, whose expertise lay in the textual aspects of the Hebrew Bible: its language, vocalization and transmission traditions.[37] The following sub-genres may be identified:

1. Biblical dictionaries and lexicons (e.g., Jonah ibn Janâh's *kitâb al-ʾuṣûl* or David ben Abraham al-Fasi's *kitâb jâmiʿ al-ʾalf âz*).
2. Works on Hebrew grammar and its verbal system.
3. Grammatical commentaries which focus on syntactical issues, rare words and etymologies, in elaborating lengthy biblical passages or books.
4. Biblical, Mishnaic, and Talmudic glossaries (cf., the fifth category of translation material mentioned above) which may also be classified as embryonic dictionaries, when viewed from the perspective of linguistics rather than that of translation.
5. Masoretic compilations on the reading traditions of the Hebrew Bible, such as Mishael ben Uzziel's *Treatise on the differences between Ben Asher and Ben Naphtali* (*Kitâb al-khilaf*).

A few words should be devoted in this context to recent discoveries based on the Cairo Genizah and Firkovitch sources that have highlighted the formative role of the early Karaite scholars in basing biblical study on the interrelated disciplines of grammar, translation and exegesis. In these studies it has been shown that the early Karaite tradition of Hebrew grammar originated in the Karaite grammatical schools that were already well-developed in Iran during the ninth century. It was later brought to Palestine by Karaite scholars who migrated there from the Persian regions, sometimes via Iraq, during the tenth and eleventh centuries.[38]

Two main traits distinguished the early Karaite grammatical tradition: First, it had a clear hermeneutic function in that its purpose was the application of grammatical analysis in order to elucidate the precise meaning of the biblical text, and not the analysis of Hebrew language *per se*. The Karaite concern with linguistic form arose from the conviction that there was a direct link between form and meaning.[39] Second, it relied on technical Hebrew terms and hermeneutic principles which are attested in Rabbinic and Masoretic sources, predating the tenth century, such as *leshon yaḥid* (= singular), *leshon ʿavar* (= past), and other such terms that are also found in the ancient Masoretic list known as *diqduqe miqra*. In particular, it applied the Hebrew term *diqduq* in the sense that it has in masoretic and rabbinic sources as: "investigating the fine points of Scripture."[40]

Despite the Karaites' ideology in rejecting the institution of Oral Law, which brought about their gradual disassociation from Rabbinic Judaism, the early Judaeo-Arabic sources teach us that the Karaite grammatical tradition was not originally isolated from mainstream Judaism. Rather, it became distinct from the tradition followed by the Rabbanites only towards the eleventh century.[41] Moreover, Karaite biblical study at large, and its grammatical emphasis in particular, grew out of a deep association with the professional bearers of the textually orientated stream of rabbinic exegesis (*peshat*), and Maoretic circles, which emphasized the disciplined analysis of the Bible's structure.[42]

Law (*halakhah*) forms the second major category of Judaeo-Arabic literature.[43] It includes the following sub-genres:

1. Continuous commentaries on the Mishnah and Talmud from the Rabbinic and Gaonic periods, such as Maimonides' *Commentary on the Mishnah*.
2. Halakhic monographs which discuss or enumerate religious laws in thematic clusters (including: divorce, inheritance, ritual slaughter etc.), such as the works of Hai Gaon, Samuel ben Hofni Gaon and Isaac Alfasi.
3. Mishnaic and Talmudic glossaries or word-lists, which are similar in style to the biblical translation glossaries mentioned above.
4. Discussions on the theory and didactic methods of halakhah.

Literature and folklore (*midrash* and *aggadah*) are related to the former category in that they correspond to the second element in the classical Rabbinic division between writings inspired by the legal corpus of the Hebrew Bible and writings inspired by its non-legal, literary corpus. In general they constitute a smaller portion of the manuscript sources, though they clearly reflect a high level of literary creativity.[44] These may be divided into four sub-genres, as follows:

1. A common source of popular and ethical legends is *The Book of Comfort* (*Kitâb al-faraj ba'd al-shiddah*) by Nissim Gaon (also called Ibn Shahin), which makes use of a known Arabic genre by this name, and also derives from Hebrew midrashic literature. Similar in popularity, though more strictly adaptive of midrashic sources is the Arabic compilation by David ben Abraham Maimonides known as *Midrash David ha-Nagid*. Proper Arabic translations of classical midrashim such as *Eikhah Rabbah* are also found in the Genizah corpus.
2. A separate genre consists of tales (*qiṣaṣ*) on biblical or apocryphal characters such as Abraham, Joseph and Hannah, sometimes in rhymed prose. These are connected to late Muslim sources, yet are not considered, for the time being, part of the Muslim literature of *qiṣaṣ al-'anbiyâ'*.[45]
3. Popular historical chronicles include the Alexander Romance and Arabic accounts of the Maccabees' history.
4. Famous works of Arabic literature such as *A Thousand and One Nights* and *Kalila wa-Dimna* are attested both in Arabic and Hebrew script. To these may be added transcribed sections of the Qur'an and the Arabic New Testament. The *maqâmah*, gird poem (*muwashshah*), love poem (*ghazal*), and rhymed prose (*saj'*) are found both in Arabic and in Judaeo-Arabic, whether as original compositions or transcriptions from known Arabic works.

Liturgy and prayer include the following sub-genres:[46]

1. Arabic translations of the Passover Haggadah, Sabbath, Festival and daily prayers, especially the *Shema'* and *'Amidah* prayers, as well as translations of Hebrew liturgy and independent Arabic liturgical compositions.
2. *Siddurim* (Prayer Books) by Saadiah Gaon and Solomon ben Nathan of Sijilmasa (South-West Morocco), in which the liturgical instructions (known as rubrics) and introductions are in Judaeo-Arabic, while the prayer text is in Hebrew.

Philosophy constitutes the third largest genre.[47] It may be divided into the following sub-genres:

1. Theology (*kalâm*), written in the outlook and style of Mu'tazilite Muslim theology yet applied to Jewish themes, such as Saadiah Gaon's *Book of Beliefs and Opinions* (*kitâb al-'amânât wal-i' tiqâdât*).
2. Ethics, such as Maimonides' *Eight Chapters* (*thamâniya al-fuṣûl*), which originally formed part of his commentary on Mishnah Avot, yet circulated separately, as an independent ethical work, or Bahyah ibn Paqûdah's *Duties of the Hearts* (*kitâb al-hidâyah 'ilâ frâ'id al-qulûb*).
3. Poetics, mostly limited to copies from the works on literary theory by Moses ibn Ezra, such as *The Book of Discussion and Conversation* (*kitâb al-muhâdara wal-mudhâkara*).
4. General philosophy, such as Maimonides' *Guide to the Perplexed* (*dalâlat al-hâ'irîn*).
5. Philosophical commentaries on the Hebrew Bible. There is some overlap between philosophy and biblical exegesis, since many a Bible commentary will discuss purely philosophical themes such as the nature of creation, while philosophical works may offer insightful literary discussions into biblical passages.[48]

Polemics is a small but significant genre in Judaeo-Arabic literature. On the one hand it may be classified as a sub-category of philosophy, since classical polemical works such as Judah Halevi's *The Book of Refutation and Proof on the Despised Faith*, known as *The Kuzari* (*Kitâb al-radd wal-dalîl fî al-dîn al-dhalîl; al-Kitâb al-khazari*) concentrate on the philosophy of religion as well as on aspects of comparative religion, between Judaism, Christianity and Islam. Lesser known anonymous anti-Christian works such as *The Polemic of Nestor the Priest* (*Qiṣṣat mujâdalat al-'usquf*) may also be placed under this category. A significant sub-genre of Judaeo-Arabic polemics, however, is devoted to internal Jewish controversy, particularly between Rabbanites and Karaites. The Cairo Genizah contains many copies of anonymous anti-Karaite treatises written by Rabbanites, or such anti-Rabbanite treatises written by Karaites, mainly on the subject of the Jewish calendar, which formed a major source for polemical strife in the tenth and eleventh centuries.

Mysticism is yet another relatively small Judaeo-Arabic genre. Due to the formative influence of rational Mutazilite philosophy in the classical period of Judaeo-Arabic literature, as reflected in the seminal works of Jewish philosophy written by Saadiah Gaon and Maimonides (see above), mystical trends were relegated to the margins. They may reflect, nonetheless, live traditions of ancient Jewish mysticism which continued into the Muslim period, as preserved in Saadiah Gaon's *Commentary on Sefer Yesirah* (*Tafsîr kitâb al-mabâdî*). As philosophical training, and, more important, the attraction to rational philosophy gradually weaken throughout the post-classical period, new works of Jewish mysticism begin to emerge in Judaeo-Arabic. These reflect the influences of Sufi Islam upon Jewish thought, as in the case of Abraham Maimonides' *Kitâb kifâyat al-ʿâbidîn* (known in Hebrew as *Sefer ha-maspik le-ʿovedey ha-shem*), or Ovadiah ben Abraham Maimonides' *Treatise on the Pool (al-maqâla al-ḥawdîyya)*.

Scientific works constitute a small but distinctive genre, which may be divided into the major sub-fields of mathematics, medicine and astronomy. The medical literature is particularly rich and its subject matter varies considerably, consisting of medicine proper (i.e., the description of diseases, diagnosis and treatment, pharmacology) and para-medical material relating to the management of patients and the medical profession. The most copied work in the medical field is ʿAli ibn ʿIsâ, *tadhkirat al-kaḥḥâlîn*, transcribed into Hebrew letters.[49]

Quasi-scientific materials form a sub-genre as well, including astrological almanacs, calendrical treatises relating to intercalation, dream interpretation manuals, magic and occultism, all of which fall under the wider conception of the sciences in the early medieval period.[50]

The functions of Judaeo-Arabic genres in the Cairo Genizah material: In general, any form of classification tends to simplify complex, multi-layered literary phenomena. The above survey only captures a glimpse of the intricate and elaborate types and genres which form Judaeo-Arabic literature. Many of the subcategories overlap in that they contain a common thematic or stylistic thread, by which they may be assigned to the same draw, or to different draws, depending on the emphasis of the classifier.

Moreover, the relative proportions suggested above do not mirror the exact dimensions of the literary repertoire of the period. This is primarily due to the haphazard nature of the disposal of material in the Cairo Genizah, and to the general preference given in this disposal process to discarded manuscripts with a conspicuous Hebrew element, such as a Bible quotation. It should be noted, therefore, that the three dominant major genres outlined above, namely, Bible translations and commentaries, law (*halakhah*), and philosophy duly reflect major types of writing typical of the religious thought of the Genizah period. Nevertheless, they do not necessarily represent the fields of interest which dominated the private library of the average Jewish intellectual, even more so, the tastes of other, popular or non-intellectual, social strata.

Notwithstanding the above reservations, three major functions emerge from the classification of the corpus:

1. The generic function defines the level of admixture between Arabic and Hebrew elements in a Judaeo-Arabic text. In other words, the genre in which the writer chooses to express himself determines his selection of a linguistic register, whether inclining towards standard or substandard middle Arabic. A Bible commentary, for instance, does not only contain Hebrew quotations but also other Hebrew phrases and loan words that are embedded in the Judaeo-Arabic discourse. This is due to the writer's discursive dependence on a Hebrew source text and to the common knowledge he shares with his audience concerning its semantic range. A medical text, on the other hand, will include very few or no Hebrew elements, since it does not discuss a Hebrew source text or derive from its conceptual world. Moreover, it is not intended for a wide Hebrew reading audience but a professional audience, familiar with general Arabic sources. In this respect, the classification of the Genizah material highlights the importance of genre as a parameter in the language definition of a Judaeo-Arabic text, alongside the formal parameters relating to the use of Hebrew script and the incorporation of Hebrew and Aramaic words.[51]

2. The educational impetus that lies behind some of the genres underscores their wider communicative function. Different discourse communities influenced the formation of diverse genres and affected the preference given to some over others.[52] The needs of educational circles explain the high proportion of Bible translations and commentaries as well as halakhic manuals and monographs. These served as basic constituents of the educational curriculum of the Genizah period, which was geared to prepare the Jewish adolescent for his religious roles, such as synagogue worship, and his advanced communal roles, such as juriconsultancy (*dayyanut*).[53]

The popularity of certain philosophical genres may also be explained by a wider pedagogical context or conception, which stressed the importance of acquiring rational modes of thought and discussion. Logic became the hallmark of the average Arab and Jewish intellectual of this period. The learning of grammar and philosophical reasoning whether applied to the biblical text or as independent fields of interest were conceived as a means of availing the mind to an admired rational (*kalâm*) type of thinking.

The dominance of Saadiah's Bible versions and commentaries in the Genizah corpus suggests that regular men and women were able to comprehend the crux of his interpretive method, which obliges knowledge of basic philosophical concepts and terminology. It appears, therefore, that these concepts were internalized through the wider educational system of the community and home, even if philosophy was only studied as an independent discipline by advanced pupils or individuals.

The popular translations and glossaries of the Hebrew Bible found in the Genizah form a distinctive genre, which tells of the Bible's function as a center-piece of basic education, more than the Mishnah or Talmud. The anonymity of the *ad hoc* translations and glossaries, as well as their unconstrained style, suggests that they were composed by teachers and pupils in classroom settings, and that they were combined with linguistic study, meant to drill the student in Hebrew, as a second language.

Certain literary types, nevertheless, did not receive expression nor legitimacy through the education system, but through other social and cultural settings. These include the popular legends, dream interpretation manuals, love poems, and other genres that tell of what was read or composed far from the supervising eye of the educator, spouse, or parent. While educational needs may explain the cultivation of some genres, different communicative needs, related to gender and class, may expound the amplification of other genres. In general, many of these genres attest to the strong links between the writers—laymen, artists and intellectuals of the period—and their discourse communities and reflect the attentive adherence of these writers to the changing collective needs of their audiences. Such adherence forms the nucleus of the communicative function; a function that has been vital to the renewal of genres in Jewish literature throughout the ages.

3. Ultimately, the generative function emerges as common to all literary types observed in the Genizah corpus. In other words, the generative function defines the transformational aspect of Judaeo-Arabic creativity, in light of the above quoted observation by Todorov that "a new genre is always a transformation of one or several old genres: by inversion, by displacement, by combination."[54]

This transformation is facilitated by the double media of translation and adaptation that operate as the main generators of new forms in Judaeo-Arabic literature. In almost every genre or class of texts it is possible to distinguish a three-layered division between a new Judaeo-Arabic composition (less accurately termed "original"), an adapted composition, and a translated one, whether from Hebrew or Aramaic into Judaeo-Arabic or from Arabic into Judaeo-Arabic. The medieval boundaries between original, translation and adaptation were far more flexible than their modern parallels.

The aspect of adaptation may explain the neglect in the study of Judaeo-Arabic as an authentic literary phenomenon, even though this process is precisely what makes it into a fascinating, complex, and incomparable literary culture. Just as the language of the Jews of Arab lands was middle Arabic, occupying the middle ground between the conservative classical forms and the innovative spoken tongue of every day life, so was their cultural world a middle world, whose members wondered comfortably between Arabic and Jewish cultures and literatures. This movement engendered modes of thinking and expression that became an inseparable part of the personal and collective identity of the men and women of the Genizah period, and for this reason it gained heightened expression in their literary tastes and needs.

Judaeo-Arabic culture relied on its ability to transfer, transmit, and filter various subject matter from language to language. The new literary forms created through this process—in fiction and non-fiction—were often born out of old forms by way of inversion, displacement, and combination. The media of translation and adaptation functioned as a sieve through which known classes of texts were passed and transformed into something different and new; the norms of the "original" genre retained visibility by being transgressed and were revitalized, simultaneously, by becoming refashioned norms. Translation and adaptation were thus the activators of the process of genre generation. The classes of texts born of this process should therefore be regarded not only as primary and authentic but also as revolutionary in respect of the cultural horizons that permitted their creation and growth.

Let us consider, first of all, the main direction of this translation process, that is, from Hebrew into Judaeo-Arabic. Apart from the Hebrew Bible, the Genizah corpus also contains fragments from a wide range of canonical Hebrew and Aramaic works that were translated into Arabic, including the Mishnah, Talmud, Passover Haggadah, the ʿAmidah and Shemaʿ prayers, liturgical and midrashic sources. These texts are usually set in the conventional mode of Bible translation, including a quotation from the beginning of a verse in the source text (incipit), followed by a literal translation of the full verse. The fact that few copies of such works (excluding the Bible translations)

have survived suggests that they did not reach the near canonization afforded to Saadiah's biblical versions but remained in the sphere of oral translation, sometimes jotted down by a teacher or pupil. Nonetheless, what survived reflects a small portion of what was actually in existence and is indicative of a wide translation culture. This culture answered the varied needs of writers and audiences who sought to understand and explain the basic contents of key works, essential to religious and spiritual life, by subjecting them to different forms of translation from Hebrew and Aramaic into Arabic.

The phenomenon of adaptation from Hebrew into Judaeo-Arabic is more complex in nature than that of translation and more difficult to trace. The Genizah corpus contains Judaeo-Arabic midrashim that were clearly translated, word for word, from Hebrew midrashim, while others do not point to a discernible Hebrew source text. It is possible that these represent novel Judaeo-Arabic works inspired by Hebrew midrash yet also derived from Arabic legendary sources, and, naturally, from the imaginative power of their composers. Works such as Nissim Gaon's kitāb al-faraj baʿd al-shiddah and the Midrash of David ha-Nagid demonstrate this phenomenon. Their many copies in the Genizah corpus reflect the immense popularity of this genre of the midrashic sermon.

The media of translation and adaptation also served in the opposite direction, from Arabic into Judaeo-Arabic. This process did not only take place on the formal level of transcription from Arabic into Hebrew letters (as in the case of the transcribed Qurʾan fragments or those of the Thousand and One Nights), but also on the level of content. Sometimes the subject matter of the Arabic text was lightly adapted or changed in order to suit a Jewish audience. In more intricate cases, entire models were adopted from Arabic literature and philosophy and then fostered in Judaeo-Arabic contexts, through which they entered Hebrew or even European literature.[55]

To the extent that we inquire whether a Judaeo-Arabic liturgical work represents a translation or an adaptation from a known

Hebrew source text, or whether it is essentially a novel composition, so we should ask whether a Judaeo-Arabic love poem, *maqâmah*, or medical work is simply a transcription from Arabic into Hebrew letters. In most cases it constitutes a more flexible form of composition, completely innovative at times, since it is adapted to the needs of a different discourse community. Only the detailed study of such texts will enable us to appreciate their true nature and the composite cultural needs they may have fulfilled.

Even more tangled is the background of those Judaeo-Arabic genres whose mutual influences are difficult to trace in the history of contacts between Hebrew and Arabic literatures. In the literary sphere, the stories (*qiṣaṣ*) of Abraham and Joseph mentioned above are a case in point, as are the adaptations of Hellenistic materials such as the Alexander romance. In the philosophical sphere, texts of a mystical inclination, combining Jewish and Sufi elements may also pose the question of who influenced whom in the chain of transmission.

In conclusion, no matter how complex the Judaeo-Arabic text under discussion, it essentially reflects a written or an oral tradition that passed through different registers of language, from classical to middle Arabic or vice versa, from Hebrew or Arabic into Judaeo-Arabic. In this process the tradition inevitably went through a change of content, however minute, that mediated between it and the target culture as a whole. The beginning and end of this process of "transculturation" are difficult to envisage, yet it was a process typical of Jewish existence in dispersion throughout the ages.[56]

From the earliest periods of encounter with dominating languages and cultures, long before the contacts with the Arabs, Jews applied the media of translation and adaptation (into Greek, Aramaic and Persian) as a means of bridging the gap between the old and the new, between the self and the other, and thus retained an independent, agile and vibrant identity. It is likely that these entrenched modes of cultural existence were regenerated in the encounter with Arabic thought and literature; translation and adaptation becoming a means of self-expression for any Jew that spoke or wrote in Arabic. If the boundaries of one's world correspond to those of his language, then one who absorbs a bilingual or multilingual atmosphere from early childhood is likely to experience a certain flexibility of mental boundaries. For such a person translation serves not only as a cultural outlet but also as a psychological outlet of primary importance, in that it enables some level of integration between different identities. It is apparent that Jewish existence in the world of Islam and the cultural flowering it inspired turned translation into an essential medium of self-expression and creativity, in all forms of Jewish language, whether spoken or written, sacred or mundane.

Summary: In discussing the question of genre in relation to medieval Judaeo-Arabic literature several ideas were raised regarding the nature of this literature and the possible paths to its comprehensive, more adequate understanding. These are dependent on the continuing work of identification and classification of Judaeo-Arabic material in the Genizah and other Judaeo-Arabic collections and will hopefully find further scope for clarification in ongoing research into this fascinating corpus. An exhaustive approach to Judaeo-Arabic literature that integrates the detailed description of its composite and illusive forms with the question of their socio-literary functions is still a *desideratum*, a challenge to all those who wish to reach a greater understanding of this unique cultural phenomenon.

As suggested above, one way of coming closer to this goal is by dissociating the narrow, technical definition of a text as "Judaeo-Arabic," whether Hebraic or Arabic in its linguistic emphasis, from the wider process of its understanding, based on a complex set of linguistic, literary, and social parameters. This understanding yields constructive insights when based on a functional model which examines the role of each genre on three separate levels, which mutually combine in the final analysis: First, the generic level, which isolates the smallest building blocks of a literary type, and studies their effects on the writer's choice of a linguistic register. Sec-

ond, the communicative level, which determines the functions fulfilled by the text in
the context of a specific discourse community, whether in educational, social or other
settings. Third, the generative level, which
investigates the transformation of old genres
into new genres through the two-way media
of translation and adaptation from Hebrew
into Judaeo-Arabic and from Arabic into
Judaeo-Arabic. In these three possibilities
there lies potential for the fruitful study of
Judaeo-Arabic literature, which transcends
classification for the sake of clarification,
and which does justice to the true dimensions of this grand oeuvre as a *sui generis*
manifestation of a particular form of life.

Bibliography

Baker. C.F., and M. Polliack, eds., *Arabic and
Judaeo-Arabic Manuscripts in the Cambridge
Genizah Collections, Arabic Old Series (T-S Ar. 1a-
54)* (Cambridge, 2001).
Blau, J., *The Emergence and Linguistic Background of
Judaeo-Arabic, A Study of the Origins of Middle
Arabic* (Jerusalem, 1981).
Halkin, A.S., "Judaeo-Arabic literature," in
Encyclopaedia Judaica (1971), vol. 10, pp. 410-
423.
Steinschneider, M., "Introduction to the Arabic
Literature of the Jews," in *Jewish Quarterly
Review* (Old Series), vols. 9-13.
Vajda, G., "Judaeo-Arabic literature," in
Encyclopaedia of Islam (1978), vol. 4, pp. 303-
307.

Notes

[1] Despite the current Israeli-Palestinian crisis,
this development is not, in my view, in jeopardy
of reverting backward, though it may be slowed
down.
[2] This medieval Hebrew adaptation represents only segments of Ibn Ezra's original mag-
num *Dissertation of the Garden on Figurative and
Literal Language*. For a detailed analysis of this
work see, P. Fenton, *Philosophie et exégèse dans le
Jardin de la métaphore de Moïse Ibn 'Ezra* (Leiden,
1997).
[3] Further on these historical-linguistic developments see, for instance, N.A. Stillman, *The
Language and Culture of the Jews of Sefrou, Morocco:
An Ethnolinguistic Study* (Louvin, 1988), p. 5.
[4] The newly-available manuscripts (also dat-
ing from the tenth-thirteenth centuries) were col-
lected in the nineteenth century from Karaite
genizot in the Middle East by the Russian
Karaite scholar and bibliophile Abraham
Frikovitch. They are now housed in the Russian
National Library. See M. Beit-Arié, "Hebrew
Manuscript Collections in Leningrad," in *Jewish
Studies* (1991), vol. 31, pp. 33-46 [Hebrew];
M. Ben-Sasson, "Firkovitch's Second Collection:

Remarks on Historical and Halakhic Materials,"
in *Jewish Studies* (1991), vol. 31, pp. 47-67
[Hebrew]; D. Sklare, *Judaeo-Arabic Manuscripts in
the Firkovitch Collections, The Works of Yūsuf al-Basīr*
(Jerusalem, 1997), pp. 7-16 [Hebrew].
[5] See the remarks concerning the study of
the Jews in medieval (Christian) Europe by the
historian I.J. Yuval, *Two Nations in Your Womb*
(Tel Aviv, 2000), pp. 11-15 [Hebrew].
[6] See J. Blau's seminal works: *The Emergence
and Linguistic Background of Judaeo-Arabic, A Study of
the Origins of Middle Arabic* (Jerusalem, 1981); *A
Grammar of Christian Arabic based Mainly on South-
Palestinian Texts from the First Millennium* (Louvin,
1966); *A Grammar of Mediaeval Judaeo-Arabic* (Jerusalem, 1961).
[7] See Blau, *A Grammar of Mediaeval Judaeo-
Arabic* (1981), p. 215: "The mixed language of
texts in which Classical, Neo-Arabic and pseudo-
correct elements alternate, I prefer now simply
to call Middle Arabic."
[8] See Blau, *Emergence*, pp. 34, 133-166.
[9] See K. Versteegh, *Pidginization and Creoli-
zation: The Case of Arabic* (Amsterdam and
Philadelphia, 1984), pp. 8f., 29-32, 42f., 116.
[10] See B. Hary, *Multiglossia in Judaeo-Arabic,
With an Edition, Translation and Grammatical Study of
the Cairene Purim Scroll* (Leiden, 1992), pp. xiii-xiv,
55-69, 71-74, 103-111.
[11] See Hary, *Multiglossia*, p. 105. Cf.,
N. Stillman, *Jews of Sefrou*, pp. 3-4: "it was the
medium of expression for one of the foremost
periods of Jewish cultural and intellectual creativity." Also consider Blau's emphasis on the
literary tradition of Judaeo-Arabic (*Emergence*,
p. 49): "it was felt by the Jews themselves to be
a distinct literary language. It was consequently
used by writers who could equally well have
written in more classical language, had they so
chosen, and its distinctive character finds expression in the possession of its own literary tradition." For an updated survey of theories on
middle Arabic and Judaeo-Arabic, see P.A.
Bengtsson, *Two Arabic Versions of the Book of Ruth,
Text Edition and Language Studies* (Lund, 1995),
pp. 85-99.
[12] For a detailed survey of these historical
stages, see Hary, *Multiglossia*, pp. 75-82. On the
orthographic distinctions between pre-classical
and classical Judaeo-Arabic, see J. Blau and
S. Hopkins, "On Early Judaeo-Arabic Orthography," in *ZAL* (1984), vol. 12, pp. 9-27;
"Judaeo-Arabic Papyri—Collected, Edited,
Translated and Analysed," in *JSAI* (1987), vol. 9,
pp. 87-160.
[13] See J. Blau, "On a Fragment of the Oldest
Judaeo-Arabic Bible Translation Extant," in
J. Blau and S.C. Reif, eds., *Genizah Research after
Ninety Years: The Case of Judaeo-Arabic* (Cambridge,
1992), pp. 31-39. For an attempt to introduce
additional social and structural criteria, see
M. Polliack, "Arabic Bible Translations in the
Cairo Genizah Collection," in U. Haxen, et al.,
eds., *Proceedings of the EAJS Copenhagen Congress
1994* (Copenhagen, 1998), pp. 35-61.

[14] See *JQR* vol. 12, p. 481.

[15] See *Encyclopaedia Judaica* vol. 10, pp. 410-423 (quote from p. 410).

[16] See *Encyclopaedia of Islam* vol. 4, pp. 303-307 (quote from p. 303)

[17] See S.D. Goitein, *Jewish Education in Muslim Countries, Based on Records from the Cairo Geniza* (Jerusalem, 1962) [Hebrew].

[18] See, nevertheless, Goitein's survey on the literary activity in his *Jews and Arabs, Their Contacts through the Ages* (New York, 1974), pp. 125-211, and, cf., his Introduction to *A Mediterranean Society, The Jewish Communities of the Arab World as Portrayed in the Documents of the Cairo Geniza* (Berkley, Los Angeles, and London, 1967), vol. 1.

[19] With regard to these collections see note 4 (above) and 26 (below). With regard to the Arabic and Judaeo-Arabic sources in the Cairo Genizah Collections, see G. Khan, "The Arabic Fragments in the Cambridge Genizah Collections," in *Manuscripts of the Middle East* 1 (1986), pp. 54-61; C.F. Baker, "Judaeo-Arabic Material in the Cambridge Genizah Collections," in *BSOAS* 58 (1995), pp. 445-454; M. Polliack, "Arabic Bible translations," pp. 35-61 and in following.

[20] See Webster's Third Dictionary.

[21] See M.H. Abrahams, *A Glossary of Literary Terms* (New York, 1981), p. 71; for an illuminating survey of the concept of genre in folklore, literary, linguistic and rhetoric studies see J.M. Swales, *Genre Analysis* (Cambridge, 1990), pp. 33-44.

[22] For examples of such letters, see S.D. Goitein, *Jewish Education in Muslim Countries*, pp. 20, 46.

[23] See his article, "The Origin of Genres," in *New Literary History* 8 (1976), pp. 161-162, and his discussion of genres as "classes of texts" on the same pages. For further elaboration, see T. Todorov, *Le genres du discours* (Paris, 1978), pp. 44-59. Also, cf., Swales, *Genre Analysis*, pp. 36-38.

[24] The search for a socio-rhetorical model in evaluating Judaeo-Arabic literature may be paralleled to attempts already undertaken to provide an alternative model for the linguistic description of Judaeo-Arabic (see above).

[25] For further information on the Cambridge Genizah Collections and the background to their discovery, see S.D. Goitein, *Mediterranean Society*, vol. 1, pp. 1-6; C. Reif, *A Guide to the Taylor Schechter Genizah Collection* (Cambridge, 1973); "The Genizah Fragments, A Unique Archive?" in P. Fox, ed., *Cambridge University Library: The Great Collections* (Cambridge, 1998); *A Jewish Archive From Old Cairo, The History of Cambridge University's Genizah Collection* (London, 2000).

[26] In addition to the Judaeo-Arabic material, the Cambridge Genizah Collections contain some 7,000 fragments in Arabic script that did not reach the Ben-Ezra loft by design but by accident; see G. Khan, "The Arabic Fragments."

[27] Some ten percent of these are in Arabic script. This classified corpus constitutes around a fifth of the Arabic material (in both scripts) preserved in the Cambridge Genizah Collections as a whole.

[28] See C.F. Baker and M. Polliack, eds., *Arabic and Judaeo-Arabic Manuscripts in the Cambridge Genizah Collections, Arabic Old Series (T-S Ar. 1a-54)* (Cambridge, 2001). On the nature of the classification process undertaken in this project, see my introduction to the volume (pp. ix-xxii). The detailed subject index appended to the volume further illustrates the complex typology of Judaeo-Arabic literature.

[29] See note 4 above.

[30] In the following categories are mentioned various Judaeo-Arabic works by medieval authors. Examples of Genizah fragments containing these works may be traced through the index of *Medieval and Classical Authors and their Works*, appended to Baker and Polliack, pp. 561-571. For modern editions of these works (when available), refer to the *Bibliography and Short Title Index* appended to the same volume, pp. 551-561.

[31] Around twenty percent of the fragments in the classified Genizah Corpus belong to this category.

[32] See further in M. Zucker, *Rav Saadya Gaon's Translation of the Torah: Exegesis, Halakha, and Polemics in R. Saadya's Translation of the Pentateuch* (New York, 1959) [Hebrew]; M. Polliack, *The Karaite Tradition of Arabic Bible Translation, A Linguistic and Exegetical Study of Karaite Translations of the Pentateuch from the Tenth to the Eleventh Centuries* (Leiden, 1997), pp. 77-90, and the additional references there.

[33] Further on Karaite translation methods, see M. Polliack, ibid.; "Medieval Karaite Views on Translating the Hebrew Bible into Arabic," in *JJS* 47 (1996), pp. 64-84; "Medieval Karaite Methods of Translating Biblical Narrative into Arabic," in *Vetus Testamentum* 48 (1998), pp. 375-398).

[34] For further details on each of these categories see M. Polliack, "Arabic Bible Translations."

[35] See, for example, M. Polliack and S. Somekh, "Two Hebrew-Arabic Biblical Glossaries from the Cairo Genizah" in *Pe'amim* 83 (2000), pp. 15-47 [Hebrew].

[36] See, for instance, D. Frank, "Karaite Exegesis," in Magne Saebo, ed., *Hebrew Bible/Old Testament: The History of Its Interpretation* (Gottingen, 2001), vol. I/2, pp. 110-128; G. Khan, ed., *Exegesis and Grammar in Medieval Karaite Texts* (Oxford, 2001); M. Polliack, "The Emergence of Karaite Bible Exegesis," in *Sefunot* 22 (1999), pp. 299-311) [Hebrew]; "On the Question of the Pesher's Influence on Karaite Exegesis," in G. Brin and B. Nizan, eds., *Fifty Years of Dead Sea Scrolls Research* (Jerusalem, 2001), pp. 275-294 [Hebrew]. For the Gaonic milieu, cf., especially D.E. Sklare, *Samuel ben Hofni Gaon and*

His Cultural World. Texts and Studies (Leiden, 1996).

[37] Around 400 fragments in the classified Genizah corpus (some five percent) belong to this category.

[38] See especially two recent works by Geoffrey Khan, *The Early Karaite Tradition of Hebrew Grammatical Thought, Including a Critical Edition, Translation and Analysis of the Diqduq of Abû Ya'qûb Yûsuf ibn Nûḥ on the Hagiographia* (Leiden, 2000) and *Early Karaite Grammatical Texts* (Atlanta, 2001). Also of relevance are his previous studies devoted to the Karaites' practice of transcribing the biblical text into Arabic characters, which reflects their wish to preserve the accurate reading tradition of the biblical text. See G. Khan, *Karaite Bible Manuscripts from the Cairo Genizah* (Cambridge, 1990); "The Medieval Karaite Transcriptions of Hebrew into Arabic Script," in *IOS* 12 (1992), pp. 157-176.

[39] See G. Khan *The Early Karaite Tradition*, pp. 9-21, 132-133.

[40] Ibid., pp. 14-15.

[41] On the differences between the early tradition and the work of later Karaite grammarians of the eleventh century, such as Abû al-Faraj Harûn, who were more deeply affected by the Arabic grammatical tradition (especially that of the Basran school), see G. Khan "'Abu al-Faraj Haran and the Early Karaite Grammatical Tradition," in *JJS* 48 (1997), pp. 314-334; N. Basal, "Excerpts from the Abridgment (*al-Mukhtaṣar*) of al-Kitâb al-Kâfî by Abû Farağ Harûn in Arabic Script," in *Israel Oriental Studies* 17 (1997), pp. 197-225 (Hebrew).

[42] For a concentrated and updated bibliographical survey of recent research on Karaism and Karaite literature (including Judaeo-Arabic texts), see D. Frank, "The Study of Medieval Karaism," in N. De Lange, ed., *Hebrew Scholarship and the Medieval World: Studies in Honour of Raphael Loewe* (Cambridge, 2001), pp. 3-22.

[43] Around fifteen percent of the fragments in the classified Genizah corpus belong to this category.

[44] Around five percent (some 200 fragments) in the classified Genizah corpus belong to this category.

[45] See H. Ben-Shammai, "Judaeo-Arabic Abraham Story of Muslim Origin—New Fragments," in *Hebrew and Arabic Studies in Honour of Joshua Blau* (Jerusalem, 1993), pp. 111-134 [Hebrew].

[46] Around 400 fragments (some five percent) of the classified Genizah corpus belong to this category.

[47] Around 800 fragments in the classified Genizah Corpus belong to this category.

[48] On this phenomenon in Saadiah's writings, see H. Ben-Shammai, "The Exegetical and Philosophical Writing of Saadya Gaon: A Leader's Endeavor," in *Pe'amim* 54 (1993), pp. 63-81 [Hebrew].

[49] See the detailed introduction to H.D. Isaacs, ed., *Medical and Para-Medical Manuscripts in the Cambridge Genizah Collection* (Cambridge, 1994).

[50] Altogether around 200 fragments (some 2 percent) of the scientific and quasi-scientific type have been identified in the classified Genizah corpus.

[51] On the "almost universal presence of Hebrew elements" in Judaeo-Arabic writings and their dependence upon the "personal style of the author, upon literary genre, and upon the presupposed Hebrew (and Aramaic) knowledge of the intended audience," see Blau, *Emergence*, pp. 44-47. Nevertheless, the inclusion of generic criteria as part of the actual language definition of Judaeo-Arabic is not addressed in Blau's discussion.

[52] According to B. Malinowski's work on folklore and genre (see *A Scientific Theory of Culture and Other Essays*, New York, 1960), "genres contribute to the maintenance of social groups because they serve social and spiritual needs" (see Swales, *Genre Analysis*, p. 35). In this respect, genres that derive from an educational communicative setting may also contribute to the survival of their social groups.

[53] For further details, see Goitein, *A Mediterranean Society*, vol. 2, chapter 4: "Education and the Professional Class," pp. 171-211.

[54] See Todorov, "Origin of Genres," p. 161. Also consider the common root of the forms "genre" and "generation," traced to the Latin noun "genus"—meaning, birth, species, or type, and the Greek verb "gignomai"—meaning, to be born, to belong to a type. This etymology illustrates the conceptual connection between creativity and typology, i.e., between the individual transformative process of creating something new and the presubjection of any novel form to a wider distinctive type.

[55] For an attempt to explain the transference of literary models from Arabic into Hebrew, see R. Drory, *The Emergence of Jewish-Arabic Literary Contacts at the Beginning of the Tenth Century* (Tel-Aviv, 1988) (Hebrew).

[56] In this respect, Judaeo-Arabic belongs to the group of Jewish languages, including Judaeo-Spanish (Ladino) and Judaeo-German (Yiddish), that functioned throughout lengthy periods and in defined geographical areas as live literary traditions and symbols of Jewish identity. On Judaeo-Arabic in relation to other Jewish languages, see Hary, *Multiglossia*, pp. 71-74, 103-111. On the term "trans-culturation" that designates transference on the combined levels of language and culture, in all that they entail, see J. Barr, *The Semantics of Biblical Language* (Oxford, 1961), p. 4.

MEIRA POLLIACK

N

NUMBERS IN JUDAISM: The book of Numbers is mediated to Judaism by Sifre to Numbers, ca. 300 C.E. Sifre to Numbers provides a miscellaneous reading of most of the book of Numbers, but examining the implicit propositions of the recurrent forms of the document yields a clear-cut purpose. The document follows no topical program; but it also is unlike Mekhilta Attributed to R. Ishmael because of its recurrent effort to prove a few fundamental points. True, these are general and not limited to a given set of cases or issues, so that the successive compositions that comprise Sifre to Numbers yield no propositional program. But the recurrent proofs of discrete propositions that time and again bear one and the same implication do accumulate and when we see what is implicit in the various explicit exercises, we find a clear-cut and rather rich message indeed.

The document as a whole through its fixed and recurrent formal preferences or literary structures makes two complementary points. [1] Reason unaided by Scripture produces uncertain propositions. [2] Reason operating within the limits of Scripture produces truth. These two principles are never articulated but left implicit in the systematic reading of most of the book of Numbers, verse by verse. The exegetical forms stand for a single proposition: the human mind joins God's mind when humanity receives and sets forth the Torah. The Torah opens the road into the mind of God, and our minds can lead us on that road, because our mind and God's mind are comparable. We share a common rationality. Only when we examine the rhetorical plan and then in search of the topical program reconsider the forms of the document does this propositional program emerge.

As with Sifra, therefore, Sifre to Numbers follows no topical program distinct from that of Scripture, which is systematically clarified, as we shall see in a sample of the document below. An interest in the relations to Scripture of the Mishnah and Tosefta, a concern with the dialectics characteristic of Sifra—these occur episodically, but scarcely define the document. Its topical program and order derive from Scripture. As with Sifra, here, too, the sole point of coherence for the discrete sentences or paragraphs derives from the base-verse of Scripture that is subject to commentary. At the same time, if we examine the incremental message, the cumulative effect of the formal traits of speech and thought revealed in the uniform rhetoric and syntax of the document, we may discern a propositional program that is implicit in the rhetoric and logic of the compilation. What is required here is the articulation of the general consequences of numerous specific exegetical exercises.

If our authorship met the sets of writers whose consensus stands behind Sifra and Sifre to Deuteronomy, the several groups would find it difficult to distinguish themselves, one from the next. For one principal point of emphasis we discern in our document takes an equally central role in the propositional, topical program of the other two compilations, Sifra and Sifre to Deuteronomy. It is the insistence on the principle that logic alone cannot suffice, and that all law must in the end derive from the written part of the Torah. The single sustained proposition of the several writings is that truth derives from Scripture, not from reason unaided by revelation. But a further proposition will attract our attention. By the very labor of explaining the meaning of verses of Scripture, the Rabbinic exegetes laid claim to participate in the work of revelation. And by distinguishing their contribution from the received text of the Torah, they announced their presence within the process of revelation. In these two ways the exegetes who made up Sifra and the two Sifre s announced not one but two fundamental propositions. The first is that God's revelation in the written Torah takes priority. The second is that man's reason in the exegesis of the written Torah enjoys full and legitimate place in the unfolding of the lessons of Sinai. No one can doubt that our authorship concurs on both principles.

The rhetorical form of both documents underlines the topical program contained in the first of the two propositions. For if I want to underline over and over again the priority of not proposition, hence reason, but process, hence the exegesis of Scripture, my best choice is an obvious one. Begin at all points with a verse of Scripture and demonstrate that only by starting with the word-choices and propositions of that verse of Scripture, all further progress of interpretation commences. But the second proposition, that man (then; now: men and women) has a place in the process of revealing the Torah of Sinai, comes to expression in the careful separation of the cited verse of the written Torah from the contribution of the contemporary exegete. In that formal preference too, the authorship made a major point and established—if implicitly— a central syllogism: God's will follows the rules of reason. Man can investigate the consequences of reason as expressed in God's will. Therefore man can join in the labor of exploring God's will in the Torah.

Consequently, the authorships of all three Midrash-compilations make their powerful case by their rhetorical program, which relies first and foremost on the citation and gloss of a verse of Scripture, as much as by their proposition and syllogism: only by Scripture does truth gain certainty. The appeal to Scripture, however, comes once the proposition is established, and that appeal then dictates the rhetoric and topic alike. Only when we know what question we bring to Scripture may we devise appropriate formal and programmatic policies for our Midrash-exegesis and Midrash-compilation alike. A second formal preference in all three documents, in addition to the exegetical form, makes the same point. The other form involves citation of a passage of the Mishnah followed by an extensive discourse on how the verse of Scripture that pertains to the topic of that Mishnah-passage must contribute its facts, revealed at Sinai, if we wish to know the truth. Reason alone, which is systematically tested through a sequence of propositions shown to fail, will not serve.

The rhetorical plan of Sifra and Sifre to Numbers and Sifre to Deuteronomy shows that the exegetes, while working verse by verse, in fact have brought a considerable program to the reading of the books of Leviticus, Numbers, and Deuteronomy, respectively. The authorships of Sifra and the two Sifre s share that program, when they cite a verse of Scripture and then a passage of the Mishnah. The proposition then in all three writings concerns the interplay of the Oral Torah, represented by the Mishnah, with the written Torah, represented by the book of Leviticus or Numbers or Deuteronomy. That question demanded, in their view, not an answer comprising mere generalities. They wished to show their results through details, masses of details, and, like the rigorous philosophers that they were, they furthermore argued essentially through an inductive procedure, amassing evidence that in its accumulation made the point at hand.

The syllogism about the priority of the revelation of the Written Torah in the search for truth is nowhere expressed in so many words, because the philosopher-exegetes of the Rabbinic world preferred to address an implicit syllogism and to pursue or to test that syllogism solely in a sequence of experiments on a small scale. The three authorships therefore find in the Mishnah and Tosefta a sizable laboratory for the testing of propositions. We have therefore to ask, "At what points do Sifra's and the two Sifres' authorships and those of the Mishnah and Tosefta share a common agenda of interests, and at what points does one compilation introduce problems, themes, or questions unknown to the other?"

The answers to these questions for the three Midrash-compilations are various. The one for Sifra will show that Sifra and Mishnah and Tosefta form two large concentric circles, sharing a considerable area in common. Sifra, however, exhibits interests peculiar to itself. On the criterion of common themes and interests, Mishnah and Tosefta and Sifra exhibit a remarkable unity. The authorships of the two Sifres in diverse measure join in that united front on a basic issue. The authorship of Sifre to

Numbers, for its part, took up a penta-teuchal book that in no way focuses upon the topics paramount, also, in the Mishnah and the Tosefta, in the way in which the book of Leviticus covers subjects that take a prominent position in the later law-codes. Consequently, we cannot find in Sifre to Numbers a counterpart to the stress on the matters we have located in Sifra. Still, the established polemic about the priority of Scripture over unaided reason does take its place. Accordingly, we can show that Sifra and the two Sifres join together in a single species of the genus, Midrash-compilation.

Let us now characterize the formal traits of Sifre to Numbers as a commentary, since, as noted at the outset, it is here that we identify the implicit propositional pro-gram of the document's compilers and the writers of the bulk of its compositions. These we have reduced to two classifica-tions, based on the point of origin of the verses that are catalogued or subjected to exegesis: exegesis of a verse in the book of Numbers in terms of the theme or problems of that verse, hence, intrinsic exegesis; exe-gesis of a verse in Numbers in terms of a theme or polemic not particular to that verse, hence, extrinsic exegesis.

The forms of extrinsic exegesis: The implicit message of the external category proves simple to define, since the several extrinsic classifications turn out to form a cogent polemic. Let me state the recurrent polemic of external exegesis.

THE SYLLOGISTIC COMPOSITION: Scripture supplies hard facts, which, prop-erly classified, generate syllogisms. By col-lecting and classifying facts of Scripture, therefore, we may produce firm laws of his-tory, society, and Israel's everyday life. The diverse compositions in which verses from various books of the Scriptures are com-piled in a list of evidence for a given propo-sition—whatever the character or purpose of that proposition—make that one point. And given their power and cogency, they make the point stick.

THE FALLIBILITY OF REASON UN-GUIDED BY SCRIPTURAL EXEGESIS: Scripture alone supplies reliable basis for speculation. Laws cannot be generated by reason or logic unguided by Scripture.

Efforts at classification and contrastive-ana-logical exegesis, in which Scripture does not supply the solution to all problems, prove few and far between. This polemic forms the obverse of the point above. So when extrinsic issues intervene in the exegetical process, they coalesce to make a single point. Let me state that point with appro-priate emphasis on the recurrent and im-plicit message of the forms of external exegesis: Scripture stands paramount; logic, reason, analytical processes of classification and differentiation, secondary. Reason not built on scriptural foundations yields uncer-tain results. The Mishnah itself demands scriptural bases.

THE FORMS OF INTRINSIC EXE-GESIS: What about the polemic present in the intrinsic exegetical exercises? This clear-ly does not allow for ready characterization. As we saw, at least three intrinsic exegetical exercises focus on the use of logic, spec-ifically, the logic of classification, compari-son and contrast of species of a genus, in the explanation of the meaning of verses of the book of Numbers. The internal dialec-tical mode, moving from point to point as logic dictates, underlines the main point already stated: logic produces possibilities, Scripture chooses among them. Again, the question, why is this passage stated? com-monly produces an answer generated by further verses of Scripture, e.g., this matter is stated here to clarify what otherwise would be confusion left in the wake of other verses. So Scripture produces problems of confusion and duplication, and Scripture—and not logic, not differentiation, not clas-sification—solves those problems.

To state matters simply: Scripture is complete, harmonious, perfect. Logic not only does not generate truth beyond the limits of Scripture but also plays no impor-tant role in the harmonization of difficulties yielded by what appear to be duplications or disharmonies. These forms of internal exegesis then make the same point that the extrinsic ones do.

In so stating, of course, we cover all but the single most profuse category of exegesis, which we have treated as simple and undifferentiated: [1] verse of Scripture or a clause, followed by [2] a brief statement of the meaning at hand. Here I see no unifying polemic in favor of, or against, a given proposition. The most common form also proves the least pointed: X bears this meaning, Y bears that meaning, or, as we have seen, citation of verse X, followed by [what this means is]. . . . Whether simple or elaborate, the upshot is the same. What can be at issue when no polemic expressed in the formal traits of syntax and logic finds its way to the surface? What do I do when I merely clarify a phrase? Or, to frame the question more logically: what premises must validate my *intervention*, that is, my willingness to undertake to explain the meaning of a verse of Scripture? These justify the labor of intrinsic exegesis as we have seen its results here:

[1] My independent judgment bears weight and produces meaning. I—that is, my mind—therefore may join in the process.

[2] God's revelation to Moses at Sinai requires my intervention. I have the role, and the right, to say what that revelation means.

[3] What validates my entry into the process of revelation is the correspondence between the logic of my mind and the logic of the document.

Only if I think in accord with the logic of the revealed Torah can my thought-processes join issue in clarifying what is at hand: the unfolding of God's will in the Torah. To state matters more accessibly: if the Torah does not make statements in accord with a syntax and a grammar that I know, I cannot so understand the Torah as to explain its meaning. But if I can join in the discourse of the Torah, it is because I speak the same language of thought: syntax and grammar at the deepest levels of my intellect.

[4] Then to state matters affirmatively and finally: Since a shared logic of syntax and grammar joins my mind to the mind of God as revealed in the Torah, I can say what a sentence of the Torah means. So I too can amplify, clarify, expand, revise, rework: that is to say, create a commentary. So the work of commenting upon the written Torah bears profound consequence for the revelation of the Torah, the sage becoming partner with God in the giving of the Torah. In that conclusion,

we find ourselves repeating the main point that Sifra yields in the description of Rabbinic literature as a whole.

What we see in Sifre's reading of Num. 7:1ff. is what we should by now expect: a systematic and close reading, verse by verse, with slight attention to issues of coherence and large-scale meaning: exegesis pure and simple.

SIFRE TO NUMBERS 44
XLIV:I.1.
A. "On the day when Moses had finished setting up the tabernacle [and had anointed and consecrated it with all its furnishings and had anointed and consecrated the altar with all its utensils, the leaders of Israel, heads of their fathers' houses, the leaders of the tribes, who were over those who were numbered, offered and brought their offerings before the Lord, six covered wagons and twelve oxen, a wagon for every two of the leaders, and for each one an ox, they offered them before the tabernacle. Then the Lord said to Moses, 'Accept these from them, that they may be used in doing the service of the tent of meeting, and give them to the Levites, to each man according to his service.' So Moses took the wagons and the oxen and gave them to the Levites]" (Num. 7:1-6):

B. Scripture indicates that for each of the seven days of consecrating the tabernacle, Moses would set up the tabernacle, and every morning he would anoint it and dismantle it. But on that day he set it up and anointed it, but he did not dismantle it. [On the prior days he set up the tabernacle and dismantled it. On the eighth day, he set it up but did not dismantle it.]

C. R. Yose b. R. Judah: "Also on the eighth day he set it up and dismantled it, for it is said, 'And in the first month in the second year on the first day of the month the tabernacle was erected' (Exod. 30:17). On the basis of that verse we learn that on the twenty-third day of Adar, Aaron and his sons, the tabernacle and the utensils were anointed."

XLV:I.2.
A. On the first day of the month the tabernacle was set up, on the second the red cow was burned [for the purification rite required at Num. 19], on the third day water was sprinkled from it in lieu of the second act of sprinkling, the Levites were shaved.

B. On that same day the Presence of God rested in the tabernacle, as it is said,

"Then the cloud covered the tent of meeting, and the glory of the Lord filled the tabernacle, and Moses was not able to enter the tent of meeting, because the cloud abode upon it" (Exod. 40:34).

C. On that same day the heads offered their offerings, as it is said, "He who offered his offering the first day..." (Num. 7:12). Scripture uses the word "first" only in a setting when "first" introduces all of the days of the year.

D. On that day fire came down from heaven and consumed the offerings, as it is said, "And fire came forth from before the Lord and consumed the burnt offering and the fat upon the altar" (Lev. 9:24).

E. On that day the sons of Aaron offered strange fire, as it is said, "Now Nadab and Abihu, the sons of Aaron, each took his censer and put fire in it...and offered unholy fire before the Lord, such as he had not commanded them" (Lev. 10:1).

F. "And they died before the Lord..." (Lev. 10:2): they died before the Lord, but they fell outside [of the tabernacle, not imparting corpse uncleanness to it].

G. How so? They were on their way out.

H. R. Yose says, "An angel sustained them, as they died, until they got out, and they fell in the courtyard, as it is said, 'And Moses called Mishael and Elzaphan, the sons of Uzziel the uncle of Aaron, and said to them, 'Draw near, carry your brethren from before the sanctuary out of the camp'" (Lev. 10:4). What is stated is not, 'From before the Lord," but, 'from before the sanctuary.'"

I. R. Ishmael says, "The context indicates the true state of affairs, as it is said, 'And they died before the Lord,' meaning, they died inside and fell inside. How did they get out? People dragged them with iron ropes."

The expansion and amplification of the base verse runs through No. 1. From that point, No. 2, we deal with the other events of that same day, surveying the several distinct narratives which deal with the same thing, Exod. 40, Lev. 9-10, and so on. This produces the effect of unifying the diverse scriptural accounts into one tale, an important and powerful exegetical result. One of the persistent contributions of our exegetes is to collect and harmonize a diversity of verses taken to refer to the same day, event, or rule.

XLIV:II.1.

A. "...and had anointed and consecrated it with all its furnishings and had anointed and consecrated the altar with all its utensils:"

B. Might I infer that as each utensil was anointed, it was sanctified?

C. Scripture says, "...and had anointed and consecrated it with all its furnishings and had anointed and consecrated the altar with all its utensils," meaning that not one of them was sanctified until all of them had been anointed. [The process proceeded by stages.]

XLIV:II.2.

A. "...and had anointed and consecrated it with all its furnishings and had anointed and consecrated the altar with all its utensils:"

B. The anointing was done both inside and outside [of the utensil].

C. R. Josiah says, "Utensils meant to hold liquids were anointed inside and outside, but utensils meant to hold dry stuffs were anointed on the inside but not anointed on the outside."

D. R. Jonathan says, "Utensils meant to hold liquids were anointed inside and not outside, but utensils meant to hold dry stuffs not anointed.

E. "You may know that they were not consecrated, for it is said, 'You shall bring from your dwellings two loaves of bread to be waved, made of two-tenths of an ephah' (Lev. 23:17). Then when do they belong to the Lord? Only after they are baked." [The bread was baked in utensils at home, so the utensils were not consecrated.]

XLIV:II.3.

A. Rabbi says, "Why is it said, '...and had anointed and consecrated it'? And is it not already stated, '...and had anointed and consecrated it'?

B. "This indicates that with the anointing of these utensils all future utensils were sanctified [so that the sanctification of the tabernacle enjoyed permanence and a future tabernacle or Temple did not require a rite of sanctification once again]."

No. 1 clarifies the rite of sanctification, aiming at the notion that the act of consecration covered everything at once, leading to the future conclusion, at the end, that that act also covered utensils later on to be used in the cult. No. 3 goes over that same ground. No. 2 deals with its own issue, pursuing the exegesis of the verse at hand. Its interest in the consecration of the utensils is entirely congruent with No. 3, because it wants to know the status of utensils outside of the cult, and, while they serve the purpose of the cult as specified, still, they are not deemed to have been consecrated.

SIFRE TO NUMBERS 45
XLV:I.1.

A. "[On the day when Moses had finished setting up the tabernacle and had anointed and consecrated it with all its furnishings and had anointed and consecrated the altar with all its utensils] the leaders of Israel [heads of their fathers' houses, the leaders of the tribes, who were over those who were numbered] offered [and brought their offerings before the Lord, six covered wagons and twelve oxen, a wagon for every two of the leaders, and for each one an ox, they offered them before the tabernacle. Then the Lord said to Moses, 'Accept these from them, that they may be used in doing the service of the tent of meeting, and give them to the Levites, to each man according to his service.' So Moses took the wagons and the oxen and gave them to the Levites]" (Num. 7:1-6):

B. May I infer that they had been ordinary people who were elevated.

C. Scripture says, "heads of their fathers' houses."

D. And they were not merely, "heads of their fathers' houses," but also "the leaders of the tribes, who were over those who were numbered.'"

E. They were leaders, sons of leaders.

XLV:I.2.

A. "... the leaders of the tribes, who were over those who were numbered:"

B. They were the same ones who had been appointed over them in Egypt, as it is said, "And the leaders of the children of Israel smote ..." (Exod. 5:14).

The interest is in showing the distinguished origins of the Israelite leadership.

XLV:II.1.

A. "... six covered wagons [and twelve oxen, a wagon for every two of the leaders, and for each one an ox, they offered them before the tabernacle]:"

B. The word "covered" means only "decorated," for they lacked for nothing.

C. Rabbi says, "The word 'covered' means only 'canopied,' and even though there is no firm proof for that proposition, there is at least some indication of it: 'And they shall bring all your brethren from all the nations as an offering to the Lord, upon horses and in chariots and in litters and upon mules and upon dromedaries to my holy mountain, Jerusalem, says the Lord' (Is. 66:20)."

XLV:II.2.

A. "... six covered wagons and twelve oxen, a wagon for every two of the leaders, and for each one an ox, they offered them before the tabernacle.

B. May I infer that there was a wagon for each one?

C. Scripture says, "... a wagon for every two of the leaders."

D. May I infer there was an ox for every two of the leaders?

E. Scripture says, "... and for each one an ox."

XLV:II.3.

A. They came and took up positions before the tabernacle, but Moses did not accept anything from them, until it was stated to him by the mouth of the Holy One, "Accept these from them, that they may be used in doing the service of the tent of meeting."

B. Lo, mortals thus brought their judgment into accord with the judgment on high.

XLV:II.4.

A. R. Nathan says, "And why in the present matter did the princes bring voluntary gifts first [rather than waiting for the community to do so], while in the work of the making of the tabernacle they in fact did not volunteer to begin with [but let the community give and only afterward they made their contribution]?

B. "Well, this is how the leaders had earlier reasoned matters out: 'Let the community contribute what they will, and what is still needed after they have given we shall make up.'

C. "When the princes realized that the community had provided all that was needed, as it is said, 'And the work was sufficient' (Exod. 34:4), the princes said, 'What is left for us to do?'

D. "So the princes brought the precious stones for the ephod.

E. "That is why, in the present case, the princes brought their voluntary offering first [so as not to be left out]."

No. 1 provides the explanation of a word, and No. 2 proceeds to a phrase. No. 3 restates what the text says and explains the implications of the matter, and No. 4 draws into relationship two distinct accounts of gifts to the sanctuary, explaining in a striking way the difference in the detail of the two pictures.

SIFRE TO NUMBERS 46

XLVI:I.1.

A. "So Moses took the wagons and the oxen and gave them to the Levites" (Num. 7:1-6):
B. Lo, Moses took them and divided them up on his own initiative.

XLVI:I.2.

A. "The two wagons and the four oxen he gave to the sons of Gershom, and the four wagons and the eight oxen he gave to the sons of Merari,"
B. Because Eleazar had sixteen sons, and Ithamar, eight.
C. As it is said, "The male heads of families proved to be more numerous in the line of Eleazar than in that of Ithamar, so that sixteen heads of families were grouped under the line of Eleazar and eight under that of Ithamar. He organized them by drawing lots among them, for there were sacred officers and offices of God in the line of Eleazar and in that of Ithamar" (1 Chr. 24:4-6).

No. 1 draws its own conclusions from the cited verse, and No. 2 proceeds to relate the present division to the materials available elsewhere, a common exegetical interest.

XLVI:II.1.

A. "He gave none to the Kohathites, because the service laid upon them was that of the holy things: these they had to carry themselves on their shoulders" (Num. 7:9):
B. R. Nathan, "On the basis of what is said here we see what David missed, for the Levites did not bear the ark, but they bore the wagon, as it is said, 'They mounted the ark of God on a new cart and conveyed it from the house of Abinadab on the hill' (1 Sam. 6:3).
C. "'The Lord was angry with Uzzah and struck him down there for his rash act, so he died there beside the ark of God' (2 Sam. 6:7).
D. "'David was vexed because the Lord's anger had broken out upon Uzzah, and he called the place Perez-uzzah, the name it still bears' (2 Sam 6:8).
E. "Ahitophel said to David, 'Should you not have learned the lesson of Moses, your master, for the Levites bore the ark only on their shoulders, as it says, "He gave none to the Kohathites, because the service laid upon them was that of the holy things: these they had to carry themselves on their shoulders."'

F. "Lo, David then sent and had it carried by shoulder, as it is said, 'And David summoned Zadok and Abiathar the priests, together with the Levites, Uriel, Asaiah, Joel, Shemaiah, Eliel, and Amminadab, and said to them, You who are heads of families of the Levites, hallow yourselves, you and your kinsmen, and bring up the ark of the Lord, the God of Israel, to the place which I have prepared for it . . . So the priests and the Levites hallowed themselves to bring up the ark of the Lord, the God of Israel, and the Levites carried the ark of God, bearing it on their shoulders with poles, as Moses had prescribed at the command of the Lord' (1 Chr. 15:11-15)."

XLVI:II.2.

A. "This was their order of duty for the discharge of their service when they entered the house of the Lord, according to the rule prescribed for them by their ancestor Aaron, who had received his instructions from the Lord, the God of Israel" (1 Chr. 24:19):
B. Where did he give a commandment? He gave nothing at all to the sons of Kohath. So lo, the sons of the Levites in no way innovated, but everything was done on the instructions of Moses, and Moses did everything at the instructions of the Almighty.

No. 1 is important in underlining David's error in not following the precedent established here by Moses and the Levites, carrying the ark not on the wagon but on their shoulders. David then corrected himself, following the proper precedent. No. 2 then underlines the matter that the precedent of the base verse guided the Levites later on. What we see then is a harmonization of diverse materials on the same important theme.

SIFRE TO NUMBERS 47

XLVII:I.1.

A. "And the leaders presented offerings for the dedication of the altar [on the day it was anointed; and the leaders offered their offering before the altar. And the Lord said to Moses, 'They shall offer their offerings, one leader each day, for the dedication of the altar.' He who offered his offering the first day was Nahshon the son of Amminadab of the tribe of Judah; and his offering was one silver plate whose weight was a hundred and thirty shekels, one silver basin of seventy shekels according to the shekel of the sanctuary, both of them full of fine flour mixed with oil for a cereal offering; one golden dish of ten shekels, full of incense; one young bull, one ram, one male lamb a year old, for a burnt offering; one male goat for a sin offering; and for the sacrifice of peace offerings, two oxen, five rams, five male goats, and five male lambs a year old. This was the offering of Nahshon the son of Amminadab]" (Num. 7:10-17):

B. The Scripture thus indicates that just as the princes made voluntary gifts for the work of building the tabernacle, so they did for the dedication of the tabernacle.

XLVII:I.2.

A. "And the leaders offered offerings for the dedication of the altar . . . and the leaders offered their offering before the altar:"

B. They came and stood before the altar, but Moses did not accept the offerings from them, until he was so instructed by the word of the Holy One: "Let them make their offerings for the dedication of the altar."

C. Moses still did not know the proper manner in which they were to make their offerings, whether by the order dictated for the journeys, whether by the order dictated by the generations in which the tribal founders had been born, until he was instructed by the explicit statement of the Holy One, blessed be he, "Let them offer in accord with the order governing their journeys," as it is said, "And it came to pass." For the words "and it came to pass" indicate solely what was said to Moses on the authority of the Holy One, so they offered in accord with the order governing their journeys.

D. But Moses still did not know how the princes were to make their offerings, specifically, whether it was to be done all at once, or each one on his own day, until he was so instructed that each was to offer on his own day, as it is said, "They shall offer their offerings, one leader each day, for the dedication of the altar."

E. The princes make voluntary offerings, but ordinary people do not do so. Why then does Scripture say, "'They shall offer their offerings, one leader each day, for the dedication of the altar" [specifying that the princes did it, when we know that only they could do it]

F. It was because Nahshon was a king, and he made the offering first. So people should not say, "Lo, because I made the offering first, I shall make an offering with everyone else, day by day. Therefore it is said, "'They shall offer their offerings, one leader each day, for the dedication of the altar.'"

We begin with the simple clarification of the donation of the princes: not only for building the tabernacle but also for dedicating the altar. Then, No. 2, we underline that each detail of the process of dedication was dictated by divine instructions. This would underline the polemic that the original work of sanctification imparted to the cult an indelible character of holiness. It is difficult to find a single point that does not begin in the amplification of the statements of Scripture.

JACOB NEUSNER

P

PARENTS, HONOR OF IN JUDAISM: Four short normative texts relevant to our discussion appear in the Torah: "Honor your father and your mother" (Exod. 20:12; Deut. 5:16); "Every one of you shall revere his mother and his father" (Lev. 19:3); "He who curses his father or his mother shall be put to death" (Exod. 21:17; see Lev. 20:9); and "He who strikes his father or his mother shall be put to death"

(Exod. 21:15). Despite the texts' dispersion throughout the Torah, they seemingly make a similar point, that honoring one's parents consists of reverence, and this reverence is derived from honor. Consequently, cursing that detracts from the honor and reverence of one's parents is forbidden, and striking them is certainly prohibited. Interestingly, every Israelite is similarly commanded to honor, revere, and not to curse the Lord.

Thus we find: "Honor the Lord with your wealth" (Prov. 3:9);[1] "You must revere the Lord your God" (Deut. 10:20); and "Whoever curses his God shall bear his sin" (Lev. 24:15).

The norms of honoring and revering one's parents, of not cursing them, and the punishing of the child who strikes them all have a common basis, the necessity of imposing parental authority upon sons and daughters.[2] This is just as the commandments to honor the Lord, to revere him, and not to curse him all originate in the biblical ideal of the believer's submission before the omnipotent Lord. Consequently, according to this worldview, the honor due one's parents and obedience to them does not serve the egotistical interest of the minor and his welfare (that present-day legal systems term "the good of the child"), just as, in the eyes of Judaism, the obligation of *Qiddush Hashem* (sanctifying the divine name) and the obligation of honoring the Lord were not intended specifically to benefit believers. And in the same manner that the individual must believe in God and adhere to his ways, "even if he takes away your soul,"[3] and is not permitted to flee from his obligations to honor him, revere him, and refrain from cursing him, since "his presence fills all the earth" (Is. 6:3), he is not free to evade the honor and reverence of his parents nor to curse or strike them, even if they patently do not have his good in mind.

This equation of a person's obligations to God and to his parents has been discussed by Jewish religious authorities throughout the ages. Of special interest is the question, just what is the meaning of "honoring one's father and mother"? Is this in accordance with an objective criterion, just as every believer honors God as mandated by the halakhah and its fixed ritual, or does this correspond to the parents' own subjective judgment of what constitutes honor? And, as a general rule, since the parents are subordinate to God, is the child permitted not to honor them if they are, for instance, Sabbath violators, *mumarim le-tayavon* (rebels against Jewish law on account of an irresistible appetite), or *mumarim le-hakhis* (rebels in a spirit of defiance), even if they do not tell their children to do anything counter to Judaism? Or, possibly, are the children obligated to honor them and do as they wish only when they do not seek to reject the observance of any commandment? Tannaitic sources, further, define honoring one's parents as providing them "food, drink, and a clean garment" (B. Qid. 32a; Y. Pe. 1:1). This gives rise to the question of whether or not children are obligated to maintain parents from their own resources, and to what extent. Does the obligation to honor one's parents more than other people, including oneself, require a son, for instance, to maintain them even if he does not have the means to provide for his wife and minor children? In the following, we deal with these several issues on the basis of Judaism's halakhic sources.

Is the obligation of honoring one's parents enforceable? A tannaitic statement cited at B. Hul. 110b and 142a (a textual variant appears at Y. B.B. 5:5) teaches: "Every positive commandment that bears its reward by its side does not fall within the jurisdiction of the earthly court." According to the Talmuds, the commandments that "bear their reward by their side" are: the commandment of honoring one's parents (B. Hul. 110b), regarding which Scripture states: "that you may long endure, and that you may fare well, in the land that the Lord your God is giving you" (Deut. 5:16; see also Exod. 20:11); the commandment of letting the mother bird go from the nest (B. Hul. 142a), as the verse mandates: "Let the mother go, and take only the young, in order that you may fare well and have a long life" (Deut. 22:7); and the commandment to measure and weigh (Y. B.B. 5:5) with "completely honest weights and completely honest measures, if you are to endure long on the soil that the Lord your God is giving you" (Deut. 25:15).

Other commandments deemed by the Rabbinic literature to bear their reward by their side, and whose observance cannot be enforced by the court, are: the returning of a pledge,[4] as it is written: "you must return the pledge to him at sundown, that he may sleep in his cloth and bless you; and it will be to your merit before the Lord your God" (Deut. 24:13); and the commandment of charity, as it is said: "Give to him readily and have no regrets when you do so, for in return the Lord your God will bless you in all your efforts and in all your undertakings" (Deut. 15:10). Notwithstanding this, regarding the commandment of *mezuzah*, concerning which it is said: "to the end that you and your children may endure, in the land . . ., as long as there is a heaven over the earth" (Deut. 11:21), *Minhat Hinukh* states "that we have never heard nor seen in the decisors of Jewish law that *mezuzah* is not enforced because it bears its reward by its side."[5]

The Talmuds themselves do not explain the absence of an obligation to compel the recalcitrant to observe these commandments. Rashi, however, argues[6] that "bearing its reward" means that "if you do not observe it, this is its punishment, that you shall not take this reward." It would seem, according to his interpretation, that the court or any individual in Israel is enjoined from enforcing the observance of these commandments.

The Tosafists, however, question how, if it is so that a positive commandment that "bears its reward by its side" is not enforced, we find at B. B.B. 8b that Rabbah "compelled Rav Nathan b. Ammi to give four hundred *zuz* to charity"?[7] Several answers appear in the name of the Tosafists.[8] The first of two resolutions offered in the name of Rabbenu Tam holds that the incident involved only compulsion through words and not any court action. This understanding was rejected by medieval authorities as based on an unreasonable assumption.[9] The second answer in Rabbenu Tam's name asserts that the compulsion was by the charity official and so was acceptable. This answer seems forced, since it limits the compulsive ability of most townspeople. Another answer is cited in the name of Rabbenu Isaac of Dampiere: "As regards charity, compulsion is applied, because it is written concerning it: 'do not harden your heart and shut your hand' (Deut. 15:7)." This answer seems equally unconvincing, since the other commandments in this category similarly are enjoined by Scripture and yet are not subject to compulsion. A different answer is offered in the name of Isaac ben Abraham (*Rizba*):

> Here, the court is not enjoined concerning a commandment that bears its reward by its side, that is, punishment is not delivered. . . . This means you are not enjoined to compel him until he complies, as [you are enjoined] regarding other positive commandments; for if one is told, "Perform [the commandment of] *sukkah* and the *lulav* [i.e., the taking of the Four Species on Sukkot]," and he does not do so, he is lashed until he expires.

This interpretation requires further explanation. *Rizba*, in contrast with Rashi, holds there is nothing preventing the court from enforcing the observance of a positive commandment "that bears its reward by its side." In this, it is like the other positive commandments in the Torah. But, according to him, as regards a positive commandment "that bears its reward by its side," the application of compulsive authority is at the court's discretion; the court is not obligated to use this authority, as it is in the case of other positive commandments. We must, therefore, examine why the court is not enjoined to punish one who refrains from giving charity, as it is mandated to compel one who refrains from performing other positive commandments.

Study of other commandments that bear their reward by their side reveals arguments both favoring and opposing the obligation to compel their performance. Thus, B. Hul. 10a-b relates that the commandment of honoring one's parents is a positive commandment "that bears its reward by its side," so that when a man was brought in to the court for not honoring his parents and bound up to be whipped, Hisda instructed the court to let him go. Y. Pe. 1:1, on the other hand, cites different traditions in the name of Yannai and Jonathan that a son is forced to support his father,[10] and Yose of the school of Bun states there: "Would that every tradition were as clear to me as this one, that the son is compelled to support his father." And supporting one's father is included in the commandment of honoring him.

When is a "positive commandment that bears its reward by its side" not enforced? Several of the later authorities have discussed the inconsistency between the absolute rule that exempts the court from enforcing any "positive commandment that bears its reward by its side," on the one hand, and, on the other, the detailed halakhot that indicate the frequency with which the recalcitrant individual was in fact compelled. While they resolved these seemingly contradictory texts in various ways,[11] it appears, in our opinion, that the exemption from enforcing these commandments is not freestanding but, rather, ensues from the nature of the commandments themselves, which differs from that of the other positive commandments in the Torah. This is insofar as the scope of the obligation to honor one's parents or to send the mother bird from its young cannot be objectively assessed and varies from one individual to another, in accordance with the circumstances. It thus is at the discretion of the one performing the commandment.

Thus, regarding the commandment of honoring one's parents, defined in the sources as a "most stringent" commandment,[12] Y. Pe. 1:1 (with a textual variation at B. Qid. 31a-b) elaborates:

> There are some instances in which a person feeds his father fat [chickens] but is destined for Gehenna, and there are other instances in which he yokes him to a millstone but is destined for heaven. How so? A person would feed his father fattened chickens. Once his father asked him: "My son, where did you get these [fine ones]?" He replied, "Old one, old one, eat and care not, for dogs eat and care not." Consequently, he feeds his father fattened [chickens], but is destined for Gehenna. . . . Another person was grinding in a mill, when an order came to grind [at the royal mill]. [The son] said [to his father]: "Father, assume the yoke of the milling in my place. [Thus], should we [at the royal mill] come to be dishonored], it would be better that I, and not you, [be so disgraced]." . . . Consequently, he yokes him to a millstone but is destined for heaven.

Fulfillment of the commandment of honoring one's parents thus depends in great measure on intentions and attitudes rather than actions. It consequently is not *incumbent* upon the court to determine who has violated the law and to punish that person. When, however, it is clear to the court, by objective criteria, that a violation has occurred, for example, if a father demands food and a son does not support him, the court is mandated to compel the son to provide for his father.[13]

The same applies to the sending of a bird forth from the nest, which the Talmuds deem an "extremely minor" commandment (Y. Pe. 1:1, M. Hul. 12:5). One who refuses to send a mother bird forth is not compelled, for at any moment he could change his mind and do so. If, however, he slaughtered the mother without sending her forth, he has transgressed the negative commandment "do not take the mother together with her young," and he is punished with lashes, like all who transgress such a prohibition (M. Hul. 12:4; B. Hul. 141b). Accordingly, if a person neither sent the mother from the nest nor slaughtered her, the court is not enjoined to punish him with lashes. If, however, a person finds a birds' nest and patently refrains from observing the commandment according to its plain intent, for example, if he tears off the bird's wings so that it cannot fly away even if he were later to send it forth, this, according to Judah, is sufficient reason to administer lashes and order him to wait until the mother's feathers grow back so that he can send her away.[14]

The commandment of proper measures and weights is similar. The Amoraim distinguished between measures that are fixed and known to all and measures that change from one day to the next, in accordance with conditions in the marketplace. An official must be appointed over the former, to supervise and enforce their correct maintenance. But the latter cannot be so enforced, and so the court is not obliged to attempt to do so.[15]

The commandment of honoring one's parents according to their subjective judgment: "Honoring," as defined by Jewish law, is "feeding and giving drink, clothing and covering, bringing in and taking out," while "fear" is "not to stand in his place, not to sit in his place, not to contradict his words, nor tip the scales against him" (B. Qid. 32a; Y. Pe. 1:1). The Talmuds stress the subjective nature of these obligations, insofar as honoring and fearing might include compliance with strange demand that accord with parents' subjective judgment. Thus the Talmud asks: "Has [the father] then thrown a purse before you into the sea without your shaming him" (B. Qid. 32a; Y. Pe. 1:1); and the rabbis in B. Qid. 31a praise Dama son of Nethinah (a non-Jew, whose conduct towards his father the rabbis viewed as paradigmatic) who "was once wearing a silken cloak with gold embroidery and sitting among Roman nobles. His mother came, tore it off him, struck him on the head, and spat in his face, yet he did not shame her."[16] The Talmudic sources contain narratives that describe the subjective nature of the commandment to honor one's parents. Thus Y. Pe. 1:1 speaks of the mother of Ishmael, who complained that her son did not treat her with honor, since he did not allow her to wash his feet and then drink the water. His colleagues told Ishmael, "Since this is her desire, this is her honor."

Y. Pe. 1:1 also tells of non-Jews who observed the commandment of honoring parents to excess, such as a non-Jew from Ashkelon "who was the chief of the magistrates and never sat on the stone on which his father had sat. When his father died, he turned it into an object of veneration." This commandment of honoring one's parent was regarded by the Tannaim and Amoraim as so individualistic that several Amoraim prided themselves on not having seen their parents, because they assumed that if they had seen them, they would never have been able to fully understand the latter's wishes, and therefore would have failed properly honor to them.[17] Needless to say, the obligation of honoring one's parents continues the entire life of the father and mother and, in certain respects, even after their death.[18] Only a married woman who "is not free to engage in this because others have authority over her" (T. Qid. 1:11; Y. Pe. 1:1) is exempt from the honor and fear due her parents. If, however, she is divorced or widowed, this obligation arises once again.[19]

From whose resources are parents to be maintained? In B. Qid. 31b-32b the Amoraim discuss whether a father is to be given food and drink from his property or from that of his son. Proofs are provided for each position, and no decision is reached. One proofs cited is a *baraita*:

> It is said, "Honor your father and your mother" (Exod. 20:12), and it is said, "Honor the Lord with your wealth" (Prov. 3:9): just as the latter means at monetary loss, so, too, the former is at monetary loss. But if you were to say, "At the father's [expense]," what loss is there for him?

The Talmud rejects this objection, because there still is a loss for the son: "Lost [time from] work." In my opinion, however, a *baraita* at Y. Pe. 1:1 implies that the obligation to honor one's parents is to be filled specifically from the son's property:

> R. Simeon b. Yohai says: Great is honoring one's father and mother, for the Holy One, blessed be He, preferred it to his own honor, as it is said: "Honor your father and your mother," and it is said, "Honor the Lord with your wealth." With what do you honor him? With what he graciously endows you. One sets aside the gifts to the poor from one's field; one sets aside heave-offering, first tithe, second tithe, poor man's tithe, and dough-offering; he performs [the commandments of] *sukkah*, *lulav*, the [blowing of the] ram's horn [on Rosh Hashanah], *tefilin*, *tzitzit*, and feeds the poor and the hungry, and gives the thirsty to drink—if you have [the means], you are obligated for them all, and if you do not have, you are not obligated for any of them. When, however, one is confronted with honoring one's father and mother, whether you have wealth or whether you do not, "Honor your father and your mother," even if you must beg.

The early talmudic commentators, such as Yom Tov ben Abraham Ishbili in his novellae, and Asher ben Jehiel in his *Tosafot* and halakhic rulings, resolve the dictum of Simeon bar Yohai in other fashions, such as: "Not that he must give him of his money, and beg, rather, he honors him with his body [i.e., personally engages in this] at the expense of his work, thereby resulting in his having to beg." The forced nature of this explanation is obvious and is not consistent with the plain meaning of the passage in Y. Peah. We may also conclude from the silence of the Tosafists in Qiddushin and of Meir ben Isaac Arama in his commentary there, who cites this passage from Y. Peah without resolving it with the passage in B. Qiddushin, that these authorities did not see fit to resolve the dictum of Simeon bar Yohai in this manner.

If we follow the view of the Yerushalmi that a child is obligated to provide for a parent from the child's property, this obligation takes precedence over the maintenance of young children, for, according to the Yerushalmi, the obligation of sustaining the parents applies regardless of whether the child has wealth or not and must be fulfilled to the satisfaction of the parent; providing for small children, by contrast, accords with the ability of the provider: if he is wealthy, he must give in accordance with his abilities; if not, he need not beg. Even, however, halakhic authorities such as the author of She'iltot and several of the Tosafists[20] who follow the orientation of the Bavli and obligate a son to maintain his father "from that of the father" emphasize that, "if the father has no money and the son does," the son must provide for his parents from his own property, for the right of the father to receive charity from his son is not inferior to that of any other person.

A woman is exempt from honoring and fearing her parents if "others have authority over her," and this exemption includes supporting her father and mother. This is because her husband's authority over her includes his ability to prevent her from giving her handiwork to her parents. This is similar to a married woman's exemption from providing for her children in any instance, even when their father has no resources or no interest in sustaining them. If she is not under the authority of others, however, a great difference separates the mother's obligation to provide for her children and to maintain her parents. While she remains exempt from providing for her sons and daughters, her obligation to honor and fear or parents again applies. She consequently must provide for her father and her mother, whether she has wealth or not, and even if she is required to beg.

Limitations on the obligation to honor one's father and mother: Understanding that the halakhah defines the obligation to honor one's parents as subjective, following the judgment of the parents, we can now explain the instances in which a son is not required to obey his parents. B. B.M. 32a raises this issue as follows:

> From where is it derived that if his father [who is of the priestly class] said to him [who accordingly also of priestly stock], "Defile yourself," or if he said to him, "Do not return [a lost article]," that he is not to heed them? As it is said, "You shall each revere his mother and his father, and keep my Sabbaths: I the Lord am your God" [Lev. 19:3]—you are all obligated to honor me.

The son is exempt from obeying his father's demand that he sin because the obligation to honor God through observance of all the commandments has priority. The same principle is the basis of the following (B. Qid. 32a), given in the name of Eleazar b. Mathia:

> If my father says, "Give me water to drink," but I have a commandment to fulfill, I set aside my father's honor and perform the commandment, for I and my father are both obligated to fulfill the commandments.

The point may also be derived from the distinction raised by Issi b. Judah in the same Talmudic discussion:

> If the commandment can be performed by others, then he lets the others perform it, while he engages in honoring his father. If, however, there are no others who could observe this commandment, then he engages in the commandment and sets aside his father's honor, for he and his father are both obligated to fulfill the commandments.

In other words, the son is obligated to set aside his father's honor and perform a commandment only if there is no one else to do it, for the father himself, in that situation, also would have been obligated to fulfill this commandment. The following hypothetical question of a widow's son is similarly resolved (B. Qid. 31a):

> If my father says, "Give me water to drink," and my mother says, "Give me water to drink," which of them takes precedence? [Rav Eliezer] replied: "Set aside the honor of your mother and fulfill the honor due your father, for both you and your mother are obligated to honor your father."

Several *Ahronim* conclude from this "that if his father told him to do for him a task that the wife is not obligated to perform for her husband . . . [and] his mother also told him to perform for her a task," then both are equal.[21] Similarly, if the parents divorce, so that the mother no longer has an obligation to honor the father, their son is free to prefer whichever one he chooses.[22]

Another case in which the question of a son's obligation to heed his parents arises if a pupil desires to move from home to study Torah elsewhere, against which his father protests, asserting that he will constantly worry about the son's being slandered by gentiles, a frequent occurrence in the land where the proposed teacher is.[23] Isserlein rules that the son is not obligated to heed his father, since the father himself, if he were certain that he would advance in his studies under a certain teacher, would be obligated to go to him and fulfill the commandment of Torah study. According to Isserlein, not only the obligation of Torah study but also "minor [prohibitions] supersede honoring and revering one's father and mother." Following this same logic, Joseph b. Solomon Colon rules[24] "that the father is not empowered to prevent his son from marrying a woman whom the son desires," since marrying a woman one finds repulsive constitutes a transgression. Such a marriage is forbidden because it constitutes a disgraceful act, entails deception, and harms the standing of the woman; the father, as well, is forbidden to marry a woman whom he does not like.[25]

The parent's obligations to children: A new interpretation of the commandment to honor one's parents appears in the rulings of the Rabbinical courts in the State of Israel. A son's failure to fulfill this obligation is liable to revoke his right to maintenance from the father. Such is the interpretation given the following law, as formulated by Maimonides:[26]

> After the age of six years, the father is entitled to state: "If he is with me, I will provide his maintenance; and if he is with his mother, I will not provide his maintenance."

The rule "a daughter is always with her mother" also was interpreted by the Rabbinical courts as conditional upon the daughter's observance of her father's honor (as expressed by his desire that she honor him and visit him from time to time).

The question was raised in case 1964/43 (Jerusalem), PDR 7:10, whether a father could be exempted from the maintenance of his thirteen-year-old son, who had left the Satmar Yeshivah against his father's wishes that he continue studying there, and, encouraged by his mother (who was divorced from the father), had transferred to the Ponevezh Yeshivah. The father argued that since the son did not heed him and did not want to continue in his specific practices, namely, the Hasidic method of study, in Yiddish, but rather desired to study in "the holy tongue" (i.e., Hebrew), then he is exempt from providing maintenance, following the principle of "If he is with me, I will provide his maintenance." For the purposes of the specific case, the maintenance that the father was required to pay consisted of the son's living expenses at the yeshivah and his tuition.

Mordecai Eliyahu, (the former Sephardic Chief Rabbi of Israel) ruled[27] that according to the law of honoring one's parents, the son is not obligated to heed his father, but rather may study Torah wherever he desires. The father in this case "cannot say to him: 'If you are not with me, then I will not provide your maintenance,' since the entire rationale [of this claim] is that [the son] does not want to heed him." The law, accordingly, is with the son: "it is incumbent upon the father to teach him Torah in a place and in a manner that he desires, and [the father] must aid and assist him in this. Consequently, the father must provide for him, maintain him, and fill his every need where he is studying."

In my view, Rabbi Eliyahu's decision breaks new ground and requires further study. The idea that the son is not obligated to heed his father and may study wherever he desires was stated only regarding the obligation of honoring one's parents. On what basis, however, can we conclude from Maimonides or other sources that this right of the son to refuse his father's wishes and not heed him also entails the right of the refusing son to be supported by the father? Furthermore, the obligation of the father to

teach his son Torah does not consist specifically of hiring a teacher for him. Avraham
Schapira, (the former Ashkenazic Chief
Rabbi of Israel), who also sat on the panel
of that Rabbinical court, was more reserved
in his ruling:[28]

> Let us return to the argument of the father
> that since the son is not with him, [the
> father] is to be exempted from supporting
> him. According to the reasoning of *Helkat
> ha-Mehokek* in the opinion of Maimonides,
> that the father is right, since [the son] must
> be with him to study Torah, it should be
> said that this applies specifically to one who
> demands that [the son] be with him, but
> the son refuses. In the instance, however, in
> which both agree that [the son] will not live
> with the father but someplace else, since in
> this case there is no argument that [the
> father] desires to teach him Torah himself,
> the father is not necessarily exempt from
> providing maintenance.

We may therefore surmise that if the father
in this case wanted to teach his son Torah
himself, the court would not be empowered
to obligate him to maintain his son, despite
the justified refusal of the son and his wish
to study someplace else.[29]

Israeli Rabbinical courts similarly have
reevaluated the rules for the maintenance of
daughters. My view is that when Maimonides stated that "a daughter is always with
her mother," he meant that the father
intends to maintain his daughter (until
the age of 12 1/2), even if she is in her
mother's custody. He does not insist that
the daughter be in his custody, since the
handiwork of this daughter always belongs
to him. Even the later *Rishonim*, however,
who regarded this rule by Maimonides as
referring to custody, limited their discussion
to the rivalry between the mother and the
husband's heirs or the administrators who
were appointed by him before his death.
Accordingly, the disagreement among the
early *Ahronim*, whether the principle of "a
daughter is always with her mother" is an
inflexible and unchanging rule or whether it
is a standard intended for the good of the
daughter, in which case the heirs could
argue that the daughter should be with
them and not with her mother, does not
relate to the right in principle of the father
to deny his daughter maintenance pay-

ments if her conduct, when she is with her
mother, is unsatisfactory to him.[30]

A new spirit, however, infuses the rulings
of the Israeli Rabbinical courts, according
to which the principle of "a daughter is
always with her mother" does not prevent
the court from considering the cancellation
of maintenance payments to the daughter if
she does not heed her father and does not
desire to visit him. This interpretation was
explained in various ways. Rabbi Ovadiah
Yosef compares the case of this daughter to
the ancient question of whether the mother
is entitled to remove the daughter from the
father's city and keep her away from the
family of the wife's dead husband. He
decides this on procedural grounds, based
on the halakhic uncertainty of whether the
mother is permitted to remove her daughter from the father's place. Rabbi Eliezer
Judah Waldenberg, on the other hand,
holds that we are to decide on the cancellation of the daughter's maintenance on the
basis of the moral corruption of this daughter who does not want to meet her father.
According to Waldenberg and other panels
of Rabbinic judges, the daughter's refusal to
visit her father constitutes moral corruption,
because "even when the father is not religiously observant," he is to be honored.[31] I
doubt whether this ruling would have been
written in such a decisive manner if the
court had been requested to rule on the
question of the basic right to custody of a
non-observant father, and not only on the
issue of visiting rights.

Notes

[1] On this verse, see Tosafot to B. Ber. 32a,
s.v., *Kabed*. I believe the subject of honor similarly stands behind the prohibition at Deut.
12:3-4.
[2] On the law in Scripture and the Ancient
Near East, see J. Fleishman, *Parent and Child in the
Ancient Near East and the Bible* (Jerusalem, 1999),
pp. 200-243 (Hebrew).
[3] M Ber. 9:5; B. Ber. 61b; Sifre Deut. 32 (ed.
L. Finkelstein [New York and Jerusalem, 1993],
p. 55).
[4] See *Teshuvot Rashba* (attributed to Nahmanides) 88; Shulhan Arukh, *Hoshen Mishpat* 97:16;
Sefer Me'irat Einayim, Hoshen Mishpat 97:35-36;
Shakh (Shabbetai ben Meir ha-Kohen), *Hoshen
Mishpat* 97:10.
[5] Commandment   479   (photocopy   edition,
Israel, 1959), 60a.

[6] Rashi, B. Hul. 110b, s.v., *She-Matan Sekharah*. *Levush*, *Yoreh Deah* 240:5 provides a fuller explanation: "The rabbis, of blessed memory, accepted that any positive commandment regarding which it is written 'its reward is at its side,' the court is not enjoined to enforce. The logical reason is that since the Torah explicitly revealed the reward for this commandment, his action, and its accompanying reward or punishment, are before him. From the affirmative [here] we derive a negative, and why should we further compel him, for 'the wicked man shall die for his iniquity' [Ezek. 3;18] if he will not observe [the commandment]."

[7] This instance falls within the context of community regulations that enable townspeople to compel observance upon each other.

[8] See B. B.B. 8b, s.v., *Akhpeih*; B. Ket. 49b, s.v., *Akhpeih*, *Mordekhai*, B. B.B., 490; *Or Zaru'a*, 1, Laws of Charity 4.

[9] *Mordekhai*, *Or Zarua*, loc. cit.

[10] The narrative reads: "R. Jonathan and R. Yannai were in session. A person came and kissed R. Jonathan's feet. R. Yannai asked him: 'What favor did you ever do for him, that he repays you in this manner?' [Jonathan] replied: 'Once he came to complain to me about his son, that [I compel the latter] to support him. I told him to cry out in the synagogue and disgrace him.' [Yannai] asked him: 'Why did you not [simply] compel him?' [Jonathan] answered: '[Is it possible to] force him?' [Yannai] said to him: 'Are you still [in doubt] regarding this?' R. Jonathan retracted, and established the tradition in his [Yannai's] name. R. Jacob ben Aha came forward: 'R. Samuel b. Nahman, in the name of R. Jonathan, said: "The son is compelled to support the father."'"

[11] See, e.g., *Kitzvot ha-Hoshen*, *Hol ha-Moed* 97:16; *Minhat Hinukh*, Commandment 479.

[12] *Midrash Tanhuma*, *Ekev* 3 (ed. Buber, p. 79), from the exposition by Simeon bar Yohai that "regarding two commandments for which the Holy One, blessed be He, revealed their reward, and they are: extremely minor, [and] most stringent [. . .]—they are equivalent in this world regarding the reward given [for their observance]."

[13] See *Sefer ha-Hinukh*, Commandment 33: "If the court has the power, he is compelled, as we have written above, for the negation of a positive [commandment], the court enforces." This was already questioned by Judah b. Samuel Rosanes at the end of the book *Parashat Derakhim*; *Minhat Hinukh*, Commandment 33; see also *Sedeh Hemed ha-Shalem*, 4, *Ma'arekhet Mem*. In our opinion, however, this can be resolved in accordance with our hypothesis.

[14] See *Sedeh Hemed ha-Shalem*, 4, *Ma'arekhet Mem*, 108, who resolves this in a similar manner. For the difference between lashes and whipping, see Maimonides, *Mishneh Torah*, Laws of Ritual Slaughtering 13:3-4. He states that lashes are administered by the authority of the Torah for the violation of a negative commandment, even if one is ultimately prevented from observing the commandment due to circumstances beyond his control; lashes, administered on the authority of the rabbis, however, are applied only when the motive of the offender is improper, such as in the case in which he "tears off the bird's wings."

[15] See a similar explanation by Aaron b. Moses Fuld, Y. fol. 12, s.v., *Ve-Hawi Mehi*.

[16] See Maimonides, *Mishneh Torah*, Laws of *Mamzerim* 6:7, who derived fixed laws from these one-time narratives; see also the commentaries on Maimonides, loc. cit.

[17] See also B. Qid. 31b.

[18] See also the law as set forth in Maimonides, *Mishneh Torah*, Laws of Mamzerim 6:4-5.

[19] B. Qid. 30b; Maimonides, *Mishneh Torah*, Laws of *Mamzerim* 6:6.

[20] Tosafot, Qid. 31a, s.v. *Kevar*; idem, 32a, s.v. *Oro*.

[21] *Pit'hei Teshuvah*, *Yoreh Deah* 240:9.

[22] The Talmud formulates the answer as follows: "Pour some water for them in a basin, and screech for them like chickens!" See the commentary of Rashi, ad loc.

[23] *Terumat ha-Deshen* 40, cited in *Beit Yosef*, *Yoreh Deah* 240, s.v. *Katuv be-T[erumat] h[a-Deshen]*; *Shulhan Arukh*, *Yoreh Deah* 240:25.

[24] Cited the name of Israel Isserlein, *Terumat ha-Deshen*, Para. 167; also cited in *Darkei Moshe*, *Yoreh Deah* 240:10; *Hagahah* on *Shulhan Arukh*, *Yoreh Deah* 240:25.

[25] This is indicated by B. Qid. 41a: "A man may not betroth a woman until he sees her, lest he find something repulsive in her, and she become detestable to him, and the all merciful said, 'Love your fellow as yourself' [Lev. 19:18]." See also the formulation by Maimonides, *Mishneh Torah*, *Hil. Ishut* 3:19: "Lest she not find favor in his eyes, and he consequently divorces her, or has relations with her while hating her."

[26] Maimonides, op cit., 21:17. For the interpretation of this law as applied by Rabbinical courts, see my *The Relations between Parents and Children in Israeli and Jewish Law* (Tel Aviv, 2000), pp. 202-203, 391-396, 473-475, 530-532 (Heb.).

[27] Idem, p. 32.

[28] Idem, p. 28.

[29] In the beginning of his opinion (p. 17), however, Schapira wrote differently, asserting that it would seem that the father does not have preferential standing over the mother in the case that the child is over six years old, since the rule of "[from the age of six, a teacher may accept pupils, and] stuff them with Torah like an ox" applies to such a son. This means, as understood by Schapira, that the father does not have preference over the mother as regards custody. See my *Relations between Parents and Children*, pp. 511-513.

[30] See *Relations between Parents and Children*, pp. 397-410, regarding the dissenting views of Joseph b. David Ibn Lev (1500-1580), Meir b.

Isaac Katzenellbogen of Padua (1473-1565), Samuel b. Moses Di Medina (1503-1590), and Moses b. Joseph Trani (1500-1580).

[31] For their exact views, with quotations, see *Relations between Parents and Children*, pp. 432-435.

ISRAEL ZVI GILAT

PSEUDO-PHILO, BIBLICAL CHARAC-TERS IN: The *Liber Antiquitatum Biblicarum* (LAB) of Pseudo-Philo retells the biblical story beginning with Adam and ending with Saul's death. Its genre is "rewritten Bible."[1] Its author is called Pseudo-Philo because the text was passed down with the Philonic corpus, although it is clearly not by Philo of Alexandria. There is general agreement that it comes from the first century C.E., but scholars debate whether it was written before or after the destruction of the Jerusalem Temple in 70 C.E.

LAB freely rewrites the biblical story. In so doing, it uses a variety of biblical and non-biblical materials. The author applies the sacred text to his own situation. Alterations to the biblical story result in a coherent narrative conveying a particular point of view. Therefore, it is appropriate to analyze LAB using the tools of literary criticism—analysis of plot, characterization, setting, and so on.[2] This article investigates the way Pseudo-Philo rewrites biblical characters. It will not engage in detailed, tradition-critical work, although parallels will be noted occasionally.[3] Rather, the narrative will be engaged as story, seeing both how it is similar to and differs from the biblical story, and how the narrative advances Pseudo-Philo's central themes. The dominant theme in LAB is God's unconditional faithfulness to Israel. This is in some tension with another main theme—moral causality, that one gets what one deserves. The same tension exists within the biblical text. Pseudo-Philo also shows God's control of human events.

Since we cannot here analyze every biblical character in LAB, we concentrate on those whose portrayal sheds most light on Pseudo-Philo's method and point of view. Pseudo-Philo is particularly interested in Israel's leaders.[4] As we analyze each biblical character, we will look particularly at the roles of God and Israel.

Joktan and Abraham: The episode of the tower of Babel in LAB interweaves the stories of Abraham and Joktan. Except for the basic narrative framework, most of the material is the author's creation.

Pseudo-Philo adds many names of his own devising to the genealogies of Genesis. He also adds the idea that each of humanity's three divisions has a leader. Joktan is the Shemites' leader. In Genesis, Joktan is Shem's grandson (10:25-26, 29; cp. 1 Chr. 1:19-20, 23), but we hear no more of him in the Bible.

In LAB, Abraham first appears when humanity decides to build the tower, while in Genesis he appears immediately afterward. Genesis sees the building as the culmination of human rebellion against God. Against this backdrop, God chooses Abraham to make of him a righteous people. In Genesis, Abraham has done nothing that explains his election. Pseudo-Philo, noting that Abraham's election is contiguous to the tower of Babel episode in the Bible, creates a connection between them—Abraham's election results from his refusal to participate in the building.

The story follows a pattern found elsewhere in LAB (chapters 9, 10, and 44).[5] First, humans plot evil; second, others oppose that plot and form a counter-plan; third, someone dissents from the counter-plan; fourth, God intervenes on the side of the dissenter. The pattern contrasts those who propose the counter-plan and the one who dissents. The evil plot in this case is the proposal to build the tower. Abraham and twelve other Shemites refuse to participate, and Joktan plans to save them. Abraham does not cooperate with Joktan's plans. Finally, God intervenes, proving Abraham right. Joktan and Abraham are both Shemites who want to do the right thing, but Abraham is most in tune with God's will.

When brought before the chiefs, the resisters declare that the tower affronts God. This is a typical trial scene.[6] One expects them either to be executed or saved by divine intervention. But Joktan diverts the expected flow of the action, suggesting a seven-day delay so that the defendants might repent of their "evil plans." The narrator discloses Joktan's motivation: "He was of their tribe and served God" (6:6).[7] Joktan provides for their escape and tells them to trust in God (6:9).

Joktan seems admirable in wanting to rescue the resisters. But Abraham refuses to cooperate with Joktan's plans, saying that he trusts God. He continues, "If there be any sin of mine so flagrant that I should be burned up, let the will of God be done" (6:11). He is confident that God is just.

Next morning, Abraham tells his interrogators that when he awoke, his companions were gone. This is a clever answer, since it is true. Joktan must now execute Abraham's sentence. "With great emotion," he casts him into the fire. God rescues Abraham and destroys the bystanders. This is typical for a trial scene, and it vindicates Abraham. This story makes important points about the nature of leadership and the proper way to serve God. Human action, even when done in the service of God, is valid only if God initiates it.

In Pseudo-Philo, the contrast between Abraham and the rest of humanity is clearer than in the Bible. First, God delivers a speech denigrating humanity. Then, God decides to bring Abram into the land that God protected from the flood. The contrast between the land of Israel and the rest of the world enhances the contrast between Abraham and the rest of humanity. God continues, "For there I will have my servant Abram dwell and I will establish my covenant with him and will bless his seed and be lord for him as God forever" (7:4). As is regularly the case in Pseudo-Philo, God's role in the narrative is enhanced. The reader hears God's own reasoning about the faithlessness of humanity and the election of Abraham.

Amram: In the Bible, Moses' birth to Amram is gratuitous. Not so in Pseudo-Philo, where the story of Moses' birth displays the same structure as Abraham's story. Pharaoh hatches an evil plan, the elders propose a counter-plan, Amram dissents, and God intervenes, proving Amram right. The elders are well-intentioned, but only Amram really trusts in God. LAB thus implicitly draws a parallel between Amram and Abraham. That the Israelites decide to

remain celibate to thwart Pharaoh's plans is common in midrashic texts, but elsewhere Amram participates in the plan.

The Israelite elders learn that pharaoh is about to kill their male newborns, marry the females to their slaves, and reduce all of Israel to slavery. They decide to stop marrying and having intercourse. They say, "For it is better to die without sons until we know what God may do" (9:2). The elders connect intermarriage with idolatry, and Pseudo-Philo condemns idolatry.[8] But Amram disagrees with this plan. He agrees that God will respond to the situation in due time, but to forego procreation would harm Israel. His speech reads like a précis of Pseudo-Philo's views. He says that God's promises to Abraham will be fulfilled, that God will not let his plans for Israel be foiled, and that the covenant with Israel's fathers will not be "in vain" (9:3-4).

Tamar: Amram invokes the memory of Tamar as one who took extreme measures to avoid separation from Israel and intercourse with gentiles (9:5). For Pseudo-Philo and other Jewish interpreters, Tamar is a positive figure, as in Gen. 38. Pseudo-Philo exculpates her for sleeping with her father-in-law (Lev. 18:15; 20:12): "Her intent was not fornication, but being unwilling to separate from the sons of Israel . . ." (9:5).[9] He quotes her as refusing "to have intercourse with gentiles," words not present in the Bible. Pseudo-Philo often expresses disapproval of intermarriage.

Moses: The author simultaneously exalts Moses and stresses God's initiative. In 9:7-8, God speaks of Amram's son, saying that Moses will serve him forever.[10] Through him, God will work signs and wonders such as have been done for no one else (see Deut. 34; Exod. 4:21; 34:10; Ps. 105:26-27). Because of Moses, God will show Israel his glory (see Exod. 33-34).[11] God will "kindle for him my lamp that will abide in him," words often taken to refer to the Law.

God then says, "I will show him my covenant that no one has seen." This may refer to the Sinaitic covenant.[12] God declares that he will show his "Law and statutes and judgments" to Moses.[13] God declares that he will create an eternal light for Moses and that his illumination of Moses will never cease. God finishes by saying that he thought of Moses long before, when limiting human life to 120 years (Gen. 6:3; LAB 3:2). In the Bible, Moses does live for 120 years (Deut. 34:7).[14]

Through Moses God will reveal his ways and the Law.[15] In 9:16, the narrator says that God freed Israel through Moses as he said, so God is faithful to his promises.

In 9:10, Moses' sister, Miriam, has a dream prophesying Moses' birth.[16] An angelic figure tells her to tell her parents, "Behold he who will be born from you will be cast forth into the water; likewise through him the water will be dried up. And I will work signs through him and save my people, and he will exercise leadership always (*ducatum*)" (9:10). The symmetry between the Nile and the Red Sea implies God's control of history. Pseudo-Philo often posits such symmetries (as do other Jewish interpreters). The author stresses God's action and sees Moses as a divine instrument. Here Moses exercises "leadership." *Dux, ducatum,* and *ducere* are applied to many characters in LAB, but only of Moses is it said that he is leader always.[17]

In LAB, pharaoh's daughter comes to the Nile because of her dreams, so again God directs the action.[18] As in the Bible, she finds Moses and recognizes that he is a Hebrew child. Her recognition of Moses as a Hebrew goes unexplained in the biblical text. Pseudo-Philo explains it by saying Moses was circumcised, an explanation found in the midrash as well.[19] This indicates Moses' special character. Pharaoh's daughter calls him Moses as in the biblical text, but LAB has Moses' mother call him Melchiel, which in Hebrew means "God is my king."[20] Moses' very name attests to God's sovereignty. The last sentence of the chapter indicates Moses' status because God acts through him, but it simultaneously affirms that God, not Moses, is ultimately responsible for freeing the Israelites. All this happens "as he (God) had said."

The story of Moses' birth sets out the themes that dominate Moses' story. Throughout the story, the focus is really on God. Through Moses, God gives the Torah and communicates with Israel, so Moses is God's instrument. Moses takes initiative only in interceding for Israel, which he does frequently. His intercessions stress characteristic points—Israel's unworthiness and God's faithfulness to the covenant.

Pseudo-Philo summarizes Exod. 2-13 in a single sentence (10:1). God sends Moses, frees the Israelites, and sends the ten plagues. Again, the focus is on God's action. In Exod. 14, when the people are trapped between the Red Sea and the Egyptians, they cry out to God and then complain to Moses. LAB 10:2 develops the people's words. They accuse God of not honoring his covenants with their fathers. This makes the people seem arrogant and also serves to heighten their confrontation with God.

Chapter 10 exhibits the same structure found in the stories of Abraham and Amram. In this case, the structure is more complex.[21] First, the Egyptians pursue Israel. Then the tribes, in three groups of four each, devise three strategies. One is to commit suicide in the sea, another is to return to slavery in Egypt, and the last is to fight, trusting in God's help. The last plan seems good, since it shows faith in God and courage before enemies. But Moses ignores all the plans, thus rejecting them, and prays. God responds by saving Israel. Because of the pattern, Moses is implicitly compared to Abraham and Amram. Each displays trust in God that goes beyond that of their fellows.

This, Moses' first intercession, occurs at the Red Sea. In the Bible, Moses does not intercede at this point. But God does ask Moses, "Why do you cry out to me?" (Exod 14:15). Pseudo-Philo notices that Moses has not cried out to God, and so he adds Moses' intercessory prayer.

LAB rewrites the story of the Red Sea to emphasize God's role. Exod. 14:21 says that Moses stretched out his hand, and God drove the sea back by a wind. LAB says that God "rebuked" the sea, that it was God's "fearful din" that and the breath of God's anger (perhaps a reference to the wind in the biblical text; cp. Exod. 15:8) that drove back the sea and caused the world's foundations to be laid bare. In Exod. 14:24, God panics the Egyptians and then clogs their wheels. In LAB, he hardens the perception of the Egyptians so that they do not even know they are entering the sea. Finally, in Exod. 14:26-28, it is said simply that God orders Moses to stretch out his hand and when he does so the sea returns. Pseudo-Philo is clearer about God's role in this final action, since he says twice that God commanded the sea itself to return, once before and once after God tells Moses to raise his staff.

When God informs Moses that he is about to promulgate the Torah through him, the accent is clearly on God's initiative (11:1-3). God says, among other things, that he will put his words in Moses' mouth. Pseudo-Philo transfers the command for sexual abstinence before the Sinai theophany from Moses to God (11:2). After God's words about the giving of the Torah, LAB says, "And Moses did what God commanded him" (11:3; see Num. 17:26; Exod. 7:6; 40:16). Later in the book, sinners from the tribe of Benjamin say, "We decided in this time to investigate the book of the Law, whether God had really written what was in it or Moses had taught these things by himself" (25:13). LAB 11 leaves no doubt about the Law's divine origin.

On Mount Sinai, Moses sees the tree of life, said to be the origin of the wood that Moses threw into the bitter water to make it drinkable (11:15; Exod. 15:25). Seeing the tree of life is in other texts an apocalyptic vision. In chapter 19 God grants Moses further such revelations.

In 12:1, Moses descends the mountain, and his face shines with glorious light that outshines the sun and moon, a detail added to the biblical story. This serves less to glorify Moses than to underline God's majesty and the revelation's authenticity. The people do not recognize Moses because of the light. The lack of recognition, followed by recognition when Moses speaks, is unique to Pseudo-Philo. The author has a predilection for such recognition scenes. The device casts human perception into doubt. The author also uses the incident to draw another of his analogies, in this case between this scene and Joseph's brothers' recognition of Joseph in Egypt.

There is a slight change in the way that the people ask Aaron to make the calf. In Exodus, the people say that they do not know what has become of Moses, "the man who brought us up out of the land of Egypt" (Exod. 32:1). In LAB, they say that Moses is "the one through whom wonders were done before our eyes." The change is enough to shift the focus away from the role of Moses as leader ("brought us") to Moses as God's instrument ("through whom"). In both the Bible and LAB, Moses smashes the tablets of the Law, but in LAB he does so only after seeing that the writing on the tablets was gone, a detail absent from the biblical story. LAB and other Jewish authors could not accept the idea that Moses destroyed God's writing.

LAB 12 streamlines and gives more logical order to the story of the golden calf. In Exodus, Moses intercedes twice. Between the two intercessions, he descends to punish the people. He calls on those loyal to God and they put many in Israel to the sword. In LAB, Moses descends the mountain as soon as God tells him of the golden calf and deals with the people. Only then does he return and intercede. While Exodus showcases Moses' anger, Pseudo-Philo pays more attention to his distress, comparing him to a woman in labor for the first time. Then the reader hears Moses' own thoughts, as he rejects despair and decides that despite the people's sin, what God had declared to him could never be in vain. Pseudo-Philo omits the slaughter that Moses causes in Israel. There is punishment for those who sinned, but only after Moses identifies the guilty though in a way that leaves the decision up to God. Those forced to participate are not punished.

Moses' intercessory prayer in LAB 12:8-9 corresponds to the prayers in Exod. 32:11-13 and 33:12-16. In Exod. 33 the prayer gives greater attention to the fact that Moses is in God's favor than that Israel is God's chosen (33:13). God responds, "I will do the very thing that you have asked; for you have found favor in my sight, and I know you by name" (33:17). In LAB, Moses never mentions that he is in God's favor, so it is similar to Moses' earlier intercession (Exod. 32). Rather, the lengthy prayer recites God's labors for Israel, notes Israel's unfaithfulness, and warns God that if he is not merciful, he will have no one to glorify him and no one will trust him in the future. He says, "Do not let your labor be in vain." God relents, saying, "Behold I have been made merciful according to your words" (12:9). There is no reference to God's favor for Moses, or his knowing Moses by name. The rewriting de-emphasizes Moses and shifts the focus to God.

LAB's version of the spy story and the people's rebellion from Num. 13-14 omits the words of Aaron and Moses to the people (Num. 14:7-9). Rather, as soon as the people rebel, God appears and launches into a speech about his faithfulness, their disobedience, and his anger (LAB 15:5-6). This amplifies God's speech in Num. 14:11-12. Moses answers with an intercession emphasizing his own insignificance and begging for mercy, claiming that no human could exist were it not for God's mercy. Moses says that it is God who is the creator, not himself. This contrasts with Moses' intercession in Num. 14:13-19, where Moses does not speak of his insignificance. Pseudo-Philo's changes decrease the roles of Moses and Aaron and emphasize God's role, stressing humanity's sinfulness, including that of Moses.

Korah's rebellion (Num. 16) is rewritten to minimize Moses' role and sharpen the confrontation between Korah and God (LAB 16). Pseudo-Philo excises the sharp confrontations between Moses and Korah found in Num. 16.[22]

At the end of his life, Moses delivers a speech (19:2-5; cp. Deut. 31-34; *Jub.* 1; *Assumption of Moses*; *Ant.* § 302-326). He says that the people will lament his passing and wish for another shepherd like him, who will "pray always for our sins and to be heard for our iniquities" (19:3). It is as an intercessor that they will miss him.

As in the Bible, Moses can see the promised land only from a distance. God tells him that he may not enter lest he see the idolatry the people will commit there (LAB 19:7). This contrasts with the Bible, which says Moses was unable to enter because of his lack of faith when he struck the rock twice for water (Deut. 32:48-52; see Num. 20:1-13; Exod. 17:1-7; Ps. 106:32). Pseudo-

Philo avoids any impression that Moses does not fulfill his mission perfectly. Pseudo-Philo never narrates Moses' lack of faith in Num. 20. By blaming Moses' exclusion from the land on the people's sins, the author also emphasizes Israel's unfaithfulness. Moses answers God by interceding yet again for the people (19:8-9).

God shows Moses more than the land. He also grants him a vision of a sort often granted to apocalyptic seers. Other ancient Jewish texts also credit Moses with reception of esoteric knowledge (e.g., *Testament of Moses*, 4 Ezra). God says that he will keep Moses' staff before him as a reminder of the covenant, as the rainbow reminds him of Noah's covenant. Moses' intercessory function essentially extends beyond his death, and the covenant will continue at least partly because of him.

The rest of the chapter glorifies Moses above all others. God tells him that even the angels will mourn his death, and that he will be glorified with his fathers and await God's visitation of the world. When the eschaton comes, Moses will be raised to dwell "in the place of sanctification." Moses' response is like that of an apocalyptic seer. He asks how much time has passed and how much remains, receiving an enigmatic answer that would easily fit an apocalypse (19:15). Then he is "filled with understanding" and his appearance becomes "glorious." The song of the heavenly hosts stops at his death, which has never happened before, nor will it happen again. God himself buries Moses "on a high place and in the light of all the world."

Pseudo-Philo's focus on Moses is fitting, given his interest in the covenant, the people's failure to live up to it, God's faithfulness, God's mercy as motivated by his promises to Israel's ancestors, leadership in Israel, and his contrast between divine and human initiative. All these themes come through in Moses' portrayal. The attention given to Moses is notable given the fact that, aside from the stories of Abraham and Moses, Pseudo-Philo concentrates on material from the books of Judges and Samuel.

The glorification of Moses in LAB 19 might seem inconsistent with the author's desire to enhance God's role in the narrative, even when that means de-emphasizing the initiative of biblical heroes. The inconsistency is only apparent. It is precisely because Moses has complete trust in God, displays no presumption, looks to God to determine his every move, and teaches the people to obey God and to blame their own sinfulness for their suffering, that he now, at the end of his life and after his task is completed, receives such glory in the eyes of humanity, the angels, and God.

Aaron: Aaron's role in the episode of the golden calf reflects a desire to exculpate him somewhat. In the Bible, Aaron promptly complies with the people's request that he make a golden idol. In LAB, he reasons with them, urging them to wait for Moses who "will explain from his own mouth the Law of God" (12:2). He gives in only because he fears the people's strength (12:3). Similarly, LAB omits the confrontation in Exodus between an angry Moses and an Aaron who ducks his own guilt and blames the people (32:21-24).

Joshua: Joshua succeeds Moses, but Moses takes no active role in the transition. The succession is purely God's work. This contrasts with the Bible where Joshua has the spirit "because Moses had laid his hands on him" (Deut 34:9). It contrasts also with the *Testament of Moses*, which is a long testamentary speech by Moses to Joshua in which he commissions Joshua.

As in the Bible, the account of Joshua's career begins with God's speech to Joshua, but Pseudo-Philo goes beyond the Bible in saying that God establishes a covenant with him (20:1). God tells Joshua to don Moses' "garments of wisdom." He does so and becomes a fit successor to Moses. Joshua delivers a speech to the people full of typical Deuteronomistic theology. The people remember the prophecy of Eldad and Modad, prophesying that Joshua would succeed Moses, and they remember that Moses was not jealous. In the Bible, Moses' lack of jealousy refers to the prophesying of the other two, but in LAB it refers to his knowledge of Joshua's succession. Leadership is not for self-aggrandizement but for the good of God's people.

In LAB 21, God tells Joshua that Israel will sin after his death. Joshua utters an intercessory prayer, asking God to give the people "a wise heart and a prudent mind" and requesting that God supply for the people a good ruler, in fulfillment of the promise in Gen. 49:10. God later answers Joshua's prayer by appointing Kenaz. Once the land is apportioned, the people declare that God has fulfilled all of his promises. Joshua blesses them, prays that they may remain faithful to God, and that a temple may be built in fulfillment of God's promise. Israel's history has culminated in the fulfillment of God's vision for it. It needs only remain faithful for this situation to be permanent.

In Josh. 22, a crisis arises when the tribes in Transjordan build an altar. The other tribes confront them, accuse them of idolatry, and threaten war. The Transjordanian tribes protest that they merely want to prevent the tribes west of the Jordan from excluding them from worship. Ultimately the tribes in Transjordan relent. In the Bible, the entire episode is presented as an interaction between the tribes as a whole, except where Phineas acts as spokesman for the majority of the tribes and accepts the explanation of the tribes and their decision to cease their cultic activity. Pseudo-Philo rewrites this episode so that Joshua plays the key role, thus presenting Joshua as a true leader. Joshua and the elders are the ones who protest the building. They hear the explanation of the altar builders, and then Joshua explains that loyalty to God consists not in sacrifices but in obedience to Torah. He counsels them to meditate on the Law day and night. This takes God's words to Joshua in Josh. 1:8 and makes them Joshua's advice to the tribes. He is wise leader who leaves ultimate judgment to God. He says that if they are guilty, they will be punished, and if only ignorant, God will be merciful. He then prays for them. He demonstrates a balance of firmness, humility, and deference to God's judgment that makes him an ideal leader.

In both the Bible and LAB, Joshua ends his career with a covenant-making ceremony. Pseudo-Philo adds that Joshua has a dream the night before the ceremony in which he is told all that he is to say. This is typical of Pseudo-Philo. He makes absolutely clear that it is God, not Joshua, who is behind things. As in the Bible, Joshua delivers God's words to the people with the prophetic messenger formula, "Thus says the Lord."

Kenaz: Kenaz is barely mentioned in the Bible, where he is father to the first judge, Othniel, about whom little is said. In LAB, Kenaz becomes the first judge, and Pseudo-Philo fabricates a long and complex narrative about him (chapters 25-28). Because he is a character largely of Pseudo-Philo's own making, his story clearly reveals Pseudo-Philo's portrait of a good leader.

Kenaz is chosen by lots to lead the people and to determine whether they are pure enough to go to war. His first act is to remind the people of Moses' and Joshua's admonition to obey the Law. He tells the people that God has declared that some of them are guilty of disobedience, and that they must cast lots to find the guilty party, and they do so. This is based on the Achan episode in Josh. 7, to which the author refers in LAB 25:7. As did Joshua in the Achan episode, Kenaz burns the offenders. He addresses the people, calling them those who have seen God's wonders, and cursing those who, like the sinners, do not believe.

Kenaz is very successful militarily against the Amorites (LAB 27). Then some begin to murmur against him. He imprisons the troublemakers and decides to win a battle with only a few soldiers, thus proving his courage and trust in God. What follows echoes Gideon's story in Jdgs. 7. Kenaz prepares three hundred soldiers with trumpets and then enters the Amorite camp. Before doing so, he prays, asking God to send a sign. Kenaz plans to draw his sword in the midst of the camp. If the Amorites recognize him, that will mean that God is with him. If they do not recognize him, he will be killed. His willingness to embrace death is remarkable: "Even if I be handed over to death, I know that the Lord has not heard me because of my faults and has handed me over to my enemies. But he will not destroy his inheritance by my death" (27:7). This is the sentiment voiced by Abraham in LAB 6:11. Both have ultimate faith in God's justice.

Kenaz asks for a sign as does Gideon, but while Gideon asks for a sign because he is reluctant to engage in battle, Kenaz simply wants to know whether God will bring him victory. The sign is to take place within the enemy camp itself, so even before receiving the sign, Kenaz demonstrates trust by venturing into the camp.

God is with Kenaz. The Amorites recognize his sword. An angel confuses them and they kill each other in great numbers. Kenaz also kills many. Toward the end of the battle, Kenaz cannot release his grip on his sword (cp. 2 Sam. 23:10). Pseudo-Philo turns this detail into a commentary on his own times. Kenaz asks an Amorite what he ought to do. The man tells him he must wash his hand in a Hebrew's blood. Kenaz instead kills the Amorite and washes his hand in his blood, thus releasing his hand. The message is that foreigners will use Israelites against one another, and that an Israelite ought not be fooled. Kenaz proves himself a shrewd defender of Israel.

The Israelites survey the battlefield in the morning and are astonished. Kenaz says, "Why are you amazed? Is the way of men like the ways of God? For among men a great number prevails, but with God whatever he has decided" (27:12). Kenaz voices one of Pseudo-Philo's favorite themes—the ways of God are not those of humans. God's attitude to Kenaz's plan to defeat Israel's enemies is complex. God does approve his plan to enter the Amorite camp and seek a sign. But God bypasses Kenaz's preparations involving three hundred soldiers with trumpets. Kenaz makes those preparations without consulting God, and that they prove to be superfluous. God goes Kenaz one better. While Kenaz aims to demonstrate that God can save by a few, God shows that he does not even need these few.

Israel now glorifies God, not Kenaz (27:13-14). They realize that God deserves belief, and they proclaim God's wonders. They now believe that God intends to save his people and that he does not need great numbers, but only holiness.

Kenaz calls from prison those who had doubted him and condemns them to death. They confess that they committed the same sins as the earlier sinners (chapter 25)—lack of trust in God, expressed, for example, by doubting God's wonders for Israel or suspecting that what was written in the Law was Moses' invention. Kenaz's trust in God contrasts with the sinners' skepticism.

Kenaz's final words, a vision he sees (cp. Moses' vision before his death), and his death are related in chapter 28. He says that he has seen the wonders God will work for them "in the last days," establishes a covenant with them so that they will obey the Law, and reminds them of the sinners' fate. Kenaz is filled with a holy spirit and prophesies. He sees the creation and humankind. The outcome of human history is humanity's sin against God. Kenaz's last words are: "If the repose of the just after they have died is like this, we must die to the corruptible world so as not to see sins" (28:10).

Deborah: Deborah fascinates commentators because she is a leader, even though she is a woman. True, she does not fight. She needs Barak for that. But Barak is clearly subject to her. In Jdgs. 5, Deborah's words are important. In LAB, those words become still more important. Deborah becomes a teacher comparable to Moses. Much of her story (chapters 30-33) contains her instruction of the people. God says that she will "enlighten" Israel. This word is used elsewhere in the work mostly with God or Moses as the subject.[23] As in Judges so in LAB, when the people are without a leader, they stray. This is the situation in which God appoints Deborah. The people recognize that their sins cause their current oppression.

Of all the judges, only Deborah is appointed through a direct speech of God.[24] When Deborah becomes leader, she immediately instructs Israel in a long speech. She delivers no such speech in the Bible. Deborah tells of God's deeds for Israel, stressing the giving of the Law. She shows that Israel has disobeyed God whenever they have been without a good leader. She announces that God will come to their aid, not because they deserve it, but because of the covenant God established with their fathers. Deborah has full knowledge of what is to happen. She even quotes Sisera, so she knows what he is thinking (31:1).

Judges does not say explicitly that God's spirit comes upon Deborah. LAB corrects this. In the hymn Deborah and the people sing in LAB 32, Deborah is told to praise God so that the holy spirit will awaken in her and to witness that she saw the stars fighting for Israel. The emphasis throughout the hymn and particularly on the parts concerning Deborah is on witness and praise for God's actions for Israel. As usual in Pseudo-Philo's, the emphasis is not on glorification of the characters, but on God's glorification.

Deborah delivers her final testament in chapter 33. There she is called a "woman of God," a phrase Harrington considers the female counterpart to "man of God."[25] She says that she "enlightens" the people "as one of the female race." Then she says, "Obey me like your mother and heed my words. . . ." Deborah's gender is highlighted here. It is precisely as a woman that she leads Israel. When Deborah dies, the people say, "Behold there has perished a *mother from Israel*, and the holy one who exercised leadership in the house of Jacob" (33:6).

Jael: When Barak proves reluctant to fight Sisera without having Deborah with him, Jdgs. 4 says that for this reason Sisera will be defeated by a woman, Jael. Pseudo-Philo avoids the idea that being defeated by a woman is shameful. Instead he reinforces the idea of moral causality by saying that a woman defeats Sisera because he intended to steal Israelite women (31:1). Pseudo-Philo, influenced by the story of Judith, adds to the biblical story the idea that Jael was beautiful and used her beauty to trap Sisera. This fits the sexual element in the story of Sisera.

The author emphasizes Jael's dependence on God. Jael prays, reminding God of the harm Sisera has done to Israel, and she tells God of her plans. She seeks a sign that God approves of her plans, and it is granted. She later asks for a second sign, which is also granted. There is an implicit contrast with Gideon. Whereas Gideon asks for two signs because he is reluctant to follow God's instructions, Jael seeks assurance that she is acting in accord with God's will, as did Kenaz earlier. The second sign that

Jael requests, where she rolls Sisera off the bed without awakening him, is another allusion to Judith's story.

Samuel: Samuel's story also begins with a notice that leadership is lacking in Israel. The people voice their need for a leader like Kenaz to deliver them from distress and say, "It is not appropriate for the people to be without a ruler" (49:1). They then cast lots but are unsuccessful. No one is chosen. They interpret this as God's abandonment of them because of their unworthiness, and they think they must choose their own leader. They are wrong on both counts. Although God occasionally turns a deaf ear to Israel because of its unfaithfulness, he never abandons it. And it is always a mistake for the people to choose their own leader. Nethez, not present in the Bible, insists that Israel trust God and cast lots again. This time the lot falls on Elkanah, who refuses to become leader. Israel accuses God of neglecting his chosen people. God reacts angrily. He then tells the people that the son of Elkanah's sterile wife will become a prophet. This strengthens Pseudo-Philo's theme that left to itself, Israel makes the wrong choices, and that God sometimes communicates with Israel in unambiguous ways because of Israel's limitations and sinfulness.

There follows the story of Samuel's conception and dedication to the sanctuary. Unlike in the Bible, Eli knows that the one to be born of Hannah will be a prophet (50:8). Later, he tells Hannah that her son is the one for whom the people have prayed and the one "previously promised to the tribes" (51:2). The point is supported when in Hannah's song she says that the psalmist predicted Samuel's coming and associated him with the "priests," Moses and Aaron (Ps. 99:6; LAB 51:6). All of this makes clear that Samuel comes because of God's will and stresses both his prophetic role and connection with Moses. God's initiative is also stressed through the omission of the biblical idea that Hannah promised to dedicate her child to God's service. Samuel is born not because of Hannah, but because God has planned it. The story of Samuel's birth ends with a remarkable scene, not in the Bible, in which the people bring Samuel to Eli with joy: "They stood Samuel before the LORD, anointed him, and said, 'Let the prophet live among the people, and may he be a light to this nation for a long time!'" (51:7).

As with the other good leaders in LAB, Samuel's main task is to convey God's will and judgments to the people. God and Eli have already proclaimed him a prophet, and in Hannah's song, she sings that since Samuel is to born from her, the "ordinance of the Lord" and "the truth" will come through her (50:4). Samuel is to be a light for both Israel and the nations (51:6; see Is. 49:6; 51:4). The words for prophet and prophecy are repeated throughout these chapters.

As in the Bible, Samuel plays a crucial role in the advent of the monarchy. But throughout this story, his dependence on God is never in question. Samuel misunderstands numerous things: he knows nothing at first of his role (52:1), a role of which Eli, Hannah, and the people are aware. Later Eli explains to him his chosenness (53:12), which frightens Samuel (as in the Bible—1 Sam. 3:15, 18); he needs to be instructed by Eli about distinguishing between God and demons (chapter 53; as in the Bible); he is unaware that the ark has been stolen by the Philistines, because God has sent him away; when he finds out about the ark, he thinks it means Israel's destruction, which is untrue; he thinks that God cannot appoint a king "before the time," although God does so; even after his death, when called up by Saul he is confused, thinking it the last judgment. None of this detracts from his stature, however. Rather, it makes him a better example of how humans must defer to God. This attitude is enshrined in Samuel's first words to God, when he receives his first revelation: "If I am capable, speak; for you know more about me (than I do)" (53:7). Samuel is exemplary in that he is always open to God's will, is willing to abandon his own ignorance, never acts out of presumption, and conveys God's word to the people fearlessly.

Samuel begins his prophetic ministry remarkably early in Pseudo-Philo, at the age of eight. Josephus says that he was twelve

(*Ant.* 5 § 348), while the Bible leaves his age unstated. Samuel's age is the more remarkable given that God did not approach Moses until he was eighty, according to LAB (53:2). Pseudo-Philo's comparison of Samuel to Moses is high praise.

As in the Bible, Samuel's first prophetic task is unpleasant—the announcement of punishment on Eli's house. While 1 Sam. 3:15 briefly notes Samuel's reluctance to prophesy against Eli's family and 3:17 equally briefly has Eli persuade him, Pseudo-Philo plays up both of these elements. Samuel laments having to prophesy against the one who nourished him and to "prophesy evil as if it were good" (53:11). Eli counters that God foretold Samuel's advent as prophet, that he, Eli, knew that Hannah would bear Samuel, and that God has always guided Samuel. He then orders Samuel to do his duty. Samuel's pain here recalls Moses' reaction to the golden calf earlier.

Pseudo-Philo fabricates an interaction between God and Samuel when God tells him of the theft of the ark (55:1). Again, Samuel is full of distress, and he sounds much like the Ezra of 4 Ezra. He protests that cannot understand the destruction of his people, that he will end his days in sorrow, and that there is no reason to go on living. God assures him that he will rescue the ark, but Samuel objects that the present generation will still suffer. Pseudo-Philo's God offers more satisfaction than does the God of 4 Ezra, for he tells Samuel that he will witness God's vengeance within his lifetime.

When the people approach Samuel to request a king, he knows of God's plan for monarchy, but he knows also that this request comes too early. Therefore, he thinks that is impossible for God to appoint a king now. He thus demonstrates an ironic combination of knowledge and ignorance about God's ways. God tells him that he will appoint a king, but one who will harm the people.

Pseudo-Philo rewrites the story of Saul looking for his father's donkeys so as to stress God's direction of the action. Samuel prays, "Direct your people, Lord, and tell me what you have planned for them" (56:5). He tells Saul that God has chosen

him "and has directed all your ways, and your future will also be directed" (56:5). Although God does appoint Saul king, Samuel does not anoint him. This puts Samuel at a greater remove from Saul's kingship than in the Bible. In 57:1, Samuel presents to the people "your king" and says that he is there "as God commanded me." This also distances Samuel from the proceedings. In a key address (57:1-3), Samuel wishes to prove that it is not due to his lack of leadership that the people ask for a king. In the Bible, the people admit that Samuel has done no wrong and that they have sinned in asking for a king. In LAB, they go further, saying that their actions prove that they "are not worthy to be governed by a prophet" (57:4). At the end of the scene, the people and Saul proclaim, "Long live Samuel the prophet!" (57:5). The entire scene establishes prophecy, as embodied in Samuel, as superior to kingship, and it emphasizes Samuel's prophetic role.

In the Bible, there are two versions of why Saul loses God's favor. In one, Saul offers sacrifice without Samuel. In the other, Saul does not execute the Amalekite king Agag after defeating him, nor does he treat all the spoils as *herem*. In the Bible, God reveals Saul's misdeed to Samuel and says he regrets making Saul king. Samuel then castigates Saul. There follows a lengthy interaction between Samuel and Saul in which Samuel actually shows some sympathy for Saul, since once Saul confesses his sin Samuel "turns back" to him while Saul worships. Samuel then slaughters Agag, although God does not explicitly tell him to do so.

Pseudo-Philo rewrites this scene, increasing God's role. LAB 58 chooses the second story of Saul's sin, the one concerning Agag. He lengthens God's speech to Samuel. God accuses Saul of greed, a charge not explicit in the biblical text, and he tells Samuel to allow Agag to be with his wife so that he can produce an heir who will cause Saul harm. He then omits the lengthy interaction between Saul and Samuel. Samuel simply carries out God's judgment. This is made clearer when LAB says that God orders Samuel to kill Agag, a command not recorded in the Bible.

God now tells him that the time has now come to appoint a king. This reinforces the idea that Samuel was right in that Saul's kingship comes too early. As in the Bible, Samuel does not know which of Jesse's sons to anoint. In LAB, God almost taunts Samuel: "Where is your vision that your heart sees? Are you not the one who said to Saul, '*I am the one who sees*'? And why do you not know whom you should anoint? And now this reproach is sufficient for you" (59:2).

Samuel now disappears from the action until his death in 64:1. The Philistines recognize that Samuel's death leaves Israel vulnerable, because it has been protected by the intercession of "Samuel the prophet." As in the Bible, Saul uses a medium to call Samuel up for consultation. LAB places in Samuel's mouth a speech in which he says that God has allowed him to be raised only so that he can pronounce God's judgment on Saul. Since Saul has now sinned a second time, he and his sons will die the following day. Samuel says that Saul's "jealousy" will result in his losing everything. So Samuel's final appearance emphasizes God's control.

Hannah: As with all the positive characters in LAB, Hannah is a mouthpiece for Pseudo-Philo's views. Her hymn demonstrates knowledge of Samuel's significance. Her role is decreased in ways that enhance God's role. Pseudo-Philo omits her oath to dedicate Samuel to God's service, so that Samuel comes in fulfillment of God's long-standing purpose.

Pseudo-Philo enhances the cruelty of Peninnah and the piety of Hannah. Peninnah says that a woman's beauty and a husband's love are worth nothing, and that the only thing that counts is having children. Ironically, she refers to Rachel and Jacob to make her point. The irony consists in the fact that Hannah resembles Rachel. Both are barren at first, both are beautiful and loved by their husbands, and, later in the story, Hannah is like Rachel in that God gives her a child. Hannah is like Rachel in these ways in the Bible, too, but there Peninnah does not refer to Rachel. Eli attests to Hannah's piety, saying that her conduct is better than that of Peninnah and

that is more important than having children (50:3). He generalizes by saying that richness consists not in abundance of children but in abounding "in the will of God" (50:5).

Saul: Saul typifies bad leadership. He ascends the throne only because the people demand it, contrary to God's will. His reign is marked by his "greed" in the case of Agag the Amalekite and his jealousy of David. His removing wizards and mediums from the land is attributed to his desire for fame (64:1). Saul himself testifies to his own wickedness and expresses that hope that his own death will atone for his sins (64:9).

In the Bible, Saul kills himself. In LAB, Saul is killed by the son of Agag, as foretold by God. The fulfillment is acknowledged by Saul (65:4). He then instructs his killer to inform David of his death and to say, "Be not mindful of my hatred or my injustice" (65:5).

The main difference in Saul's portrait in LAB and the Bible is the clearer focus in LAB on Saul's sin through the choice of only one act as responsible for his loss of kingship, the characterization of that act as greed, the explanation that the calling up of Samuel is a second offence, requiring Saul's death, Samuel's condemnations of Saul with respect to greed, using the medium, and jealousy, and Saul's own admissions of his wickedness. The author has made the story a clear example of moral causality.

David: LAB ends with Saul's death and does not recount David's reign. Although Pseudo-Philo is concerned with leadership in Israel, he is not interested in kingship as such or with messianic hope. Several of the leaders in the book are model leaders—Moses, Joshua, Kenaz, Deborah, and Samuel, but they are not kings. The story of Samuel seems to promote prophecy over kingship. But certainly the signs are good for David's rule. His kingship is predicted by God (62:2) and by a spirit possessing Saul (62:2). God predicts David's future victories (59:5). Pseudo-Philo adds a psalm of David acknowledging God's protection and favor (59:4).[26] The song David sings to relieve Saul of his evil spirit evinces a sophisticated knowledge of the origin of demons and predicts Solomon's power over demons, a theme found in other Jewish traditions.

The account of the battle between David and Goliath enhances God's role. David connects the coming battle with God's earlier prediction of victory (61:3; see 59:5). Before killing Goliath, David tells him that their mothers were sisters, Ruth and Orpah, and that while Ruth followed God, Orpah chose the Philistine gods. Then Goliath perceives that David is accompanied by God's angel and declares that his death is not due to David alone. The detail in the Bible that Saul does not recognize David after the battle is explained by David's association with the angel. Since he has just participated in a joint operation with this superhuman figure, he is transformed, just as Moses was transformed on Sinai and was not recognized by the people. These details reinforce the idea that it is God who conquers Goliath and the Philistines.

Since the book ends abruptly, some speculate that its original ending has been lost. The present ending functions somewhat as does the ending of the gospel of Mark. Both works lay the groundwork for what is to come. In doing so, they challenge their respective communities. For Mark, it is the challenge to take up discipleship and to live it in a more successful way than the first disciples have done. For LAB, it is the challenge to find leaders in the Jewish community that understand the relationship between strong leadership and trust in God. Pseudo-Philo is less concerned that the Davidic monarchy be the form of that leadership than that future leaders follow the example of figures like Moses, Joshua, Kenaz, and Deborah.

Women: Women in Pseudo-Philo appear mainly in a positive light,[27] but it would be too much to say, as some have done, that Pseudo-Philo is a "feminist." That is an anachronism, and it would be too much to claim that Pseudo-Philo has overcome his patriarchal culture. But it is noteworthy that while he might have abbreviated or even deleted Deborah's story, he enhances it, adding considerably to her portrait in Judges. The same is true of his treatment of Jael. Other details of the narrative reinforce the point.

Israel: To the extent that the people of Israel are a composite character in LAB, they are portrayed pessimistically. They act much as they do in the book of Judges. Without a good leader, they go wrong. When they try to choose their own leaders, they also err. And they are prey to bad leaders, as well as to temptations from outside Israel. God frequently displays impatience with them, often wishing to give up on them entirely, were it not for the covenant with the ancestors. Even when they are well-intentioned, the people often err. This is the case, for example, when they react to the pharaoh's wicked plot, or when they devise plans to deal with the crisis at the Red Sea.

Key aspects of Pseudo-Philo's portrait of Israel appear in the story of Kenaz. Kenaz's first act as leader is to discover who is sinning and so preventing Israel from being successful in battle. The episode recalls the Achan episode of Josh. 7. Kenaz's casting of lots determines that there are sinners in every tribe, where in Josh. 7, only one family is guilty. Israel's sins are described generally as not believing in the wonders God has done for Israel (25:6). Many of them are skeptical about the Torah, and some even think that it is an invention of Moses and not truly divine.

God: God is really the main character in LAB.[28] Every character is rewritten to enhance God's role. Pseudo-Philo praises good characters, but mainly insofar as they exemplify subjection to and trust in God. Their main accomplishments are credited to God. This point has been reinforced above, so here the results are simply summarized.

Pseudo-Philo makes few abstract statements about God. God is defined by his action within Israel's history. God frequently speaks in the narrative, and his words in LAB are often not found in the corresponding biblical stories. God gives commands, directs the action, judges the characters' actions, predicts what is to come, and so on. The reader often hears God's thoughts which react to and determine events. Good leaders are dependent on God. Bad leaders inevitably fail. God's plans are never in vain, so to oppose them is to fail. Prophecy proves God's control of history.

LAB examines Israel's history (chapters 1-5 are a prologue to Israel's history) and proves that any oppression or failure it has suffered has been its own fault. God, in every case, has been faithful to Israel and to the covenant. Even when God would have been justified in rejecting Israel, he has never done so. Good leaders often make this point, and the people occasionally admit it. God punishes Israel, but never to the extent of destroying it. So LAB functions as a theodicy. The problem it addresses is not so specific as the destruction of the temple, as in 4 Ezra or 2 Baruch, for example. Rather it is the general situation in first-century Jewish Palestine, where Israel is dominated by foreign powers and must strive for a way to find effective leadership and to remain loyal to God.

Summary: Pseudo-Philo systematically rewrites the Bible to advance his own themes. This is seen clearly in his treatment of biblical figures. He is particularly interested in leadership. A good leader is determined by his or her trust in God. Biblical traits such as courage are prized, but underlying such traits must be a total lack of presumption. Whether the leader goes to war against Israel's enemies is less important than whether he or she depends completely on God not only for the success of specific actions but also for their very conception. When it comes to the internal affairs of Israel, the leader must be a teacher of God's ways and one who constantly reminds the people of their covenantal obligations and of God's faithfulness to them. Pseudo-Philo uses its portrayal of biblical characters to advance other themes as well. Among them are that God's ways are not human ways, moral causality, God's unconditional faithfulness to Israel, disapproval of intermarriage, and so on.

The Bible is consistently rewritten to enhance God's role in the story. Characters are enhanced in ways that demonstrate their trust in and reliance on God. The people of Israel are portrayed somewhat pessimistically, but they are capable of being faithful to God if they have a good leader.

Comparison with Josephus: Feldman has produced several studies of characters in Josephus.[29] From his studies it is clear that Josephus exalts individual characters more than does Pseudo-Philo. In many cases, he provides summaries of a character's traits and accomplishments. Feldman considers this typically Hellenistic. Similar treatments of biblical characters are found in Philo. In contrast, Pseudo-Philo seems interested in characters only insofar as they support the sorts of themes outlined above, such as God's sovereignty and control of history. This is not to say, of course, that Philo and Josephus do not treat such themes, or that Pseudo-Philo is completely uninterested in human characters. But there is a difference of approach between Pseudo-Philo on the one hand and Josephus and Philo on the other. Characterization in Pseudo-Philo remains closer to that of the Hebrew Bible itself. Pseudo-Philo develops themes found in the Bible, and he does so in a way that makes them applicable to his own day.

Bibliography
Brown, Cheryl Anne, *No Longer Be Silent: First Century Jewish Portraits of Biblical Women* (Louisville, 1992).

Jacobson, Howard, *A Commentary on Pseudo-Philo's Liber Antiquitatum Biblicarum: With Latin Text & English Translation* (2 volumes; Leiden, 1996).

Murphy, Frederick J., *Pseudo-Philo: Rewriting the Bible*, (New York, 1991).

Nickelsburg, George W.E., "Good and Bad Leaders in Pseudo-Philo's *Liber Antiquitatum Biblicarum*," in George W.E. Nickelsburg and John J. Collins, eds., *Ideal Figures in Ancient Judaism: Profiles and Paradigms* (Chico, 1980), pp. 189-221.

Van der Horst, Pieter Willem. "Portraits of Biblical Women in Pseudo-Philo's *Liber Antiquitatum Biblicarum*," in *Journal for the Study of the Pseudepigrapha* 5 (1989), pp. 29-46.

Notes
[1] Other examples of the genre are Josephus's *Biblical Antiquities*, *Jubilees*, and the *Genesis Apocryphon*.

[2] For a narrative analysis of the work, see Frederick J. Murphy, *Pseudo-Philo* (New York, 1991).

[3] For more on the traditions Pseudo-Philo uses, see Howard Jacobson, *A Commentary on Pseudo-Philo's* Liber Antiquitatum Biblicarum (Leiden, 1996); M.R. James, *The Biblical Antiquities of Pseudo-Philo* (New York, 1971), especially Louis Feldman's "Prolegomenon" there; Daniel Harrington, *et al.*, *Les Antiquités Bibliques* (Paris, 1996).

[4] See George W.E. Nickelsburg, "Good and Bad Leaders in Pseudo-Philo's *Liber Antiquitatum Biblicarum*," in George W.E. Nickelsburg and John J. Collins, eds., *Ideal Figures in Ancient Judaism* (Chico, 1980), pp. 189-221.

[5] Frederick J. Murphy, "Divine Plan, Human Plan: A Structuring Theme in Pseudo-Philo," in *Jewish Quarterly Review* 77 (1986), pp. 5-14.

[6] Cp., for example, 2 Macc. 6-7.

[7] The translation used here is Daniel J. Harrington, "Pseudo-Philo," in James H. Charlesworth, ed., *Old Testament Pseudepigrapha* (Garden City, 1985), vol. 2, pp. 297-377. Italics within the quotes indicate text that agrees with some ancient biblical manuscript.

[8] See Frederick J. Murphy, "Retelling the Bible: Idolatry in Pseudo-Philo," in *Journal of Biblical Literature* 107 (1988), pp. 275-287.

[9] The rabbis also justify Tamar's action. See also Jub. 41:23.

[10] Jacobson, p. 412, finds verbal parallels in 1 Sam. 27:12 and Exod. 21:6. He also notes a similarity with Hannah's words regarding Samuel. The midrash parallels Moses and Samuel.

[11] Following Jacobson's suggestion (pp. 412-413) for the sense of *faciam in eis gloriam meam* in 9:7.

[12] Jacobson thinks that these words have been corrupted in transmission.

[13] The word translated "Law" here is actually *superexcellentia*. See Jacobson, pp. 415-417) for alternative translations.

[14] The midrash also connects Gen. 6:3 and Moses; see Jacobson, pp. 417-418.

[15] Note the parallel between God's words to Amram here and the speech to Amram by God in *Ant.* 2 §§ 212-216 (Jacobson, p. 412).

[16] In later Jewish sources, Miriam also has a dream concerning Moses' birth (Jacobson, pp. 417-418). In Josephus, Amram has the dream.

[17] Jacobson (p. 420) cites later Jewish sources

to the effect that Moses leads Israel even in the world to come.

[18] There is only one parallel to this, found in the midrash (Jacobson, p. 427).

[19] Jacobson, p. 425.

[20] There are some parallels to this in Jewish tradition (Jacobson, p. 430).

[21] For a full discussion of this story including its parallels in the midrash, see Saul Olyan, "The Israelites Debate Their Options at the Sea of Reeds: *LAB* 10:3, Its Parallels, and Pseudo-Philo's Ideology and Background," in *Journal of Biblical Literature* 110 (1991), pp. 75-91; Murphy, "Divine Plan;" Jacobson, pp. 435-438.

[22] Frederick J. Murphy, "Korah's Rebellion in Pseudo-Philo 16," in Harold W. Attridge, John J. Collins, and Thomas H. Tobin, Jr., eds., *Of Scribes and Scrolls* (New York, 1990), pp. 111-120.

[23] Ibid.

[24] Pieter Willem van der Horst, "Portraits of Biblical Women in Pseudo-Philo's *Liber Antiquitatum Biblicarum*," in *Journal for the Study of the Pseudepigrapha* 5 (1989), p. 34.

[25] "Pseudo-Philo," p. 347.

[26] See John Strugnell, "More Psalms of David," in *Catholic Biblical Quarterly* 27 (1965), pp. 207-216. He suggests the psalm comes from a non-canonical collection of David's psalms.

[27] See Cheryl Anne Brown, *No Longer Be Silent* (Louisville, 1992); van der Horst.

[28] See Frederick J. Murphy, "God in Pseudo-Philo," in *Journal for the Study of Judaism* 19 (1988), pp. 1-18.

[29] See, for example, Louis Feldman, "Hellenizations in Josephus' *Jewish Antiquities*: The Portrait of Abraham," in Louis H. Feldman and Gohei Gata, eds., *Josephus, the Bible, and History* (Detroit, 1989), pp. 133-155.

FREDERICK J. MURPHY

R

RABBINIC LITERATURE, LOGICS OF:

The word "logic" here stands for the determinative principle of intelligibility of discourse and cogency of thought. Logic is what tells people that one thing connects, or intersects, with another, while something else does not, hence, making connections between this and that, but not this and the other thing. And logic further tells people what follows from the connections they make, generating the conclusions they are to draw. Governing logic tells us what is thinkable and what is not, what can be said intelligibly and what cannot. Accordingly, the first thing we want to know about any piece of writing is its logic of cogent discourse. Logic is what joins one sentence to the next and forms the whole into paragraphs of meaning, intelligible propositions, each with its place and sense in a still larger, accessible system. And logic as a matter of fact makes possible the sharing of propositions of general intelligibility and therefore forms the cement of a whole literature, such as the Rabbinic canon of Judaism's formative age.

The matter of defining the governing logic bears more than formal consequence. It also introduces the social side of a literature. Specifically, because of shared logic, one mind connects to another, yielding self-evidence, so that, in writing or in orally formulated and orally transmitted teaching, public discourse becomes possible. Because of logic, debate on issues of general interest takes place. Still more to the point, because of logic a mere anthology of statements about a single subject becomes a composition of theorems about that subject, so that facts serve to demonstrate and convey propositions. Through logic, the parts, bits and pieces of information, add up to a sum greater than themselves, generate information or insight beyond what they contain. What people think—exegesis of discrete facts in accord with a fixed hermeneutic of the intellect—knows no limit. How they think makes all the difference. Since each of the documents of Rabbinic literature sets forth a cogent statement, a clear picture of the conventions of logic that permits cogent discourse is required.

Modes of patterned thought form propositions out of facts, turning information into knowledge, knowledge into a system of sense and explanation and therefore composing a shared structure of sensibility and meaning for the social order. The logic of coherent discourse exhibited by the writer of a given document is what tells people about how to make interesting connections between one thing, one fact, for instance, and some other, therefore instructing them on what deserves notice, and what can be ignored. Every document in the Rabbinic literature selects a particular means of holding together two or more sentences and forming of them a coherent thought, that is to say, of making the whole more than the sum of the parts. There are, in fact, four such logics, three of them entirely familiar, one of them not.

First, let us consider a concrete example of how a logic of coherent discourse turns facts into propositions, information into

truth. The simple sequence moves us from two unrelated facts to two connected facts and thence to a proposition. Here is one example of a possible logic of coherent discourse:

[1] I threw a rock at a dog. It rained.
[2] I threw a rock at a dog, then it rained.
[3] If I throw a rock at a dog, it will rain.

The first set of sentences contains no link, so no conclusions are to be drawn. No unstated premise tells me how the two sentences relate, or whether they relate at all. The second item presents a temporal, narrative link; this happened, then that happened. Conclusions may or may not be drawn. Two events are juxtaposed, but the "then" carries with it no judgment on causation or other modes of explanation, that is, of coherence between sentences. A narrative line extends from the former to the latter sentence. The third formulation of course establishes a conditional link between two facts, forming of them an allegation as to what will happen if one does such and so. The "if" of course may be replaced with a "since," and a variety of other joining language will establish a connection between the two sentences (or clauses of one sentence). The third case shows us how the sum of the whole exceeds the parts.

This simple set of sentences shows what I mean when I point out that some facts are inert, others bear consequence. Facts that fail to intersect with others in general gain slight notice; those that form structures and convey sense gain systematic consequence and ultimately form an encompassing account of how things are and should be, why we do things one way and not another: an ethos, an ethics, an account of a "we," altogether, a system. The convention of a shared logic of coherent discourse moreover explains to people about the consequences of the connections that they are taught to perceive, yielding conclusions of one sort, rather than another, based on one mode of drawing conclusions from the connections that are made, rather than some other.

Making connections and drawing conclusions represent abstractions. Let me give a concrete example of what is under discussion. It is, very simply, what constitutes the "and" and the "equals" of thought, e.g., in the sentence, "two and two equal four." The way in which people add up two and two to make four always requires the appeal to the *and*, and that is what endures, that *and* of the two and two equal four, and, too, the *equal*, which is to say, the conclusion yielded by the *and*. The logic lasts: the *and* of making connections, the *equal* of reaching conclusions. This endures: the certainty that—to shift the symbols that serve to clarify this simple point—X + Y are connected and generate conclusion Z, but that (for purposes of discussion here) the symbol # and the number 4 are not connected and therefore, set side by side, produce a mere nonsense-statement, e.g., # and 4 equal *. The conventions that govern thought and discourse permit us to make one such statement but not the other.

The Propositional Logic of Philosophical Discourse: Propositional and syllogistic logic is the most familiar to us in the West, and it also is the most commonplace in the Rabbinic literature, though the forms that convey the proposition or syllogism are unfamiliar to us. Philosophical discourse is built out of propositions and arguments from facts and reason. The cogency of discourse—the *and* that joins two sentences together into a cogent statement—derives from the argument we wish to make, the fact we wish to establish, the proposition we wish to prove. The tension in this mode of thought arises from the trait of mind that derives from two facts a third, one that transcends the givens. The resolution, then, comes from the satisfying demonstration, out of what we know, of something we did not know but wish to find out, or of something we think we know and wish to prove.

The syllogistic character of philosophical discourse is familiar to us all. That is why commonplaces such as "[1] All Greeks are liars, [2] Demosthenes is a Greek, [3] (therefore) Demosthenes is a liar," need not detain us. In that sequence, fact [1] and fact [2] come together to prove a fact that is not contained within either [1] or [2]. Syllogistic logic yields a sum greater than the parts. From our perspective, we want to identify the connection between two facts.

And what matters in the famous syllogism at hand is that proposition [3] is what joins fact [1] to fact [2] into joined and cogent sentences, that is, the *equal* generates the *and*. In the texts before us, the idiom is exceedingly odd, which makes all the more valuable the exemplification of what is, in fact, a perfectly routine mode of thought. For the issue at hand is one of connection, the *and* of the *two and two*, that is, not of fact (such as is conveyed by the statement of the meaning of a verse or a clause of a verse) but of the relationship between one fact and another. And at stake in the connection is the proposition, the *equal* of the *two and two* equal *four*.

The critical point is in the *equals*, since it is at that result that the point of the connection is both realized but also established. We see a connection between one item and the next because of the third item that the first two generate. In the logic at hand, connection rests upon conclusion. And let me with emphasis state the central point: *that relationship, connection, is shown in a conclusion different from the established facts of two or more sentences that we propose to draw when we set up as a sequence two or more facts and claim out of that sequence to propose a proposition different from, transcending, the facts at hand.*

We demonstrate propositions in a variety of ways, appealing to both a repertoire of probative facts and also a set of accepted modes of argument. In this way we engage in a kind of discourse that gains its logic from what, in general, we may call philosophy: the rigorous analysis and testing of propositions against the canons of an accepted reason. The connection produced by the cogent discourse of philosophy therefore accomplishes the miracle of making the whole more—or less—than the sum of the parts, that is, in the simple language we have used up to now, showing the connections between fact 1 and fact 2, in such wise as to yield proposition A.

Before we move to our concrete example, let me introduce a secondary, but, in our context, important, alternative way for conducting philosophical argument—a way at the foundation of all scientific inquiry. It is the demonstration we know, in general, as comparison and contrast, the search for the rules that express the order and sense of diverse facts. We seek to identify what discrete facts have in common and thereby to state the rule common to them all, e.g., to identify a genus, then its species, and on downward. The fundamental logic of cogency here is simple: something is like something else, therefore it follows the rule of that something else; or it is unlike that something else, therefore it follows the opposite of the rule governing that something else. The way in which the result is presented tells us the principle of cogency. When we classify, we identify a genus and its species and lay them forth in their nomothetic system. The layout often takes the form of a list. The logic before us on that account is called the science of making lists, that is, *Listenwissenschaft*, a way to classify and so establish a set of probative facts, which compel us to reach a given conclusion.

These probative facts may derive from the classification of data, all of which point in one direction and not in another. A catalogue of facts, for example, may be so composed that, through the regularities and indicative traits of the entries, the catalogue yields a proposition. A list of parallel items all together point to a simple conclusion; the conclusion may or may not be given at the end of the catalogue, but the catalogue—by definition—is pointed. All of the catalogued facts are taken to bear self-evident connections to one another, established by those pertinent shared traits implicit in the composition of the list, therefore also bearing meaning and pointing through the weight of evidence to an inescapable conclusion. The discrete facts then join together because of some trait common to them all. This is a mode of classification of facts to lead to an identification of what the facts have in common and—it goes without saying—an explanation of their meaning. These and other modes of philosophical argument are entirely familiar to us all. In calling all of them "philosophical," I mean only to distinguish them from the other three logics we shall presently examine.

The first document to yield a concrete example for our purposes is not in a readily accessible form, e.g., a propositional argument or a list; it is not an essay or a well-composed philosophical argument, but rather a document in the form of a commentary. The choice of this rather odd way of setting forth a proposition, of joining two facts into a cogent statement or linking two sentences into a paragraph (in literary terms) is critical to my argument. For I maintain that the form, commentary, bears no implications for the logic of discourse contained within that form. Arrangements of words by themselves tell us little about the logic that operates therein. To demonstrate the irrelevance of mere form in the analysis of logic, I choose a commentary. In general, a commentary works its way through discrete entries and does not necessarily propose to prove large-scale propositions. On formal grounds, therefore, we should not anticipate a fine example of propositional argument to emerge from writing in such a form. But we now see that a commentary can put together facts into arguments and propositions, sentences into paragraphs, as much as an essay.

We turn to Sifre to Deuteronomy, a systematic commentary on much of the book of Deuteronomy,. The pertinent verse is the following: "For the Lord will vindicate his people and repent himself [JPS: take revenge] for his servants, when he sees that their might is gone, and neither bond nor free is left" (Deut. 32:36). The proposition is not explicitly stated but it is repeatedly implied: when the Israelites are at the point of despair, then God will vindicate them. We shall now see a systematic demonstration of the proposition that, when things are at their worst and the full punishment impends, God relents and saves Israel. And what is critical is at the pivots and the joinings of sentences (Sifre to Deuteronomy CCXXVI:II.):

> 1.A. ". . . when he sees that their might is gone, and neither bond nor free is left:"
>   B. When he sees their destruction, on account of the captivity.
>   C. For all of them went off.

Let me make explicit, in terms of the first case, how I conceive the connections to be established, the conclusion to be drawn. A

PLATES

ותבנית חשמים

לסרת חלבנה

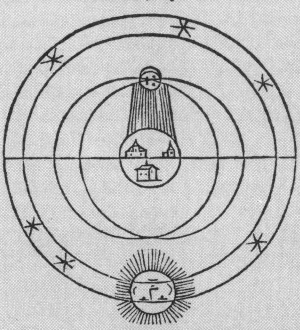

Item eclipsis lunæ fit
secundum uerum op-
positum: situm lumina-
rium, solis autem deli-
quium fit iuxta appa-
rentem & non ueram
coniunctionem, nisi cõ
tingeret in nonagesi-
mo gradu ab ascen-
dente.

In

אֵלֶּה הֵן הָעִנְיָנִים אֲשֶׁר חַלְקוּת הָאֶחָד
רוֹמֵז בָּהֶן אֶל חַלְקוּת הַשֵּׁנִי .
וְיֵשׁ בֵּינֵיהֶן תִּפְרֹשׁ גָּרוֹל מְאֹד אַחֵר
וְהוּא שֶׁלְקוּת הַלְּבָנָה פֶּגַם נִמְצָא
בְּגוּפָהּ שֶׁהוּא מַאֲבִיר אֶרֶץ אוֹרָהּ וּ
וּמַאֲפִיל אֶת גוּפָהּ מִכָּל רוּחוֹתֶיהָ כִּי
הַלְּבָנָה בְּכָל תֵּימִים חֲצִי גוּפָהּ מ
מַאֲפִיל וְהֶחֱצִיו מֵאִיר וּבְעֵת חַלְקוּת
יִהְיֶה הַמַּחֲצִית הַמֵּאִיר מַאֲפִיל בְּלֹי
ר ב אוֹ

Astronomy: An eclipse of the moon, in *Tzurat ha-Aretz* (Form of the Earth), by Abraham b. Hiyya Ha-Nasi.

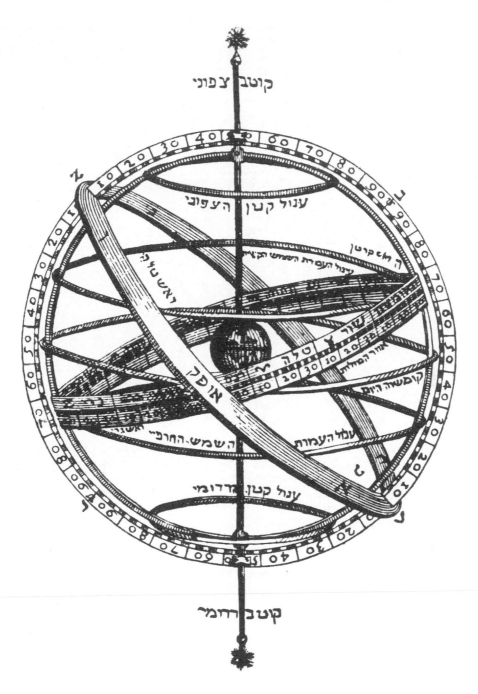

Astronomy: Image of an astrolabe, taken from *Ma'aseh Tuviyyah* by Tobias Cohn,
Venice, Italy, 1708.

Astrology: Mosaic from the synagogue of Beit Aleph, with sun, moon, stars, zodiac, and, in the corners, images of the four seasons. Taken from *Denkmäler der Jüdischen Antike* by Adolf Reifenberg, Berlin, Germany, 1937.

Astrology: Painted ceiling, Chodorov, Ukraine. By Israel Lisnicki, 1714.

Astrology: Porcelain wedding cup from Denmark (1856). Hebrew inscription says: "4 Tevet, sign of Capricorn, on the day of his wedding and the day his heart rejoiced; and this is the Torah Moses gave to the children of Israel." (Torben Samson Collection, Efrat, Israel)

Honor of Parents in Judaism: "The Examination" by Moritz Daniel Oppenheim (Germany, 1800-1882). In a traditional Jewish home the father reviews what the child has learned, while the mother looks on proudly.

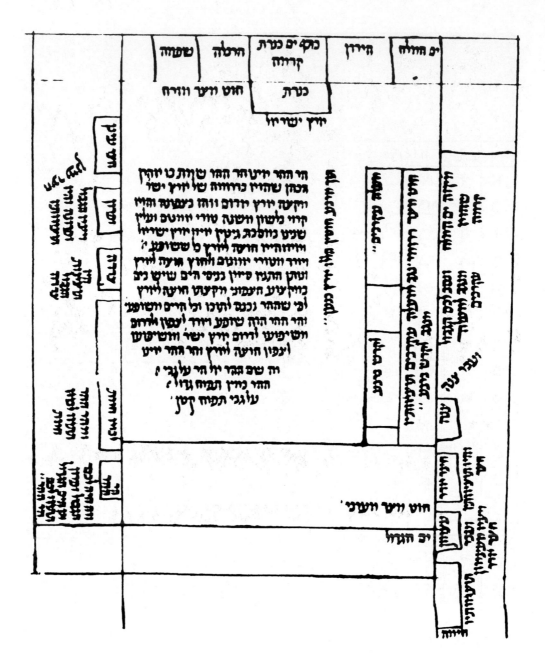

Rashi: Rashi's map of the boundaries of the land of Israel from his commentary to Num. 34:11, according to Vienna Hebrew ms. 220, folio 79r. (Photo courtesy Österreichische Nationalbibliothek, Vienna, Austria)

The Samaritan Scripts

	I	Majuscule				Minuscule				X	
	I	II	III	IV	V	VI	VII	VIII	IX	X	
א	⳿	ℵ	ℵ	⳥	ℵ	⳥	ℵ	ℵ	ℵ	Ӿ	ā'lāf
ב	⳥	⳥	⳥	⳥	⳥	⳥	⳥	⳥	⳥	⳥	bīt
ג	⳥	⳥	⳥	⳥	⳥	⳥	⳥	⳥	⳥	Ⳅ	gā'mān
ד	⳥	⳥	⳥	⳥	⳥	⳥	⳥	⳥	⳥	⳥	dā'lāt
ה	⳥	⳥	⳥	⳥	⳥	⳥	⳥	⳥	⳥	Ӟ	īy
ו	⳥	ℵ	ℵ	ℵ	⳥	⳥	⳥	⳥	⳥	⳥	bā
ז	⳥	⳥	⳥	⳥	⳥	⳥	⳥	⳥	⳥	⳥	zēn
ח	⳥	⳥	⳥	⳥	⳥	⳥	⳥	⳥	⳥	⳥	īt
ט	⳥	⳥	⳥	⳥	⳥	⳥	⳥	⳥	⳥	⳥	ṭīt
י	⳥	⳥	⳥	⳥	⳥	⳥	⳥	⳥	⳥	Ⳣ	yūt
ך כ	⳥	⳥	⳥	⳥	⳥	⳥	⳥	⳥	⳥	⳥	kāf
ל	⳥	⳥	⳥	⳥	⳥	⳥	⳥	⳥	⳥	2	lā'bāt
ם מ	⳥	⳥	⳥	⳥	⳥	⳥	⳥	⳥	⳥	⳥	mīm
ן נ	⳥	⳥	⳥	⳥	⳥	⳥	⳥	⳥	⳥	⳥	nūn
ס	⳥	⳥	⳥	⳥	⳥	⳥	⳥	⳥	⳥	⳥	sin'gāt, sin'kāt
ע	⳥	⳥	⳥	⳥	⳥	⳥	⳥	⳥	⳥	⳥	īn
ף פ	⳥	⳥	⳥	⳥	⳥	⳥	⳥	⳥	⳥	⳥	fī
ץ צ	⳥	⳥	⳥	⳥	⳥	⳥	⳥	⳥	⳥	⳥	ṣā'dīy
ק	⳥	⳥	⳥	⳥	⳥	⳥	⳥	⳥	⳥	⳥	qūf
ר	⳥	⳥	⳥	⳥	⳥	⳥	⳥	⳥	⳥	⳥	rīš
ש	⳥	⳥	⳥	⳥	⳥	⳥	⳥	⳥	⳥	⳥	šān
ת	⳥	ℵ	ℵ	⳥	ℵ	ℵ	ℵ	⳥	ℵ	Ӿ	tāf

Samaritan Judaism: The Samaritan scripts.

Samaritan Judaism: Young Samaritan studying with his teacher (Yefet Tzedaka in Nablus, Israel, c. 1960).

Die Predigt

P. G. 1. r.
ges. gesch.
19

Sermons in Modern Judaism: "Die Predigt". Paul Grödel Verlag 1890-1910. Postcard, artist unknown. (Courtesy Jewish Historical Museum, Amsterdam, The Netherlands)

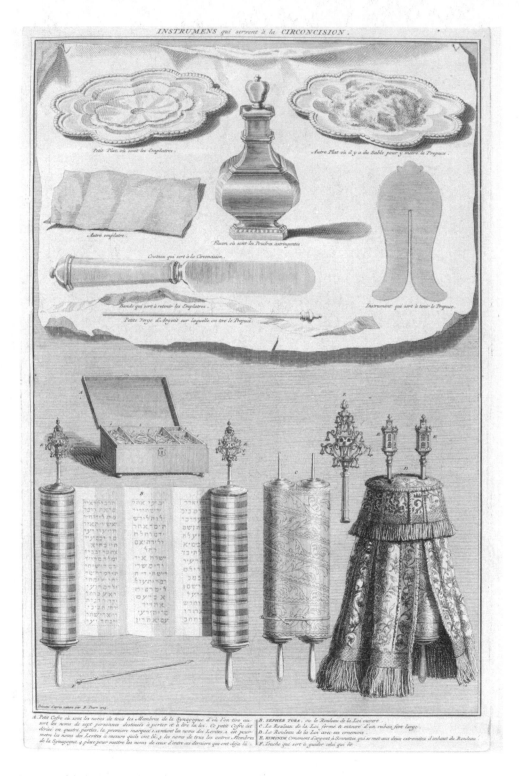

Torah and Culture: Instruments used for circumcision and a Torah scroll with decorations. Copperplate by B. Piccart, 1725. (Courtesy Jewish Historical Museum, Amsterdam, The Netherlands)

Torah and Culture: Wooden box, holding the scroll of the law, decorated with a three-pointed crown and a miniature Ark of the Covenant in copper and velvet. From the inheritance of Jacob and Isaac Henriques de Castro, The Hague, The Netherlands. (Photo courtesy Jewish Historical Museum, Amsterdam, The Netherlands)

Zionism in Moroccan Judaism: Jewish Family from Fez, Morocco, c. 1925.

Zionism in Moroccan Judaism: Membership card of the religious Zionist youth movement, BaHaD (Brit Halutzim Datiyyim), Meknes, Morocco, c. 1947. (Private collection Henry Toledano)

Le Vénérable Rabbin Amram Ben Diouan

תמונת הרה״ג המלומד בנסים מוהר״ר עמרם דיוואן
זצ״ל זיע״א מעה״ק חברון ת״ו ובא שד״ר למערב
ונתבש״ם בעיר וואדזאן בחדש אב שנת תקמ״ב פ״ק
שנמצאת בהולאנדא בין כתבים עתיקים

תמונת הרה״ג רבי עמרם בן דיוואן זיע״א

Zionism in Moroccan Judaism: Pictorial presentation of Rabbi Amram Ben Diwan, an emissary from Hebron to Morocco where he died suddenly in 1782 in the northern town of Ouezzane. His tomb became a popular place of pilgrimage for Moroccan Jews, especially on *Lag ba-Omer*. (Private collection Henry Toledano) represents the conclusion, that is, the proposition to be proved. B, C present the facts that are connected. C is the first fact, namely, all of them went off into exile. B then is the second fact, that [1] when God saw that they had gone into captivity, and [2] were without arrogance or power, yielding the unstated conclusion, [3] he had mercy on them, and that then validates the proposition, A. Turned around, the second and third of the three sentences work together so as to make a point that neither one of them by itself establishes, and that is how such a syllogism works in general. Then a sequence of syllogisms of the same kind, not all of them fully spelled out and most of them as truncated is the first, make the same point, establishing the besought theorem by setting forth numerous demonstrations of that theorem: "When he sees. . . ."

2.A. Another teaching concerning the phrase, ". . . when he sees:"
B. When they despaired of redemption.
3.A. Another teaching concerning the phrase, ". . . when he sees [that their might is gone, and neither bond nor free is left:"
B. When he sees that the last penny is gone from the purse,
C. in line with this verse: "And when they have made an end of breaking in pieces the power of the holy people, all these things shall be finished" (Dan. 12:7) [Hammer's translation].
4.A. Another teaching concerning the phrase, ". . . when he sees that their might is gone, and neither bond nor free is left:"
B. When he sees that among them there are no men who seek mercy for them as Moses had,
C. in line with this verse: "Therefore he said that he would destroy them, had not Moses his chosen one stood before him in the breach" (Ps. 106:23). . . .
5.A. Another teaching concerning the phrase, ". . . when he sees that their might is gone, and neither bond nor free is left:"
B. When he sees that among there are no men who seek mercy for them as Aaron had,
C. in line with this verse: "And he stood between the dead and the living and the plague was stayed" (Num. 17:13).
6.A. Another teaching concerning the phrase, ". . . when he sees that their might is gone, and neither bond nor free is left:"
B. When he sees that there are no men who seek mercy for them as Phineas had,
C. in line with this verse: "Then stood up Phineas and wrought judgment and so the plague was stayed" (Ps. 106:30).

Despite the form of a commentary on a verse of Scripture, we assuredly can identify the regnant proposition, which, as a matter of fact, joins the individual facts into a cogent exercise of syllogistic proof.

Among the available means of linking sentence to sentence in paragraphs, the first, now amply exemplified, is to establish propositions that rest upon philosophical bases, e.g., through the proposal of a thesis and the composition of a list of facts that prove the thesis. This is to us an entirely familiar, western mode of scientific expression, that is, through the classification of data that, in a simple way, as we noted, is called the science of making lists (*Listenwissenschaft*). No philosopher in antiquity will have found unintelligible these types of units of thought, even though the source of facts in the present instance, Scripture, not established social norms or observations of nature, and the mode of appealing to facts, citations of Scripture, rather than allusions to generally prevailing patterns and norms, would have proved alien to such a philosopher. The connection, the process of thought—these seem to me entirely commonplace in the intellectual world at large.

The Teleological Logic of Narrative: In the teleological logic of connection-making and conclusion-drawing, the logic of coherence invokes a fictive tension and its resolution. It appeals for cogency to the purpose and direction of an arrangement of facts, ordinarily in the form of narrative. Teleological or narrative logic further serves quite effectively as a mode of making connections between two facts, that is, linking two otherwise unrelated sentences and presenting conclusions based on the linkage. In this mode of thought, we link fact to fact and also prove (ordinarily implicit) propositions by appeal to teleology, that is, the end or purpose of discussion that makes sense of all detail. The tension of narrative derives from the open-endedness of discourse. We are told a series of facts, or a problem is set forth, such that, only when we see in the sequence of the series of facts the logical, inevitable outcome do we find a resolution: that sense, that fittingness of connection, which makes of the parts a cogent whole. Accordingly, a proposition (whether or not it is stated explicitly) may be set forth and demonstrated by showing through the telling of a tale (of a variety of kinds, e.g., historical, fictional, parabolic, and the like) that a sequence of events, real or imagined, shows the ineluctable truth of a given proposition. Whence the connection? The logic of connection demonstrated through narrative, rather than philosophy, is simply stated. It is connection attained and explained by invoking some mode of narrative in which a sequence of events, first this, then that, is understood to yield a proposition, first this, then that—*because of this*. That manufactured sequence both states *and also establishes* a proposition in a way different from the philosophical and argumentative mode of propositional discourse.

Whether or not the generalization is stated in so many words rarely matters, because the power of well-crafted narrative is to make unnecessary an author's explicitly drawing the moral. Narrative sees cogency in the purpose and direction and of course outcome, appealing for its *therefore* to the necessary order of events understood as causative. That is then a logic or intelligibility of connection attained through teleology: the claim of goal or direction or purpose, *therefore* cause, commonly joining facts through the fabric of a tale, presenting the *telos* in the garb of a story of what happened because it had to happen. Narrative-logic thus makes connections and draws conclusions and conveys a proposition through the setting forth of happen-ings in a framework of inevitability, in a sequence that makes a point, e.g., establishes not merely the facts of what happens, but the teleology that explains those facts. Then we speak not only of events—our naked facts—but of their relationship. We claim to account for that relationship teleologically, in the purposive sequence and necessary order of happenings. In due course we shall see how various kinds of narratives serve to convey highly intelligible and persuasive propositions.

For an example of narrative, I turn to another Rabbinic document, the Fathers According to Rabbi Nathan I:XIII. Here we have a parable that supplies a simple example of how narrative links fact to fact in cogent discourse and further conveys with powerful logic a clear proposition:

2.A. R. Simeon b. Yohai says, "I shall draw a parable for you." To what may the first man be compared? He was like a man who had a wife at home. What did that man do? He went and brought a jug and put in it a certain number of dates and nuts. He caught a scorpion and put it at the mouth of the jug and sealed it tightly. He left it in the corner of his house.

B. "He said to her, 'My daughter, [for husbands referred to wives as daughters], whatever I have in the house is entrusted to you, except for this jar, which under no circumstances should you touch.'" What did the woman do? When her husband went off to market, she went and opened the jug and put her hand in it, and the scorpion bit her, and she went and fell into bed. When her husband came home from the market, he said to her, 'What's going on?'

C. "She said to him, 'I put my hand into the jug, and a scorpion bit me, and now I'm dying.'

D. "He said to her, 'Didn't I tell you to begin with," "Whatever I have in the house is entrusted to you, except for this jar, which under no circumstances should you touch.'" He got mad at her and divorced her.

E. "So it was with the first man.

F. "When the Holy One, blessed be he, said to him, 'Of all the trees of the garden you certainly may eat, but from the tree of knowledge of good and evil you may not eat, for on the day on which you eat of it, you will surely die' (Gen. 2:17),

G. "on that day he was driven out, thereby illustrating the verse, 'Man does not lodge overnight in honor' (Ps. 49:24)."

Simeon's point is that by giving man the commandment, God aroused his interest in that tree and led man to do what he did. The explicit proposition is the first point, we sin on account of our obsession. The implicit proposition is that God bears a measure of guilt for the fall of humanity. The issue of connection should be made explicit. Let us consider the sequence of sentences of the opening unit:

1. A man had a wife at home
2. He went and brought a jug
3. . . . put in it a certain number of dates and nuts.
4. He caught a scorpion
5. . . . put it at the mouth of the jug
6. . . . sealed it tightly.
7. . . . He left it in the corner of his house.

Nos. 1, 2, 3, and 4 bear no connection whatsoever. Nos. 4-7, of course, form a single sentence, but that sentence on its own stands utterly unrelated to the earlier of the two sentences, Nos. 1-3. However, we realize, the sequence of clauses and sentences, all of them discrete, in fact form a tight fit, since they bear the burden of the narrative. At the end, then, the narrative reaches its point and, retrospectively, establishes a very close connection between clause and clause, sentence and sentence. It is the goal, the teleology, of the composition, that joins the components of the composition to one another, and that happens only at the end. Our trust in the narrator's purpose is what allows us to suspend our suspicion that we are linking things that stand out of all relationship with one another. The linkage imparted at the end then makes sense of everything from the outset, and that is what I mean by a logic of teleology, as distinct from propositional logic, which results in the making of connections and the drawing of conclusions.

The Non-Propositional Logic of Fixed Association: This brings us to an unfamiliar mode of establishing connections between sentences, which I call the logic of fixed association. Though difficult to define in familiar terms, it forms the critical and indicative logic of discourse of a variety of Rabbinic documents. It is a logic that to begin with bears a negative trait, in that in this logic we find connection *without* conclusion, that is, the *and* but not the *equals* or the *therefore*. In this logic, the two *and* the two do not *equals* anything. Then on what basis do we impute or introduce the *and* at all? The cogency of two or more facts is imputed and extrinsic. The *and* is not sensible, intrinsic, propositional, or purposive. But in Rabbinic literature, document after

document appeals to precisely this logic of fixed association. Not only so, but even highly propositional compositions, of considerable dimensions, are linked together not syllogistically but solely through extrinsic, fixed association. It follows that writers of documents of Rabbinic literature do perceive cogency through fixed association without either syllogistic or even teleological proposition. That cogency, the connection lacking all proposition, derives from a sense of the order and proportion of data extrinsic to those at hand.

What effects connection in the logic of fixed association? Fixed associations derive from an extrinsic and conventional list of items deemed joined for reasons pertinent to those items. Then, each fact or sentence joined together fore and aft with others finds its own relationship to that extrinsic connection, without the slightest connection to other facts or sentences that stand, in writing or in mental sequence, in the same context, fore and aft. Discrete facts, propositions, or sentences hang together because they refer equally to an available protocol of associations. Hence it is a logic that rests upon conventional connections. It appeals, rather, to protocols—e.g., lists of things, a given text, a sequence of facts—that are known and familiar, rather than on logico-propositional connections that are unknown and subject to discovery. It is meaning imputed, not discovered. The contrast to the logic most familiar to us in the West is readily grasped. In philosophical logic we set up a sequence of two or more facts and claim out of that sequence to propose a proposition different from, transcending, the facts at hand. Here, by contrast, we join two or more facts or sentences without pretending that any proposition whatsoever is to be demonstrated. That is why the sequence that links in one composition sentence 1, then sentence 2, then sentence 3, though there is no propositional connection between 1 and 2 or 2 and 3, rests upon principles of intelligibility practically unknown to us. It is easy to find appropriate illustrations.

For an illustration, we return to an already familiar compilation. I give a sustained passage, a sequence of freestanding sentences, bearing no relationship, sequential let alone propositional, to one another. What makes me insist that the sentences are discrete? A simple test suffices. Were the following items given in some other order, viewed in that other sequence, they would make precisely as much, or as little, sense as they do in the order in which we see them. But in syllogistic logic, all the more so in teleological logic, (though not in *Listenwissenschaft*), the order of facts bears consequence. Indeed, reversing the order of sentences yields either a proposition exactly contrary to the one that is argued, or mere gibberish. In what follows, by contrast, the order of sentences has no bearing upon any proposition, and given the power of the correct ordering of facts/sentences in both syllogistic argument and teleological logic alike, the utter incapacity of order to impart meaning shows us that we have in hand a logic other than the philosophical-syllogistic or the teleological. Now to our passage:

Sifre to Deuteronomy XXV:I

1.A. "What kind of place are we going to? Our kinsmen have taken the heart out of us, saying, ['We saw there a people stronger and taller than we, large cities with walls sky-high, and even Anakites']" (Deut. 1:25-28):

B. They said to him, "Moses, our lord, had we heard these things from ordinary people, we should have never believed it.

C. "But we have heard it from people whose sons are ours and whose daughters are ours."

XXV:II

1.A. "We saw there a people . . . taller than we:"

B. This teaches that they were tall.

2.A. ". . . and greater . . . :"

B. This teaches that they were numerous.

XXV:III

1.A. ". . . large cities with walls sky-high, and even Anakites":

B. Rabban Simeon b. Gamaliel says, "In the present passage, Scriptures speak in exaggerated language: 'Hear, O Israel, you are going to pass over the Jordan this day to go in to dispossess nations greater and mightier than yourself, cities great and fortified up to heaven' (Deut. 9:1).

C. "But when God spoke to Abraham, Scripture did not use exaggerated language: 'And we will multiply your seed as the stars of the heaven' (Gen.

26:4), 'And we will make your seed as the dust of the earth' (Gen. 13:16)."

XXV:IV

1.A. ". . . and even Anakites did we see there":

B. This teaches that they saw giants on top of giants, in line with this verse: "Therefore pride is as a chain about their neck" (Ps. 73:6).

XXV:V

1.A. "And we said to you:"

B. He stressed to them, "It is not on our own authority that we speak to you, but it is on the authority of the Holy One that we speak to you."

XXV:VI

1A. "Do not be frightened and do not be afraid of them:"

B. On what account?

C. "For the Lord your God is the one who goes before you."

D. He said to them, "The one who did miracles for you in Egypt and all these miracles is going to do miracles for you when you enter the land:

E. "'According to all that he did for you in Egypt before your eyes' (Deut. 1:30)."

F. "If you do not believe concerning what is coming, at least believe concerning what has already taken place."

That each unit of thought, signified by a Roman numeral, stands by itself hardly needs proof, since it is a self-evident fact. Were we to present the several items in a different order, that shift would have no affect whatsoever upon the meaning of the passage. That proves that the individual sentences bear no relationship to one another. Then it follows that there is no *equals*. All we have is a sequence of unrelated sentences, not a cogent paragraph; the sentences do not appeal to their neighbors, fore or aft, to prove a proposition beyond themselves; and each one, standing by itself, makes a point that bears no connection to any other in context—*except* for the verse of Deuteronomy, the base-verse, that all of them cite and claim to elucidate in one way or another. I cannot imagine how, apart from the mere statement of the facts, I can show more vividly that a sequence of utterly unrelated sentences has been laid forth before us. They occur in context of sequences of highly propositional units of thought.

The third logic therefore rests upon the

premise that an established sequence of facts, e.g., holy days, holy persons, holy words, in a manner extrinsic to the sense of what is said joins whatever is attached to those words into a set of cogent statements, even though said sequence does not form of those statements propositions of any kind, implicit or explicit. The protocol of associated items, that is, the established sequence of words, may be made up of names always associated with one another. It may be made up of a received text, with deep meanings of its own, e.g., a verse or a clause of Scripture. It may be made up of the sequence of holy days or synagogue lections, which are assumed to be known by everyone and so to connect on their own.

The fixed association of these words, whether names, whether formulas such as verses of Scripture, whether lists of facts, serves to link otherwise unrelated statements to one another and to form of them all not a proposition but, nonetheless, an entirely intelligible sequence of connected or related sentences. Fixed association forms the antonym of free association. I know no case in Rabbinic literature in which the contents of one sentence stimulate a compositor to put down the next sentence only because one thing happens to remind the compositor of something else, that is, without any reference to a principle of association external to both sentences (our "fixed association"), and also without any reference to a shared proposition that connects the two (our "propositional cogency").

To show the full power of the logic of fixed association, quite independent of the fixed associations defined by sequences of verses of Scripture and hence in no way serving as a commentary of any kind, I turn to a few lines of Mishnah-tractate Abot, The Fathers, Chapter One. That chapter is made up of three units, first, three names, then five paired names, finally, three more names. The first three names are Moses (and the following), then Simeon the Righteous, then Antigonos. The groups of pairs are the two Yoses, Joshua b. Perahiah and Nittai the Arbelite, Judah b. Tabbai and Simeon b. Shatah, Shemaiah and Abtalion, and, finally, Hillel and Shammai. Then at the end come Gamaliel, Simeon his son, and (repetitiously) Simeon b. Gamaliel. That the names are not random but meaningful, that the fixed association of name A with name B, name C with name D, name E with name F, and so on, is deemed cogent—these are the premises of all discourse in Chapter One of The Fathers. The premise rests on the simple fact that these names are announced as sequential, set by set—e.g., the first holds office M, the second, office N—and then in their unfolding, the first group is prior in time to the second, and on down. The order matters and conveys the information, therefore, that the compositor or author wishes to emphasize or rehearse. So when we claim that the logic of fixed association links sentences into meaningful compositions, even though it does not find cogency in the proposition at hand, we believe that claim rests upon the givens of reading the chapter at hand that universally prevail among all interpreters. I present in italics the apodosis—the propositions, the things that people say, which would correspond to the propositions of a syllogistic, philosophical discourse. In plain type is the attributive, or, in the less precise usage introduced earlier, the protasis.

1:1 MOSES received the Torah at Sinai and handed it on to Joshua, Joshua to elders, and elders to prophets. And prophets handed it on to the men of the great assembly. They said three things: *Be prudent in judgment. Raise up many disciples. Make a fence for the Torah.*

1:2 SIMEON THE RIGHTEOUS was one of the last survivors of the great assembly. He would say: *On three things does the world stand: On the Torah, and on the Temple service, and on deeds of loving-kindness.*

1:3 ANTIGONUS OF SOKHO received [the Torah] from Simeon the Righteous. He would say: *Do not be like servants who serve the master on condition of receiving a reward, but [be] like servants who serve the master not on condition of receiving a reward. And let the fear of Heaven be upon you.*

That the names are intended signals is shown, of course, by the reference of No. 2 to No. 1 and No. 3 to No. 2. The rest of the chapter proceeds along these same lines. No unfolding proposition emerges from what is attributed to the named sages, and, indeed, most of the assigned statements stand autonomous of one another.

Now if we ask ourselves what the italicized words have in common, how they form a cogent discourse, the answer is clear. They have nothing in common, and they certainly do not so make connections as to draw a conclusion (though some may claim they are joined in overall theme), and, standing by themselves, do not establish a proposition in common. As propositions in sequence, they do not form an intelligible discourse. But—and this must stand as a premise of all argument—in the mind of the authorship of The Fathers, which has set matters forth as we see them, those same words serve intelligible discourse. But the principle of cogency, upon which intelligibility rests, does not derive from what is said. A shared topic by itself does not in our view constitute an adequate logic of connection between two otherwise discrete sentences, though, admittedly, a shared topic is better than none at all.

To recapitulate: the principle is that things are deemed to form a fixed sequence, specifically, the list of named authorities. The premise that because Rabbi X is linked on a common list—a text, a canon of names—with Rabbi Y, and linked in that order, first X, then Y, accounts (for the authorship at hand) for the intelligibility of the writing before us: this is connected to that. That is to say, the logic joining one sentence to another in The Fathers derives from the premise of fixed associations, or, stated in more general terms, an established or classic text. This formulation of fixed associations, this received text—in this case, a list of names—joins together otherwise unrelated statements. What makes two or more sequential sentences into an intelligible statement overall (or in its principal parts) is not *what* is said but (in this context) *who* does the saying. The list of those canonical names, in proper order, imparts cogency to an otherwise unintelligible sequence of statements (any one of which, to be sure, is as intelligible as the statement, "all Greeks are philosophers").

The upshot is a statement that relies for intelligibility upon the premise of fixed asso-

ciations, e.g., an established text. The text does not have to be a holy book and it need not even be in writing. It may consist in a list of names, a passage of Scripture, the known sequence of events, as in the Pesher-writings, or even the well-known sequence of events in the life of a holy man. But the *and* of this connection—hence also mode of drawing conclusions if any—differs in its fundamental logic of cogency from one that relies for intelligibility upon either narrative, on the one side, or philosophical and syllogistic thought, on the other. What holds the whole together is knowledge shared among those to whom this writing is addressed, hence the "fixed" part of "fixed association," as distinct from (mere) free association.

Metapropositional Discourse: Despite its formidable name, this kind of logic is not difficult to grasp; essentially it amounts to making a point of an abstract character by exemplifying the same concrete fact over and over again. Then the reader can identify out of the cases the proposition that is intended. Metapropositional discourse forms a subspecies of propositional; the former is not articulated, the latter is. That is to say, propositional discourse involves setting forth facts to prove a point, such as the authorship of the Mishnah accomplished, or laying out facts to point to a conclusion, as in the case of narrative.

This sort of discourse characterizes philosophy, including of course natural philosophy. Metapropositional discourse proves the unity of diverse cases by imposing a single program of analytical questions—hence "methodical-analytical"—upon a virtually unlimited range of problems. This demonstration of the proposition, within the deep structure of argument, that all things fit into a single pattern, is accomplished through sorting out many and diverse cases and the discourse repeatedly invokes a fixed set of questions. And that kind of inquiry marks science, natural and social, as we know it today. It is the supreme effort to put two and two together and therefore to explain four.

I call this classification of logic in discourse metapropositional because the effect is to present two propositions, one immediate and at the surface, the other within the subterranean layers of thought, with the latter the more encompassing of the two, of course. The former—propositions concerning the case at hand,—may derive from familiar modes of argument, making connections between two facts and drawing a conclusion from them. Or the superficial discourse may present what appears to be merely a simple assertion of fact, with no further conclusion to be drawn or even intended. But the latter—the metapropositional level—always sets forth a fundamental proposition and proves it.

For this higher level of discourse manages time and again to make a single point even while examining many points, and it is that capacity to conduct discourse at two levels, the one near at hand, the other at the level of recurrent polemic, that I find remarkable. Metapropositional discourse does not repeat itself; there is no recourse to only one proposition in every instance. But the propositions indeed prove few, and a survey of the canonical writings underlines the limited program of thought encompassed by this mode of discourse: the propositions are few, but they recur everywhere. That is why the upshot is to prove the unities of diverse things, and to do so in such a way which, time and again, one is able to articulate the proposition that is demonstrated through recurrent proofs of little things.

Metapropositional discourse of course forms a subdivision of propositional discourse. What distinguishes this species from its genus is not only that in these cases, the compositors make two points, one on the surface, another underneath. This mode of thought, seeking unity in diversity in a highly particular way, affects a broad range of documents; it is an instance of that process that, in the aggregate, defines traits indicative not of particular documents but of large sectors of the canon as a whole. Indeed, the intellectually highly-structured character of the Mishnah, with its systematic and orderly exposition of the extension or restriction of rules, its rigorous exercise in comparison and contrast, sets the style and defines the task for later authorships, to the end of the formation of the canon in late antiquity. Not only so, but the mind trained in seeking unity in diversity, and unity susceptible of statement in proposition, works systematically through an amazingly broad program of topical inquiry and repeatedly produces that single, besought result. Out of this kind of mind, capable of making connections among wildly diverse data, science can have arisen, so far as science seeks connections and draws conclusions to explain connections. But in so stating, I have once more moved too far ahead of my argument. What of the propositional character of metapropositional discourse?

The propositions that are proven in each instance are in one case minor and in the other, encompassing. The minor proposition is on the surface, the rule prevailing in a detail of law. The encompassing generalization bears global consequence, that is, for example, reason alone bears reliable results, and the like. Commonly, the surface-generalization forms little more than a clause or a verse followed by a phrase in amplification thereof. Yet the unit of thought may be enormous, relative to the size—number of words—of the completed units of thought in our document. Reading the cases of Scripture and transforming them into general rules suitable for restatement in, and as, the Mishnah, the authorship of Sifre to Deuteronomy, for example, accomplished an amazing feat of sheer brilliance: holding many things together within a single theoretical framework. What is critical in holding together discourse in these items therefore is the imposition of a fixed analytical method, rather than the search for a generalization and its demonstration or proof. These items are topically discrete but time and again present the application of a fixed analytical system or structure or produce, in an episodic instance, a recurrent proposition of an analytical character (e.g., extension or restriction of a rule, demonstration that solely through Scripture are firm conclusions to be established).

One recurring exercise, which fills up much of the discussion of the legal passages of Deuteronomy in Sifre to Deuteronomy, for example, systematically proposes to generalize the case-discourse of the book of Deuteronomy and to reframe the case into the example of a general law. The "if a person does such and so," or the details of a case as spelled out in Scripture will be subjected to a sustained exercise of generalization. In this exercise one does two things. Either—in the process of generalization—he will restrict the rule, or he will extend it. If Scripture contains a detail, such as the statement of a case always demands, one should ask whether that detail restricts the rule to a kind of case defined by the detail, or whether that detail represents a more general category of cases and is to be subjected, therefore, to generalization. (In the unfortunate word-choice of contemporary philosophy, the fixed analytical method at hand investigates issues of *generalizability*.) Here is an example of many instances in which the authorship of a sustained discourse proposes to turn a case into a law.

> Sifre to Deuteronomy CLXVI:I
> 1.A. "[You shall also give him] the first fruits of your new grain and wine and oil, [and the first shearing of your sheep. For the Lord your God has chosen him and his descendants, out of all your tribes, to be in attendance for service in the name of the Lord for all time]" (Deut. 18:1-6):
> B. This teaches that offerings are taken up for the priestly rations only from produce of the finest quality.

The point applies to more than the case at hand. At issue is whether we extend or restrict the applicability of the rule. Here we restrict it.

> 2.A. Just as we find that as to two varieties of produce of fruit-bearing trees, priestly rations are not taken from the one to provide the requisite gift for the other as well,
> B. so in the case of two varieties of produce of grain and vegetables, priestly rations are not taken from the one to provide the requisite gift for the other as well.

No. 2 is parachuted down and has no bearing upon anything in the cited verse. But the importance is to derive a general rule, as stated at B, which applies to a broad variety of categories of priestly gifts, just as at No. 1.

> CLXVI:II
> 1.A. ". . . the first shearing of your sheep:"
> B. not the fleece that falls off when the sheep is dipped.
> 2.A. ". . . the first shearing of your sheep:"
> B. excluding a sheep that suffers from a potentially fatal ailment.
> 3.A. ". . . the first shearing of your sheep:"
> B. whether in the land or abroad.

No. 1 is particular to our verse, Nos. 2, 3 are general rules invoked case by case. These items are not coherent, one by one, and the three sentences in no way state a single proposition, explicit or otherwise. And yet the exercise of analysis is uniform—I could give many dozens of cases in which precisely the same distinctions are made—and the purpose is clear. It is to impose upon the case a set of generalizing issues, which yield either restrictive or expansive definitions. This is a fine instance of what I mean by attaining cogent discourse—linking one sentence to another—through an established methodical analysis of one sort of another.

> CLXVI:IV
> 1.A. "You shall also give him:"
> B. This indicates that there should be sufficient fleece to constitute a gift.
> C. On this basis sages have ruled:
> D. How much does one give to the priest?
> E. Five selas' weight in Judah, equivalent to ten in Galilee, bleached but not spun,
> F. sufficient to make a small garment from it,
> G. as it is said, "You shall also give him:"
> H. This indicates that there should be sufficient fleece to constitute a gift.

The same pattern recurs as before, and the interest is in an autonomous program. This represents a different kind of methodical analysis. The framer wishes to relate a verse of Scripture to a rule in the Mishnah and so asks how C-F are founded on Scripture. G-H go over the ground of A-B. The work of restriction or expansion of the rule is now implicit, of course. Metapropositional discourse takes a central place in some documents, e.g., Sifra and the two Talmuds, none at all in many others.

To conclude: metapropositional discourse brings to expression a range of logic that shows unity in diversity, demonstrates that many things follow a single rule, and demonstrates how a few simple propositions underlie many complex statements of fact. That mode of thought seeks connections at the deepest structure of thought and proposes to explain by reference to a single rule a various and vast universe of fact. Metapropositional logic makes a single fabric out of the threads of propositional logic that fill up the loom comprised by one document after another. Sifra and the two Sifres stood for that large sector of the canonical writings that, all together, serve to make a few fundamental points, applicable to many cases indeed. The two Talmuds present us with the same phenomenon: systemic and generalizing thinking about the discrete propositional statements presented by the Mishnah. And yet, while the two Sifres and Sifra (among other writings) prove essentially metapropositional in their overall structure, attaining cogency by doing one thing many times and showing the inner simplicity of the outwardly complex propositions at hand, the Yerushalmi—and by extension, the Bavli—does not follow suit. Quite to the contrary, if we had to characterize the paramount logic of cogent discourse of the Yerushalmi, we should have to identify the prevailing principle of joining one statement to another, that is, of making connection, not with propositional, let alone metapropositional, discourse, but with the connection imposed by fixed association, that alone. For while the several units of completed thought in the two Talmuds systematically connect fact to fact, sentence to sentence, through the shared proposition generated by what is reasoned and syllogistic argument, those units of thought themselves find connection only in their common reference-point, the Mishnah. The two Talmuds, as we shall see, succeed in making enormous statements because they join syllogistic logic, which stands behind the bulk of their compositions, to fixed associative logic, which holds the compositions together in huge composites.

The prevailing logics in some documents work in both the parts and the whole, in one and the same way, connecting sentence to sentence, and also paragraph to para-graph. In the Mishnah, Genesis Rabbah, and Leviticus Rabbah, the same logic of propositional discourse that links sentence to sentence also links paragraph to paragraph. That is to say, propositions join one fact or sentence to another and make of the whole a single cogent statement. Still broader propositions join one large-scale cogent statement ("paragraph" in the language of the opening sentence) to another cogent statement. The logic of the whole also defines the logic of the parts. And the same is so of the metapropositional discourse that makes the accomplishment of the authorship of Sifra so remarkable and imparts noteworthy force and sustained argument to the discrete statements of the two Sifres as well.

In all three documents, the metapropositional program of the parts imparts its character to large stretches of the whole as well. We may therefore conclude that some documents hold together, whole and also in part in one and the same way. They will find connections between their sentences and among the compositions of sentences either by systematically setting forth propositions, argued along the lines of syllogism, worked out through the analysis accomplished by classification, comparison and contrast, of genus and species, for instance, and this they will do throughout. Or authorships will impose a single subterranean program upon data of unlimited diversity and show, point by point and overall as well, the unities within diverse facts—documents that persistently make metapropositional points and all together find cogency through those recurrent exercises of deep and methodical analysis.

But the Yerushalmi and the Bavli differ in their basic logical structure from all the other documents. For the authorships of these writings compose their completed units of thought principally as propositional, or metapropositional statements. The logic, then, connects one fact to another, one sentence to another, in such a way as to form a proposition. But the joining of one completed unit of thought ("paragraph," "propositional statement") to another finds connection not in a still larger exercise of propositional discourse but rather by appeal to the connection imposed through the fixed association accomplished by the framers of the Mishnah or by the author of Scripture. That mixing of two logics, the propositional for medium-range discourse, the fixed associative for large-scale composition, differentiates the two Talmuds from all other canonical writings.

Tradition, Commentary, and Logic: The logic of fixed association clearly serves the purpose of composing in some sort of cogent way the discrete observations about this and that of which a commentary to a fixed text is made up. But, as our survey of the documents of Rabbinic literature will show us, the prevailing logic is not exegetical for the sentences or fixed associative for the logic of coherent discourse, but highly propositional. Most large-scale and sustained units of cogent discourse except for the Bavli, appeal for cogency to propositions, not to fixed associations, such as characterize commentaries of a certain sort and other compilations of exegeses of verses of Scripture.

Strictly speaking, commentary has no need for propositions in order to establish coherence among discrete sentences, though through commentary an authorship may propose to prove propositions (as is the case with methodical-analytical demonstrations via metapropositional logic). A document formed in order to convey exegesis attains cogency and imparts connections to two or more sentences by appeal to fixed associations. It makes no call upon narrative, does not demand recurrent methodical analyses. The text that is subjected to commentary accomplishes the joining of sentence to sentence, and to that cogency, everything else proves secondary. For, by definition, a commentary appeals for cogency to the text that the commentators propose to illuminate.

True, they may frame their commentary in diverse, appropriate ways. For example, they may comment by translating. They may comment by tacking paragraphs—stories, expositions of ideas, and the like—onto constituent structures of the base-verse. But, overall, the genre, commentary, dictates its own rhetoric, such as we have noticed, and its own logic. The logic of commentary, narrowly viewed, is that of fixed-associative compositions.

But, as a matter of fact, most of the Rabbinic commentaries to Scripture proved highly propositional, not only in general, but also in detail, not only in proposition, but also in process and in rhetorical pattern. What holds things together in large-scale, sustained discourse does not rely upon the verse at hand to impose order and cogency upon discourse. Writers, as in the middle and late Midrash-compilations, ordinarily appeal to propositions to hold two or more sentences together. If, by definition, a commentary appeals for cogency to the text that the commentators propose to illuminate, then far more common is a document that is in no essential way a commentary. The logic is not that of a commentary, and the formal repertoires show strong preference for other than commentary-form. So far as commentary dictates both its own rhetoric and its own logic, the documents have to be described in the aggregate as highly argumentative, profoundly well-crafted and cogent sets of propositions. Authors found a need for propositions to attain cogency or impart connections to two or more sentences, called upon narrative, demanded recurrent analyses of a single sort.

JACOB NEUSNER

RASHI: The acronym for Rabbi Shlomo Yitzhaki, that is, Solomon son of Isaac. This acronym was also popularly interpreted to mean *Rabban shel Yisrael*, that is, "*the teacher of Israel*," *par excellence*.[1] That same appraisal of Rashi is reflected in the application to him of the eptithet *Parshandatha*, the name of one of the ten sons of the wicked Haman (Est. 9:6) but treated as a combination of the Hebrew noun *parshan*, "exegete," and the Aramaic noun *datha*, meaning "Torah" (see, e.g., Ezra 7:12). Thus *Parshandatha* means "Interpreter of the Torah *par excellence*."

Rashi was born in either 1030 or 1040 C.E. in Troyes, the capital of the province of Champagne in Northern France, and he died there in 1105 C.E.[2] Of his father Isaac we know for certain only that Rashi cites and recommends his interpretation of an obscure passage in B. A.Z. 75a. Rashi's mother was the sister of Simeon b. Isaac the Elder of Mainz (b. 950 c.e.), an author of synagogue poetry. Rashi quotes this uncle in his commentary on B. Shab. 85b. It is unknown whether Rashi received his earliest education at home or in a school sponsored by the Jewish community of Troyes.

It is widely agreed that by the age of thirty Rashi had completed his monumental commentary on the Pentateuch.[3] At this point he left Troyes to study at the established Jewish academies of Mainz and Worms. At Mainz, Rashi studied at the yeshivah, which had been presided over by Rabbenu Gershom b. Judah (960-1028), "the Light of the Exile," of whom Rashi said, "All Ashkenazic Jewry are the disciples of his disciples."[4] Rashi's teachers at Mainz were Rabbenu Gershom's direct disciples, Jacob son of Yakar, whom Rashi called "my old teacher" and "my teacher in Scripture,"[5] and Isaac son of Judah, whom Rashi called "virtuous teacher."[6] In the course of time Rashi would surpass Isaac son of Judah in his expertise in halakhah, and the latter would address some thirty-eight questions on Jewish law to Rashi.[7] After the death of Jacob son of Yakar, Rashi continued his studies at the Worms yeshivah headed by Isaac b. Eliezer, whom Rashi calls "our holy teacher."[8]

In about 1070, Rashi returned from Worms to Troyes, where he is said to have founded a yeshivah.[9] This institution was located within a Jewish community numbering not more than two hundred souls, surrounded by a Christian population of not more than ten thousand.[10] Baron surmised that under these circumstances both Rashi's academy and his exegetical work were essentially leisure activities, while his principal occupations were the cultivation of grapes and the preparation of wine.[11] In fact, evidence from Rashi's responsa indicates that he had the title Gaon and that his academy bore the pretentious name *Yeshivat Geon Ya'aqov*.[12] Both of these designations suggest that Rashi was one of a number of persons throughout Europe and the Middle East who saw themselves and were seen by others as the legitimate successors of Hai Gaon (d. 1038). Hai Gaon's academy, "the Yeshivah of Pumbeditha" located at Baghdad, was alleged to have been founded by Judah b. Ezekiel (d. 299) in the third century c.e. Until the death of Hai Gaon in 1038, this academy and its rival, in Sura, alleged to have been founded by the Amora Rav in 219 c.e., had a status in Jewish intellectual life comparable to that of Oxford, Cambridge, and Harvard in modern academic life. Likewise, in the Jewish religion, the authority of those academies and their heads was analogous to that of the papacy in Roman Catholic Christianity. When Moses Maimonides (1135-1204) refers in the introduction to his *Mishneh Torah* to Geonim in Spain and France, he alludes to persons like Rashi, who had succeeded, like the Babylonian Geonim before them, in building institutions of learning, composing exegetical works, supplying authoritative answers to questions in halakhah, and raising up disciples. By so doing, these persons achieved a degree of recognition among world Jewry rivaling that of Hai Gaon in his time as both masters of and contributors to the essential literary canon of world Jewry. So well did Rashi succeed that within a few hundred years his commentaries on both Scripture and the Babylonian Talmud would be found in Jewish homes and schools throughout the world, while the name of Hai Gaon would be remembered only by specialists.

Evidence from a number of Rashi's responsa indicates that his students lived in his home and ate at his table. Some historians even hold that the yeshivah itself may have doubled as Rashi's living room This latter view may reflect a failure of older historians to recognize that Jewish civilization in both antiquity and in the Middle Ages was not confined to home and synagogue.[13]

The first disciples of Rashi included Simhah of Vitry, Shemayah, Judah b. Abraham, Judah b. Nathan, and Meir b. Samuel. Simhah of Vitry produced the important and fascinating annotated prayer book called *Mahzor Vitry*. Shemayah was for many years Rashi's personal secretary. He helped Rashi edit the final versions of his commentaries on Isaiah and Ezekiel, and

Rashi consulted him when he edited the final version of his commentary on Psalms. In addition, Shemayah produced the earliest supercommentary on Rashi's Pentateuch commentary. This supercommentary survives in a single copy contained in Leipzig Stadtbibliothek, Ms. Wagenseil, B.H. fol. 1, which was produced by a scribe named Makhir b. Creshbia.[14] Simhah's son Samuel married Rashi's granddaughter, who was the sister of Rashbam (on whom see below). Judah b. Nathan (known as Riban) wrote commentaries on most of the Babylonian Talmud, including the commentary on Tractate Nazir found in the inner margins of current editions of the Talmud. Judah b. Nathan married Rashi's daughter Miriam. Their son was Rabbi Yom Tov of Falaise, while their daughter was the famous Elvina, one of the few women in the Middle Ages whose halakhic opinion has been recorded for posterity.[15] Meir b. Samuel is regarded as one of the first authorities to compose the commentaries now printed in the outer margins of Talmud, known as Tosafot.[16] He married Rashi's daughter Jochebed. Their children were Isaac, Solomon, Rabbenu Tam,[17] and Samuel b. Meir. The latter Samuel wrote a monumental commentary on the Pentateuch, the definitive commentary on the tenth chapter of B. Pesahim, and the standard commentary on the greater part of B. Baba Batra.[18]

Rashi's Literary Output—Liturgical Poetry: Best known today for his influential commentary on the Pentateuch and his indispensable commentary on most of the Babylonian Talmud, Rashi was also a poet. At least ten liturgical poems, all of which belong to the genre of *selihot*,[19] are attributed to him. In 1865, Leopold Zunz established the accepted list of seven of these that are now commonly regarded as actually from Rashi's pen.[20] Five of these are alphabetical acrostics beginning with the first letter of the Hebrew alphabet, *aleph*, and ending with the final letter, *taw*. Two are acrostics that begin with *taw* and end with *aleph*. The closing lines of all seven contain colophons identifying Rashi as the author. In five of these, Rashi refers to himself as "the young," while in the longest of these

colophons he writes, "Solomon son of Rabbi Isaac, the young; may he grow in [mastery of] Torah and in good deeds." These colophons suggest that Rashi composed at least five of the seven poems at the dawn of his literary creativity.

One of Rashi's *selihot*, whose first line is "God of Hosts," is commonly recited on the morning before the New Year in the Ashkenazic rite shared by many Orthodox and Conservative congregations throughout the world. The poem reads:

> God of Hosts, worshipped by the supernal beings,
> You said, "Return rebellious children.
> "Come to Me with thanksgiving and songs (cf., Ps. 100:3, 4),
> "Seek My face (cf., Ps. 27:8) with crying and supplication" (Jer. 3:21).
> Even when the prayer of persons praying is silenced (cf., Lam. 3:8)
> The doors are wide open for the repentant.
> Your promise is forever (cf., Ps. 119:89).
> The paths to You kindly provided are everlasting and unchanging (cf., Mal. 3:6).
> Look! We approach You like poor (Jer. 3:22) and impoverished
> knocking on the door for charity (and) moaning like doves.
> The charity is yours (Dan. 9:7), and the iniquities are ours.
> We return to you in shame [knocking] on your doors (and) moaning like doves (Is. 38:14).
> Remember us and recall us for a full life.
> Cleanse our stains pure and white (cf., Is. 1:18).
> May the sins of our youth (Ps. 25:7) be wiped away like [passing] clouds.
> Renew our days like the former days (cf., Lam. 5:21).
> Remove uncleanness (Zech. 13:2), and put an end to malicious deeds (cf., Dan. 9:24).
> Pour pure (and) faithful water (Ezek. 36:25; Is. 33:16; Jer. 2:13; cf., Job. 6:15).
> We acknowledge (Jer. 14:20) our wickedness: (we are) thorns and thistles (Ezek. 2:6).
> Our stiff-neckedness is as [great as] the stoutness of oak trees.
> We planted a vineyard spoiled by weeds (cf., Jer. 2:21).
> Its face was covered with brambles and thorns (cf., Prov. 24:31).
> Experienced in doing evil, glued to idols,
> Avid for bribes, greedy for graft (cf., Is. 1:23),
> Quickly we polluted the marriage chamber.[21]
> From then on we have been (Is. 59:14; Jer. 7:24) steadily losing ground.

The sacrifices of doubly fat lambs ceased.
[Likewise] the fragrance of the incense,
Captain of fifty, advisor and official (Is. 3:3)
Assistant priest and high priest, Levites and
  Aaronides.
Look how we stand before you poor and
  impoverished.
Anxious in spirit (Is. 63.10), bitter like
  wormwood (Prov. 5:4),
We recall you in [our] trouble.
Worried and mournful because of the fear
  of your decree.
Make spring up for the faithful a branch of
  kindness (Jer. 33:15).
Command the expiation of former iniqui-
  ties (Job. 7:21; Ps. 79:8).
May the voice of the one who sings aloud[22]
  put an end to litigation.
Silence the prosecuting attorney, and hush
  the defamers.
May our humble spirit and our broken and
  contrite hearts
be accepted as a substitute for the fat of
  sacrifices.
Fulfill for the descendants the oath [you
  swore] to the patriarchs.
Hear from your [heavenly] abode the
  prayers of those who sing aloud[23] to you.
Prepare their hearts so that they will be
  prepared to revere you.
Make your ear hearken to their plea for
  mercy
Again extricate your people from the mire.
May your ancient love come toward us
  quickly.
May those who depend on your compassion be acquitted in their trial.
Praying for your kindness and relying on
  your mercy.

**Exegetical Compositions, Comment-
ary on the Babylonian Talmud:** Observing that Rashi's commentary on
B. M. Q. is missing from standard editions
of the Talmud but survives in a single MS.
published by Kupfer,[24] Grossman suggests
that 1) Rashi did, in fact, comment on most
and possibly all of the Bavli; 2) the commentaries on tractates Taanit, Nedarim,
Nazir, Horayot, and the latter parts of the
commentaries on Baba Batra and Makkot
were lost; 3) the vivid imagination of later
copyists, followed by the printers, supplied
the plausible explanation, eventually treated
as fact by modern scholars, that Rashi died
in the middle of his writing the commentaries on Baba Batra and Makkot and that
he simply did not live long enough to write
commentaries on the others.[25] But Abraham
Berliner has showed that Rashi composed a

frequently quoted, complete commentary
on Nedarim, which disappeared.[26] Berliner
likewise pointed out that the numerous
quotations from Rashi in Rashbam's commentary on Baba Batra and in works by
other medieval authorities prove that Rashbam and others had access to a complete
commentary by Rashi on that tractate.[27] In
the same vein, Berliner noted that numerous quotations in the responsa of Yom Tov
b. Abraham of Seville (Ritba; 1250-1330)
prove that the latter had access to Rashi's
complete commentary on Makkot.[28]

Berliner pointed out that because the
technique of preparing animal skins for
writing was not yet widely known in France
and Germany when Rashi was growing up,
books were extremely rare in those lands.
Consequently, one of Rashi's esteemed
teachers, Eliezer the Great of Mainz, testified that he had never studied B. Abodah
Zarah. It has been suggested that Rashi left
his native Troyes for Mainz primarily to
gain access to reliable copies of the Babylonian Talmud. He himself testifies that he
made use of the copy of that work that
Rabbenu Gershom (c. 1000) had copied out
from manuscripts brought to Europe from
the Middle East. Rashi took pains, mostly
on the basis of conjecture (like modern biblical scholars with the Hebrew Bible!), to
correct the text of the Talmud. In fact, all
subsequent editions bear the imprint of his
numerous conjectural emendations.

The first dictionary of the Hebrew and
Aramaic employed in Rabbinic literature
was Nathan b. Jehiel of Rome's *Arukh*,
completed in 1105, the year Rashi died. As
demonstrated by Berliner, both R. Nathan
and Rashi learned much of their talmudic
lexicography from two common sources,
(a) the Mainz Commentary on the Talmud,
which in turn was based on the commentary of Rabbenu Gershom, and (b) the
Worms Commentary on the Talmud. In
addition to establishing a usable Talmudic
text and virtually creating his own dictionary in his head or in writing (his equivalent
of index cards has not survived) at the very
same time that Nathan b. Jehiel created the
Arukh, Rashi made use of the Mainz and
Worms Commentaries and the written
commentaries of his three mentors, Jacob

son of Yakar, Isaac b. Judah, and Isaac b. Eliezer. Rashi also made extensive use of material he had committed to memory during his student days in Mainz and Worms or which he had otherwise received orally from teachers and contemporaries. Just as Rashi systematically studied the Bavli and created and made extensive use in his commentary of a Babylonian Jewish Aramaic and Rabbinic Hebrew lexicon, so did he create and utilize a dictionary of the Talmud's exegetical terminology. As in his biblical commentaries, so also in his talmudic commentary, Rashi made use of the Hebrew term *leshon*, literally "language," to designate, variously, "a synonym of," "an expression referring to," and "a cognate of." Similarly in both commentaries, Rashi takes for granted the ubiquity of biliteral roots in the Semitic languages.

As in his biblical commentaries, so also in his talmudic one, Rashi rarely identifies his sources. Nevertheless, it is known that the basis of his commentary on each talmudic tractate of is what he had learned from the particular mentor who had first guided him through that tractate.[29]

Rashi succeeded in writing his running commentary on a large part of the Babylonian Talmud in Rabbinic Hebrew liberally peppered with Aramaisms and some 1,100 glosses in French and other European languages.[30] The principle task, which the commentary continues to fulfill almost perfectly to this very day, is to lead the student, whose native language is neither Rabbinic Hebrew nor Babylonian Jewish Aramaic, through the syntax of the Talmud, indicating where a question ends and where an answer begins, defining obscure expressions, and filling in phrases and entire sentences, including allusions to Scripture, which the highly elliptical language of Mishnah and Talmud leave to the imagination of the educated reader. As in his biblical commentaries, Rashi frequently quotes the text being commented upon and incorporates his commentary into that text. While his biblical commentaries have in only a few interesting cases influenced modern Jewish and Christian Bible translators to deviate from the traditions established by the Old Greek and Jerome, his

talmudic commentary is the basis of virtually all subsequent interpretations of the Talmud.

M. Liber's biography of Rashi includes eleven pages of Talmud translation with Rashi's commentary incorporated into it, separated from the text by brackets. Liber thereby replicates in Modern French (or in Adele Szold's English translation) the experience of yeshivah students and Jewish seminarians over the last nine centuries who have read the Talmud using Rashi's commentary to fill in the ellipses. The following two excerpts from Szold's English version graphically illustrate how Rashi's works:

> However, it is taught in a Baraita: "It once happened that R. Nehorai accompanied a witness to give evidence concerning him at Usha" [at the time when the Sanhedrin had its seat in that city, and the new moon was proclaimed there]. R. Nehorai was accompanied by another witness, and if this witness is not mentioned, it is out of regard for R. Nehorai [for R. Nehorai is mentioned only that we may infer from his case that so prominent an authority inclined to leniency in the circumstances stated; but it is not fitting for us to appeal to the authority of his less important companion]. Rab Ashi replies: There was already another witness at Usha [who knew the one who was coming to give evidence], and R. Nehorai went to join him. . . . (B. R.H. 22a).[31]
> It has likewise been shown [that the motive of the Mishnah in declaring the stolen lulav unfit for use on the second day of the festival, is that it would be the fulfillment of a regulation through the commission of a transgression]. Rabbi Ammi says. . . . (B. Suk. 29b).[32]

These quotations demonstrate how Rashi composed a very sophisticated commentary that provides the information the Talmud assumes the reader has at her or his fingertips. It is no wonder, therefore, that it has been suggested that, without this commentary, the Talmud might have been forgotten.[33]

Biblical Commentaries—The Pentateuch: According to the *Shulhan Arukh*, Orah Hayyim, Chapter 285, a Jew may fulfill the obligation to read each Sabbath the weekly Torah portion twice and the officially sanctioned Aramaic translation (Targum Onkelos) once by substituting for the Aramaic version Rashi's commentary.

This law accords to Rashi's commentary a status in the liturgical life of the Jew rivaled only by the Pentateuch and the prayer book. The Jews' special devotion to Rashi's biblical commentaries inspired medieval Christians such as Nicholas de Lyra (fourteenth century), leaders of the Reformation, especially Martin Luther, and modern Jewish and Christian exegetes to go out of their way to consider and reconsider Rashi's interpretations.[34]

Rashi's commentary explains the meaning within Rabbinic Judaism of the Pentateuch's corpora of civil and criminal law (such as Exod. 21-24, Lev. 17-25, and Deut. 12-26), the prescriptions for the building of the Tabernacle (Exod. 25-31, 35-40), the sacrificial service of the Tabernacle (Lev. 1-7), and the laws of purity and diet (Lev. 11-16). In commenting on these subjects Rashi quotes verbatim, paraphrases, and summarizes the relevant commentaries found in the Mekhilta deRabbi Ishmael, Sifra, Sifre, and the Babylonian Talmud. He intersperses his quotations from these sources with lexicographical notes based primarily upon the dictionaries of biblical Hebrew produced by Menahem b. Jacob Ibn Saruq and Dunash b. Labrat in the tenth century and observations concerning Hebrew phonology, syntax, and grammar. Modern biblical exegetes find Rashi's observations on these subjects, many of which may be original, especially interesting.[35] The fascination derives from the fact that Rashi's many important insights were made without benefit of either the phenomenal developments in Semitic linguistics accomplished by Spanish Jews of the tenth century (such as Judah Hayyuj, Moses b. Samuel ha-Kohen Ibn Gikatilla, and Jonah Ibn Janah, whose Arabic writings were inaccessible to Rashi) or the rediscovery in modern times of ancient Semitic languages such as Akkadian and Ugaritic.

In his treatment of biblical narrative, Rashi summarizes numerous Rabbinic stories culled from Genesis Rabbah and the Babylonian Talmud (e.g., B. Sot. 11a-12b in elucidating Exod. 1-15; B. Hag. 12a-b in elucidating Gen. 1; B. Sot. 34-35 in elucidating Num. 13-14) as well as medieval sources, such as several versions of Midrash Tanhuma and a book composed by R. Moses the Interpreter of Narbonne (eleventh century). Frequently, Rashi notes that a particular Rabbinic story, which may be worthwhile for the ideas it conveys, assumes the deliberate misinterpretation of a biblical word or idiom. Typical is Rashi's comment at Gen. 12:5 where the Hebrew idiom *asah nephesh* meaning "acquired person(s)," i.e., "purchased slaves" could be taken to mean "made soul(s)." Rashi comments as follows:

> THE SOULS THEY MADE IN HARAN, whom they brought under the wings of the Divine Presence. Abraham would convert the men to Judaism and Sarah would convert the women to Judaism, and Scripture accorded them merit as though they MADE them.[36] The literal meaning of Scripture is "the menservants and maidservants whom they acquired." The very same usage [of the Hebrew verb *asah*, normally "make," in the rarer meaning "acquire"] is attested in "he acquired all this wealth" (Gen. 31:1); "Israel acquires wealth" (Num. 31:1). [In each of these cases the verb *asah*] is a synonym of "acquire" [*qoneh*], i.e., "collect."

When Rashi concludes this comment with the expression *wekones*, meaning, "collect," he alludes to the ambiguity of the verb *qanah*, which, being a close semantic equivalent of *asah* can, like *asah*, mean "make," as in Gen. 14:19 where, as Rashi explains in his commentary there, the locution *qoneh*, "maker" of heaven and earth, corresponds to *oseh* (from *asah*), "maker" of heaven and earth, in Ps. 134:3. In bringing to bear upon the Pentateuchal narrative gems culled from Rabbinic literature as well as philological notes, Rashi does not create a running narrative. In fact, his insightful comments on one word, phrase, or passage are often contradicted by his equally insightful comments on following words, phrases, or passages. Typical of this phenomenon is Rashi's commentary on the creation narrative, Gen. 1:1-2:3. Here he alternates between his insistence, following Genesis Rabbah 1:19, that all of creation was called into being on the first day of the week of creation (so Rashi at Gen. 1:14, 24) and his quotation of other Rabbinic sources, according to which creation took place in stages exactly as related in Gen. 1:1-2:3 (so, e.g., Rashi at Gen. 1:11-12). In his commentaries on biblical narrative Rashi succeeded in striking the perfect balance between a summary of the great ideas found in Rabbinic aggadah and the basic data concerning biblical lexicography, grammar, and syntax that are necessary to decode the biblical text. A master pedagogue, Rashi rarely loses his readers' attention.

Commentaries on the Prophets and Hagiographa: In his commentary on the Pentateuch, Rashi summarizes the extensive legacy of ancient Rabbinic commentary on both the halakhah and aggadah, interspersed with important stylistic, grammatical, and lexicographical observations. The legacy of formative Judaism provided considerably less material on the books of the Prophets and Hagiographa. Most of these books, with the notable exceptions of Ezek. 40-48 and Est. 9, have no bearing on halakhah. Consequently, in his commentaries, Rashi concentrates on the stylistic, grammatical, and lexicographical issues without having to discuss the meaning of a given phrase or verse in halakhah. Likewise, the meager amount of Rabbinic aggadah quoted in Rashi's commentaries on the Former and Later Prophets probably reflects the absence of any Rabbinic corpora that treat the narratives of Joshua-Judges-Samuel-Kings in the way that Genesis Rabbah treats the narratives of Genesis. In fact, just as in commenting on the patriarchal narratives in his commentary on Genesis Rashi draws extensively upon the narratives contained in Genesis Rabbah, so in his Psalms commentary he draws heavily upon the Midrash on Psalms.

Despite these facts, some modern scholars have concluded that Rashi's commentaries on the Prophets and Hagiographa are "rudimentary."[37] Others have concluded that the differences between the Pentateuch commentary and that on the Prophets and Hagiographa are primarily a function of Rashi's growing awareness of the difference between exegesis and eisegesis.[38] In fact, one of Rashi's last compositions, the commentary on Psalms, reveals his magnificent ability to combine midrash halakhah, midrash aggadah, source critical

observations, lexicographical, syntactical, and grammatical insights and innovations. No less fascinating is his commentary on Ezekiel, which includes detailed maps of the future Jerusalem and the future reapportionment of the land of Israel among the twelve tribes.[39]

Typical of Rashi's source-critical observations is his comment at Ezek. 1:1. Ezekiel himself begins his book, speaking in the first person, "Now it came to pass in the thirtieth year, in the fourth month, in the fifth day of the month, as I was among the captives by the river of Chebar, that the heavens were opened, and I saw visions of God." This verse is followed immediately with the following: "In the fifth day of the month, which was the fifth year of king Jehoiachin's captivity, the word of the Lord came expressly unto Ezekiel the priest, the son of Buzi, in the land of the Chaldeans by the river Chebar; and the hand of the Lord was there upon him" (Ezek. 1:2-3). Noting that while in v. 1 and vv. 4ff. Ezekiel speaks in the first person while in vv. 2-3 he is spoken about by someone else, Rashi remarks:

> The prophet spoke anonymously. He did not supply his name nor did he explain the system of chronology to which he referred [when he said, "in the thirtieth year"]. Therefore, the divine utterance [Heb. *ruah haqodesh*] interrupted his words in the two verses that follow [vv. 2-3] to identify the prophet and to explain his chronology, as it is stated, "on the fifth day of the month which was in the fifth year. . . ." These two verses are not the words of the prophet. The reasons why [these two verses] cannot be the words of the prophet are that he already said [in v. 1] that he was standing on the fifth day of the month; and that, at the beginning [of the Book], the prophet spoke in the first person, "as I was among the captives and I saw visions of God," and so also later on, "I looked, and behold a whirlwind" [vv. 4ff.] while two verses interrupt his words [in first person] as though someone else were speaking about him, "The word of the LORD came unto Ezekiel the priest . . . and the hand of the Lord was there upon him" (v. 3).[40]

In addition to writing complete commentaries on all biblical books with the exception of Ezra-Nehemiah[41] and Chronicles,[42] Rashi commented extensively on numerous biblical texts, which are quoted in the course of his monumental talmudic commentary.[43] One of the most interesting of these comments is his explanation, in Aramaic, of the dynamics of synonymous parallelism, one of the most obvious features of biblical poetry. Commenting on Ps. 33:13-14, "The Lord looks from heaven; he beholds all the sons of men. From the place of his habitation, he looks upon all the inhabitants of the earth," Rashi writes in his commentary to B.R.H. 18a: "and it [v. 14] repeats what is stated in the verse preceding it" [v. 13].

Commentary on Canticles: In his Bible commentaries Rashi frequently provides two alternative explanations of words, phrases and verses. One of the two he will label *peshuto* or *mashmao*, meaning "its literal meaning," while the other one he will label either "our rabbis interpreted" or *midrasho*, "the meaning it acquired in a Rabbinic source." Careful examination of Rashi's known sources,[44] as for example, at his commentary on Exod. 1-2, reveals that frequently both the interpretation designated as the literal meaning and the one which he seemingly marginalizes as Rabbinic are derived from the Rabbinic literature. In his commentary on Canticles, Rashi adds to literal meaning and "the meaning it acquired in a Rabbinic source" a third component, which he labels *dugmah*, "allegorical interpretation."[45] In this allegorical interpretation, the man in love who speaks, is spoken to, and spoken about is identified with God, and the woman in love is identified with the Jewish people, referred to as the Congregation of Israel. Rashi indicates both in his long introduction to this commentary and throughout the commentary itself that his allegorical reading is to be preferred over all other allegorical interpretations of Canticles for two reasons. First, it makes possible a running narrative. Second, Rashi attempts to incorporate only Rabbinic texts, whose interpretations of biblical texts accord with biblical syntax, grammar, and lexicography.

Consequently, the commentary on Canticles successfully conveys the message that the Jewish allegorical interpretation by Rashi rests on the foundation of scientific biblical exegesis. The implication is, *inter alia*, that the Jewish allegorical interpretation in which the two persons in love are God and Israel is correct because the alternative, Christian allegory, in which the woman is the Church, lacks such a scientific basis. Consequently, as demonstrated by Kamin and Saltman, an anonymous thirteenth century Christian scholar produced a new Christian allegorical exposition of Canticles based upon Rashi's understanding of the vocabulary, grammar, and syntax of the book. The design was to establish the Christian understanding of the personae upon the firm foundation of scientific philology.[46]

Commentaries on Liturgical Poetry: Rashi held that the inclusion of medieval poetry (*piyyutim*) in the liturgy was a legally sanctioned practice known to Jewish communities all over the world and not to be questioned. While Abraham Ibn Ezra (1089-1164) in his commentary on Ecc. 5:1 argued that people should not include in their prayers liturgical poems that they did not understand, Rashi held that people are obligated to learn and to teach the meaning of the liturgical poems.[47] Consequently, he himself interpreted this poetry. Grossman notes that the surviving fragments of his commentaries on liturgical poetry interpret poems by Eleazar ha-Qallir, Solomon ha-Bavli, Meshullam b. Kalonymos, and Elijah the Elder of Le Mans.[48] Moreover, Grossman points out, Rashi's "manner of expounding the *piyyut* was much akin to his manner of expounding the Bible."[49] In addition, as in his commentary on the Babylonian Talmud, Rashi, like many nineteenth and twentieth century biblical scholars, assumed that when the received text made no sense, it should be restored by conjectural emendation.[50] As in his biblical commentaries, he gave prime consideration to lexicography, grammar, and syntax, and the eisegetical interpretations of the *piyyutim*.[51] From among the six examples of his commentaries on liturgical poetry that have survived in the writings of his disciples,[52] his commentary on line 22 of *Tohelet Yisrael*, "The Hope of Israel," by Solomon the Babylonian the Younger[53] is here chosen to illustrate his approach. The poetic line reads as follows:

Our guilt has accumulated to an eighth and a twentieth. You, O Lord will not put an end to your mercy.

Rashi's comment including the lemma reads as follows:

TO AN EIGHTH AND A TWENTIETH. These two obscure terms are small measures [of quantity] as we say in [B.] Sotah [8b]. [The line, therefore means] OUR GUILT HAS ACCUMULATED TO [such an extant] that it reaches all the measures that are counted with respect to transgressions, from the largest measure to the smallest measure. . . . All the measures that they [the Tannaim in the *baraita* quoted in B. Sot. 8b] mentioned with respect to transgressions can be counted in our hands, and with respect to all of them YOU WILL NOT PUT AN END TO YOUR MERCY. [This comment is] from the mouth of *rabbi* [i.e., my mentor, Rashi].[54]

Responsa: Rashi wrote approximately 350 responsa,[55] definitive answers to or legal decisions concerning questions of law. Most of his responsa deal with the rather typical questions addressed to rabbis in every generation: whether one may slaughter with a knife that is defective in an area not used in the slaughter,[56] what should be done with the head and legs of a lamb cooked in the same pot in the case in which the head, but not the legs, had been salted to remove the blood,[57] and whether a man may appoint a gentile as his agent to deliver a bill of divorce to his wife.[58]

Others of Rashi's responsa deal with biblical exegesis, and these fall into four groups: a) #21 in Elfenbein's edition, which deals with Is. 45:1; b) the responsa addressed to Samuel of Auxerre concerning various passages in Jeremiah and Ezekiel;[59] c) the responsa concerning the Book of Psalms, which were recently edited and published by Jordan Penkower;[60] and d) the long responsum addressed to Nathan b. Makhir concerning the variety of meanings of the ubiquitous particle *ky* in Biblical Hebrew.[61] The latter responsum, is, in fact, a programmatic essay on the problem of homonymy in both Biblical Hebrew and Targumic Aramaic. Rashi demonstrates that the primary means for determining the meaning of any word in any text is its usage in context.

Typical of Rashi's responsa addressed to Samuel of Auxerre is the following, #1 in all editions:

[He replied]: "Money shall be purchased" (Jer. 32:43). [In this clause the verb *weniqnah*] is future tense. [The clause means], "A FIELD shall again be purchased IN THIS LAND." [The verbal form] *niqnah*, "it was purchased," is the same grammatical form as are *nibnah* "it was built," *na'asah*, "it was done," *niglah*, "it was revealed." When [this verbal form] has no [prefixed] *waw*, it is past tense. Examples of this latter grammatical form [include]: "It was built [*nibnah*] of whole stone brought [from the quarry]" (1 Kgs. 6:7), ". . . a vision [*hazon*] was revealed [*niglah*] to Daniel" (Dan. 10:1). Now the *waw* turns it [the perfect form of the verb] into future tense. Examples of this latter grammatical form [include]: "The Glory of the Lord shall be revealed [*weniglah*]" (Is. 40:5), [wherein the verb *weniglah* means] "and it shall be revealed." Likewise *weniqnah* [in Jer. 32:43 means] "and it shall be purchased."

This responsum shows that, in Rashi's time as now, a proficient practicing rabbi, such as Samuel of Auxerre, might be ignorant of one of the most ubiquitous features of biblical Hebrew, the *waw* conversive. What the latter term means is that forms that would be construed as past in post-Biblical Hebrew are often in fact future in Biblical Hebrew and vice versa; and the main key to the identification of such forms is a prefixed *waw*. Rashi exemplifies the patience that ought to characterize the best of modern academicians. The latter are often surprised to find themselves explaining to advanced students or colleagues data one should have learned in elementary school. Ironically, the very questioner, Samuel of Auxerre, was able to show Rashi that he had contradicted himself on another matter in his commentary on Ezekiel. Consequently, Rashi, the patient respondent to Samuel's elementary questions, was prompted to correct his originally errant explanation of an obscure point.[62]

No less brilliant is Rashi's responsum concerning a grammatical problem in the liturgy of the Ten Days of Repentance.[63] The question is why during the High Holy Days one concludes the eleventh blessing of the weekday Amidah with the strange, seemingly ungrammatical formula *hammelek hammishpat* when elementary Hebrew grammar would seem to require *melek hammishpat,* "the just King." Rashi remarks that the accepted formula, in which the definite article precedes both of the two elements in the construct genitive chain, is probably a mistake and that the correct and original form indeed was probably *melek hammishpat.* He suggests that the accepted but ungrammatical formula was probably based on the analogy of the conclusion of the third blessing of the Amidah during the Ten Days of Repentance, *hammelek haqqadosh,* "the Holy King." There, however the syntax is different, since the two elements are not a construct genitive chain but a noun and adjective. However, Rashi, argues, in order not to change established practice, we should rely on exceptional cases in biblical Hebrew in which, as in this problematic benediction, the prefixed definite article appears before both elements of a construct chain. Such cases include *ha'emeq happegarim* at Jer. 31:40, *hammizbeah hannehoshet* at 2 Kgs. 16:14, and *hasseper hammiqnah* at Jer. 32:12.

Rashi as Storyteller: Experts in the history of Hebrew literature cite as many as eighteen narratives found in the commentary printed in the inner margins of the Talmud for which that commentary is the oldest known source.[64] In fact, most of these stories belong to Talmud commentaries that are commonly known not to be from the pen of Rashi. It is proper, therefore, to speak of a maximum of four stories for which our oldest source is Rashi's commentary on the Babylonian Talmud. Three of these stories in their respective contexts are as follows:

1. B. Qid. 80b discusses whether or not grief sufficiently suppresses what moderns would call the libido (Heb.: *yetser*) so that a mixed group of men and women may carry a dead infant to the cemetery without being led to engage in illicit sex on the way. By association the Talmud points out a *ma'aseh,* "legal precedent/ story:" Ten [men] carried her [i.e., an unnamed woman] in a bier.

Rashi comments as follows:

TEN MEN TOOK HER [a certain woman] OUT IN A BIER relying on the assumption [of the bystanders] that she was dead. They had sex with her, and she was [in fact] a married woman.

2. In B. San. 19a we read: Rammi bar Abba reported that R. Yose [b. Halafta] legislated in Sepphoris that a woman should not go around in the marketplace with her child following her because of a *ma'aseh,* "legal precedent."

Rashi comments as follows:

WITH HER CHILD FOLLOWING HER. Her little son should not walk behind her but in front of her. BECAUSE OF A LEGAL PRECEDENT: Licentious men kidnapped him [her child] from behind her back, and they put him in a house. When she returned home and did not see him, she began to cry out and weep. One of them [the licentious kidnappers] came and said, "Come, and I will show him to you." She entered his house after him, and they had sex with her.

3. The Story of Beruria: It is reported in B. A.Z. 18b that Meir (fl. c. 135-175 C.E.) suddenly fled from Palestine to Babylonia. It is further reported that it is a matter of controversy why he did so: There are some who say that it was because of the *ma'aseh,* "what happened with" Beruria.

Rashi comments:

AND THERE ARE SOME WHO SAY THAT IT WAS BECAUSE OF WHAT HAPPENED WITH BERURIA. Once she made fun of the sages' dictum (B. Qid. 80a), "Women are light headed." He [Meir, her husband] said to her, "I swear by your life that ultimately you will agree with their words." He commanded one of his disciples to test her with respect to fornication. [The disciple] pressured her for many days until she agreed. When she came to her senses she strangled herself. Rabbi Meir ran away because of [his] shame [at what he had perpetrated].

Not surprisingly, in three of the four instances Rashi understands the term *ma'aseh* in the very limited sense it has in the Mishnah, namely, "legal precedent" rather than in the wider sense that it acquired in Yiddish, where *ma'aseh* came to mean "story." Consequently, except for the famous Beruria legend, there is hardly anything in Rashi's attempts to answer the exegetical question, "What precisely was the legal precedent?" that would qualify as a contribution to the history of Hebrew *belles lettres.* In fact, aside from the appearance in the Beruria legend of a named hero and heroine of Rabbinic literature, Meir and his wife Beruria, the Beruria legend would also hardly qualify as a narrative rather than as simply an anecdote. Interestingly, Jacob Neusner demonstrated in his *Rabbinic Narrative: A Documentary Perspective. Volume One. Forms, Types, and Distribution of Narratives in the Mishnah, Tractate Abot, and the Tosefta* (Leiden, 2003) that in the Mishnah *ma'aseh* simply means "legal precedent" while in Tosefta it can have the wider meaning of "story."

The last of the four narratives, for which Rashi's commentary on the Babylonian Talmud seems to be the oldest source, is his version of the Fable of the Fox and the Wolf. It is noted in B. San. 38b that Yohanan b. Napha (d. 279 C.E.) reported that Meir had in his repertoire three hundred fox fables, of which only three are extant. Yohanan, in turn, tells us only that one fox fable (or perhaps all three) was associated with the following three biblical verses: "Parents ate sour grapes, and children's teeth are in pain" (Ezek. 18:18); "Scales are honest, and weights are honest" (Lev. 19:35); "A virtuous one is rescued from trouble, and a wicked one is below him" (Prov. 11:8). Apparently, Yohanan and the anonymous editor of the Talmud relied on the Jewish people's collective memory to preserve all three of Meir's fables associated with the three biblical verses. Unfortunately, none of these tales has so far been recovered from ancient manuscripts. Consequently, Rashi, in his commentary at B. San. 38b, supplies the following fable in which Meir, as it were, composes a story utilizing the previously quoted verses from the Prophets, Torah, and Hagiographa respectively:

> "PARENTS ATE SOUR GRAPES" (Ezek. 18:18). The fable is as follows: The fox deceitfully persuaded the wolf to enter the Jewish quarter [of the town] on the eve of the Sabbath and to prepare with them what is required for [the three festive Sabbath] meal[s] and to eat with them on the Sabbath. However, when he was about to enter [the Jewish quarter] they [the Jews] beat him with clubs. He [the wolf] went [with intent] to kill the fox. He [the fox] explained to him: "They only beat you because of your father, who once went to help them [the Jews] to prepare a meal and he ate every good dish." He [the wolf]

asked him, "Am I being beaten up because of my father?" He [the fox] replied, "Yes. 'The parents ate sour grapes...' (Ezek. 18:18), but come with me and I will show you a place to eat to satiety." He came to a well at whose edge was located a tree on which a rope was hung, and at each end of the rope was tied one of two pails. The fox entered the upper pail so that it became heavy and descended, while the [previously] lower pail ascended. The wolf asked him, "Why do you enter there?" He [the fox] replied, "Here there is meat and cheese to eat to satiety." He [the fox] showed him the reflection of the moon in the water. It was a round image that looked like round cheese. He [the wolf] asked him, "How can I descend?" He [the fox] said to him, "Get into the upper pail." He [the wolf] entered so that it became heavy and descended while the pail in which the fox was located ascended. He [the wolf] said to him, "How can I ascend?" He [the fox] said to him, "A virtuous one is rescued from trouble, and a wicked one is under him" (Prov. 11:8). Is it not thus written [in the Torah], "Scales are honest and weights are honest" (Lev. 19:35)?

The lesson taught here by Rashi, if not by R. Meir, is that, contrary to appearances, justice ultimately does prevail.[65]

Rashi in Poetry: As early as the fifteenth century, Rashi was known in Spain as *Parshandatha*, Torah commentator *par excellence*. This idea was expressed in two famous poems from the fifteenth and sixteenth centuries. For example, Hayyim Joseph David Azulai (c. 1724-1807) in his monumental work on medieval Jewish sages, *The Names of the Great Ones*, quotes the fifteenth century Moses Ibn Danon to the effect that those who came after Rashi said:

> All the French commentaries throw into the trash [Heb.: *'ashpatha*]
> Except for Parshan Datha and Ben Poratha

In addition, Oxford Bodleian Library Ms. Pococke 74[2], whose *terminus ab quo* is 1586 C.E., records the following frequently quoted poem, which the manuscript itself wrongly attributed to Abraham Ibn Ezra (1089-1164):

> A star arose from France; he pitched his camp at Jotbathah.
> Blessed be the arrival of him and his host. He has come from Sinai or from Zin.

From Ithiel and Jekuthiel he came like
   Samuel from Ramah.
Through him there is light for every blind
   person. Through him every thirsty per-
   son drank honey from his sweet water.
He provided for the Torah an awesome
   commentary. Therefore, they named him
   Parshan Datha.
His book provides answers to all who ask,
   and in all Israel it is the accepted solution.
The endeared solves. He breaks through the
   wall.
The Lord's secret he saw.
Divine wisdom was spread out for him.
Also kingship was for him appropriate.
An angel of the creator abides with him,
   [and he says to that angel, which is per-
   sonified wisdom]:
"Be strong in Mishnah."

Rashi in Legend: Rashi, whose contributions to Torah-literature were known
and read by literate Jews throughout the
world, was the subject of numerous legends. For example, it is said that his father
was an extremely poor man who sought a
way other than philanthropy to honor the
Torah. Therefore, Rashi's father would
sweep the floor in front of the Holy Ark
in the synagogue with his beard. The
prophet Elijah informed him that in consideration of his thus honoring the Torah,
he would father a son who would enlight-
en the entire world with his knowledge.
The prophet asked one favor, namely, that
he be privileged to hold that son in his
lap at his circumcision. As one might
expect, Elijah arrived late, and the impatient guests pressured Rashi's father,
Isaac, to go ahead with the ceremony
without waiting for the honored guest.
Isaac, however, insisted on waiting just a
bit longer. Elijah arrived and thus demonstrated the virtue of Isaac *vis-a-vis* the
impatient guests.[66]

Probably the most famous legend about
Rashi pertains to his alleged encounter with
Godfrey of Bouillon. According to this
story, when Godfrey was about to wrest the
land of Israel from the Muslims in the
course of the First Crusade, he wished to
ask Rashi if he would succeed. At first
Rashi refused to meet him, and when
Godfrey went to Rashi's academy, Rashi
made himself invisible. Rashi eventually
informed Godfrey that he would indeed

conquer the land of Israel but that he
would only hold it for three days, after
which it would be reconquered by the
Muslims. Moreover, Rashi foresaw that
Godfrey would return home with only two
surviving soldiers from his vast army.
Godfrey responded that if the prophecy
should not be fulfilled to the last detail, he
would throw Rashi to the dogs and put to
death all the Jews of France. Ultimately,
Godfrey returned to France with three soldiers rather than two and was prepared to
punish Rashi for prophesying falsely. However, just as he passed through the gates of
the city, a heavy rock fell upon one of the
three soldiers and killed him. Godfrey went
to Rashi's academy to acknowledge the
veracity of the prophesy but learned that
Rashi was no longer alive.[67]

It has long been observed that this legend
is rooted in a tendency to enhance Jewish
cultural heroes by asserting that they inter-
acted with and were recognized by heroes
of the larger gentile world.[68] In fact, this
same tendency is reflected in many modern
studies of Rashi, which emphasize less the
cogency of his exegesis than the fact that he
was admired and quoted by Christian
scholars.

Rashi's Drawings: When Abraham
Berliner (1833-1915) was examining medieval manuscripts for the preparation of a
critical edition of Rashi's commentary on
the Pentateuch,[69] he called attention to
maps and other diagrams that accompanied
the commentaries. Because the common
printed editions were based upon inferior
manuscripts that did not include these pedagogical devices, it was almost forgotten
that Rashi's commentaries, like many other
medieval Hebrew exegetical works, originally included line drawings. In fact, the
printed editions of Rashi's commentary on
the Bavli includes more than a hundred
drawings, while medieval manuscripts include many more; the common printed
editions of Rashi's biblical commentary
include an illustration at 1 Kgs. 6:31.[70] The
illustrations found in medieval manuscripts
include, *inter alia,* 1) a combination map and
ladder to accompany Rashi's exegesis of
Gen. 28:17;[71] 2) a picture of the lampstand
or *menorah* described in Exod. 25;[72] 3) an

illustration at Exod. 29:2 of the gesture to be performed while anointing with oil the unleavened wafers for the ceremony of consecration of the Aaronide priesthood;[73] 4) a crown indicating the hand motion to be performed at the anointing of a king of Israel (1 Kgs. 1:34);[74] 5) an illustration of the interpretation Rashi rejects concerning the shape of the entrance to the Inner Sanctum of Solomon's Temple (1 Kgs. 6:31);[75] 6) a map showing the location of Shiloh (Jdg. 21:19);[76] 7) an illustration of the circuitous route by which the Israelites went from Egypt into the Promised Land (Num. 34);[77] 8) a schematic map of the boundaries of Canaan described in Num. 34;[78] 9) a map of the future Jerusalem, illustrating Ezek. 45;[79] 10) a map of the future restoration of the all the twelve tribes of Israel to Cisjordan Palestine, illustrating Ezek. 48, with the assigning of equal portions to each tribe.[80]

Initially modern scholars encountered skepticism when they argued that these and other illustrations were an integral part of Rashi's exegesis. People often assume that what they have never seen before cannot be real. One of the classic arguments employed by scholars who sought to restore the drawings to modern editions of the commentaries was that Rashi himself testified to his use of illustrations in a responsum addressed to Samuel of Auxerre. There he stated, "I will make a drawing and send it to you."[81] Jordan Penkower actually found a copy of that drawing in the medieval Ms. Evr. I C 6, p. 93b in the National Library at St. Petersburg, Russia, and he published it together with a modern rendition of it prepared by Menachem Cohen.[82]

Rashi explains in the block of text contained within the map of the boundaries of the land of Canaan (Num. 34; see illustration) that the purpose of the map described in Num. 34 and illustrated graphically by Rashi is to provide a legal definition of "the land of Israel" with respect to those regulations of the Torah that apply only therein (see M. Qid. 1:9; T. Ter. 2:12; T. Hal. 2:11). In fact, in supplying this map with precisely that justification, Rashi was responsible for the

view within the realm of halakhah that the map of the land of Israel found in Num. 34 is operative with respect to the Mishnaic Law of Agriculture.

Bibliography

Banitt, Menahem. *Rashi: Interpreter of the Biblical Letter* (Tel Aviv, 1985).
Sed-Rajna, Gabrielle. "Some Further Data on Rashi's Diagrams to his Commentary on the Bible," *Jewish Studies Quarterly* 1 (1993/94), pp. 149-157.
Touito, Elazar. "Rashi's Commentary on Genesis 1-6 in the Context of Judeo-Christian Controversy," in *Hebrew Union College Annual* 61 (1990), pp. 159-183.

Notes

[1] See, *inter alia*, V. Aptowitzer, *Introductio ad Sefer Rabiah* (Jerusalem, 1938), p. 395; this interpretation of the acronym recognizes that during the past nine centuries Rashi's commentaries on the Bible and Babylonian Talmud have been the two most influential corpora of Jewish sacred texts after the Bible and the Talmud themselves. The apostate Raymond Martini (1220-1285) seems to have been the first to misinterpret the initials *Rshy* as Rabbi Salomo Yarhi, which is the name given Rashi in the Latin translations of most of his Bible commentary produced by Johann Friedrich Breithaupt (2 vols.; Gotha, 1710-1713) and which appears even in some Jewish sources; for various views concerning the meaning of the acronym, see Avraham Grossman, *The Early Sages of France* (Jerusalem, 1996), p. 122, n. 2.

[2] See Mayer I. Gruber, *Rashi's Commentary on Psalms* (Leiden, 2004); see also Grossman, op. cit., p. 122.

[3] On the relative dating of Rashi's various commentaries, see Benjamin J. Gelles, *Peshat and Derash in the Exegesis of Rashi* (Leiden, 1981), pp. 138-139.

[4] J. Mueller, ed., *Teshuvot Hakeme Sarephat weLutir* (Vienna, 1881), #21.

[5] Esra Shereshevsky, *Rashi: The Man and His World* (New York, 1982), p. 26.

[6] See Rashi's commentary to B. Yom. 16b; for additional sources, see Shereshevsky, p. 34, n. 63.

[7] For the list, see Israel Elfenbein, *Responsa Rashi* (New York, 1943), p. xxii.

[8] For the sources see I. Ta-Shma, "Isaac Ben Eliezer," in *Encyclopedia Judaica*, vol. 9, pp. 18-19.

[9] Herman Hailperin, *Rashi and the Christian Scholars* (Pittsburgh, 1963), p. 27.

[10] Salo Baron, "Rashi and the Community of Troyes," in H.L. Ginsberg, ed., *Rashi Anniversary Volume* (New York, 1941), p. 59; similarly, L. Rabinowitz, *The Social Life of the Jews of Northern France in the XII-XIV Centuries* (New York, 1972), pp. 30-32.

[11] Baron, "Rashi and the Community of Troyes," p. 60.

[12] See the responsum addressed to Azriel son of Nathan in Joël Müller, *Réponses faîtes de célèbres rabins français et lorrains du XI. et XII. siècle* (Vienna, 1881), p. 9b; and see also the responsum addressed to Joseph son of Judah in Müller, p. 4a.

[13] M. Breuer, "Toward the Investigation of the Typology of Western Yeshivot in the Middle Ages," in E. Etkes and Y. Salmon, eds., *Studies in the History of Jewish Society in the Middle Ages and in the Modern Period Presented to Professor Jacob Katz on his Seventy-Fifth Birthday* (Jerusalem, 1980), pp. 49-53 (Hebrew); contrast the evidence assembled by Norman Golb, *The Jews in Medieval Normandy* (Cambridge, 1967), pp. 192-198, 563-576, for the medieval yeshivah as an independent institution with its own architecturally distinct building. For antiquity, Dan Urman, "The House of Assembly and the House of Study: Are They One and the Same?" in *JJS* 44 (1993), pp. 236-257; Bruce Chilton, *The Glory of Israel: The Theology and Provenience of the Isaiah Targum* (Sheffield, 1982); idem, *The Isaiah Targum. Introduction, Apparatus, and Notes* (Collegeville and Edinburgh, 1987); Steven Fine, *Jewish Archaeology: Art and Judaism during the Greco-Roman Period* (Philadelphia, 2004).

[14] See Grossman, *The Early Sages of France*, pp. 358-365.

[15] For the reference, see Gruber, *Rashi's Commentary on Psalms* and the literature cited there.

[16] Grossman, *The Early Sages of France*, pp. 168-170, and the extensive literature cited there.

[17] See E.E. Urbach, *The Tosaphists* (Jerusalem, 1980), pp. 41-45 (Hebrew).

[18] Concerning R. Samuel b. Meir, commonly known as Rashbam, see especially Sara Japhet and Robert B. Salters, *The Commentary of R. Samuel ben Meir Rashbam on Qoheleth* (Jerusalem, 1985); Martin I. Lockshin, *Rashbam's Commentary on Exodus* (Atlanta, 1997).

[19] *Selihot* are liturgical poems that precede and follow the recitation on the Day of Atonement and various other fasts of the so-called thirteen attributes of God (Exod. 34:6-7), conceived as a reminder to God of his promise made at the time of the golden calf episode to forgive collective Israel for backsliding.

[20] Leopold Zunz, *Literaturgeschichte der synagogalen Poesie* (Berlin, 1865), pp. 252-254; for the complete text of the poems, see A.M. Haberman, *Piyute Rashi* (Jerusalem, 1940).

[21] Here Rashi alludes to the worship of the golden calf at the very foot of Mt. Sinai, conceived metaphorically as the site of the marriage of God and Israel. Israel's worship of the calf is therefore compared, as it were, to a bride's committing adultery during her honeymoon; see Rashi at Cant. 1:12 following Canticles Rabbah; cf., B. Shab. 88b; B. Git. 36b.

[22] The *hazzan* who intones the prayers on behalf of the congregation.

[23] The plural form here refers to all *hazzanim* in all synagogues.

[24] Efraim F. Kupfer, *R. Salomon Izhaqi (Rashi) Commentarius in Tractatum Mo'ed Katan ad Fidem Codicus Hispansiensis* (Jerusalem, 1961); for a summary of the extensive literature reflecting the ongoing debate on whether or not the latter publication is, in fact, Rashi's commentary on B. M.Q., see Gruber, *Rashi's Commentary on Psalms*.

[25] Grossman, *The Early Sages of France*, pp. 217-218.

[26] Abraham Berliner, "Beiträge zur Geschichte der Raschi Kommentare," in *Jahresbericht des Rabbiner-Seminars zu Berlin für 1901/1902*, p. 15.

[27] Ibid.

[28] Ibid.

[29] Ibid., pp. 7-8.

[30] Moche Catane, *Recueil Des Gloses* (Jerusalem, 1988), p. 252.

[31] Maurice Liber, *Rashi* (Philadelphia, 1938), pp. 144-145.

[32] Ibid., p. 117.

[33] Menahem b. Zerah (c. 1312-1385) in his *Zedah la-Derek*, quoted by Liber, p. 158.

[34] See Hailperin, *Rashi and the Christian Scholars*; for the modern period, see Harry M. Orlinsky, *Notes on the New Torah Translation* (Philadelphia, 1969), p. 40.

[35] See, e.g., Chaim (Harold) Cohen, "Elements of 'Peshat' in Traditional Jewish Bible Exegesis," in *Immanuel* 21 (1987), pp. 30-42; idem, "Jewish Medieval Commentary on the Book of Genesis and Modern Biblical Philology: Gen 1-18," in *JQR*, n.s., 81 (1990), pp. 1-11.

[36] This part of the comment is based upon Genesis Rabbah 39:14.

[37] Hayyim Soloveitchik, "Rashi," in *Dictionary of the Middle Ages* (New York, 1988), vol. 10, p. 259.

[38] Gelles, p. 139.

[39] See below.

[40] Biblical quotations are based upon KJV; the text of Rashi's commentary is the one established by Jordan Penkower and published in Menachem Cohen, *Mikra'ot Gedolot 'HaKeter': Ezekiel* (Ramat-Gan, 2000), p. 2; other examples of Rashi's source-critical comments are found at Josh. 1:1; Jdg. 5:31; Is. 8:19; Ps. 37:25; 45:2. Modern source criticism sought by reference to contradictions either 1) to debunk the authority of Scripture by arguing, for example, that Moses alone could not have written the Pentateuch (Spinoza); or 2) to distinguish between authoritative prophetic voices and spurious additions (see *passim* in the various critical commentaries on Jeremiah and Ezekiel). Rashi, and his Rabbinic forbears sought instead, by pointing to two or more divinely commissioned voices within a given Scriptural text, to *eliminate* the possibility that a single authoritative voice would contradict itself.

[41] The commentary on Ezra-Nehemiah wrongly attributed to Rashi in standard editions

of the Rabbinic Bible shares Rashi's exegetical terminology. However, unlike Rashi, whose telegraphic style replicates that of Rabbinic Midrash, the author of Pseudo-Rashi on Ezra-Nehemiah is one of the most verbose Hebrew exegetes of the Middle Ages. Demonstrating great familiarity with Rashi's discussion of many texts from Ezra-Nehemiah, this unnamed commentator tends to contradict Rashi as, for example, at Ezra 2:2; 4:12; 6:4; Neh. 3:2; 10:39; see the extensive discussions in Gruber, *Rashi's Commentary on Psalms*; Joel Florsheim, *Rashi on the Bible in His Commentary on the Talmud* (Jerusalem, 1981-1991), vol. 3, pp. 264-285.

[42] J.N. Epstein, "L'auteur du commentaire des chroniques," in *REJ* 58 (1909), pp. 189-199, went beyond Joseph Weisse (1841), Leopold Zunz (1845), and V. Aptowitzer (1908), showing that the author of the commentary on Chronicles could not be Rashi and assigning it rather to Samuel the Pious of Speyer. This twelfth century commentator employs exegetical terminology distinct from that of Rashi. The teachers he mentions were not Rashi's mentors but, frequently, lived two generations after Rashi, such as Isaac b. Samuel of Narbonne and Eliezer b. Meshullam of Narbonne. At 2 Chron. 3:15 and 22:11, he cites Rashi's comments at 1 Kgs. 7:15 and 2 Kgs. 2:11, referring to Rashi as "Rabbenu Solomon, may the memory of the righteous be for a blessing." At 2 Chron. 35:18, he cites and explicitly rejects an interpretation known to be Rashi's at 2 Kgs. 23:22. Epstein's arguments were anticipated already by the seventeenth-eighteenth century Chalifa b. Malka of Morocco; see Shlomo Elkayam, "The Liturgy of the Jews of Morocco according to Kaph Naqi by R. Halifa b. Malka," in *Peamim* 78 (1999), p. 66, n. 39 (Hebrew).

[43] Rashi's comments on biblical texts incorporated in the Talmud have been collected Florsheim; see above, n. 41.

[44] See modern annotated editions of Rashi's commentaries, such as Charles Chavel, *Rashi's Commentaries on the Torah* (Jerusalem, 1983) (Hebrew); Aryeh Bodenheimer, *Ha'Elef LiShlomo On Rashi's Commentary to Song of Songs* (Beer Sheva, 2001) (Hebrew); Gruber, *Rashi's Commentary on Psalms*; I. Maarsen, *The Commentary of Rashi on the Prophets and Hagiographa*, vol. 1 [the Minor Prophets] (Amsterdam, 1930); vols. 2 and 3 [Isaiah and Psalms] (Jerusalem, 1935-1936) (Hebrew); Mordechai Leib Katzenelenbogen, *Joshua and Judges with the Commentary of Rashi* (Jerusalem, 1987) (Hebrew); see also Menahem Zohory, *Rashi's Sources* (17 vols.; Jerusalem, 1986-1994).

[45] See Sarah Kamin, "*Dugmah* in Rashi's Commentary on Song of Songs," in *Tarbiz* 52 (1983), pp. 41-58 (Hebrew).

[46] See Sarah Kamin and Avrom Saltman, *Secundum Salomonem* (Ramat-Gan, 1989).

[47] See E.E. Urbach, *Arugat Habosem* (Jerusalem, 1963) pt. iv, pp. 6-7 (Hebrew) and the literature cited there.

[48] See Avraham Grossman, "Exegesis of the Piyyut in Eleventh Century France," in Gilbert Dahan, Gérad Nahon, and Elie Nicolas, eds., *Rashi et la culture juive en France du Nord au moyen âge* (Paris, 1997), p. 263.

[49] Ibid., p. 264.

[50] Cf., Grossman, *The Early Sages of France*, p. 527.

[51] Grossman, "Exegesis of the Piyyut in Eleventh Century France," p. 264; idem, *The Early Sages of France*, p. 250.

[52] See Grossman, *The Early Sages of France*, pp. 249-250; 522-528.

[53] Solomon b. Judah was a tenth century Hebrew liturgical poet who appears to have lived in Northern Italy. It is surmised that he is called "the Babylonian" because his family was of Iraqi origin.

[54] Grossman, *The Early Sages of France*, p. 525.

[55] See Israel Elfenbein, *Responsa Rashi* (New York, 1943). Grossman, *The Early Sages of France*, pp. 239-243, cites additional unpublished manuscript responsa. On the other hand, Grossman, there, shows that various responsa treated as authentic by Elfenbein are spurious.

[56] Elfenbein, *Responsa Rashi*, #133.

[57] Ibid., #138.

[58] Ibid., #203.

[59] A new edition of these responsa, edited by Jordan Penkower, is found in Cohen, *Mikra'ot Gedolot 'HaKeter': Ezekiel*, p. 321.

[60] See ibid.

[61] For the Hebrew text see, *inter alia*, Elfenbein, *Responsa Rashi*, #251, pp. 293-297; for additional literature and an annotated English translation see Gruber, *Rashi's Commentary on Psalms*.

[62] See Jordan Penkower, "Rashi's Commentary on Ezekiel," in *Studies in Bible and Exegesis* (Ramat-Gan, 2004), vol. 7 (Hebrew).

[63] Elfenbein, *Responsa Rashi*, #18, pp. 12-13.

[64] For a complete survey of the scholarly literature and an important original contribution to this subfield of the discipline Hebrew Literature, see Luis Landa, "Rashi's Stories in the Rashi Commentary Printed in the Babylonian Talmud," in *Eshel Beer Sheva* 3 (1986), pp. 101-117 (Hebrew); see also Eli Yassif, *The Hebrew Folktale: History, Genre, Meaning* (Jerusalem, 1994), pp. 288-290.

[65] Concerning the assertion in Rabbinic literature that justice prevails on earth within historical time, see Jacob Neusner, *How the Rabbis Liberated Women* (Atlanta, 1998), pp. 80-83; concerning Rabbinic Judaism's recognition that, in fact, justice does not always prevail, see also idem, *The Halakhah and the Aggadah: Theological Perspectives* (Lanham, 2001), pp. 192-193; for the sources of the fable see Haim Schwarzbaum, *The Mishle Shu'alim (Fox Fables) of Rabbi Berechiah Ha-Nakdan* (Kiron, 1979), pp. 550-555.

[66] For literary analysis of the story, see Eli Yassif, *The Hebrew Folktale: History, Genre, Meaning* (Jerusalem, 1994), pp. 368-369; for the written sources, see p. 656, n. 83.

[67] See Yassif, p. 360; for the sources, see, p. 654, n. 77; cf. Liber, pp. 69-70.

[68] See Liber, pp. 68-69; for detailed literary analysis of the story, see Yassif, pp. 360-362.

[69] See A. Berliner, *Raschi (Salomonis Isaacidis) in Pentateuchum Commentarius* (Berlin, 1866) (Hebrew); idem, *Raschi: Der Kommentar des Salomo b. Isak über den Pentateuch* (Frankfurt-am-Main, 1905) (Hebrew).

[70] For the meaning of this illustration and its origins, see below and Mayer I. Gruber, "Notes on the Diagrams in Rashi's Commentary to the Book of Kings," in *Studies in Bibliography and Booklore* 19 (1994), pp. 29-34.

[71] See Menachem Cohen, *Mikra'ot Gedolot 'HaKeter': Genesis, Pt. II* (Ramat-Gan, 1999), p. 230.

[72] See Mayer I. Gruber, "What Happened to Rashi's Diagrams?" in *Bodleian Library Record* 14, no. 2 (1992), p. 120.

[73] See Mayer I. Gruber, "Light on Rashi's Diagrams from the Asher Library of Spertus College of Judaica," in Mayer I. Gruber, ed., *The Solomon Goldman Lectures VI* (Chicago, 1993), pp. 73-85.

[74] See Mayer I. Gruber, "Notes on the Diagrams in Rashi's Commentary to the Book of Kings," in *Studies in Bibliography and Booklore* 19 (1994), pp. 29-34.

[75] Ibid., pp. 34-36.

[76] See Gruber, "What Happened?" p. 119, fig. 6.

[77] Catherine Delano Smith and Mayer I. Gruber, "Rashi's Legacy: Maps of the Holy Land," in *The Map Collector*, no. 59 (summer, 1992), pp. 3-35.

[78] Ibid.

[79] See now Cohen, *Mikra'ot Gedolot 'HaKeter': Ezekiel*, p. 324

[80] See ibid., p. 325; and see the discussion in Mayer I. Gruber, "The Sources of Rashi's Cartography," in Norman Simms, ed., *Letters and Texts of Jewish History* (Hamilton, New Zealand, 1999), pp. 61-67.

[81] For the argument, see Delano Smith and Gruber, p. 7; for the text of the responsum, see Cohen, *Mikra'ot Gedolot 'HaKeter': Ezekiel*, p. 321, #9.

[82] See *Mikra'ot Gedolot 'HaKeter': Ezekiel*, pp. 322-323.

MAYER GRUBER

S

SAMARITAN JUDAISM: The Samaritans today are a tiny monotheistic community numbering a few more than six hundred, though at the beginning of the twentieth century they numbered less than two hundred. The growing community today is in two approximately equal parts, one living in the shadow of their sacred mountain, Gerizim, in their ancient, urban nucleus, Shechem, that is today the modern Palestinian and Arab city of Nablus, or in latter years at Kiryat Luzza on the slopes of Gerizim. The other part of the community lives in Israel proper, at Holon, a suburb of Tel Aviv. This settlement was established in the 1930s, but Samaritans have been encouraged to live there in concentrated housing units since 1952, when, under the Law of Return, a special Samaritan neighborhood was established. This allowed the Samaritans in Israel to function and develop as a community. In both locations they are subject to local and influential daily pressures, in the one case Moslem and political and in the other secular and Jewish. They are the remnant of a more extensive nation that numbered more than one million in its heyday in biblical and post-biblical Samaria, in particular in Ephraimite and Manassite territories.

In many books and articles, Samaritans are depicted as a sect of Judaism, the earliest Jewish sect, famous for their yearly Passover sacrifice on Mount Gerizim. They reject that designation in favor of their being known as Israelites. Whether Samaritanism is an intrinsic or adopted culture, or both, is a matter of dispute and discussion. What is beyond dispute is that the Samaritan experience, which encompasses at two least thousand years of history, has been more than enough to endow them with their own linguistic, religious, cultural, and ethnic identity differing from that of Jews in many respects. It can be argued that the loss of a diaspora has meant that they have a Gerizim-centered religion that has left them with limited means of halakhic development, hence one source of its difference from Judaism. It is interesting that the establishment of the State of Israel has not led to a fusing with the Jews but to coexistence and occasional intermarriage.

The real answer to the question of Samaritan identity in the current era lies both in their religious and ethnic identities, which allow a Hebrew speaking Samaritan from Holon and an Arabic speaking Samaritan from Nablus to feel more affinity towards each other than towards their Israeli and Palestinian neighbors. The sense of community between the groups is based upon a shared kinship, a member's birth into and natal identification with his or her particular community, a special religious tradition, a separate language, and similar social practices. At the same time, in contrast, while the Samaritans in Shechem have political difficulties with their Palestinian neighbors, those of Holon make use of the Law of Return to justify their community's living in Holon.

Whatever the precise nature of their identity, the Samaritans manifest a developed form of the biblical, Israelite religion and tradition that has maintained parallels with the Jewish religion through continuing interaction.[1] The survey that follows of Samaritan history, literature, religion, and contemporary problems underlines this conclusion.

The name *Shomeronim*: The name *Shomeronim*, Samaritans, appears first in 2 Kgs. 17:29, where it is associated with the worship of idols. This name was adopted by Josephus (*AJ* 9.29), whereas in the Rabbinic literature we find instead the pejorative term, Cuthean, after Cuthah, from which place, according to biblical tradition (2 Kgs. 17), idolatrous settlers were brought to replace the Israelites exiled in consequence of the Assyrian conquest of Israel in 721 B.C.E. Josephus' words seem to depend directly on the biblical view of Samaritan syncretism.

The Samaritans identify themselves as Israelites and guardians, *shamerem* the true guardians of the law, the preservers of the proper text of the Torah, which the Jews have corrupted. The Samaritans' claim about the meaning of their name has

ancient antecedents. A comment of Jerome indicates that he accepted this interpretation, and Bar Hebraeus calls them *Shomrayye*—in Origen's Commentary on John there is an appreciation of the meaning of their name in line with the Samaritans self-assessment. The antiquity of this interpretation might also have been recognized by Meir in his quotation of Gen. 46:13 (Gen. Rabbah 94) to indicate that the Samaritans were descended from the tribe of Issachar.

Samaritan History and Religion: At least until Moslem times Samaritan history interlocked not only with that of the numerous conquerors of their homeland but with that of the indigenous Jews. While the Samaritans were principally an offshoot of the Israelite peoples, they developed their own identity, which was different from that of the Jews. Recent studies have shown that in the second and first centuries B.C.E. neither the Samaritans nor their religion were homogeneous, some of them being descendants of Greek colons who settled in Samiritis following the Alexandrine conquest,[2] intermarrying with the natives of the land. Mt. Gerizim was not the holy place of these settlers; ultimately the temple at Samaria established by Herod became their central place of worship. Other Samaritans were natives of the part of Palestine that had been Israel and seemed to be the heirs and products of evolutionary Israelitism developed from biblical times. How then can one reconcile Samaritan claims, the literary evidence, and the historical evidence?

The prime source of information for the early period, the Hebrew Bible, gives contradictory information. On the one hand, 2 Kgs. 17 (especially at verse 18) relates that the population of Israel in its totality was deported and exchanged for an alien population;[3] and on the other hand, Ezek. 27:17 depicts a prosperous land of Israel joining Judah in the export of goods via Tyre early in the sixth century. Between these polarized views are repeated hints, in both pre-exilic and exilic sources,[4] that there is some degree of continuity between Israel before 721 B.C.E. and after this critical date. It is one polarity in this prime source that is drawn upon by Josephus to support his views of Samaritan origins, and these views have tended to become the standard that affects Jewish assessments.

The internal conflicts in the text stem from editorial processes. Parts of 2 Kings 17 belong to an earlier Deuteronomic redaction and parts to an exilic rewriting.[5] The older verses[6] indicate that there was no complete exile, and they provide synchronisms with Assyrian annals that show something of the true situation after 721 B.C.E. and demonstrate the bias in the sources.[7] The probable purpose of the rewritten account was to provide data for a polemic of returned Judeans after 521 B.C.E., aimed neither at Judah nor at Israel but at the remnant of both who had stayed in situ. These people were the *amei-ha'aretz*,[8] the people of the land, including those who were given the derogatory name Samaritans.

There is tangible evidence that shows the absurdity of the prime source in Kings. Estimates of the population of Samaria in the period[9] range from 600,000 in the late eighth century B.C.E. to 140,000 in the same period.[10] The survey of Judea, Samaria, and the Golan carried out in 1967-1968[11] suggests a total of 560,000.[12] The Assyrians numbered their deportees. Sargon II, who completed the work of Shalmaneser V in reducing Israel,[13] records that he deported 27,290 or 27,280 prisoners from Samaria, indicating a depopulation of the order of some 14% of Israel's population: in other words, 86% of the people remained. This is prima facie evidence that the greatest concentration of people remained in the province until at least the sixth century B.C.E. Clearly the story of Samaritan origins in the Bible must be viewed with caution.

Prophetic concern for Israel-Samaria, particularly that of Jeremiah, seems to support a hypothesis that there was a sixth-century rapprochement between Israel and Judah. Jeremiah regarded Samaria as peopled by legitimate Yahwists, sons of Israel (Cap. 3:6, 11 i.e. 16 ET), a view doubtless colored by the fact that Samarians were living as resident aliens or refugees in Judah (2 Chron. 30:25) and the process of the intermingling of the fraternal nations was continuing. The archaeological evidence[14] indicates that refugees from the north flooded south to the Judean hills.[15] The strict separation of Judeans and Samarians, which had been the situation, pertained no longer.

The new commingling raised hopes of a united kingdom in the reign of Josiah, who was able to control, if not formally annex, the Assyrian provinces of Samaria and Megiddo[16] of the former Israelite kingdom. The mother of Josiah's son, Jehoiakin (2 Kgs. 23:26), was from Rumah, a township of Israel. Thus the future king was born of the dual nation. In the accounts of Josiah's Passover, in both Kings and the Chronicles, the uniting of Samaria and Judah in the celebration is emphasized. The words of 2 Kgs. 23:22-23 underscore that this was a new beginning. The amplification of 2 Chron. 35:18 implies that Josiah was king of a united Samaria/Judah. He is the only Judean king after the schism to be described by the Chroniclers as King of Israel. Thus, almost at the end of the monarchy, the rule of Jerusalem over a united people was restored.

Information about the relationships between those Judeans and Samarians who survived the series of deportations between 597 and 582 B.C.E. is conjectural. While the juxtaposition of the terms Israel/Judah and Jerusalem in the writings of the prophets of the early post-exilic period indicates that an ideology of a united nation centered on Jerusalem was still extant, it is clear that the prophets looked for a return from the Babylonian captivity. In the course of the sixth and fifth centuries B.C.E., the returned remnant became the community with whom the spiritual (eschatological) future of the nation lies. The old Israel was set aside. Religious ideology was interwoven, henceforth, with political reality, in the denouement of events, which lead to the development of a Samarian body politic, which became the Samarian nation, then the Samaritan heresy, and ultimately the Samaritan sect of the Jews before developing a more complex identity.

Prophetic ideology found its consummation in the missions of Ezra and Nehemiah, whose political role was to provide a stable base for the Persian military occupation of southern Palestine as a defense against Egypt. The fortification of Jerusalem as a secure center for troops and tax raising, and a sharpening of the ethnic identity of the Judeans, was strictly in line with Persian policy in such matters.[17] The work of Ezra-Nehemiah was a vital factor in the Samarian-Samaritan national identification, but it was the final stage in a political process that took nearly a century to work out, from Darius I and onwards.

In keeping with Achaemenid practice, Ezra, a *sofer*, i.e., *mar shiprum*, a royal messenger, was given authority to reform the legal system in Judea so that the community could be tied more closely into the Achaemenid administrative system.[18] Changes to the marriage laws, determination of who was within and who was outside the community, put property and inheritance rights, land and economic opportunity, in the hands of a group that accepted the Torah as law and who could be relied on to be loyal to the Empire. Ezra's work disestablished the *'am-ha'aretz*. The New Israel was in effect exclusively returned Judeans.

It is interesting to note that Rabbinic tradition lays emphasis on Ezra's role in changing the script of the Torah from the biblical cursive to square Aramaic, so that the Torah could be kept from the Hedyotot who are defined as Samaritans. Ezra's work marked the end of a hope for national unity between old Israel and old Judah.

In 445 B.C.E., in the wake of Megabyzus' revolt, Nehemiah became *pehah* with authority in Yehud. Sanballat (Sin-u-ballit), almost certainly, in the light of Persian policy of appointing locals to office, a local either from Beth Haran in Samaria, or even an Aharoni, an Aaronite priest, was made *pehah* in Samaria; Judea and Samaria thus were separated from each other administratively. Nehemiah was charged with the task of physically reinforcing Jerusalem to ensure the safety of the capital and to underpin the administrative and legal reforms of Ezra by supervising the application of the law. Sanballat probably had a similar charge to ensure the loyalty of Samaria.[19]

Neh. 7 implies that there was still a considerable feeling in Judea/Yahud for main-taining an active relationship with Samaria. Sanballat had the support of the Tobiads, a leading Judean family, and perhaps Eliashib, the priest. Sympathizers of the Samarian party must have been discouraged when Manasseh, grandson of Eliashib, was driven from Jerusalem for his marriage to the daughter of Sanballat. As Josephus is inclined to stress this incident, it may well have been the consummating act in the rift that continued to develop between the parties. The separatist pattern forced on the heirs of Israel and Judah by the new Judean leaders and Sanballat of Samaria led eventually to the establishment of a second sanctuary in Palestine, on Mt. Gerizim: the Israelites—Samarians, in consequence, became the Samaritan nation.

The building of a sanctuary was the culminating stage in the process of political separation that also involved the adoption by a Samarian leader, who became either priest or governor, or both, of the royal name, Jeroboam,[20] and the reintroduction of the paleo-Hebrew script, perhaps an outcome of the insistence of the Samarians that they were the true lineage of ancient Israel, the *Bnei Yisrael*. The Judeans probably felt obliged to follow the same pattern. The shift from Aramaic script to paleo-Hebrew in the late Persian period and on through the Hasmonean eras is to be noted on the Yahud coins at a time when the Aramaic script was employed in daily affairs.[21] Hence, the shift to palaeo-Hebrew must have been politically motivated.

In 400 B.C.E. the Samaritans were still considered to be Jewish and were approached as such by the Jews of Yeb/ Elephantine. Within seventy years, by the time of the invasion of Alexander the Great (333 B.C.E.), the Samaritan schism was well advanced and the Judean-Samaritan rift was in place

The question of whether the Samaritan sanctuary became a temple at this time,[22] which is crucial to the matter of their separation as a nation, seems to have been solved by the excavations on Mt. Gerizim and the soundings through the floor of the church of Mary Theotokos.[23] By early Hellenistic times a temple city was in existence on Mt. Gerizim, and a temple seems to have been built (*AJ* xi 342). The very existence of the temple at Gerizim was a challenge to Jerusalem.[24] Whereas other Jewish temples promoted by Greek rulers as a counter to the authority of Jerusalem (*AJ* xiii 54) in the late Hellenistic period[25] were outside Palestine, the Gerizim temple was inside and hence a dangerous rival, especially since it was proximate to the ancient sacred city of Shechem, albeit just rebuilt. The Samaritan temple stood on a site made sacred by the Patriarchs. There are ample indications, especially from the comments of the Hellenistic Jewish writers, Theodotus and Ezekiel, that the equation Gerizim = Bethel = Moriah that is common in Samaritan literature was already being made in the second century B.C.E. (and probably before). This was the basis of the claim for Gerizim's being *the* sacred mountain.[26]

The Samaritans were conscious of their continuity with the Israelites-Samarians, as demonstrated by the iconography of the fourth century B.C.E. seals found in the Wadi Daliyeh cave. Two of the bullae used to seal the papyri (WD 22 & 23) belong to the old Israelite seal tradition, and it has been suggested that they were either maintaining an ancient practice or consciously making a nationalistic statement.[27]

An additional basis for rivalry between the temples at Gerizim and Jerusalem must have lain in the similarity of their sacrificial rites. Josephus' account (*AJ* xii. 8-10) of controversy in Egypt between Jews and Samaritans over the destination of the sacrifices from Egypt—whether to Jerusalem or Gerizim—implies that the Samaritan sacrificial rites were considered equivalent to the sacrifices offered at Jerusalem. The writers of the second century B.C.E. Delian inscriptions were of the view that the Samaritans, like the Jews, were Israelites. Despite the fact that the Samaritans of Delos had their own synagogue, they were regarded as differing from the Jews on the island only because of their affinity for Mt. Gerizim and its sanctuary and not because of other distinguishing characteristics that defined them as Samaritans. Josephus freely admitted that the Samaritan temple was the Temple of the God Most High in a passage where he accused the Samaritans of trying to hide this fact during the Antiochan persecutions.[28] He quoted a letter that they wrote to Antiochus in which, according to Josephus, they said that the Royal officers were persecuting them because their practices were the same as those of the Jews.[29]

The Samaritan temple (or at least the sanctuary central to the temple) is represented on the numerous oil-lamps that have currently been identified as Samaritan. Cult objects that are known to have been in use in Jerusalem—the menorah, shofar, etrog, *mahta/*fire shovel, perpetual light, shew bread table, two heaps of twelve loaves each, musical instruments, and a knife (perhaps used for slaughtering animals)—were also used at Gerizim. The style of these objects is identical with what is depicted on the mosaic floors of the Jewish synagogue at Bet Alpha and the Samaritan one at Beth Shean. Even the facade of the temple is almost identical with the building familiar to us from Jewish silver coins, which have a tetrastyle facade on the obverse, now identified as the entrance to the temple, with the sacra showing within the portico. These pictorial representations support Josephus' observation that Sanballat was to build a temple similar to that in Jerusalem.

In the period of the Samaritan temple and down to Herodian times, when there is little other information about the Samaritans, there was a flowering of Samaritanism, which is seen in Samaritan Hellenist writing. The immediate effect of John Hyrcanus' destruction of their temple in 128 B.C.E. on the political, social, and literary life of the Samaritans is unclear. When the Hasmonean renaissance in Palestine was at its height, the Samaritans were at their nadir. The destruction of Shechem at the time of Hyrcanus' campaign against Samaria is recorded archaeologically and, it seems, the Samaritans of that city were forced to move elsewhere. Some may have left the country. There was a substantial diaspora throughout the Mediterranean islands by the second century CE.

In the short term, it is probable that, after a brief lapse, the pilgrim festivals, which were normally observed on the mountain, continued. If there had been a considerable hiatus it is likely that the tradition of the pilgrimage would have been lost, yet the Passover pilgrimage and the sacrifice of the lambs is still observed today; the Sukkot pilgrimage in its original form was observed until Byzantine days. Only under later political stress did the form of that pilgrimage change. The Samaritan chronicle, admittedly a late document, indicates that Hyrcanus' support of the Sadducees extended to the Samaritans and that he restored the pilgrimages to the sacred mountain and provided tithes, votive offerings, and gifts.

Josephus relates that during the revolutionary wars, in July, 67 c.e., a substantial group of Samaritans ascended Mt. Gerizim. The Romans interpreted this gathering as a hostile threat and surrounded the mountain. After a "siege" of two days they put the gathering to death, killing nearly twelve thousand men. Josephus is likely to be correct in attributing a hostile intent to the Samaritans, who ascended the mountain for some sort of religious ceremonial, perhaps a sacrificial rite before going into battle, and were caught before their preparations were complete.

It may also be assumed that the Samaritans looked for a restoration of their temple. Not being exempt from the eschatological currents wracking the Jewish world at the time, they apparently saw the contemporary turbulence as part of the messianic pangs that precede the restoration of Israel, i.e., themselves. They apparently saw that restoration as coming in the near future. In 35 c.e. Samaritans gathered at Gerizim in search of the sacred vessels; this episode must be seen in the light of the Samaritan belief expressed in later writings (see below) that the world's history was structured in epochs of favor and disfavor. For the episode to have happened as described, it indicates that the Samaritans had already adopted a theory of the periodicity of the world, in an eschatological connection that we note in other writings of the period. Though there is no trace in the early Samaritan eschatological writings of the specific terminology for the periodicity of the world and the eschaton that is found in later Samaritan writings, there is ample evidence of their belief in Moses as a mes-

sianic figure, in the Tibåt Marqe, and in his accompaniment by Aaron, Eleazar and Joshua, and the seventy elders, when the Day of Vengeance comes. There is also clear evidence in John 4:24-25 of Samaritan messianic expectation, perhaps in some figure other than Moses. By the end of the first century c.e. there can scarcely be any doubt of the Samaritan messianic views and activities.

While the loss of their temple may well have lead the Samaritans, like the Christians, in the direction of seeing themselves as a spiritual temple, the idea of being a spiritual temple never became fully blown. The Samaritans prayed facing Gerizim and recited blessings in the name of Gerizim, subsuming to themselves a form of spirituality.

Their view of the continued existence of a house of worship in Jerusalem was one of jealousy: they despised the Jerusalem temple and did their best to pollute it. Josephus relates a story of Samaritans who entered the temple on the eve of Passover and scattered human bones in there, thus rendering the temple unclean. The Samaritan chronicle tells of the substitution of rodents for a cage of doves destined for a temple (freewill) offering. It is alleged that Samaritans interfered with the priestly fire signals to the diaspora, though it has been argued that this was not deliberate but a Samaritan signal to their own diaspora that was misread by the Jewish community.

Rivalry was kept within reasonable bounds until the mid-second century c.e. onwards, when there was a marked increase in polemic on both sides. It is possible that the Samaritans saw a manifestation of divine activity in this second subjugation of Judea, and a claim to superiority within the Jewish world might appear to have been justified by events. The intensity of the polemic has led scholars to argue that the Samaritans took no part in the struggles against the Romans, a view supported by the statement of Abbahu that "thirteen towns were absorbed by the Cutheans in the days of Hadrian's persecutions." There is every likelihood that the Samaritans did take up arms against the Romans. Hadrian built a pagan temple on Gerizim, turned

Neapolis into a polis, and forbade Samaritan natives to circumcise. Eusebius points to Samaritan participation in the revolt in his words that, "these two mountains (Gerizim and Jerusalem) were destroyed and besieged in the days of Titus and Vespasian and in the days of Hadrian."

Ties with the Jews were not broken until the third century C.E. Throughout the first century, the Samaritans were no less Jews than the Essenes and the early Christians, Jews bound by the Torah, both oral and written, and a form of the written Torah, at that, which was well established and is represented at Qumran (4Q Paleo ExM, 11Q Paleo Lev) among types of the Masoretic text and types of the Septuagint. Samaritan observance of the written Torah was both known and widely accepted, though there was some suspicion of their oral tradition. That Samaritan oral tradition has considerable antiquity is made clear by the statement that where Jewish halakhah derives directly from the Torah, the Samaritans would observe the halakhah in a like way, and their observance is reliable and is acceptable to the Jews.[30] However, where Jewish halakhah is based only on oral tradition, the Samaritan halakhah will deviate, as they too will have a tradition in this matter, and it will be different. Implicit in these arguments is that the Samaritan Torah version was regarded as a reliable source of halakhah, and it was not to be lightly set aside, or viewed with the same suspicion as expressed by the Amoraim, who deemed the Samaritan version corrupt.

Throughout the period of the Tannaim there was division on the issue of the Samaritans' status as Jews, a matter determined by halakhic definitions found in Tannaitic texts. The Samaritans appeared to be neither in nor out, and their identity and legal status continued to perplex the Tannaim, who could not decide whether they were to be considered gentiles or Israelites until at least the third century C.E.[31] The usual view was that the Samaritans were not Jews by origin but that they were to be considered as true proselytes and, therefore, Jewish. There is adequate evidence from the Mishnaic texts that Samaritans were treated as Jews by the first generation of the Tannaim. Thus, in M. Ket. 3:1-2 the fact that a Samaritan girl requires a monetary fine of fifty shekels from her seducer puts her on the same level as a Jewess, whereas non-Jewish girls are excluded from this law. This text is instructive, for one can trace the levels of the law's development, and it is clear that until the mid-second century C.E. the Samaritans are considered to be Jews in the halakhah pertaining to marriage. Within this general attitude, one sees a range of particular viewpoints. Simeon b. Gamaliel, the father of Judah the Patriarch, took the view that a Samaritan is like a Jew in all respects,[32] whereas Judah held that they are to be considered like non-Jews. On the other hand, a Tanna of the previous generation, Eliezer b. Hyrcanus, put Samaritans in the class of people of doubtful status for the purposes both of tithing[33] and the marriage laws.[34] Aqiba, who bridges the generation between Hyrcanus and Simeon b. Gamaliel, argued that the Cutheans were true proselytes and that the priests who were mixed with them were true priests. Yet a disciple of Aqiba, Simeon b. Yohai, of the third generation, is more positive about the Jewishness of the Samaritans in the matter of tithing and states that they are to be compared with a Jewish 'am-ha'aretz and can be relied upon not to replace tithed with untithed produce.

Not only the Tannaim were uncertain of the Samaritans' status. The early Church Fathers, who were concerned with the heresies of their day, identified the Samaritans with Sadducees. It is not impossible that the Samaritans had cordial relationships with the Sadducees[35] and that there was some degree of co-operation between them. Be that as it may, the fact that some of the Fathers identified the two sects with each other speaks for the Jewishness of the Samaritans and their practices.

The hardening of Rabbinic attitudes and their excluding the Samaritans from the status of Jews was probably triggered by the development of heretical, rather than schismatic, Samaritanism. This was marked by the adoption of a Pentateuch version that included the specific characteristics that we come to recognize as Samaritan, the development of a chain of synagogues, and the establishment of a liturgy and a series of Midrash schools for the expansion of the Samaritan halakhah. These developments, parallel with the work of the Tannaim for the Jews, began under the aegis of the third century (235-238 C.E.) Samaritan hero, Baba Rabba, a younger contemporary of Judah the Patriarch, and were continued by the Samaritan council—the *Hukama*—that Baba restructured.[36] The Council's function was not only to dispense justice and advice but was to guide the people in the interpretation of the law. The revival of the council was followed by the building of a number of synagogues in Beth Shean/Scythopolis, at Nebo/Siyagha in Moab, and elsewhere in Palestine Prima. It was during this period that their great religious reformers worked, their liturgy began to take shape, and they developed the first stages of their massoretic traditions relating to the copying of their unique version of the sacred text. In this period of the "time shadow" of the compilation of the Mishnah we see the beginning of Samaritan "philosophical" literature that to some extent should be seen as halakhic literature, especially the Memar or Tibåt Marqe and other works, which were to lead to the fifth century work of Marinus, the neo-Platonist Samaritan philosopher. During this period the Samaritans in the large cosmopolitan cities developed pagan tendencies that took them further away from their Jewish roots than their brethren in the smaller towns and the villages. Wherever ambiguity among Jews remained as to the religious identity of the Samaritans it was because of the difference between the cosmopolitanism of the urban Samaritans and the conservatism of the agrarian ones.

At the beginning of the Byzantine era, the Samaritans comprised about one third of the population of Caesarea, Gaza, Antipatris, Ascalon, Nicopolis/Emmaus, and the whole of the coastal strip from Castra Samaritanorum southwards. Early in the Byzantine period, Yamnia was almost entirely Samaritan. The division into Palestine Prima and Secunda (and Tertia) virtually unified the Samaritans into a region whose geographical characteristics lent itself to dense settlement in small farming villages across the Sharon, Shephelah, and into the hill country of Samaria. The Samaritans of the later Roman Empire and the period of Byzantine rule became reasonably well entrenched in the civil service. In the large Greco-Roman cities such as Scythopolis/Beth Shean and Caesarea, they were quick to convert to Christianity, or at least to adopt the outward style of Christians, if not the inner spirit, with the intention of obtaining preferment. Their conversions were not regarded as sincere.

The Samaritans engaged in several rebellions in the Byzantine period, each of which had its own causes; overall there were two factors that provoked the Samaritans. The first was their military strength, the second, the attitude of the rulers towards them. Because the Samaritans were not considered by the Byzantine rulers to be Jews they were not exempted from military service until Justinian removed this obligation in the wake of their repeated revolts. Thus, until Justinian's day, the Samaritans had numerous, trained, battle-seasoned soldiers living on home ground, able to take the field whenever it was deemed to be necessary.

The geography of the Samaritan home territory made it difficult to defend, especially Shechem/Neapolis, which sat astride a road network that gave easy access, rendering the city vulnerable, which meant that the city must fall in the face of a persistent frontal attack. In every attested instance, the Samaritans lost the advantages gained from their preparedness and logistic situation and from the fact that they could always win the initial advantage in the event that there were no local garrisons.

The Christianization of the Empire brought significant changes to the status of Jews and Samaritans and considerable discontent. Constantine began to translate Christian prejudices into legal disabilities. Biblical sacred sites were seen as Christian sacred sites, and Constantine and his successor Constantius, who saw the land to be a Holy Land, encouraged the building of churches at the holy places. This course of action led to violent collisions. Constantius gave a converted Jew, Josephus of Tiberias, a mandate to build churches in places in which none had been built hitherto, in exclusively Jewish settlements. Relationships between the populace and the government were already strained because of the marauding activities of soldiers gathered to attack the Persians. A rebellion broke out. In the ensuing fighting, which encompassed Sepphoris and Lydda, both towns with Samaritan populations, many Samaritans were slaughtered alongside the Jewish rebels, though there is no certainty that the Samaritans themselves were actively involved in the rebellion.

The Samaritan chronicle gives the impression that the early years of the reign of Arcadius (395-408 C.E.) were years of relative peace, in which they continued to embellish their new synagogue building, adding a valuable set of doors, which, apparently, had been looted from Jerusalem. The lack of notice of Palestine in Byzantine chronicles of the period, and the wording of the Samaritan chronicle, conveys an impression that the toleration of the Byzantine emperors for the Samaritans, at least until 400 C.E., was not matched by many in the royal entourage and by the Christians of Palestine, who are reported as having informed on the Samaritans. The internal Samaritan evidence would seem to be in accord with the mandate of Theodosius I, Arcadius and Honorius of 393 C.E. (CT. 16.8.9.) that forbade acts of Christian anti-Semitism, indicating in the very need for the mandate that there were clashes among the populace.

There is ample evidence that, in the last decades of the fourth century, the seeds of conflict between the Samaritans and the Byzantines began to germinate with some rapidity.[37] The church began to entrench itself in the Holy Land: bishops were appointed in predominantly Samaritan places and many of the sacred sites were colonized by monastic groups who were the hated spearhead of Christian intolerance. The tone of imperial legislation became increasingly menacing as perceptions strengthened, mistakenly, that the Samaritans were the source of the Gnostic movements troubling Christianity. Only bitter internecine conflicts within the church staved off violence between the Samaritans

and the church. It is probably no coincidence that between the Synod of Jerusalem in 415 C.E. and the Council of Lydda at the end of the same year, excavations by a Byzantine expedition for the bones of Joseph at Shechem brought a foretaste of the major revolt that was to flare in the middle of the century.

The affair of Joseph's bones is recorded both in Samaritan and Christian sources. Theodosius II charged a special commission with recovering the remains of the Old Testament patriarchs, and they began to excavate at the site of the tomb of Joseph. The Samaritans were outraged. Veneration of the elders and the concept of the merit of the fathers was already an important element in the Samaritan theology of religious causation (hence, of free will), as was the special role of Joseph in that theology. The attempt to plunder their sacred site struck both at their national pride and their religion.

The Samaritan account of the affair in the Chronicle of Abu'l Fath[38] is the most detailed available. The trigger for the conflict was the erection of a building (church?) over the site by the government commission, which the Samaritans promptly demolished. The Samaritans killed a number of the Byzantines who retaliated by seizing and hanging the High Priest and the Samaritan Council. The Samaritans then bribed the remaining officials with an unspecified sum, and they left the site. It may well have been this episode that provoked Theodosius into further anti-Samaritan legislation. According to Samaritan sources, he left a garrison in Neapolis and banned prayer towards the sacred mountain.

A new attempt to excavate at Awerta, the traditional home and burial place of the Samaritan priests, for the bones of the Old Testament priests Eleazar, Ithamar, and Pinhas touched off another episode of conflict in 450/451 C.E., all but unrecorded in non-Samaritan sources. The Samaritans, provoked to the point of violence, found themselves caught up in the Monophysite or Eutychian struggle. They chose the opportunity to fall on rival parties, destroying churches and monasteries, burning and pillaging, and in the end were ordered to join the Byzantine troops to help in the re-establishment of government authority. This, apparently, they did with bloodthirsty zeal.

The events of 454 C.E. were a precursor of the great revolt of 484 C.E. The Samaritan revolt was a manifestation of a more general movement. However, the immediate cause was probably that the public authorities sought, once again to exhume sacred relics for removal to Constantinople. The revolt flared at Gerizim, where five churches built on sites sacred to the Samaritans were burned. The Samaritans then advanced on Caesarea, where many Christians were murdered, and a victory celebration was held in the circus. According to Malalas, the Samaritans were beaten in battle by Asclepiadus, and the dux Zeno himself campaigned against the Samaritans. The first stage of their punishment was forcible conversion, fire torture, death by burning or being squeezed to death. Seventy of the *Hukama* and priests were executed, apparently at a public market where there were several colonnades.[39] The synagogue built by Aqbun at the *Helqat Hasadeh* was confiscated and turned into a convent, while the synagogue built by Baba was confiscated. The Samaritans were denied access to the mountain and some sort of signaling device was installed atop the tower to alert the garrison troops in the city below or at Caesarea in case of civil unrest. The countryside was pillaged and female Samaritans raped.

Procopius records another, abortive rebellion during the reign of Zeno's successor, Anastasius, (491-518).[40] It is stated that a group of Samaritans, led by an unnamed woman, scaled the sacred mountain and took the guards by surprise and slew them. The garrison commander at Neapolis put down the revolt.

The two rebellions that flared in the reign of Justinian were the principal events in reducing the Samaritans numerically. The revolt of 529 C.E. was provoked, apparently, by Justinian's adoption of anti-Samaritan legislation, especially his rescript of *De Haereticis et Manichaeis et Samaritis*, first promulgated in 527 C.E. The revolt may have been touched off not only by the restrictive anti-Samaritan legislation but also by the Persian advance to the gates of Constantinople in 529. In 530 C.E. the Samaritans do seem to have made contact with the Persians, but this was fully a year after the rebellion and may have been a consequence rather than a direct cause thereof. The rebellion was of major proportions.

Led by one Julian, who was crowned as king and who evidently had Messianic pretensions,[41] it was marked by the butchery of Christians, the burning of churches across a large area of the countryside, and widespread devastation. The local officials were slow to react, so the rebels were able to do maximum damage. However, vengeance, if delayed, was bloody. Some 20,000 Samaritans were killed in one battle alone, and many fled across the Jordan, where they were captured and sold as slaves from the west to the east of the Fertile Crescent.

In the aftermath of the rebellion, Justinian hounded the Samaritan refugees across the Samarian hills, executing leading citizens. Synagogues were razed beyond hope of repair. As many as 50,000 Samaritans fled and joined the Persian emperor, who seems to have transported them as slaves to Armenia, where they worked the mines for precious metals.

The fourth and final rebellion of the Samaritans during the Byzantine period in Palestine, that of 556 C.E., seems to have been a continuation of the former. Justinian tightened repressive legislation against the Samaritans until they were virtual outlaws; even his own followers protested against the severity of the legislation. The actual trigger for the rebellion might have been the renewal of war between Byzantium and Persia in 556 C.E., when the five-year armistice between the countries came to an end. On this occasion the Jews and the Samaritans seem to have made common cause, beginning their rebellion in Caesarea and spreading as far south as Bethlehem, where the Church of the Nativity was burned. The sources declare that either 100,000 or 120,000 Samaritans were butchered in the aftermath of the rebellion, many were tortured, and others were driven into exile; however, this may be an exaggeration, as the punishment of the Samaritans seems to have been limited to those in the district of Caesarea, and they were not yet subdued by the Byzantine emperors.

The Samaritan chronicle suggests that shortly before the accession of Heraclius, during the Palestinian campaign of Chosroes II, a large number of Samaritans were slaughtered. Heraclius followed the policy of his predecessors in forcibly baptizing and converting the Samaritans; a contemporary royal edict on baptism, of which there is no other direct evidence, was put into effect in Carthage in 632 C.E. by George, Prefect of Africa.[42]

Though the advent of the Moslems posed some initial problems for the Samaritans, including a considerable loss of life, there was considerable sympathy between them and the Samaritans, and there was a limited but renewed flowering of Samaritan life and letters, between the end of Byzantine rule and the Crusades.

When Abu Bekhr invaded Palestine in 633 C.E. at the head of the Arab armies, the defenders conscripted some 5,000 Samaritans as unwilling soldiers and put them in the van where they died. The Samaritan chronicles say that Samaritan captives were taken from Caesarea and they were never heard of again. It is clear that the Samaritans functioned as a fifth column, and they were freed from all land taxes in exchange for their services as guides and spies. The sequence of the Moslem conquests in the Holy Land indicates that towns that had substantial Samaritan populations fell first to the invaders, perhaps justifying the view that the Samaritans earned their freedom from taxation, except for the capitation tax, by helping the invading forces.

Until the coming of the Crusaders, external data for the relationships between the Samaritans and the Moslems are limited. According to Samaritan sources, by 639 C.E. the Samaritan council seems to have been re-established, under the aegis of the High Priest. The description of the council suggests that the Samaritans were re-establishing themselves up the coast from Beit Dagan and Gaza through to Aleppo.

Under the Omayyede caliphs, from the days of al-Walid I, the Samaritans seem to have been at peace, and the only incidents recorded by them are the incident during the rule of el-Mansur (754 C.E.), when an expedition was dispatched to Neapolis where the tomb of Zeno on Mt. Gerizim, with the associated complex of buildings, was burned during a midnight onslaught. All the churches and cemeteries of the Christians on the slopes of Gerizim were also destroyed.

Sometime in the middle of the eighth century, perhaps in the decade from 760-770 C.E., the succession to the Samaritan High Priesthood was disputed and the Samaritans appear to have fallen into schism over the matter of the religious calendar controlled by the priest, Nathaniel. He had been deposed by his brother, who espoused the Byzantine calendar, resulting in the observance of the New Year festival on a Tuesday, and on a Wednesday by the rival groups. Eventually the matter was settled in favor of Nathaniel's view, with the aid of one of the members of the Samaritan council, Darta. This man was probably the father or grandfather of the well-known liturgist and grammarian, Tabiah ibn Darta. The eighth century is too early to suppose that there was a Samaritan literary flowering, but the Aramaic elements in Ibn Darta's work suggest that he wrote not too late into the Moslem period. The period of ease during the Fatimid caliphate, which saw some of the administration in Samaritan hands, was also a period of literary resurgence.

The chronicles leave us with very uncertain chronology. It seems that during the period of the civil war between Hadi and Ar-Rashid, c. 786 C.E., the Samaritans suffered a number of natural calamities, including a major locust plague that resulted in many deaths from famine, with a subsequent outbreak of bubonic plague. The fratricidal struggle between al-Amin and al-Ma'mun, the sons of Ar-Rashid is noted in the chronicles, since it resulted in the destruction of some of the Samaritan centers of population in Palestine. The Samaritans are described as having to take to the caves in the hills to save lives and possessions, and the women are said to have been raped in a campaign of looting and pillage that lasted a whole year. The situation of the Samaritans seems to have changed for the better shortly before the Fatimid conquest of Egypt. The literary advances made by the Samaritans in this period may have been possible because of the renewed, but short-lived, prosperity.

Crusader rule had relatively little impact, though at some time during in the Crusader occupation of Nablus, their buildings were destroyed, and, shortly before the collapse of the Frankish kingdom, Samaritan inhabitants of the coastal towns may have been abducted to Europe. It has been argued that the Samaritans enjoyed special status under the Crusaders, which would account for the substantial literary activity of the twelfth and thirteenth centuries. Major damage to the Samaritan community during the period undoubtedly came from Muslims. According to the *Tulidah*, some five hundred people were taken captive and transported to Damascus by Bazoka of Sidon (i.e., Bazwadj, commander of the Damascene army), who raided Nablus in 1137. More prisoners were taken in a raid by Saladin in 1184.

The Mamluk Caliphate (1260-1516) was a period of relative peace, when Samaritans saw advancement as administrators and scribes in the royal service, but an era of demographic depletion. Though they were actively creating literature and liturgy, they gradually disappeared from their centers of population, for physical conditions in Palestine were harsh—there were outbreaks of plague, an economic crisis, and Bedouin raids on the cities. On the coast, the concentrations of Samaritans at Caesarea, Ascalon, and Acco disappeared, and the Nablusi Samaritans fell under the jurisdiction of Egyptian Jewry. From now on they were increasingly isolated so that in some respect they lived the life of Marranos in their home environment.

The Samaritans seem to have had a political involvement in events in Egypt, which preceded the Ottoman invasion of Palestine, and the Ottoman Turks deported many of them to Damascus. Though they were allowed to return in 1538, the com-

munity may have suffered in a destruction of the city in the mid-sixteenth century. From this time on we are given vastly more information than ever before about the affairs of this diminishing community, because they became an object of interest for European scholars, who actively sought their manuscripts and made contact with them either in person or by letter.

Though no reasons are adduced, the High Priest was deported to Damascus in 1584 and for the following half-century the Samaritans suffered oppression, confiscation of land, and many converted to Islam. The Aaronite line died out in 1624, though the Levitical line soon adopted the family name Cohen, transferring the Aaronite descent to themselves.

The Samaritan community in Damascus disappeared by 1625 and in Egypt by 1708, from Gaza by 1829 and from Jaffa in 1806. Only the Nablus community remained of a once mighty Samaritan nation. Despite the influence of the Samaritan scholar Ibrahim al-'Ayya, access to the sacred places on Gerizim was forbidden from 1785-1820, and the sect had to sacrifice the Passover lambs on the lower slopes of the mountain. In 1841 a conspiracy was formed to murder or convert all Samaritans, since they had benefited from the unpopular period of Egyptian rule (1831-1840). They were saved by the chief rabbi of Jerusalem, Abraham Chaim Gagin, who certified that the Samaritan people were a branch of the Children of Israel, who acknowledged the Torah and were thus entitled to his protection. They also paid substantial bribes to local Arab leaders. In 1854 they received the protection of the British consulate in Jerusalem, which preserved them until they came directly under British protection after World War I. Nablus was seriously damaged by an earthquake in 1927, and so the Samaritans moved from their residential district to their present neighborhood. In 1948 the two communities in Nablus and Holon were cut off from each other by the partition and the war, although radio communication was permitted and ultimately allowed the two sections of the community to make contact for the annual Passover ritual. From 1948-1951 the Jordanian authorities refused to allow the Samaritans from Israel to cross the border. In 1951 they permitted a joint celebration of the Passover sacrifice. In 1967, the Six Day War, which put the West Bank into Israeli hands, saw the Samaritans reunited as they wished.

Samaritan Literature and Their Torah: A survey of Samaritan literature shows that there are many parallels with Jewish literature. The Samaritans claim to have had an extensive early literature that was lost in the course of various oppressions, particularly at the hands of the emperor, Hadrian.[43] Three factors lead us to consider this claim seriously. First, there was indeed a Samaritan Hellenistic literature. Second, references to Samaritan writings appear in some of the Church Fathers, including some discussion of content.[44] Third, there are a number of independent traditions in Samaritan chronicles, some of which have considerable antiquity.

There is no consensus on which Hellenistic authors were of Samaritan origin, and scholars have changed their minds after having once thus identifying one or other author.[45] Criteria for identifying Samaritan texts are not clear. References to Mt. Gerizim are no longer accepted as best evidence of Samaritan authorship.[46] Suffice it to say that there was a substantial midrashic-aggadic literature, which may have been Samaritan or Jewish. For example the matter of whether Pseudo-Eupolemus was Samaritan or Jewish is not settled. Heinemann[47] demonstrated that the question of Melchizedek, which is central in Pseudo-Eupolemus, became an important issue in the Rabbinic-Samaritan polemics, which surfaced both in Talmudic and Aggadic literature. Wacholder[48] may well be correct in his assessment that the Samaritan known as Pseudo-Eupolemus "must be counted among the earliest Biblical historians writing in Greek."

There is no doubt that the Samaritan version of the Torah has the same status among Samaritans as the massoretic version has among Jews. Its variants and format, with the exception of the tenth commandment, reflect versions current before the adoption of a standard Jewish text. The earliest manuscripts from Qumran relating to the Samaritan Pentateuch include some, both in the cursive-Hebrew script and the square Hebrew script that are akin to the Samaritan text type as it must have been before being fixed.[49] These pre-texts are what Qumran scholars call "authentic" texts as against "reworked" texts, into which category it might be possible to put parts of the Samaritan Pentateuch, such as the tenth commandment.[50] That they existed before the reworking by third-century C.E. Samaritan sages is clear. Among the surviving manuscripts that belong to this group are 4QpaleoExod^m and 4QNum^b, 4QExod-Lev^f. There are related manuscripts that make substantial use of the Samaritan text-type, viz., 4Q158 and 4Q364.

These pre- or proto-Samaritan texts preserved at Qumran and dating from perhaps the third century B.C.E.[51] are significant in that they are at times as expansionist as the Samaritan Pentateuch and may almost exactly coincide with it.[52] They are of the genre that grew into the Samaritan Pentateuch, in which the greater part of the differences between the Massoretic text and the Samaritan text rose through the influence of later currents of thought,[53] that is, they were rewritten.

It is clear enough today that a substantial number of the Samaritan variants relate to Samaritan hermeneutics, exegesis of the text, and theories as to the nature of the text. They are not only the crystallization into a particular type of textual variants, such as one finds in some of the Qumran pre-massoretic texts, though there are many of these relating to old Samaritan rituals. Some of the variants and rewording are intended to "impart a more perfect and internally consistent structure to the text."[54] Furthermore recent studies make clear that the Samaritan tendency to remove anthropomorphisms in the Pentateuch came about under the influence of the fusion of Samaritan and Hellenistic cultures and that their hermeneutic style developed in an Aramaic milieu and follows rather than precedes the Septuagint.[55] Macuch[56] concludes that the Samaritan Pentateuch was fixed over a period that extended into the first

Christian centuries. Macuch's conclusions could be supplemented with a statement of the obvious, that while the Samaritan-Qumran materials may have been proto-Samaritan, they were not the Samaritan version in the forms in which it is now known.[57]

The Samaritan version was formulated in the fashion found today at some time later than the direct textual evidence from Qumran allows us to see. Because there is no other evidence from Qumran for this version, we may be justified in arguing that it took place some time after the Qumran site was deserted for the second time, in other words in the period between 135 C.E. and Origen's citation of the Samareitikon, which would put its reformulation squarely into the period of intensive activity of the Samaritan sages during Baba's lifetime. Baba Rabba's sages canonized a distinctive version of the Pentateuch with some 6,000 variants from the Massoretic text[58] and established the traditions by which it was to be copied henceforth.[59] There is reasonable evidence that some of the features of the arrangement of the Samaritan text that seem to be specifically Samaritan—the decorative finials of Samaritan manuscripts and the layout of some parts of the same manuscripts—were established by the time the great uncial manuscript, Codex Alexandrinus, was copied, perhaps in Caesarea.[60]

Works of the Aramaic Period: Samaritan literature from the fourth to the tenth centuries was almost certainly composed in Aramaic, with perhaps a little liturgical material in Hebrew and some writings in Arabic at the end of this time. Three most important types of literature are known from this period. The first is the translation of the Pentateuch into Aramaic, the Samaritan Targum, an obvious parallel to the Jewish Targum; the second is philosophical, in the form of Pentateuch commentary, with clear parallels with Midrash and Aggadah; and the third is liturgical, again with clear parallels with Jewish writings.

Until recently the Targum was known as either a single version, a translation of the Samaritan Pentateuch to Aramaic,[61] or as a text so diverse that it seemed that there had never been a single version. A critical edi-tion by Abraham Tal[62] has made it possible to see that the Targum had a development history and went through several translation processes, despite the diversity of the manuscripts. The Targum is now known to scholars in three fundamental text types. The oldest is probably of the same age as the canonization of the Samaritan Pentateuch. Tal[63] argues for a date close to the writing of Targum Onkelos.[64] The second text type, representing a stage of Aramaic used in Palestine from the fourth century onwards, was composed close to the period of the invasion of the Moslems, before Arabic came into common use among the Samaritans. The third type should be seen as a product of scribes who no longer understood Aramaic and therefore made many errors, producing a bastardized text in a new hybrid language with elements of Hebrew, Aramaic, and Arabic.

The only other extant large work of this period is the Tibåt or Mimar Marqe, really a collection of writings of different ages and origins.[65] The component parts of the collection are: Book I: The Book of Wonders of between the eleventh and thirteenth centuries C.E.; Book II: A commentary on Exodus 15, The Song of the Sea, of Marqah's day (late third or early fourth century); Books III-V: Commentaries on Deuteronomy; and Book VI, a series of Midrashim on the twenty-two letters of the alphabet, from sometime between the sixth and the tenth centuries, but most likely the ninth century.

The Defter: Tal[66] traces the beginning of Samaritan prayer to the substitution of prayer for the *Tamid* sacrifice, though this must be dated some centuries earlier than he suggests (i.e., to the period of the rapprochement between the Samaritans and Hyrcanus after the latter had destroyed their temple).[67] It is very probable that at this time the liturgy was principally a series of appropriate readings from the Torah selected to match the occasion. As these were replaced by texts written for the occasion, the readings were abbreviated into single sentences or even words representing paragraphs strung together in a qatena called a *qataf*.[68] The term defter is used to describe the core corpus of the liturgy.[69] It had ninety-three poems and served the liturgical needs of the community until the fourteenth century, when separate books began to be written for the festival services. Liturgies for Passover, Shavuot, and other occasions are written separately, independent of the defter.

Shortly after the Moslem conquest of Palestine, the Samaritans became bilingual, using Aramaic for religious purposes and Arabic for secular ones. Samaritan writing again paralleled that of the Jews and in some ways intermeshed, since there was a Samaritan-Karaite dialogue. On the whole, the Samaritans faced the same religious and literary needs as the Jews, but their literary responses were a century or so later. By the end of the tenth century, Samaritan works were written in Arabic, including a series of grammatical works and an anonymous lexicographical dictionary, *haMelits*, which relates the Hebrew of the Samaritan Pentateuch with equivalents in Aramaic and Arabic. The grammatical works, which have been edited by Z. Ben-Hayyim, include Ibn Darta's Rules Regarding the Reading, probably called forth by the breakdown of the traditions among the Samaritan scribes about the diacritical marks inserted into codices. A Treatise on the Vowels (early twelfth century) and the Prolegomenon, *Sefer al-Tautiyah*, is the first true Samaritan grammar, written by Abu Ibrahim b. Faraj b. Maruth in the twelfth century. Abu Saʿid b. Abu'l-Hasan b. Abi Saʿid wrote a guide for students for reading the Torah. The first Samaritan Arabic translation of the Pentateuch was a version based primarily on the *Tafsir* of Saʿadyah Gaon (882-942). It was succeeded by the Old Arabic translation of the Samaritan Pentateuch, which was replaced by the revised text of Abu Saʿid b. Abu'l-Hasan b. Abi Saʿid (thirteenth-century).

A second period of liturgical writing began in the tenth century, when Aramaic was still in use for the synagogue service but was starting to be contaminated by Arabic. Hebrew was beginning to penetrate the sacred poetry, and for the first time Hebrew was used for the liturgy, but Aramaic and Hebrew were never mixed in a single composition. In the thirteenth century literary

flowering, the liturgy was a hybrid of Hebrew and Aramaic with a strong admixture of Arabic, which is identified by grammarians as "Samaritan." At this time, the register of liturgical works in the defter began to be restricted to the Sabbath and weekday services. The festival services were supplied with special prayer books, and a new collection was written for weddings and circumcisions (the Book of Joyous Occasions = *Memar Hasameah* or *Mimar Ashama*).

Chronicles, Theological and Polemic Works of the Arabic Period: Several basic chronicles stem from the period in which Arabic began to displace Aramaic in Samaritan literature and from the literary renaissance of the fourteenth century.[70] They include the *Asatir*,[71] a midrash on the life of the Patriarchs including Adam, Noah, Abraham, and Moses, not dissimilar in style and content to parts of the *Tibât Marqe*[72] and the *Tulidah* or "genealogy," written in Aramaic and Hebrew by Eleazar b. Amram in 1149. Related to the *Tulidah* is the *Shalshalat* or Chain of the High Priests, which is the list of High Priests to the time of the scribe who updated the text, Jacob b. Aaron. Jacob may well have been the compiler rather than merely a copyist.

The *Kitab al-Tarikh* of Abu'l-Fath was written in Arabic by Abu'l-Fath in 1355 at the instigation of the High Priest, Pinhas b. Joseph. This chronicle uses sources now lost and has been drawn on by the Samaritans who have built round it by continually adding material to bring it up-to date, so that there is a shorter, original version and a longer, extended and much glossed one. It has been abstracted and paraphrased for several other works that have been misrepresented as old chronicles.

The Book of Joshua, sometimes identified as the Arabic Book of Joshua to distinguish it from the Hebrew text, was compiled from a number of sources and translated into Arabic by an unnamed Samaritan scholar in the thirteenth century. The text was edited by Juynboll,[73] and an English translation by Crane[74] has been published. Moses Gaster[75] published what he claimed to be the Hebrew source of this work. It is a modern compilation based on a transla-tion from the Arabic version of Joshua, with some additional material from the extended version of Abu'l-Fath.[76] It is in biblical Hebrew contaminated by Samaritan forms that Ben-Hayyim showed to have devel-oped in the period of the Samaritan literary renaissance. However, preserved in the text are some Christological elements found in an Ethiopic parallel text.[77] This chronicle, which brings the history up to date from Joshua to modern times, was published sep-arately as the New Chronicle by Adler and Seligsohn.[78]

The so-called Chronicle II is extensively excerpted and reprinted in some modern collections of Jewish documents. While a fourteenth century C.E. date has been sug-gested for the work, in fact it is a modern compilation: no old manuscripts are known, and it was compiled, apparently, by the priestly scribes of Nablus at the end of the last century. It is closely related to the ex-tended, Samaritan Hebrew Joshua version and New Chronicle of Adler. It contains some material that can be traced to nine-teenth-century European textbooks.[79]

Commentaries, Halakhic/legal, and Polemical texts: A canonical Samaritan halakhah resembling the Jewish compila-tions never existed, though the reasons are not clear, since there were ancient halakhic differences between Samaritans and Rabbi-nic Jewry.[80] It may be that the halakhic differences were enshrined in the Samaritan Pentateuch and no need was felt for addi-tional commentary. The very existence of halakhah in the community in ancient times is indicated by several precepts "concealed" behind various passages of the Targum in which the Aramaic translation does not follow the Hebrew original or where the original has a peculiar form.[81] Certainly the rabbis had no hesitation in pointing up the differences between their rituals and practices and those of the Samaritans. In the years before the Rabbinic recognition that the Samaritans were no longer Jews, few if any Samaritan halakhic treatises were written. All of them were composed after the language shift from Aramaic to Arabic, and some scholars doubt that the term "halakhic" can be applied legiti-mately to any extant Samaritan religio-legal literature.

The oldest halakhic/legal and polemical texts thus belong to the period when Arabic was penetrating Samaritan religious writ-ings. They appear at the beginning of the Samaritan renaissance and continue to be written at intervals throughout the period. The first to appear were the *Kitab al-Kafi*, written by Yusuf ibn Salama b. Yusuf al-'Askari, in 1041/2, and the *Kitab at-Tabbah*, composed by Abu'l-Hasan as-Suri between 1030-1040. They may have been written as part of the general Samaritan response to Karaism and Islam.[82] These works were followed by the *Kitab al-Khilaf* (the Book of Differences [between Samaritans and Jews]), written by Munajjah ibn Tsedaqa in the mid-twelfth century, and the *Kitab al-Mirat* (Book of Inheritance, a juridical treatise dealing with the precepts of inherit-ance), written by Saladin's personal physi-cian,[83] Abu Ishaq Ibrahim ibn Faraj ibn Maruth, the son of Abu'l-Hasan of Tyre, also known for his grammatical study *Kitab at-Tautiyya* and the *Kitab al-Fara'id*. Two different versions exist of the *Kitab al-Itiqadat*, the Book of Principles, known by Gaster as the *Hillukh*, which were composed in the late nineteenth century.

Finally, one should note the exegetical works written in Arabic by the few Samaritan scholars who wrote commen-taries on the Torah. As far as is known, a complete commentary on the Torah penned by one author is not available, despite the fact that the Torah is the begin-ning and end of law and religion. Yet such works did exist, as is explicitly stated in some Samaritan and non-Samaritan sources. Thus, the eleventh-century scholar Yusuf b. Salama al-'Askari, in his *Kitab al-Kafi*, affirmed that he had written an exegetical commentary on the Torah. On the evidence of Ibn abi-Usaybya (1203-1269), a thirteenth-century physician, Tsedaqa b. Munajjah b. Tsedaqa as-Samiri ad-Dimasqi, known as Tsedaqa al-Hakhim, had written such a commentary, and this Tsedaqa confirmed that his father, Munaj-jah, composed a commentary on the Torah. Today only the commentary on Genesis 1:2-50:5 is extant,[84] but there are excerpts of other books, such as the commentary on the life of Moses, which survive in a single manuscript.[85] Most Samaritan exegesis of the text is in the form of halakhic commentary. Abu'l-Hasan as-Tsuri appears to have begun a commentary on Genesis in 1053 as part of his writings on religio-legal subjects,[86] and he wrote a commentary on the Decalogue, *Kitab fi Suruh al-'asr kalimat* and a commentary on Deut. 32 known as *al-Khutba al-gami'a* or *Sharh 'zinu*, which is usually included in copies of *at-Tabbah*. Among the incomplete extant works, one of the earliest is that of Nafis al-Din Abu'l-Faraj ibn Ishaq ibn Al-Kathar, the thirteenth century author who wrote a commentary on Lev. 26 called *Sharh am baqquti*,[87] i.e., *im behuqotai*. Among his other writings known to us were a proof of the existence of the world to come, his *Kitab al-Dalail*, in which he made critical use of the writings of his predecessors.[88] Isma'il ar-Rumayhi of the sixteenth century wrote a commentary on Deuteronomy and halakhic comments on *terumah* and *niddah*,[89] and Ghazal b. Abi as-Sarur (Ab Zehuta) al-Matari al-Ghazzawi (1702-1759) wrote commentaries, on Exodus, Leviticus, and Numbers.[90]

Other commentaries were by Muslim/ Meshalma ibn Murjan, a renowned liturgist and scribe (1699-1738) and his nephew Ibrahim Ibn al-'Ayyah who wrote a lengthy commentary on the first four books of Moses.[91] None of the commentaries is as yet properly published[92] though this is one of the major tasks still facing Samaritan scholars. From the late nineteenth century onwards new commentaries have been written. Amram b. Salama, the High Priest (1809-1874) wrote a commentary in two parts on Exodus; Pinhas (Khidr) b. Isaac, the High Priest (d. 1898) composed a commentary on Lev. 18, named *Tafsir surat al-irbot* or *Sharh utsul az-zawag*, on the principles of marriage, and recently 'Abd-al-Mu'in (Eleazar) Tsedaqa (born 1927) wrote an interpretation of the names occurring in the Torah, *Tafsir al-asma' al-werida fi t-tawra*.

Beliefs and Practices: The Samaritan creed touched on above has been succinctly stated in letters from the Samaritans to inquiring Western scholars: "We say: My faith is in Thee, YHWH; and in Moses son of Amram, thy servant, and in the Holy Law; and in Mount Gerizim Bethel and in the Day of Vengeance and Recompense."

The Samaritan concept of God has shaped itself in the direction of the rigorous monotheism of Islam, and they may have first used in their liturgy the slogan later adopted by Islam, "There is no God, but God." The tetragrammaton, YHWH, is in regular use. Samaritans, like Jews, avoid making images of God, whom they see as the ineffable and incorporeal creator and sustainer who has entered into unique covenant with Israel. The Law of God emanates from the divine fire as part of the covenant. The practical and legal aspect of Torah has been emphasized to elevate its interpreters, the priests, to unique authority. Moses, as mediator of the Torah, deserves adoration as the third focus of Samaritan faith. Blessings are offered "in the name of Moses the faithful," the last and most exalted of the prophets. His birth is exalted in a treatise, the *Molad Mosheh*. He is depicted as a pre-existent primordial light who came to illuminate the world.

Mt. Gerizim, in the Samaritan view, is the navel of the world, where Abel built the first altar and where God told Abraham to sacrifice Isaac. The Memar Marqe enumerates thirteen honorific names for the mountain. Tradition calls it the oldest and highest mountain in the world, and its peak survived the flood in the time of Noah. Here the Samaritans have built a series of altars and sanctuaries at three major sacred spots and continue to celebrate their festivals. In the matter of the sanctity and centrality of Mount Gerizim, the Samaritan belief may be more primitive than innovative. If one reads the patriarchal accounts with a critical eye, Bethel and Shechem seem to be proximate places. The association of Bethel—and all the events in the patriarchal accounts linked with Bethel—Shechem, Moriah, and Gerizim can be made directly from the Pentateuch. The Septuagint reading of Shiloh instead of Shechem (Josh. 24) and the statement in the Testament of Joseph (2:6) that Joseph was buried in Hebron, rather than near

Shechem, suggest that the Jewish authorities were already troubled by Samaritan interpretations of the sacred writ in favor of Shechem and Mt. Gerizim. In addition to the textual evidence that Gerizim was the sacred mountain on which God dwelt, the traditional sites of the tombs of some of the High Priests, such as Abisha and Pinhas, are near Gerizim at Awerta, and of course Joseph was buried at Timnat Serah (or Kfar Haris), in the same region. Jacob's well is traditionally located at the Helqat Hasadeh, the "Parcel of Ground" near Shechem, and Jacob is also held to have been buried near Shechem. As noted elsewhere, claims for Mt. Gerizim have helped distinguish Samaritanism from Judaism.

The notion of a Day of Vengeance and Recompense is based on the Samaritan text of Deut. 32:35: "To the day of vengeance and recompense, at the time when their foot shall slide: For the day of their calamity is at hand, and the things that are to come upon them shall make haste." The coming Day of the Lord will be ushered in by the Taheb, a messianic figure, unlike the Jewish, Davidic messiah, a prophet like Moses, whose role is modeled on Deut 18:18. The day of Vengeance and Recompense is characterized by a long period of peace and security before the final end. The Samaritan periodization of the history of salvation includes an epoch of *panutha*, disfavor, preceding Moses, an epoch of *rahuta*, grace, lasting 260 years after Moses, a further epoch of disfavor initiated by the evil priest Eli[93] and the final period of grace to be initiated by the Taheb.

The calendar by which the feasts are determined originated with the Jewish calendar, and the Samaritan festivals relate to those Israelite (Jewish) ones that have a warrant in the Torah. Jewish festivals that have no warrant in the Torah, such as Hanukkah and Purim, are not celebrated. The calendar has become so complex through the centuries of alien influences that only the priest can calculate the appropriate feast days for any given year. On the Day of *Tsimmuth*, (meaning not certain), sixty days before Passover, each member of the community pays a half shekel and receives the calendar in which the priest has

calculated the festivals for the next six months.[94] During the year, the Samaritans celebrate seven festivals, that is, the three pilgrim *haggim*, festivals, and the four seasonal festivals, the *moʿadim*. These are the *Moʿed* of Passover, the *Hag* of Unleavened Bread, the *Hag* of Weeks (Shavuot), the *Moʿed* of the Seventh Month, the *Moʿed* of Yom haKippurim, the *Hag* of Booths (Sukkot), and the *Moʿed* of the eighth day of Solemn Assembly. The Festival of Unleavened Bread, the Feast of Weeks, and the Feast of Booths are celebrated on Mt. Gerizim. Although Passover is distinct from the Feast of Unleavened Bread, the Samaritans remain on the mountain through the days of each. There is a special liturgy for each of the services and associated days such as the nine penitential days and the ten days of *selihot*, which precede the *Moʿed* of Yom haKippurim.

During each festive service, the Torah is read in the synagogue. The annual cycle begins on the Sabbath following the *Moʿed* of the eighth day of Solemn Assembly, and the weekly selections are divided into portions as in the Jewish synagogue. Most lections are named with a lemma rather than a single word as in the Jewish tradition. As in the Jewish synagogue, there are a number of "special" Sabbaths, such as the "Sabbath of the Sea" or the Sabbath of "Amalek," relating to the content of the Torah reading. On the Day of Atonement, the main festival of the synagogue, the law is read and the Abisha Scroll is displayed for adoration.

The Sabbath day is rigidly observed and is almost a festive day. Young people dress up, the boys go to synagogue to pray and afterwards come home to eat together. Unlike their Israeli counterparts, young people do not go out on Friday nights. Women do not have a place in the synagogue for fear of rendering it unclean through menstrual impurity. Because no *erub* is available, cold food is eaten; Sabbath timers or any other modern means of alleviating Sabbath stringencies are not utilized.

Ritual purity and impurity retains its significance for the Samaritans. A *niddah*, a menstruant woman, is unclean for seven days and forbidden to touch furniture, family chattels, husband or children because of the fear of secondary contamination. Purification takes place at the end of the seventh day. After the birth of a male child, she is impure for forty days with the addition of the day of the circumcision; after the birth of a daughter eighty days.

Circumcision is practiced on the eighth day and is never postponed, which posed problems for the Samaritans of Holon, who relied on Jewish *mohalim*, who would not act on the Sabbath. Jewish doctors were permitted to perform the operation on their behalf.

The contemporary situation: The twentieth century has been marked by revi-

In the past, elders viewed such marriages with disfavor, but once the barriers were breached, mixed marriages were accepted, provided the Jewish woman accepts Samaritan religious forms.[95] In contrast, Samaritan women are rarely allowed to marry Jewish males. There remains an imbalance in the community with a shortage of females, predicating that the old custom of early marriage is maintained to a substantial degree. Though women have more rights today and there are fewer arranged marriages, it is still the case that many girls are engaged or betrothed as infants. Statistics for the late 1980s-1990s show the following imbalance:

Proportion of males to females over five years

Year	Holon males	Holon females	Shechem males	females	total
1987	145 (27.4%)	109 (20.6%)	146 (27.6%)	129 (24.4%)	529
1988	146 (27.7%)	109 (20.6%)	146 (27.7%)	127 (24.0%)	528
1989	148 (27.9%)	110 (20.7%)	144 (27.1%)	129 (24.3%)	531
1990	153 (28.1%)	113 (20.8%)	147 (27.0%)	131 (24.1%)	544
1991	153 (28.0%)	116 (21.2%)	147 (26.9%)	131 (23.9%)	547

talization through measures designed to preserve the Samaritan people. They have been able to reverse their population decline, so that they are no longer in danger of imminent extinction, and they have been able to reassert their distinct identity, even mobilize in the face of an uncertain future, for those who live in Nablus. This is exemplified by the fact that the drop-out rate of the Samaritan community in the past sixty years has been less than two percent, despite their partial modernization within their own parameters and extensive social and economic contact with secular Israeli and Palestinian culture.

The Samaritans have been virtually an endangered people until the twentieth century. Their habit of marrying only within the group, often by arranged marriage within the same family, made for excessive child mortality, a high proportion of Rh-babies and inbreeding. This situation changed within the twentieth century, when the Samaritans received genetic counseling and the late Yitzchak ben Zvi encouraged Samaritan males to marry Jewish females.

The Samaritans' relationship with the State of Israel has been fostered through their friendship with the late president, Yitzchak ben Zvi, and is still colored by the view of Rabbi Abraham Chaim Gagin that they believe in the sanctity of the Torah. In 1951, they were given the same status as oriental Jews.

Since early after the establishment of the State of Israel there has been a special committee of four Samaritan males to represent them to the various state foundations and to create bridges between them and the State. The question of the Samaritans' identity as Jews became an issue in 1955 when the head of the *Hevra Qadishah* in Tel Aviv wanted to allocate them a piece of the Christian Burial ground. Representations to the Rabbinate and to President Ben Zvi resulted in the allocation of a separate Samaritan burial ground in Kiryat Shaul, Tel Aviv, on the grounds that the Samaritans viewed themselves as "complete Israelis, not only in citizenship but in their spiritual relationship to the rest of Israel." At the beginning of the 1960s, a separate department was created in the Ministry of Religion to deal with Samaritans, Karaites, and the Jews of India. The committee was not only concerned with spiritual and religious matters but with other aspects of Samaritan life. It dealt with the task of finding jobs for the young, influenced payments from the state to the High Priest and to teachers, was instrumental in opening a club for the young, and helped educate the young in modern Hebrew.

Holon and Nablus: The Samaritans of Holon found themselves separated from their community in Nablus for nineteen years after the state of Israel's establishment; the impact of division left a profound impression upon them. In Nablus, the Samaritans remained in their age-long dilemma of living almost as Marranos in their native city, as relationships with their Palestinian neighbors were badly troubled. They had better relations with the Hashemite monarchy than with any other preceding government. Some of the policies of the Jordanians were helpful, in particular the acquisition of land around the holy sites on Mount Gerizim. A high proportion of the Samaritans of Nablus work in state offices and this generates Arab hostility. Intifada leaders wanted them to give up state service, but they refused on the grounds that their work serves to facilitate contact between Jews and Arabs. The Arabs burned some Samaritan houses in response. While some Samaritans argue that there is no difference in life style for the Samaritans between Holon and Nablus, there are educational differences in that in Holon students learn Tanakh in Jewish schools, whereas in Nablus they read the Qur'an in Moslem schools.

After the Six Day War, when direct contact between Holon and Nablus was established, a democratic committee was set up to represent the families who had differed in role in both places during the separation. In Nablus, where the priesthood[96] was centered throughout the period of separation, priests remain the leaders and source of living religion, representing the community to the outside. The priests act as precentors, fix the law, and a most senior priest is chosen as High Priest, chosen for his seniority, knowledge, and wisdom. Because this priest has public functions outside the community,

there have been times when he has not been available to serve as a leader at home. The priests resisted this challenge to their authority through the spreading of leadership tasks but eventually accepted a committee run by a member of the Altif family and representing all the families. It was agreed from the outset that no one would challenge the spiritual leadership of the priests. Subsequently the idea has been raised by the Holon-Samaritans of a committee with a supervisory role over religion in Shechem and Holon. But this seems beyond the realm of current possibilities. In 2003, the Israeli High Court granted two Samaritan priests who serve as cantors in the Holon Synagogue the status of local rabbis, equivalent to the status of local Jewish rabbis.

The Samaritan conflict with modernity: The Samaritans face particular pressures from modernity, related both to their environment and to their mingling with Israelis, which allows young Samaritans to see alternatives to their own rigid religious life. Ironically this pressure comes from the fact that the Samaritans are now living in a state that gives them equal rights with the majority and imbues in them strong feelings of patriotism.

Contact with Israeli society has exposed Samaritan customs to closer scrutiny than ever was the case at Shechem. The failure of the Samaritans to develop a halakhic system that might ameliorate some particularly stringent religious requirements has created a number of problems for Samaritans in Holon who are integrated within the Israeli community (less so, though, for those who serve in the army, where they are allowed to remain indoors on Shabbat and follow a vegan kosher diet). In general there is a tendency for the Samaritans to keep to themselves and to live their lives within their own community, as there is a fear that outside influences will interfere with traditions. There have been conscious efforts to prevent young people from living outside the community, so as to keep them within the tradition; so far there have been few defections from the community. However, young Samaritans go to state schools and kindergartens and so are able to judge that their Jewish sister tradition has developed facilities for coping more readily with modernity.

Among demands for reform are for the abridgement of the liturgy, especially for that of the Sabbath. Some Samaritans argue that electronic timers should be acceptable for operating lights and the like on the Sabbath and that one should be permitted to turn on a light before the Sabbath for Sabbath use (as is done within traditional Judaism): others maintain their opposition to such modernisms. There is a desire to differentiate between the Sabbath and festivals, which, at the moment, are subject to the same restrictions. According to current practice, on the Sabbath one cannot journey even by foot. Some want to permit this, and they want to allow cooking on festivals, including the baking of *matzoth* on Passover itself. However there is the fear that reform will open the gates to undesired changes.

Notes

[1] The Samaritans have argued in recent years that there are four major differences between themselves and the Jews: 1. their unbroken connection to the land of Israel; 2. their continuation of the sacrificial ritual, in the form of the Passover sacrifice; 3. their refusal to make use of an *erub* to ameliorate some of the stringencies of the Sabbath; and 4. the universal preservation among the Samaritans of rules of menstrual purity.

[2] See Rita Egger, *Josephus Flavius und die Samaritaner: eine terminologische Untersuchung zur Identitätsklarung der Samaritaner* (Freiburg and Göttingen, 1986); and "Josephus Flavius and the Samaritans," in A. Tal, ed., *Proceedings of the First International Congress of the Société d'Études Samaritaines* (Tel Aviv, 1991), pp. 109-114.

[3] C.S. Chang, *A New Examination of Samaritan Origins and Identity in the Light of Recent Scholarship* (Sydney, PhD dissertation), 1990.

[4] One must assume that Is. 63:17f. is a pre-exilic source, despite its position in the book.

[5] Chang, *Samaritan Origins*, has a substantial discussion of the Deuteronomic redactions in relation to 2 Kgs. 17.

[6] Vv. 1-6, 24, 30-31 and 34a.

[7] B. Oded, "Observations on Methods of Assyrian Rule in Transjordania after the Palestinian Campaign of Tiglath Pileser III," in *JNES* 29 (1970), pp. 177-186, gives reason to believe that even the source that, by common consensus in 2 Kgs. 17 is secondary, has elements that match known Assyrian policies.

[8] Aharon Oppenheimer, "The 'Ammei Ha'aretz, the Christians and the Samaritans," in *The 'Am Ha'aretz. A Study in the Social History of the Jewish People in the Hellenistic-Roman Period* (Leiden, 1977), pp. 218-238.

[9] See Y. Shiloh, "The Population of Iron Age Palestine in the Light of a Sample Analysis of Urban Plans, Area and Population Density," in *BASOR* 239 (1980), pp. 25-35.

[10] See M. Broshi and R. Gophna, "Middle Bronze Age II Palestine: Its Settlements and Population," in *BASOR* 261 (1986), pp. 73-90.

[11] M. Kochavi, et al., *Judaea, Samaria and the Golan* (Jerusalem, 1972).

[12] See the calculations in Chang, *Samaritan Origins*.

[13] J.H. Hayes and J.K. Kuan, "The Final Years of Samaria (730-720 BC)," in *Biblica* 72:3 (1991), pp. 153-181.

[14] See M. Broshi, "The Expansion of Jerusalem in the Reigns of Hezekiah and Manasseh," in *IEJ* 24 (1974), pp. 21-26.

[15] About 50% of the late iron age sites in Judea seem to have been established between 700 and 600 B.C.E. according to the survey of Judea and Samaria.

[16] From 2 Kgs. 23:4, 15, it would appear that Bethel was under his control and, from the accounts of his death in 2 Kgs. 23:29 and 2 Chron. 35:11, the country as far as, and probably including, Megiddo was in his hands. An ostracon discovered at Mesad Hashavyahu on the coast seems to indicate that this fortress too was in Josiah's hands.

[17] Kenneth J. Hoglund, *Achaemenid Imperial Administration in Syria-Palestine and the Missions of Ezra and Nehemiah* (Atlanta, 1992).

[18] Hoglund, p. 244.

[19] Idem, and H.H.M. Williamson, "Sanballat," in *Anchor Bible Dictionary*, vol. 5, pp. 973-975.

[20] Y. Meshorer and Shraga Kedar, *The Coinage of Samaria in the Fourth Century B.C.E.* (Jerusalem, 1991). They argue that it was Manasseh who assumed this name as his official title. Governors in parts of the Persian Empire seem to have adopted the status of king even though they were not independent of Persia. See Diodorus Siculus XVI, 42.4-9 and his description of the *kings* of Cyprus. Some Phoenician governors minted coins with their own crowned busts.

[21] N. Avigad, *Bullae and Seals from a Post-Exilic Judaean Archive*, Qedem 4 (Jerusalem, 1976), reconstructs the list of governors, p. 36.

[22] See Y. Magen, "Mt. Gerizim—A Temple City," in *Qadmoniot* 33:2 (120) (2000), pp. 74-118, and other statements in the same issue of *Qadmoniot*. See also R.T. Anderson, "The Elusive Samaritan Temple," in *BA* 54:2 (June 1991), pp. 104-107. Idem, "Josephus' Accounts of Temple Building: History, Literature or Politics?" in *Proceedings, Eastern Great Lakes and Midwest Biblical Societies* 9 (1989), pp. 246-257.

[23] See Y. Magen, "Mt. Gerizim—A Temple City," in *Qadmoniot* 23:3-4 (91/92) (1990), pp. 69-96 (Hebrew).

[24] R.T. Anderson, "Temple and Tabernacle as Symbols in Jewish Samaritan Polemics," in *Proceedings of the Eastern Great Lakes and Midwest Biblical Societies* 8 (1988), pp. 23-33.

[25] See E.F. Campbell, Jr., "Jewish Shrines of the Hellenistic and Persian Periods," in F.M. Cross, ed., *Symposia Celebrating the Seventy-Fifth Anniversary of the Founding of the American Schools of Oriental Research (1900-1975)* (1975), pp. 159-167.

[26] A writer of the period, Theodotus, not certainly a Samaritan despite claims that his description of Shechem, preserved by Alexander Polyhistor and quoted in Eusebius' *Praeparatio Evangelica*, indicates authorship by a Samaritan, stated in his poem, *On the Jews*, that Shechem was a holy city. In his views of Shechem, he seems to espouse the Bethel = Shechem equation. If this claim indeed was made by a non-Samaritan, it underscores the intensity of the rivalry between Jerusalem and Gerizim.

[27] Mary Joan Wynn Leith, *Greek and Persian Images in Pre-Alexandrine Samaria: The Wadi ed-Daliyeh Seal Impressions* (Harvard University PhD dissertation, 1990), p. 48.

[28] AJ xii. 256-260, referring to the year 168 B.C.E. Josephus reported that the Samaritans asked that their temple, hitherto unnamed, be named the Temple of Zeus Hellenios. 2 Maccabees 6:2 links the renaming with the enforced pollution of the Jerusalem Temple and indicates that the temple was renamed after Zeus Xenios, "after the manner of the local usage" perhaps, as suggested by J.A. Montgomery, *The Samaritans* (Philadelphia, 1907), p. 77, because the name Mt. Gerizim indicated such a name (i.e., the local usage).

[29] Ibid.

[30] On the Samaritan Halakhah at Qumran, see A.D. Crown, "Qumran, Samaritan Halakhah and Theology and pre-Tannaitic Judaism," in M. Lubetski, Claire Gottlieb, and Sharon Keller, eds., *Boundaries of the Ancient Near Eastern World; A Tribute to Cyrus Gordon* (Sheffield, 1998), pp. 420-441.

[31] L.H. Schiffman, "The Samaritans in Tannaitic Halakhah," in *JQR* lxxv (1985), pp. 323-350.

[32] "Every precept the Cutheans have adopted, they observe with minute care, even more than the Israelites," B. Qid. 75b, 76b.

[33] T. Dem. 5:21-24, Erfurt MS.

[34] M. Qid. 4:1.

[35] See James D. Purvis, "The Samaritans and Judaism," in R.A. Kraft and George Nickelsburg, eds., *Early Judaism and its Modern Interpreters* (Philadelphia, 1986), p. 83.

[36] On the Samaritan Council, see A.D. Crown, "Samaritan Religion in the Fourth Century," in *NTT* 41:1 (1986), pp. 29-47.

[37] For the Byzantine period of Samaritan history see A.D. Crown, "Samaritans in the Byzantine Orbit," in *BJRUL* 69, 1 (Autumn, 1986), pp. 96-138, and A.M. Rabello, *Giustiniano, Ebrei E Samaritani*, 2 vols. (Milan, 1987-1988).

[38] For the chronicle of Abu'l Fath, see P.L. Stenhouse, *Kitab al-Tarikh of Abu'l Fath* (Sydney, 1985).

[39] These are to be seen at the extreme left of the presentation of Neapolis on the Madeba map.

[40] Procopius, *Buildings* V, vii.10.

[41] The Samaritan chronicles (Abu'l Fath iv 228-229) regard Julian as the leader of their seventh sect.

[42] Cf., R. Devreese, "La fin inédite d'une lettre de Sainte Maxime," in *Revue des Sciences Religieuses* XVII (1937), pp. 25-35.

[43] According to the *Book of Joshua*, chapter 47. Abu'l-Fath places the loss of books in the reign of Commodus (*AF* cap. 37). The books lost are claimed to have been *The Book of Choice Selections* (some sort of land register?); Hymns and praises that were used when the sacrificial rite was offered; the *Book of the Imams* (*Tulidah?*), and the *Annals*. It is interesting that the extant Samaritan works are of the types mentioned by Abu'l-Fath, i.e., liturgies, the genealogical register, and chronicles.

[44] Photius says (in the name of Eulogius), "He (Dositheus, the Samaritan) adulterated the Mosaic octateuch with myriads of spurious changes of all kinds, and he also left behind with his believers certain other works he had composed—foolish and outlandish and contrary to the laws of the spirit." For further discussion of early patristic views of Samaritan writings, see Bruce Hall, *Samaritan Religion from Hyrcanus to Baba Rabba* (Sydney, 1987). Reinhard Pummer is producing a new study of Samaritan references in Patristic writings.

[45] See C.R. Holladay, *Fragments from Hellenistic Jewish Authors* (Chico and Atlanta, 1983-1989), 2 vols.

[46] R. Pummer, "Argarizin—A Criterion for Samaritan Provenance," in *JSJ* 18 (1987-1988), pp. 18-25.

[47] Joseph Heinemann, "Anti-Samaritan polemics in the Aggadah," in *Proceedings of the Sixth World Congress of Jewish Studies* (Jerusalem, 1977), pp. 57-69.

[48] Ben-Zion Wacholder, "'Pseudo-Eupolemus.' Two Greek fragments on the life of Abraham," in *HUCA* 34 (1963), pp. 83-113.

[49] For these texts see P.W. Skehan, E. Ulrich, and J.E. Sanderson, *Qumran Cave IV Palaeo-Hebrew and Greek Biblical Manuscripts* (Oxford, 1992). Emanuel Tov has observed that "in view of the recent finds in Qumran it is now believed that at the base of the Samaritan Pentateuch lies a non-sectarian Palestinian text similar to several texts that have been found at Qumran and which for this purpose are named 'proto-Samaritan.' These sources contain early non-sectarian texts on one of which the Samaritan Pentateuch was based." In its present form, the Samaritan Pentateuch contains a clearly sectarian text. However, when its thin sectarian layer is removed, together with that of the Samaritan phonetic features, the resulting text probably did not differ much from the texts, now labelled "proto-Samaritan." See E. Tov, "Samaritan Pentateuch," in A.D. Crown, R. Pummer, and A. Tal, eds., *A Companion to Samaritan Studies* (Tübingen, 1993), pp. 177-183.

[50] See, for example, Emanuel Tov, "Re-

written Bible Compositions and Biblical Manuscripts, with Special Attention to the Samaritan Pentateuch," in *DSD* 5:3 (1998), pp. 334-354.

[51] For a brief evaluation of these texts in the light of the problems of Samaritan origins, see F. Dexinger, "Samaritan Origins and the Qumran Texts," in M. Wise, N. Golb, et al., "Methods of Investigation of the Dead Sea Scrolls and the Khirbet Qumran Site," in *Annals of the New York Academy of Sciences*, vol. 722 (New York, 1994), pp. 231-250.

[52] On this point, see Kyung Rae Kim, "Studies in the Relationship Between the Samaritan Pentateuch and the Septuagint" (Hebrew University, PhD dissertation, 1994). Unfortunately Kim did not deal with the similarities between the pre-Qumran and Samaritan texts, which might reflect older halakhic traditions.

[53] See R. Macuch, "Hermeneutical Divergences between the Samaritan and Jewish Versions of the Blessings of the Patriarchs (Genesis 49 and Deuteronomy 33)," in A.D. Crown and Lucy Davey, *New Samaritan Studies of the Société d'Études Samaritaines, III & IV. Essays in Honour of G.D. Sixdenier* (Sydney, 1996), pp. 365-380.

[54] Cf., Tov, "Rewritten Bible Compositions," p. 341.

[55] Cf., R. Macuch, "Les bases philologiques de l'herméneutique et les bases herméneutique de la philologie chez les Samaritaines," in Jean-Pierre Rothschild, and Guy Sixdenier, eds., *Études samaritaines Pentateuque et Targum, exégèse et philologie, chroniques* Actes de la Table Ronde, Paris (7-9 Octobre 1985) (Louvain and Paris, 1988), pp. 149-158. John Lightfoot, *Horae Hebraicae et Talmudicae* (Oxford, 1859), makes an interesting observation (p. 358) on the exchange of the names Ebal and Gerizim in Deut. 11:29 and 27:12-13. Having drawn our attention to Rabbinic complaints about the expansion of Deut. 11:30, he suggests that the reason no complaints were heard about the exchange of Gerizim and Ebal is that these changes were made after the lifetime of Eliezer b. Yose, i.e., after the second century C.E. The argument from silence is dangerous, but not without merit.

[56] "Les bases philologiques," p. 154.

[57] Cf., D.N. Freedman and K.A. Mathews, *The Palaeo-Hebrew Leviticus Scroll* (Winona Lake, 1985). where the words "proto-Samaritan" regularly indicate that the text is not the Samaritan Pentateuch. Judith E. Sanderson, *An Exodus Scroll from Qumran* (Atlanta, 1986), seems to find 4QpalaeoExod^m rather close to the Samaritan version but not identical with it.

[58] Cf., F. Dexinger, "The Limits of Tolerance in Judaism: The Samaritans," in E.P. Sanders, ed., *Jewish and Christian Self-Definition* (Philadelphia, 1981), pp. 88-114. Dexinger correctly points out (pp. 108-109) that the additional commandment making Mt. Gerizim the sacred mountain was the limit of tolerance for the Jews of the Samaritans. James D. Purvis, "The Samaritans and Judaism," in *Early Judaism and its*

Modern Interpreters, pp. 81-98, reaches a similar conclusion about the role of the Samaritan Pentateuch in forcing a breach with the Jews. His neat summary reads (p. 89):

> At some time subsequent to the building of their temple the Samaritans produced an edition of the Pentateuch in which their theological legitimacy was decisively declared and through which the cultic traditions of Jerusalem were declared illegitimate. This was accomplished by deliberate textual manipulation to underscore the sanctity (and necessity) of Shechem/Gerizim as the divinely ordained center of Israel's cultic life . . . It was this contention, not simply the existence of a Samaritan temple, which drove the permanent wedge between Samaritans and Jews.

[59] Recent discussion of the activity of the Samaritan sages (see "Samaritans in the Byzantine Orbit," pp. 111-112) has been extended by I.R.M. Bóid, "Use, authority and exegesis of Mikra in the Samaritan tradition," in M.J. Mulder, ed., *Mikra* (Assen, 1988), pp. 595-633. There is a clear implication that Samaritan sages' halakhic exegetical activity included the fixing of the text.

[60] The evidence for this suggestion has been examined in my Studies in Samaritan Manuscripts III, "Columnar writing and the Samaritan Masorah," in *BJRUL*, 67:1 (1984), pp. 349-381. Note S. Lieberman's words about scholarly co-operation in Caesarea at this time, "The Martyrs of Caesarea," in *Annuaire de l'Institut de philologie et d'histoire orientales et slaves*, vii (1939-1944) (New York, 1944), pp. 345-446, at 398.

[61] See Julius Petermann and K. Vollers, *Pentateuchus Samaritanus ad fidem librorum manuscriptorum apud Nablusianos repertorum, edidit et varios lectiones adscripsit* (Berlin, 1872-1891) and Samuel Kohn, *Zur Sprache, Literatur und Dogmatik der Samaritaner. I. Aus einer Pessach Haggadah der Samaritaner. II. Das samaritanische Targum. III. Die Petersburger Fragmente des samaritanische Targum. IV. Nachträge* (1876), pp. 1-238. (Reprint: Lichtenstein, 1966).

[62] Abraham Tal, *The Samaritan Targum of the Pentateuch: A Critical Edition* (Tel Aviv, 1983). See especially vol. 3, *An Introduction*. See also, idem, "The Samaritan Targum of the Pentateuch," in Mulder and Sysling, *Mikra*, pp. 189-216: idem, "The Samaritan Targum to the Pentateuch, Its Distinctive Characteristics and Its Metamorphosis," in *JSS* 21 (1976), pp. 26-38; idem, "The Samaritan Targum to the Torah—Its Unity and Metamorphosis," in *Proceedings of the Sixth World Congress of Jewish Studies*, 1973 (Jerusalem, 1977), vol. 1, pp. 111-117 (Hebrew); idem, "The Samaritan Targumic Version of the 'Blessing of Moses' (Deut. 33) according to an Unpublished Ancient Fragment," in *AN*, 24 (1986), pp. 178-195; idem, "Towards a Critical Edition of the Samaritan Targum of the

[63] Abraham Tal, "Samaritan Literature," in
A.D. Crown, ed., *The Samaritans* (Tübingen,
1989), pp. 447-448.

Pentateuch," in *IOS* 8 (1978), pp. 107-128; idem,
"The Hebrew Pentateuch in the Eyes of the
Samaritan Translator," in Joze Krasovec, ed.,
The Interpretation of the Bible (Sheffield, 1988), pp.
341-354.

[64] For a good discussion of the date of
Targum Onkelos, see *Encyclopaedia Miqra'it* 8
(1982), pp. 742-748.

[65] On the keeping of Samaritan manuscripts
in chests, see A.D. Crown, "Studies in
Samaritan Practices and Manuscript History; V.
Samaritan Bindings: A Chronological Survey
with Special Reference to Nag Hammadi
Techniques," in *BJRUL* 69:2 (Spring, 1987), pp.
425-491.

[66] "Samaritan Literature," p. 450.

[67] See the discussion of the end of the
Samaritan temple in my "Redating the Schism
between the Judeans and the Samaritans," in
JQR, 82:1/2 (1991), pp. 17-50.

[68] J. Macdonald, "Comprehensive and Thematic reading of the Law by the Samaritans," in
JJS 10:1-2 (1959), pp. 67-74, suggests that the
word is derived from the Arabic, *qatf*, curtailment.

[69] The word derives from the Greek, *diftera*,
and then its Arabized form, *defter*.

[70] Cf., P.L. Stenhouse, "The Reliability of the
Chronicle of Abu'l Fath with Special Reference
to the Dating of Baba Rabba," in *Etudes samaritaines*, pp. 235-257. Idem, "Samaritan Chronicles," in *TS*, pp. 218-265. Idem, "Samaritan
Chronology," in Tal and Florentine, *Proceedings*,
pp. 173-188. Idem, "Source and Purpose of the
Chronicle Sections of the John Rylands Hillukh
MSS 182, 183" (University of Sydney, M.A.
thesis, 1972).

[71] Moses Gaster, *The Asatir, The Samaritan Book
of the Secrets of Moses together with the Pitron or
Samaritan Commentary and the Samaritan Story of the
Death of Moses* (London, 1927). Mills, op. cit.,
p. 318, calls the work the *Kitab es Sateer*.

[72] The title of the work seems to mean "The
Book of the Ancestors," in keeping with its con-
tent. See József Szengellér, *Gerizim Als Israel*
(Utrecht, 1998), p. 17.

[73] T.W.J. Juynboll, *Chronicon Samaritanum
Arabice conscriptum, cui titulus est liber Josuae*
(Luchtmans, 1848).

[74] Oliver T. Crane, *The Samaritan Chronicle or
the Book of Joshua, the Son of Nun* (New York,
1890); a translation of the Scaliger codex.

[75] Moses Gaster, "Das Buch Josua in hebrä-
isch-samaritanischer Rezension. Entdeckt und
zum ersten Male herausgegeben," in *ZDMG* 62
(1908), pp. 209-279, 494-549 (reprint: Leipzig,
1908), p. 127.

[76] For an edition of the text and discussion of
the problems, see A.D. Crown, "A Critical Re-
evaluation of the Samaritan Sepher Yehoshua"
(University of Sydney PhD dissertation, 1966). A
note attached to Dropsie/Annenberg MS NS2

of 1907 says "Murjan ist der eizenliche verfasser
des Samarit. Joshua Buches ed. Gaster." Which
Murjan is not clear, but presumably it was someone who had been a recent scribe, perhaps Ab
Sakhwa/Murjan b. Asad (1901). The Ben-Zvi
Institute has a manuscript of Joshua said to have
been translated by Jacob b. Aaron in 1908. This
is too late a date for it to have been the first
translation. Note, however, MS 7042 in the Ben-
Zvi Institute, which alleges to be of fourteenth-
century provenance but which is certainly a
forgery, as noted by Ben-Zvi in "The Samaritan
Book of Joshua and Its Recent Forgery,"
in *Knesset* 10 (1945), pp. 130-153 (Hebrew). The
author's theories about the Book of Joshua and
in general on the inter-relationships of Samaritan
chronicles are discussed by Zsengellér, op. cit.

[77] On this point, see Georg Graf, "Zum alter
das samaritanischen Buches Josue," in *Biblica* 23
(1942), pp. 62-67.

[78] E.N. Adler and M. Seligsohn, "Une nou-
velle chronique samaritaine," in *REJ* (1902-
1903), vol. 44, pp. 188-222; vol. 45, pp. 70-98,
160, 223-254; vol. 46, pp. 123-146 (reprint:
Paris, 1903).

[79] The so-called twelve tables of Roman law
represented in Gaster MS 863 (utilized as a base
manuscript by Macdonald for his edition) are
translated directly from a textbook of Roman
law. The tables are found in my transcript of this
manuscript in my Sydney Ph.D. thesis.

[80] Differences in practice between Samaritans
and Pharisaic Jews are to be noted in the matters of purity, especially regarding the menstruant, work performed on the eve of the Sabbath,
objects that may not be handled on the Sabbath,
the calendar, the kashrut of a foetus, tithes, marriage to a niece, consanguinity rules for priests,
and sexual relations on the eve of the Sabbath.
On these see A.D. Crown, "Qumran, Samaritan
Halakha and Theology and Pre-Tannaitic
Judaism," in *Boundaries of the Ancient Near Eastern
World*, pp. 420-441, and Magen Broshi, "Anti-
Qumranic Polemics in the Talmud," in J.
Trebolle Barrera and L. Vegas Montaner, eds.,
The Madrid Qumran Congress (Leiden, 1992), vol. 2,
pp. 589-600.

[81] See A. Tal, "Halakhic Literature," pp.
108-111. One can see very clearly from the pre-
Samaritan texts at Qumran that they were formulated to support halakhic differences between
Samaritans and Jews. It can be shown that the
Samaritan halakhah, like that of the other bibli-
cist sects, has a distinct proximity to that at
Qumran, and one is forced to consider the probability that pre-Mishnaic Judaism had a latitudi-
narian form. The details of this picture may
begin with the examination of the relationship
between 4QMMT and the Samaritans, but it is
of course to be extended to the true Pentateuch
texts.

[82] See Gerhard Wedel, "The *Kitab at-Tabbah*,"
in Crown, ed., *The Samaritans*, pp. 468-480. See
also Shehadeh's notes on Ben-Zvi MS 7046.

The name *Kitab al-Kafi* is an abbreviation of the longer title, which makes it clear that the work was a response to Islam.

[83] See Leon Nemoy, "Abu Ishaq Ibrahim's *Kitab al-Mirath*," in *JQR*, 66 (1975), pp. 62-65.

[84] On this material, see Haseeb Shehadeh, "Commentaries on the Torah," in *CSS*, pp. 59-61.

[85] Ben-Zvi Institute 7072.

[86] See A. Neubauer, "Un commentaire samaritain inconnu," in *JA* (April, 1873), pp. 341-368.

[87] On Nafis al-Din, see *LOT* 1:45 and *SL*, 425.

[88] Ben-Zvi Institute 7048.

[89] Ben-Zvi Institute 7053.

[90] Ben-Zvi Institute 7004a, 7005, and 7006, respectively.

[91] Among his works is a guide for understanding the *Sidre miqrata.*

[92] See G.L. Rosen, "The Joseph cycle (Gen. 37-45) in the Samaritan Arabic Commentary of Meshalmah ibn Murjan" (Columbia University PhD dissertation, 1951). M. Klumel, *Mischpâtim, ein samaritanisch arabischer Commentar zu Ex. 21-22,15 von Ibrahim ibn Jakub* (Berlin, 1902), and S. Hanover, *Das Festgesetz der Samaritaner nach Ibrâhîm ibn Ja'kûb. Edition und Uebersetzung seines Kommentars zu Lev. 23: nebst Einleitung und Anmerkungen* (Berlin, 1904). These works represent the sum total of what has been published from the commentaries.

[93] According to this tradition, the sacred vessels were hidden in the time of Eli, when the period of Divine Disfavor commenced.

[94] For some years, a printed version was available as a supplement to the Samaritan newspaper, *Aleph Bet.*

[95] The Samaritans have no fixed conversion process, but a Jewish woman coming into community must learn the rules and customs. For six months she attends Sabbaths and festivities and learns the Samaritan way of life. She is examined to test her knowledge. Before the wedding arrangements can proceed, the Samaritan male must acknowledge that children will be brought up in the Samaritan tradition.

[96] The Aaronite priesthood died out in the sixteenth century and has been replaced by a Levitical one.

A.D. CROWN

SERMONS IN MODERN JUDAISM: The focus here is on preaching in Britain and the United States by representatives of the Orthodox, Conservative, and Reform movements (though not by the Ultra-Orthodox, whose Yiddish and—in Israel—Hebrew preaching is a very different tradition).[1] Limits of space in comparison to the breadth of the topic make it is unrealistic to attempt to survey all of Jewish preaching in the modern period. From the middle of the eighteenth century to the beginning of the twenty-first, there is such a multitude of diverse material that some selectivity is necessary, and this means excluding some of the great Jewish preaching traditions of the modern period, including the celebrated preachers of Germany, Austria, and France, the Hasidic and non-Hasidic preachers of eastern Europe, the Zionist and ultra-orthodox preachers in the land of Israel, and the rabbis of Middle Eastern countries who addressed their people in Arabic. In addition, while I will address several major themes of modern Jewish preaching—Jewish doctrine as reflected in internal and external conflicts, war and peace, social consciousness—treatment of other important topics—including sermons responding to Jewish suffering, pulpit debates over Zionism and the State of Israel, and the role and status of women and the emergence of women's voices in pulpits[2]—are beyond my present scope. This overview therefore is not intended to be complete; it is a survey of a limited but significant sample.

Changes in the Modern Sermon—From Exegesis to Exposition: Perhaps the greatest transformation in the sermon of the modern period is that the exegetical dimension lost its centrality and often became peripheral or disappeared entirely. In the Middle Ages and early modern periods, the interpretation of biblical verses and Rabbinic statements was such an integral component of the sermon that in some cases the boundary line between the genres of sermon and commentary were blurred.[3] Indeed many medieval sermons contain extensive passages in the "homily" form, in which the preacher discusses a series of consecutive verses from the biblical lesson or one of the Psalms. One of the favorite rhetorical forms used by preachers and commentators alike was to raise a series of exegetical and conceptual problems in a Scriptural passage or Rabbinic aggadah and then to resolve each problem in the course of the ongoing discussion.[4]

In the nineteenth century, whether in Sephardic or Ashkenazic, Orthodox or Reform preaching, this exegetical impulse diminished dramatically. It is not that the textually based sermon was completely abandoned (although, in some cases, in the late-nineteenth and twentieth century, it was, as will be noted below). Many nineteenth century and some twentieth century sermons begin with a biblical verse, called by the preacher his "text," though the verse is not necessarily from the Torah lesson of the week. Isaac Mayer Wise, leader of the American Reform movement, counseled, "Never preach a sermon without a text from the Bible, a text containing the theme which you can elaborate. The text is the best proof in support of your argument. A sermon without a text is an argument without a proof."[5] The preacher may spend some time discussing the original context of the verse before applying it to the main issue he wants to address. Occasionally the preacher will use the various parts of the verse as headings that structure the divisions of his sermon. Absent in the mainstream sermons, however, is the preoccupation of medieval and early modern preachers with exegetical problems: identifying the linguistic or theological difficulties in the verse, reviewing the attempts by earlier commentators to resolve the problems before the preacher suggests his own solution, proposing various interpretations of the verse, each with its homiletical significance. Where homiletical exegesis had been the center of gravity for the earlier preachers, now the verse becomes a springboard catapulting the preacher into the central topic for his address.[6]

The detailed exploration and exegesis of Rabbinic texts plays even less of a role in the modern sermon. In the classical Sephardic form, a Rabbinic dictum was cited at the beginning of the sermon immediately after the "text" from the Scriptural lesson, and the dictum, homiletically interpreted, was eventually incorporated into the sermon.[7] A few of the Sephardic preachers at the Bevis Marks Synagogue in London continued this tradition into the eighteenth and early nineteenth century. But by the middle of the century, this homiletical tradition was largely ignored or forgotten.[8] Where Rabbinic statements appear in the sermons, they are simply cited, rarely analyzed or probed.

New Occasions: The traditional occasions—Sabbath, holy days, life-cycle events, dedication of a new synagogue building—remain. But in some environments associated with new movements in Judaism, the context for the major weekly sermon shifted dramatically. In late nineteenth century America, many large Reform congregations began to hold weekday worship services on Sunday mornings, the only day of the week when all would be free to attend. Since the liturgical component of such gatherings was significantly curtailed in comparison with Sabbath worship, the major focus of the gathering was a rather lengthy sermon, lecture, or address delivered by the rabbi. Some of the most celebrated, eloquent, and influential liberal Jewish preachers in the United States, including Stephen S. Wise, drew their largest audiences on Sunday mornings.

By the middle of the twentieth century, this practice had all but disappeared, to be replaced by a new focus for American Jewish preaching: the late Friday evening service. Traditionally, the Friday evening service was relatively brief; its timing depended upon the sunset, to be followed by the Sabbath evening meal in the home. As the mandated Scriptural readings occurred in the morning, sermons were rarely included in the evening service.[9] In the twentieth century, Reform and many Conservative synagogues began to set the Friday evening service at a fixed time, unchanging throughout the year, late enough to follow rather than precede the evening meal. The idea was that this service would be the central activity for families on Friday nights. Since the liturgy remained fairly brief, there was ample time for a twenty or twenty-five minute sermon.[10]

These new contexts affected the substance of the discourse. Most rabbis who gave a major address on Sunday morning or Friday night also had Shabbat services on Saturday morning, when the Torah was read and when their message was generally connected with the Scriptural reading. This liberated the addresses on Sunday or Friday from the need to be anchored in a fixed Scriptural passage. The Sunday morning or Friday evening discourse could be on any topic the preacher considered of interest and concern to the listeners, opening up a wide range of political and cultural as well as religious themes. With titles often announced in advance, a controversial topic became a major motivation for coming to the synagogue.

In addition, from the eighteenth century on, we find sermons delivered by Jewish preachers on occasions not of specifically Jewish concern but rather pertaining to the wider society in which Jews are living. On such occasions both Jews and Christians would be in their respective places of worship listening to the religious message of their respective leaders; this sense of a shared experience influenced the identity of Jewish communities in their various countries. Through the first third of the nineteenth century, when synagogues in both Britain and the United States had no established tradition of a regular weekly Sabbath sermon, the occasional sermon on dates established by governmental authorities was one of the most important opportunities for pulpit discourse.

One such occasion was a Day of Fast, Humiliation, and Intercession proclaimed by the government. The causes of such proclamations could be natural events, such as the Lisbon Earthquake, a cholera plague, or the potato famine. All too common was the outbreak of war or a defeat of the nation's armies (see below). In America, Gershom Mendes Seixas, Hazzan of New York's Shearith Israel Synagogue, preached there on May 9, 1798, a day of fasting and national humiliation proclaimed by President John Adams in the context of an unofficial naval war with France.[11] A "National Fast Day" was proclaimed for January 4, 1861, and Jewish preachers used the occasion not only to express their hope for the preservation of the Union, but also to stake their position on the incendiary issue of slavery (see below).

The death of a monarch or member of the royal family was an occasion for shared mourning, articulated through pulpit discourse. One of the most challenging such tasks for the preacher was the 1780 death of the Austrian Empress Maria Theresa, widely known as perhaps the most anti-Jewish monarch of the eighteenth century. Yet at a solemn memorial service, Prague Rabbi Ezekiel Landau eulogized the Empress in flattering terms that appear to express a genuine admiration for qualities appreciated by contemporaries in the larger community.[12] At the death of Kaiser Wilhelm I in 1888, Moritz Levin, the preacher of the Berlin Reform-Gemeinde, delivered a eulogy at the memorial service entitled "Kaiser Wilhelm: ein Messias unserer Zeit."[13]

Jewish preachers in Britain eulogized every British monarch, and many of these sermons were published. Not surprisingly, special eloquence was inspired at the death of Queen Victoria. Her long reign, earlier commemorated in sermons at her diamond jubilee in 1897, allowed Jewish leaders to review and to celebrate the dramatic improvements in Jewish status during her reign. As one preacher put it, "We Jews shall never forget that it was during her reign that we lost the Ghetto bend and learned to stand erect. Sixty-four years ago, the Jew, even in this land of enlightenment, was a barely tolerated alien. He was excluded from the boon of a liberal University education. He was ineligible for State Service. He was debarred from Parliamentary representation. What a marvelous change has taken place in two short generations, thanks largely to the example of good Queen Victoria."[14]

In the United States, the most poignant inspiration for preaching in the nineteenth century was the assassination of Abraham Lincoln. This occurred on Friday night; Isaac Leeser in New York learned of the shooting from newspapers the following morning while walking to the synagogue, and the news of Lincoln's death was disclosed during the Shabbat morning worship service. Virtually every American rabbi spoke on the following Wednesday, April 19, a National Day of Mourning, as Lincoln's body was being brought to its burial place in Illinois.[15] These sermons reveal a sustained effort to articulate the special qualities of Lincoln as human being and political leader—sometimes using explicitly messianic rhetoric—and later to apply these qualities to the contemporary challenges of the body politic.

Almost a century later, President John F. Kennedy was killed in the middle of the day on Friday, at a time at which most rabbis were well along in preparing what they planned to say that evening or the following morning. Suddenly, to preach the planned sermon seemed inconceivable. The challenge was to decide what to say a few hours later, when synagogues throughout the country would be filled to overflowing with Jews who expected and needed to hear from the pulpit some articulation of the meaning of this disaster.[16]

Occasionally, sermons were delivered at the death of non-Jewish figures beyond the category of national leadership. A striking example is the tribute by Reform Rabbi Abba Hillel Silver to Pope Pius XI on February 19, 1939.[17] Needless to say, the death of a leading rabbi, or of a non-Rabbinical Jewish leader, was an occasion for homiletical oratory, the continuation of a tradition going back for centuries.

Other government-mandated occasions for preaching were times for celebration and thanksgiving: military victories, an abundant harvest following a famine, the escape from an epidemic ravaging other areas. The earliest known English sermon delivered on the American continent, on August 15, 1763, was occasioned by a day of thanksgiving proclaimed by the civil authorities of New York following the peace treaty that ended the French and Indian War.[18] When George Washington proclaimed a national day of thanksgiving, following the request by both houses of Congress, for Thursday, November 26, 1789, Gershom Mendes Seixas, was requested by the lay leaders of Shearith Israel to provide an appropriate service of thanksgiving, and the discourse he delivered was printed a few weeks later.[19] Another day of thanksgiving, though in a more somber mood, was designated for Thursday, November 29, 1860, on which Isaac Leeser and other Jewish preachers delivered special discourses.[20]

Other celebratory preaching occasions include the coronation of a new monarch, the Jubilee anniversary of a monarch, the birth of a child in the royal family, and the recovery of a monarch from a serious ill-

ness. In addition, there were occasions of celebration internal to the Jewish community: the installation of a new Chief Rabbi, the inaugural sermon of a rabbi coming to an important new position, the laying of a cornerstone for a new synagogue building, or the consecration of the synagogue when the building is completed. In Britain, the Chief Rabbi was frequently invited to preach for such occasions; in America, well-known preachers were asked to travel some distance to grace the new pulpit. Frequently such occasions were used to define publicly the principles for which the rabbi or the synagogue stood.

Different Media for Preservation: A third transformation in the modern Jewish sermon pertains not to the sermon itself but to its influence after it was delivered. The extant texts of pre-modern sermons are predominantly the preacher's collections of his own work, copied by scribes and either safeguarded in libraries (occasionally in private collections) or printed. This format was relatively unusual in the first half of the nineteenth century; it regained popularity in the late nineteenth and twentieth centuries, with hundreds of such collections in many different languages. (In the English language, the first published collection of Jewish sermons was apparently the two volumes of Isaac Leeser's *Discourses on the Jewish Religion*, published at Philadelphia in 1837, followed by an 1839 translation of sermons delivered by Gotthold Salomon in the Hamburg Temple during the 1820s, and then the 1851 volume by David Woolf Marks of the West London Synagogue of British Jews, containing sermons from the 1840s. Collections by German preachers preceded these.)[21]

Related are collections of contemporary sermons by different rabbis. A striking nineteenth century example is *The American Jewish Pulpit: A Collection of Sermons by the Most Eminent American Rabbis* (Cincinnati, 1881), including examples by eighteen different rabbis (some translated from German) representing a spectrum of theological positions. In the twentieth century, similar collections cut across denominational lines.[22] The Reform Movement in the United States began to publish an annual "Set of

Holiday Sermons" in pamphlet form, representing the preaching of the Reform rabbinate on the holy days of the Jewish calendar; this was published from 1906 to 1965. The Orthodox Rabbinical Council began publishing a *Manual of Holiday and Sabbath Sermons* in 1943 and continued virtually every year from 1951 through its Jubilee Anthology of 1985.

Beginning in the eighteenth century, options other than books became available for the preservation and dissemination of the sermon text. Especially appropriate for the occasional sermons described above, we find an increasing number of sermons printed in pamphlet form and sold or otherwise distributed soon after their delivery. Some were translated from the language of delivery into the language of the host country. Publication was often at the initiative of the lay leadership of the synagogue where the sermon was delivered, reflecting a desire on the part of this lay leadership to give wider exposure to the sentiments expressed from their pulpits.

Some of these printed sermons were used for political purposes. When Morris Raphall of New York delivered his famous (or infamous) "pro-slavery" sermon on January 4, 1861, arguing that slavery was not considered a sin in the Bible, it was reprinted in pamphlet form and distributed by the Unionist party leaders, according to a contemporary diarist, in "hundreds of thousands of copies . . . in all the states of the Union," generating an enormous controversy.[23] After the British Chief Rabbi Hermann Adler's patriotic sermon of November 4, 1899, following serious military reverses suffered by British troops in South Africa (see below), six hundred copies were circulated to the press, and bound copies were sent to the Queen and leading ministers of the government.[24] What was said in the synagogue pulpit was thought to be of interest beyond its walls.

Printing sermons in ephemeral form continued into the twentieth century. Some rabbis (Joseph Krauskopf in Philadelphia, J. Leonard Levy in Pittsburgh) had their weekly addresses transcribed and printed, in Krauskopf's case over a period of thirty-six years.[25] A different yet related pattern, still

current though going back to the nineteenth century, is for a congregation to subsidize the publication of its rabbi's sermons for the Days of Awe in a particular year or on a regular basis. Such pamphlets are generally distributed to the membership of the congregation and to Rabbinical colleagues.[26]

Jewish periodicals and journals of the nineteenth and first part of the twentieth century regularly printed sermons by leading preachers.[27] The general press also showed occasional interest in Jewish sermons. Raphall's "pro-slavery" sermon was printed in the New York *Herald*; newspapers carried other rabbis' forceful rebuttals to the thesis of the sermon. Some of the sermons delivered at the time of the assassination of Abraham Lincoln were preserved in newspaper articles.[28]

Sermons by southern rabbis Max Heller of New Orleans and William Fineshriber in Memphis in the first decades of the twentieth century were summarized and cited, often quite sympathetically, in the local press.[29] On December 21, 1925, "The New York Times" reported on a sermon by Stephen S. Wise entitled "Jesus the Jew," which argued that Jesus was a great moral leader, whose faith and life are "a part of the Jewish possessions and of the very fiber of our Jewish heritage." In response, the Union of Orthodox Rabbis demanded Wise's resignation as national chairman of the United Palestine Appeal.[30] New York Reform Rabbi Louis I. Newman's strong pulpit condemnations of British policy toward Palestine following the 1939 White Paper, extensively reported by "The New York Times," led to pressure from the board of his synagogue for him to resign from his leadership position in the militant revisionist Zionist organization.[31]

The final decade of the twentieth century witnessed a new mode of preserving and disseminating sermon texts: placing them on the website of the congregation in which they were delivered. Whether this should be classified in the ephemeral or more permanent category of sermon preservation remains to be seen.

Themes in Modern Jewish Preaching—Jewish Doctrines in Internal and External Conflicts: Many sermons delivered in the nineteenth and first half of the twentieth century were devoted to an exposition of Jewish doctrine. Not infrequently, these discussions have an apologetic or polemical purpose, either with regard to internal Jewish divisions or the pressure of Christian missionaries.

Eight years after his installation as Chief Rabbi, Nathan Adler published a sermon delivered at the Great Synagogue on the Sabbath of Chanukah entitled "Solomon's Judgment: A Picture of Israel." Noting his general reluctance to print his sermons, "because the spoken word must always lose much of its original warmth thereby," he decided to publish this because of the crucial importance of its topic: the belief in the oral law. After briefly referring to the "struggle without," against Christianity and Islam, he focused on the "struggle within," against Jews who believe in the divine revelation of Scripture but who "deny the divinity of the oral law." His position is relatively moderate in tone: "not all is divine which is found in the writings of our sages . . . yet the existence of an oral law cannot be denied." Those who reject this "attempt to divide Judaism [and] extinguish its vitality."[32]

Within a few months the same printer published four lectures delivered by David Woolf Marks at the West London Synagogue on the "sufficiency of the Law of Moses as the Guide of Israel," described in the first lecture as his response to Adler's sermon. Marks had already argued against the divine character of the oral law in his 1842 consecration sermon; here he seized on Adler's statement that "not all is divine" in the Rabbinic literature and probed the problematics of differentiating between what is and what is not. His most powerful rhetorical argument is that Adler's insistence that the oral law is necessary to understand Scripture is analogous to the Roman Catholic claim that Scripture is impenetrable without the authoritative tradition of the Church. Yet Adler expects Jews to read this "impenetrable" Scripture every week in the synagogue without the accompanying interpretation of the oral law that he claims is necessary to understand it. This, Marks claims, is less consistent than the Catholic

practice, which discourages the ordinary believer from reading and studying Scripture. Thus sermons, in their oral and published form, became part of an ongoing polemic between the two streams of British Judaism, engendering considerable discussion in articles and letters to the Jewish press.[33]

In addition to the oral law, the Sabbath became a major issue of contention between the movements. This institution came under great pressure in the nineteenth century as Jewish workers became more integrated into the general economy. British and American preachers across the spectrum tried to defend its integrity and railed against its violation. The similarity in their rhetoric of rebuke bespeaks a serious underlying social problem that the pulpit alone was incapable of redressing.

Already in 1841, a sermon delivered in Charleston, South Carolina, where the first Reform synagogue in the United States had been established, railed against the "new ways, including the violation of the festivals and Sabbaths," by those who "fear being impoverished by our forsaking our daily toil."[34] A generation later, Isaac Mayer Wise in a Rosh Hashanah sermon insisted that the proper observance of the Sabbath was one of the absolute obligations of the Jew. Other rabbis recognized with empathy the problem of those who cannot control their work schedule. Therefore the option of shifting the main weekly worship service to Sunday became a polarizing issue even within the Reform movement, not to mention between Reform and Orthodox Rabbis. In his inaugural sermon at Chicago's Sinai Congregation on Rosh Hashanah, 1880, Emil G. Hirsch explained why he wanted services on Sunday. In 1888, Kaufman Kohler preached at Temple Beth-El of New York on the topic, "Are Sunday Lectures Treason to Judaism?" and Joseph Krauskopf of Philadelphia, who had instituted a Sunday morning service at congregation Kneseth Israel, devoted one of his Sunday morning lectures to the topic "The Saturday and the Sunday Sabbath."[35]

Such tinkering with the rhythms of the Jewish calendar infuriated the traditionalists. On December 15, 1888, Benjamin

Szold of Baltimore, preaching in German, perhaps responding to Krauskopf, announced in advance that he would preach on the topic "Sabbath or Sunday," and a large audience therefore was present. Rehearsing the reasons for the traditional observance of the Sabbath, the heart of the sermon was a polemic against synagogues that hold "public divine service" on Sunday, even if they retain the Shabbat on its traditional day. These, he maintains in his rhetorical climax, are like politicians who straddle the fence, bigamists, or "Jews who, in order to keep on good terms with both Jews and Christians, wind the *Tephilin* about their left hand and with the right grasp the rosary."[36] The text of the sermon was published shortly after. The same year, another pamphlet was published with the title "Sabbath or Sunday," three sermons delivered by David Davidson at a Cincinnati congregation. Although a preceptor at the Hebrew Union College, he took the same position as Szold, denouncing those rabbis who would abolish the Sabbath in favor of Sunday but also excoriating the rabbi who preaches on both days as "the veritable double-faced Janus," guilty of making "war against Judaism, principle, self-respect."[37] This was a battle being waged from the pulpits and from the printing press, with considerable interest in the community.

Another doctrine that aroused considerable controversy, not only in the context of internal Jewish clashes but also in the ongoing tension with Christian missionaries, was the doctrine of the messiah and the ultimate redemption of the Jewish people. David de Sola, preaching at the Bevis Marks Synagogue on Shabbat *Nahamu* (following Tisha b'Av) of 1833, noted that it has been an "invariable custom" in this congregation and others that sermons on this Sabbath be devoted to the subject of the "future restoration." He therefore set out to provide "clear proofs"—from Scripture, plain reasoning, and historical sources—that this restoration is yet to come. The sermon was published in pamphlet form soon after.[38]

A sermon for the same Sabbath delivered in the early 1840s by David Woolf Marks, and published in the American *Occident* of November 1843, reveals the transition from inner Jewish debate to the external context. In some ways it is quite traditional, echoing a famous statement by Moses Mendelssohn, that "the Scriptural view of Israel's restoration does not in the remotest degree affect us in any of the duties we, as good and loyal citizens, owe to our country, nor does it in any way prevent us from rendering ourselves useful in the land of our birth."[39]

Marks's conclusion that the redemption will be achieved "through the immediate and miraculous work of God, and not by the combination of human powers" is then mobilized for polemic. He refers to "many hundreds of enthusiasts [in this country], who fancy themselves the immediate agents of God for bringing about the salvation of Israel," in contradiction to "plain Scriptural doctrine." Responding to the charge "that we do not take to heart the consequences of the societies that are forming about us, and that we make no effort to oppose the attempts that are made to convert [us]," he continues,

> My friends, we do take these things to heart. We deeply lament that, in days of such universal privation and distress . . . the vast sums which are annually expended upon an attempt which eighteen centuries have proved to be vain and hopeless, are not directed to a quarter where sorrow might be alleviated, where the hungry might be fed, the naked clothed. . . . But as regards Judaism itself, we have no fears from such societies. . . . [W]e rely principally upon the truth of the word of God, that He will ever be a wall round his people, that He will preserve them in their faith and identity as his great witnesses to the end of time.

Thus, with considerable rhetorical skill, the theological claim that redemption is a supernatural event that cannot be effected by human initiatives is used to undermine the efforts of Christian "enthusiasts," within a context of concern for victims of socioeconomic deprivation, for whom the resources mobilized to convert the Jews could more humanely be directed.[40]

Sometimes, rabbis felt compelled to transcend the niceties of allusion and euphemism to address the Christian challenge directly. Beginning in October, 1835, Isaac

Leeser devoted a series of seven sermons to the Jewish concept of the messiah, which he published in the second volume of his *Discourses* in 1837. Near the beginning of the first, he spends more than a full page summarizing the "Nazarene" doctrine of the messiah held by "our opponents," before outlining the Jewish teachings, which itself is interspersed with an ongoing polemic: "The absurdity of a divided deity is thus made perfectly manifest, it being so completely disconsonant with common sense." The doctrine of the incarnation is "an invention of heathen poets." Much of these long discourses repeat arguments made by Jewish authors over many centuries; perhaps the most interesting passage is his defense of his outspoken, even belligerent pulpit style.[41]

In England, both Nathan Adler and David Woolf Marks published collections of sermons responding to missionary arguments that they must have felt were taking a toll. Adler's was first, published in 1869. Here he mentions specifically the Societies for Promoting Christianity among Jews, which, he maintains, turn "bad Jews into worse Christians."[42] Marks waited until 1885 before publishing nineteen lectures that focus on issues that divide Christians and Jews, one of them a response to the February, 1872, issue of the journal "Hebrew Christian Inquiries" that had criticized him.[43] American rabbis of the next generation also argued openly against Christian doctrines, undoubtedly in response to missionary efforts directed against the wave of east European immigrants. Thus Joseph Krauskopf of Philadelphia devoted major addresses to the topic "Jesus—Man or God" both in 1900 and in 1915 and gave a series of six lectures in 1901 (later published as a book) on "A Rabbi's Impressions of the Oberammergau Passion Play."[44]

War and Peace: War became an important theme in Jewish preaching in the eighteenth century, and sermons delivered on occasions connected with war reveal Jewish attitudes in the context of the new roles Jews were expected to play as citizens of the state.

Hirschel Levin (Hart Lyon), recently arrived at the Great Synagogue in London from Germany, delivered several sermons connected with the Seven Years' War. The first was on a national day of fasting in response to military reverses and severe economic hardship; a second is in a different mood, delivered on a day proclaimed by the Crown following a military victory. They reflect a new kind of awareness: rarely before had the battles between gentile kings become a matter of Jewish concern in a context devoid of any messianic speculation.[45] A year or so after these sermons were delivered, there appeared in London an English translation of a sermon written by Moses Mendelssohn but delivered by Rabbi David Fraenkel in Berlin as a sermon of thanksgiving following the victory of Britain's Prussian allies over the Austrian forces at Leuthen. It contains a powerful evocation of the ravages of war, its patriotic fervor tempered by enlightened universalistic sentiments.[46]

Following the outbreak of "revolt of the American colonies," a day of national fasting and prayer was proclaimed, and Moses Cohen de Azevedo preached in the Bevis Marks Synagogue, evoking the ravages of war, and especially of internecine violence:

> War is a scourge and punishment to mankind, let the cause be ever so just. . . . If these are calamities that are experienced in a foreign war, how much greater are those attendant on a domestic or civil war. . . . [We therefore pray to God] to dispose the hearts of the insurgents that this unhappy war may be soon ended and that they may embrace the indulgence offered them by His Majesty's Commissioners, which they have hitherto refused, and return to their duty.[47]

There is little else in the sermon, however, that addresses the actual circumstances of the fighting or the political issues behind it; the discourse is addressed almost entirely to a discussion of the Rabbinic dictum cited by the preacher at the beginning.

In 1854, Britain joined the forces opposing Russia in the Crimean War. Once again, the Crown ordained a day of humiliation and prayer, and on April 26 churches and synagogues were filled. The *Jewish Chronicle* carried reports of the sermons delivered by British rabbis for several weeks following. For example, the Sephardic Rev. A.P. Mendes of Birmingham, after once again evoking the horrors of war, turned to the "motives that could urge civilized nations to this evil." Two themes pertain to the specifics of the conflict as they relate to a Jewish audience: the tolerance of Turkey toward the Jews (following the recent reforms promulgated by the Sultan) as contrasted with the "atrocities" of Russia; and war as fulfillment of Ezekiel's prophecy in chapter 37.[48] The first of these themes was highlighted by the Rev. N.B. Levy of the Western Synagogue, according to the *Chronicle* report of the following week: the preacher noted that "the Sultan of Turkey had caught the sympathizing spirit of the age, that he had bestowed liberty upon our heretofore persecuted brethren." By contrast, Russia was known as "the modern Pharaoh."[49]

Less than three years later, October 7, 1857, was proclaimed as yet another day of humiliation and prayer following the outbreak a rebellion in India. D.W. Marks's sermon on this occasion is a fascinating text. The significance of the occasion is emphasized: a time of "private grief and of national calamity," a "national disaster," when the state is plunged into affliction. Although the selected day falls during the week of Sukkot, a time of rejoicing, nevertheless it is appropriate "as true Israelites and devoted patriots, to unite with our fellow countrymen of all sects and creeds, in sending up a national cry to Heaven for support, when calamity befalls, or danger threatens, our common Fatherland."

Marks expresses sentiments strikingly similar to those in the sermons by Mendelssohn and Azevedo, mentioned above, although he actually quotes from the Unitarian minister William Ellery Channing. "Of the many afflictions to which humanity is exposed, war, under any circumstances, may be considered amongst the most trying and severe.... But deplorably great as these evils are, they are multiplied tenfold in a case of civil war." Yet in applying this message to the situation at hand, there is no sense of identification with the rebels as fellow subjects, or even as human beings with legitimate grievances. The preacher's rhetorical power is unrestrained in attacking the rebels:

> Against this merciful and human rule, however, an alarming rebellion has broken out, accompanied by deeds of horror to which it would be difficult to find a parallel in modern times. It might have been hoped that we had survived the age when acts of atrocity like those of which we have recently heard were capable of being committed. The outrages that have been perpetrated on defenseless women and children make the heart turn sick.... There is scarcely a deed of horror familiar to savage life that has not been practiced by the rebels in their sanguinary career.

The continuation of the sermon, however, implies that attitudes at home were not unanimous. "Whatever opinions we may entertain with respect to the causes which have produced this serious rebellion"— among which, unmentioned, were the British annexation of the Oudh homeland and the issuance of cartridges greased with beef and pork fat to Indian soldiers—"it is our duty as good citizens to practice self-denial and to refrain from indulging in harsh and intemperate criticisms." The preacher then anticipates military reprisals that some would consider as brutal as the provocation: "Nor must we display a hostile front to the government, if the humane principles applied to legitimate warfare fail to be employed, in every instance, on the present occasion.... [T]o indulge a maudlin sentimentality for those, in comparison with whose crimes cannibalism itself almost becomes tolerable, is to betray great folly and unmanly weakness." Although the sermon is entitled "God Protects the Fatherland," here the absolute patriotic identification is not just with nation, but with Empire.[50]

Similar was the Chief Rabbi Hermann Adler in the context of the South African War. On November 4, 1899, preaching at the North London Synagogue, Adler alluded to "the reverse which our troops have unhappily sustained during this week." Therefore, "our minds are absorbed, even as it becomes loyal Englishmen and Englishwomen, by the critical position of a portion of her Majesty's forces, on whose behalf our prayers have just ascended." He then pulls out all the stops in his assertion of Englishness, quoting from Milton's *Areopagitica* ("Methinks I see in my mind a noble and puissant nation, rousing herself like a strong man after sleep. . . ."), and invoking the great military victories of the previous generation in conjunction with Jewish triumph of a more distant past:

> Was God on the side of the biggest battalions on the day that Judas the Maccabee defeated the drilled legionaries of Antiochus? . . . on the days when [George Lucan, Earl of] Scarlett's Dragoons rode through the Russians at Balaklava, and a handful of [Sir Henry] Havelock's heroes saved our Indian Empire? Our troops and their commanders have already shown by their splendid courage that they worthily uphold the traditions of British valour and British chivalry. And our hearts must be filled with mingled sadness and satisfaction, knowing, as we do, that among the brave men who have fought gallantly, and among those who have fallen in the battle, dying a soldier's honourable death, there have been a goodly number of our brethren in faith who have cheerfully sacrificed their lives in the service of their Queen and of their flag, feeling that it is sweet and glorious to die for one's country.

The appeal at the end of the sermon mentions "the sick and the wounded—both British and Boer;" there is no dehumanization of the enemy as in Marks's discourse about the Indian revolt. But the patriotic commitment to nation and empire are every much as manifest.[51]

Given this nineteenth century background, the sermons delivered at the outbreak of the Great War come as something of a surprise. Rare is the patriotic fervor of Marks and Adler that recognizes no ambiguity in the conflict and proclaims that "God Will Protect the Fatherland." Instead, the dominant motif—undoubtedly influenced by the German origins of many in the congregation—is one of dismay, discouragement, confusion, a sense of devastating failure that undermines cherished beliefs in progress, even possibly in divine providence. This is in striking contrast with the patriotic élan in the sermons by German and Austrian rabbis at the beginning of the war.[52] Thus the report by the *Jewish Chronicle* on August 21, 1914:

Devoting his sermon to the subject of the War, the Rev. Morris Joseph preached as follows from his pulpit at the Berkeley Street Synagogue last Saturday [August 15]: We resume our Sabbath Services this week in circumstances all but unparalleled in the history of mankind. . . . The lust to destroy and slay has taken possession of minds hitherto chiefly concerned to heal the hurt of the world, and to set the feet of mankind more firmly on the high-way of progress. It is a terrifying paradox, a cruel blow to our optimism and our most cherished ideals. It makes us doubt the value, the reality of our civilization, the stability of righteousness, the fixity of purpose of God himself.

Not unexpectedly, Joseph insists that our first duty is to "brush such doubts aside," to keep one's faith in God, and to "rally to the help of our beloved country in her hour of need."[53]

Two months later, reports of the German invasion of Belgium and atrocities against civilians helped solidify a sense of the justice of the British cause. Yet Hermann Gollancz at the Bayswater Synagogue, preaching on October 24 on "The War and the Belgian Refugees," condemned not Germany alone but all who were responsible for the catastrophe:

> Shame on the world as a whole; shame on the sham term "civilization"; shame, above all, on those rulers of the world who have "God" on their lips at every turn, and are themselves the devil incarnate! Shame, shame upon the hypocritical leaders and counselors of nations who have thrown the firebrand into the midst of the peoples, and caused the conflagration that is now bringing disaster and desolation upon the whole earth! Shame again upon those so-called men of science whose inventions, if not by design yet in practice, have become the curse of the world![54]

The devastating carnage of human lives on both sides appears to have taken a toll in religious faith. The loss of trust in God and presumptuous claims of God's favor were both reflected in the sermons. At the Intercession Services of January 1, 1916, A.A. Green, minister at Hampstead, complained about the improper invocation of God in the present context:

> Throughout the whole of this War there has been too much mention of God amidst

conditions as ungodlike as can possibly be conceived. . . . Hymns of hate, creeds of cruelty and religions of reprisal have hidden the sunshine of religious civilization behind a dark cloud of international misunderstanding. . . . In such circumstances many of the appeals to God have seemed but mockery and blasphemy, while there are times when the oft-repeated prayers of intercession convey repugnance instead of comfort, and their well-intentioned sanctity fades away before their well-defined sacrilege.[55]

On the other side of the Atlantic, in a Rosh Hashanah sermon from 1915 or 1916, the liberal rabbi Leon Harrison of St. Louis articulated the theological questions in many minds:

But, if the Lord be with us, they bitterly ask today in the bloody shambles that now cover Europe, Why then have all these horrors come upon us? Can there be a God in heaven if He suffers this deviltry upon earth? Why does He not blight and blast the evildoers that have brought about this cataclysm? Can we believe in any Providence that governs human events, seeing that these abominations are allowed to be? . . . In view of this horrible blasphemy and travesty of religion, can one not hear the great chorus of indignation that swells up from millions of hearts, and breaks forth in the poignant cry of Gideon, "O my Lord, if the Lord be with us, why then have all these things come upon us?" (Jud. 6:13).[56]

And late in 1917, Morris Joseph returned to the impact of the war on religion: "We begin to question our most fundamental convictions. We ask ourselves, "Where is God in all this terrifying upheaval? Where is His goodness, His omnipotence?"[57]

Occasionally, we even find an element of self-criticism of British society, suspicion of the extreme nationalism that many thought to be responsible for the war. Following the sinking of the "Lusitania" on May 7, 1915, hostility toward Germany spilled over to attacks against aliens in Britain. According to the *Jewish Chronicle*, Rev. D. Wasserzug of the orthodox Dalston Synagogue said in his sermon for the first day of Shavuot, "In our battles with wrongdoing and injustice, we can win only by love, never by hate. To oppose crime by crime, to loot the shops of the alien enemy as a reprisal for

the unspeakable crime—the destruction of the 'Lusitania'—is, alas!, worse than useless. We only add to the crime."[58] A few months later, Hermann Gollancz raised "the question, as to how far the share of our country in the cruel war in which we are now engaged, is justified, " though he went on to insist that "we have entered into the War, and it has to be ended."[59] One is struck on the whole by lack of vindictiveness and demonization of the enemy. Only rarely are the traditional motifs of "the new Egypt" or "Amalak" exploited.

The catastrophic bloodbath of the Great War led many rabbis, especially in the more liberal branches of Judaism, to adopt commitments to a pacifist ideology, concluding that war was the greatest possible evil, that nothing could justify ever traveling that route again. Young rabbis from the Jewish Institute of Religion, influenced by Stephen S. Wise (who had modified his anti-war views to justify American entry on the side of the Allies, but later conceded he had erred) preached pacifism in their synagogues during the 1920s and 1930s, despite the looming specter of Fascism, certainly recognized by Wise and his disciples (see below). Not untypical was Harold Saperstein, a Reform rabbi on Long Island who—drawing from the experience of the Great War—preached pacifism both in general and in specifically Jewish terms:

When the Germans took Poland, the Jews were attacked as Russian agents. And when the Russians took it, they were hounded as German spies. No people suffered more than did the Jews during the last war. And so it will ever be. War means certain destruction to the Jews. And the horror of war is intensified by the fact that the Jew, dwelling as he does in every nation, must inevitably find himself fighting against his brother.[60]

In Britain, one graduate of Jews' College chose to submit for inclusion in a volume dedicated to Rabbi Samuel Daiches a sermon lauding the Patriarch Jacob's "pacifist view and practice," warning that increasing our defenses only further provokes aggression, for "every weapon of defense is a potential weapon of attack," and urging that we must be "sufficiently strong to withstand the alarms of the scaremongers, and the harangues of the false prophets of jingoism."[61] A few of these rabbis retained their pacifist commitment even during the Second World War; for others, including Wise, it was a wrenching, agonizing process to admit they had been wrong, to justify the war effort against Nazi Germany, in many cases to serve in the war as chaplains.

The recognition of Nazism as an evil that validated an effort of total war to destroy was transferred by many rabbis to Stalin's Soviet Union in the years following 1945. There does not seem to have been a significant movement of condemnation of the Korean War from the pulpits of the United States or Britain. This changed, however, during the Vietnam War. While we cannot document it here in detail, many leading American rabbis condemned the Vietnam War from their pulpits, often arousing significant antagonism within their congregations.[62]

Once again issues of war presented a challenge to Jewish preachers during the High Holy Days immediately following the terrorist attacks in the U.S.A. on September 11, 2001 upon the World Trade Center and other targets. Among the themes addressed was the nature of the appropriate response. A few rabbis tried to distance themselves from American militancy: "By the following morning, a voice of anger, outrage and retribution had been discovered. America would avenge the deaths of its thousands. Retaliation would be its bitter-sweet comfort and solace in its hour of loss . . . An eye for an eye, a tooth for a tooth, a life for a life. . . . It was an instinctive attempt at self-preservation at a time of intense vulnerability and profound fear."[63] Others spoke of the circumstances that may have produced the terrorist mindsct, including policies of the American government. Yet most seem to have emphasized the threat to civilization posed by suicide bombers, the "inescapable duty to take strong action against the perpetrators and those who have in any manner aided and abetted them," both for the sake of justice, and "for the sake of our own safety and that of generations to come."[64] The delicate balance in expounding Jewish views of war and peace had shifted again.

Social Justice: Traditional Jewish preaching in the medieval and early modern periods showed relatively little concern for what we would call "social justice." When preachers employed the rhetoric of rebuke, it was applied to sins internal to Jewish society. From the perspective of Jews dependent upon the protection of royal power, movements of social unrest, peasants' uprisings, revolutionary challenges to the existing power structure, were terrifying, as they often began or ended with attacks upon Jews as visible, accessible, and vulnerable representatives of the forces of oppression.

This pattern changes in the modern period for several reasons. First, Jews began to identify more with the states in which they were being granted citizenship and with the societies into which they aspired for integration. Gathered together on national days of prayer under conditions of war while their neighbors were in their churches, it seemed natural to have an appeal for funds that would support the victims of war—the widows and orphans of soldiers who would not return, the wounded and disabled veterans—no matter what their religion. Second, the Reform movement highlighted universalistic elements of Jewish tradition— God's concern for all human beings, and especially for the down-trodden and disenfranchised. This doctrine was associated with the biblical prophets, whose denunciations of sacrificial rituals performed in obliviousness to the injustices of the surrounding society were invoked as support for the central Reform principle that ethical behavior is more important than ceremonial observance.

We find indications of this new consciousness in the first half of the nineteenth century. Gershom Mendes Seixas, preaching in December, 1804, on a day of thanksgiving proclaimed by the government of New York City for being spared an epidemic that ravaged other parts of the country, said that "Among the various duties we owe to our heavenly Father, there are none perhaps more important than attending to the poor, the widow, and the orphan." Several of his other sermons are devoted to the theme of charity.[65] D.W. Marks, on the Sabbath preceding the national day of thanksgiving for an abundant harvest (October 16, 1847), reflected upon the potato famine of the previous year and emphasized the importance of benevolence and philanthropy, especially the obligation of his congregants to give to the poor.[66] In the Bevis Marks Synagogue, David de Sola preached on another thanksgiving day two years later, this one in response to the end of the recent cholera epidemic. His sermon underscored the listeners' obligation of gratitude to God, which must be fulfilled through the support of "sanitary committees" and assistance to the poor that will improve the conditions of their health.[67]

The high point of Jewish social preaching came in the late nineteenth and early twentieth centuries. Forceful, eloquent orators—Joseph Krauskopf in Philadelphia, Emil G. Hirsch in Chicago, J. Leonard Levy in Pittsburgh, Leon Harrison in St. Louis, and Stephen S. Wise in New York—most of whom delivered their message of social justice at Sunday services, spoke at times to as many as a thousand worshippers. It has been argued that such preachers, who had little use for ritual or ceremony, disciplined Jews in their growing affluence, laid the foundations for new institutions of Jewish philanthropy, and inculcated an awareness that responsibility for workers, the poor, and the oppressed was an integral part of what it meant to be a Jew. This often entailed criticizing from the pulpit governmental policies or even the practices of wealthy Jewish employers—an act that required considerable courage and generated vigorous controversy and antagonism. The "Social Gospel" ideal of their Protestant colleagues provided a natural context in which these preachers could claim the mantle of "prophetic Judaism."[68]

Thus J. Leonard Levy justified talking about economic issues as an "unavoidable duty" by claiming the precedent of Jeremiah's application of religion to the economic life; so the contemporary synagogue and church must take on the role of the prophets. He criticized "the present tariff system," though conceding that such criticism is "political heresy."[69] He also addressed issues of poverty and socialism, and

specific scandals of government corruption.[70] Leon Harrison, of St. Louis, devoting his March 27, 1914, sermon to the theme "What Would Lincoln Do in the White House Now?" made Lincoln into a spokesman for the current liberal agenda. He maintained that Lincoln would defend the small trader against the monopolist, promote reform in the selection of candidates, and oppose the influence of the bosses, favor national legislation for the protection of women and for women's suffrage, oppose child labor in New England and the South, endorse a law mandating compulsory arbitration of industrial disputes, honor international treaties, and foster peaceful union with all great Powers, including arbitration of issues not vital to national existence. In short, he concludes, Lincoln would have a profile very much like President Wilson.[71]

Civil rights for African Americans became a defining issue for many twentieth century American preachers. Rabbis (especially those of northern backgrounds) serving congregations in the south were in an especially challenging position, and their position on civil rights and integration often became a source of considerable tension both within their synagogues and in the larger communities. The sermon was by no means the only, or perhaps even the most important, vehicle for addressing this issue, but some of the southern rabbis spoke out from their pulpits with impressive courage.

Max Heller, a German-speaking immigrant from Prague, came to Temple Sinai, the largest synagogue of New Orleans, in 1887. Disillusioned by a wave of prejudice and violence in the 1890s and into the new century, he exclaimed in his sermon on Yom Kippur, 1909, "Why today there are people, right around us, who are too stupid or too inhuman to understand that the Negro has a soul, with the same rights as our own, to all of God's truth and beauty." Because the Jew was "the oldest and most unflinching victim of persecution," it was his obligation to "frown down every inhuman barrier that separates races, ranks, and creeds."[72] William Fineshriber brought a commitment to social justice with socialist inclinations to the Memphis congregation he served from 1911–1924. The local newspapers frequently reported, summarized, and quoted from his sermons, especially one on the Ku Klux Klan delivered in October, 1921, in which he asserted that the "mob law" of the Klan was "far more dangerous than Bolshevism."[73]

Jacob M. Rothschild, a Reform Rabbi who had recently come to the oldest and most influential synagogue in Atlanta, addressed racial segregation directly in his Yom Kippur sermon of 1948. Mentioning a series of specific incidents that illustrate "the growing race hatred that threatens the South," he rebuked both the militant bigots and his own people. It is not that Jews have committed overt offences against the Negroes, he said. "I feel certain that we have treated them fairly; certainly we have not used force to frighten them. . . . No, our sin has been the deeper one, the evil of what we didn't do. . . . Millions of us must know the truth—but we keep silent, even though the word is in our own hearts. The problem is ours to solve, and the time for solution is now. . . . There is only one real issue: civil rights."[74] Ten years later, "the Temple" of Atlanta would be bombed, partly in anger at the rabbi's leadership.

During the 1954-1965 height of the Civil Rights movement, some southern rabbis opposed militant challenges to the status quo, but others condemned segregation strongly from their pulpits. Perry Nussbaum insisted to his Jackson, Mississippi, congregation in his Rosh Hashanah sermon of 1955 that "[the Negro] believes what you and I as Jews have hungered for ourselves during 1900 years of history—that every man has a natural right to share in God's gifts: the right to life himself, and to give his children the best possible training; the right to economic security, the right to political equality."[75] William Silverman, of Nashville, Tennessee, denounced in early 1958 the policy of public silence both as a violation of the moral ideals of "prophetic Judaism" and as strategically misguided:

> The Negro is the symbol to galvanize the mobilization of the bigots for warfare against all spiritual values. The ultimate objective is to attack the principles and precepts of the Judeo-Christian way of life.

> There s a time when silence is cowardly. There is a time when our faith must commit us to moral action. Now is such a time.[76]

This was an inversion of an argument used a generation earlier by Jewish leaders warning against Nazism: "don't think they are only against Jews; they are opposed to the core values of our civilization." Here it is the Negro in the American South who is the visible victim of a bigotry that ultimately endangers Jews and others as well.

A high point was the "March on Washington" of August 28, 1963, climaxed by the "I Have a Dream" speech of Martin Luther King. Reporting to his congregation the following Sabbath, Harold Saperstein cited not only King's famous peroration but also another speech, by a colleague, Joachim Prinz, who had been rabbi of a Berlin congregation during the Hitler regime. Prinz said to the enormous crowd that the most disgraceful problem of the Hitler era was silence. "America must not be silent," he said; "[We must speak up and act,] not for the sake of the Negro, but for the sake of America."[77] Among many other rabbis, Jacob Rudin made this the theme of his Rosh Hashanah evening sermon a few weeks later, saying "This isn't the other fellow's fight. It is our fight—here in Great Neck [an affluent Long Island, New York, suburb]. . . . Because Jews are Jews, we need to be in this struggle."[78]

Three years later, this was still a burning issue for many Jewish preachers, although the Civil Rights Movement had changed to some extent. The articulation of a new ideology of "Black Power" by Stokeley Carmichael and others in the spring of 1966 raised a dilemma: was this a legitimate form of group pride and assertiveness, comparable to the Zionist revolution, or was it a dangerous abandonment of the principle of non-violent resistance that had made the Civil Rights movement so inspiring? Eugene Lipman, previously director of the Reform Movement's Commission on Social Action, addressed "Black Power" in his Yom Kippur 1966 sermon at Temple Sinai of Washington, D.C.:

> Black Power was an inevitable development so long as violent White Power refused to

accept any of society's decisions—legislative, judicial, or moral—and continued its naked violence against everyone who does not advocate White supremacy. Black Power was inevitable so long as respectable middle-class White citizens continued to insist on their right to make a mockery of human equality by fleeing from integrated housing, by fleeing from integrated schools, by fleeing from an integrated economy, by indifference or open sabotage. . . . Black Power is inevitable when the real situation of Negroes—social, economic, educational—is shown to be worse than in 1954: more unemployment, more segregated housing, more segregated schools. That's where Black Power came from, from our hatred, hypocrisy, and indifference. . . .[79]

His refrain in this passage, "Black Power was inevitable . . ." is not a ringing endorsement of the new program. It is, rather, a powerful criticism of forces in American society that naturally led to this development, a condemnation of the failures of Jews to pursue sufficiently the goal of social justice—failures that require confession and atonement—and a call to concrete action to promote the cause of equality. The modern Jewish preacher, like predecessors in previous centuries, still felt impelled "to tell My people its sin" (Is. 58:1); now, however, the sins were conceived in a broader context.

Notes

[1] See the important studies by Kimmy Caplan, *Orthodoxy in the New World: Immigrant Rabbis and Preaching in America (1881-1924)* (Jerusalem, 2002) (Hebrew), treating sermons preached in Yiddish and published in Yiddish and Hebrew, and "God's Voice: Audio Taped Sermons in Israeli Haredi Society," in *Modern Judaism* 17 (1997), pp. 253-280.

[2] Records of western Jewish women preaching go back at least to the 1890s, with Ray Frank in the U.S., continuing in the twentieth century with Lily Montague in England, Regina Jonas in Germany, and Helen Hadassah Levinthal in the United States. In the last quarter of the twentieth century, women have exerted a significant influence on many aspects of Jewish pulpit discourse. See, for example, the passage from Margaret Moers Wenig's 1990 Kol Nidre sermon, "God Is a Woman, and She Is Growing Older," in Marc Saperstein, "Five Sermons No One Slept Through," in *Reform Judaism* 29 (Fall 2000), pp. 33-37. The sermon has been included in several anthologies.

[3] See Marc Saperstein, *Jewish Preaching, 1200-1800* (New Haven, 1989), p. 74, n. 26. Some famous preachers (Moses Alsheikh of Safed is a prime example) published biblical commentaries

using material from their sermons re-organized in accordance with the order of biblical verses.

[4] See Marc Saperstein, "The Method of Doubts: The Problematizing of Scripture in the Late Middle Ages," in J.D. McAuliffe, B.D. Walfish, and J.W. Goering, eds., *With Reverence for the Word* (New York, 2003), pp. 133-156.

[5] Wise in *American Israelite*, September 21, 1899, p. 4, cited by Robert Friedenberg, *"Hear O Israel"* (Tuscaloosa, 1989), p. 71.

[6] See on this change the classical study by Alexander Altmann, "The New Style of Preaching in Nineteenth-Century German Jewry," in *Studies in Nineteenth-Century Jewish Intellectual History* (Cambridge, 1964), pp. 65-116.

[7] This form may be seen in the 1756 Fast Day sermon of Isaac Nieto (see Cecil Roth, *Magna Bibliotheca Anglo-Judaica* [London, 1937], p. 323, no. 17), the sermon that Haim Isaac Carigal delivered in Newport on Shavuot 1773 ("Rabbi Carigal Preaches in Newport," [Cincinnati, 1966]), the fast day sermon of Moses Cohen de Azevedo in 1776 (Roth, p. 325, no. 26) (but not in the Thanksgiving Day sermon of November 26, 1789, by Gershom Mendes Seixas [below, n. 19]).

[8] David de Sola, preaching on March 24, 1847, in Bevis Marks on the day of a general fast because of the potato famine (not listed in Roth; I used the copy in the British Library), exemplifies the tradition, beginning by citing Is. 16:9, followed by B. Shab. 55a ("Death is the result of sin"). But the continuation of the sermon had little to do with either of these texts. Abraham P. Mendes of Birmingham, England, began his published sermons (London, 1855) with a Torah text but without a Rabbinic dictum.

[9] For unusual evidence of Friday night preaching in certain eighteenth century European communities, see Saperstein, *Jewish Preaching*, p. 28.

[10] On the late Friday evening service, see the sources listed in Kimmy Caplan, "The Life and Sermons of Rabbi Israel Herbert Levinthal," in *American Jewish History* 87 (1999), p. 12, n. 40.

[11] See on this Friedenberg, *"Hear O Israel,"* pp. 13-16.

[12] Marc Saperstein, *Your Voice Like a Ram's Horn* (Cincinnati, 1996), pp. 445-484.

[13] "Kaiser Wilhelm ein Messias unserer Zeit. Rede bei dem Trauer-Gottesdienst der juedischen Reform-Gemeinde zu Berlin zum Gedaechtnis Sr. Majestaet des hochseligen Kaisers und Koenigs am 18 Maerz gehalten von M. Levin" (Berlin, 1888), Leo Baeck Institute pamphlet DD 223.9 L4 K3. Fifty years later (April 6, 1934), in a Passover sermon criticizing the super-patriotism and assimilationist aspirations of German Jewry, Chief Rabbi Joseph Hertz exemplified by referring to "the Rabbi of the Berlin Liberal Synagogue who published a sermon under the title, *Kaiser Wilhelm: ein Messias unserer Zeit* (*Sermons, Addresses and Studies*, [London, 1938], vol. 1, p. 156).

[14] Rev. Moses Hyamson, *The Oral Law and*

Other Sermons (London, 1910) (Dayan of the United Synagogue), eulogy delivered February 2, 1901, p. 165. See also the eulogy of the Chief Rabbi, Hermann Adler, in *Anglo-Jewish Memories and Other Sermons* (London, 1909), pp. 117-125.

[15] Some fourteen of these sermons—in English and in German, some published immediately as pamphlets, others preserved in different forms—were gathered together with dozens of sermons from the following Sabbath and on subsequent anniversaries of Lincoln's births in a marvelous collection called *Abraham Lincoln: The Tribute of the Synagogue*, edited by Emanuel Hertz ((New York, 1927).

[16] See, for example, Jacob Rudin, *Very Truly Yours* (New York, 1971), pp. 273-274; Harold Saperstein, *Witness from the Pulpit* (Lanham, 2000), pp. 226-229; John Raynor, *A Jewish Understanding of the World* (Oxford, 1998), pp. 102-103; Immanuel Jakobovits, *Journal of a Rabbi* (London, 1967), pp. 271-275; Israel Brodie, "Tribute to the late President John Fitzgerald Kennedy. Spoken . . . at the Marble Arch Synagogue, London, on Sabbath, 30th November, 1963" (London, 1963). Unfortunately, no systematic effort has been made to collect the records of what was said on that Shabbat. At an analogous situation in France—the assassination of the president by an anarchist in 1894—the Chief Rabbi Zadoc Kahn preached at the memorial service (Michael Marrus, *The Politics of Assimilation* [Oxford, 1971], p. 145).

[17] Abba Hillel Silver, *A Word in Its Season* (New York, 1972), pp. 359-365. There has been controversy in recent years about the role of this pope with regard to the Jews, but Silver, a strong leader of American Zionism, shows no ambivalence. The deceased was "not given to adroitness or evasion. He was not a diplomat. He was a man of God." He denounced "the false Christianity of the Nazis," "extreme nationalism," "anti-Semitism." He was, in short, one of the "righteous among the Gentiles." Of course, the eulogy is a genre not given to a balanced evaluation of strengths and weaknesses of character, but there was no need for Silver to devote his sermon to the late pope at all. Hermann Gollancz eulogized Cardinal Manning in 1892, and Frederick, late Emperor of Germany, in 1888: *Sermons and Addresses* (New York, 1909), pp. 315-317, 270-272.

[18] Joseph Jeshurun Pinto at New York's Shearith Israel Congregation; see Friedenberg, "*Hear O Israel*," pp. 5-6.

[19] Gershom Mendes Seixas, "A Religious Discourse: Thanksgiving Day Sermon, November 26, 1789" (New York, 1789, republished by the Jewish Historical Society of New York in 1977), pp. ix, 12-14. On this sermon, see Raphael Mahler, "Yahadut Ameriqah ve-Ra'ayon Shivat le-Tsiyon bi-Tequfat ha-Mahpekhah ha-Ameriqanit," in *Zion* 15 (1950), pp. 106-134, and Friedenberg, "*Hear O Israel*," pp. 10-12.

[20] Isaac Leeser, *Discourses on the Jewish Religion* (Philadelphia, 1827), vol. 9, pp. 148-163, address at the Franklin Street Synagogue, Philadelphia. In 1863, Thanksgiving was made into an annual national holiday.

[21] Leeser, *Discourses*, vols. 1 and 2; on the original 1937 publication of these volumes, see Sussman, *Isaac Leeser*, p. 88. Gotthold Salomon, *Twelve Sermons Delivered in the New Temple of the Israelites at Hamburgh* (London, 1839). (Three of Salomon's sermons had been translated and published in Dutch in 1825: Wallet, "Religious Oratory," p. 174). D.W. Marks, *Sermons Preached on Various Occasions* (vol. 1) (London, 1851). This volume is said to have been "undertaken at the request of the Council of Founders" of the West London Synagogue, considered important because of a "dearth of Jewish discourses in the English language." According to Curtis Cassell's unpublished biography of Marks (loaned to me by the author's son, David Cassell), the book was extensively reviewed both in the Jewish press and in the "Christian Reformer" and "Kitto's Journal of Sacred Literature." ("David Woolf Marks: Father of Anglo-Jewish Reform," p. 37.)

[22] Saul I. Teplitz, ed., *The Rabbis Speak: A Quarter Century of Sermons for the High Holy Days from the New York Board of Rabbis* (New York, 1986); the *Best Jewish Sermons* series, ed. by Saul I. Teplitz (New York); *Living Words: Best High Holy Day Sermons, 5759, 5760, 5761, 5762* (NY: Sh'ma).

[23] The text of the sermon is accessible at: www.jewish-history.com/raphall.html; a diarist on the printing of sermons: www.jewish-history.com/Salomon/salo14.html (January 7, 1861). Cf., Friedenberg, "*Hear O Israel*," pp. 46-52; Bertram Korn states that, "This sermon aroused more comment and attention than any other sermon ever delivered by an American Rabbi," in *American Jewry and the Civil War* (Philadelphia, 1951), p. 17.

[24] Geoffrey Alderman, *The Jewish Community in British Politics* (Oxford, 1983), pp. 43-44. For the text of sermon, see Adler, *Anglo-Jewish Memories*, pp. 106-116.

[25] According to Israel Levinthal, who reported on Krauskopf's Sunday lectures for a Philadelphia newspaper as a high school student, the entire text of each lecture was written in advance and memorized by Krauskopf, who spoke pacing from one end of the pulpit to the other (*The Message of Israel* [New York, 1973], pp. 145-146). On Levy, see Solomon B. Freehof and Vigdor W. Kavaler, eds., *J. Leonard Levy: Prophetic Voice* (Pittsburgh, 1970), pp. xi, 41. In addition to the sixteen cycles of his Pittsburgh sermons, eight cycles of Philadelphia sermons were published in this form. Needless to say, the historical value of such texts is considerable.

[26] E.g. "On the Height: Five Sermons Delivered on New Year's Eve and Morning, September 21st and 22nd; on the Eve, Morning,

and Evening of the Day of Atonement, October 1st and 2nd, 1892," by Isaac S. Moses, Rabbi of Kehillath Anshe Mayriv, Chicago (JTSA digital copy at http://sefer.jtsa.edu:4505/ALEPH/-/start/PAMPHLETS).

[27] For example, the first Jewish periodical in the German language, *Sulamith*; Isaac Leeser's *Occident*; Samuel Isaacs' *Jewish Messenger*; Isaac Mayer Wise's *American Israelite* and its rival *Jewish South*; the *Jewish Chronicle* all printed full texts of sermons on a regular basis.

[28] A particularly moving example is an article in the *San Francisco Daily* of April 16, 1865, apparently written by a member of Congregation Emanuel, which reports that the rabbi, Elkan Cohn, was handed a note informing him of Lincoln's death as he ascended the pulpit to deliver the sermon he had prepared. Initially overcome with emotion, the rabbi recovered and spoke extemporaneously, the correspondent recording for his article the "substance" of the words that, he confesses, does not do justice to the eloquence of the moment, yet retains its power in print. *Tribute of the Synagogue*, p. 138.

[29] See the essays by Bobbie Malone and Berkley Kalin in Bauman and Kalin, *The Quiet Voices: Southern Rabbis and Black Civil Rights, 1880s to 1990s* (Tuscaloosa, 1997), and citations below.

[30] Carl Voss, ed., *Stephen S. Wise: Servant of the People* (Philadelphia, 1970), pp. 132-133.

[31] Rafael Medoff, *Militant Zionism in America* (Tuscaloosa, 2002), pp. 65-66, reference to Times articles on p. 237, n. 73.

[32] Nathan Adler, *Solomon's Judgment: A Picture of Israel, A Sermon Delivered at the Great Synagogue . . . 31 December 4615 [1853]* (London, 1854). I used the copy at the Cambridge University Library.

[33] Marks, *Torah 'Or: The Law is Light: A Course of Four Lectures on the Sufficiency of the Law of Moses as the Guide of Israel* (London, 1854), pp. 5, 19, 23, 10. For examples of some withering polemical sermons against liberal Judaism from the twentieth century, see Joseph Hertz, *Sermons, Addresses, and Studies* 1:305-311, 26 April 1914, "The 'Strange Fire' of Schism," and "The New Paths: Whither Do They Lead (Three Sermons by The Chief Rabbi)" (London, 1926).

[34] "The Dangers of Israel," February 19, 1841, www.jewish-history.com/Occident/volume1/june1843/danger.html

[35] Emil G. Hirsch, "Crossing the Jordan," Rosh Hashanah even, 1880, in *The American Jewish Pulpit* (Cincinnati, 1881), p. 152 ("I deny that this step [to provide services on Sunday morning for those unable to attend on the Sabbath] is a surrender of Jewish principles"); Kaufmann Kohler, *A Living Faith* (Cincinnati, 1948), pp. 19-30; Joseph Krauskopf, *Sunday Lectuyres Delivered before the Reform Congregation Keneseth Israel, January 22, 1888 (until) January 4, (1891)* (New York, 1891), sermon no. 9.

[36] "The Sabbath: Sermon Delivered Saturday, December 15, 1888, by Benjamin Szold," (Baltimore, 1889), pp. 6, 12; Jewish Theological Seminary digital version at http://sefer.jtsa.edu:4505/ALEPH/-/start/PAMPHLETS

[37] Jewish Theological Seminary digital version at http://sefer.jtsa.edu/aleph/images/pamphlets/128846.pdf. Cf. also Hermann Gollancz's 1895 sermons on "The Sabbath," and "Which Is the True Sabbath?" (*Sermons*, vol. 1, pp. 75-87).

[38] David de Sola, "Consolation of Jerusalem" (Roth, p. 327, no. 41), pp. 4, 17, 20; I used the copy of this sermon in the British Library.

[39] On the Sabbath before Passover, 1842, the Rev. Abraham Rice of Baltimore delivered a sermon on "The Messiah" with the same assertion: "The idea of Messiah has nothing to do with the state; we can and should do nothing to hasten the time of his coming; all we have to do is to observe our laws in such a manner that it may be the pleasure of the Most High, to hasten the approach of this time. But so long as we live among the gentiles, we are commanded to obey the laws of the respective states. A clear proof of the truth of this position is furnished us by the prophet Jeremiah;" www.jewish-history.com/Occident/volume1/sept1843/messiah.html. For Mendelssohn's statement about the belief in Jewish redemption and duties as a citizen, see *The Jew in the Modern World* (Oxford, 1995), pp. 48-49. Unlike Marks, Rice does not include any clear allusion to Christian doctrines or missionary efforts; his argument in this sermon is against Jews who question the need for, or reasonableness of, this belief.

[40] Marks, Sermon for "The Sabbath Nahamoo," www.jewish-history.com/Occident/volume1/nov1843/marks.html. Cf. sermon 14 in the first volume of Marks's *Sermons* (1851), dated Sabbath Nahamoo, August 12, 5603 (1843), quite similar in theme, but with a different biblical text and virtually no actual verbal repetition. The sermon published in the November, 1843, *Occident* must therefore have been delivered earlier, perhaps in the summer of 1842. For the Christian missionary Societies focused on Jews, see Mel Scult, *Millennial Expectations and Jewish Liberties: A Study of the Efforts to Convert the Jews in Britain up to the Mid-Nineteenth Century* (Leiden, 1978), chapter 6; Todd M. Endelman, *Radical Assimilation in English Jewish History, 1656-1945* (Bloomington, 1990), chapter 5.

[41] Leeser, *Discourses*, vol. 2, pp. 254, 269, 270-271 (the entire series, delivered over a period of fourteen months, is printed on pp. 253-372).

[42] Nathan Adler, *Naftulei Elohim: A Course of Sermons on the Biblical Passages Adduced by Christian Theologians in Support of the Dogmas of Their Faith* (London, 1869), p. 2.

[43] David Woolf Marks, *Sermons Preached on Various Occasions* (London, 1885), vol. 3, p. 132.

[44] In the foreword to his book (Philadelphia, 1901), Krauskopf referred to "the widespread interest which the treatment of the subject awakened, and the keen desire of large audiences, and of a yet larger reading public—both of Jews

and non-Jews—to hear and read more and more" (p. 11).

[45] Saperstein, *Jewish Preaching*, pp. 347-358; JTSA Ms R 79 (Adler, 1248), fol. 23b; Saperstein, *"Your Voice Like a Ram's Horn,"* pp. 6-7.

[46] *A Thanksgiving Sermon for the Victory [of Leuthen]* (London, 1758) (Roth, p. 324, n. 18). I used the copy in Harvard's Houghton Library; see Saperstein, *"Your Voice Like a Ram's Horn,"* pp. 7, 13-14.

[47] Moses Cohen de Azevedo, cf., Roth, p. 325, no. 26, Hyamson, p. 136; copy in British Library. Copies of the order of service and the sermon were published immediately in the original Spanish and in English translation. On this publication, cf., also David S. Katz, *The Jews in the History of England, 1485-1850* (Oxford, 1994), p. 280.

[48] *Jewish Chronicle*, vol. 10, no. 31, pp. 261-262.

[49] Ibid., vol. 10, no. 32, p. 273. Reference is to the Ottoman legislation that granted civil equality to non-Muslims (notably the Khatt-i Sherif of 1839).

[50] D.W. Marks, *Sermons Preached on Various Occasions: Second Series* (London, 1885), pp. 155-165.

[51] Hermann Adler, *Anglo-Jewish Memories*, pp. 106-116. Geoffrey Alderman describes Adler as "a pillar of the establishment and a staunch Conservative," whose defense of the Salisbury government's policy in this sermon meant taking a strong stand on what was very much a political issue. *The Jewish Community in British Politics* (Oxford, 1983), pp. 43-44.

[52] Amos Elon, *The Pity of It All: A History of Jews in German, 1743-1933* (New York, 2002), p. 305; Paul Mendes-Flohr, "The *Kriegserlebnis* and Jewish Consciousness," in Wolfgang Benz, et al., eds., *Jews in the Weimar Republic* (Tubingen, 1998), e.g., pp. 227-228, on Leo Baeck's sermon delivered at the day of prayer proclaimed by the Kaiser for August 5, 1914, on which all Berlin's synagogues were filled to capacity.

[53] *Jewish Chronicle*, August 21, 1914, pp. 11-12. This sermon was not included by Joseph in the last volume of his sermons, but he did include several others on the war, and in one, delivered after the Armistice, he proclaimed that only Jews and Quakers "dared to preach peace during the past period of strife when most other men were for war" and that his pulpit was consecrated to preaching peace throughout the five years of awful conflict. "Peace and Goodwill," in *The Spirit of Judaism*, p. 224.

[54] Gollancz, *Sermons and Addresses (Second Series)* (London, 1916), p. 203.

[55] A.A. Green, *Sermons* (London, 1935), pp. 138-139.

[56] Leon Harrison, "Tragedies and Providence," in *The Religion of a Modern Liberal* (New York, 1931), pp. 251-253.

[57] Joseph, "The War and Religion," in *The Spirit of Judaism*, p. 199.

[58] *Jewish Chronicle*, May 28, 1915, p. 16.

[59] Gollancz, "The War and the Jews of Eastern Europe," in *Sermons and Addresses, Second Series* (London, 1915), pp. 239-240.

[60] "Can Jews Afford to Be Pacifists?" December, 1937, in *Witness from the Pulpit*, p. 59. See also the previous sermon, "Must There Be War?" November 11, 1936, pp. 50-55.

[61] L.M. Sanker, of "The Synagogue," Bristol, "Children of Israel," in J. Israelstam and L. Wiewow, eds., *"Ye Are My Witnesses:" Sermons and Studies by Former Students of Dr. Samuel Daiches at Jews' College, London* (London, 1936), pp. 48-51. Thought undated, the book was published in 1936, and the preacher says that "A year ago the cult of internationalism was not an unpopular one." We should probably date the sermon in 1934 or 1935.

[62] See, for example, Roland B. Gittelsohn, *Fire In My Bones* (New York, 1969), pp. 1-19 (November 1965 and November 1966); Saperstein, *Witness from the Pulpit*, pp. 252-258 (June 10, 1966). For more radical pulpit attacks on American militarism in Vietnma, see Michael E. Staub, *Torn At the Roots: The Crisis of Jewish Liberalism in Postwar America* (New York, 2002), pp. 171-172, 320, n. 13.

[63] Alexandra Wright, cited in *European Judaism* 35:1 (Spring, 2002), p. 24.

[64] John Rayner, cited in *European Judaism* 35:1 (Spring, 2002), p. 25.

[65] Friedenberg, "*Hear O Israel*," pp. 13, 17.

[66] Marks, *Sermons* (vol. 1), pp. 124, 130-131

[67] David de Sola, above, n. 8, pp. 4-5, 9.

[68] Solomon B. Freehof and Vigdor W. Kavaler, introduction to *J. Leonard Levy: Prophetic Voice* (Pittsburgh, 1970), pp. 25, 31; cf. p. 206.

[69] Levy, pp. 199-207 (December 3, 1916).

[70] Ibid., pp. 139-145.

[71] Harrison, in *Abraham Lincoln: The Tribute of the Synagogue*, pp. 452-456.

[72] Cited by Malone in Bauman and Kalin, *The Quiet Voices*, p. 34, from *American Israelite*, September 16, 1909. See also the description of Heller's 1898 sermon "Modern Intolerance," on the Dreyfus trial and racial prejudice, and his memorial sermon following the assassination of President McKinley, decrying—among the other evils he had seen during the previous decade— "the drunken mob that kindles a pyre around a chained negro" (ibid., p. 27, from *Times Democrat*, February 19, 1898, and p. 32, from *Daily Picayune*, September 20, 1901).

[73] Cited by Berkley Kalin in Bauman and Kalin, *The Quiet Voices*, p. 59.

[74] Rothschild, "The Greater Sin," unpublished Yom Kippur sermon, October 13, 1948 (in the context of the Dixiecrat presidential campaign), cited by Melissa Fay Greene, *The Temple Bombing* (Reading, 1996), pp. 173-174. Rothschild's widow wrote that he "gradually accustomed his congregation to hearing his opinion on the segregation issue by speaking of it at least once during each High Holy Day season and on two or three other occasions every year." Janice Rothschild Blumberg, in Bauman and Kalin, *The Quiet Voices*, pp. 263-264.

[75] Cited by Gary Zola in Bauman and Kalin, *The Quiet Voices*, p. 242.

[76] Cited in Staub, *Torn at the Roots*, p. 58, from *American Judaism* 7 (January, 1958), p. 11. See the other examples also cited by Staub on that page.

[77] Saperstein, *Witness from the Pulpit*, pp. 222-223. For a recent discussion of Prinz's address to the rally, see Staub, *Torn at the Roots*, pp. 45-48.

[78] Jacob Philip Rudin, "The March on Washington (Rosh Hashanah, 1963), in *Very Truly Yours*, p. 158. Cf., his powerful defense of the Civil Rights movements on Yom Kippur eve three years later, ibid., pp. 259-269.

[79] Eugene Lipman, "Black Power Slogans" (Yom Kippur, 1966), in *Yamim Nora'im: Sinai Sermons* (Washington, D.C., 1987), pp. 40-44. See also his strong sermon from Yom Kippur, 1963, called "Racial Justice: A Pledge of Conscience," addressing his congregants about their apparent uneasiness over the March on Washington a few weeks earlier: "I am ashamed for you, because you have to be pushed and cajoled and begged and occasionally shouted at to accept the smallest, most insignificant kind of responsibility in the most important American movement of the twentieth century, in solving the deepest religious problem we face in our society. I am ashamed for you because you are so determined to do nothing" (ibid., pp. 23-24).

MARC SAPERSTEIN

T

TORAH AND CULTURE: Does culture express or defy the religious imperative? Do the patterns of the social order realize the divine plan, or do they represent that from which religion must separate itself, upon which religion stands in judgment? This inquiry pertains in particular to religions engaged in constructing norms for the social order of the faithful. The matter, then, concerns the relationship between the generative symbol of a religion and the ambient culture that forms the framework in which that religion constructs its holy society. Does culture form a medium of religion or an obstacle thereto?

Religions that speak to, make provision for, communities of the faithful respond to the issue. They further mediate relationships between those communities and the ambient universe beyond their limits—that is, all religions that rise above the utterly idiosyncratic and private[1] must address the same issue.

Torah and Culture: A Contemporary Debate in the Torah Camp: The contemporary question may be framed very simply. It is "Torah along with secular learning" as against "Torah but no secular learning," and that issue is framed in the world of the Orthodox Yeshivot. Proof-texts for both sides derive from the canonical writings of normative Judaism. Indeed, the debate involves Yeshiva University in the U.S.A. and Bar-Ilan University in the State of Israel, as against the Yeshiva worlds of Brooklyn and Bene Beraq: Does the study of Torah prevent the study of any other subject, as the Yeshiva-world maintains, or does the study of Torah encompass all learning, as Yeshiva and Bar-Ilan aver? If the former, then the Torah stands in opposition to, in judgment upon, secular sciences, and, if the latter, then the Torah represents the apex and realization of all learning. As to the conflict between Torah and secular learning, it may be framed very simply. Is it permitted for a pious Jew to study mathematics, biology, or history, or must he devote all of his time and energy to study of the Torah? The curricula of the great Yeshivot, centers of Torah-study, and of the schools that prepare young men for study in those Yeshivot, answer that question in different ways. Some accommodate secular studies, others do not.

Now there is no more blatant formulation of the debate on the interplay of religion and culture than the issue as it is articulated, to begin with, in contemporary Judaic Orthodoxy. In its interior debates on the value of a secular education, the Torah-camp of contemporary Judaism today carries forward a debate that first came to the surface in the formation, in the nineteenth century, of integrationist Orthodox Judaism, which held that study of Torah does not preclude study of secular sciences, broadly construed, including literature, philosophy, and natural science. Is Torah in conflict with culture, or does Torah infuse culture, so that those that study nature enter into the realm of Torah-learning? From the time of Samson Raphael Hirsch in the nineteenth century to the present time in Yeshiva University and Bar-Ilan University, the debate has gone forward on whether or not Israelites faithful to the Torah may devote any amount of time to other-than-Torah-learning. Integrationist Orthodoxy affirmed, and segregationist-Orthodoxy denied, that proposition. The contemporary debate serves only to show how the basic question animates interior debate in the Torah-camp of Judaism. In these corresponding terms, the issue addressed by Christianity is not only *not* alien to, but quite commonplace in, the debates of the continuators of Torah-learning in Judaism. Now to consider matters in greater particularity.

Torah as a Component of Culture or Torah as the Entirety of Culture: When Torah is a chapter of life, then Torah is integrated into the affairs of the everyday, a component of the whole. When Torah commands the entirety of the human situation, it contrasts with all other forms not only of learning but of human engagement. So at issue, as I shall show, is whether Torah is represented as a component of culture, to be sure, hierarchically at the apex of the social order, or is portrayed as the entirety of culture, in competition with the other, competing and also illegitimate demands that culture makes: Torah versus culture, or Torah as harmonious with culture.

What I shall now show is that the categorical conflict is native to Rabbinic Judaism. The matter is framed in diverse ways. In normative law, the opposition of Torah and culture comes to concrete expression in the conflict between the natural family and the supernatural relationships brought into being by Torah-study. How, then, does Torah imposes itself upon familial ties? One way the halakhah finds to express the position that the Torah stands against all other (natural, social) relationships is as follows (M. B.M. 2:11):

A. [If he has to choose between seeking] what he has lost and what his father has lost,
B. his own takes precedence.
C. . . . what he has lost and what his master has lost,
D. his own takes precedence.
E. . . . what his father has lost and what his master has lost, that of his master takes precedence.
G. For his father brought him into this world.
H. But his master, who taught him wisdom, will bring him into the life of the world to come.
I. But if his father is a sage, that of his father takes precedence.
J. [If] his father and his master were carrying heavy burdens, he removes that of his master, and afterward removes that of his father.
K. [If] his father and his master were taken captive,
L. he ransoms his master, and afterward he ransoms his father.
M. But if his father is a sage, he ransoms his father, and afterward he ransoms his master.

The point is made explicit at G-H: the master takes precedence over the father, because the master has brought him eternal life through Torah-teachings, so the natural relationships of this world are set aside by the contrasting ones of the world to come, family by Torah.

In the next statement of the same view, social relationships—the hierarchy of the castes—are reframed in the same way. Now the castes are at issue, priest, Levite, Israelite, mamzer (an outcaste, e.g., the offspring of a union that violates the law, for instance, of a married woman and a man other than her husband), and so on down. These are contrasted with disciple of a sage in relationship to one who is not a disciple of a sage but, by contrast, an *am ha'ares* (in context: ignorant man). Here knowledge of Torah overrides the hierarchy of castes and transcends it (M. Hor. 3:8).

A. A priest takes precedence over a Levite, a Levite over an Israelite, an Israelite over a mamzer, a mamzer over a Netin, a Netin over a proselyte, a proselyte over a freed slave.
B. Under what circumstances?
C. When all of them are equivalent.
D. But if the mamzer [outcaste] was a disciple of a sage, and a high priest was an

am ha'ares [unlettered in the Torah], the mamzer who is a disciple of a sage takes precedence over a high priest who is an *am ha'ares*.

In both contexts, Torah stands over against the social order and disrupts its natural arrangements, both in family and in caste. What about the conflicting responsibilities of devoting time to Torah-study and devoting time to earning a living? The same view predominates when it comes to earning a living: Torah competes with other components of the ambient culture. That conflict comes to expression in the following:

What is explicit here is that knowledge of the Torah does not change one's caste-status, e.g., priest or mamzer or Netin, and that caste-status does govern whom one may marry, a matter of substantial economic consequence. But it does change one's status as to precedence of another order altogether—one that is curiously unspecific at M. Hor. 3:8. Hierarchical classification for its own sake, lacking all practical consequence, characterizes the Mishnah's system, defining, after all, its purpose and its goal! Along these same lines, the premise of tractate Sanhedrin is that the sage is judge and administrator of the community; knowledge of the Torah qualifies him; but knowledge of the Torah does not provide a living or the equivalent of a living. No provision for supporting the sage as administrator, clerk, or judge is suggested in the tractate.

Study a craft and also study Torah versus study Torah only: What about knowledge of Torah as a way of making one's living? Here is a fine occasion on which to say, there is knowledge that possesses value but is not part of the Torah. Or only knowledge of the Torah registers. In the former case, study of Torah represents one component of legitimate learning and livelihood, but there are other things to be learned and to be practiced, and these do not come into conflict with Torah-study. In the latter instance, study of Torah competes with, stands over against, study of all other matters, e.g., of trade or commerce. The issue is joined in a systematic way in the Halakhic system, where some authorities recognize the value of

studying a trade, while others insist that one should study only Torah, which will provide a livelihood through supernatural means.

We see in the normative law more than a single viewpoint. In the list of professions by which men make a living we find several positions. That underscores my basic point: within the framework of Judaism diverse positions register. The issue is common to both traditions, but each frames it in its natural language and category-formations. First is that of Meir and Simeon (M. Qid. 4:14):

> E. R. Meir says, "A man should always teach his son a clean and easy trade. And let him pray to him to whom belong riches and possessions.
> G. "For there is no trade which does not involve poverty or wealth.
> H. "For poverty does not come from one's trade, nor does wealth come from one's trade.
> I. "But all is in accord with a man's merit."
> J. R. Simeon b. Eleazar says, "Have you ever seen a wild beast or a bird who has a trade? Yet they get along without difficulty. And were they not created only to serve me? And I was created to serve my Master. So is it not logical that I should get along without difficulty? But I have done evil and ruined my living."

One's merit makes the difference between poverty and wealth, or one's sinfulness. This simply carries forward the curse of Eden: Adam must work because he has rebelled against God, and that is the human condition. A more practical position is that which follows in the continuation of the passage:

> K. Abba Gurion of Sidon says in the name of Abba Gurya, "A man should not teach his son to be an ass driver, a camel driver, a barber, a sailor, a herdsman, or a shopkeeper For their trade is the trade of thieves."
> L. R. Judah says in his name, "Most ass drivers are evil, most camel drivers are decent, most sailors are saintly, the best among physicians is going to Gehenna, and the best of butchers is a partner of Amalek."

The third view is that of Nehorai, who holds that Torah suffices as a means for making a living, and Torah-study defines all that man should do, in utter rejection of the imperatives of culture, e.g., mastering a trade and earning a living:

> M. R. Nehorai says, "I should lay aside every trade in the world and teach my son only Torah.
> N. "For a man eats its fruits in this world, and the principal remains for the world to come.
> O. "But other trades are not that way.
> P. "When a man gets sick or old or has pains and cannot do his job, lo, he dies of starvation.
> Q. "But with Torah it is not that way.
> R. "But it keeps him from all evil when he is young, and it gives him a future and a hope when he is old.
> S. "Concerning his youth, what does it say? 'They who wait upon the Lord shall renew their strength' (Is. 40:31). And concerning his old age what does it say? 'They shall still bring forth fruit in old age' (Ps. 92:14).
> T. "And so it says with regard to the patriarch Abraham, may he rest in peace, 'And Abraham was old and well along in years, and the Lord blessed Abraham in all things' (Gen. 24:1).
> U. "We find that the patriarch Abraham kept the entire Torah even before it was revealed, since it says, 'Since Abraham obeyed my voice and kept my charge, my commandments, my statutes, and my laws' (Gen. 26:5)."

Precisely why Torah works as it does is made explicit at R: "It keeps him from evil when he is young." That is to say, the position of Meir and Simeon is repeated, only in a fresh way. If I know the Torah, I will not sin. Meir and Simeon concur in denying conflict between earning a living and studying the Torah, and Nehorai sees a choice to be made.

The first apologia for the Mishnah, tractate Abot, takes the view that one should *not* make one's living through study of the Torah. One should both practice a trade and also support himself, and there is no conflict between the one and the other. That is made explicit in Torah-sayings of tractate Abot, where we find explicit rejection of the theory of Torah-study as a means of avoiding one's obligation to earn a living. Torah-study without a craft is rejected, Torah-study along with labor at a craft is defined as the ideal way of life. No one then concedes that one should do the one and not the other: study the Torah but not practice a trade. The following sayings make that point quite clearly (M. Abot 2:2 and 3:17):

> 2:2.A. Rabban Gamaliel, a son of Rabbi Judah the Patriarch says: Fitting is learning in the Torah along with a craft, for the labor put into the two of them makes one forget sin. And all learning of the Torah which is not joined with labor is destined to be null and causes sin.
> 3:17.A. R. Eleazar b. Azariah says, ". . . If there is no sustenance [lit.: flour], there is no Torah-learning. If there is no Torah-learning, there is no sustenance."

The way of virtue lies in economic activity in the conventional sense, joined to intellectual or philosophical activity in sages' sense. The labor in Torah is not an economic activity and produces no solutions to this-worldly problems of getting food, shelter, clothing. To the contrary, labor in Torah defines the purpose of human life; it is the goal; but it is not the medium for maintaining life and avoiding starvation or exposure to the elements. So too, Tosefta's complement to the Mishnah is explicit in connection with M. Git. 1:7A, "a commandment pertaining to the father concerning the son" (T. Qid. 1:11E-G):

> It is to circumcise him, redeem him [should he be kidnapped], teach him Torah, teach him a trade, and marry him off to a girl .

There clearly is no conception that if one studies Torah, he need not work for a living, nor in the Tosefta's complement to the Mishnah does anyone imagine that merit is gained by supporting those who study the Torah.

Cited in Abot 2:8, Yohanan b. Zakkai speaks of Torah-study as the goal of a human life, on the one side, and a reward paid for Torah study, clearly in a theological sense and context, on the other. That the context of Torah-study is religious and not economic in any sense is shown by Hananiah's saying, which is explicit: if people talk about the Torah, the Presence of God joins them and participates (M. Abot 2:8, 2:16, 3:2):

2:8.A. Rabban Yohanan b. Zakkai received [the Torah] from Hillel and Shammai. He would say: "If you have learned much Torah, do not puff yourself up on that account, for it was for that purpose that you were created. "

2:16.A. [Tarfon] would say: "It's not your job to finish the work, but you are not free to walk away from it. If you have learned much Torah, they will give you a good reward. And your employer can be depended upon to pay your wages for what you do. And know what sort of reward is going to be given to the righteous in the coming time."

3:2.B. R. Hananiah b. Teradion says, "[If] two sit together and between them do not pass teachings of the Torah, lo, this is a seat of the scornful, as it is said, 'Nor sits in the seat of the scornful' (Ps. 1:1). But two who are sitting, and words of the Torah do pass between them—the Presence is with them,

C. "as it is said, 'Then they that feared the Lord spoke with one another, and the Lord hearkened and heard, and a book of remembrance was written before him, for them that feared the Lord and gave thought to his name' (Mal 3:16).

D. "I know that this applies to two. How do I know that even if a single person sits and works on the Torah, the Holy One, blessed be He, set aside a reward for him? As it is said, 'Let him sit alone and keep silent, because he has laid it upon him' (Lam. 3:28)."

Do worldly benefits accrue to those who study the Torah? The rabbi cited in the following statement maintains that it is entirely inappropriate to utilize Torah-learning to gain either social standing or economic gain (M. Abot 4:5):

B. R. Sadoq says, "Do not make [Torah-teachings] a crown in which to glorify yourself or a spade with which to dig. So did Hillel say, "He who uses the crown perishes. Thus have you learned: Whoever derives worldly benefit from teachings of the Torah takes his life out of this world."

This calls to mind the immediate debate I cited at the outset: May Yeshiva-students study biology or computer science, or does Torah-study constitute the whole of the appropriate curriculum in opposition to secular studies? The contemporary issue surfaces in comparable terms here. Torah-study forms only a chapter in the proper education of a man. It is the simple fact that the bulk of opinion in the Mishnah and in tractate Abot identifies Torah-learning with status within a system of hierarchical classification, not with a medium for earning a living. And learning a trade and earning a living form harmonious obligations with Torah-study.

Admittedly that is not the only position that is represented. The following seems to me to contrast working for a living with studying Torah and to maintain that the latter will provide a living, without recourse to hard labor (M. Abot 3:15):

A. R. Nehunia b. Haqqaneh says, "From whoever accepts upon himself the yoke of the Torah do they remove the yoke of the state and the yoke of hard labor. And upon whoever removes from himself the yoke of the Torah do they lay the yoke of the state and the yoke of hard labor."

But the prevailing view, represented by the bulk of sayings, treats Torah-study as an activity that competes with economic venture and insists that Torah-study take precedence, even though it is not of economic value in any commonplace sense of the words. That is explicitly imputed to Meir and to Jonathan in the following (M. Abot 4:9-10):

4:9.A. R. Jonathan says, "Whoever keeps the Torah when poor will in the end keep it in wealth. And whoever treats the Torah as nothing when he is wealthy in the end will treat it as nothing in poverty."

4:10.A. R. Meir says, "Keep your business to a minimum and make your business the Torah. And be humble before everybody. And if you treat the Torah as nothing, you will have many treating you as nothing. And if you have labored in the Torah, [the Torah] has a great reward to give you."

Torah-study competes with, rather than replaces, with economic activity. That is the simple position of tractate Abot, extending the conception of matters explicit in the

Mishnah. If I had to make a simple statement of the situation prevailing at ca. 250 C.E., sages contrast their wealth, which is spiritual and intellectual, with material wealth; they do not deem the one to form the counterpart of the other, but only as the opposite.

Wealth, Material and Spiritual: Real Estate versus Torah: The rational disposition of scarce resources forms a chapter of culture, which defines what is rational and determines therefore what constitute scarce resources. If we wish to construct a contrast between Torah and culture, then we should do so by pointing to a choice between Torah and other valued things and by contrasting two rationalities, that of the Torah and that of other things that people value. Here we have a story that sets the value of Torah into opposition with the value of real estate, which in antiquity was deemed the preferred form of wealth. To be sure, the tale carries forward the view that a man should study Torah to the exclusion of all else, and that action secures his material needs as well. But the conflict between Torah and culture is expressed in more explicit ways here. Wealth in the form of real estate and income derived therefrom, which conventionally defined a secure investment in antiquity, conflict with the value of Torah-study, the source of supernatural riches. So the conflict is between two rationalities, two definitions of what constitute scarce resources. But there is a twist, which I shall point out (Lev. Rabbah XXXIV:XVI):

> 1.B. R. Tarfon gave to R. Aqiba six silver centenarii, saying to him, "Go, buy us a piece of land, so we can get a living from it and labor in the study of Torah together."
>
> C. He took the money and handed it over to scribes, Mishnah-teachers, and those who study Torah.
>
> D. After some time R. Tarfon met him and said to him, "Did you buy the land that I mentioned to you?"
>
> E. He said to him, "Yes."
>
> F. He said to him, "Is it any good?"
>
> G. He said to him, "Yes."
>
> H. He said to him, "And do you not want to show it to me?"
>
> I. He took him and showed him the scribes, Mishnah teachers, and people who were studying Torah, and the Torah that they had acquired.
>
> J. He said to him, "Is there anyone who works for nothing? Where is the deed covering the field?"
>
> K. He said to him, "It is with King David, concerning whom it is written, 'He has scattered, he has given to the poor, his righteousness endures forever' (Ps. 112:9)."

Instead of defining wealth as land, this story defines land as not-wealth, and something else is now defined as wealth in its place.

The transformation from real estate to Torah is made explicit when we are told how we turn real estate into Torah. That transvaluation of values is worked out, once more quite explicitly, in the statement (Y. Meg. 4:1.IV.P-Q): "'I can write the whole Torah for two hundred copper coins.' What did he do, he went and bought flax seed worth two hundred copper coins, sowed it, reaped it, made it into ropes, caught a deer, and wrote the entire Torah on the deer hide." The three operative components here are money (capital) converted into land converted into (a) Torah (scroll). In context, the ambient culture comes to expression in the definition of real wealth. In the world at large, as I said, that was real estate. So we transform money into land. But then the definition of wealth is shifted, and the symbolic shift is blatant: turn money into real wealth, then real wealth produces the wherewithal of making a Torah. And with that rather stunning symbolic transformation, we find ourselves in a world wholly different from the one in which scarce resources are identified with matters of material, palpable value, and in which economics is the theory of the rational disposition of scarce resources of capital, labor, movables, real estate, and the like. Now Torah is opposed to the regnant rationality of worth, which is real estate, and Torah stands in judgment of real wealth.

Why do I insist there is an antimony between Torah and culture? The reason is that there are passages that are quite explicit: land is wealth, or Torah is wealth, but not both; owning land is power and studying Torah permits (re)gaining power—but not both. To take the first of the two propositions in its most explicit formulation (Lev. Rabbah XXX:I):

4.A. R. Yohanan was going up from Tiberias to Sepphoris. R. Hiyya bar Abba was supporting him. They came to a field. He said, "This field once belonged to me, but I sold it in order to acquire merit in the Torah."

B. They came to a vineyard, and he said, "This vineyard once belonged to me, but I sold it in order to acquire merit in the Torah."

C. They came to an olive grove, and he said, "This olive grove once belonged to me, but I sold it in order to acquire merit in the Torah."

D. R. Hiyya began to cry.

E. Said R. Yohanan, "Why are you crying?"

F. He said to him, "It is because you left nothing over to support you in your old age."

G. He said to him, "Hiyya, my disciple, is what I did such a light thing in your view? I sold something that was given in a spell of six days [of creation] and in exchange I acquired something that was given in a spell of forty days [of revelation]."

H. "The entire world and everything in it was created in only six days, as it is written, 'For in six days the Lord made heaven and earth' [Exod. 20:11].

I. "But the Torah was given over a period of forty days, as it was said, 'And he was there with the Lord for forty days and forty nights' [Exod. 34:28]."

J. "And it is written, 'And I remained on the mountain for forty days and forty nights' (Deut. 9:9)."

5.A. When R. Yohanan died, his generation recited concerning him [the following verse of Scripture]: "If a man should give all the wealth of his house for the love" (Song 8:7), with which R. Yohanan loved the Torah, "he would be utterly destitute" (Song 8:7). . . .

C. When R. Eleazar b. R. Simeon died, his generation recited concerning him [the following verse of Scripture]: "Who is this who comes up out of the wilderness like pillars of smoke, perfumed with myrrh and frankincense, with all the powders of the merchant?" (Song 3:6).

D. What is the meaning of the clause, "With all the powders of the merchant"?

E. [Like a merchant who carries all sorts of desired powders,] he was a master

of Scripture, a repeater of Mishnah traditions, a writer of liturgical supplications, and a liturgical poet.

The sale of land for the acquisition of "merit in the Torah" introduces two principal systemic components, merit and Torah.[2] For our purpose, the importance of the statement lies in the second of the two, which deems land the counterpart—and clearly the opposite—of the Torah.

Now one can sell a field and acquire "Torah," meaning, in the context established by the exchange between Tarfon and Aqiba, the opportunity to gain leisure to (acquire the merit gained by) the study of the Torah. That the sage has left himself nothing for his support in old age makes explicit the material meaning of the statement, and the comparison of the value of land, created in six days, and the Torah, created in forty days, is equally explicit. The comparison of knowledge of Torah to the merchandise of the merchant simply repeats the same point, but in a lower register. So too does the this-worldly power of study of the Torah make explicit in another framework the conviction that study of the Torah yields material and concrete benefit, not just spiritual renewal. Thus Huna states, "All of the exiles will be gathered together only on account of the study of Mishnah-teachings" (Pesiqta deRab Kahana VI:III.3.B).

I portray the opposition as a matter of culture, expressed through economic theory. But the conflict between Torah-study and all else cuts to the bone. For the ultimate value—Torah-study—surely bears comparison with other foci of value, such as prayer, using money for building synagogues, and the like. It is explicitly stated that spending money on synagogues is a waste of money, while spending money supporting Torah-masters is the right use of scarce resources. Further, we find the claim, synagogues and school houses—communal real estate—in fact form the property of sages and their disciples, who may dispose of them just as they want, as any owner may dispose of his property according to his unfettered will. In Y. Sheqalim we find the former allegation, Y. Megillah the latter:

Y. Sheqalim 5:4.II
A. R. Hama bar Haninah and R. Hoshaia the Elder were strolling in the synagogues in Lud. Said R. Hama bar Haninah to R. Hoshaia, "How much money did my forefathers invest here [in building these synagogues]!"
B. He said to him, "How many lives did your forefathers invest here! Were there not people who were laboring in Torah [who needed the money more]?"
C. R. Abun made the gates of the great hall [of study]. R. Mana came to him. He said to him, "See what I have made!"
D. He said to him, "'For Israel has forgotten his Maker and built palaces'! (Hos. 8:14). Were there no people laboring in Torah [who needed the money more]?"

Y. Sotah 9:13.VI
C. A certain rabbi would teach Scripture to his brother in Tyre, and when they came and called him to do business, he would say, "I am not going to take away from my fixed time to study. If the profit is going to come to me, let it come in due course [after my fixed time for study has ended]."

Y. Megillah 3:3:V
A. R. Joshua b. Levi said, "Synagogues and schoolhouses belong to sages and their disciples."
B. R. Hiyya bar Yose received [guests] in the synagogue [and lodged them there].
C. R. Immi instructed the scribes, "If someone comes to you with some slight contact with Torah learning, receive him, his asses, and his belongings."
D. R. Berekhiah went to the synagogue in Beisan. He saw someone rinsing his hands and feet in a fountain [in the courtyard of the synagogue]. He said to him, "It is forbidden to you [to do this]."
E. The next day the man saw [Berekhiah] washing his hands and feet in the fountain.
F. He said to him, "Rabbi, is it permitted to you and forbidden to me?"
G. He said to him, "Yes."
H. He said to him, "Why?"
I. He said to him, "Because this is what R. Joshua b. Levi said: 'Synagogues and schoolhouses belong to sages and their disciples.'"

Not all acts of piety, we see, are equal, and the one that takes precedence over all others (just as was alleged at M. Pe. 1:1) is study of the Torah. But the point now is a much more concrete one, and that is, through study of the Torah, sages and their disciples gain possession, as a matter of fact, over communal real estate, which they may utilize in any way they wish; and that is a quite concrete claim indeed, as the same story alleges.

No wonder, then, that people in general are expected to contribute their scarce resources for the support of sages and their disciples. Moreover, society at large was obligated to support sages, and the sages' claim upon others was enforceable by Heaven. Those who gave sages' disciples money so that they would not have to work would get it back from Heaven, and those who did not would lose what they had (Y. Sotah 7:4.IV):

F. R. Aha in the name of R. Tanhum b. R. Hiyya: "If one has learned, taught, kept, and carried out [the Torah], and has ample means in his possession to strengthen the Torah and has not done so, lo, such a one still is in the category of those who are cursed." [The meaning of "strengthen" here is to support the masters of the Torah.]
G. R. Jeremiah in the name of R. Hiyya bar Ba, "[If] one did not learn, teach, keep, and carry out [the teachings of the Torah], and did not have ample means to strengthen [the masters of the Torah] [but nonetheless did strengthen them], lo, such a one falls into the category of those who are blessed."
H. And R. Hannah, R. Jeremiah in the name of R. Hiyya: "The Holy One, blessed be he, is going to prepare a protection for those who carry out religious duties [of support for masters of Torah] through the protection afforded to the masters of Torah [themselves].
I. "What is the Scriptural basis for that statement? 'For the protection of wisdom is like the protection of money'" (Ecc. 7:12).
J. "And it says, '[The Torah] is a tree of life to those who grasp it; those who hold it fast are called happy'" (Prov. 3:18).

Such contributions form the counterpart to taxes, that is, scarce resources taken away from the owner by force for the purposes of the public good, that is, the ultimate meeting point of economics and politics, the explicit formation of distributive, as against market, economics. Then what is distributed and to whom and by what force forms the centerpiece of the systemic political economy, and the answer is perfectly simple: all sorts of valued things are taken away from people and handed over for the support of sages.

That extends to freeing sages from the obligation to pay taxes, e.g., for the defense of the city. I cannot imagine a more extreme claim than that not walls but sages and their Torah-study form the strongest defense for the city. Therefore sages should not have to pay for the upkeep of the common defense. Since people took for granted that walls were the best defense, Torah here confronts the common culture with its uncommon claim.

So it is alleged that sages are the guardians of cities, and later on that would yield the further allegation that sages do not have to pay taxes to build walls around cities, since their Torah-study protects the cities (Pesiqta deRab Kahana XV:V):

1.A. R. Abba bar Kahana commenced discourse by citing the following verse: "Who is the man so wise that he may understand this? To whom has the mouth of the Lord spoken, that he may declare it? Why is the land ruined and laid waste like a wilderness, [so that no one passes through? The Lord said, It is because they forsook my Torah which I set before them; they neither obeyed me nor conformed to it. They followed the promptings of their own stubborn hearts, they followed the Baalim as their forefathers had taught them. Therefore these are the words of the Lord of Hosts the God of Israel: 'I will feed this people with wormwood and give them bitter poison to drink. I will scatter them among nations whom neither they nor their forefathers have known; I will harry them with the sword until I have made an end of them]' (Jer. 9:16)."

B. It was taught in the name of R. Simeon b. Yohai, "If you see towns uprooted from their place in the land of Israel, know that [it is because] the people did not pay the salaries of teachers of children and Mishnah-instructors.

C. "What is the verse of Scripture that indicates it? 'Why is the land ruined and laid waste like a wilderness, [so

that no one passes through?'] What is written just following? 'It is because they forsook my Torah [which I set before them; they neither obeyed me nor conformed to it.]'"

2.A. Rabbi sent R. Yose and R. Ammi to go and survey the towns of the land of Israel. They would go into a town and say to the people, "Bring me the guardians of the town."

B. The people would bring out the head of the police and the local guard.

C. [The sages] would say, "These are not the guardians of the town, they are those who destroy the town. Who are the guardians of the town? They are the teachers of children and Mishnah-teachers, who keep watch by day and by night, in line with the verse, 'And you shall meditate in it day and night' (Josh. 1:8)."

D. And so Scripture says, "If the Lord does not build the house, in vain the builders labor" (Ps. 127:1).

7.A. Said R. Abba bar Kahana, "No philosophers in the world ever arose of the quality of Balaam b. Beor and Abdymos of Gadara. The nations of the world came to Abnymos of Gadara. They said to him, 'Do you maintain that we can make war against this nation?'

B. "He said to them, 'Go and make the rounds of their synagogues and their study houses. So long as there are there children chirping out loud in their voices [and studying the Torah], then you cannot overcome them. If not, then you can conquer them, for so did their father promise them: "The voice is Jacob's voice" (Gen. 27:22), meaning that when Jacob's voice chirps in synagogues and study houses, The hands are not the hands of Esau [so Esau has no power].

C. "'So long as there are no children chirping out loud in their voices [and studying the Torah] in synagogues and study houses, The hands are the hands of Esau [so Esau has power].'"

The reference to Esau, that is, Rome, of course links the whole to the contemporary context and alleges that if the Israelites will support those who study the Torah and teach it, then their cities will be safe, and, still more, the rule of Esau/Rome will come to an end; then the Messiah will come, so the stakes are not trivial. That claim, contrary to the intuited givens of the common culture, places Torah over against that culture, and does so in an extreme manner.

What we see are two distinct positions, Torah-study within the framework of the culture of economics, Torah-study as against the culture of conventional economics. There is no harmonizing the two. Economics deals with scarce resources, and the disenlandisement of economics has turned upon its head the very focus of economics: scarcity and the rational way of disposing of what is scarce. To land rigid limits are set by nature, to the Holy Land, still more narrow ones apply. But to knowledge of the Torah no limits pertain. So we find ourselves dealing with an economics that concern not the rational utilization of scarce resources, but the very opposite: the rational utilization of what can and ought to be the opposite of scarce. In identifying knowledge and teaching of the Torah as the ultimate value, the successor-system has not simply constructed a new economics in place of an old one, finding of value something other than had earlier been valued; it has redefined economics altogether. It has done so, as a matter of fact, in a manner that is entirely familiar, by setting forth in place of an economics of scarcity an economics of abundant productivity. Disenlandising value thus transvalues value by insisting upon its (potential) increase as the definition of what is rational economic action. The task is not preservation of power over land but increase of power over the Torah, because one can only preserve land, but one can increase one's knowledge of the Torah.

The Harmony of Torah and Culture: So much for the position that recognizes only conflict between Torah and culture. Is there no view that finds culture in the Torah, that identifies the Torah as the source of culture? I can show how the identification of Torah and culture comes to expression in the same documents as contain the opposite theory of matters. The aspect of culture that is identical to Torah is what we should call natural science. The Torah is represented as fully realized by the creation of the world, so that, by extension, the study of creation carries us deep into the mysteries of the Torah as the record of creation. This view I find in a classic, famous passage, which alleges in so many

words that God created the world by looking into the Torah. Then creation comes about by reference to the design set forth in the Torah. That bears the message: creation forms a guide to the fullness of the Torah, and all natural science forms a chapter in the revelation of the Torah that creation realizes. No. 2 below states that proposition in so many words (Gen. Rabbah I:I):

l.A. "In the beginning God created" (Gen. 1:1):

B. R. Oshaia commenced [discourse by citing the following verse:] "'Then I was beside him like a little child, and I was daily his delight [rejoicing before him always, rejoicing in his inhabited world, and delighting in the sons of men]' (Prov. 8:30-31).

C. "The word for 'child' uses consonants that may also stand for 'teacher,' 'covered over,' and 'hidden away.'

D. "Some hold that the word also means 'great.'

E. "The word means 'teacher,' in line with the following: 'As a teacher carries the suckling child' (Num. 11:12).

F. "The word means 'covered over,' as in the following: 'Those who were covered over in scarlet' (Lam. 4:5).

G. "The word means 'hidden,' as in the verse, 'And he hid Hadassah' (Est. 2:7).

H. "The word means 'great,' in line with the verse, 'Are you better than No-Ammon?' (Nah. 3:8). This we translate, 'Are you better than Alexandria the Great, which is located between rivers.'"

2.A. Another matter:

B. The word [for child] in fact means "workman."

C. [In the cited verse] the Torah speaks, "I was the work-plan of the Holy One, blessed be he.

D. In the accepted practice of the world, when a mortal king builds a palace, he does not build it out of his own head, but he follows a work-plan.

E. And [the one who supplies] the work-plan does not build out of his own head, but he has designs and diagrams, so as to know how to situate the rooms and the doorways.

F. Thus the Holy One, blessed be he, consulted the Torah when he created the world.

G. So the Torah stated, "By means of 'the beginning' [that is to say, the Torah] did God create..." (Gen. 1:1).

H. And the word for "beginning" refers only to the Torah, as Scripture says, "The Lord made me as the beginning of his way" (Prov. 8:22).

The matter is explicit: the Torah forms the key to the creation of the world, and, working back from nature to the Torah, man penetrates the mysteries of the Torah by investigating the traits and properties of nature. Botany, biology, physics, chemistry—these form media of revelation of God's plan and will, as much as does the Torah in its specific formulation. Here Torah forms a harmonious union with culture. In that capacious vision, one cannot distinguish secular from sacred science, for all learning, all chapters of culture, embody God's plan and program for creation, which to be sure comes to its most authentic expression in the words of the Torah itself.

Why the Persistence of the Dialectics? In Scripture, God is represented, sometimes by the same theologian in the same piece of writing, as both immanent and transcendent, both "with us" and "wholly other." The same God who makes himself known and hides his face, who shelters his prophet in the cleft of the rock as his glory goes by, is the God who is both at home in humanity and different from humanity. Then the issue of how God takes up his abode in the midst of humankind, and when his thoughts are not our thoughts at all, will come to expression in details, as much as in the main point. In that setting, why should culture differ? Culture both embodies the faith, reminiscent of God's immanence in the world, and culture also is contradicted by faith, recalling God's transcendence over the world. It is hardly surprising, then, that culture is to be abandoned by the faithful and also to be shaped as their primary medium, opposed but also co-opted. The generative theology not only sustains but defines the binary opposite realized in the dialectics that comes to expression here too. It is in the conception of Torah as part of culture and separate from culture. And that explains why some Yeshiva-masters counsel studying mathematics and astrophysics along with Torah, and many do; and others advise studying only Torah, wherein all worth knowing is contained, and many more do.

Notes

[1] We know the social from the solipsistic by reference to the language rules that prevail. One can say, "My Judaism," meaning, one's private belief and practice, called, idiosyncratically, "Judaism," which is not uncommon, and "My Torah," which in most contexts of Judaic society would constitute an oxymoron. One can say, "the Torah of Moses," or "the Torah of Rabbi Aqiba," but the only "my" that works with "Torah" in Hebrew, the sole language that is native to Judaism, is God's, as in "It is My Torah, do not abandon it," of the governing liturgy.

[2] In a well-crafted system, of course, principal parts prove interchangeable or closely aligned, and that is surely the case here. But I have already observed that the successor-system is far more tightly constructed than the initial one, in that the politics and the economics flow into one another, in a way in which, in the initial, philosophical system, they do not. The disembedded character of the Mishnah's economics has already impressed us.

JACOB NEUSNER

Z

ZIONISM IN MOROCCAN JUDAISM: Defined in broad religious and nationalistic terms, Zionism is the attachment of Jews to the land of Israel, *Eretz Yisrael*, the messianic yearnings for redemption, the prayer and hope for the restoration of the national homeland, and the ingathering of exiles. Such Zionism is as old as exile itself and has been widespread among all Jews at all times. It antedates the political Zionism of Herzl as well as the spiritual Zionism of Ahad Ha'am. It may be called pre-Herzlian Zionism. A midrash states that the messiah was born on the very day the Temple in

Jerusalem was destroyed (Num. Rabbah 7). Clearly, the general idea conveyed by this midrash seems to be that the messianic yearning for redemption set in as soon as the Jews found themselves in exile, outside their homeland, with the symbol of their national existence, the Temple, in ruins.

In Arab lands, Zionism was generally conceived in religio-messianic terms. It was inspired by the traditional yearning for redemption and reinforced by the fiercely Zionistic poems of Judah Halevi, which form an integral part of Sephardic liturgy. The Jews of the Arab world had also maintained direct ties with the land of Israel due in part to the physical proximity of most Arab lands to the Holy Land and the fact that, until colonial times, the majority of those Jews lived in the Ottoman Empire, of which Palestine was a part.

The Jews of North Africa, and those of Morocco in particular, have been known for their deep attachment to the land of Israel. The love of *Eretz Yisrael* and the messianic yearnings for redemption were always in the forefront of their religious consciousness. The eyes of Moroccan Jews, like those of Jews everywhere, were forever turned towards Jerusalem in prayer for and in anticipation of the coming of the messiah. This love for *Eretz Yisrael* permeated all aspects of Moroccan Jewish life including prayer, poetry, customs and rituals, humor and folklore. It found expression in a number of specific and concrete manifestations, the most striking of which are:

1. The generosity and readiness with which they extended financial assistance to the old *yishuv* (Jewish settlement) in the land of Israel.
2. The messianic-nationalistic motif of the Moroccan *piyyutim* and the important role these *piyyutim* played in spreading and intensifying the Zionist or messianic fervor among Moroccan Jews, due in great measure to their popular aspect.
3. Customs unique to Moroccan Jews that were based from their inception on the attachment to and love for *Eretz Yisrael*.
4. Actual immigration, *aliyah*, to *Eretz Yisrael*, which dates back to the earliest days of the *yishuv*, an *aliyah* that really never stopped.

This essay deals with Moroccan Zionism both before and after Herzl. It first dis-cusses briefly the financial help extended by Moroccan Jewry to the old *yishuv* and focuses on their immigration to Palestine during the pre-Herzlian period. Next, it deals in broad outline with the response of Moroccan Jews to modern Zionism and their massive immigration to the State of Israel.

Financial Assistance to the Old Yishuv: One of the expressions of Moroccan Jewry's attachment to the land of Israel was the generosity and readiness with which they extended financial help to the old *yishuv*, which, as is well known, depended for its livelihood and sustenance on the generosity of diaspora Jews. Emissaries were sent from the main centers of the *yishuv* on a mission (*shelihut*) to various Jewish communities to collect funds for the yeshivot (known also as *kolelim*; sing., *Kolel*) in the Holy Land. This practice was fairly institutionalized by the beginning of the seventeenth century. The emissaries were known as *shadarim* (the singular *shadar* being an acronym of *shaliah de-rahamana*, lit., an envoy or emissary of God). Initially, emissaries were sent from Jerusalem, Hebron, and Safed. After the Jewish settlement in Tiberias was renewed in 1740, it was added to the list. Together these cities became known as "the four holy cities" or *arba' ha-'aratzot*.

The Jews of North Africa, and particularly the Jews of Morocco, maintained very strong and close ties with the *yishuv*. Their rabbis corresponded with rabbis in *Eretz Yisrael* and at times even sought their halakhic guidance. Naturally, the emissaries played a significant role in strengthening these ties. They acted as a living bridge between the *yishuv* and the North African communities. In fact, according to Abraham Ya'ari in his monumental historical study, *Sheluhe Eretz Yisrael* . . . (Jerusalem, 1950/1951), the Jewish communities of North Africa constituted one of the four most important regions of *shelihut* activity, that is, countries visited by these emissaries (the others being Turkey/Bukhara, Holland, and Italy).

The Jews of Morocco always responded generously to the regular solicitations of funds by these emissaries, whose frequent visits were awaited with much anticipation. They received them with great warmth, honor, and respect, and accorded them all the affection they felt for the land of Israel itself. Moreover, since these emissaries were usually men of learning and scholarship, the Moroccans looked up to them for spiritual inspiration and even guidance in matters of Torah and halakhah. They firmly believed that "Torah shall go forth from Zion and the word of God from Jerusalem." Incidentally, these *shadarim* were also instrumental in spreading the latest developments in Moroccan Rabbinic thought and literature to other Sephardi communities. In discussing the experience of emissaries who were sent to Morocco, Ya'ari writes:

> The Jews of North Africa were always distinguished with a great measure of love for *Eretz Yisrael*, and the degree of success of the mission of the emissaries in these communities did not depend on the good will of these communities, for they were always well disposed to all matters having to do with *Eretz Yisrael*; rather, it depended on the political and economic conditions of the time, over which the Jews had no control.

Similarly, Rabbi Jacob Moshe Toledano, the first historian of Moroccan Jewry, in discussing the attitude of Moroccan Jews to emissaries from *Eretz Yisrael*, states:

> Their love for *Eretz Yisrael* is marvelous and awe-inspiring. They donate their last "pennies" to Rabbi Meir Ba'al Hanes and Rabbi Shim'on Bar Yohai; and the emissary who visits them, be he Sephardi or Ashkenazi, is received with great honor and respect and is accorded hospitality and given contributions way beyond their means.

In support of this statement, Toledano published in his *Otzar ha-Genazim* (Jerusalem, 1960) an agreement-document (*haskamah*) made by the Jewish community of Fez in 1797 on the division of funds collected for the land of Israel between the four holy cities, Jerusalem, Hebron, Tiberias, and Safed. He adds:

> This agreement proves how much and to what extent the Jews of Morocco remembered Jerusalem and the other three cities, Hebron, Tiberias, and Safed on every happy occasion; and if, by chance, the

groom [who was called to the Torah] forgot to make a donation to *Eretz Yisrael*, the entire congregation would immediately shout, "Ah! *Arba' ha-aratzot!*" (meaning, "what about the four cities!") to remind him of his obligation.

An examination of the sources reveals that emissaries from the *yisuhv* were sent to Morocco as early as the end of the sixteenth century. In a recent article on the relations between Moroccan Jewry and the land of Israel, Haim Bentov shows that not only were emissaries sent to Morocco as early as the end of the sixteenth century but that by then Morocco already was considered one of the central regions of *shelihut* activity. From then on, emissaries continued to visit Morocco on a regular basis until 1936-1939, when Rabbi Jacob Hay Abikhzir made what would be the last visit.

The number of emissaries who visited Morocco at the end of the eighteenth century and during the nineteenth century was especially impressive compared with the number of emissaries who were sent to the rest of the diaspora. Thus, between 1778 and 1878, twenty emissaries went from Safed to Morocco and other Jewish communities in North Africa. Most of these emissaries were themselves of Moroccan origin. Likewise, between 1837 and 1880, twenty-seven emissaries went from Tiberias to the entire diaspora; of these, twenty went to Morocco, two went to Tunisia, Algeria and Tripoli, and only five to the rest of the Jewish world. Between 1830 and 1862, more than fifteen emissaries went from Jerusalem to North Africa, and ten of them went to Morocco. From 1862 to 1900, eleven emissaries were sent by the Sephardi Community Council of Jerusalem to Morocco. Ten more were sent there by the Moroccan community in Jerusalem, which by then had secured the right to send its own emissaries.

These numbers are very instructive as to the centrality of Moroccan Jewry in *shelihut* activity as well as to the relatively large number of Moroccan Jews involved in the settlement of the land of Israel. Abraham Ya'ari makes an astute and telling observation regarding the significance of these numbers. He points out, for example, that in the last quarter of the seventeenth century, emissaries went from Jerusalem to North Africa one after another. Ya'ari adds that, "if, notwithstanding their number, each emissary managed to get a considerable contribution, it is because Jerusalem itself was the home of a large colony of North African Jews whose ties with their native communities remained very strong." It seems reasonable to assume that Ya'ari's observation and conclusion are as applicable to the number of emissaries who went from Jerusalem to Morocco in the second half of the nineteenth century (1862-1890) as well as those who went then from Tiberias and Safed to Morocco. That is, if, notwithstanding their number, they all managed to make sizable collections, it is because these cities were the homes of large communities of Moroccan Jews who maintained strong ties with their native communities.

Emissaries continued to visit Morocco and other communities in North Africa as late as the middle of the twentieth century. With the outbreak of World War I, *shelihut* activity stopped altogether. At the end of the war, the Sephardi Community Council of Jerusalem began to reorganize the institution. But income from the *shelihut* during the period between the two World Wars dwindled considerably compared to what it had been previously. Nonetheless, the *shelihut* of North Africa continued to constitute the major share of the Council's income. Thus, during this period, the Council sent thirteen emissaries to North Africa, approximately half the total number of emissaries it sent to the entire diaspora.

As stated above, Moroccan Jews extended the love and affection they felt for *Eretz Yisrael* to its emissaries. This was expressed in several ways, including warm receptions, lavish hospitality appropriate to the status of the emissaries, honors bestowed in the synagogue, and the extent to which the Rabbinic and communal leaders extended themselves on their behalf in order to spare them hard work and to ensure that their mission met with success.

More important, the love and affection shown the emissaries by the Jews of Morocco are reflected in the number of *piyyutim* (religious poems) composed in their honor by Moroccan rabbis and by the number of *kinot* (elegies) composed to mourn their death. Thus, Rabbi David Ben Hassin, the renowned and popular Moroccan *paytan* (religious poet) from Meknes, composed poems in honor of six emissaries, and one *kinah* to mourn the death of Rabbi Amram Ben Diwan, an emissary from Hebron who died suddenly in Morocco in 1782.

Finally, in addition to funds raised by the emissaries, there were other forms of financial assistance extended to the old *yishuv* by Moroccan Jews. Wills and trusts made in favor of Jews living in *Eretz Yisrael* constituted another source of income for the Jewish settlement there. A number of responsa indicate that some Moroccan Jews left a share of their estates (and in some cases entire estates) to Jews living in Jerusalem and the other holy cities. At times, they established trusts the income of which was earmarked for helping the needy and scholars of one of the four holy cities.

Aliyah—Sixteenth-Nineteenth Centuries: The generous response of Moroccan Jews to the continuous influx of *shadarim*, the messianic yearning and deep love for the land of Israel permeating Moroccan *piyyutim*, and some of the unique customs that are tied up in one way or another with the land of Israel and the messiah all illustrate the degree to which the love of *Eretz Israel* filled the entire existence and religious experience of Moroccan Jewry. Yet, it seems that this nationalistic fervor found its ultimate and fullest expression in *aliyah*, immigration to Israel, an immigration that really never stopped.

In reviewing the sources, one is struck by the incredible continuity of the presence of Moroccan Jews in *Eretz Yisrael* beginning with the sixteenth century and continuing to the present. The Jews of North Africa in general and those of Morocco in particular immigrated continuously and constituted a significant segment of the old *yishuv*. They strengthened it numerically and morally, helped consolidate it, and in many cases were among its leaders. From the sixteenth century onwards, we find Moroccan Jewish communities all over Israel's urban centers.

Moreover, after the sixteenth century, the *Maghrebi* community (*'Adat ha-Ma'aravim*), as North African Jews called themselves, was second in size and importance only to that of the Spanish speaking Sephardim, both in Jerusalem and the Galilee.

Early Years: As early as the tenth and eleventh centuries, we encounter Jews from what later became known as Morocco, Tunisia, Algeria and Libya. One of the rabbis appointed to the *gaonate* in Israel in the eleventh century was Rabbi Shelomo ben Yehuda al-Fasi of Fez. In his responsa, Maimonides mentions Rabbi Moshe Ed-Dar'i who immigrated to Israel in the second half of the twelfth century. In Jerusalem, Al-Harizi (1170-1235) found a significant *Maghrebi* community headed by Rabbi Eliyahu ha-Ma'aravi.

Following the expulsion of Jews from Spain in 1492, many Spanish exiles went to Morocco. But for many of them, Morocco was only a stop on their way to Israel. [Such for example, were Rabbis Abraham Zakkut, Jacob Berab, and Abraham Azulay as well as other equally renowned spiritual leaders of the time.] During the sixteenth and seventeenth centuries, following the conquest of the land of Israel by Sultan Selim in 1517, immigration increased considerably. Continuing for two to three generations, it greatly increased the Jewish settlement and advanced its consolidation. While this immigration consisted mostly of Spanish and Portuguese exiles, we learn from various sources that North African Jews' share in this immigration was not insignificant. We find them especially in the Galilee and in Jerusalem, organized in separate and distinct *Maghrebi* communities (*'Adat ha-Ma'aravim*).

Moroccan Jews in Safed: After 1517, the majority of both the Spanish and Portuguese exiles and North African immigrants settled in Safed, which developed into an important commercial and industrial town as well as a center of Jewish mysticism. Various sources attest to the presence of Moroccan rabbis and mystics there as early as the beginning of the sixteenth century. A petition sent from Safed to Jerusalem in 1504 regarding the matter of *shemittah* (sabbatical year) includes the name of a Moroccan rabbi among its signatories. Rabbi Jacob Moshe Toledano relates that Rabbi Yissakhar Sussan, who had emigrated with his father from Fez to Jerusalem in 1530, settled in Safed in 1546 where he joined the *Maghrebi* community and became one of its dignitaries. Toledano relates further that, in 1577, a group of *mekubbalim* (mystics) from southern Morocco immigrated to Safed, joining other Moroccan rabbis who were studying Qabbalah under the famous mystic master Rabbi Isaac Luria, known popularly as the Ari.

In a letter dated 1603, Rabbi Shelomo Shlumil from Moravia mentions that his teacher of Qabbalah was Rabbi Mes'od Azulay from Fez who was "famous in all Israel for his great piety and saintliness and for his mastery of all the secrets of the Torah." Finally, Rabbi Moshe Basula who was in Safed in 1522 records that he found there more than three hundred families as well as three synagogues: one for the Spanish speaking Sephardim; a second one for the *Moriscim* (local Jews who were there before the Sephardim); and a third for the *Ma'aravim* (North African Jews). He adds that the latter group called theirs Elijah's Synagogue, because it was very old, and tradition has it that Elijah prayed in it.

From another source we learn that the *Maghrebi* community in Safed not only had their own synagogue but their own dwelling quarters as well. Thus, in a government census prepared in 1526, mention is made of four separate quarters in Safed as follows: *Musta'rabim* (same as *Moriscim*) quarter, 130 families; Frank quarter, 48 families; Portuguese quarter, 21 families; and *Maghrebi quarter*, 33 families. It shows that outside the indigenous group of *Musta'rabim*, the *Maghrebi* community constituted the second largest group.

Both the Spanish and Portuguese exiles and the North Africans included not only scholars and mystics but also wealthy merchants, and various craftsmen and artisans, all of whom contributed to the flourishing of Safed and the consolidation of its Jewish settlement. Interestingly, we learn from various sources that even during its years of decline (1800-1900), Safed still had two thousand Jewish families, again separated into four groups (Sephardim, *Parushim*, Hasidim, and *Ma'aravim*), and that they continued to live their separate lives in separate quarters and synagogues.

Moroccan Jews in Tiberias: An early attempt, in the middle of the sixteenth century, by Dona Gracia Mendes and her nephew Don Yoseph Nasi, the wealthy Marrano statesman and leader, to rebuild the city and renew its Jewish settlement met with some initial success. The rebuilt Tiberias began to attract Jewish settlers from Safed and from the diaspora. Their success, however, was short lived, and by the time of Don Yoseph Nasi's death in 1579 Tiberias was again in decline. As a result of various political and economic factors, the deterioration continued, and, by 1644 it lay again in ruins.

It was not until 1740 that the Jewish settlement in Tiberias was renewed by Rabbi Hayim Abulafia. The Turkish governor at the time, Zahir al-Omar, had extended his rule over the Galilee. He invited the Jews of Turkey and especially Rabbi Abulafia to come to Tiberias and renew its Jewish settlement. Rabbi Abulafia accepted the invitation and arrived in 1740. Seizing this historic opportunity, he immediately and energetically set about renewing the Jewish settlement. In a relatively short time, he managed to build houses, stores, a synagogue, and even a bathhouse. He apparently saw in this renewal the beginning of *kibbutz galuyot* (the ingathering of exiles) and the resettlement of the land of Israel as a whole.

Many of the Jews of Safed, in decline at the time, moved to Tiberias, *Maghrebi* Jews among them. Rabbi Abulafia's efforts had impressed many Jews who saw in his initiative "*athalta de-geulah* (the beginning of redemption)." As a result, Tiberias again began attracting Jews from the diaspora including those of North Africa. But the immigration of North African Jews, especially those from Morocco, reached serious proportions only in the nineteenth century. In the second half of the nineteenth century, it reached relatively speaking massive proportions.

Tiberias apparently had a special attraction for Moroccans because of its sanctity

and because of the tomb of Rabbi Meir Ba'al Hanes and other saintly rabbis buried in and around the city. Moroccan rabbis flocked to Tiberias to study in its yeshivot. Its emissaries were the most popular among Moroccan Jews, because of the tomb of Rabbi Meir Ba'al Hanes. Rabbi David Ben Hassin, the renowned Moroccan *paytan*, expressed Moroccan Jews' love for Tiberias in his popular *Piyyut*, "*Ohil yom yom 'eshta'eh.*"

In his *Otzar ha-Genazim* Rabbi Jacob Moshe Toledano states that the number of immigrants to Israel from Morocco in general, and from the city of Meknes in particular, reached the hundreds in 1860 and that three hundred of them went to Tiberias. He further states that until 1840-1860, Tiberias was settled mostly by Turkish Jews who spoke Spanish or Ladino, but after 1860, when hundreds of Jews from Meknes arrived, Ladino and Spanish were replaced by Moroccan Arabic, and Tiberias was nick-named "*Meknes ha-ketanah* (the small Meknes)." He also relates that after 1860, the leadership of the Jewish community in Tiberias was taken over by Moroccan rabbis.

Toledano's claim regarding the large number of Moroccan Jews who arrived in Tiberias after 1860 is confirmed by another source. From Ya'ari's list of emissaries who went from Tiberias to Morocco, we learn that between 1837 and 1900, of the twenty seven emissaries sent from Tiberias to the diaspora, twenty went to Morocco, two to Tripoli, Tunisia and Algeria, and only five to the rest of the diaspora. Moreover, of the twenty who went to Morocco, many went more than once (some even three to four times). Finally, of the twenty, twelve were Moroccan natives who were now being sent there by the community in Tiberias.

From Ya'ari's list as well as many other sources cited by Toledano and Y. Ben Tzvi, it is clear that during the nineteenth century, the greatest support for Tiberias came from the Jews of Morocco. It is equally clear that the reason for this was that the Jewish community in Tiberias at the time was made up mostly of Moroccan Jews.

Moroccan Jews in Jerusalem: Because of its holy character, Jerusalem had always attracted Jews from all the diaspora. But as in the Galilee, immigration to Jerusalem reached serious proportions only after its capture by the Turks in 1517. Since then, it has never stopped. Among the immigrants to Jerusalem during the sixteenth and seventeenth centuries were North African Jews, who constituted one of the more important communities in the city. Rabbi Jonathan ben Hayim Sholal, a rabbi from Tlemcen, Algeria, who immigrated to Jerusalem in the last quarter of the fifteenth century, was chosen Chief Rabbi and Rosh Yeshiva in Jerusalem in 1479.

Rabbi Aryeh Lev Frumkin, in his book, *The History of the Rabbis of Jerusalem* (Jerusalem, no date), mentions many North African (and especially Moroccan) rabbis who lived and were active in Jerusalem from the sixteenth century through the end of the nineteenth century. Among the most famous of these were:

1. Issakhar ben Susan, who emigrated from Fez to Jerusalem in 1530 and was one of the disciples of Rabbi Levi ben Habib.
2. Abraham ben Rabbi Mordekhai Azulay (of Fez), a Spanish rabbi who settled in Morocco after 1492 and from there immigrated to Israel. He is the author of *Hesed le-Abraham* and grandfather of the famous Rabbi Hayim Yosef David Azulay, known popularly as the *Hida*.
3. Hayim ben Attar of Sale, Morocco, author of the biblical commentary *Or ha-Hayim*, known popularly as the *Or ha-Hayim ha-kadosh* ("the saintly *Or ha-Hayim*"). He arrived in Jerusalem in 1742, where he founded *Yeshivat Kenesset Israel*.
4. Judah 'Iyyash, who emigrated with his four sons from Algeria to Jerusalem in 1758. He was later chosen as the *Av Bet Din* (presiding judge) and Chief Rabbi of Jerusalem.
5. Jacob Moshe 'Iyyash, one of the sons of Rabbi Judah, who founded *Yeshivat Hayim va-Hesed* in Jerusalem. In 1806, he was elected as *Rishon le-Tzion* and Chief Rabbi of *Eretz Yisrael*.
6. David ben Shim'on (known as *Tsuf Devash*), Chief Rabbi and founder of the independent *Maghrebi* community in Jerusalem. He immigrated to Jerusalem from Rabat, Morocco, in 1854.
7. Raphael ben Shim'on, son of Rabbi David and his successor as Chief Rabbi of the *Maghrebi* community.

We know of the existence of a separate community of *Maghrebi* Jews in Jerusalem from as early as the beginning of the sixteenth century. Rabbi Moshe Basola who visited Jerusalem in 1522 relates that at the time the Jewish community in Jerusalem was made up of four distinct groups: Ashkenazim, *Musta'rabim* (or *Moriscim*), Spanish speaking Sephardim, and the *Ma'aravim* (*Maghrebi*). He notes that the rabbis and judges (*dayyanim*) represented all groups.

The seventeenth century was marked by difficult economic conditions as well as a harsh attitude on the part of the local rulers. Nonetheless, the Jewish population succeeded in consolidating its position in Jerusalem. Jerusalem even regained the spiritual leadership, which it had lost to Safed during the previous century. It was now the center of most of the scholars of the land of Israel. Also, Jerusalem continued to attract many pilgrims who came to pray in its holy places. Many of these pilgrims ended up staying. Some even wrote to their relatives in the Diaspora encouraging them to join them. As a result, the various groups of the Jewish community in Jerusalem, including the *Maghrebi* one, were strengthened. As mentioned above, during the last quarter of the seventeenth century, emissaries went from to Jerusalem to North Africa one after another. And as Ya'ari points out, notwithstanding their number, each managed to collect a considerable contribution because Jerusalem itself was the home of a large colony of North African Jews whose ties with their native communities remained very strong.

In 1742, Rabbi Hayim ben Attar arrived in Jerusalem with a group of thirty students and founded the yeshivah *Kenesset Israel*. While monetary support for his yeshivah came mainly from the Jews of Italy, we know from the sources that the scholars who came with him were mostly former students and colleagues from Morocco. As a result, his *aliyah* strengthened the *Maghrebi* community in Jerusalem both spiritually and numerically.

The first years of the nineteenth century were difficult for Jerusalem. Nonetheless, the *Maghrebi* community held its own. Emissaries continued to go to North Africa and especially to Morocco. Between 1830 and 1860, more than fifteen emissaries went from Jerusalem to North Africa, and, of these, ten went to Morocco. Again, the number of emissaries and the success of their mission is indicative of the presence of a sizable group of *Maghrebi* Jews in Jerusalem and of the strong ties they maintained with their native country.

While it is rather difficult to establish with absolute certainty the exact number of either *Maghrebi* Jews or the general Jewish population in Jerusalem at this time, it can be safely stated that the Jewish population of Jerusalem towards the middle of the nineteenth century numbered anywhere from five to seven thousand souls. Likewise, all the sources agree that the majority of the Jews of Jerusalem at this period were Sephardim and that these included a sizable *Maghrebi* community. Abraham Ya'ari puts the number of *Maghrebi* Jews in Jerusalem in the middle of the nineteenth century at one thousand souls. At any rate, the immigration of Moroccan Jews to Jerusalem increased considerably following that of Rabbi David ben Shim'on from Rabat, Morocco, in 1854. In fact, the immigration of Moroccan Jews to Jerusalem, as in the case of Tiberias, reached serious proportions in the second half of the nineteenth century due no doubt to the impact of Rabbi David ben Shim'on and his leadership.

Rabbi ben Shim'on, who became known affectionately as *Tsuf Devash* (lit., drink of honey, *devash* being an acronym of his Hebrew name), was a great scholar as well as a man of action. He was an inspiring and effective leader. Shortly after his arrival, he was appointed first rabbi and presiding judge (*Av Bet Din*) of the *Maghrebi* community. In this capacity, he reorganized the community, establishing for it independent religious, educational, and communal institutions. He even secured for it the right to send its own emissaries to the diaspora, a right denied the Moroccan community by the Sephardic council until 1860. Under the able and forceful leadership of Rabbi David ben Shim'on, it established its own communal, religious, and educational institutions, including its own *shelihut*, i.e., the

sending of its own emissaries to the diaspora. Following 1860, emissaries of the new *Maghrebi* community went to Morocco one after another. Between 1862 and 1900, ten visited Morocco in addition to eleven who went there on behalf of the Sephardi community.

In order to enlarge and consolidate the now independent community, David ben Shim'on tried to build it a new neighborhood. For that purpose, he bought a parcel of land outside the old city in 1870. A year later, he sent emissaries to Europe to collect money for his project. At that time, two wealthy and prominent Moroccan Jewish families, the 'Amiels and Abishdids, immigrated to Jerusalem, where they played an active role in the affairs of the *Maghrebi* community. They built synagogues in the old city, including the large synagogue of the *Ma'aravim*, which was named *Tsuf Devash* in honor of Rabbi David ben Shim'on. Rabbi ben Shim'on died in 1880 and was succeeded in the leadership of the community by his elder son, Rabbi Raphael ben Shim'on, a scholar and a leader in his own right.

A document published recently by Ruth Kark in the journal *Pe'amim* proves that Moroccans were the first local Jewish residents of Jerusalem to purchase land (in 1866) and build a neighborhood outside the walled city. The same document shows that the initiative for building this neighborhood was taken by individual Moroccan Jews even before David ben Shim'on embarked on his project. In fact, it was from one of these individuals, Eliyahu Ezra, that Rabbi ben Shim'on purchased the land for his project. At any rate, it was on the land purchased by these Moroccan Jews that the *Maghrebi* neighborhood, *Mahaneh Israel*, known as *shekhunat ha-Ma'aravim*, the first neighborhood outside the walled city, was built.

Moroccan Jews in Other Cities: It is clear that beginning with the sixteenth century through the end of the nineteenth century, North African and especially Moroccan Jews constituted an important community both in the Galilee and in Jerusalem. It must be added, however, that beginning with the nineteenth century, we find Moroccan Jews not only there but in other places as well, most notably in Jaffa, Shefar'am, Gaza, and Ramleh.

Of particular interest is a story connected with the renewal of the Jewish settlement in Jaffa by *Maghrebi* Jews. S. Ben Tzion relates, on the authority of the elders of Jaffa, that in 1838 a boat sailed from Morocco with many Moroccan Jews who wanted to settle in the land of Israel. They had apparently intended to settle in the Galilee, but their boat was wrecked before they reached the Carmel. Twelve drowned, but the others were miraculously saved and managed to get to Haifa. Later, however, they decided against staying. They were businessmen, and at the time Haifa was no more than a deserted village. They went first to Nablus and then to Jerusalem, but stayed in neither. Even Jerusalem was no place for commerce, for its Jewish residents "look to the *halukah* (money collected by emissaries)" for their livelihood. They finally settled in Jaffa. Among them was the family of Abraham Shloush from Tlemcen, Algeria, who was to play a vital role in the renewal of its Jewish settlement. Aaron Shloush, barely eleven when he arrived with his family, would later buy most of the land surrounding the city. It was on this land that the new Jewish neighborhoods of *Neveh Tsedek* and *Neveh Shalom* were built. According to M.D. Gaon (in his book *Yehude ha-Mizrah be-Eretz Yisrael*, vol. II), Aaron Shloush developed an interest in the development of the Jewish settlement in Jaffa in 1898. For that purpose, he bought all the land in the center of the city as well. He divided it into small lots that he sold at affordable prices to the Jewish residents. Ze'ev Vilna'i relates that a list of the Jewish residents of Jaffa submitted to M. Montefiori in 1839 already included the names of *Maghrebi* Jews from Rabat, Sale, Marrakesh, Oran, and Algiers. He adds that the Arabic-speaking *Maghrebis*, whose way of life resembled that of the Arabs in many ways, adjusted to their new surroundings in no time. They engaged in crafts, commerce, and shop-keeping. They even opened shops in the Arab market.

Likewise, Moroccan Jews played an important role in the renewal of the Jewish settlement in Shefar'am. Ben Tzvi writes that according to the report of the English commission, which researched and measured the land of Israel in the 1870s, "thirty Moroccan Jewish families settled in Shefar'am in the 1840s and engaged in agriculture." Ben Tzvi adds that the settlement of these Moroccan Jews "prolonged the existence of the Jewish settlement in Shefar'am by fifty years." This settlement, however, declined gradually, so that by 1870 only six Jewish families (thirty persons) remained there. Again, immigrants from Morocco came to the aid of the dwindling community. In 1890, responding to an appeal by the local *Hakham Bashi* for the strengthening of the Jewish settlement in Shefar'am, twelve more Moroccan Jewish families joined the Jewish community in Shefar'am. Ben Tzvi notes that these Moroccan immigrants included shoemakers, blacksmiths, peddlers, and one physician.

Moroccan Jews also helped renew Jewish settlements in Gaza and Ramleh towards the end of the nineteenth century. Following Napoleon's invasion of Palestine in 1799, Gaza's Jewish settlement declined considerably, until, by 1811, it ceased to exist. However, it was renewed after 1870, and among its first settlers were two Moroccans. This settlement increased appreciably during the ten years preceding the First World War, when it numbered two hundred Jews half of whom were Moroccans. Similarly, one of the sources quoted by Ben Tzvi relates that the first Jews who settled in Ramleh at the end of the nineteenth century were six Moroccans who had businesses in Athens and Damascus and who returned to their homes in Jaffa for Shabbat and holidays. It is clear from all the above that North African Jews and particularly Moroccan Jews played a significant role in the renewal of the Jewish settlement in *Eretz Yisrael* not only in the Galilee and Jerusalem but in other cities as well.

Distinguishing Features of the Aliyah of Moroccan Jews to *Eretz Yisrael*: A number of important sources published in recent years provide a wealth of information about the immigration of Moroccan Jews to the land of Israel during the second half of the eighteenth and the nineteenth century. From these sources we learn not only about the immigration of Moroccan Jews during this period but also about various spiritual, cultural, and social features that characterized this immigration. Based on these and other sources, it is possible to identify five such features:

1. *Commitment to Aliyah in legal deeds*. Moroccan Jews wrote legal deeds in which a number of individuals committed themselves to emigrate together. Anyone changing his mind would have to pay a fine. Some of the compelling reasons for these legal contracts were considerations of safety as well as the desire to insure the success of their *aliyah* and the ease of their absorption in the land of Israel. It was safer and more pleasant to travel in a group and in the company of relatives and friends than to do so alone. Likewise, they were convinced that it would be much easier for them to adjust to a new life in a strange environment if they were with friends and relatives rather than cut off from all family and social ties—a factor likely to cause them to return to Morocco. But these legal contracts also show the seriousness of purpose with which Moroccan Jews undertook *aliyah*. By entering into legally binding contracts, they assured each other of their determination to emigrate, thus enabling each other to prepare seriously for the long journey without the fear of anyone else's sudden change of heart.

2. *Aliyah Ordered in Wills as a Religious Duty*. Another feature of *aliyah* was fathers' inclusion in their wills of orders to their sons to emigrate to the land of Israel, thereby making *aliyah* a religious duty incumbent on their children by virtue of the religious obligation to honor one's parent's will (*mitzvah le-kayyem divre ha-met*). This shows that Moroccan Jews regarded *aliyah* as an essential religious duty. Similarly, an examination of the responsa of Moroccan rabbis shows that nearly all of them, especially during the eighteenth and nineteenth centuries, held that residence in the land of Israel (and by implication *aliyah*) was an important obligation incumbent on each Jew even during the period of exile.

3. *Continuous and Massive Aliyah*. Another important feature of this *aliyah* was its continuous and massive character as well as the persistence, energy, and determination with which Moroccan Jews approached it. It took place in every generation, sometimes involving large numbers. It did not remain a dream but became a reality. Thus, as soon as someone decided on *aliyah*, or following the legal commitment of several individuals to emigrate together, they would immediately take concrete steps towards the implementation of their decision, selling homes, liquidating businesses, packing belongings, preparing provisions for the long journey, and setting out on the journey. Even when people failed to reach their destination because of factors beyond their control, they tried again and again and did not give up until they eventually realized their dreams. And while during the sixteenth and seventeenth centuries Moroccan immigration was limited to individuals and small groups, beginning with the end of the eighteenth century and throughout the nineteenth century it reached relatively serious and massive proportions.

4. *Social and Professional Diversity of Immigrants*. A fourth feature of this immigration was the social and professional diversity of the groups that emigrated from Morocco. This *aliyah* was not limited to the elderly wishing to spend their last years in the Holy Land; nor was it confined to rabbis and scholars desiring to study Torah and live on charity. Rather, the immigrants included entire families, men, women, and children, young and old. Similarly, among the immigrants were people of many trades and professions, as well as merchants and farmers. This was especially true of those who settled in Jaffa, Shefar'am, and Ramleh.

5. *Religious and Nationalistic Motivation for Aliyah*. A final feature of this *aliyah* was that it was motivated by the strong nationalistic feelings of Moroccan Jews. From the various sources at our disposal, it is clear that while certain local difficulties, such as political instability, economic hardships, and Arab hostility, occasionally hastened Moroccans' departure, these were not the chief factors responsible for their *aliyah*. After all, the political and social conditions of the Jews in the Holy Land were not much better than those prevailing in Morocco. In fact, economic opportunities and sources of livelihood were much more limited in the land of Israel then. Rather, the decisive motivation for the continuous and persistent immigration of Moroccan Jews to *Eretz Yisrael* was their strong attachment to and deep love for it, their fervent messianic and nationalistic yearnings for redemption, and their

strong desire to live in the vicinity of the holy places in the land of Israel. These strong nationalistic feelings were reinforced by the strong ties Moroccan Jews maintained with the Jewish settlement in *Eretz Yisrael*, which included sizable Moroccan communities, throughout the centuries. Likewise, the emissaries who visited the Moroccan Jewish communities helped strengthen these ties by their enthusiastic and inspiring preaching for *aliyah*. Finally, as mentioned above, the messianic and nationalistic *piyyutim* popular among Moroccan Jews helped spread and intensify their nationalistic feelings and keep the love of *Eretz Yisrael* in the forefront of their religious consciousness.

The relatively large scale immigration of Moroccan Jews to the land of Israel that characterized their *aliyah* during the second half of the eighteenth and the nineteenth centuries continued unabated through the end of the nineteenth century. Large groups from most cities in Morocco continued to make their way to the land of Israel throughout the end of the nineteenth century and the beginning of the twentieth century. But with the outbreak of World War I, contact with *Eretz Yisrael* was explicitly prohibited by the French authorities, on the pretext that Palestine was Turkish territory. Between World War I and World War II, a number of internal and external factors (totally beyond Moroccan Jews' control) converged to discourage and even put a stop to the immigration of Moroccan Jews to Israel.

Moroccan Jewry's Response to Modern Zionism: The news of the founding of the Zionist movement spread rapidly throughout Morocco and triggered great enthusiasm among the small elite who could read Hebrew and/or European languages. Within a few years of the First Zionist Congress in Basel, chapters or "cells" of the Zionist movement sprang up all over the major cities in Morocco. The first was founded in the coastal city of Mogador (Essaouira) in 1900 and was called *Sha'are Tzion* (Zion's Gates). The society in Mogador was headed by David Bohbot and Samuel Bendahan and by the community's spiritual leader, Rabbi Jacob Ifargan. It was the first group that popular-

ized the *shekel* (the official membership dues established by the Zionist movement) in North Africa. It transmitted to the Zionist Federation in Cologne over two hundred *shekels*, which entitled the Mogador chapter to send two delegates to the Fifth Zionist Congress, although it did not take advantage of this opportunity. Its president wrote Theodor Herzl asking him for literature (in Hebrew) on the new movement. It is to be noted that it is no accident that the first Moroccan chapter of the Zionist movement was founded in Mogador, for Mogador was a Moroccan center of *haskalah* (Jewish enlightenment) and the cultivation of Hebrew culture. The *haskalah* had made inroads in Mogador in the latter part of the nineteenth century. Its *maskilim* were in direct contact with Europe. They received Hebrew books and newspapers, and some of them even contributed articles to European Hebrew periodicals of the time.

At the same time, and with no coordination with the association in Mogador, a second association, *Shivat Tzion* (Return to Zion) was founded in Tetouan in northern Morocco through the initiative of Dr. Y. Berdiawsky, a Russian Jew who had settled in the north. This association set up a Hebrew library to propagate the language and the Zionist idea among members of the larger community. Four years later, a third association, *Ahavat Tzion* (Love of Zion) was founded in the coastal town of Safi. In a letter to Theodor Herzl, Meir bar Sheshet and Jacob Murciano, the officers of the association, expressed the readiness of their society to serve Zionism, although they confessed, "its members do not have yet a clear notion of what the movement is all about." In the same letter, the association asked Herzl to send them a Hebrew translation of his book, *The Jewish State*, as well as any other reading material in Hebrew on the nature and goals of the new movement, so that they too "will be able to help this great undertaking" with all their might.

The news and message of Zionism took a few more years to reach the cities in the interior of Morocco, which had not been as exposed to European influence and languages. Accordingly, it was only in 1908 that a Zionist association, *Hibbat Tzion*

(Love of Zion), was founded in Fez. The new association in Fez sent letters to Cologne and began disseminating the *shekel*. It expanded its activities to Sefrou and Meknes where it opened chapters or sections in 1909 and 1910 respectively. The chapter of *Hibbat Tzion* in Meknes was headed by the city's Chief Rabbi, Joshua Berdugo who was to become the Chief Rabbi of Morocco in 1941. In one of his early letters to the Zionist leaders in Cologne, Rabbi Berdugo expressed great enthusiasm for the movement and a determination to work tirelessly in order to spread the message of Zionism throughout Morocco. "Would that all the people of Israel love and magnify this grand idea with one heart and one mind," he prayed. In the same letter he expressed his eagerness to learn more about Zionism and requested that the Zionist leaders send "books on Zionism to all *shekel*-paying members."

The organization of so many Zionist chapters or associations in Morocco in such a relatively short time after the First Zionist Congress is the more remarkable when it is realized that at the time there were no Jewish (or non-Jewish) newspapers in Morocco at all. To be sure, these early associations were no more than embryonic cells; nonetheless, they were beginning to play an active role in the communities, enough at any rate to alarm the French authorities and the representatives of the Alliance Israelite Universelle (AIU). Another remarkable aspect of these early Zionist associations in Morocco is the active and supportive role played by rabbis in the leadership of the movement. There was simply nothing resembling the anti-Zionism of much of Europe's Orthodox and Reform leadership. Not only did Moroccan rabbis not oppose the movement, they were actually its leaders. Thus, the chief rabbis of Mogador, Safi, and Meknes headed their respective associations, while in Fez all the rabbis in the city including the most prominent spiritual leaders at the time, Rabbis Raphael Aben-Tzur, Mordekhay Serero, Shelomo Ibn-Danan and Vidal Tzarfati belonged to the association *Hibbat Tzion*.

The reason for this is that most Moroccan Jews were not at all familiar with the political and secular nature of Herzl's Zionism. Rather, they conceived Zionism in purely religious and messianic terms, in accordance with their long tradition of longing for redemption and the ingathering of exiles. They perceived Zionism as a thoroughly natural expression of Judaism. To them, Zionism seemed simply the realization of their centuries-long messianic dreams; it was seen as *athalta de-geulah* (the beginning of redemption). Above all, they saw Zionism as a means of facilitating *aliyah*, a fact not appreciated by the Zionist leaders in Europe until many years later. It is no wonder that when the Zionist secretariat advised the Zionist associations of Fez and Meknes to join the Mizrahi Religious Zionist movement, the rabbis of both cities were surprised and perplexed. While accepting the advice, they could not understand how there could be any kind of Zionism other than a religious one. To them, the terms seemed synonymous, and therefore they failed to see the need for a specific religious Zionist movement.

The establishment of the French Protectorate over Morocco in 1912 did not enhance the Zionist movement in Morocco. Likewise, the outbreak of World War I put an end to the attempt of Zionism to establish itself there. It also brought a total halt in communications between Morocco and the land of Israel, which was under Turkey's rule and therefore considered enemy territory. When, at the end of World War I, contact was resumed between the Zionist movement and Moroccan Jewry, conditions had completely changed. A number of internal and external factors converged to slow and limit the further development of the Zionist movement until the end of World War II. The same factors discouraged and even militated against the immigration of Moroccan Jews to the land of Israel between the two World Wars.

Aliyah after World War II: Immediately following World War II, Moroccan Jews resumed emigration to Israel. The establishment of the State of Israel in May, 1948, was followed by successive waves of ever-increasing numbers of emigrants, reaching massive proportions after the independence of Morocco in 1956 and the Arab-Israeli wars of 1967 and 1973. Between 1948 and 1956, about 70,000 Moroccan Jews left for Israel, and by the late 1960s that number reached 200,000. Thus, Moroccan Jewry, which had numbered close to a quarter million souls after World War II, declined to approximately 50,000.

Until the establishment of the State, this *aliyah* was mostly clandestine; indeed, because the French refused to grant exit visas, it was doubly clandestine. Jews needed first to get out of Morocco, and then they had to get into Palestine. Some people used semi-legal methods of emigration, obtaining exit visas for France and continuing from there to Palestine. But, the most popular way of leaving Morocco was by crossing the Algerian border from Oudjda. A transit camp was set up in the region of Algiers, attracting hundreds of young people who converged from all over Morocco. All sorts of ingenious ruses and stratagems were used to cross the Algerian border. In 1947, three ships bearing the symbolic names of *Shivat Tzion*, *Yehudah Halevi*, and *Haportzim* left from Algiers with 1,500 emigrants. However, the Algerian police, alerted by the British, managed to find the camp and close it. Indeed, most of the early immigrants were arrested by the British authorities and interned in Cyprus until the establishment of the State of Israel. Still, hundreds, motivated by the ideology of political Zionism, managed to make it to Palestine in time to participate in the War of Independence. The Negev Battalion, known as the "French Battalion," that liberated Beersheba was composed mostly of North Africans. Many died in the battles of Latrun and Jerusalem.

Reaction to Israeli Independence in Morocco: The Saturday Israel was declared a state, a joyous mood gripped the Jews in the *Mellahs*. Fortunately, the French were still in Morocco and the Jewish quarters were well guarded, so that the Jews had no reason to fear any adverse Arab reaction. A kind of a messianic fervor seized everyone in the *Mellahs*, with celebrations everywhere. In the synagogues, a festive atmosphere filled the air. There was singing and dancing with the Torah, as on *Simhat Torah*. In the homes, the mood was more like Purim, with eating, drinking, embracing, and singing. In the streets, the youth of such new Zionist movements as *Bnei Akiva*, *Habonim*, and others danced the hora. Most of the songs sung in the synagogues, in the homes, and in the streets were modern Zionist ones as well as Moroccan *piyyutim* about the messiah, redemption, and *Eretz Yisrael*. In short, the mood was electrifying. Immigration to Israel was on everyone's mind. The awaited moment had come.

And the moment had also become more propitious for *aliyah*. Without its being officially legalized, the Zionist movement enjoyed great tolerance on the part of the French authorities. After 1948, Zionist activities were conducted almost openly under the guise of social welfare. Envoys of the Jewish Agency were allowed into Morocco to organize *aliyah* and youth movements. Immigration had become the top priority for the Zionist movement. Following the armistice agreement in March, 1949, between Israel and its Arab neighbors, an agreement was reached between the French authorities in Morocco and representatives of the Jewish Agency. It permitted the creation of Cadima, a Zionist organization in charge of *aliyah*, which was to process the emigration of thousands of Moroccan Jews during its existence between 1949 and 1956. The French also allowed a monthly emigration quota of six hundred, which number was increased to nine hundred soon thereafter. Yet, even the higher number proved inadequate in meeting the pressure of the increasing number of candidates eager to emigrate. To meet this challenge, Cadima opened a large transit camp near Casablanca. It housed thousands of emigrants from all over Morocco for weeks at a time until their departure for France, where they stayed even longer at an old military camp near Marseille, where the conditions were truly unbearable.

Notwithstanding these difficulties, enthusiasm for *aliyah* remained at a peak. In 1949 alone, the number of emigrants from Morocco reached 13,920, representing 9% of all immigrants arriving in Israel that year. Discouraging news about difficulties of integration encountered in Israel dampened this enthusiasm somewhat, causing the number of emigrants in the years 1950-1953 to drop to anywhere from 4,980 in 1950 to 2996 in 1953. But even during these lean years of 1950-1953 another 17,340 emigrants left for Israel.

It must be pointed out that this initial Moroccan *aliyah* after 1948 was not the result of any sense of fear for physical security or outright political oppression. Nor was it motivated by the ideologies of modern political Zionism, as was the case of the clandestine emigration between 1945 and 1948. Rather, it was an expression of a quasi-messianic fervor that swept the *Mellahs* (as it did the rest of North African Jewry) in the wake of the stunning Israeli victory in the War of Independence.

Emigration rose dramatically as Morocco neared independence. Once again, the number of emigrants swelled into the thousands. Fearing that Moroccan independence might trap them in Morocco, many Jews decided to emigrate. Cadima offices were inundated with applicants for *aliyah*, and in 1954 the number of emigrants reached 8,171. In 1955, the number reached 24,994, and in 1956 it reached the historical peak of 36,301.

But Moroccan independence put an end to all organized emigration. On June 11, 1956, barely three months after independence, the Moroccan government ordered all *aliyah* offices closed. Twenty-five Israeli envoys were ordered to leave the country within eight days. This led to a second wave of clandestine emigration, organized by agents of the Israeli Mosad, lasting from 1957 to 1961. Representatives of the Mosad, aided by local Zionists, used all possible means to smuggle Jews out of the country. Using Moroccan and European passports provided by a special lab set up in France by the Mosad for that purpose, and relying on the assistance of the Spanish authorities in the enclaves of Malaga and Algeciras as well as that of the British in Gibraltar, they managed to spirit nearly 18,000 Jews out of the country. Throughout the 1950s, the emigrants were smuggled in ferryboats from the northern coast of Morocco to Gibraltar. In September, 1960, the small boats were supplemented by the

mid-size Pisces (a former mine sweeper renovated and converted to transport illegal emigrants), which was capable of carrying larger numbers of people. By the end of 1960, the Pisces had ferried hundreds of Moroccan Jews in twelve successful missions.

But on the night of January 10, 1961, disaster struck. The Pisces left Morocco with forty-two Moroccan Jews (men, women, and children). Barely several hours after sailing, a vicious storm broke out. The most prudent course would have been to turn back and seek help, but the Spanish captain, afraid of being discovered, forged ahead towards Gibraltar. Soon the Pisces foundered at sea, drowning all the forty-two emigrants as well as Hayim Tsarfati, the Israeli radio operator who was also of Moroccan origin. Only the Spanish captain and his mechanic survived, having abandoned the ship before it sank.

Operation Yakhin: The tragic Pisces incident put the problem of the emigration of Moroccan Jews into the international limelight. To counter the negative international publicity engendered by the drowning of the forty-two Jews who were attempting to flee the country, the Moroccan government decided to relax its restriction of Jewish emigration. Thus, shortly after the Pisces incident, in the summer of 1961, a number of critical discussions between a representative of the Mosad and a senior Moroccan official were held in Europe. After six meetings, a formula was agreed upon whereby the Jews would officially be allowed to emigrate to the United States and Canada but not to Israel. Also, the process of organizing the emigration was to be carried out by the American Jewish organization, the United HIAS Service, and not by the Jewish Agency. In reality, however, HIAS served as a cover for the Mosad and the Jewish Agency. Thus began "Operation Yakhin," which in the course of the following three years (1961-1964) processed the emigration of over eighty thousand Jews from Morocco. This was a veritable exodus. The majority of Moroccan Jews (about 200,000) had left for Israel between 1948 and the end of 1964. The number dropped between

1964 and 1967, but the downward trend was reversed drastically following the Six Day War in 1967. Between 1968 and 1969, emigration to Israel reached approximately five thousand per year, dropping again to 200-250 per month in 1970. By then, the 35,000 Jews remaining in Morocco, reassured by the Moroccan authorities' solicitousness on their behalf during times of crisis (such as the Arab summit in Rabat in 1969 following Al-Aqsa fire), reconsidered staying in Morocco and postponed emigrating to Israel or elsewhere. They might have been convinced by the leaders of AIU and French Jewry of the importance of maintaining a Jewish presence in Morocco. Rene Cassin, the president of AIU in 1970, went as far as to suggest that the presence of Jews in Morocco was vital for future rapprochement between Israel and Morocco. King Hasan's support for Egyptian President Anwar Sadat's peace initiative in November 1977, and his invitation to Moroccan Jews living in Israel to visit Morocco or resettle there, further reassured Moroccan Jews and enhanced their trust in the King.

Conclusion: A detailed description of the successive waves of Moroccan *aliyah* as well as a comprehensive account of the vicissitudes of the various Zionist activities in Morocco between 1912 and the establishment of the State of Israel are beyond the scope of this essay. Yet, the above survey provides an overview of the deep attachment of Moroccan Jews to the land of Israel, manifested in their generous financial help to the old *yishuv* and their vital role in its settlement and consolidation; the impact of the influx of their immigrants in the nineteenth century on the revival of Jerusalem, Tiberias, and Jaffa; their spontaneous and enthusiastic response to modern Zionism; and their massive immigration to the State of Israel, which they regarded as the fulfillment of their centuries-long dream and hope for redemption and the ingathering of exiles. In addition, it is clear that Moroccan rabbis not only did not oppose Zionism but were its most ardent supporters, often acting as its leaders. It is also of note that not all Moroccan Jews who settled in Palestine during the eighteenth and nineteenth centuries devoted themselves to study and prayer, living on charity. Many of them earned a livelihood by engaging in commerce, handicrafts, manual labor, and in some cases in agriculture. All in all, it is abundantly evident that Moroccan Jewry's contribution to the old *yishuv* and to the State of Israel was truly considerable.

Bibliography

Laskier, Michael, *North African Jewry in the Twentieth Century: The Jews of Morocco, Tunisia, and Algeria* (New York and London, 1984).

Messas, Joseph, *Otsar ha-Mikhtavim*, vol. I (Jerusalem, 1968).

Toledano, Henry, "*Yahadut Maroko ve-Yishuv Eretz Yisrael: Toledot ha-ʿaliyot ha-Shonot shel Yehude Maroko meha-Meʾah ha-Shesh ʿEsreh ve-ʿad Reshit ha-Meʾah ha-ʿEsrim*," in Zohri, Menahem, et al., eds., *Hagut ʿIvrit be-Artzot ha-Islam* (Jerusalem, 1981), pp. 229-252.

Toledano, Henry, "The Attachment of Moroccan Jewry to the Land of Israel according to Rabbinic Literature," in Angel, Marc, ed., *Haham Gaon Memorial Volume* (New York, 1997), pp. 197-221.

Yaʾari, Abraham, *Sheluhe Eretz Yisrael: Toledot ha-Shelihut meha-Aretz la-Golah me-Hurban Bayit Sheni ʾad ha-Meʾah ha-Teshaʾ ʿEsreh* (Jerusalem, 1950/51).

HENRY TOLEDANO

LIST OF ILLUSTRATIONS

1) Astronomy: An eclipse of the moon, in *Tzurat ha-Aretz* (Form of the Earth), by Abraham b. Hiyya Ha-Nasi.
2) Astronomy: Image of an astrolabe, taken from *Ma'aseh Tuviyyah* by Tobias Cohn, Venice, Italy, 1708.
3) Astrology: Mosaic from the synagogue of Beit Aleph, with sun, moon, stars, zodiac, and, in the corners, images of the four seasons. Taken from *Denkmäler der Jüdischen Antike* by Adolf Reifenberg, Berlin, Germany, 1937.
4) Astrology: Painted ceiling, Chodorov, Ukraine. By Israel Lisnicki, 1714.
5) Astrology: Porcelain wedding cup from Denmark (1856). Hebrew inscription says: "4 Tevet, sign of Capricorn, on the day of his wedding and the day his heart rejoiced; and this is the Torah Moses gave to the children of Israel." (Torben Samson Collection, Efrat, Israel)
6) Honor of Parents in Judaism: "The Examination" by Moritz Daniel Oppenheim (Germany, 1800-1882). In a traditional Jewish home the father reviews what the child has learned, while the mother looks on proudly.
7) Rashi: Rashi's map of the boundaries of the land of Israel from his commentary to Num. 34:11, according to Vienna Hebrew ms. 220, folio 79r.
8) Samaritan Judaism: The Samaritan scripts.
9) Samaritan Judaism: Young Samaritan studying with his teacher (Yefet Tzedaka in Nablus, Israel, c. 1960).
10) Sermons in Modern Judaism: "Die Predigt". Paul Grödel Verlag 1890-1910. Postcard.
11) Torah and Culture: Instruments used for circumcision and a Torah scroll with decorations. Copperplate by B. Piccart, 1725.
12) Torah and Culture: Wooden box, holding the scroll of the law, decorated with a three-pointed crown and a miniature Ark of the Covenant in copper and velvet. From the inheritance of Jacob and Isaac Henriques de Castro, The Hague, The Netherlands.
13) Zionism in Moroccan Judaism: Jewish Family from Fez, Morocco, c. 1925.
14) Zionism in Moroccan Judaism: Membership card of the religious Zionist youth movement, BaHaD (Brit Halutzim Datiyyim), Meknes, Morocco, c. 1947. (Private collection Henry Toledano)
15) Zionism in Moroccan Judaism: Pictorial presentation of Rabbi Amram Ben Diwan, an emissary from Hebron to Morocco where he died suddenly in 1782 in the northern town of Ouezzane. His tomb became a popular place of pilgrimage for Moroccan Jews, especially on *Lag ba-Omer*. (Private collection Henry Toledano)

GENERAL INDEX
(Volumes I-V)

Aaron   2205
Abba Mari ben Moses ben Joseph Astruc
   1617
Abbadan   198
Abd el-Jabbar ibn Mohammad al-Hamdani
   1826
Abd al-Mu'in Tsedaqa   2257
Abel, K.   1052
Aben-Tzur, Jacob   1849
Abikhzir, Jacob Hay   2295
Aboab, Isaac   255, 1899, 1904 n. 76
Abodah Zarah   354
Abogard, Archbishop of Lyon   1905
abortion   350, 856, 859-862, 1654
Abraham   1730, 1779-1780
   as an astrologer   2031-2032
   converting gentiles   2046-2047
   and the history of Israel   2115-2116
   in *Liber Antiquitatum Biblicarum* (Pseudo-Philo)
   2200-2201
Abravanel, Isaac   270, 1618, 1900, 1904 n. 78
Abravanel, Judah   732-733
Abu Bekhr   2251
Abu Ibrahim b. Faraj b. Maruth   2255
Abu Ishaq Ibrahim ibn Faraj ibn Maruth
   2256
Abu Sa'id b. Abu'l-Hassan b. Abi Sa'id   2255
Abu-Zaid   1631
Abu'l Fath   2249, 2255, 2256, 2262 n. 43
Abu'l-Hasan as-Suri   2256, 2257
Abu'l-Hasan of Tyre   2256
Abulafia, Abraham   1773
Abulafia, Hayim   2298
Abyss of Despair (Hanover)   216
acculturation   1492, 1493, 1495
Acharonim   1674
Ad convincendum perfidiam judaeorum (de Santa Fe)
   1680
Adam   465, 471
adaptations, of texts into Judaeo-Arabic   2180
Adelman, H.   1501 n. 37, 1501 n. 44
Adelman, P.V.   1502 n. 82
Aderet Eliyahu (The Cloak of Elijah, Gaon of
   Vilna)   275
Aderet Eliyyahu (The Cloak of Elijah, Bashyazi)
   1818
Adler, E.N.   2256

Adler, Hermann   2269, 2273-2274,
   2282 n. 51
Adler, Nathan   2270, 2272
Adler, R.   565, 1483, 1500 n. 16, 1502 n. 86
admonition, words of   2097-2100
Admonition (Cairo manuscript)   190
Adret, Shelomo ben (*Rashba*)   235, 342, 343,
   1617, 1906
adultery, excusing of   2145
Aegean diaspora   1763-1764
Aegean synagogues   1764, 1765, 1777 n. 7
Afes   2040
After Auschwitz (Rubenstein)   416
afterlife *see* eternal life
Against Apion (Josephus)   1791
Aggadah *see* Haggadah
Aggadic discourse   1593
Aggadic literature   2047
Aggadic midrash   1893
agricultural species, mingling prohibited   1754,
   1757
agriculture
   in ancient Israel   1626, 1727-1728
   in Judean Hills   1719-1721, 1726
   rule of diverse kinds   1727
   sabbatical year   1726
Agudah   427
Agudat Israel   1673
agunah problem   1804
Agus, Jacob B.   768, 1738
Ahab   1789
Ahad Ha'am (Asher Ginzberg)   758-759
Ahai   1659
Aharonim   342
Ahavat Tzion (Love of Zion)   2303
Ahmad ibn Muhammad ibn al-Faqih
   al-Hamadhani   1826
Ai Tien   1632, 1636
Akedah   35, 406-408
Akiba   110
Alans   1829
Albo, Joseph   162, 206, 505-506
Albornoz, Claudio Sánchez   2090-2091
Alconstantin, Solomon   1616
Ale hen sandek   93-94
Alemán, Mateo   2081, 2086
Alexander the Great   199

Alfasi, David 1810, 1820
Alfasi, Isaac (*RIF*, Rabbi Yitzhak ben Ya'acov
    Alfasi) 342, 1657, 1660, 1848
aliyah 684
    by Beta Israel (Ethiopia) 1751-1752
    of Chinese Jews 1644
    of Moroccan Jews 2294, 2296-2303,
        2304-2307
Alkalai, Yehuda 685, 756-757
allegorical exegesis 1893, 1902 n. 37
Almohad persecutions, of Jews in North Africa
    1848
Almohades dynasty, ruling Al-Andalus 1677
Almosnino, Moses 1897
Alpert, R.T. 1240
Alphonsi, Petrus 1686
Alshekh, Moses 275
Altabib, Abraham 1618
altar 361, 469, 526, 528, 545, 585, 591, 598,
    610, 620, 622, 815, 877-878, 896, 1291,
    1292, 1293, 1297, 1299, 1301, 1389, 1393,
    1434, 1444
Alter, Abraham Mordechai 223
Alter, Judah Aryeh Leib 277
Altschuler, David and Hillel 275
Aly, W. 1051
Ambrose, St 75, 77
*The American Jewish Pulpit: A collection of Sermons
    by the Most Eminent American Rabbis* 2268
American Judaism 563, 668, 670-672, 674,
    695, 704, 706-707, 764, 768, 831, 922,
    977-993
    Conservative movement 512, 1797-1798,
        1799, 1803-1805
    feminist influence on 1804
    of Holocaust and Redemption 666-667,
        671, 986-990
    Karaite communities 1813
    non-Orthodox Jews 1799, 1801, 1802
    Orthodoxy 124, 209, 1795, 1796-1797,
        1798, 1799, 1800-1801
    practice of 1794-1796, 1798-1807
    preaching in 2267-2268, 2270-2271, 2275,
        2276, 2277-2279
    Reconstructionism 1804
    Reform movement 209, 510-511, 764,
        1795, 1799-1800
    synagogues 1795
Americas, conversos in 2082
Amidah (standing prayer) 44, 818-820
Amiel, M.A. 1405, 1409 n. 26
Amis des Judaism 304-305
Amoraim 341
    and astrology 2033-2034
    and astronomy 2038, 2039-2040
    on commandment of proper measures and
        weights 2194
    on honoring of parents 2195
Amorites
    fights against 2206
    practices 1905

amputees 1707
Amram 649, 2201
Amsterdam, Jewish community in 1896,
    1897, 1903 n. 61
amulets, use of 1617, 1905-1907, 1908
analogical-contrastive reasoning, in Mishnah
    1832-1847, 1926-1931
Anan ben David 651, 1808, 1809, 1813,
    1817, 1818
Ananites 1808
Anchias, Juan de 2085
ancient Israel, agriculture in 1626, 1727-1728
ancient Judaism 13, 82, 180, 186, 1605-1611
    astrology in 2031-2037
    astronomy in 2037-2044
Al-Andalus, ruled by Almohades dynasty
    1677
angels 131
    in Beta Israel literature 1743
    of Darkness/Death 204, 262, 1910
    help against forces of the dark 1913
    as treated by Josephus 1791
aniconism 1440
animals
    allowed for husbandry 1723, 1728
    clean and unclean 1723-1725, 1729 n. 14
    offering of (*Zebahim*) 1296-1300
annual holidays, of Beta Israel 1746-1747
An answer to the Jews (Tertullian) 91
antagonism, to non-Jews 1817
anthropological approaches, to religion
    1870-1871, 1880 n. 9
anthropology, theological 1419-1428
anti-Christian polemics, by Jews 1013-1014,
    1817, 1895-1896, 2176
anti-converso movement 1682, 1683-1689
anti-Islamic polemics, by Jews 461-462, 1817
anti-Jewish polemics
    by Muslims 461
    during Enlightenment 1866, 1879 n. 1
anti-Karaite polemics 2176
anti-Samaritan legislation, adopted by Romans
    2249-2250
Das antike Judentum (Weber) 236
Antiochus IV (Seleucid king of Syria)
    199-200
Antiquities of the Jews (Josephus) 203, 1778,
    1782, 1786, 1791
antisemitism
    in antiquity 1026, 1027, 1028, 1029, 1032,
        1033, 1037, 1039, 1043
    Christian 541, 633-634, 643, 1022-1023
    during Second Temple period 610
    in Eastern Europe 215, 1273, 1335, 1336
    in France 296, 299, 300, 303, 306, 308
    and idea of chosen people 1730, 1738 n. 3
    of Nazis 86-87, 421, 675, 1022-1023, 1277
    as a political and social movement 662,
        663, 736, 1078, 1242
    Zionism confronting 668, 671
anusim (forced converts) 1772, 2077

anuss concept (someone forced by heredity or environment to sin) 2152
apikoros 368
Apiryon Asah Lo (He Made himself a Palanquin, Solomon ben Aaron) 1811
apocalypse 381-382, 613, 650, 678, 714
apocalyptic literature 527, 882
apocalyptic visionaries 385-388
apocalypticism 1445, 1446
Apocrypha 170, 200, 269, 878, 882, 1313, 1318, 1319
apostasy 366-380, 1440, 1873
Apple, R. 1397 n. 23
Aqiba, R. 52, 236, 253, 278, 317, 323, 340, 404, 444, 453
 on Samaritans 2247
Arab countries, Zionism in 2294
Arabian Judaism 454
Arabic culture, new openness towards 2168
Arabic language
 Christian 2170
 Jewish 2169-2170
 medieval 2167, 2169
 'middle' 2169, 2179, 2181 n. 7
 'neo' 2169
 translations
  of the Bible into 1207
  into Judaeo-Arabic 2179
 use
  by Jews 1855, 2168, 2169, 2171
  by Samaritans 2255
Arabic writings
 medieval, by Jews 2167-2181
 Samaritan 2255, 2256
 translated into Hebrew 1820
Die arabische Literatur der Juden (Steinschneider) 2170
Arama, Isaac 478, 1618, 1898-1899, 1900
Aramaic language, use of 2244
Aramaic texts
 Samaritan 2254
 translated into Judaeo-Arabic 2179
Arba'ah Turim (*TUR*, Jacob ben Asher) 342, 1657, 1658, 1660, 1667, 1668
archaeological evidence, of Khazar Jewish practices 1827-1828
Archives israëlites 304, 306
Arendt, Hannah 421
Arieti, S. 1107
Aristotelian philosophy 274, 481, 1760
Aristotelian science 132, 478, 482, 1661
Aristotelianism 132, 133, 1820
Aristotle 76, 132, 135, 624-627, 712-714, 721-724, 726-727, 729-732, 953, 967, 970
 on embryogenesis 1624-1625
 Historia animalium 1625
Ark of the Covenant 528, 596-599
Arnold, M. 1090
Arpad (king of Hungary) 1830-1831
arrogance 244-245
Artapanus 1789

artificial insemination 857, 1757, 1916-1917, 1919 n. 3
Aruch, S. 1464
Arugat Ha-bosem (Moses Ibn Ezra) 2168
Arukh HaShulhan (Epstein) 344, 1675-1676
Arukh (Nathan ben Jehiel) 2229
Asara Levushim 216
Asatir 2255
asceticism 612, 638, 650-652, 658, 827, 933, 1019, 1486, 1489, 1492
 ascetic 926, 954, 1013
Asherah 437, 519
asherah-tree 354
Asheri *see* ben Yehiel, Asher
Ashkenaz, Hasidei 255, 270
Ashkenazi, Meir 1640
Ashkenazic communities 8
Ashkenazic Judaica 4, 6
Ashkenazic Judaism 342, 425, 1948
 and Sephardic Judaism 344, 681, 955
Ashkenazic music 911-916, 921-923
Ashkenazic orientation, of Zionism and State of Israel 2168
Ashkenazic scholars 480
Ashkenazic synagogues 311
Ashkenazim 2, 432, 1364, 1465 n. 13
 in Hong Kong 1647
 migrating to China 1637-1638
 in Shanghai 1638-1639, 1640
Ashmedai 1908
Ashton, D. 1501 n. 49, 1502 n. 58
askara (diphtheria) 1707-1708
assimilation 607, 697, 701, 708, 756, 982, 989, 1004, 1274, 1279, 1492, 1493, 1495
astral magic, in medieval Judaism 480, 1612-1620
astrological theology 1615-1616
astrology 269, 481-482, 837-843, 964-965, 1911-1912
 in ancient Judaism 2031-2037
astronomers, and priests 2037
astronomy
 in ancient Judaism 2037-2044
 and astrology 2031
Atil 1822, 1830
atonement 361, 600, 610, 748, 805, 812-813, 820, 867-868, 875, 900, 1019, 1172, 1180, 1183, 1188, 1193, 1195, 1197
 see also Day of Atonement
Attar, Hayyim ben Moses 275, 1849
Atzeret 35, 36, 42
auctor 2052
Auerbach, Shlomo Zalman 1757
Augustine, St 396, 713
Auschwitz 407-408, 410-414, 416-417, 421-422, 429
 see also Holocaust
Ausmus, Harry J. 772
authorship, of biblical books 2052-2055
autonomy 475
 human 2138, 2145

Auxerre, Samuel of   2234
Avars   1828
Avery-Peck, A.J.   1500 n. 11
Avodah Zarah   439
Axelrod, Rabbi Gedalyahu   379
Azharot   1858
Azulai, Abraham ben Rabbi Mordekhai   2299
Azulai, Hayyim Joseph David   2236
Azulay, Mes'od   2297

Baal   153, 437
Baal Ha-Turim see ben Asher, Jacob
Ba'al Hanes, Meir   2298
Baal Shem Tov   217
Ba'alei Ha-Tosafot   273, 279
Baalei Teshuvah (people who repent)   1796-1797
Baba Qamma (Asher ben Yehiel)   1664
Baba Rabba   2248, 2254
Babel, Tower of   2200
Babovich, Simhah   1811
Babovich, Tobiah   1812
baby-selling   1918, 1920 n. 7
Babylonian academies   1809
Babylonian astrology   2031, 2032
Babylonian astronomy   2037, 2041
Babylonian exile *see* exile
Babylonian Talmud *see* Talmud
Bachrach, B.   1051
Bacon, G.C.   1397 n. 32
Baeck, Leo   752, 1738
Baer, Yitzhak   1679, 1900
BAH see Sirkes, Joel (*BAH*)
Bahya ben Asher   270, 1891, 1902 n. 25
Bahya ben Joseph ibn Paquda   254
Bainish, Eisik   1911
Bakan, D.   1108
bakkashot service   1854
Al-Bakri   1823-1824
Balaam   1790
Balanjar, Christianity in   1823
baldness   1708
Balkan rites   1769
Baltanas, Fray Domingo de   1689
Bamberger, Bernard J.   1731, 1736, 1737
ban
    on bigamy   1848
    on homosexuality   2139-2140, 2141, 2146
    on raising small cattle   1728
Bandura, A.   1103, 1109
Banitt, Menahem   790-791
banquets   2127
baptism   65-68
bar Helbo, Menahem   273, 2046, 2050
bar Hiyya, Abraham   473, 476, 1613
Bar Kappara   2040
Bar Kokhba   44, 73, 142, 248, 262, 316, 367, 380, 382, 431, 499
bar Sheshet, Meir   2303
bar Yohai, Simeon   227, 1731, 1738-1739 n. 11, 1857
bar Zadok, Shimson (*Tashbetz*)   1665

Bar/Bat Mitzvah   94, 308, 425, 427, 567-568, 683, 689, 694, 696, 699, 702, 709, 799, 800, 915, 984, 1498
    among Karaites   1815
    children with disabilities participating in 1705
Baraita deMazalot   2035, 2042
Baraita deShmuel   2035, 2043-2044, 2049, 2050
al-Bargeloni, Isaac ben Reuben   1858
Barnabas   67-68, 77
Baron, Salo   2227
Barr, James   197
Barret, W.   1090
Barrientos, Don Lope de   1685
Barth, Karl   86
Barthes, Roland   943, 2171
Bashyazi, Elijah   1811, 1816, 1818
al-Basir, Joseph   1810, 1818, 1819
Baskin, J.R.   1500, 1500 n. 3, n. 11, 1501 n. 29, n. 32, n. 36, n. 37, 1502 n. 66
Basola, Moshe   2299
Bassan, E.   1272
Basser, Herbert   951
Bateson, G.   1090, 1109
Baur, F.C.   83
Bavli *see* Talmud
Beattie, D.R.G.   1320
Beaugency, Eliezer de   271, 2050-2051, 2052-2053, 2056, 2057-2060
Becker, G.   237
Beer, M.   1109
Beginning of Wisdom (Vidas)   255
Beijing, Jewish community in   1646
Bein Hamatzarim   37
Beit Avraham (Danzig)   1670
beit din   309, 312, 351, 476, 1850, 1918
Beit Hadash (Caro)   343
Beit Yosef (Caro)   343, 1665, 1666, 1667, 1674, 1946
Bekhor Shor of Orleans, Yosef (Joseph ben Isaac)   271, 273, 2054-2055, 2056
belief systems   26
Bellah, Robert   708
ben Aaron, Jacob   2255
ben Abdimi, Rabbi Isaac   2033
ben Abraham, Isaac (*Rizba*)   2193
ben Abraham of Seville, Yom Tov   2229
ben Ahaba, Ada   2041
Ben-Ami, Issakhar   1857
ben Amram, Eleazar   2255
ben Asher, Jacob   270, 342, 1657, 1658, 1660, 1665, 1667, 1668
ben Attar, Hayim   2299
ben Azariah, Eleazar   228
Ben Azzai, Rabbi   253
ben Diwan, Amram   1857, 2296
ben Eli, Yefet   1810, 1818-1819, 2174
ben Eliezer, Isaac   2227, 2230
ben Eliezer, Israel *see* Shem Tov, Israel Baal (*Besht*)
ben Eliezer of Kastoria, Tobias   1767

ben Elijah, Aaron 1811, 1818, 1819, 1820
Ben-Ezra Synagogue (Cairo) 2172
ben Gamaliel, Simeon 2039, 2247
ben Gershom, Levi (Gersonides) 254-255,
    274, 481, 483, 725-728, 731, 735, 965
Ben-Gurion, David 1776
ben Hananel, Jacob 1894
ben Hananiah, Joshua 1786
ben Hanina, Hama 2034
ben Hanina, Sherira 342
ben Hassin, David 1849, 2296, 2298
Ben-Hayyim, Z. 2255, 2256
ben Helbo, Menahem 271, 273
ben Hillel, Mordecai 1665
ben Hyrcanus, Eliezer 2247
ben Isaac, Hayyim 221
ben Isaac, Joseph (Yosef Bekhor Shor of
    Orleans) 271, 273, 2054-2055, 2056
ben Isaac, Pinhas (Khidr) 2257
ben Isaac, Simeon 2227
ben Isaac, Solomon 271
ben Jehiel, Nathan 2229
ben Joseph, Aaron 1811, 1820
ben Joseph, Saadiah 206
ben Joseph of Trani, Moses (Mabyt) 1667
ben Judah, Eleazar (Rokeah) 1908
ben Judah, Gershom 2227
ben Judah, Isaac 2227, 2230
ben Judah, Solomon 2233-2234
ben Judah, Yeshua 1810, 1819
ben Levi, Joshua 2033-2034
ben Levi, Yefet 1810
ben Mali di Trani, Isaiah 274, 1764
ben Manoah, Hezekiah 271
ben Mazliah, Sahl 1810
ben Media, Yohanan 2041
ben Meir, Samuel (Rashbam) 271, 272, 273,
    275, 2047-2048, 2050, 2052, 2053-2054,
    2056-2057, 2228, 2229
ben Moses, Aaron 1819
ben Moses, Tobias (the Translator) 1810,
    1819
ben Nahman, Moses see Nahmanides (Ramban)
ben Nahshon, Hai 2042
ben Nathan, Judah 2228
ben Paroah, Eliezer 2042
ben Reuben, Jacob 1819, 1826
ben Salama, Amram 2257
ben Samuel he-Hasid of Regensburg, Judah
    255
ben Samuel, Meir 2228
Ben Sasson, H.H. 882
Ben Sasson, M. 1396 n. 1
ben Shetah, Simeon 1808
ben Shim'on, David 2299, 2300
ben Shim'on, Raphael 2299, 2300
Ben Sira 166, 878
ben Solomon, Elijah see Vilna, Elijah ben
    Solomon Gaon of (GRA)
ben Solomon, Joseph (RIK) 1666
ben Tsion, S. 2301

ben Uziel, Jonathan 2043
ben Yakar, Jacob 2227, 2230
ben Yakar, Judah 269
ben Yefet, Levi 1818
ben Yehiel, Asher (Rosh) 255, 342, 1658,
    1660, 1663-1664, 1665, 1947, 1952 n. 56
ben Yehiel, Jacob 1660
ben Yehuda al-Fasi of Fez, Shelomo 2297
ben Yeruhim, Salmon 1810
ben Yohai, Simeon 2247
ben Yosef, Simon Akiva Baer 1832
ben Zakkai, Yohanan 1786, 2039, 2286
ben Zvi, Yitzchak 2259, 2298, 2301
benai yisrael 113-114, 501-502
    see also Children of Israel
Benedict XIII (Pope) 1687
benediction 175
Benevisti, Hayyim 1666
Benjamin of Tudela 1767
Benjamin, Walter 943, 949
Bentov, Haim 2295
Berab, Jacob 1772
Berchman, R.M. 1052
Berdiawsky, Y. 2303
Berdugo, Joshua 2304
Berger, David 378-380
Berger, Peter 683
Berghe, Pierre L. van den 502
Bergier, Nicholas 82
Bergman, H. 1100
berit 15
Berkovits, Eliezer 265, 408, 412, 768-769,
    1022-1023
Berlin, Naphtali Zevi Judah 277
Berliner, Abraham 2229, 2237
Bernstein, D.S. 1496, 1502 n. 70
Bernstein, G. 1396
Berossus 13
Bershady, H.J. 1410 n. 36
Besht see Shem Tov, Israel Baal
bestiality, taboo on 2146
Besula, Moshe 2297
Beta Israel (Falasha) 795, 1741-1753
Beth Aaron Synagogue (Shanghai) 1640
Bethel 2257
Bettelheim, Bruno 421
Between East and West: A History of the Jews of
    North Africa (Chouraqui) 1857
Beur (Mendelssohn) 275
Bevis Marks Synagogue (London) 2266, 2279
    n. 8
Biale, D. 1492, 1501 n. 53
Biale, R. 1500 n. 14, 1501 n. 18
Bialik, H.N. 265
Bibago, Abraham 1618
Bible 604, 617-618, 711-715, 718, 720, 734,
    914, 940-942, 953, 1077, 1078, 1080
    ban on homosexuality 2139-2140, 2141,
        2146
    of Beta Israel (Orit) 1749
    Christian 169, 401, 1049

commandments in 855
ethical teachings of 252-253, 510
Ethiopian 1741, 1749
exegesis of 266, 269, 274, 277, 278, 604, 859
  French medieval 2045-2060
Hebrew 601, 633, 637, 752, 832, 837, 1302, 1321, 1323, 1342-1343, 1458
  on chosen people 1730
  Christian interpretations of 1011-1012, 1013-1016
  the messiah in 874, 878
  miracles in 889, 894
  mythology in 945-948
  textual aspects of 2175
  translations of 1207, 1309-1312, 1318, 1319, 1490
    in Judaeo-Arabic 2170, 2173-2174, 2177, 2178
  women in 1479-1481
Josephus' interpretation of 555-556
miracles in 776, 892-893
and natural science 960-961
philosophy of 779
and the Quran 453, 454-455
Rabbinic 728, 2124
redaction of 2051-2060, 2243
rewritings of 1788-1789, 2243
on Samaritans 2242-2243
women's stories 572
see also Scripture; Torah
Biblia Poliglota Complutense (de Nebrija) 2087
biblical cantillation 908-909
biblical characters
  described by Josephus 1778-1794
  described by Pseudo-Philo 2200-2212
biblical Hebrew 790
biblical Judaism 314, 502, 1869, 1874
  astrology in 2031-2033
  astronomy in 2037
biblical medicine 1705-1706
biblical monotheism see monotheism
biblical philology 1761
biblical poetics 2052
biblical religion, secular understanding of 1866
bigamy, ban on 1848
biography, in Rabbinic Judaism 2061-2076
biology, and Judaism 1620-1629
biotopes, protection of 1725-1726
birds
  clean and unclean 1723-1724, 1725, 1729 n. 14
  commandment of sending of 2194
birkat ha-minim 1876
Birkat Ha'aretz see Grace after Meals
birth
  death during 1715
  defects 1708
  of Moses 2201, 2202
  superstitions about 1908-1909

Black Power, Jewish preaching on 2278-2279, 2283 n. 79
blasphemy 369
Blau, Joseph C. 790
Blau, Joshua 790, 2169, 2181 n. 11, 2183 n. 51
Bleich, J. David 1944, 1945, 1950 n. 23, n. 27, 1951 n. 41, n. 43
Bleich, M. 859, 1409 n. 27
blessings 592, 597-598, 646, 649, 679, 688, 799-800, 802-803, 805, 807-808, 812, 815, 817, 824-825, 827, 829, 832, 948, 974, 1001, 1004, 1080, 1139, 1171, 1173, 1193, 1232, 1702
blindness see visual disabilities
Bloch, A.I. 1405
Bloch, J.L. 1405, 1406, 1409 n. 25
blood, purity of (limpieza de sangre) 1685, 2078, 2080, 2088
Blumenkranz, B. 1676
Blumenthal, Michael 1639
Boccarat, Abraham 272
bodily harm, punishments for inflicting of 1702
Boer War, sermons on 2273-2274
Böhm, G. 1397 n. 21
Bohr, Niels 975
boils 1708
Boleslav (Prince of Great Poland and Kalisz) 214
Bonafed, Salomón 1680
Bonafós, Saltiel 1680
Bonfils, Joseph (Tov Elem) 1616
Book of Beliefs and Options (Joseph) 206
Book of Commandments (Sefer haMitzvot) (Maimonides) 1661
Book of Foundations (Libro de las fundaciones, Saint Theresa) 2089
Book of Gardens and Parks (al-Qirqisani) 1826
Book of Kingdoms and Roads (Al-Bakri) 1823-1824
Book of the Pious (Regensburg) 255
Book of Principles (Albo) 206
Boorstein, Sylvia 576
Borowitz, Eugene B. 576, 769-770
botany, Talmudic 1626-1627, 1629 n. 5
Bouzaglo, David 1854
Boyance, P. 1051
Boyarin, Daniel 949, 951, 1483, 1501 n. 17, 1941, 1942, 1949 n. 6
Boyden, Edward A. 964
bread from heaven (manna), Jesus presented as 2135
Breffny, B. de 1396, 1397 n. 17, n. 20, n. 33, n. 35
Breithaupt, Johann Friedrich 2238 n. 1
Brenk, F.E. 1052
Breslauer, S. Daniel 775, 782
brit 137
Brit Milah see circumcision
British Judaism 20-31

preaching in 2267, 2270, 2271, 2272-2275
Brock, S. 1320 n. 1
Brodsky, Garry M. 512-513
Brontologion (Qumran text) 2032
Brooke, G.J. 1320 n. 2
Brooten, B. 1501 n. 26, n. 27
Brown, F. 1332 n. 5, 1465 n. 9
Brown, Norman O. 926
Brueggemann, W. 1447
Buber, Martin 408, 410, 428, 564, 566, 568, 571, 573, 740, 751-753, 759, 941-942, 956, 1021-1022, 1092, 1100, 1101
Buber, Solomon 1767
Buchenwald 430
buggery 2140
Bulan (king of Khazaria) 1824-1825
burial rituals
  of Beta Israel 1749, 1753
  flutes and wailer women 2125
  of Kaifeng (China) Jewry 1636-1637
  of Khazars 1828
  and superstition 1910
burial societies 8
Burner, J. 1090
Burns, R.I. 1501 n. 34
business transactions, superstitions about 1914
Byzantium
  Karaites in 1767-1768, 1810-1811
  Rabbanites in 1768
  relations with Khazars (*Kuzarim*) 1829
  Samaritans in 2248-2251

Caballería, Don Vidal de la 1678
Caballería, Fernando de la 1677-1678
Cabrera, Andrès 1681
Cadima 2305, 2306
Cairo Geniza 120, 1809, 2036, 2170
  Bible translations and commentaries in 2173-2174, 2177, 2178
  classification of Judaeo-Arabic sources of 2172-2181, 2182 n. 28
  collections 2171, 2172-2173, 2182 n. 19, n. 26, n. 27
  fragments 119, 2173, 2182 n. 30, n. 31, 2183 n. 37, 2183 n. 43, n. 44, n. 46, n. 47, n. 50
  grammar and massorah 2175
  legal texts 2175, 2177, 2178
  literature and folklore texts 2175-2176, 2178
  liturgy and prayer texts 2176, 2179-2180
  mysticism texts 2176-2177
  philosophy texts 2176, 2177, 2178
  polemic texts 2176
  scientific works 2177
Cairo manuscript (Qumran writings) 190
calendar 32-33, 37, 179, 188, 192, 194
  awareness of 2037
  Ethiopian 1746
  Jewish 2040-2042, 2043, 2044

observance by Kaifeng (China) Jewry 1634-1635
  Karaite 1813-1814
  lunar 1746, 2039
  Rabbinic calculations of 2038, 2039
  Samaritan 2258
  solar 2037, 2039
  used in Qumran 2037-2038
Calmet, Abbot Augustin 81
Calvin, J. 78
Cambridge University Library, Geniza collections at 2172, 2182 n. 19, n. 26, n. 27
Camino de perfección (The Road to Perfection, Saint Theresa) 2089
Canaan 13, 153, 491
Canaanites 68, 517, 520, 522
Candelabrum of Illumination (Aboab) 255
Canon 14, 15, 19, 166, 169, 246-247, 248, 327, 341, 487
Canticles *see* Song of Songs
cantillation 908-909, 917
Cantor, A. 1501 n. 42
cantoral music 1860
Cardoso, Isaac 1689
Carmelite order 2088
Caro, Isaac 1899, 1904 n. 76
Caro, Joseph 343, 932-933, 968, 1657, 1658, 1660, 1667-1668, 1772, 1946
  Beit Yosef 1665, 1666, 1667, 1674, 1771, 1944, 1946
  on homosexuality 2141
  Shulhan Arukh (Set Table) 1665, 1666, 1668, 1669-1670, 1671, 1674, 1771, 1853, 1854
Carta-enciclica (Severus) 1676
Cartagena, Alonso de 1683, 1684-1685, 1689-1690
Cartagena, Pedro de 1681
de Cartegena family 1680-1681
Cassin, Rene 2307
Cassuto, Umbretto 276
Casti, John L. 975
Castile, conversos in 1682
Castro, Américo 2083, 2085, 2090
category formations
  in Haggadah 1595-1596
  halakhic 1595, 1883, 1887
  in Midrash 1595
  in Mishnah 1595
Catholics 77, 79, 81, 86-87, 122, 151, 1676-1677
cattle, ban on raising small 1728
celebrations, among Beta Israel 1746
celebratory preaching 2268
Celestina (de Rojas) 2087
celibacy, practised by homosexuals 2140
cemeteries, Jewish, in China 1649-1650
ceremonies, and rituals 798-803, 1799-1800
Cervantes, Miguel de 2085, 2089-2090
Chabad Hasidism 1735
Chabad-Lubavitch movement, in Asia 1648

Channing, William Ellery 2273
Chanukah see Hannukah
charity 50-62, 566, 577, 810, 872, 878, 1014,
 1067
 commandment of 2193
 Jewish preaching on 2276-2277
Charles I (king of Spain, Holy Roman emperor
 Charles V) 2081-2082
chauvinism, in Judaism 1731, 1733-1734,
 1737, 1738, 1740 n. 50, n. 51
chavurah see Havurah
cheresh, shoteh v'katan category (deaf-mute, mental
 disability and pre-verbal minor) 1696,
 1698-1700, 1705
Chichek (Khazar princess) 1829
childbirth, death during 1715
childlessness 1708-1709, 1716
 see also surrogate motherhood
children
 custody over, and Jewish law 1918-1919,
 2197-2198, 2199 n. 29
 rights of 1918, 1920 n. 9
Children of Israel 455-457
 see also benai yisrael
Chilton, B.D. 1320 n. 3
China, Judaism in 1630-1652
chiromancy 1911
Chmielkicki massacres 256
Chmielnitski, Bogdan 216
Choice of Pearls (ibn Gabirol) 254
Chosen People 597, 736, 766-768, 770, 777,
 1005, 1234, 1235, 1729-1741
 and antisemitism 1730, 1738 n. 3
 burden of 1731, 1735, 1738 n. 10
 Christian claim to 1732, 1739 n. 23
 Conservative Judaism on 1740 n. 44, n. 47
 and covenant 1730, 1738 n. 5, 1873,
 2092-2093, 2094-2095
 medieval Judaism on 1732-1735
 and promise of the land 1730-1731, 2093
 Rabbinic literature on 1731-1732
 Talmud on 1731, 1738 n. 7
Chouraqui, Andre 1857
Christ 69, 87, 488, 492, 497-498, 503
 see also Jesus
Christian Arabic 2170
Christian church 488, 498
Christian doctrine 1895-1896
Christian exegesis 2052
Christian Hebraism 77, 79, 81, 1811, 1817
Christian Judaism 70, 192
Christian literature 2073
Christian martyrs 71
Christian scholarship 169-170, 1867-1870,
 2045, 2075
Christian of Stavelot 1826
Christian theology 1866, 1900
Christian-Jewish dialogue 2060
Christianity 63, 69, 72, 151, 153, 166, 190,
 270, 330, 366, 391-392, 491, 544
 adopted by Roman Empire 2112, 2116

 among Khazars 1823-1824, 1829
 antisemitism of 541, 633-634, 643
 early, study of 2073-2074
 in the Holy Land 2249
 origins of 1868-1869
 relationship with Judaism 77, 79-80, 83,
 87, 1874-1876, 1878
 and Samaritanism 2247, 2249-2250
 views
 of salvation 2115
 of women's sexuality 1948
Christians 66, 118-119, 122, 401, 493, 499,
 501, 503, 505, 507-508
 claiming to be the Chosen People 1732,
 1739 n. 23
 distrust of conversos 1678
 Ethiopian 1741
 seen as idolators by Jews 1732, 1739 n. 24
chronicles, Samaritan 2255-2256, 2264 n. 76,
 n. 79
chronological order, in the Bible
 2055-2056
Chubb, Thomas 80
churches, Jews seeking refuge in 1665-1666
circumcision 89-95, 139, 287, 493, 592, 798,
 826, 848, 915, 947, 984, 990, 1010, 1015,
 1026, 1028, 1030, 1033, 1036, 1041, 1049,
 1068, 1095, 1188, 1194, 1278, 1413, 1768
 of Beta Israel boys 1748-1749
 in the Bible 89-90
 of females among Beta Israel 1749
 Josephus on reasons for 1780
 night before 1909
 as part of conversion to Judaism 114, 123,
 804
 performed by women 1952 n. 52
 ritual of 90-94, 813-815
 on Sabbath 2131
 of Samaritan boys 2259
'civil Judaism' 1796, 1801-1802
Civil Rights Movement (United States), Jewish
 preaching about 2277-2278
classical Judaism 149, 281, 290, 295, 369,
 443-444, 462-472, 1302, 1304, 1307, 1349,
 1410, 1448, 1506, 1516
classifications
 of data 2216, 2217
 in Mishnah 1834
 hierarchical 1837, 2155, 2285
 of Judaeo-Arabic sources of Cairo Geniza
 2172-2181, 2182 n. 28
 in Scripture 2159, 2161
 in Sifra 2160-2167
cleanness see purity
Clement of Alexandria, St 74
Clements, R.E. 1447, 1447 n. 11, n. 12,
 n. 15
cloning 1652-1655, 1655 n. 6, n. 16
Cochin (India), synagogue in 1634
Code of Discipline 262
Codex Theodosius (CTh) 1765

codifications of Jewish law 343, 1656-1668,
  1668-1676, 1816, 1818
Cohen 1827
Cohen, Arthur A. 210, 412, 770, 1090
Cohen de Azevedo, Moses 2272
Cohen, Gerson D. 1804, 1805
Cohen, Hermann 135, 737, 747-749, 754,
  779
Cohen, Mark R. 1012-1013
Cohen, Meir Simha 277
Cohen, Menachem 2238
Cohen, Moise 313
Cohen, R.I. 1397 n. 28, n. 30
Cohen, S.J.D. 1484, 1489, 1501 n. 22, n. 41
Cohen, Steven 701, 982, 984-985, 1796,
  1805, 1806
collections
  of Cairo Geniza 2171, 2172-2173,
    2182 n. 19, n. 26, n. 27
  Firkovich (Russian National Library) 1811,
    2168, 2171, 2173, 2181 n. 4
  preacher's 2268, 2272, 2280 n. 21
  of wise sayings 2065, 2070-2071, 2073
Columbus, conversos connected with 2082
Comedia 2086
comets 2040
commandments 599, 657, 713, 741, 751, 756,
  799, 804, 810, 817, 826, 854-857, 871, 873,
  880, 883, 888, 947, 1004-1007, 1012, 1015,
  1194, 1220, 1229, 1230, 1231, 1234, 1256,
  1257, 1259
  astral-magical explanations of 1616
  not enforceable by the court 2192-2194,
    2199 n. 6
  observance of 1803
  positive 2192-2194
  prohibition to reproduce 1779, 1793 n. 4
  of the sons of Noah (7) 1731, 1739 n. 19
  ten 5, 43, 100, 163, 251, 288, 354,
    595-596, 606, 869, 906, 908, 988, 1013,
    1663
  of Torah 536, 1072, 1258, 1474,
    1503-1504, 1512-1513, 1727
commentaries 2216, 2226
Commentary to the Mishnah (Maimonides) 204,
  254, 1661
Community Rule 190-192, 495
compositional techniques, in the Bible
  2056-2060
compositors, of the Talmud 2063-2065
conception, superstitions about 1908
concubinage, in biblical times 1919
confession, of sins 2127
conflicts, resolution of 1883-1884
Conforte, David 1770
congregation
  disabled people participating in 1700
  Rule of 193
conquistadores, conversos among 2082
Conservative Judaism 95-105, 107-112, 165,
  257, 345, 511, 693, 696, 702, 705-707, 766,

769, 796, 798, 922-923, 977-978, 980-982,
  1005, 1332, 1335, 1347, 1352, 1361, 1362,
  1394, 1478 n. 2, 1492, 1496
  in America 1797-1798, 1799, 1803-1805
  on Chosen People 1740 n. 44, n. 47
  on homosexuality 2139
Conservative movement 96, 107, 209, 211,
  695-696, 699, 706-707, 800, 828, 830-831
Constantine Porphyrogenitus (emperor of
  Byzantium) 1829, 1830
Constantinople, leader of Jewish community
  1688-1689
Constantius (Roman emperor) 2248-2249
contextual reading methodology 2045, 2046-
  2051, 2060
Contra algunos cizanadores de la nacion de los conver-
  tidos del pueblo de Israel (Barrientos) 1685
contraception 855-857
contracts, illegal 1917-1918, 1920 n. 7
conversion 1663, 1664, 1676
  to Beta Israel 1749
  as a condition for forgiveness 2130
  from Beta Israel to Christianity or Islam
    1749, 1752
  requirement of Jewish tradition 2131
  to Christianity
    of Jews 644, 1765
      in medieval Spain and Portugal
        1676-1690, 2077-2091
    of Samaritans 2248
  to Islam, of Jews 461, 1773
  to Judaism 112-126, 1734, 1735, 1795-
    1796
    from Christianity 2079
    of Khazars 1823-1827
    see also proselytes
conversionary sermons 1889
conversos 2077-2091
  internal prosecution of 2082-2083
  Judaizers 1679, 2079, 2080, 2081
  in medieval Spain 1676-1690, 1772, 1900,
    1904 n. 78
convivencia (coexistence of Christians, Moors and
  Jews) 2080
Cooley, C. 1103
Cordovero, Moses ben Jacob 255, 479, 930
cosmology, and Judaism 126-136
cosmopolitanism 234
cosmos, Jewish concepts of 2038
Council of Trent 79
covenant 14, 15, 17, 18, 19, 37, 69-70, 78,
  88, 89-91, 95, 114, 136, 137, 142, 186-188,
  190, 191, 192, 367, 414, 435, 472, 508, 534,
  554, 572, 582, 584, 591-592, 594-596,
  598-600, 620-621, 707, 736, 741, 753-754,
  766-770, 779, 785, 798, 800, 813-816,
  825-826, 829, 838, 840-841, 846, 893, 896,
  1009, 1013, 1080, 1082-1087, 1171, 1172,
  1173, 1190, 1193, 1196-1199, 1436-1443,
  1445-1447, 1455, 1525, 1534, 1535, 1538
  Ark of 528, 596-599

and chosen people   1730, 1738 n. 5, 1873
between God and all other nations (Noahide
    Covenant)   1732, 1735
between God and the Jews/Israel (Sinai
    Covenant)   139-141, 1079, 1439-1441,
    1730, 1735, 1869, 1872-1873, 2092-2093,
    2094-2095
and possession of the land   1885, 2093
of salt   2050
Cover, R.   1321, 1332 n. 1
Cowan, Paul   571
Crane, Oliver T.   2255
creation   588-589, 621, 652, 712, 714, 735,
    749, 783-784, 812, 815-818, 820-821,
    825-826, 892, 896, 900-901, 905, 939-940,
    945-948, 950, 952-955, 1046, 1049, 1059,
    1085, 1108, 1141, 1146, 1176, 1178, 1179,
    1198
    as described in Genesis   972, 974-975,
        1627-1628, 2054
    disabled persons being part of   1702-1703
    ex nihilo   719-721, 725-731, 1437
    through God's Word   2133-2134
    holistic view of   1627-1629
    man being active partner in   1755-1757
    and salvation of Israel   2114
    special rank of humanity in order of nature
        1721
    Torah on   722, 725-731, 1722-1723,
        2292-2293
creatures   2127
creeds   151, 154, 161-162
Crescas, Hasdai   161-162, 206, 728-731, 733,
    736, 953, 967, 969
Crimean peninsula   1811, 1830
Crimean War, sermons on   2272-2273
Cronbach, A.   1252, 1253
Cross, Frank Moore   517, 948-949
cross-cultural experiences, of Judaism
    1865-1866
crucifixion   80, 408-409
Crusader rule, Samaritans under   2252
Crusades   406, 531-532, 637, 641-643, 664,
    825, 868, 1013
Culi, Jacob   1771
cultic rites   1599
    see also Temple cult
cultural relativism   1870
cultural-spiritual styles, and religion
    1870-1871
culture
    Arabic   2168
    and identity   2180
    Judaeo-Arabic   2179
    polytheistic   1763
    and religion   1864, 2283
    and Torah   2283-2293
    Yiddish   222
cursing, of deaf persons   1703
Curtis, Edward   437
Curzon, David   574

custody, of children of divorced couples
    1918-1919, 2197-2198, 2199 n. 29
Cutheans see Samaritans
cyclical character, of Israel's history   2094
Cyril, Saint   1824
Czerniakow, Adam   424

da'at   1696, 1697-1698, 1699, 1700
Dahlquist, A.   1051
Dalian (China), Jewish community in   1643
Damascus Document (Qumran writings)   19,
    185-187, 189-194, 1809
Damascus Rule   495
Damascus sect   186, 190
Dan, Joseph   253
Daniel, as described by Josephus   1788
Danzig, Abraham   1669-1671
Darkei Moshe (Isserles)   1666, 1668
Darkhé hammishnah (Frankel)   100
Darmesteter, James   296, 300-301
Darwin, Charles   972
Dasxuranc'i, Movses   1823
Daum, A.   1502 n. 80
David
    adultery of   1097-1100
    as described by Josephus   1785-1786
    in Liber Antiquitatum Biblicarum (Pseudo-Philo)
        2210-2211
Davidman, L.   1502 n. 89
Davidson, David   2271
Davidson, Herbert A.   967
Davies, W.D.   882
Davila dynasty   1681
Davis, N.Z.   1501 n. 43, 1501 n. 50
Dawidowicz, Lucy S.   422, 1339, 1342 n. 17
Day of Atonement (Yom Kippur)   22, 24-26,
    33-38, 44-49, 83, 89, 178, 358-359, 362-364,
    424-425, 429, 430-431, 449, 455-459, 513,
    531-532, 659, 695, 715, 757, 801, 810,
    820-821, 980, 982, 986-987, 1019, 1030,
    1035, 1126, 1127, 1140, 1185-1187, 1189,
    1215, 1217, 1255, 1256, 1257, 1329, 1330,
    1433, 1490, 1546, 2130
    celebrations among Moroccan Jews
        1859-1860
Day of Judgement   34, 40, 45
Days of Awe   34, 36, 38, 45, 46, 364
    sermons for   2269
dayyanim (judges), in Morocco   1850
Dead Sea scrolls see Qumran, texts
Dead Sea Sect   1303
deafness see hearing disabilities
Deah, Y.   1464
death
    and afterlife, Judaic doctrines of   196-212
    during childbirth   1715
    penalty   2151
    superstitions about   1910, 1913
Deborah   2207
Decalogue see Commandments, ten
Décret Crémineux   308

Defensorium unitatis christianae (Alonso de Cartagena) 1683, 1689
definitions
  of genres 2171-2172, 2178, 2183 n. 52, n. 54
  of Judaism 579-588, 1866
  of religions 1863, 1871-1872
  of sermons 1887
  of Zionism 2293
Defter 2254-2255
Deists 81, 83, 415
Delitzsch, Franz 85
Dellapergola, S. 1272
Delmedigo, Joseph Solomon (*YASHAR* of Candia) 733, 970-971, 1770, 1811
Demiurgos (Plato) 415
demons 261, 1906, 1907-1908, 1913
  astral-magical explanations of 1616
Denkart 1826
derash 271, 273, 2047, 2048
derech emet 270
Derenbourg, Hartwig 297-298
Derenbourg, Joseph 297
Derrida, Jacques 956
Descartes, René 134, 734, 961
desertification 1728, 1729 n. 22
The Destruction of the European Jews (Hilberg) 421
determinism 313, 315-316, 318, 321
Deuteronomy 582
  in Judaism 2091-2101
devekuth 219
Dewey, J. 1231
Dexinger, F. 2263 n. 58
dhimma 460-461
d'Holbach, Paul 81-82
dialectics 1092, 1093, 1095-1097
  in Judaism 1690-1696
Dialogue with Trypho, A Jew (Justin Martyr) 73
Dialogus (Alphonsi) 1686
diarrhoea 1709
diaspora 17, 32, 41, 43, 47, 50, 367, 371, 588, 602-603, 608-610, 612, 615, 620, 635, 647-649, 678, 684, 688-689, 736-737, 746, 756-758, 760-761, 778, 785, 796, 1078, 1079, 1081, 1086, 1463, 1485, 1536
  Aegean 1763-1764
  influence of local culture 1763
  Jewish law in 1657
  support for old *yishuv* 2294-2296
Didascalicon (Hugh of St. Victor) 2045
dietary laws 343, 596, 602-603, 646, 651, 947, 982, 1026, 1029, 1031, 1037, 1041, 1044, 1484, 1542, 1763
  Karaite 1813
  see also kashrut; kosher
Dillon, J. 1052
Dimashqi 1823
Dinur, Benzion 662-663, 676, 1241, 1242, 1254

diphtheria 1707-1708
disabilities
  disqualifying priests from officiating the cult 1701
  Judaism and 1696-1705
disabled people, treatment of 1703
discourse
  Aggadic 1593
  focusing on Sages 2065-2073
  halakhic 1593
  logics of, in Talmud 1934-1938, 1940
  metapropositional 2222-2225
  mode of
    in Mishnah 1833, 2223, 2225
    in Pentateuch 1833-1834
  philosophical 2215
Discourses on the Jewish Religion (Leeser) 2268, 2272
diseases
  causes of 1707
  in Jewish sources 1705-1718
Dishon, J. 1501 n. 40
dislocations 1710
diversity, within Judaism 579-580, 876-877, 1545, 1605-1611, 1879
divination, Talmud on 1913
divine providence 2129
divinization of humans 1875
divorce 80, 285, 292-294, 347-348, 369, 379, 1815
  custody of children 1918-1919, 2197-2198, 2199 n. 29
  serving writ of 2129-2130
Documentary Hypothesis 516
Dod Mordecai (The Beloved of Mordecai, Kokizow) 1811
dodder, fruit of 1622
Dodds, J. 1396 n. 3, n. 4, n. 6
Doenme movement 1773-1774
Dohm, Christian Wilhelm von 507
Domestic Judaica 8
Dominican order, intolerance towards conversos 2080
Don Quijote (Cervantes) 2085, 2089-2090
Don-Yehiyah, E. 1374
Doppelt, Frederic A. 1740
Douglas, Mary 961
Douglas, W. 947
Dov Ber of Mezeritch (*Maggid*) 218, 219
Dover Mesharim 1899
drawings, by Rashi 2237-2238
dreams, interpretation of 1915
dropsy (hydrops) 1710
Drosnin, Michael 971
drought 1603
Drury, Shadia B. 781
dual Torah *see* Rabbinic Judaism
dualism 191, 210
Dubb 1350
Dubno, S. 276
Duran, Simon ben Zenach 505

Durkheim, E.   297, 302, 1102, 1232
Duties of the Heart (Paquda)   254
dwarfism   1710
The Dwelling Places (*Las moradas*, Saint Theresa)
   2089

Easter, importance for Christians   1766
Eastern Europe
   education of Jews in   1266-1272
   Judaism in   213-224, 1272-1290, 1335-1337
   Karaite communities in   1811
Ebreo, Leone   *see* Abravanel, Judah
Ecclesiastes, redaction of   2052
eclipse   2043
Eco, Umberto   939
ecology
   in ancient Judaism   1718-1729
   of Nile delta   1620-1621
economics
   and Halakhah   1771-1772
   and Judaism   224-240
   and study of Torah   2292
ecstasy   658, 678, 920, 931, 936, 1020,
   1104-1106
Ed-Dar'i, Moshe   2297
Edelstein, L.   1052
Eden   36, 38, 48, 128, 131, 164, 196, 224,
   260, 294, 462-465, 471, 521
Edict of Expulsion (1492)   1688, 2081
education
   of American Jews   702, 763
   of Jews in China   1635, 1640, 1648
   of Jews in Eastern Europe   1266-1272
   of Moroccan Jews   1851-1853
   role of Judaeo-Arabic texts   2178
Egypt
   fertility of the soil   1719
   Karaite communities in   1812
   prophecy against   2056
Egyptian plagues, sequence of   1620-1622
Ehrlich, Arnold Bogumil   276
Ehud, L.   1538
Eibeschutz, Jonathan   1755
Eichhorn, Johann G.   83
Eichmann in Jerusalem (Arendt)   421
Eilberg, Amy   1805
Eim Habanim S'mechah (Teichtal)   411
Einhorn, David   208
Eisen, Arnold M.   1737, 1740 n. 47, 1803,
   1806
Eisenberg, Shaul   639
Eisenstein, J.   1093
Elazar, Daniel   1089, 1357, 1374, 1797
election of Israel *see* chosen people
Elementary Forms of the Religious Life (Durkheim)
   302
Eli   2208, 2209, 2258
Eliade, Mircea   938, 941
Eliezer the Great of Mainz   2229
Elijah   1717, 1908-1909, 2132
Elisha   1716-1717, 2132

elites   1863-1864
Eliyahu, Mordecai   2197
Ellis, Albert   2147
Elohist   518-521
Elon, Menaham   1850-1851
Emancipation   661-663, 739, 755, 994, 1241,
   1392, 1492, 1493
embryology   1623-1625
Emden, Jacob   1906
Emet ve-Emunah   165
emissaries (*shadarim*), seeking support in
   diaspora for old *yishuv*   2294-2296, 2298,
   2299-2300
emotions, in Judaism   240-250
empires of antiquity, and Rabbinic Judaism
   2062
Encyclopaedia of Islam   2171
Encyclopaedia Judaica   2171
encyclopedia of Judaism, scriptural   2102,
   2103
end of times   603, 621, 685, 714, 812, 820,
   826, 876, 1019, 1172, 1188
Enlightenment   80-82, 85-86, 102, 123, 165,
   207, 257, 507
   anti-Jewish themes of   1866, 1879 n. 1
Enoch, books of   2037, 2038
entertainment function, of Jewish preaching
   1897
Enuma Anu Enlil (Babylonian text)   2032
epilepsy   1710
Epstein, M.M.   1340, 1342 n. 1, n. 26, 1405,
   1407, 1410 n. 29
Epstein, Baruch   277, 2142
Epstein, C.   1397 n. 22
Epstein, Yechiel Mechel   344, 1675-1676
Erasmus, Desiderius   2088
Erdal, Marcel   1827
Erek Apayim   411
Eruv-ceremony   1622
Esau, as described by Josephus   1780-1781
eschatological doctrines   201, 204
eschatological literature   179-181
eschatology   195, 211, 212, 539, 613-614, 750,
   783, 826, 880, 902, 949, 1019, 1183, 1204,
   1205
eschaton   192, 202
Eshkol ha-Kofer (The Cluster of Henna, Hadassi)
   1818
Espina, Alonso de   1685
Essay on Resurrection (Maimonides)   204-205
Essays in Jewish Biography (Alexander Marx)
   105
Essenes   84, 183-184, 203, 486, 494, 549,
   551-553, 555-556, 558, 561, 612, 614, 1019,
   1451
   library at Qumran   497-498
*The Establishment of Proofs for the Prophethood of
   Our Master Muhammad* (al-Hamdani)   1826
Esther
   Fast of   49, 1748
   women reading Scroll of   1947, 1952 n. 67

eternal life   195-197, 200, 202-204, 205,
   209-212, 291-292, 294, 552, 575, 613, 905,
   951, 1068, 1110, 1173, 1204, 1247
Ethical Manual of the Rosh (ben Yehiel)   255
ethics   251, 253, 259
   of human cloning   1652-1655
   Kabbalistic   255-256
   medical   854-873
   and rituals   1799-1800
Ethiopia, Judaism in   1741-1753
Ethiopian Bible   1741
Ethiopian calendar   1746
Ethiopian Christians   1741
ethnic Jewish identity   1795, 1800, 1805
'ethnolects'   2170
Etkes, I.   1501 n. 52
Etsi doctoris gentium (Benedict XIII)   1687
Etz Hayyim (The Tree of Life, Aaron ben
   Elijah)   1820
Etzioni, Amitai   708
eulogies   1889-1890, 1901 n. 10
European Jewish refugees, in China   1638,
   1639, 1651
Eusebius   546
euthanasia   862-864, 951
Eutyphro   252
evil eye, beliefs among Moroccan Jews   1862
exaltation, acts of   2110
Exalted Faith (ibn Daud)   131
Las excelencias de los Hebreos (Cardoso)   1689
exclusion   671, 675, 986
exclusiveness, Jewish   303
exegesis   474, 481, 627, 635, 637, 640,
   644, 647, 651-652, 655-656, 715, 725, 746,
   748, 773, 777, 790-791, 845, 898, 905,
   1132, 1135-1139, 1147, 1150, 1151, 1153,
   1155-1157, 1159, 1160, 1161, 1164, 1165,
   1169, 1174, 1176, 1177, 1179, 1184, 1189,
   1199, 1209, 1227, 1255, 1257, 1266
   allegorical   1893, 1902 n. 37
   astral-magical   1616, 1618
   of Bible   266, 269, 274, 277, 278, 604, 859
      French medieval   2045-2060
   Christian   2052
   contextual   2046-2051
   extrinsic   2186
   intrinsic   2186-2187
   in Jewish preaching   1892-1893, 2265-2266
   Kabbalistic   280
   Karaite   1818-1819
   midrash   2046, 2047, 2184-2185
   peshat   2045, 2047-2049, 2050, 2051, 2060
   of Quran   2173
   of sage-stories   2065-2068
   Samaritan   2256-2257
   Sifra on   2049, 2057
   traditional rationalist   1618
   typological   1893
exemptions, from honoring of parents
   2196-2197
exilarch   646-647, 651

exile   33, 35, 40, 43, 48, 83, 139, 145, 172,
   186-187, 207, 331, 370, 439, 454, 462,
   465-466, 469, 475, 480, 504, 516-517,
   519-523, 527, 530, 533, 550, 555, 579, 581,
   586-588, 594, 600, 610, 620-621, 634, 650,
   736, 760, 796, 812-813, 818, 823, 830,
   837, 875-876, 883-890, 892, 900-901,
   939, 944-946, 1088, 1176, 1191, 1193,
   1194-1196, 1201, 1219, 1265, 1429, 1431,
   1436, 1441, 1468, 1525, 1528, 1529,
   1532-1534, 1536
   Babylonian   2242-2243
Exodus   34, 36, 38, 70, 224, 319, 472, 573,
   595-597, 600, 816, 818, 822, 827, 892-893,
   948-949, 1016, 1025, 1027, 1028, 1030,
   1032, 1035-1037, 1053-1060, 1062, 1183,
   1187, 1189, 1233, 1439, 1441, 1445, 1447,
   1541, 1547
   in Judaism   2101-2111
exorcism, in Judaism   1910-1911
Expositio in Matthaeum Evangelistam (Christian of
   Stavelot)   1826
Expulsion, Edict of (1492)   1688, 2081
extrinsic exegesis   2186
Eybeschütz, Jonathan   1906
eye diseases   1711
Eyn Sof   417, 503 (infinite Deity)
   see also God
Ezekiel
   Greek translation of   1763
   Rashi's commentaries on   2232
Ezra   2244
Ezra, Eliyahu   2300

The Face of God After Auschwitz (Maybaum)
   408
Fackenheim, Emil L.   413, 767, 771, 988,
   1022-1023
Faith After the Holocaust (Berkovits)   265, 408,
   412
A Faith for Moderns (Gordis)   209
Faitlovitch, Jacques   1751
Falasha (Beta Israel)   121-122, 1741-1753
Falk, M.   1498, 1502 n. 81
fall of fortune   2081
family relations
   in Judaism   281, 285, 287
   and study of Torah   2284
Fast of Esther   49, 1748
Fast of Gedaliah   38, 45
fasting
   among Beta Israel   1746, 1747
   national days of   2267
   and rainfall   1604
   in times of crisis   1600, 1601, 1605
fathers, obligations of   1918-1919
Feïn, Leonard   563, 704
Feiner, H.   1240
Feinstein, Moshe   1917, 1942, 1944, 1945,
   1947, 1949, 1949 n. 7, 1950 n. 17, 1951
   n. 41, n. 49, 1952 n. 54

Feldman, L.H.   857, 859, 1026, 1032, 1037, 1038, 2212
female circumcision, among Beta Israel   1749
female homosexuality   2141
female purity   1479, 1748, 1753, 1815, 1845, 1943, 1947
feminism   572-573, 768
and Judaism   707, 777, 1804
militant   2145
Fenton, Paul   658
Ferdinand (king of Aragón and Castile)   1677, 2079, 2081, 2085
Ferrer, Vicente   2079
fever   1711-1712
Fez
    center of Jewish learning   1847
    Jewish community supporting old *yishuv*   2295
    Zionist movement in   2303-2304
financial law   343, 348
Find, M.   1290
Fineshriber, William   2269, 2277-2278
Finkelman, Eliezer   2140, 2152
Finkelstein, Louis   1804
Fioretti (Francis of Assisi)   1897
Firkovich, Abraham   1811
Firkovich collections (Russian National Library, St. Petersburg)   1811, 2168, 2171, 2173, 2181 n. 4
Fishbane, Michael   946
Fishbane, Simcha   1674
Fishman, S.B.   1272, 1497, 1500, 1502 n. 77, 1502 n. 88, 1502 n. 91
fixed association, logic of   1934-1935, 1936-1937, 1940, 2159, 2219-2222, 2226
Flesher, P.V.M.   1320
Fletcher, Joseph   2146
floods   1597
flutes, at funerals   2125
folkist definition of Judaism   1866
folkist religions   1864
formal Judaism   1489
formative Judaism   282, 1515
Formstecher, Solomon   743-745, 747, 1018
Fortalitium fidei (de Espina)   1685
fortune, fall of   2081
Foucault, M.   1092, 1104
Fourth Lateran Council   118, 1663
fox, fable of   2236
Fox, Everett   574
Fox, Marvin   259
Foxbrunner, Roman A.   1735
Fraenkel, David   2272
Fraga, Astruc Rimoch de (Magister Francesch de Sant Jordi)   1680
France
    biblical exegesis, medieval   2045-2060
    Judaism in   295-313
Francis of Assisi, St   1897
Franco, Solomon   1618
Frank, Jacob   217

Frankel, Zechariah   100-102, 106, 108-109, 796, 1005
Frankfort, Henri   940-941
Frankiel, T.   1499, 1502 n. 90
fraternal warnings, before punishment   2129-2130
Frede, M.   1052
Freud, S.   942, 960, 1091, 1094, 1095, 1096, 1107
Freundel, Barry   2140, 2152
Friedman, M.A.   1501 n. 30, n. 31, 1538
frogs   1723
Fromm, Erich   942, 2144
fruits, prohibition to harvest during first three years   1727-1728
Frumkin, Aryeh Lev   2299
Frydman-Kohl, Baruch   1734
Frymer-Kensky, T.   1479, 1480, 1481, 1500 n. 2, n. 7
fundamentalism   699
funerals, weepers and flutes at   2125
fungi   1622-1623
fur trade, Jews engaging in   1643

Gaddin, R.   1356
Gagin, Abraham Chaim   2259
Galchinsky, M.   1493, 1502 n. 57, n. 59
Galen   964, 967
galut see exile
Gamaliel II   2039
Al-Gamil, Joseph   1812
Gan Eden (Garden of Eden, Aaron ben Elijah)   1818
Gans, David   969-970
Ganzfried, Solomon   1671-1673
Gaon, M.D.   2301
Gaon, Hai   342, 2227
Gaon, Nissim   2179
Gaon, Saadiah   254, 267, 1660, 1768, 2170
    on ban on homosexuality   2142
    criticism of Karaites   1810, 1818
    and the Jewish calendar   2042, 2044
    Judaeo-Arabic texts written by   2174, 2177, 2178
    Tafsîr   2174, 2255
Gaon of Vilna *see* Vilna, Elijah ben Solomon Gaon of (*GRA*)
Gaon, Yehudai   1660
Gaster, Moses   2255-2256, 2264 n. 79
Gastor, Theodore   1768
Gates of Prayer (Einhorn)   208
Gates of Repentance (Gerondi)   255
Gaventa, Beverly R.   113
gay militants   2138, 2144, 2148
gay synagogues   2139, 2153
Gaza, Jewish community in   2301
Gedaliah   1832
Geertz, Clifford James   1870-1871
Geffen, Rela Mintz   1797
Gehenna   164

Geiger, Abraham   100, 103-104, 208, 297,
   1004, 1018, 1656-1657, 1735
Geller, L.   1502 n. 78
gematria   270
gender, in Judaism   844-854
Genesis
   describing the creation   972, 974-975,
      1627-1628, 2054
   image/likeness of God   1758-1762
   in Judaism   2111-2124
   on proper use of natural resources   1721
Genesis Rabbah   388-389, 489, 495,
   2111-2124, 2225
genethlialogy   2034, 2035
genetic engineering, and Judaism   1627, 1653,
   1754-1757
Geniza *see* Cairo Geniza
genocide   407, 423
   and ecumenicism   86
genres
   definitions of   2171-2172, 2178, 2183 n. 52,
      n. 54
   generation of   2178-2179, 2181
   of Judaeo-Arabic literature   2172-2181
gentiles   65-67, 355-357, 369, 486, 489,
   492-494, 497, 525, 532, 553-554, 556,
   558-561, 602, 607, 610, 654, 657, 680,
   682-683, 692, 704-705, 739, 750, 769, 774,
   797, 815, 831, 838, 840, 842, 875, 900, 984,
   987, 994, 1003, 1008-1011, 1015-1019,
   1096, 1112, 1117, 1118, 1123, 1135, 1182,
   1184, 1189, 1192, 1195, 1198, 1205, 1295,
   1411, 1417, 1427, 1428, 1432, 1545
   and commandments of the sons of Noah (7)
      1732
   converting to Judaism   1734
   greeting of   2130
   Jews pretending to be   1664-1666
   lust of   1731-1732, 1733-1734
   Samaritans equalled to   2125
   studying Torah   1739 n. 17
Geonim   2227
Gereboff, Joel   101
gerey sedeq   119
gerim   187
Gerizim (mountain), holy place for
   Samaritanism   2241, 2244-2246, 2257-2258,
   2262 n. 26, n. 28, 2263 n. 58
Gerondi, Jonah ben Abraham   255
Gershevich, Leo I.   1643
Gershom, Rabbenu   2229
Gersonides *see* ben Gershom, Levi
Ghazal b. Abi as-Sarur (Ab Zehuta) al-Matari
   al-Ghazzawi   2257
Gibbor, Judah   1819
gigantism   1712
Gikatilla, Joseph   270
Gillman, Neil   212
Gilman, Stephen   2081
gilulim   436
Ginzberg, Asher (Ahad Ha'am)   758-759

Ginzberg, Louis   106, 108-111, 458
Girard, Rene   942
Gitelman, Z.   1290
Glatzer, Nahum   778
gnosis   472
gnosticism   72
Gobineau, Joseph Arthur de   84
God
   as an astrologer   2034
   astronomy as a way of knowing   2037
   Christian conception of   1875
   honoring of   2127, 2192
   image of   1758-1762
   Jewish conception of   324-340, 1652,
      1757-1762, 1883-1885
   keeping Israel's peace   1883-1884
   Kingdom of   2131, 2132
   in *Liber Antiquitatum Biblicarum* (Pseudo-Philo)
      2211-2212
   measuring man   2127
   punishments of   2104, 2111
   rationality of   2184, 2185
   relationship with Israel (people)   2115
   Samaritan concept of   2257
   traits of   2092
God in Search for Man (Heschel)   408
Godfrey of Bouillon, alleged encounter with
   Rashi   2237
Goitein, S.D.   650, 657, 659, 793, 1081,
   1396 n. 2, 1501 n. 30, 2168, 2171
Golb, Norman   184, 1827
Goldberg, H.   1409 n. 8, 1410 n. 32
golden calf   36, 37, 43, 44, 46, 363, 437,
   1296, 1613, 1618, 2100
   in *Liber Antiquitatum Biblicarum* (Pseudo-Philo)
      2203, 2205
Goldenberg, Robert   18795
Goldman, Ari L.   572, 983
Goldman, Bernard   842-843
Goldscheider, Calvin   506, 979-980
Goldschmidt, D.   1062
Goldsmith, E.   1240
Gollancz, Hermann   2274, 2275
Gombiner, Abraham Abele ben hayyim Halevi
   343
gonorrhea   1712-1713
Goodblatt, D.M.   1132, 1500 n. 15
Goodenough, Edwin R.   617-618, 843,
   1383
Goodman, M.   1132
Gordis, Robert   110, 209, 1740 n. 44
Gordon, Aaron David   758
Gordon, Albert I.   1804
Gospels   539-542, 544-545
   absence of, in Rabbinic Judaism   2063,
      2064, 2077 n. 4
   oral traditions of the Mishnah in
      2124-2136
   Samaritans in   2125
   Synoptic   69, 77, 102
gout   1713

GRA see Vilna, Elijah ben Solomon Gaon of (*GRA*)
Grace after Meals (*Birkat Ha'aretz*) 91, 815-816, 1060-1061
  women reciting 1945-1946, 1948
Graetz, Heinrich 100-103, 106, 108-109, 213, 276
grammar, Judaeo-Arabic writings on 2175
Grammatica sobre de la lengua castellana (de Nebrija) 2087
Granzfried, Solomon 1671-1672
Great Court *see Beit Din*
Great Sabbath 1889
Great Sanhedrin 32, 33
Greece, Judaism in 1763-1778
Greek language, use by Jews in Greece 1764, 1766, 1769, 1770, 1775
Greek nationalism 1774-1775
Greek Orthodox Church 1775
Green, A.A. 2274-2275
Green, Arthur 571, 767
Green Book of Aragón (*Libro Verde de Aragón*, Anchias) 2085
Green, Kenneth Hart 781
Green, William Scott 992
Greenberg, E. 1397 n. 43
Greenberg, Yitzchak (Irving) 40, 413-414, 1332 n. 11
Greenblum, Joseph 1794-1795
Greenspan, Leonard 771
Greenstone, J.H. 1465 n. 12
greetings, importance of 2130
Grodzinski, Hayyim Ozer 223
Grossfeld, B. 1320 n. 4
Grossman, Avraham 1948, 2229, 2233
Grossman, S. 1500, 1500 n. 5
Guénée, Abbé Antoine 82
Guerra de las Comunidades (war of the communities) 2081
Gugenheim, Ernest 309
Gugenheim, Michel 309
Guide for the Perplexed (*Moreh Nevukhim*, Maimonides) 79, 204, 254, 263, 505, 1820
Gumbiner, Abraham 1951 n. 44
Gunkel, Hermann 83
Gur Aryeh 272
Guttmann, Julius 733, 1383, 1397 n. 32
Guzmán de Alfarache (Alemán) 2086

Ha-Ketav ve-Ha-Qaballah (Koenigsberg) 276
Ha-Lorqui, Yehoshua (Jerónimo de Santa Fe) 1679-1680, 1686-1687
Ha-Qalir, Eleazar 2035, 2042
ha-Shomer ha-Tsair 426
Ha'amek Davar (Berlin) 277
Habad Hasidism *see* Chabad Hasidism
Habiba, Joseph (Nimukei Yosef) 1662
HaCohen, Hayim Yeshayah 1672
Had Gadya song 40, 42
Hadad-Ishi 1758-1759
Hadassi, Judah 1810, 1818, 1819-1820

Hadrian (Roman emperor) 2246-2247
Haftarot 43-46, 49, 174
Hag hakatzir festival 43
Hagahot Maimunniyot 1658
Hagar 1919
Haggadah 1, 2, 3, 34, 35, 41, 42, 267, 350-351, 354-357, 365, 646, 650, 755, 778, 811, 827, 1215, 1219, 1221, 1226, 1228, 1428, 1430-1435
  category formations in 1595-1596
  in the Halakhah 1593-1605
  in the Mishnah and Gospels 2128-2129
Haggadah (Passover) 1052-1062, 1806, 1855
hagigah 364
Hagim u-Mo'adim (Maymoun) 1858
Hagiographa 906
hair, covered by women 1944
Hakkafot ceremony 1860
Halachot Gedolot (Kayyara) 1660, 1947, 1952 n. 62
Halachot Pesukot (*sefer re'u*, Yehudai Gaon) 1660
halakhah 24, 26-28, 107, 127, 148, 165, 223, 229, 233, 234, 251, 252, 254, 255, 257-258, 259, 267, 275, 340-366, 368, 369, 414, 429, 431-432, 472-477, 509, 512, 530, 580, 640, 647, 654-655, 677, 680, 682, 689, 744, 753-754, 755, 759-761, 779-780, 785, 788, 790-791, 811, 825, 869, 878, 882, 883, 886, 964, 969, 974, 985, 1003, 1068, 1078, 1082, 1088, 1110-1114, 1116, 1117, 1120, 1123, 1124, 1125, 1127-1130, 1132, 1137, 1139, 1206-1217, 1219, 1221-1225, 1227, 1231, 1233, 1273, 1293-1296, 1298, 1300-1302, 1357, 1360, 1365, 1372, 1397, 1399, 1401, 1403, 1405-1409, 1428, 1430-1435, 1470, 1488, 1496, 1499, 1530, 1532, 1533
  and economics 1771-1772
  in Gospels 2129-2131
  Haggadah in 1593-1605
  on homosexuality 2141-2142, 2149-2151
  Karaite interpretation of 1813
  and Orthodox Judaism 1796
  Samaritan 2247, 2256, 2260, 2264 n. 80, n. 81
  on suicide 2150
  texts in Judaeo-Arabic 2175, 2177, 2178
  used for Jewish preaching 1894
halakhic category formations 1595, 1883, 1887
halakhic codes, reliance on 1800-1803
halakhic discourse 1593
halakhic injunctions 231, 232
Halevi, David ben Samuel 343, 968
Halevi, Jacob 800
Halévi, Joseph 1751
Halevi, Judah (Judah the Prince) 263, 276, 473, 476, 483, 504, 506, 513, 715-717, 719, 780, 782, 955, 965
  astral-magical convictions of 613
  on Chosen People 1732-1733, 1734

Kuzari   79, 120-121, 473, 482, 683,
    1732-1733, 1825, 1832, 2176
  on lunar calendar   2039
  Mi Kamokha   1861
  on proselytes   1733
  on Samaritans   2247
  suffering from scurvy   1716
  Zionistic poems by   2294
Halevi, Salomon (Pablo de Santa María)
    1679-1680
Halevy, Z.   2172
Halkin, Abraham   2171
Hall, C.S.   1109
Hallel-Psalms   264, 825-827, 907, 1059-1060,
    1061-1062
Hallo, William W.   784
Halperin, S.   1227
Ham   2140
Haman, as an astrologer   2034
Hameln, Gluckel   265
Hangzhou (China), Jewish community in
    1631-1632
Hannah, mother of Samuel   2208, 2210
Hanover, Nathan Nata   216
Hanukkah   2, 9, 39, 40, 48, 49, 513, 609,
    649, 695, 701, 826, 913, 980, 982-985,
    1284, 1661
  celebration by American Jews   1805
  celebration by Moroccan Jews
    1860-1861
Haran, made in   2046
Harbin (China), Jewish community in
    1641-1642, 1645
Haredi groups   29
al-Harizi, Judah   1767
Harlow, J.   1332 n. 10, n. 13
Harrison, Leon   2275, 2277
Hartman, David   761-763
Hartshorne, Charles   415
Harun, Abu-l-Faraj   1810, 1820
Hary, Benjamin   2170
Hasdai ibn Shaprut   1822, 1824, 1825-1826,
    1831-1832
Hasidic leadership   218, 220
Hasidic music   564, 565, 914, 916, 922, 923
Hasidic rabbis   218, 408, 432, 576
Hasidic spirituality   753
Hasidism   212, 217-220, 221, 224, 256, 303,
    369, 428, 501, 506, 535, 565, 571, 574, 657,
    690, 742, 743, 752, 772, 780, 801, 883, 910,
    1360, 1398, 1399, 1401, 1491, 1492, 1529,
    1549
  on Chosen People   1735
Haskala *see* Jewish Enlightenment
Hassan (king of Morocco)   2307
hatafat dam   89
hathalot   161
Hauptman, J.   1483, 1500 n. 14, 1501 n. 19,
    n. 20
Haut, R.   1500, 1500 n. 5, 1502 n. 73, n. 87
havdala   1799, 1951 n. 44

havurah   26, 283, 564-565, 566-570, 574,
    575-576, 694-695, 702, 707, 824, 922
Hawking, Stephen   975
Hayei Adam (Danzig)   1669-1671
Hayyuj, Judah ben David   267
Al-Haziri   2297
Hazleton, L.   1502 n. 69, n. 71, n. 72
headaches   1713
hearing disabilities   1703, 1705
heaven *see* eternal life
Hebrew alphabet, belief in power of letter
    combinations   1906
Hebrew language
  Biblical   790
  grammar, study of   1848, 2175
  use
    by Karaites   1820
    by Samaritans   2255
    in Judaeo-Arabic texts   2177, 2183 n. 51
Hebrew script, used in Judaeo-Arabic literature
    2169, 2170
The Hebrew Scriptures (Sandmel)   1869
Hegel, Georg W.F.   83, 742, 744-746, 749-
    750, 771, 1002, 1052, 1094, 1095, 1096,
    1100
Heidegger, M.   754
Heilman, Samuel   695, 1796, 1798, 1806
Heinemann, I.   1051, 1056, 1062
Heinemann, Joseph   1888, 2253
Heinze, A.   1502 n. 68
Hellenistic Judaism   1310, 1313
Hellenistic origins, of Samaritan writings   2253
Heller, Max   2269, 2277, 2282 n. 72
Hellinization
  of Jews in Greece   1775
  of Judaism   607-610
hemophilia   1713-1714
hemorrhoids   1714
Hengel, M.   1051
henna, used against evil spirits   1909
henotheistic   606
Her Life (*Su vida*, Saint Theresa)   2089
Heraclius (Roman emperor)   2251
Herberg, Will   210, 767, 771-772
Herder, Johann Gottfried von   82
hereditary diseases, and Jewish law   1654
heresy   366-380
hermeneutics   752, 898, 927, 956, 1092, 1093,
    1097, 1098, 1099, 1106, 1232
Hermetic influences, on the Muslim world
    1613
Hermetic literature, astral magic in   1612-
    1613
Herodotus   1719
Hertz, D.   1397 n. 28, 1492, 1501 n. 55
Hertz, J.H.   972
Hertzberg, Arthur   99, 107, 706, 1729,
    1879 n. 1
Herzl, Theodore   675, 686, 756-757, 2303
Herzog, I.H.   1399
Herzog, Isaac   1705

Heschel, Abraham Joshua   408, 563, 566, 577,
    702, 706, 753, 772-773, 1401, 1409 n. 13,
    1760
Heschel, S.   1501 n. 42
Hevra Qadishah   2259
hevrot (study groups)   1852
Hezekiah   394, 521
hezkat hayishuv   231
Hibbat Tzion (Love of Zion)   2303-2304
hidalgo class, of aristocracy in Spain   2085
hiddushim   107
Hidushei HaRashba (Adret)   343
hierarchical classifications   1837, 2155, 2285
High Holidays   33-38, 40, 45, 46, 209
high priesthood   1027
high priests   34, 175, 535, 541, 554, 561, 605
    rules of   1835-1836, 1929-1930
Hilberg, Raul   421
Hildesheimer, Rabbi   105
Hillel   349, 1657, 2041
Hillukh   2256
Hillula (*Lag ba-Omer*, Morocco)   1857
Himmelfarb, M.   1290
Hirsch, Emil G.   2270
Hirsch, Samuel Raphael   97, 103-104, 110,
    174-1755, 277, 508-510, 513, 675, 747,
    1002-1007, 1018, 1744-1745
Hisda   1624
Historia animalium (Aristotle)   1625
historical events, used for Jewish preaching
    1896-1897
The Historical School   95-101, 103-104, 106
historical thought   1921
history
    and biography   2062, 2063
    of Israel (people)   2093-2095, 2114,
        2115-2116, 2119-2124
    of Judaism   588-710
        affected by its environment   1870
        in Christian scholarship   1867-1870
    theology of   2113
History of the Caucasian Albanians (Dasxuranc'i)
    1823
History of the Jewish People (Alexander Marx)
    106
A History of the Jewish People in the Time of Jesus
    (Schürer)   84
History of the Jews in Christian Spain (Baer)   1679
*History of the Jews from the Earliest Times to the
    Present* (Graetz)   100
History of the Origin of Christianity (Renan)   84
History of the People of Israel (Renan)   84
The History of the Rabbis of Jerusalem (Frumkin)
    2299
Hitler, Adolf   407, 411-414, 416, 420-422,
    426, 428
Hizqia   2040
Hizzekuni (Manoah)   271
Hizzuq Emunah (Faith Strengthened, Isaac ben
    Abraham of Troki)   1811, 1817
Hobbes, Thomas   729, 734, 780, 1866

Hochmat Adam (Danzig)   1670
Hoffman, Lawrence   704, 1409
Hoffmann, David Zevi   105, 277, 2142
Hok le-Yisra'el   1853-1854
holiness   280, 526-527, 529
Holland, conversos in   2082
Hollekreisch   1909, 1910
Holocaust   44, 88, 149, 213, 306, 308, 312,
    406-432, 513, 570, 581, 586, 588, 674-675,
    693, 705, 708, 736, 763, 767-771, 778-780,
    810, 830-831, 885-887, 956-958, 961,
    985-989, 1022-1023, 1372, 1398, 1497,
    1540, 1541, 1547
    in Greece   1776-1777, 1778 n20
    see also Shoah
Holon, Samaritan community in   2260
Holy days   8
Holy of Holies   46, 176, 194
Holy Land
    Christianity in   2249
    Muslim conquests in   2251
holy places, building of churches at
    2248-2249
Holy Spirit   331, 447
Homberg, Herz   162
Homberg, N.   276
homiletical excellence, centers of   1892
homosexuality
    and celibacy   2140
    female   2141
    in Judaism   872, 2136, 2138-2142,
        2145-2146, 2149-2153
    permissiveness towards   2138-2139,
        2144-2146
    practical attitudes towards   2143-2144
    psychological attitudes towards   2146-2148
    repressive attitudes towards   2137, 2143
    reversibility of   2139
    statistics   2137-2138
homosexuals, marrying   2138-2139
Hong Kong, Jewish community in   1647-1648
Hongkou Ghetto (Shanghai)   1641
Honi, stories about   1599, 1600, 1605
honor, Spanish terms for   2085
honoring
    God   2127, 2192
    of parents   2191-2200
Hooker, Evelyn   2146
hope   240-241
Horowitz, Isaiah ben Abraham ha-Levi   122,
    432
Horowitz, S.   1497, 1502 n.75
hospitality   538, 1067
Hotz, L.   1357
houses, superstitions about   1910
Hoyle, Fred   973
Huberband, Simon   422
Hugh of St. Victor   2045
Hukama (Samaritan council)   2248, 2251
hukkim   1755, 1757 n. 4
Hullin   351

human autonomy 2138, 2145
human cloning 1652, 1654-1655, 1655 n. 6
human reproduction 1623-1625, 1702
humanism 79
humanists 275
humanity, and nature 1721-1722
humans 1761
Hume, D. 729, 972
humility 240-241
Hungary, Khazar influences 1830-1831
'Huns', Christianity among 1823
Hurba de Moshe (The Sword of Moses) 1906
Hurban 423
husbandry, animals allowed for 1723
hybridization of plants, prohibited 1757
Hyman, P.E. 1493, 1495, 1500, 1501 n. 49,
    1502 n. 58, n. 60, n. 62, n. 64, n. 65, n. 67,
    n. 92
Hyrcanus, John 2245, 2246

I-thou doctrine 941-942, 1091, 1092, 1100,
    1101
Ibn abi-Usaybya 2256
ibn Adham, Ibrahim 1897
ibn Athri, Mash'allah 2036
ibn al-'Ayyah, Ibrahim 2257
ibn Battuta, Abu Abdullah Mohammad 1632
ibn Bilaam, Judah ben Samuel 268
ibn Danon, Moses 2236
ibn Darta, Tabiah 2251, 2255
ibn Daud, Abraham 131, 1830
ibn Ezra, Abraham 206, 224, 267-270, 274,
    473-474, 476, 1767, 1832, 2236
    on astral magic 1613-1614
    on including liturgical poems in prayer
        2233
    on prohibition on interbreeding and
        mingling of agricultural species 1754
ibn Ezra, Moses 1613, 2168
ibn Gabirol, Solomon ben Judah 254,
    715-716, 1858
ibn Geat, Isaac ben Judah 268
ibn Gikatilla, Moses ben Samuel Ha-Kohen
    267
ibn 'Isa, Ali 2177
ibn Ishaq an-Nadim, Muhammad 1826
ibn Janah, Jonah 267
ibn Labrat, Danash 271
ibn Mayor, Shem Tov 1616
ibn Moskoni, Judah 1767
ibn Murjan, Meshalma 2257
ibn Nuh, Joseph 1810, 1820
ibn Salama ben Yusuf al-'Askari, Yusuf
    2256
ibn Saruk, Menahem 271, 2049, 2050
ibn Shaprut, Shem Tov 1616
ibn Shem Tov, Joseph 1891, 1896, 1898
ibn Shem Tov, Shem Tov 1832, 1893, 1896,
    1898, 1900-1901, 1904 n. 76
ibn Tsea, Munajjah 2256
ibn Tsedaqa, Munajjah 2256

ibn Zimra, David (*Radbaz*) 1663, 1664, 1667,
    1816
iconography 5, 7
icons 435
Idelsohn, Abraham Zvi 906, 912, 919
identity
    and culture 2180
    Jewish 1795, 1796, 1800, 1801, 1805, 1878
idolaters, Christians seen as 1732, 1734, 1739
    n. 24
idolatry 6, 56, 57, 82, 355-357, 369, 377,
    379, 434-443, 481, 1417, 1422, 1427, 1428,
    1431, 1445, 1474, 1475, 2095
    astral magic seen as 1614, 1616, 1618
    Jewish 1869
Iggerot Moshe 1917
Ikriti, Shemarya 1767
Ilan, T. 1500 n. 10
image of God 1758-1762
imitatio dei 252, 345, 476
immigration 213
    see also aliyah
immortality 201, 205-206, 210, 507, 589
    of the soul 195, 200, 202, 203, 208
impurity 529, 538, 543, 621-622, 857, 859,
    869, 877, 907, 1110-1118, 1120-1124, 1140,
    1145, 1146, 1159, 1187
    Levitical uncleanness 621
    maddaf-uncleanness 1838-1847
    see also purity
incest 1943
    Karaite laws on 1813, 1815
incipit 2173, 2179
inclusio pattern, compositional technique of
    2059-2060
India, rebellion in, sermons on 2273
individualism, in America 1795
individuals, place within Rabbinic Judaism
    1882
infertility *see* childlessness
The Informed Heart (Bettelheim) 421
Inner Mongolia, Jewish communities in 1643
Inquisition 2079, 2082, 2083-2084, 2085
insanity (*shiga'on*) 1714
insects, allowed for human consumption 1724
Instruccion de Relator (de Toledo) 1684
integration 739
intellect, image of God metaphor for 1758,
    1759-1760
interbreeding, prohibition of 1627, 1754,
    1756-1757
intercalations 2041, 2043
intermarriages 124, 370, 501, 513, 1493
    between Jews and Chinese 1649
    between Karaites and Rabbanites
        1815-1816, 1821
    between Samaritans and Jews 2259, 2265
        n. 95
    of Esau, described by Josephus 1780-1781
    of Solomon, as described by Josephus 1788
intertestamental literature 202

intrinsic exegesis   2186-2187
Introduction (Geat)   268
Introduction to the Arabic Literature of the Jews
   (Steinschneider)   2170-2171
inyan terminology, use of   2049-2050, 2051
irrationality, of repentance   1898-1900
Isaac, as described by Josephus   1780
Isaac of Corbeil   1658
Isaacs, Nathan   348
Isabella I (Queen of Castile)   2079
Isaiah, prophecies of   1720
Iser, W.   1109
al-Isfahani, Abu Isa Ovadia   1817
Ishbili, Yom Tov ben Abraham   342
Ishmael   1624
Islam   119, 151, 166, 459
   conversion of Jews to   461, 1773
   influencing Jewish philosophy   1894
   Jews living under medieval   2169
   Kalam theology   1816
   Khazars practising   1823
   and Samaritanism   2251
   Sufi, influence on Jewish thought   2177,
      2180
Israel (corporate, society)   1881-1882,
   1883-1884, 1886
Israel, Jonathan   968
Israel (land)   462-484, 1441-1442
   and acceptance of Torah   1873
   and Chosen People   1730-1731
   and covenant with God   1885, 2093
   geology of   1719
   Judaism in   1357-1374
   Kabbalistic conceptions of   473-474,
      479-481, 483-484
   Karaite communities in   1809-1810, 1812
   maps of   2238
   old *yishuv*   2294-2303, 2307
   population density in   1718, 1729 n. 2
   union with   1885
   and Zionism   2293
Israel (people)   484-516, 1440, 1872, 1873,
   1875-1876, 1878
   history of   2093-2095, 2114, 2115,
      2119-2124
   leaders of   2095
   in *Liber Antiquitatum Biblicarum* (Pseudo-Philo)
      2211
   relationship with God   2093, 2115
   Rome as part of   2116
   salvation of   1934, 2112-2113, 2114, 2115,
      2119
Israel (person), deafness and blindness of   1703
Israel (state)
   Ashkenazi-centric orientation of   2168
   declaration of   2305
   Jews migrating to
      Beta Israel (Ethiopia)   1751-1752
      from China   1644
      from Morocco   2294, 2296-2303,
         2304-2307

Josephus on   1780
   Rabbinic courts in   2197
   Samaritans and   2259-2260
Israeli army, women serving in   1944-1945
Israelite religion   516-525
   and Judaism   1868, 1879 n. 6
Israelites
   conflicts between   1882-1884
   and corporate Israel (society)   1881-1882
   Samaritans describing themselves as   2242,
      2245
   sustained management of environment
      1718-1719
Israyel, Bishop   1823
Isserlein, Israel   1666, 2197
Isserles, Moses (*REMA*)   343, 863-864, 1666,
   1668, 1946, 1947, 1950 n. 18
Italy
   Jewish legacy   1767, 1777 n. 10
   Jewish preaching in   1892
De Iudaicis Superstitionibus (On the Superstitions
   of the Jews, Abogard)   1905
Ivry, A.   1347 n. 3
'Iyyash, Jacob Moshe   2299
'Iyyash, Judah   2299

Jabotinsky, Ze'ev   1776
Jacob
   as described by Josephus   1781
   and disabilities   1704
   and history of Israel   2119-2124
   and idea of chosen people   1730
   vow taken by   2116-2118
   wounded sciatic nerve   1715
Jacob, Benno   276
Jacobs, Louis   211
Jael   2207-2208
Jaffa, Moroccan Jews in   2301
Jakobovits, I.   859, 863
James, William   926
Jamesian community, in Jerusalem   1876
Jamill, E.   1392, 1397 n. 31, n. 36, n. 38
Janet, Paul   298
Jaroslaw, A.   276
Jastrow, M.   1347 n. 1
Jehoash (king of Israel)   1789
Jehoiachin (king of Israel)   1789
Jellicoe, S.   1320
Jeroboam   2244, 2261 n. 20
Jerome   1793
   Order of St   1685
Jerusalem   1, 19, 43, 44, 48, 64-65, 68, 72,
   129, 142, 152, 181, 184, 189, 194, 199, 290,
   350, 370, 467, 469, 471-472, 478, 498
Jamesian community in   1876
   in Judaism   525-534
      Karaite community in   1810
      North African Jews in   2296, 2298-2300
      rivalry with Mt Gerizim   2262 n. 26
Jesuit order, tolerance towards conversos   2080
Jesus   56, 63-67, 69-74, 76, 81, 84, 102, 392,

408, 534-546, 875, 879, 1010-1012, 1015,
  1017-1019, 1021-1022
  descent from David 1785-1786
  on observance of the Sabbath 2130, 2131
  putting himself above the Torah 2132-2136
  sermon by Stephen S. Wise about 2269
  as teacher of Torah 2129
  theology of 2131-2136
Jewish- Americans 1806
Jewish doctrine, sermons about 2270-2272
Jewish Enlightenment 195, 204, 207, 221,
  276, 686, 739, 913, 996, 1398, 1399-1401,
  1405-1407, 1492-1495
Jewish feminists 958
Jewish identity 1795, 1796, 1801, 1806, 1878
  ethnic 1795, 1800, 1805
  of karaites 1811-1812, 1815-1816, 1821
  religious 1795, 1800
Jewish law 29, 51, 127, 151, 165, 166, 202,
  213, 340, 343-348, 379, 432, 443, 501-502,
  505-506
  on abortion 1654
  amputation as punishment, absence of
    1707
  changes in 1949
  codifications of 343, 1656-1668, 1668-1676,
    1816
  development of 2095-2096, 2186
  and hereditary diseases 1654
  and homosexuality 2139-2140, 2141, 2146
  origins of 1659
  Rabbinic interpretation of 1817, 1887
  responsa 2234-2235, 2240 n. 55
  and surrogate motherhood 1917-1920
Jewish migrations
  to China 1630, 1637-1638, 1641
  to Greece 1768, 1769
  to Morocco 1848
  see also aliyah
Jewish philosophy 710-783
  influenced by Islam 1894
Jewish preaching 1888-1904, 2265-2283
Jewish Renewal movement 574-577, 696, 699
Jewish Socialism 662, 666-668, 670-672, 675,
  680, 957, 1333, 1334, 1336-1339, 1341,
  1342
Jewish spirituality 210
Jewish studies, developments in 2168-2169
Jewish Theological Seminary (JTS,
  Conservative Movement) 1798, 1803-1804,
  1805
Jewish theology 1606-1607, 1608, 1610
Jewish Theology: Systematically and Historically
  Considered (Kohler) 208
A Jewish Theology (Jacobs) 211
Jewish universalism 299
The Jewish War (Josephus) 203, 1792
The Jewish way: Living the Holidays (Greenberg)
  40
Jewish-Christian dialogue 2060
John, Gospel of 2133

John of the Cross, Saint (Juan de Yepes)
  2088
Joktan 2200-2201
JONAH (Jews Offering New Alternatives to
  Homosexuality) 2139
Jones, A.H.M. 1051
Joseph
  as described by Josephus 1781-1782
  search for his bones at Shechem (Nablus)
    2249
  sold as a slave 2140
Joseph, Morris 2274, 2275, 2282 n. 53
Joseph Solomon see Delmedigo, Joseph
  Solomon
Josephus, Flavius 65, 168, 184, 202, 262, 270,
  278, 315, 608, 823, 875, 878, 905, 1763
  Against Apion 1791
  Antiquities of the Jews 1778, 1782, 1786,
    1789, 1791
  apologetics of 1789-1790
  appeal to Greek readers 1792
  biblical characters described by 1778-1794
  on circumcision 1780, 1790
  compared to Pseudo-Philo 2212
  as a historian 1792, 1793
  on homosexuality of Herod's son Alexander
    2141
  on intermarriages and assimilation 1780-
    1781, 1788, 1790
  The Jewish War 203, 1792
  and Judaism 546-563
  omissions from bible 1778-1779, 1792
  on Palestine and Philistines 1879 n. 4
  political philosophy of 1784-1785
  on politically independent land for the Jews
    1780, 1790
  as a priest 1793
  on proselytism by Jews 1791
  on Samaritans 1779, 1793 n. 3, 2242,
    2244, 2245, 2246, 2262 n. 28
  treatment of miracles 1791
Joshua 1603
  as described by Josephus 1783
  in Liber Antiquitatum Biblicarum (Pseudo-Philo)
    2205-2206
  Samaritan book of 2255-2256, 2264 n. 76
Josiah (king of Israel) 2243, 2261 n. 16
JTS see Jewish Theological Seminary (JTS,
  Conservative Movement)
Jubilee years 33
Jubilees, book of 2037
Judaeo-Arabic literature, medieval 2167-2183
Judaeo-Spanish literature 1771
Judah the Prince see Halevi, Judah
Judah (region), and Samaria 2243-2244
Judaica 4, 6, 8
Judaism in the First Centuries of the Christian Era
  (Moore) 1607
Judaism and Modern Man (Herberg) 210
Judaizer conversos 1679, 2079, 2080, 2081
Judean Hills

agriculture in 1719-1720, 1726
  in Iron age 2243, 2261 n. 15
Die Juden und das Wirtschaftsleben (Sombart)
  237
Judenrat 423-426, 432
Judeoconversos see conversos
judicial autonomy, of Moroccan Jews 1850
Jung, Carl 942, 954
justice of God, governing principle of Judaism
  1610-1611
Justin Martyr 72-74, 76-77
Justinian I (Byzantine emperor)
  Code of 2137
  edicts of 1766
  and Samaritans 2250
Juynboll, T.W.J. 2255

Ka'ba 459
Kabars 1829-1830
Kabbalah 128, 133, 206, 207, 264, 268, 474,
  477, 479, 483-484, 571, 575, 641, 678-680,
  733, 827-828, 875, 883, 932, 956, 958, 972,
  1667
  astral magic in 1619
  popularization in America 1803
  used for Jewish preaching 1895
  view of the Jewish people 1734
Kabbalism 1104-1108, 1221-1223, 1489
  Salonika centre of 1772-1773
Kabbalistic conceptions, of land of Israel 473-
  474, 479-481, 483-484
Kabbalistic doctrines 94, 753, 758, 886, 932
Kabbalistic ethics 255-256
Kabbalistic exegesis 280
Kabbalistic influences 43, 784
Kabbalistic literature 479, 794, 928, 934
Kabbalistic views, of proselytes 1735
Kabbalists 275, 783, 910, 930, 931, 933, 935,
  936
  Karaite 1820
Kad ha-Qemah (The Jar of Flour, Bahya ben
  Asher) 1891, 1902 n. 25
Kaddari, Menahem Zevi 792
Kaddish 44, 429, 809-810
  used by Kaifeng (China) Jewry 1636-1637
kadesh (ritual male homosexual prostitute)
  2140
Kadish, S. 1396, 1397 n. 22
Kadushin, Max 773-774, 785
Kagan, Israel Meir Hakohen 344, 1673-1675,
  1949 n. 7
Kahan, Abraham 277
Kahle, P. 1409
Kahn, Jean 313
Kaifeng (China), Jewish community in 1631,
  1633-1637, 1650-1651
Kalam, Karaite 1816, 1819-1820
Kalimat As-Shahadat 151
Kalisher, Zvi Hirsch 756
Kalmin, R. 1125, 1132
Kalonymos 274

Kamin, Sarah 2233
Kant, Emmanuel 82-83, 251, 713, 741-742,
  746-747, 767, 771, 779, 973, 1002
Kapach, J. 1396 n. 16
Kaplan, Aryeh 571
Kaplan, Chaim A. 424
Kaplan, Jacob 308
Kaplan, Joseph 970
Kaplan, L. 1409 n. 14, n. 27
Kaplan, Mordecai 565, 734, 766, 774-775,
  778, 800, 831, 1231, 1235, 1238, 1493, 1502
  n. 56, n. 61, n. 62
  on Chosen People 1737, 1740 n. 50, n. 51
  Reconstructionism 209, 1804
Kapparah ceremony 1912-1913
Kapsali, Moses 1769
Kara, Joseph 272-273, 2046, 2047, 2050,
  2051, 2053
Karaimic language 1820
Karaism 651, 653-655, 657
Karaite historiography 1808-1809
Karaite Judaism 152, 161, 473, 636, 650-653,
  1767-1768, 1807-1821, 2175
Karaite Kalam 1816, 1819-1820
Karaite law 1816, 1818, 1821
Karaite literature 1809, 1811, 1812, 1818
Karaite philosophy 1819-1820
Karaite scholarship
  biblical studies 2174, 2175, 2183 n. 38, n.
    41
  Byzantine 1767, 1811
Karaite theology 1816-1817, 1819-1820
Karaites 213, 650, 652, 968, 1660
  Jewish identity of 1811-1812, 1815-1816,
    1821
  use of Hebrew 1820
Kark, Ruth 2300
Karlen, Arno 2145
Karlinsky, Ch. 1409 n. 6
Karo, Joseph *see* Caro, Joseph
Kasher, M.M. 500-501, 1409 n. 10
kashrut 24, 28, 232-234
  observed by Kaifeng (China) Jewry 1636
  see also dietary laws; kosher
Kashtan, A. 1397 n. 24, 1397 n. 27
Kasovsky, Chayim Yehoshua 1842
Kaspi, Joseph ben Abba Mari ibn 274
Kaspi, Nethanel 482
katan (minor) 1698-1699, 1700
Katz, J. 166, 224, 232, 234, 1003-1004, 1464,
  1465 n. 11, 1501 n. 52
Kaufman, Abraham 1642
Kaufman, D.R. 1499, 1502 n. 89
Kaufmann, Yezekhel 940, 1059
kavanah 254, 445, 828
Kayyara, Shimon 1660
Kazimir the Great 214
Kebrä Nagast (The Glory of Kings) 1741
kedushat 'am Yisrael 433
Kehillah 214, 215
kelippot 483

Kelsen, H. 1408, 1410 n. 37
Kenaz 2206-2207, 2211
Kennedy, John F., assassination of 2268, 2280 n. 16
Kerch 1822
Keset Sofer (Ganzfried) 1672
Kesil 2040
Keter Torah (Crown of the Torah, Aaron ben Elijah) 1819
ketubbah 802, 1858
Khanfu (China), massacre of 1631
Khazaria
   collapse of 1830
   kingdom of 1822, 1832
   struggles with neighbouring countries 1829-1830
Khazars (*Kuzarim*) 1821-1832
Kiddush ha-shem: Kitavim mi-yame ha-Shoah (Huberband) 422
Kierkegaard, S. 749, 753, 771, 779, 1096
Kiev, Khazars in 1822, 1827
Kievan Letter 1827, 1828
Kilayim 351, 1767
Kima 2039-2040
Kimhi, David (*Radak*) 274, 345, 1717
Kimhi, Joseph 273, 1013
Kimhi, Moses 269, 270, 273
Kindbettzettel (*Kimpettzetl*) 1908-1909
king, rules of 1836, 1929-1930
King, Martin Luther 2278
kingdom
   of God 2131, 2132
   of heaven 1880
kingship, Germanic concept of 1721-1722
Kinnot 44
kinot 1862, 2296
Kinsey, Alfred Charles 2137-2138, 2141, 2143-2144
Kitab al-Anwar wa'l-Maraqib (The Book of Lights and Watchtowers, al-Qirqisani) 1818
Kitab al-Buldan (al-Hamadhani) 1826
Kitab al-Dalail (Nafis al-Din) 2257
Kitab al-Fara'id (Abu'l Hasan) 2256
Kitab al-Kafi (ibn Salama) 2256
Kitab al-Khilaf (the Book of Differences, ibn Tsedaqa) 2256
Kitab al-Mirat (Book of Inheritance, Abu Ishaq) 2256
Kitab al-Murshid (The Guide, ha-Ma'aravi) 1818
Kitab al-Tabbah (Abu'l Hasan) 2256
Kitab al-Tarikh (Abu'l-Fath) 2255
Kitab al-Tautiyya (Abu'l Hasan) 2256
Kitzur Shulhan Arukh (Granzfried) 1671, 1672-1673
Klausner, I. 1409 n. 2, n. 3
Klausner, Joseph 734, 2132, 2133
Kleeblatt, N.L. 1396 n. 9
Klezmer music 923
Kli Yakar (*The Precious Vessel*, Luntschitz) 272, 1663

Knesset 1357, 1359, 1363, 1371, 1373, 1530
Knesset haGedolah (Benevisti) 1666
knesset yisrael 121, 504
Koenigsberg, Jacob Zevi Meklenburg of 276
kofer 368
kohanim 409
   see also priests
Kohler, Kaufman 208, 775-776, 1019, 2270
Kokizow, Mordecai ben Nissan 1811
Kol Bo 1666
Königsheil 1721-1722
Kook, Abraham Isaac 757-758, 2141
Korah 1793, 2204
Kore ha-Doroth (Conforte) 1770
Koren, S. 1501 n. 39
Korey, W. 1272
kosher 25, 49, 96, 104, 108, 233, 577, 982-983
   food 1801
   slaughter 1946
   see also dietary laws; kashrut
Kraemer, D. 1501 n. 30
Kraemer, R.S. 1485, 1501 n. 24, n. 27, n. 28
Krauskopf, Joseph 2269, 2270, 2272, 2280 n. 25, 2281 n. 44
Krausz, Michael 512
Krautheimer, R. 1396 n. 11
Kravitz, Leonard 149
Krinsky, C. 1396, 1397 n. 18, n. 24, n. 25, n. 29, n. 37
Kristallnacht 4, 420
Krochmal, Nachman 100, 101, 735, 745-746
Kroll, E. 1047
k'tatsah', ritual of 1701
Ku Klux Klan, Jewish preaching on 2278
Kuntris Matzevat Moshe (Danzig) 1670
Kupfer, Ephraim 969
Kushner, Harold 265
Kushner, Lawrence 568, 571
Kutscher, E.Y. 787
Kuzari (Halevi) 79, 120-121, 473, 482, 683, 1613, 1732-1733, 1825, 1832
Kuzarim see Khazars
Kuzmack, L.G. 1494, 1502 n. 63
Kuznetz, Simon 236-237
kvatter 93
Kybalová, H. 1396 n. 15
Kybalová, L. 1396 n. 14

Labowitz, Shoni 576
Lacquer, Richard 547
Lag ba-Omer, celebration in Morocco (*Hillula*) 1857
Laing, Ronald 2146
Lambert, Ph. 1396 n. 1
Lamentations, Book of 1862
Lamphere, L. 1501 n. 21
Landau, Ezekiel 2267
languages, in Judaism 783-797, 2183 n. 56
Laqish, Simeon b. 263
lashes 2199 n. 14

Late Judaism   83-85
law
  Maimonides on   2139
  repressiveness of   2146
  'to do the'   2126-2127
  see also Jewish law
Law of God   57, 136, 145, 321, 346
  observance of, and Kingdom of God
    2131
  see also Torah
Lazarillo de Tormes (novel)   2086
Lazarus, Moritz   746-747, 1740 n. 43
Leach, Edmund   946
leaders, of Israel (people)   2095
learning
  as a child or adult   2128-2129
  secular, and study of Torah   2283,
    2285-2288, 2292, 2293
Leeser, Isaac   2267, 2268, 2271-2272
legal deeds, commitment to aliyah in   2302
legends, Rashi in   2237
Legends of the Jews (Ginzberg)   458
Leibnitz, Gottfried Wilhelm   82, 718, 730,
    734, 738
Leibowitz, Yeshayahu   760-761, 974, 1405
León, Fray Luis de   2089
Leon, Moses de   270
Lerner, A.L.   1502 n. 66
Lerner, Michael   577
lesbianism   2141
Levenberg, S.Z.   1335, 1342 n. 8
Levenson, Jon D.   1729
Levi, A.   1396 n. 8
Levi, Hayyim   1812
Levi, Solomon   1893
Lévi, Sylvain   298, 300
Levi-Strauss, Claude   938
Levin, Hirschel   2272
Levin, Moritz   2267
Levin, N.   1342 n. 27
Levinas, Emanuel   136, 734, 740, 755,
    943-944
Levinthal, Israel   2280 n. 25
Levirate marriages   369, 803-804
Levites   173, 187, 295, 383, 486, 528, 581,
    596-598, 604, 907, 1141, 1264, 1290, 1291,
    1294, 1515
  priestly title   1827
Levitical piety   1309
Levitical religion   876-878, 1303
Levitical uncleanness   621
Leviticus, in Judaism   2153-2167
Leviticus Rabbah   2153, 2225
Levy, J. Leonard   2277
Lévy, Louis-Germain   301-302
Levy, N.B.   2273
Lewy, J.   1051
Liber Antiquitatum Biblicarum (Pseudo-Philo)
    2200-2212
Liber, M.   2230
liberal Judaism   1493, 1546

Libro de las fundaciones (Book of Foundations,
    Saint Theresa)   2089
Libro Verde de Aragón (Green Book of Aragón,
    Anchias)   2085
Lichtenstein, Aaron   780
Lieberman, Saul   1804
Liebes, Yehuda   952, 956
Liebig, Justus von   1623
Liebman, Charles   982, 1374, 1798-1799,
    1806
life
  beginning of   1623-1624
  Jesus as the giver of   2134
  sacrificing of   1662
  Torah as   2134-2135
Life of Constantine   1822, 1823, 1824
life cycle   797-811, 1889
Life of Jesus (Renan)   84
Life of Jesus (Straus)   84-85
Life of the Scroundel (Vida del Buscón, de Quevedo)
    2086
light-headedness, of women   1946, 1948, 1951
    n. 49
Lilith   1908, 1909
limpieza de sangre (purity of blood)   2078, 2080,
    2088
Lincoln, Abraham, assassination of   2267,
    2269, 2280 n. 15, 2280 n. 28
Lindars, B.   1320 n. 2
Lindzey, G.   1109
linguistic analysis, of Judaeo-Arabic Bible
    translations   2174
linguistic comparisons, between Gospels and
    Mishnah   2126-2128
linguistic perspective, of studies of
    Judaeo-Arabic literature   2169, 2177-2181
Lipkin, Israel (Salanter)   221, 742
Lipman, Eugene   2278-2279, 2283 n. 79
Listenwissenschaft   1833, 1834, 1926, 1927,
    1929, 2154, 2156, 2159, 2161, 2216,
    2217
literate civilizations, religions of   1864
literature
  apocalyptic   527, 882
  of Beta Israel   1743, 1749-1750
  eschatological   179-181
  Judeo-Arabic   2167-2183
  Judeo-Spanish   1771
  Kabbalistic   479, 794, 928, 934
  Karaite   1809, 1811, 1812, 1818
  Midrashic   1888
  mystical   206
  Rabbinic see Rabbinic literature
  Samaritan   2253-2257, 2262 n. 43, n. 44
Lithuania, Karaite communities   1811
liturgical cycle, of Beta Israel Judaism   1746
liturgical poems
  Rashi's commentaries on   2233-2234
  selihot   2228, 2239 n. 19
liturgy   169, 202, 208, 462, 811-832
  feminist influence on   1804

Samaritan 2254-2255
texts in Judaeo-Arabic 2176, 2179-2180
livelihood, and study of Torah 2285-2288
Löb, A. 1405
Locke, John 740
locusts 1724
Loew, Judah 272, 1734, 1756
logics
of coherent discourse, in Talmud
1934-1938, 1940
of fixed association 1934-1935, 1936-1937,
1940, 2159, 2219-2222, 2226
propositional 1934, 1935, 1938, 1940,
2215-2217, 2226
of Rabbinic literature 2213-2226
taxonomic 2156, 2157, 2159
teleological 2217-2219
'logos' 1610
Low Countries, conversos in 2082
*Lumen ad revelationem gentium et gloriam plebis Dei
Israel de unitate fidei et de concordi et pacifica
aequalitate fedelium* (de Oropesa) 1685
luminaries 2037, 2043
lunar calendar 1746, 2039
lunar eclipse 2043
luni-solar calendar 2040
Luntschitz, Solomon Ephraim 272, 1663
Luria, Isaac (Ari) 207, 264, 275, 1772, 1773,
2297
Luria, Solomon 2141
Luther, Martin 78, 2231
Lutherans 82
Lutzki, Simhah Isaac 1811, 1820
Luzzatto, Moses Hayyim 256
Luzzatto, Samuel David (*Shadal*) 276
Lyra, Nicholas de 2231

ha-Ma'aravi, Eliyahu 2297
ha-Ma'aravi, Samuel 1818
Ma'ase Bereshit 127
Ma'ase Ha-Merkavah 127
Ma'aseh he-Shem (Simon Akiva Baer ben Yosef)
1832
ma'aseh (legal precedent) 2235-2236
Mabyt see ben Joseph of Trani, Moses
Maccabean revolt 199
Maccabean Wars 174
macchia 1720
McKenzie, John L. 941
McNamara, M.J. 1320
Macuch, R. 2253-2254, 2263 n. 55
maddaf, uncleanness 1837-1847
Magen Abraham (Gombiner) 343, 1670
Maggid 1667
Maghrebi communities, in Israel 2297, 2299,
2300, 2301
magic 301, 832-844, 889, 950, 961, 963,
990-991
in medieval Judaism 1612-1621
relation with superstition 1904
Maharal of Prague *see* Loew, Judah

Mahberet (dictionary of biblical Hebrew, ibn
Saruk) 2049
Mahzor Vitry (Simhah of Vitry) 2227
Maidanek 430
Maimonides, Moses (*Rambam*) 57, 59, 60,
78-79, 120, 163, 206-207, 228, 264, 268,
270, 275, 342, 345, 379, 431, 472-473,
475-476, 481-483, 504-507, 513, 528-531,
573, 640, 645, 655, 657, 659, 717-724, 726,
728-733, 735-736, 745, 760, 777, 780, 782,
790-791, 795, 804, 843, 854-855, 860, 863,
866, 868-869, 873, 882, 907, 935-936, 955,
964-969, 1014-1016, 1657, 1658, 1949
on astrology and magic 1613, 1614-1615,
1617
Book of Commandments (*Sefer haMitzvot*)
1661-1662
on Chosen People 1733-1734, 1739-1740
n. 31
on Christians as idolaters 1734, 1739 n. 24
Commentary to the Mishnah 204, 254, 1661
on custody of children 2198, 2199 n. 26
Essay on Resurrection 204-205
fleeing Spain 2079
Guide for the Perplexed (*Moreh Nevukhim*) 79,
204, 254, 263, 505, 1733, 1820
Helek 204-205
on homosexuality 2141-2142
on Jewish superstitions 1905, 1906
on law 2139
on love of God 1652
on lunar calendar 2039
on martyrdom 1662-1663
Mishneh Torah (*Yad haHazakah*) 57, 204,
206, 254, 263, 343, 431, 476, 505, 1658,
1660-1661, 1662, 1897, 2227
on prohibition on interbreeding and
mingling of agricultural species 1627,
1757 n. 4
on proselytes 1734, 1739 n. 15,
1739 n. 28
on rules regarding women 1943, 1944,
1945, 1946, 1947, 1949 n. 4, 1950 n. 25,
1951 n. 49, 1952 n. 54
on sanctification of God's name 1662
Thirteen Principles of Faith 205
Mainz Commentary on the Talmud 2229
Malchuyot 45
mamzer 295, 372, 502
man, measured by God 2127
Manasseh 2244, 2261 n. 20
mandate, of Theodotius I (Roman emperor)
2249
Manichean tradition 172
Mann, T. 1095
Mann, V.B. 1396 n. 8, n. 9, n. 28, n. 30,
n. 32
manna (bread of heaven) 2135
Man's Quest for God (Heschel) 408
Manual of Holiday and Sabbath Sermons 2269
Mapa (*Table Cloth*, Isserles) 1668

Marcus, J.R. 1252, 1253
Marcus, R. 1465 n. 5
Margaliouth, M. 1227
Margoliouth, David Samuel 1631
Maria Theresa (empress of Austria) 2267
Marinus 2248
Marks, David Woolf 2268, 2270, 2271, 2272, 2273, 2276-2277, 2281 n. 40
Marmor, Judd 2148
marranos 2078
marriages
  homosexual 2138-2139
  in Judaism 800-805
  Karaite 1815
  Levirate 369, 803-804
  see also intermarriages
Martini, Raymond 2238 n. 1
Martola, N. 1062
martyrology 46, 199, 406, 424, 431-432
martyrs 74, 200, 413, 423, 483
  Christian 71
  Jewish 1662-1663, 1664-1665
Marx, Alexander 105, 106, 111
Marx, Karl 236, 663, 1094
Marxist schools 224
Marzuk, Elijah 1812
Marzuk, Moses 1812
Masada 431
maskil 178
Masoretic texts 461, 607, 1312
  in Judaeo-Arabic 2175
material wealth, versus spiritual wealth 2288-2292
Matt, Herschel 210
matzot 40
Maxwell, Nancy Kalikow 709
May, Rollo 2148
Maybaum, Ignaz 408
Maymoun, Rabbi 1858
mazal tov 2036
Mead, G.H. 1103
Mead, Sidney E. 764
Me'am Lo'ez (Culi) 1771
'measure for measure', idea of 1704
measures and weights, commandment of proper 2194
Medding, P. 1357
medical ethics, of Judaism 854-873
medical literature, in Judaeo-Arabic 2177
medicine
  biblical 1705-1706
  practised by conversos 2090
medieval Judaeo-Arabic literature 2167-2181
medieval Judaism 366, 525, 1486
  astral magic in 480, 1612-1620
  on Chosen People 1732-1735
  codification of Jewish law 1656-1668
  in France 2045-2060
Medina, Shmuel di (Rashdam) 1770
A Mediterranean Society (Goitein) 2168, 2171
Megillah, reading of 1861

megorashim 1848
mehaye hametim 202
Meier, R. 1394, 1397 n. 34, 1397 n. 41
Meir Leibush ben Yechiel Michel (Malbim) 277
Meir, Rabbi 2033
Meir of Rothenberg 1665, 1911
Meiselman, M. 1947, 1948
Mekhilta, attributed to R. Ishmael 2101-2111, 2131, 2133, 2135
Melammed, R.L. 1501 n. 33
melancholy 1714
Melchizedek, question of 2253
haMelits 2255
mellah (Jewish quarter) 1850
Memar Hasameah 2255
Memar Marqe 2254, 2257
Mendelsohn, E. 1335, 1336, 1342 n. 10
Mendelssohn, Moses 162, 207, 275, 276, 507-510, 513, 734-735, 737-738, 740-742, 749, 1017-1018, 1247, 2271, 2272, 2281 n. 39
Mendes, A.P. 2273
Mendes, Dona Gracia 2298
mental disabilities (shoteh) 1698, 1699, 1700, 1714
mental illnesses 1714-1715
Meri, Menahem 342
merit, and Torah 2289
Merneptah, inscription on stele 519
meserat nefesh 428
Meshech Hochmah (Meir Simha Cohen) 277
meshumadim 368, 372, 2077-2078
messiah 95, 120, 189-190, 205-206, 247, 365, 384, 387-388, 394, 472, 525, 545, 579, 613, 623, 650, 736, 756, 759, 776, 816, 820, 826, 844, 874-888, 890, 897, 951, 999, 1001, 1011, 1014, 1018-1019, 1046, 1048, 1049, 1084, 1172, 1173, 1179, 1183, 1189, 1190, 1191, 1192, 1193, 1197, 1225, 1228, 1240, 1245, 1246, 1247, 1250, 1252, 1290, 1319, 1431, 1434-1436, 1456, 1510, 1525, 1528, 1532
  prophecies of 1720, 2128
  sermons about 2271, 2272, 2281 n. 39
Messiah Apocalypse (Qumran Text) 200
messianic activism 474, 479, 678
messianic age/era 54, 164, 504-505, 525, 533-534, 714, 776, 797, 816, 1016
messianic expectations, Samaritan 2246
messianic myths 948-949, 955, 958
messianic redemption 683, 684, 760, 926
messianic rejoicing 472
messianism 217, 476, 1015, 1365, 1529, 1532, 1773, 1786, 1793-1794, 1794 n. 9, n. 10
metaphors, in Biblical texts 1760, 1762 n. 22
metapropositional discourse 2222-2225
Metaxas, John 1776
metsitsah 89
Mettinger, T.N.D. 1447 n. 7

Metzudot David 275, 1717
Metzudot Zion 275
Meyer, Michael A. 506, 1247, 1254
Meyer, Michael M. 1017
Meyers, C.L. 1383, 1480, 1500 n. 4, n. 6, n. 7
Meyers, E.M. 1383
Mez, Adam 653
mezuzah, commandment of 2193
Mi Kamokha (Halevi) 1861
Michaelis, Johann David 82
midah k'neged midah ('measure for measure') 1704
'middle Arabic' 2169, 2181 n. 7
midras-uncleanness 1843
midrash 91-92, 127, 262-263, 266, 269, 277, 405, 433, 457, 458, 474, 487, 510, 532, 574, 619, 641, 748, 777, 784, 789, 791, 811, 844, 867, 905, 919, 956, 962, 1052, 1057, 1062, 1082, 1092, 1093, 1096, 1097, 1098, 1099, 1106, 1137, 1161, 1162, 1163, 1164, 1169, 1174, 1175, 1179, 1184, 1186, 1188, 1189, 1191, 1199, 1206, 1208, 1317, 1397, 1398, 1459, 1481, 1529
  on astrology 2034-2035
  on astronomy 2039, 2042-2043
  on baldness 1708
  category formations in 1595
  compilations 2102, 2186, 2226
  exegesis 2046, 2047, 2184-2185
  in Judaeo-Arabic 2179
  Samaritan 2255
  sermons in 1888
  syllogisms in 2217
  on Zionism 2293-2294
  see also Genesis Rabbah; Leviticus Rabbah; Mekhilta; Sifra; Sifre to Deuteronomy; Sifre to Numbers
Midrash Lekah Tob (Tobias b. Eliezer) 1767
midrashic literature 1888
Mikhlol (David Kimhi) 274
mikveh 26, 369
Milah 89
Milhamot Adonai (Gersonides) 481
'milk and honey' metaphor 1719, 1720
Mill, J.S. 729
Miller 1020-1021
milling, women's work 2126
mimouna celebration 1856-1857
Minhat Shai (Norzi) 268
Minhat Yehudah (The Offering of Judah, Gibbor) 1819
minors 1696, 1815
minyanim 28
Mipnei Chataeynu 410
Miqraot Gedolot 266, 268
miracles 776, 880-897, 903-904, 950, 1717, 1791
Mirre Yeshivah 1639
Mishkinsky, M. 1342 n. 16
mishloah manot (exchange of gifts) 1861

Mishnah 19, 46, 53, 63, 73, 90, 92, 94, 101, 117, 142-143, 161, 202-203, 232, 234, 241-242, 244, 252-253, 282-283, 325-331, 341, 361, 367, 377, 404-405, 430, 442, 485-488, 492, 494-495, 497-498, 502, 528, 530-535, 537-538, 540, 564, 619-630, 633, 722, 784-790, 792, 796-797, 801, 804, 810, 844, 851, 853, 875, 879-881, 905, 964, 1008-1011, 1014-1015, 1052, 1070, 1072, 1073, 1074, 1076, 1077, 1110, 1112, 1114, 1129, 1133, 1135, 1136, 1138, 1139, 1140-1144, 1146-1160, 1165-1170, 1176, 1177, 1180, 1189, 1199, 1200, 1202, 1206, 1207, 1210, 1211, 1212, 1214, 1217, 1219, 1220-1226, 1253, 1256, 1257, 1260, 1263, 1275, 1398, 1405, 1430, 1432-1435, 1477, 1481, 1485, 1503, 1507-1510, 1513, 1514, 1516, 1524, 1549, 1596, 1659, 1694
  analogical-contrastive reasoning in 1832-1847, 1926-1931
  book of lists 1926, 1929
  category formations in 1595
  classifications in 1834, 1837, 2285
  on clean and unclean animals 1725
  on disabilities 1698, 1704
  divine character of 2270
  halakhic focus of 1597
  history in 380-388
  on homosexuality 2141
  logic of fixed association in 2221-2222
  mode of discourse 1833, 2223, 2225
  oral traditions of 2124-2136
  origins of 1816-1817, 1846, 2064, 2124
  and Pentateuch 1925-1927, 1928, 2154
  philosophical view of 2112
  rules in 2091
  and Scripture 2154-2157
  small cattle ban 1728
  systemic document 1925-1932, 1941 n. 3
  and Talmud 1933-1934, 2064, 2075-2077
  and Torah 1148-1149, 1155, 1200-1201, 1448-1465, 1846-1847, 2185
Mishnah Berurah (Kagan) 344, 1673-1675
Mishnaic Judaism 1927
Mishneh Torah (Maimonides) 57, 204, 206, 254, 263, 343, 431, 476, 505, 1658, 1660-1661, 1662, 1897
mishpat ivri school on Jewish law 349
Mishpatim 14
misoxenia *see* xenophobia
missionary efforts, by Christians among Jews 2271-2272
mitnagdim 220, 221, 223
mitzvot 22, 116, 505, 511, 707, 1799, 1803
modern Orthodox Judaism 1796, 1797, 1798, 1801
modernity, and Samaritanism 2260-2261
Mocllin, Jacob 1892
Mogador 1854, 2303
mohel 8, 89-90, 93-94

Moisses, Asher 1770
Molad Mosheh 2257
molad (nativity) 2032
Momigliano, A. 1051
monasteries 184, 1744
monasticism, in Ethiopian Judaism 1743, 1744
monism 734
monotheism 80, 83, 367, 439, 459, 521, 555, 579, 602, 606, 643, 897-905, 940, 951, 1002, 1014-1015, 1025-1027, 1029, 1037, 1039, 1369, 1410, 1428, 1432, 1440, 1480, 1539
   ethical 1736
monothetic taxonomy 2156
Monson, R.G. 1502 n. 79
Montanino, F. 1097
Montemayor, Jorge de 2087
months, intercalation of 2039
Montoro, Antón de 1690
Moore, George Foot 1607
Moorish rule, of Spain 1677
Las moradas (The Dwelling Places, Saint Theresa) 2089
morality 2146
Moreh nebukhe hazzeman (Krochmal) 100
Moreh Nevukhim (Guide for the Perplexed, Maimonides) 79, 204, 254, 263, 505, 1820
Morgan, L. 771
Morgan, Thomas 81
Moriah 463
Morocco
   Judaism in 1847-1863, 1909
   Zionism in 2294-2307
Morteira, Saul Levi 1892, 1895, 1896, 1897
Mosad, helping Moroccan Jews to go on *aliyah* 2306
Mosaic Law 66, 164, 190, 506
   see also Torah
Moses 722, 1025-1028, 1031, 1035, 1039, 1046-1048, 1050, 1129, 1155, 1172-1174, 1183, 1603
   admonishment of Israel 2097-2100
   birth of 2201, 2202
   as described by Josephus 1782-1783
   focus of Samaritanism 2257
   in *Liber Antiquitatum Biblicarum* (Pseudo-Philo) 2201-2205
   prophecies of 1733
   as redactor of the Torah 2053-2054, 2055
   speech impediment 1701-1702
Moses ben Jacob of Coucy 1657-1658, 1665
moshav kavod 93
motherhood, surrogate 1916-1920
mothers, and child custody 1918
Mourners of Zion 1809, 1818
mourning practices 806-811
   described in Torah 806-807
   flutes and wailer women 2125
   forbidden 1600-1601
   shaving one's head as sign of 1708

Muhammad 453, 455-457, 460, 462
Müller, Joel 657
multiple Judaisms, claim of 1870
mumar concept (heretic who violates the law out of 'appetite') 2152
Munk, Solomon 297-298, 300
Munzer, Z. 1396 n. 12
Murciano, Jacob 2303
Musar movement 221, 254, 256
music
   Ashkenazic 911-916, 921-923
   cantoral 1860
   Hasidic 564, 565, 914, 916, 922, 923
   Sephardic 916-921
Muslim rule
   Jews under 2169
   Samaritans under 2251-2252
Muslims 152, 453-454, 459, 462
   conquests in Holy Land 2251
   Hermetic influences on 1613
   in Yangzhou (China) 1632
mystical elements, in contemporary Jewish thought 767, 775
mystical literature 206
mystical meaning of prayer 827-828
mysticism 126, 131, 134, 206-207, 212, 255, 264, 503-504, 571, 576, 657-659, 678-679, 688, 779-780, 792, 836, 926-936, 1104-1107, 1489, 1491
   appeal to conversos 2088
   in Greece 1772-1773
   Jewish 2031
   texts in Judaeo-Arabic 2176-2177
mystics 134, 206, 658, 886, 930-931, 951, 953, 956
mythic Judaism 662
mythical statements 211
mythology, and Judaism 938-960

Nablus *see* Shechem
Nadell, P.S. 1502 n. 76
Nafha, Isaac 2042
Nafis al-Din Abu'l-Faraj ibn Al-Kathar 2257
al-Nahawendi, Benjamin 1819
Nahmanides (*Ramban*) 75-77, 206, 268, 269-270, 342, 479, 481, 1667, 1894
   on astral magic 480, 1619
   on prohibition of interbreeding and mingling of agricultural species 1754
   on surrogate motherhood 1919
   on use of amulets 1906
nakedness 1944, 1950 n. 24
names, superstitions about 1910
The Names of the Great Ones (Azulai) 2236
Nanjing (China), treaty of 1637, 1647
Napoleonic Code, legalising homosexuality 2137
Naqedimon, aggadic story of 1603, 1604
Narkiss, B. 1396 n. 3
narrative, teleological logic of 2217-2219

narrative order, in the Bible 2055-2056
Nasi, Don Joseph 2298
Nathan, Sir Matthew 1647
nativity (*molad*) 2032
natural parents, suppression of identity of
   1917
natural philosophy 2111-2112
natural science, and Judaism 960-977, 2292
nature
   and humanity 1721-1722
   importance in Judaism 1628
Nazis 86-87, 149, 213, 411-413, 418, 423,
   427-430, 432-433, 511, 763, 767-768,
   778-779
Nazism, Jewish preaching on 2276, 2278
Nebrija, Antonio de 2087
Negev, use for farming 1719
Nehemiah 2244
Néher, René 969
neo-Arabic 2169
nephilim 260-261
neshekh 232
Netanyahu, Benzion 1689, 2083
Netherlands, Jewish community in
   2082-2083
Netivot Ha-Shalom 276
Neusner, Jacob 184, 707, 709, 773, 787, 789,
   875, 880-882, 975, 1051, 1160, 1176, 1206,
   1254, 1419, 1481, 1482, 1500 n. 10, n. 11,
   n. 13, n. 14, 1609-1611, 1628-1629
   on image of God 1759
   on Judaism in America 1794, 1795, 1805
   on *ma'aseh* (legal precedent) 2236
   on teachings of Jesus 2129, 2131, 2132
   on women in Judaism 1942
Neusner, Noam 773
New Age Judaism 563, 576-578
New Testament 63-64, 70-71, 77, 84, 169,
   190, 401, 1319, 1379
The New Union Prayer Book (Einhorn) 208
New Year 364, 424, 430
   see also Rosh ha-Shanah
Newman, Louis 259, 2269
Newman, M. 1409 n. 9
newspapers, printing sermons 2269,
   2280 n. 28
Neziqin tractate, of Mekhilta 2103
Nicholas I Mystikos (Patriarch of
   Constantinople) 1829
Nicholson, G. 771
Nickelsburg 114
Niditch, S. 1479, 1480, 1500 n. 3, n. 7
Niger, S. 1501 n. 43, n. 47
Nile delta, ecology of 1620
Nimukei Yosef (Joseph Habiba) 1662, 1663,
   1664, 1665, 1666
Ningpo (China), Jewish community in 1632
Ningxia (China), Jewish community in
   1632-1633
nishmat hayyim 201
nizozot 483

Noah 1597
   commandments of the sons of (7) 1731,
      1739 n. 19
Noahide covenant 1732, 1735
nobility in Spain, and conversos 2085
Noeldeke, Th. 1527
nominal orthodox 24
non-Israelites 355-357
   see also gentiles
non-observant Orthodox Judaism 1796
non-Orthodox Jews, in America 1799, 1801,
   1802
non-Rabbinic Judaism 1809
non-Talmudic Judaism, practised by Falasha
   1741
Norich, A. 1502 n. 66
normative Judaism 1499, 1607, 1863-1864,
   1865-1866, 1869, 1872-1874, 1878-1879,
   1920
norms
   of Judaism 1864-1865
   for social order, and religions 2283
North Africa
   Almohad persecutions of Jews in 1848
   Jewish communities in, ties with old *yishuv*
      2296
Northern Kingdom 521
nosei 1891, 1902 n. 22
Notes from the Warsaw Ghetto (Ringelblum) 422
Noth, Martin 517, 1879 n. 2
Novak, David 259, 767, 952, 1009,
   1015-1016, 1020-1021, 1734
Noveck, Simon 780
Numbers, in Judaism 2184-2191
Nussbaum, Perry 2278

oaths, media for resolution of social conflict
   1883
oekumene of the Hellenes 1763
Ofer, D. 1502 n. 74
offering see sacrifice
official Judaism 1479
Ohel Leah synagogue (Hong Kong) 1647,
   1648
Ohel Moshe synagogue (Shanghai) 1640,
   1651
Ohel Rachel Synagogue (Shanghai)
   1639-1640, 1646-1647, 1651
Olat Tamid: Book of Prayers for Jewish Congregations
   (Einhorn) 208
Old Testament 77-78, 80-82, 381, 390, 401,
   2116
   scholarship 1867-1870
Olesnicki, Zbigniew, Cardinal 215
al-Omar, Zahir 2298
omens 1913-1914
   interpretation of 2033-2034
On the Improvement of the Moral Qualities (ibn
   Gabirol) 254
On the Jewish Question (Karl Marx) 236
ones (duress) 2149-2150, 2152

'Operation Yakhin'   2306
Or Ha-Hayyim (Attar)   275, 1849
Oral Torah *see* Mishnah
oral traditions
    of Beta Israel   1750
    of the Mishnah   2124-2136
    of Samaritans   2247
Orel, Vladimir   1827
Orient, Jews of the   2168
*The Origins of the Spanish Inquisition in the Fifteenth
    Century* (Netanyahu)   1689
Orit (Bible of Beta Israel)   1749
orlah   90, 351-354
Orleans, Yosef Bekhor Shor of (Joseph ben
    Isaac)   271, 273, 2054-2055, 2056
Ornstein, D.   1502 n. 83, n. 85
Oropesa, Fray Alonso de   1685
Orpheus (Reinach)   302
Orthodox Judaism   28, 59-97, 99-102, 105,
    108, 111, 223, 311, 345, 350, 379, 533, 664,
    673, 675, 693, 696, 704-706, 769, 829, 922,
    977-981, 993-1008, 1332, 1406, 1478 n. 2,
    1507
    in America   699, 702, 766, 983, 1795,
        1796-1797, 1798, 1799, 1800-1801
    education   702, 794, 1495
    on homosexuality   2139
    in Israel   1360-1361, 1369-1373, 1527
    leaders of   884, 965
    and *mitzvot*   1803
    and natural science   971, 972, 973
    and secular learning   2283-2284
    sermons in   2269
    in South Africa   1349-1351, 1352-1353
    women in   1495-1499
    and Zionism   781, 885, 1529, 1531, 1535,
        1536
    see also modern Orthodox Judaism; non-
        observant Orthodox Judaism; ultra
        Orthodox Judaism
Orthodoxy   536, 565, 571, 574, 579-580,
    602, 618, 657-658, 663, 665-666, 671, 676,
    759-761, 796, 798, 1133, 1134, 1242, 1243,
    1244, 1249, 1270, 1275, 1280, 1284, 1335,
    1339, 1341, 1347, 1349, 1350, 1351, 1355,
    1361, 1408, 1492, 1499, 1535, 1545-1548
oscillating patterns of settlement   1718, 1729
    n. 1
Osuna dynasty   1681
Ottoman Caliphate, diversity of Jewish commu-
    nities in   1769-1770, 1771
Otzar he-Genazim (Toledano)   2295, 2298
Otzar Nehmad (The Desirable Treasure, Tobias
    ben Moses)   1819
An Outline of Jewish Eschatology (Matt)   210

pacifism, in Jewish preaching   2275-2276,
    2282 n. 61
pagan historians, on Judaism   1025-1038
pagan origins, of dying and rising god   1875,
    1880 n. 14

pagan philosophers, on Judaism   1038-1052
pagan rites, included in Judaism   38, 198
Palamas, Gregory   1773
Pale of Settlement   1267, 1273, 1274, 1275,
    1283
paleo-Hebrew   2244
Palestine
    origins of   1868, 1879 n. 4
    see also Israel (land)
Palestinian Talmud *see* Talmud
Palm Tree of Deborah (Cordovero)   255
pamphlets, sermons published as   2269
Pan Guangdan   1632
pantheism   757-758, 926, 1020, 1030, 1040
parables   540, 1102, 1103, 1202, 1203
paradigmatic thinking   2062
paralysis   1715
parents
    honoring of   2191-2200
    see also fathers; mothers
Pareto Optimum   231, 235
Paris, John   1653
Parshandatha, name used for Rashi   2226, 2236
paschal lamb   70-71, 92-93, 95, 361
passivism   424
Passover   25, 33-36, 38-44, 48, 50, 71, 90, 92,
    94, 116, 357-359, 361-364, 401, 424, 429,
    529, 540, 552, 573, 592, 595, 597, 609, 638,
    650, 688, 695, 696, 701, 705, 801, 807, 810,
    823, 827, 877, 887, 980, 982-985, 988, 991,
    1052-1060, 1109, 1140, 1184, 1185, 1215,
    1219, 1220, 1221, 1225, 1233, 1275, 1284,
    1297, 1298, 1300, 1301, 1316, 1350, 1359,
    1433
    observance in American Judaism
        1805-1806
    observance in Morocco   1854-1856
    see also Haggadah (Passover)
Passover seder   1, 364, 513, 1805
The Path of the Upright (Moses Luzzatto)   256
Patmos   70
patriarchs   488, 493, 2115
patterns of religion   1609
Paul   65-68, 74, 91, 156-157, 492-494, 497,
    499, 1764, 1875, 1876
Paul and Palestinian Judaism (Sanders)   1608-
    1609
paytanim   1851, 1854
peah   1704
Pe'amim (journal)   2300
Pedersen, Johannes   1879 n. 6
Pelliot, Paul   1631
Peninnah   2210
Penkower, Jordan   2234, 2238
Pentateuch   527, 579-589, 602, 604, 606-607,
    620, 624-626, 653, 730, 739, 784-785,
    787-789, 795-796, 811, 876-877, 906, 911,
    1047, 1073, 1074, 1133, 1136, 1146, 1147,
    1164, 1184, 1194, 1208, 1213, 1215, 1219,
    1223, 1226, 1308-1310, 1312, 1314-1317,
    1349, 1447-1449, 1455, 1458

and Mishnah 1925-1927, 1928, 2154
mode of discourse in 1833-1834
Rashi's commentary of 2227, 2230-2232
Saadiah Gaon's Arabic translation and
  commentary of 2174
Samaritan 2253-2254, 2255, 2262 n. 49,
  2263 n. 55
Pentecost 42, 43, 177, 424
La perfecto casada (The Perfect Wife, de León)
  2089
periyah 89
Perls, F. 1094
perush 188
Perush le-Sefer Mishlei (Joseph Kimhi) 273
Perush le-Sefer-Iyov (Joseph Kimhi) 273
Pesach *see* Passover
Pesahim 357, 363
pesharim 170, 190
peshat exegesis 2045, 2047-2049, 2050, 2051,
  2060
Pesher 171, 173, 179, 180, 181
Peshitta 1313, 1318
Peshuto shel Miqra (Torczyner) 276
Peskowitz, M. 1500 n. 10, 1500 n. 12
Petuchowski, J.J. 1250, 1254
Phaedo 201, 207
Phaedon or On the Immortality of the Soul
  (Mendelssohn) 207
Pharisaic purity 538
Pharisaic-Rabbinic tradition 174
Pharisaism 1847
Pharisees 19, 69, 84, 115, 143, 202-203, 499,
  541-543, 546-547, 553, 555, 557, 561, 614,
  1018, 1109, 1303, 1459
phenomenology of Judaism 1863-1880
philanthropy 560, 1469, 1478
Philo of Alexandria 13, 72-73, 154-155,
  184, 270, 278, 494-495, 497-498, 602, 604,
  608-609, 711-713, 732, 737, 782-784, 875,
  905, 953
    on prohibition to mix meat and milk 1763
    and Pseudo-Philo 2212
    on work forbidden on Sabbath 2130
philology, biblical 1761
philosophical discourse 2215
philosophy 134, 253, 267-268, 1921
    Aristotelian 274, 481, 1760
    of Judaism 710-783
    Karaite 1819-1820
    natural 2111-2112
    pre-Socratic 2031
    Stoic 1792
    texts in Judaeo-Arabic 2176, 2177, 2178
    used for Jewish preaching 1894, 1900,
      1904 n. 76
    young Jews being forbidden to study 2083
Photius 2262 n. 44
phylacteries, worn by women 1946-1947,
  1952 n. 53
physical wholeness 1701, 1702
physiognomy 1911

picaros 2086
Piera, Salomón de 1680
piety 268, 407, 424, 1062-1069
    acts of 2290
pigs 1723
pilgrimages 1697
    to gravesites of ancestors and *zaddikim* 679,
      1857
    to Mount Gerizim 2246
pilgrims 152
pinkasim (records) 1850
Pinkerfeld, J. 1396 n. 10
pinot 161
Pirqe de Rabbi Eliezer 2035, 2042-2043
'Pisces', sinking of 2306
Pishra de-Rabbi Hanina ben Dosa 2036
Pitzele, Peter 574
Pius XI, Pope, death of 2268, 2280 n. 17
piyyutim (religious poems) 679, 825,
  1849-1850, 1851, 1854, 1855
    and astrology 2035
    and astronomy 2042
    French medieval 2016
    included in liturgy 2233
    Moroccan 2294, 2296, 2298, 2303
    Rashi's commentaries on 2233-2234
plagues
    in Apocalypse of St. John 1621-1622
    Egyptian 1620-1621
plants 1622
Plaskow, Judith 776-777, 1499, 1502 n. 86,
  1950 n. 10
Plato 132, 415, 625, 713-714, 720, 727, 732,
  780, 952-953, 956
Platonism 72-73, 76
pledge, returning of 2192
Pliny 183-184
pluralism 149, 563, 569, 575, 664, 766, 767,
  776, 782, 1092, 1247
poetics, biblical 2052
poetry
    biblical 2052
    by Moroccan rabbis 1849-1850, 1851
    by Rashi (Solomon Yitzhaki) 2228, 2229
    Hebrew 910
    liturgical 2228, 2233, 2239 n. 19
    Rashi described in 2236-2237
    see also piyyutim
pogroms 1274
Polak, Jacob 216
polemics
    anti-Christian 1013-1014, 1817, 1895-1896,
      2176, 2272
    anti-Islamic 461-462, 1817
    anti-Jewish 461, 1866, 1879 n. 1
    in Judaeo-Arabic 2176
Polish Jewish community, in Shanghai 1639
politics
    and Judaism 1069-1089
    sermons used in 2269, 2280 n. 23
pollination 1757

Pollnoe, Jacob Joseph of   218
polygamy   281, 283, 287, 579, 610, 897, 940,
    1025, 1026, 1028, 1410, 1428, 1480, 1917
polytheistic cultures   1763
polythetic taxonomy   2156, 2161
Popkin, Richard   970
population density, in Israel   1718, 1729 n. 2
Porton, Gary   949
Portugal
    forced conversion of Jews in   2081
    Karaites in   1810
    receiving Jews expelled from Spain   2082
poshe'a yisra'el   368
positive commandments, in Torah   2192-2194
The Positive-Historical School   97, 100, 103,
    108, 111
poskim   1666, 1668
postmodernism, and religion   767
poterim   2046
Potiphar, purchase of Joseph as slave   2140
prayer books   208, 209, 827
    feminist influence on   1804
prayer houses, of Beta Israel   1745
prayers   28, 537, 539, 564, 572, 575, 603,
    612, 637-638, 649, 658, 684, 694, 696,
    702-704, 748, 750-752, 755, 759, 774, 796,
    800, 807-809, 811, 816, 820-821, 823,
    825-830, 843, 848, 887, 907-908, 910-912,
    917, 919, 922, 931-933, 950, 968, 1003,
    1063, 1064, 1069, 1095, 1171, 1178, 1189,
    1215, 1223, 1228, 1232, 1234, 1238, 1248,
    1249, 1254, 1275, 1278, 1288
    of Beta Israel   1745, 1750
    Karaite   1814
    mystical meaning of   827-828
    women's obligations   1945, 1951 n. 46
pre-Aristotelian philosophers   1625
pre-astrology   2031
pre-Socratic philosophy   2031
preaching, Jewish   1888-1904, 2265-2283
preaching aids   1891, 1902 n. 25
pregnancy, superstitions about   1908, 1914
Prell, R.-E.   1502 n. 61
pretending to be a gentile   1664
Preuss, H.D.   1447 n. 2, n. 5, n. 8, n. 11,
    n. 20
priesthood   18, 596, 600, 604, 625-626, 1019,
    1084, 1109, 1140, 1141, 1145, 1179, 1180,
    1181, 1184, 1264, 1290, 1292, 1293, 1444
    Samaritan   2260, 2265 n. 96
priests   173, 175, 187, 295, 486, 532, 537,
    542, 544, 546, 551-552, 554, 556, 581, 586,
    597, 624, 877, 907
    and astronomers   2037
    in Beta Israel Judaism   1744, 1752
    disabled   1701
    Zadokite ('sons of Zadok')   166, 178, 496
print, sermons appearing in   2268-2269, 2270,
    2271, 2272
Prinz, Joachim   2278
Pritsak, Omeljan   1827

private Judaism   1806-1807
Procopius   2250
procreation   855, 1908
Progressive Judaism   1349, 1351, 1352
prolepsis, compositional technique of   2056
prophecies   257, 381, 388, 1720
prophetic Judaism   301
prophetic writing   380
Prophets   1308, 1311-1313, 1315, 1317-1319,
    1436, 1450, 1490, 1521, 1541, 1730
    exemplifying leaders of Israel (people)
        2095
    Rashi's commentaries on   2232
propositional logic   1934, 1935, 1938, 1940,
    2215-2217, 2226
proselytes   114-116, 122, 187, 785, 804-805,
    1029, 1035, 1037, 1189, 1190, 1192, 1485,
    1739 n. 14, n. 15, n. 26, n. 28
    acceptance of   1732, 1733, 1734, 2118
    Kabbalistic view of   1735
    Samaritans seen as   2247
    Zohar on   1740 n. 38
proselytism
    by Christians   644
    by Jews   603, 690, 1791
Protestant biblical criticism   268
The Protestant ethic (Weber)   236
Protestants   77-79, 81, 86-88, 123
proto-Samaritan texts   2253, 2262 n. 49, 2263
    n. 57
providence   315, 320-321, 507-508
    divine   2129
Psalms   909, 1730
    Book of   1859, 1907
    Hallel   264, 825-827, 907, 1059-1060, 1061-
        1062
    Rashi's commentaries on   2232
Pseudepigrapha   170, 182, 200, 878, 882,
    1313, 1318, 1319, 1449
pseudo-corrections, used in classical Arabic
    2169
Pseudo-Eupolemus   2253
Pseudo-Philo   2200-2212
psychoanalysts   2138
psychology, and Judaism   1089-1109
Ptolemy (Claudius Ptolemaeus)   2031, 2038,
    2039, 2042
public Judaism   1806-1807
Public Preaching in the Talmudic Period
    (Heinemann)   1888
puerperal illness   1715
Pulgar, Fernando del   1688
Pulgar, Isaac   1618
punishments   199, 260, 265, 365, 550,
    552-555, 589-590, 600-601, 804, 899-900,
    904, 1254, 1257, 1258, 1259, 1261, 1262,
    1263
    amputation   1707
    for blaspheming God   1702
    by God   2104, 2111
    death penalty   2151

fraternal warnings before 2129-2130
for homosexuality 2151-2152
for inflicting bodily harm 1702
lashes 2199 n. 14
purification 529, 565, 596-597, 757, 806, 860,
886, 933, 989, 1112-1114, 1118, 1119, 1123,
1140, 1181
Purim 10, 11, 39-40, 48-50, 429, 477, 649,
785, 1284, 1861
puritanism, new 2148
purity 527, 535-539, 542-543, 545, 596, 637,
682, 756, 801, 815, 964, 1109, 1110-1124,
1140, 1145, 1187, 1433, 1479, 1484, 1543,
1544, 1546
of blood (*limpieza de sangre*) 2078, 2080,
2088
female 1479, 1748, 1815, 1845, 1943, 1947
rituals
of Beta Israel 1748-1749, 1752-1753
Karaite 1815
of Samaritans 2258-2259
see also impurity
Purvis, James D. 2263 n. 58
Putnam, Robert 708

Qara, Joseph 272-273, 2046, 2047, 2050,
2051, 2053
qataf 2254, 2264 n. 68
Qimron, E. 785
Qingdao (China), Jewish community in
1644
al-Qirqisani, Jacob 1810, 1818, 1819,
1826
Querido, Jacob 1773, 1774
Quevedo, Francisco de 2086, 2089
quietism 424
al-Qumisi, Daniel 1809, 1819
Qumran 15, 19, 56, 166, 168, 182-186, 193,
194, 534, 607, 785-786, 1011
calendar used in 2037-2038
Community 168, 177, 183-186, 193-194,
486, 494-499, 2130
Essenes library at 497-498
scrolls 17, 185, 606, 612, 614, 905, 1809
texts 166-195, 607, 878, 1309
on astrology 2032
on astronomy 2038
Brontologion 2032
Cairo manuscript 190
Damascus Document 19, 185-187,
189-194, 1809
Messiah Apocalypse 200
Samaritan 2247, 2253, 2254, 2262 n. 49,
2264 n. 81
Quran 712-713, 782, 790
and the Bible 453, 454-455, 461
exegesis 2173
and the Torah 461, 712-713

Rabanism *see* Rabbinic Judaism
Rabbinic authorities 317, 442

Rabbinic Bibles 728, 2124
Rabbinic courts 1850-1851
in State of Israel 2197-2198
Rabbinic Judaism (Judaism of the dual
Torah) 14, 53, 56, 80, 82, 84, 87-88, 101,
110, 131-132, 143-145, 155, 176, 190, 219,
241, 243, 249, 255, 280, 316-323, 367,
371-372, 376, 378, 388, 391-392, 396, 401,
404-405, 471, 484-485, 492, 494, 498, 502,
525, 529-530, 533-535, 617-619, 631, 654,
661, 663, 665-666, 670-671, 674, 773,
822, 833, 851, 878, 888, 890-891, 961,
986-987, 1010, 1018, 1092-1093, 1132-1206,
1243-1246, 1290, 1293, 1302, 1303,
1305-1307, 1309, 1313, 1325, 1329, 1337,
1341, 1343, 1397, 1434, 1448-1450,
1459-1462, 1481, 1482, 1484, 1485, 1491,
1593, 1594
biography in 2061-2076
normative dogmas of 2104
opposed by Karaites 1807-1809, 1821,
2175
practised by Kaifeng (China) Jewry 1635
social teaching of 1880-1887
theology of 1161-1174, 1251-1254
views on teachings of Jesus 2132
Rabbinic law 123, 136, 145, 164, 269
Rabbinic literature 77, 79, 144, 162, 164,
214, 252-253, 263, 266-267, 277, 320, 368,
371, 377, 401, 485, 1135-1139, 1206-1227
astrology in 2033-2036
astronomy in 2038-2044
biography in 2063
chauvinistic statements in 1731
on Chosen People 1731-1732
on disabilities 1696
homogeneity of 1607
on homosexuality 2140-2142
Jewish law in 1657
logics of 2213-2226
and records of early Christianity
2073-2074, 2075
study of 2076
wise sayings collections 2065, 2070-2071,
2073
Rabbinic Narrative (Neusner) 2236
Rabbinic teaching 196, 269-270
Rabbinic Torah interpretation 1817
Rabbinical Assembly (Conservative Movement)
1804-1805
Rabbinowitz, H. 1405
Rabbinowitz, J.I. 1405
rabbis 218, 379, 408, 579, 680-681,
1124-1132
Ethiopian 1752
Hasidic 218, 408, 432, 576
of the Kaifeng Jewish community 1635
Moroccan 1849-1850, 1851, 2299
support for Zionism 2304, 2307
women 1804-1805
rabies 1715

Rabin, Yitzhak 785
Rabin, Chaim 789
racial theories 84
racism *see* antisemitism
Rackman, Emmanuel 1738
Radak see Kimhi, David (*Radak*)
'Radanites' 1630
Radbaz see ibn Zimra, David
Rader, L.W. 1397 n. 39, 1397 n. 42
rainfall 1596, 1597, 1601, 1602-1603, 1604
Ralbag 1717
Ramadan 459
Rambam see Maimonides, Moses
Ramban see Nahmanides
Ramle
  Jewish community in 2301
  Karaite headquarters 1812
Ramsey, Paul 1654
Rank, O. 1095, 1109
Raphael, Marc Lee 764
Raphael, Simcha Paull 212
Raphall, Morris 2269
Rapoport-Albert, A. 1489, 1491, 1501 n. 37,
  n. 51
Ras Shamra tablets 197
Rashba see Adret, Shelomo ben
Rashbam see ben Meir, Samuel
Rashdam see Medina, Shmuel di
Rashi (Solomon Yitzhaki) 105, 162, 230,
  232, 268, 270, 271-272, 278-280, 342, 787,
  790-791, 908, 963, 968, 1013, 1015, 1102,
  1663, 1664, 1945
  acronym 2226, 2238 n. 1
  on commandments not enforceable in court
    2193, 2199 n. 6
  commentaries
    Biblical 2227, 2230-2233, 2237-2238,
      2239 n. 40, n. 41, n. 42
    on Canticles 2233
    on liturgical poetry 2233-2234
    on the Talmud 2045-2046, 2229-2230,
      2235
  on contextual reading methodology
    2046-2047, 2048, 2050
  disciples of 2227-2228
  drawings by 2237-2238
  on guarding from evil spirits 1909,
    1913
  on humanity and nature 1721-1723
  in legends 2237
  life of 2226-2227
  in poetry 2236-2237
  poetry by 2228-2229
  on prohibition of interbreeding and mingling
    of agricultural species 1754
  on redaction of the Bible 2052, 2053,
    2055-2056, 2058
  responsa written by 2234-2235,
    2240 n. 55
  as storyteller 2235-2236
  Yeshiva founded by 2227

rationalism 222, 477, 482, 775, 1866
rationality, of God's will 2184, 2185
Rava 2038
Ravid, Benjamin C.I. 778
Ravitzky, Aviezer 884, 1538
Rawidowicz, Simon 777-778
reading, texts on 2045
realia 2125-2126
reconciliation 2130
Reconstructionist Judaism 564, 574, 693,
  696, 699, 705-707, 734, 800, 829, 831, 978,
  980-981, 1227-1240, 1478 n. 2, 1497, 1804
Reconstructionist synagogues 573
Red Sea, parting of 2202-2203
redaction
  of the Bible 2051-2060, 2243
  of the Talmud 2063-2065
redeemer 600-601, 825, 874-875, 877-880,
  888
redemption 575, 577, 581, 586, 590, 592,
  594-595, 598, 600, 667, 672, 683-685,
  714, 736, 750, 756, 758-760, 779, 796-799,
  815-818, 820-821, 826, 846-847, 849, 876,
  880-884, 886-887, 893-894, 896, 926,
  944-946, 950, 952, 955-956, 972, 974,
  986-989, 1021, 1093, 1132, 1163, 1173,
  1176, 1178, 1179, 1180, 1181, 1184, 1187,
  1188, 1189, 1191, 1193, 1194, 1195, 1196,
  1198, 1199, 1219, 1233, 1235, 1258
  of Israel 2164-2165
  sermons about 2271, 2281 n. 39,
    n. 40
Reform Judaism 96-98, 100-101, 109-111,
  257, 345, 369, 411, 532, 563-564, 565,
  568, 572, 574, 662-664, 668, 673, 675, 680,
  693, 702-705, 707, 736, 743, 746, 766, 769,
  795, 922-923, 943, 957, 977-981, 995-997,
  999-1000, 1002, 1004, 1006-1007, 1240,
  1242-1244, 1246, 1247-1253, 1332, 1335,
  1341, 1347, 1351, 1352, 1361, 1362, 1478
  n. 2, 1492-1494, 1496, 1497, 1537
  on Chosen People 1735, 1736
  on homosexuality 2138, 2153
  sermons in 2266, 2268-2269
Reform Movement 163, 208, 211, 572-573,
  744-745, 800, 805, 830-831, 920, 1351,
  1494, 1497, 1498, 1545, 2276
  in America 1795, 1799-1800
reformist religions 1864
Reggio, Isaac Samuel 276
Reich, Wilhelm 2138
Reik, Theodor 946-947
Reinach, Salomon 301-302, 304
Reines, Isaac Jacob 884, 1405, 1406,
  1409 n. 9
religions
  anthropological approaches to 1870-1871,
    1880 n. 9
  and cultural-spiritual styles 1870-1871
  and culture 1864, 2283
  definition of 1863, 1871-1872

determination of superstition 1904
folkist 1864
of literate civilizations 1864
and norms for social order 2283
origins of 1877, 1880 n. 18
religious Jewish identity 1795, 1800
religious norms 1864
religious systems 1922-1923
REMA see Isserles, Moshe (*REMA*)
Renan, Joseph Ernest 84, 300-301, 308
repentance 369, 552-553, 598, 684-685, 810,
812-813, 818-820, 826, 848, 872, 881-883,
886-887, 900-901, 968, 1091, 1094, 1096,
1098, 1099, 1100, 1173, 1174, 1184, 1185,
1186, 1191, 1195, 1254, 1255, 1256, 1257,
1258, 1261
  Sabbath of 1889, 1901 n. 7
  theme in Jewish preaching 1895,
    1897-1901, 1904 n. 78
  tradition of 2130, 2151
reproduction techniques 1653-1654
responsa, written by Rashi 2234-2235,
2240 n. 55
resumptive repetition, compositional technique
of 2058-2059
resurrection 63, 64, 76, 164, 195, 199, 200,
202-203, 205-212, 575, 582, 586-587, 613,
620, 714, 808, 813, 875, 905, 1228
Resurrection of the Dead (Arthur Cohen) 210
Resurrection (Wyschogrod) 211
Reuchlin, Johannes 275
revealed regulations 176
Revelation Restored (Weiss Halivni) 1798
revelation of Torah 950-951, 954-955, 1133
  man's place in 2185, 2187
Réville, Albert 301
Revue de Paris 301
Revue des études juives (Zadoc-Kahn) 299, 305
Rice, Abraham 2281 n. 39
Ricoeur, P. 1096
RIF (Isaac Alfasi) 342, 1657, 1660, 1848
righteousness, and physical wholeness 1701
RIK see ben Solomon, Joseph (*RIK*)
Ringelblum, Emanuel 422
Ringelheim, J. 1497, 1502 n. 74
rishonim 187, 342, 344
rites
  Balkan 1769
ritual 647, 695, 748, 751, 757, 798, 801,
805, 808, 813-815, 825, 831, 859-860,
867, 877, 899, 947, 964, 972, 984, 986,
988, 991, 1297, 1320, 1330, 1343, 1353,
1370, 1382, 1393, 1394, 1424, 1433, 1460,
1465 n. 13, 1478, 1480, 1483, 1484, 1489,
1490, 1493, 1494, 1498, 1499, 1543, 1546,
1548
ritual purity, among Beta Israel 1748-1749,
1752-1763
rituals 798-803, 1798-1799
  burial 1828, 1910
  and ethics 1799-1800

observance of 1801
performed by women 1945, 1947, 1948,
  1951 n. 44, n. 46, 1952 n. 55
Tannaitic 92
Rizba see ben Abraham, Isaac
The Road to Perfection (*Camino de perfección*, Saint
Theresa) 2089
Robinson, Joan 231
Rohling, August 85
Roiphe, Anne 571
Rojas, Francisco de 2086-2087
Rokeah see ben Judah, Eleazar
Rolling Stone Magazine 1796
Roman Catholics 78, 88
Roman Empire
  influence on Genesis Rabbah 2112, 2115,
    2116
  Judaism in 1605
Roman laws 1765
Romaniotes 1766, 1773
Romans 1781, 1790
  and Samaritans 2246-2247
Romantic Movement 102
Romanus I (Romanus Lekapenos, emperor of
Byzantium) 1766, 1829
Rome 64, 73, 193, 386-387, 389-391, 398,
400, 404, 466, 485, 488, 491, 501
Roof, Wade Clark 698
roofs, used for drying agricultural produce
2126
Rosaldo, M.Z. 1484, 1501 n. 21
Rosenberg, Joel 574
Rosenbloom 509
Rosenzweig, Franz 135, 566, 749-752, 754,
780-781, 943, 961, 974-975, 1019-1022,
1803
Rosh see ben Yehiel, Asher
Rosh ha-Shanah 22, 24-26, 28, 33-35, 38, 45,
364, 424, 827
  celebrations among Moroccan Jews
    1859-1860
  determining date of 2040
  tractate of 2042
  see also New Year
Rosner, Fred 859
Rotenberg, M. 1105, 1109
Roth, C. 1397 n. 24, n. 31
Roth, Jeff 575
Rothschild, Baron Alain de 308
Rothschild, Fritz A. 773
Rothschild, Jacob M. 2278, 2282 n. 74
Rousseau, Jean Jacques 81
Routtenberg, Max J. 1737
Rozin, J. 1405, 1406, 1409 n. 9, n. 10,
n. 15
Rubenstein, Richard 416, 419, 767, 778-779,
950-951, 1022-1023
Ruderman, David 969-970
Rudin, Jacob 2278
Rueda, Lope de 2086
rulers 175

rules, search for   2216
ar-Rumayhi, Isma'il   2257
ruminants   1723
Russel, D.E.   1052
Russia, Khazar influences   1831
Russian Chronicle   1831
Russian Jews, in China   1641-1642, 1643,
    1645
Russian Orthodox Christians   84
Russo, Baruchya   1774

Saadiah Gaon *see* Gaon, Saadiah
Saba, Abraham   1899-1900
Sabbateanism   875
Sabbath   3, 5, 6, 8, 9, 17, 18, 22, 24-28, 30,
    43, 89, 94, 97, 99, 114-116, 178, 187-188,
    232, 234, 351, 370, 377, 401-402, 422, 424,
    429, 448, 456, 509, 526, 528, 530, 564,
    567-568, 570, 586, 596, 602-603, 611, 613,
    615, 621, 637, 646, 649, 651, 657, 682, 750,
    776, 795, 798-801, 805, 807, 809-811, 818,
    821, 826-828, 834, 839, 860, 869, 873,
    877-878, 881, 908-913, 917-919, 930, 962,
    982-983, 986, 989, 994, 1007, 1026, 1029,
    1030, 1032, 1033, 1034, 1044, 1054, 1061,
    1064, 1068, 1140, 1141, 1142, 1146, 1184,
    1185, 1186, 1214, 1228, 1232, 1250, 1263,
    1265, 1274, 1276, 1277, 1278, 1284, 1286,
    1287, 1302-1304, 1343, 1350, 1351, 1359,
    1362-1365, 1368, 1370, 1371, 1379, 1394,
    1433, 1434, 1437, 1445, 1483, 1484, 1486,
    1488, 1490, 1493, 1499, 1503-1505, 1511,
    1535, 1542-1544, 1546, 1547
    Great   1889
    observance of   1629, 2130-2131, 2270
        among Beta Israel   1746
        among Samaritans   2258, 2261
        Karaite   1815
    of repentance   1889, 1901 n. 7
Sabbath Prayer Book (Mordecai Kaplan)   209
sabbathical year   51, 52, 349, 351-352, 467,
    1726-1727
Sabians   1613
Sachar, Abram L.   778
Sacks, M.   1502 n. 58
sacrifices   118, 360-361, 446, 524, 528, 541,
    543-544, 546, 551-552, 577, 591-592, 596,
    598, 610, 620-621, 804, 810, 815, 823-824,
    826-827, 836, 877, 882, 890, 907, 947, 964,
    1004-1005, 1039, 1114, 1119, 1136, 1139,
    1140, 1144, 1145, 1185, 1186, 1189, 1192,
    1256, 1258, 1263, 1264, 1266, 1291
    of animals (*Zebahim*)   1296-1300
    in Beta Israel Judaism   1745
    one's life to sanctify God   1662
    Samaritan   2245
    teruma (heave-offering)   1698-1699
Sadducees   69, 84, 186, 203, 547, 555, 614,
    651, 1303, 1459, 1816
Samaritans identified with   2247
Safed

center of mysticism   678
    Moroccan Jews in   2297-2298
Safir, M.   1500, 1502 n. 71
sages   1608, 1888
    on astrology   2036
    biographies of   2061-2062, 2063, 2064,
        2068, 2077 n. 1
    on biological species   1626-1627
    discourse that focuses on   2065-2073
    exempt from paying taxes   2292
    and the norms of Israelite social order
        1885-1887
    on participants in Jewish life   1696-1697
    Samaritan   2254, 2263 n. 59
    on study of Torah   2118
    support of   2290-2291
    used by medieval Jewish preachers   1893
The Sages: Their Concepts and Beliefs (Urbach)
    1608
Sagi, Avi   259
St Petersburg Manuscript   1902 n. 17
Saint Veneration among the Jews of Morocco
    (Ben-Ami)   1857
St. Victor, Hugh of   2045
Salanter *see* Lipkin, Israel (Salanter)
Salmon, Y.   1409 n. 11
Salomon, Gotthold   2268
Salonika   1770-1776
salt, covenant of   2050
Saltman, Avrom   2233
salvation   389, 493, 508, 552, 587, 594-595,
    598, 620-623, 627, 667, 800, 818, 826, 843,
    875, 880, 885, 955, 988, 990, 1001, 1019,
    1102, 1176-1181, 1184, 1189, 1197, 1198,
    1206, 1231
    Christian views of   2115
    of Israel (people)   1934, 2112-2113, 2114,
        2115, 2119
Samaritan views of   2258
Samandar   1822
Samaria, and Judea   2243-2244
Samaritan council (*Hukama*)   2248, 2251
Samaritanism   1874, 1876-1877, 2241-2265
    beliefs and practices   2257-2259
    contemporary   2241-2242, 2259-2261
    halakhah in   2247, 2256, 2260, 2264 n. 80,
        n. 81
    history of   2242-2253
    and Judaism   2244, 2247-2248, 2256, 2258,
        2259, 2261 n. 1, 2263 n. 58, 2264 n. 80,
        n. 81
    literature   2253-2257, 2262 n. 43, n. 44
Samaritans   16, 372, 486, 527, 552, 646, 653,
    1877, 2241
    in the Gospels   2125
    in the Mishnah   2125-2126
    and Romans   2246-2247
    in writings of Josephus   1779, 1793 n. 3,
        2242, 2245, 2246, 2262 n. 28
Samizdat   1279
Samkarsh al-Yahud   1822

Samson, as described by Josephus   1783-1784
Samuel
    book of   2053
    as described by Josephus   1784-1785, 2209
    in *Liber Antiquitatum Biblicarum* (Pseudo-Philo)
        2208-2210
Samuel of Auxerre   2234
Samuel the Pious of Speyer   2240 n. 42
Samuel, Rabbi   2034, 2039-2040, 2041
Samuelson, Norbert   661, 802, 813, 868, 877,
    912, 974-975, 986, 988, 990, 999, 1001,
    1123, 1124, 1140-1143, 1179-1182, 1184,
    1245, 1252
Sanballat   2244, 2245
sanctification   290, 293, 575, 587, 620-622,
    630
    centrality in Mishnah   1928-1929
    of God's name   1662
sanctuaries   190-191, 470, 1616
Sanders, E.P.   1606, 1608-1609, 2077 n. 6
Sanders, Jack T.   1010-1011
Sandmel, Samuel   1869
The Sane Society (Fromm)   2144
Sant Jordi, Magister Francesch de (Astruc
    Rimoch de Fraga)   1680
Santa Fe, Jerónimo de   1679-1680, 1686-1687
Santa María, Pablo de (Salomon Halevi)
    1679-1680
Saperstein, Harold   2275, 2278
Sarah   1919, 2046-2047
Sarkel   1822, 1830
Sarmiento, Pedro   1682, 1683
Sarmiento Rebellion   1682-1683
Saron, G.   1357
Sassoon family   1638, 1639-1640, 1647
Satan   261-262, 335, 407, 885, 970, 1106,
    1321, 1530
Satinover, Jeffrey   2147
Saul
    as described by Josephus   1785
    in *Liber Antiquitatum Biblicarum* (Pseudo-Philo)
        2209, 2210
Savior   325
Savoraim   341
Savunarola, Girolamo   2143
Schachter, Herschel   1949
Schachter, Lifsa   813
Schachter-Shalomi, Zalman   564, 575-576,
    767
Schäfer, P.   1026, 1027, 1028, 1029, 1033,
    1034, 1037
Schafer, R.   1098
Schapira, Avraham   2198, 2199 n. 29
Scharz, S.H.   1240
Schechter Letter   1822, 1825, 1827, 1829
Schechter, Solomon   105, 107, 1606-1607,
    2172
Scheler, M.   753-754, 1408
Schelling, Friedrich Wilhelm Joseph von
    742-743, 745-746
Schiffman, Laurence H.   194

Schindler, Alexander   124, 428
Schneersohn, Shalom Dov Baer   885, 887
Schneur Zalman of Liadi   1735, 1740 n. 39
Schoeps, Hans Joachim   749
scholars
    among Greek Jews   1766, 1767, 1770
    Ashkenazic   480
    Christian   169-170, 1867-1870, 2075
    historicistic and relativistic   1870
    of Jewish legal traditions and codifications
        1656
    of Judaism   1606
        in Morocco   1847-1848, 1849
    Karaite   1767, 1811
        biblical studies by   2174, 2175, 2183 n.
            38, n. 41
    Sephardic   1770-1771
    Zoroastrian   301
scholastic argumentation, modes of   1899
Scholem, Gershom   207, 264, 759, 883, 928,
    932, 943, 949, 952, 1347 n. 4, 1410 n. 32,
    1489, 1501 n. 38
    on Doenme movement   1774
    on Jewish mysticism   2031
schools *see* education
Schorsch, Ismar   101, 103
Schpiegel, S.   1109
Schullenberg, Jane Tibbets   1948
Schulweis, H.   566, 763, 1238
Schumpeter, Joseph   1922
Schürer, Emil   84, 1051
Schwarzschild, Steven   259
sciatic nerve, consumption prohibited   1715
sciatica   1715-1716
science
    Aristotelian   132, 478, 482, 1661
    astrology as a   2031
    natural
        and the Bible   960-961
        and Orthodox Judaism   971, 972, 973
        and Torah   2292
scientific research, and Jewish religion   1628-
    1629
scientific works, in Judaeo-Arabic   2177
scientists, religious motivation of   1628
Screech, M.   1104, 1105
scribes   1850
scriptor   2052
scriptural encyclopedia of Judaism   2102
scriptural traditions   1864
Scripture   266-267, 277, 282, 367, 387, 388,
    391, 401, 525, 527-531, 537, 579, 582,
    584-589, 619-620, 625, 627, 652, 654-655,
    665, 670, 719-720, 783-789, 792, 794-795,
    797-798, 801-802, 806, 811, 817, 826-827,
    832, 833, 845, 849, 851, 874-875, 889,
    892-894, 897-901, 903-904, 928, 935,
    960-963, 972, 980, 1002, 1009, 1014, 1077,
    1096, 1109, 1110, 1112, 1113, 1116-1119,
    1122, 1124, 1125, 1130, 1132, 1133, 1135-
    1138, 1146, 1147, 1148, 1149, 1153-1158,

1160-1163, 1165-1171, 1174, 1175, 1177,
1178, 1179, 1180, 1182, 1184, 1185, 1186,
1189, 1190, 1192, 1198, 1200, 1202, 1203,
1204, 1212, 1223, 1230, 1243, 1254, 1255,
1256, 1258, 1259, 1260, 1261, 1266,
1290, 1293, 1294, 1296, 1298, 1301-1310,
1320-1325, 1330, 1343-1345, 1410,
1412-1414, 1416, 1417, 1419, 1422, 1425,
1428, 1430, 1434, 1436, 1437, 1442, 1444-
1447, 1449-1451, 1454-1456, 1458-1464,
1466, 1467, 1469, 1505, 1510-1516, 1519,
1522, 1528, 1539, 1542, 1543, 1545
  classifications in 2159, 2161
  criticism of 1866
  description of social order 1886, 1887
  and Mishnah 2154-2157
  translations of 1309-1320
  see also Torah
scriptures 1864, 1865
A Scroll of Agony (Chaim Kaplan) 422
scrolls
  at Qumran 17, 185, 606, 612, 614, 905,
    1809
  of Torah 810, 878, 1384, 1385, 1388,
    1450, 1456, 1476, 1489
Scult, M. 1240
scurvy 1716
Second Temple
  destruction of 1927
  Judaism 527, 529, 601, 606, 614-616
  period 32, 38, 41, 47, 48, 84, 439, 534,
    546, 557, 601-617
Second Vatican Council 87
secular learning, and study of Torah 2283,
  2285-2288, 2292, 2293
secular understanding, of biblical religion
  1866
secularism 234, 1866
Seder 24-28, 41
  right of women to recline at 1946,
    1952 n. 51
Seder Amram Gaon 1768
Seder ha-Olam 2039
sefer al-Tautiyah (Abu Ibrahim) 2255
Sefer ha-Azamim (Ibn Ezra) 1616
Sefer Ha-Brit (Joseph Kimhi) 273
Sefer Ha-Maqneh (Joseph Kimhi) 273
Sefer Ha-Mitzvot (David ben Anan) 1818
Sefer ha-Mivhar (The Choice Book, Aaron ben
  Moses) 1819
Sefer Ha-'Osher (The Book of Richness, Jacob
  ben Reuben) 1819, 1826
Sefer ha-Razim (Book of Secrets) 1906,
  2034-2035
Sefer ha-Rikma (Janah) 267
Sefer ha-Shorashim (Janah) 267
Sefer Ha-Torah (Joseph Kimhi) 273
Sefer Ha-Zikharon 272
Sefer haBahir 207
Sefer Hagalui (Joseph Kimhi) 273
Sefer haHalachot (Alfasi) 1660

Sefer Hahinnuch 229
Sefer HaLevushim (Yoffe) 1668
Sefer haMitzvot (Book of Commandments,
  Maimonides) 1661
Sefer Hasidim 56, 57, 1666, 1906, 1908, 1910,
  1912, 1913, 1915
Sefer Meirat Einayim (Falk) 343
Sefer Mitzvot Gedolot (SMAG, Moses of Coucy)
  1657-1658, 1665
Sefer Mitzvot Ketanot (SMAK, Isaac of Corbeil)
  1658
Sefer Razi'el 1906, 1907
Sefer Yetzirah (Book of Creation) 133, 1906,
  2035
Sefer Yosippon 1767
sefirot 479, 503-504
Segal, Alan 113, 787, 942
segregation 634, 664, 667, 743, 994, 996
segullot, doctrine of 1615
self correction 1102, 1103
self-enclosure 742, 754
selichot 45
Seligsohn, M. 2256
Seligson, David J. 121-122
selihot
  poems 2228, 2239 n. 19
  service 1859
Seltzer, Claudia 1010, 1011, 1012
Seltzer, R.M. 1240
semikha (Rabbinic ordination) 1772
separateness see xenophobia
Sephardic communities 272
Sephardic customs 309, 680, 1853-1854, 1855
  of Moroccan Jews 1848-1850
Sephardic Judaism 680, 681-683, 686, 687
  and Ashkenazic Judaism 344, 681, 955
Sephardic music 916-921
Sephardic preaching 2266, 2279 n. 8
Sephardic scholarship 1770-1771
Sephardim 2, 460, 676-678, 688-690, 1359,
  1361, 1364, 1452, 1465 n. 13, 1537, 1546
  in Hong Kong 1647
  migrating to Ashkenazic lands 1667
  migrating to China 1637
  migrating to Greece 1768, 1769
  in Salonika 1770
  in Shanghai 1638, 1639
September 11 terrorist attacks, Jewish
  preaching on 2276
Septuagint 461, 550, 604, 607-608, 784, 787,
  789, 1028, 1309-1314, 1318
Sered, S.S. 1478, 1500 n. 1
sermons
  by Jesus 2129
  conversionary 1889
  definition of 1887
  eulogies 1889-1890, 1901 n. 10
  in Judaism
    medieval and early modern 1887-1904,
      2265, 2268, 2276
    modern 2265-2283

life cycle 1889
of rebuke 1895
written 1890
settlements
in Judean Hills 1719
oscillating pattern of 1718, 1729 n. 1
se'udat mitzvah 89
The Seven Books of Diana (*Los siete libros de la Diana*, de Montemayor) 2087
Severus, Bishop 1676
sexes, separation of, in synagogues 1942-1943, 1950 n. 11, n. 13, 1951 n. 49, 1952 n. 59
Sexias/Seixas, Gershom Mendes 763-765, 2267, 2268, 2276
sexual deviancy, in Judaism 2137
sexual impropriety, seen as source of disabilities 1704-1705
sexual relations 188, 192, 281, 284, 855, 1943, 1948
superstitions about 1908
sexual revolution 2138
sexuality 1479, 1481, 1483-1485, 1488
Sforno, Obadiah ben Jacob 275
Sha'are Tzion (Zion's Gates) 2303
Shabbetai Tzvi 1773, 1906
Shabriri 1906
Shadal see Luzzatto, Samuel David
shadarim (emissaries), seeking support in diaspora for old *yishuv* 2294-2296, 2298, 2299-2300
Shaddai 1755
Shaffer, Aaron 512, 784
Shahat 198
Shain, M. 1357
Shakhna, Shalom 216
Shalom Zakhar 94
Shalshalat (ben Aaron) 2255
shamash (sexton) 1851
Shammaites 346
Shanghai, Jewish communities in 1638-1641, 1645, 1646-1647
Shanghai Volunteer Corps, Jewish platoon 1641
Shanghai Zionist Association (SZA) 1640
Shapiro, L. 1290
Shapiro, M. 216, 1410 n. 31, n. 38
Shapiro, Saul 982
al-Shaqer, M. 1944
Sharh am Baqquti (Nafis al-Din) 2257
Sharú (Saadiah Gaon) 2174
Shavua Haben 94
Shavuot 33, 35, 36, 40, 42-44, 1858
she'alot u'teshuvot (Adret) 343
Shebiit (tractate) 351-353
Shechem (Nablus)
Joseph's bones at 2249
sacredness in Samaritanism 2257-2258
Samaritan community in 2260
sheep, cloning of 1653
Shefar'am, settlement of 2301

shekels (membership dues to Zionist movement) 2303
shekhina 133-134, 331, 504
shekhita 220, 1946
Shelah (Horowitz) 432
shelihut 2294-2296, 2300
Shem Tov, Israel Baal (*Besht*) 217-218, 1105, 1735
Shema 46, 425, 448, 452, 464, 805, 816-818, 824, 825-826, 848, 907, 951, 1944
and protection against demons 1907-1908
Shemayah 2227-2228
Shemini Atzeret 46-48
Sheney Lukoth Ha-Berit (Horowitz) 122, 432
Sheol 198
Shepard, Jonathan 1828
Shepard, Sanford 2080, 2084
shevirat ha-kelim 503
Shibbolei Haleket 93
shiga'on (insanity) 1714
Shimmush Tehillim 1907
Shimoni, G. 1357
Shir ha-ma'alot 425
Shivat Tzion (Return to Zion) 2303
Shivhay ha-Besht 218
Shkop, Shimon 1405, 1406, 1409 n. 19
Shloush, Aaron 2301
Shloush, Abraham 2301
Shlumil, Shelomo 2297
Shmeruk, Ch. 1342 n. 14
Shoah 86, 406-407, 409-414, 417-418, 420-421, 423, 427-428, 432-433, 753-755, 810
see also Holocaust
shofar 37, 40, 382
sounding of 1596, 1601-1602, 1603, 1913
Shofarot (Shofar verses) 45
Shomeronim (Samaritans), origins of name 2242
Shorashim (David Kimhi) 274
Shoteh (mental disability) 1698, 1699, 1700, 1714
shtetl 215, 220, 425, 429
shtibl 28, 424-425
Shulhan Arukh (*Set Table*, Caro) 343-344, 347, 349, 1657, 1658, 1659, 1665, 1666, 1667, 1668, 1669-1670, 1671, 1674, 1853, 1854, 2230
Sibylline Oracles 878
Siegel, Seymour 258
Los siete libros de la Diana (the Seven Books of Diana, de Montemayor) 2087
Sifra 853, 1153, 1164, 1165, 1166, 1167, 1169, 1170, 1175, 1176, 1179, 1186, 1223, 1225, 2126, 2185
classifications in 2160-2167
metapropositional logic in 2225
on principles of Rabbinic exegesis 2049, 2057
topical program of 2158-2159
as a union of the two Torahs 2153-2158, 2159

Sifre 1153, 1164, 1165, 1167, 1170, 1179, 1186, 1210, 1223, 1225
  metapropositional logic in 2225
  to Deuteronomy 2091, 2092, 2096-2101, 2111, 2126, 2216, 2223-2224
  to Numbers 2184-2191
Siftei Hakhamim 272
Sigd festival 1747-1748, 1753
Sihat HaGeullah 378
Silberman, Charles 567, 1802
Silk Road, used by Jewish merchants 1630
Silver, Abba Hillel 2268, 2280 n. 17
Silver, Lee 1652
Silverman, William 2278
Simeon b. Eleazar 244, 262
Simhah of Vitry 2227
Simhat Torah 35, 36, 38, 47, 48, 1860
Simon, Erward H. 972
Sinai covenant 139-141, 1079, 1439-1441, 1730, 1735, 1869, 1872-1873
Singer, Peter 2146
Sinim 1630
sins 146, 207, 361, 365, 407, 410-411, 445, 449-450, 453, 479, 590-591, 594, 596, 599-601, 610, 625, 643, 748, 753, 756, 760, 800, 805, 812, 818, 820-821, 829, 838, 843, 855, 875, 889, 892, 899-901, 968, 1010, 1014, 1058, 1070, 1072, 1091, 1095, 1096, 1097, 1098, 1099, 1110, 1119, 1145, 1171, 1172, 1173, 1174, 1179, 1180-1184, 1187, 1188, 1189, 1191, 1193, 1194, 1195, 1196, 1197, 1198, 1201, 1254, 1255, 1256, 1257, 1258, 1259, 1260, 1261, 1262, 1263, 1264, 1265, 1266, 1320-1326, 1328, 1331, 1410-1413, 1428, 1429, 1431, 1432, 1466, 1468, 1472, 1475, 1516, 1517, 1519, 1522, 1524, 1525
  confession of 2127
  and interaction between sexes 1943, 1950 n. 14
  offerings 360, 450-451
  and sacrificial offerings 1290, 1295, 1296-1302, 1329
Sirkes, Joel (*BAH*) 1666, 2141
Sisera 2207-2208
Sitruk, Joseph 312
skin afflictions, biblical 1708
Sklare, Marshall 1794-1795, 1797
slaughter of animals (*shekhita*) 220
  performed by women 1946
slavery, Jewish preaching on 2269, 2280 n. 23
slaves, women and minors category 1696
SMAG see Sefer Mitzvot Gedolot (*SMAG*, Moses of Coucy)
SMAK see Sefer Mitzvot Ketanot (*SMAK*, Isaac of Corbeil)
Smith, Daniel L. 370
Smith, John E. 764
Smith, Jonathan S. 493, 941
Smith, M. 1465 n. 4

Smith, W. Robertson 947
Socarides, Charles W. 2148
social justice, Jewish preaching on 2276-2279
social order
  of Israel 351, 354
  norms for, and religions 2283
  and Torah 2284-2285
social organization 282
social preaching, Jewish 2276-2279
social relationships, and study of Torah 2284-2285
social teachings, of Judaism 1881
socialism 220, 427
Socialist Zionism 426, 736
Société des études juives 299-301
socio-linguistics, as a model to study Judaeo-Arabic literature 2170
socio-rhetorical model, to study Judaeo-Arabic literature 2172, 2182 n. 24
sociological dimension, of Judaism 1872
Socrates 201
Sodom and Gomorrah 1597, 2128
sodomy 2140
Sofer, M. 1944
Sofer, rabbi Hatam 231
soil, protection of 1726-1727
Sokoloff, N. 1502 n. 66
Sola, David de 2271, 2277
solar calendar 2037, 2039
solar eclipse 2043
Solomon, as described by Josephus 1786-1788
Solomon, N. 1409 n. 1, 1409 n. 16
Soloveitchik, Haym 1404, 1405, 1406, 1407, 1408, 1409, 1409 n. 5, n. 9, n. 22, 1800
Soloveitchik, J.B. 779-780, 974, 1049, 1099, 1755-1756, 1942, 1947, 1948, 1950 n. 12, n. 24, 1952 n. 59, 1952-1953 n. 67
Soloveitchik, Joseph Dov 753-754
Sombart, Werner 236, 237
Some Aspects of Rabbinical Theology (Schechter) 1606
Song of Songs, Rashi's commentaries on 2233
sorcery 1616
Sorsky, A. 1409 n. 7
souls 552-553, 575, 657, 714-716, 734, 750, 805, 852, 859, 863-864, 867-868, 917, 933-934, 954, 961, 992, 1342-1347
  doctrine of the transmigration of 1895
  fate after death 1750
  Jewish, innate divine nature 1735, 1740 n. 39, n. 44
  judgement of 1743
Souls on Fire (Wiesel) 571
South Africa, Judaism in 1347-1357
Spain
  conversos in 1676-1690, 2077-2091
  expulsion of Jews from (1492) 1685, 1688, 2081
  Golden Age of culture 2086-2091

Jews migrating to Morocco (*megorashim*) 1848
  Karaites in 1810
speech impediments 1701-1702, 1705
Spero, M. 1092, 1109
Spinoza, Baruch de 78, 102, 135, 718, 729-730, 733-735, 736-738, 740-741, 743, 780, 782, 967, 970, 972
  excommunication of 2082, 2083
  on Jewish law 1867
The Spirit of Capitalism 236
spiritual wealth, versus material wealth 2288-2292
spirituality
  in American Judaism 1802-1803, 1807
  Hasidic 753
  Jewish 210
Spitzer, Robert L. 2139
Stace, William 926
Stampfer, S. 1409 n. 4, n. 8
stars, names of 2037
Statman, Daniel 259
Staub, J.J. 1240
Stein, Sir Marc Aurel 1630
Steinheim, Solomon Ludwig 749
Steinschneider, Moriz 2170-2171, 2173
sterility *see* childlessness
Stern, David 949, 1009
Stern, Kenneth 512-513
Stern, M. 1026, 1027, 1028, 1030, 1031, 1032, 1033, 1034, 1037, 1038, 1051, 1052
Stertz, S.A. 1038
stoicism 131, 135, 1792
Storr, A. 1107
Stow, K.R. 1501 n. 35
Straus, David 84-85
Strauss, Leo 737, 767, 780-781
Stuart, C. 1089
Study as a Form of Worship (Isaacs) 348
Su vida (Her Life, Saint Theresa) 2089
Suffering Servant 35, 50, 261, 408-409, 1703-1704
Sufi Islam, influence on Jewish thought 2177, 2180
suicide 430, 867-868
  halakhah on 2150
Sukkot 33, 36-38, 46, 47, 362-365, 1860
summary-elaboration patterns, compositional technique of 2056-2057
Sun Fo 1651
Sun Yat-sen 1651
Sunday, synagogue services on 2266, 2267, 2270-2271
sundials, use of 2038
sunstroke 1716-1717
superiority *see* chauvinism
superstition 217, 301
  in Judaism 1904-1916
Sura, Yeshiva in 2227
surgery, in biblical and talmudic times 1717
surrogate motherhood, in Judaism 1916-1920

Sussan, Yissakhar 2297, 2299
Svei, Elya 1949 n. 7
Swirsky, B. 1500, 1502 n. 71
syllogisms
  philosophical logic of 1833, 2215
  used in midrash 2217
  used in Talmud 2097, 2098, 2100
  used in Torah 2186
symmetry, biblical principle of 1704
synagogue services
  on Friday evening 2266-2267
  modelled on Temple cult 1768
  in Morocco 1851, 1853-1854, 1859
  of non-Orthodox American Jews 1799, 1802, 1803
  on Sunday 2266, 2267, 2270-2271
synagogues 23, 28-31, 47, 174, 462, 530, 564-568, 603, 610, 618, 637, 640, 649, 656-657, 659, 676, 688, 693, 695, 700-705, 709, 750, 787, 795-796, 799-800, 808, 811, 821-827, 833, 842, 875, 900-901, 907, 913-915, 922-923, 980-983, 989, 1010, 1023, 1304, 1314, 1319, 1326, 1338, 1348-1356, 1361, 1367, 1374-1396, 1476, 1478, 1484-1494, 1496, 1498, 1500, 1510, 1512, 1524, 1528, 1546-1548
  Aegean 1764, 1765, 1777 n7
  American 1795
  Ashkenazic 311
  Ethiopian 1752
  gay 2139, 2153
  Karaite 1815
  money spent on building of 2289-2290
  Moroccan 1851
  Reconstructionist 573
  Samaritan 2248
  separation of sexes in 1942-1943, 1950 n. 11, n. 13, 1951 n. 49, 1952 n. 59
  with zodiac signs 2036
syncretism 521, 617-618, 679, 1025, 1035
Synoptic Gospels 69, 77, 102
system, and tradition 1921, 1922, 1924-1925
systemic writing 1922-1924
Szaz, Thomas 2146
Szold, Adele 2230
Szold, Benjamin 2270-2271

Tabernacles 1, 35, 178, 363, 401, 424, 526, 528, 530, 539, 596, 609, 806, 810, 827, 848, 907, 1004, 1109, 1140, 1186, 1187, 1395, 1480, 1541
Tadhkirat al-kaúúâlîn (ibn 'Isa) 2177
Tafsir al-asma' al-werida fi t-tawra (Abd al-Mu'in Tsedaqa) 2257
Tafsîr (Saadiah Gaon) 2174, 2255
Tafsir surat al-irbot (Pinhas b. Isaac) 2257
Taitz, E. 1501 n. 36, n. 44, n. 47
Taiwan, Jewish community in 1648-1649
takkanot 1848
Tal, Abraham 2254

Tallan, Ch. 1501 n. 34
Tallit 44, 1947, 1952 n. 59
Talmud 4, 43, 45, 52, 60, 61, 75, 78-80,
  82, 85, 88, 99-101, 103, 107, 110-111,
  112, 116-117, 118-119, 123, 204, 206, 213,
  245-246, 252-253, 263, 266, 269, 273, 282,
  285, 301, 319, 325, 326, 328, 330, 333-335,
  341, 342, 346-350, 367, 373, 376-377, 386,
  388, 405, 430, 432, 442, 480, 487, 510, 531,
  536, 564, 601, 617-619, 622-623, 626-627,
  631, 633, 637, 645-649, 682, 689, 697, 755,
  784-785, 787-789, 795, 799, 801, 807, 811,
  826, 835, 844, 851, 853-857, 859-860,
  867-868, 871-872, 905, 908, 961-969, 975,
  980, 1008-1009, 1011, 1013-1014, 1052,
  1057, 1062, 1067, 1074, 1075, 1076, 1077,
  1079, 1092, 1093, 1094, 1097-1100, 1115,
  1125, 1130, 1133, 1136, 1138, 1139, 1148,
  1150-1160, 1168, 1176, 1186, 1206-1223,
  1225, 1226, 1227, 1253-1257, 1263, 1266,
  1277, 1280, 1304, 1305, 1313, 1316-1320,
  1338, 1348, 1353, 1386, 1397, 1398, 1403,
  1404, 1406, 1412, 1418, 1433, 1447-1449,
  1451, 1454-1457, 1459, 1599-1600, 1656,
  1659, 1462-1464, 1481, 1486, 1490, 1509,
  1528, 1533, 1542, 1544, 1549, 1550
  on amputations 1707
  attacks on 1686-1687
  on Chosen People 1731, 1738 n. 7
  commentaries on 2229, 2235
  compositors of 2063-2065
  dialectical argument in 1691-1696
  on divination 1913
  on embryogenesis 1624-1625
  on homosexuality 2140-2141, 2142
  on honoring of parents 2194-2196
  logics used in 2225-2226
  on lunar calendar 2039
  and Mishnah 1933-1934, 2064,
    2075-2076
  on pretending to be a gentile 1664-1665
  redaction of 2063-2065
  rules regarding fertility of land 1728
  study of, in Morocco 1853
  syllogism used in 2097, 2098, 2100
  systemic and traditional document
    1932-1940
  and Torah 1154, 1155, 1159
  on women's head covering 1944
  zodiacal signs in 1911-1912
Talmud Torah, in Morocco 1851-1852
Talmudic botany 1626-1627, 1629 n. 5
Talmudic Judaism 1463, 1948
Tam, Jacob ben Meir 342, 1015, 1949
Tamar 2201, 2213 n. 9
tamid 189
Tanakh 199
Tang Dynasty, Jewish presence in China
  during 1630-1631
Tannaim 341, 1611 n. 4, 1763
  and astrology 2033

  on lunar calendar 2041
  on Samaritans 2247
Tannaitic Judaism 1607
Tannaitic rituals 92
Tanya (Schneur Zalman) 1735, 1740 n. 39
taqqanat hashavim 347
taqqanat hashuk 347
Targum Onqelos 273, 279, 2173
Targumim 269, 271, 274, 1309, 1311,
  1313-1320, 1656, 1947, 1952 n. 57, 2173
  Samaritan 2254, 2256
Ta'rikh-i Fakhr ad-Din Mubarak Shah
  1826-1827
Tashbetz see bar Zadok, Shimson
Tashlikh 45, 1800
tax collectors, associated with sinners 2125
taxes 2291-2292
  imposed on Jews 1663
taxonomic logic 2156, 2157, 2159
taxonomy 2156, 2161
Tcherikover, V. 1051
Teacher of Righteousness 180
Tedeschi, Moses Isaac ben Samuel 276
tefillin 44, 2048
Teharot 177
Tehilah le-David (ben Hassin) 1849
Tehilim (Book of Psalms) 1859
tehiyat hametim 202
Teichtal, Isaachar 411
Teitelbaum, Joel 411
Teitelbaum, Moshe 885
tekufot (solstice) 1912
teleological logic 2217-2219
teleology 1833
Tell Fekheriyeh inscription 1758-1759
Temple 1, 5, 7, 13-16, 19, 34, 46-47, 61,
  64-66, 70, 77, 114-115, 143, 147, 176, 186,
  189-191, 290, 295, 350, 351, 359-362, 370,
  382, 385, 387, 389, 402-405, 455, 467, 469,
  472, 474, 518, 526-533, 535-537, 540-546,
  548-552, 557, 561, 581-582, 584-585, 597,
  599-605, 608-616, 620, 623, 625, 641,
  647-649, 652, 689, 741, 757, 799, 801-803,
  810, 815, 823-824, 826, 868, 875-878, 881,
  888-890, 906-907, 913, 929, 964, 1010-1011,
  1026, 1028, 1030, 1033, 1034, 1036, 1037,
  1040, 1048, 1050, 1054, 1055, 1057, 1059,
  1060, 1062, 1063, 1067, 1070, 1071, 1073,
  1085, 1086, 1109, 1111, 1116, 1123, 1124,
  1140, 1141, 1142, 1515, 1516, 1523,
  1541-1543, 1144, 1145, 1146, 1159, 1161,
  1172, 1176, 1178, 1179, 1180, 1183, 1193,
  1194, 1196, 1205, 1206, 1221, 1225, 1226,
  1228, 1230, 1255, 1256, 1263, 1265,
  1290-1296, 1303, 1305, 1309, 1323, 1329,
  1330, 1379, 1381, 1392, 1396, 1413, 1423,
  1429, 1433-1435, 1440-1445, 1460, 1461,
  1471, 1479, 1480, 1503, 1505
  architecture of 1942, 1950 n. 11
  cult 112, 144-1445, 187, 189, 194, 533,
    535, 545, 581-582, 596-597, 601-605, 610,

619-622, 625, 650, 659, 823-824, 826-827, 877, 888, 1006, 1291, 1296-1302, 1329, 1440, 1443
    synagogue services modelled on 1768
    obligation to appear at 1697-1698
    and observance of Sabbath 2131
    rivalry with temple at Mount Gerizim 2244-2245, 2246, 2262 n. 26
    utensils 1616
Tendler, Moshe 865, 871
tephillin 44, 2048
Tertullian 91
teruma (heave-offering) 1698-1699
Terumat haDeshen (Isserlein) 1666
teshuvah (repentance/rehabilitation), tradition of 2130, 2151
Testament of the Rosh (ben Yehiel) 255
Testament of Shem, astrology in 2033
Testament of Solomon, astrology in 2032-2033
Tetrateuch 517
Teutsch, D. 1240
Tewodros (Davidic messiah) 1743
textile industry, in Salonika 1771
Thackery, Henry St. John 547, 1465 n. 3
thanksgiving, national days of 2268, 2276-2277
thanotology 212
themes, in modern Jewish preaching 2269-2279
theodicy, in Judaism 1410-1419
Theodosius I (Roman emperor), mandate of 2249
Theodosius II (Roman emperor) 1765, 2249
Theodotus 2262 n. 26
theological anthropology, of Judaism 1419-1428
theology
    astrological 1615-1616
    Biblical 1436-1447
    Christian 1866, 1900
    of history 2113
    of Jesus 2131-2136
    of Judaism 710-783, 1606-1607, 1608, 1610
    of Karaite Judaism 1816-1817, 1819-1820
    of Rabbinic Judaism 1161-1174, 1251-1254
    of Torah 1410-1414, 1417-1434, 1436-1439
The Theology of the Oral Torah (Neusner) 1609-1610
Theophrastos 2037
Theresa of Avila, St 2088-2089
Thirteen Principles of Faith (Maimonides) 205
Thomas Aquinas 76, 1625
Tianjin (China), Jewish community in 1643-1644, 1645-1646
Tibåt *see* Memar Marqe
Tiberias
    Moroccan Jews in 2298

    Yeshiva in 2043
Tigay, Jeffrey H. 1759, 1760
Tikkun Hatzot 1854, 1862
Tikkun (magazine) 1806
Tindal, Matthew 80
Tinterow, G. 1396
tiqqun 207, 419
tiqqun 'um Yisrael 433
tiqqun Hatzot 226
tiqqun olam 345, 504
Tish'a be-av 1861-1862
Tishre 33, 35, 46, 364, 459
tithes 228, 529, 538, 1139, 1185, 1264
to'aliyot 254
Todorov, Tzvetan 2172, 2178
to'evah (abomination) 2142, 2150
Tohelet Yisrael (The Hope of Israel, Solomon ben Judah) 2233-2234
Toland, John 507
Toledano, Jacob Moshe 2295, 2297, 2298
Toledo, Fernán Díaz de 1684, 1685
Toledo massacre 1683
Toledot Adam (Danzig) 1670
Toledoth Yaakov Yosef (Pollnoe) 218
tolerance, in Judaism 1736, 1738
Tolkes, Y. 1342 n. 25
Torah 318, 402, 718, 770, 1093, 1147, 1301-1306, 1447-1458
    allegiance of Jews to 740-741, 756-757, 766, 893, 1171-1174, 1182, 1193, 1292-1294, 1296, 1298, 1299, 1441, 1475, 1505, 1541
    ban on homosexuality 2141-2142
    Christian view of 1179, 1875
    commandments of 536, 1072, 1258, 1474, 1503-1504, 1512-1513, 1727
        positive 2192-2194
    commentaries 1217, 1218, 1219, 1225, 2256-2257, 2265 n. 92
    and covenant of God and Israel 2093, 2094-2095
    on creation 722, 725-731, 1722-1723, 2292-2293
    and culture 2283-2293
    dual *see* Rabbinic Judaism
    on family relations and marriage 281, 285, 287
    God's revelation 257, 323, 619, 633, 745, 751-752, 833, 895-896, 971-972, 1133, 1151, 1167, 1229, 1232, 1290, 1360, 2157
    importance of 192, 582-589, 615, 772-782, 993-1007, 1133-1134, 1872-1873
    interpretations of 1444-1447
    Jesus seeing himself as replacement of 2132-2136
    kabbalistic interpretation of 935-936
    kept by Abraham 2115
    on land of Israel 1719-1721
    laws of 1072, 1076, 1080, 1083,

1092-1093, 1139, 1178, 1323, 1324,
1404-1409, 1470-1471, 1514-1515
as life 2134-2135
meaning of 1867-1868, 1871
and merit 2289
and Mishnah 1148-1149, 1155, 1200-1201,
1448-1465, 1846-1847, 2185
mode of discourse in 1833
monotheism in 900-905
Moses as redactor of 2053-2054, 2055
mourning practices described in 806-807
and natural science 2292
Oral see Mishnah
on parents, honor of 2191
prophecies of 722-723
protected birds 1723-1724
and the Quran 461, 712-713
reading of 826, 828, 911
references to tefillin 2048
revelation of 950-951, 954-955, 1133,
2185, 2187
Samaritan 1877, 2247, 2253-2254, 2255,
2262 n. 49, 2263 n. 55
scrolls 810, 878, 1384, 1385, 1388, 1450,
1456, 1476, 1489
sole source of reliable information 2095
study of 295, 627-631, 794, 833-835,
851-852, 854, 881, 891, 996, 1069,
1327-1329, 1397-1401, 1476-1478,
1506-1511, 1515-1516, 1542, 2093
by women 1483, 1941-1942, 1949 n. 4,
n. 6, n. 7
and material wealth 2288-2292
obligation of father to assist son in
2197-2198
and secular learning 2283, 2285-2288,
2292, 2293
views of sages 2118
and Talmud 1154, 1155, 1159
theology of 1410-1414, 1417-1434,
1436-1439
translations of 1314, 1318-1320, 2174
two competing voices in 577
see also Scripture
Torah ark 1385, 1386, 1388, 1391-1396
Torah binders 7-8
Torah Shrine 1376, 1378, 1382, 1383
Torah Teminah (Epstein) 277
Torat Habayit LeRashba (Adret) 343
Torpusman, Avraham 1827
Torquemada, Juan de 1683-1684
Torquemada, Tomás de 2083
Torrance, Thomas 961
Tortosa Debate (1413-1414) 1686-1687
Tosafists 33, 279, 635-636, 1661, 1945-1946,
2045-2046
Tosefta 116, 244-245, 371, 377, 379, 405,
530-531, 787-788, 791, 853, 1008, 1112,
1136, 1139, 1148-1153, 1155, 1158, 1160,
1168, 1169, 1177, 1186, 1206, 1207, 1208,
1212, 1223, 1224, 1260, 1320, 1398, 1430,

1433, 1449, 1459, 1513, 1596-1597, 1599,
1939, 2228
on commandments not enforceable in court
2193
on disabilities 1699
on maddaf-uncleanness 1838
on women 1946, 1947, 1948
Tov, Emanuel 2262 n. 49
Tower of Babel 2200
Towner, W.S. 1062
Tractatus contra madianitas et ismaelitas adversarios
et detractores filiorum qui de populo israelitico
originem traxerunt (de Torquemada)
1683-1684
Tractatus theologico-politicus (Spinoza) 736-737
trade relations, between Mediterranean region
and Far East 1630
tradition
in Judaism 1458-1466, 1798-1800,
1920-1941, 2131
Manichean 172
oral 1750, 2124-2136, 2247
Pharisaic-Rabbinic 174
scriptural 1864
and system 1921, 1922, 1924-1925
traditional Judaism 31, 302, 1406, 1499
traditional Orthodox Judaism see ultra
Orthodox Judaism
tragedians 1792
Tragocomedia de Calisto y Melibea (Tragicomedy of
Calisto and Melibea, de Rojas) 2086-2087
traif 96, 104, 108
transculturation, processes of 2180,
2183 n. 56
translations
from Arabic 1207
into Judaeo-Arabic 2179
from Hebrew
of the Bible 1207, 1309-1312, 1318, 1319,
1490, 2178
into Judaeo-Arabic 2170, 2173-2174, 2177,
2179
as a means of self-expression 2180
of Scripture 1309-1320
of Torah 1314, 1318-1320, 2174
transmigration of souls, doctrine of 1895
Treblinka 408
Tree of Knowledge 264
Trembling Before God (film) 2139
The Tremendum: A Theological Interpretation of the
Holocaust (Arthur Cohen) 421
Trinity 409
Trokai, Lithuania 213
Troki, Isaac ben Abraham of 1811, 1817
Troki, Joseph ben Mordecai of 1811
Troki, Solomon ben Aaron of 1811
Trop, N. 1405, 1406, 1409 n. 19, n. 24
Trumpeldor, Joseph 1643
Tsabra, Abba 1743-1744
Tsedaqa al-Hakkim 2256
Tsimmuth, Day of 2258

tsimtsum 503
Tu Bishvat 1861
Tulida (ben Amram) 2255
TUR see Arba'ah Turim (Jacob ben Asher)
Tur Sinai, N.H. (Torczyner) 276
Turei Zavah (Poland) 343
Tustari family 1812
Twersky, Isadore 782
typological exegesis 1893
Tyre, prophecy against 2056
tzara'at, disease of 1706
tzedakah 230

Ullendorff 1741
Ulrich, E.C. 1320 n. 2
ultra Orthodox Judaism 690, 707, 742, 1796,
  1797, 1801
ululations 1909
Umansky, E.M. 1493, 1501 n. 49, 1502 n.
  57, n. 61, n. 64, n. 84
uncleanness *see* impurity
uniformity 1608
Union Prayer Book (Einhorn) 208
Union for Traditional Judaism (UTJ) 1798
United States, homosexuality in 2137
United Synagogue 21, 29, 30, 109,
  1804-1805
Urbach, Ephraim E. 1607-1608, 1731
Urschrift und Uebersetzungen der Bibel (Geiger)
  100

Vaad Arba Aratzoth 214
Vajda, George 2171
vegetable gardens 1719
vengeance and recompense, Samaritan notion
  of day of 2258
Verdict Statute (Sarmiento) 1683
Verein für Cultur und Wissenschaft der Juden (Zunz)
  297
Versteegh, Kees 2170
via iluminativa 2088
via purgativa 2088
via unitiva 2088
Victoria, British Queen 2267
Vida del Buscón (Life of the Scoundrel, de
  Quevedo) 2086
Vidas, Elijah ben Moses de 255
Vieira, Antônio 2080
Vietnam War, Jewish preaching on 2276
Villena dynasty 1681
Vilna, Elijah ben Solomon Gaon of (*GRA*)
  220, 221, 275, 276, 1668, 1906, 1949
Vilna'i, Ze'ev 2301
Vinogradoff, Hieromonach Alexei 1630
virtue, in Judaism 1466-1478
Visigoth kings 1676-1677
visual disabilities 1699, 1703, 1705
Viterbo, Carlo Alberto 1751
Vitry, Simhah of 2227
Vives, Juan Luis 2088
Vladimir (Russian prince) 1831

Volhynia, Karaite communities 1811
Völkerpsychologie 1735, 1740 n. 43
Voltaire 81-82, 1867
vow-taking, as a religious act 2116-2118

Wach, Joachim 1871
Wachnacht 1909
Wacholder, Ben-Zion 2253
Wahrhafting, Zerah 1639
Waldenberg, Eliezer Yehudah 862-863,
  2198
Walzer, R. 1051, 1052
War, in Jewish preaching 2272-2276
The War Against the Jews (Dawidowicz) 422
war of the communities (*Guerra de las
  Comunidades*) 2081
The Warsaw Diary of Chaim A. Kaplan 422
Waskow, Arthur 576-577, 696, 767
Wasserfall, R. 1501 n. 39
Wasserman, E.B. 1404, 1409 n. 23
Wasserzug, D. 2275
water, image of, associated with life of Jesus
  2134, 2136 n. 6
Ways of Life (ben Yehiel) 255
Ways of the Righteous 255
wealth
  material versus spiritual 2288-2292
  pursuit of, as sign of Jewishness 2084
Weber, Max 236, 969, 1090, 1104, 1628
websites, used for publishing sermons 2269
weddings, superstitions about 1909-1910
weepers, at funerals 2125
Wegner, J.R. 1485, 1501 n. 23
Weinberg, Dudley 1737
Weinberg, Jacob J. 1950-1951 n. 28
Weinberg, Sheila Peltz 575
Weinberg, Y.Y. 1409
Weinfeld, M. 1085, 1447
Weisel, E. 1279
Weiss, A. 1502 n. 87
Weiss Halivni, David 1798
Weiss, I. 1950 n. 11
Weissler, Ch. 1491, 1501 n. 44, n. 45,
  n. 48
Weitsman, I.J. 1502 n. 74
Wellhausen, Julius 83
Werner, A. 1397 n. 40
Wertheimer, Jack 706, 980-981, 983,
  1409 n. 27, 1795
Wessely, N. 276
wheat 1726-1727
When Bad Things Happen to Good People (Harold
  Kushner) 265
Whitehead, A.N. 415, 1231
Wiener, M. 1251, 1254
Wiesel, Elie 571-572, 941
wild animals 1725
Wilhelm I (German emperor) 2267
Wilken, R. 1052
Willadsen, Steen 1653
Williams, George H. 782

Willis, Ellen   1796
wills, *aliyah* ordered in   2302
wine, parables of   2128-2129
Wisdom literature   2134
Wise, Isaac Meyer   1018, 2266, 2270
wise sayings, collections of   2065, 2070-2071,
   2073
Wise, Stephen S.   2269, 2275, 2276
Wisse, R.R.   1333, 1334, 1341, 1342 n. 2
witchcraft   1914
Witschnitzer, R.   1396, 1397 n. 24, n. 26,
   n. 33
Wittgenstein, Ludwig   926
Wolf, Immanuel   297
Wolf, Rabbi Arnold Jacob   567
Wolff, Christian   738
Wolfson, Elliot   952
Wolfson, Harry Austryn   733, 781-782
women
   in *Liber Antiquitatum Biblicarum* (Pseudo-Philo)
      2211
   milling   2126
   in Samaritanism   2259
   wailing at funerals   2125
women in Judaism   1478-1501, 1548, 1625,
   1941-1953
   exemptions from honoring of parents
      2196
   hair covering   1944, 1951 n. 35
   light-headedness of   1946, 1951 n. 49
   participation in Jewish life   1705, 1804
   piety of   1064-1065
   preaching by   2265, 2279 n. 2
   purity of   1479, 1748, 1815, 1845, 1943,
      1947
   rabbis   1804-1805
   reading Scroll of Esther   1947
   serving in Israeli army   1944-1945
   singing in presence of men   1944,
      1950-1951 n. 23, n. 27, n. 28
   in slaves and minors category   1696
   study of Torah   1941-1942, 1949 n. 4,
      n. 6, n. 7
   wearing phylacteries   1946-1947, 1952
      n. 53
Woocher, Jonathan   708, 1796
wood offerings   1597-1598, 1599
work, in Judaism   1502-1516
World Council of Churches   87-88
world to come *see* eternal life
World War I   44, 303
   Jewish preaching on   2274-2275,
      2282 n. 53
World War II   20, 44, 220, 306, 308,
   406-432
   Jewish preaching on   2276
Worms Commentary on the Talmud   2229
wounds   1717-1718
writing, systemic   1922-1924
Writings   1308, 1311, 1316-1318, 1436, 1450,
   1521

Wurzburger, Walter   995, 1005
Wyschogrod, Morton   211

xenophobia   583, 1026, 1027, 1028, 1029,
   1032, 1033, 1037, 1039, 1040, 1089, 1235,
   1241

Ya'ari, Abraham   2294, 2295-2296, 2298,
   2299, 2300
Yad haHazakah see Mishneh Torah (Maimonides)
Yaffe, Mordecai   1668
Yagod, L.   1465 n. 1
yahad   191-193
Yahweh, use of   1868
Yahweh Alone Movement   521-523
Yahwistic religious practices   516-520
Yamim Noraim, *see* Days of Awe
Yanagimachi, Ryuzo   1652
Yangzhou (China)
   Jewish community in   1632
   Muslim community in   1632
Yarhi, Rabbi Salomo *see* Rashi
YASHAR of Candia *see* Delmedigo, Joseph
   Solomon
Yehi Ratzon ceremony   1859
Yemenite Jewish communities, using *Tafsîr*
   2174
Yerushalmi see Talmud
yeshivot   107, 256, 344, 349, 1852-1853
   centres of excellence   2227
   medieval   2239 n. 13
   in Tiberias   2043
Yeshua Haben   94
Yesode ha-Torah   431
yetzer hara   263
Yiddish culture   222
Yiddishism   1332-1334, 1337-1342, 1874,
   1877-1878
Yihud (clandestine male/female unions)
   1943-1944
yishuv, old   2294-2303, 2307
Yitzhaki, Solomon *see* Rashi
yizkor prayer   422, 1637, 1859
Yoffie, Eric   708-709, 1736
Yohanan   1662, 1692-1693, 1893-1894, 2040,
   2121
Yom Haatzma'ut   50
Yom Habikkurim   43
Yom Hadin   45
Yom Hateruyah   45
Yom Hazikaron   50
Yom Kippur *see* Day of Atonement
Yosef (king of Khazaria)   1824-1825, 1827,
   1828
Yosef, Ovadia   2198
Yosef, Y.   1102, 1103
Yovel, Y.   733

Zab/Zabah, uncleanness   1110-1124,
   1837-1847
Zaddikim   428, 1808-1809, 1857

Zadoc-Kahn 299, 305
Zadokite Documents 166, 170, 177
Zadokite priests ('sons of Zadok') 166, 178, 496
zar (hostile) spirits 1743
Zealots 552
Zebahim (animal offerings) 359, 1296-1300
Zedckiah 1789
zekhut 337, 389-390, 433, 630-631, 851-853, 1516-1525
Zichronot 45
Zichru Torat Moshe (Danzig) 1670
Zionism 20, 86, 97, 220, 222, 265, 302, 305-306, 411, 461, 471, 532, 577, 662, 666-673, 675, 680, 683-687, 755-761, 875, 884-888, 943, 957, 986, 1525-1538
  in Ashkenazic Jewish community of Shanghai 1639, 1640-1641
  Ashkenazic orientation of 2168
  Chinese support for 1651
  confronting antisemitism 668, 671
  definition of 2293
  in Jewish communities in Greece 1776
  in Jewish community in Harbin (China) 1642
  in Moroccan Judaism 2294-2307
  and Orthodox Judaism 781, 885, 1529, 1531, 1535, 1536
  pre-Herzlian 2293-2294
Zionist movement, in Morocco 2303-2304, 2305
Zionists 344, 424, 427, 688, 707, 751-752, 775, 778, 781, 924, 945, 956, 958
Zipor, M. 1109
Zipperstein, S.J. 1501 n. 37
zodiac signs
  mentioned in *piyyutim* (religious poems) 2035
  synagogues with 2036
Zohar 121-122, 133, 207, 264, 268, 277-278, 504, 513, 527, 641, 678, 688, 791-792, 843, 927, 930, 935, 955, 1652
  astra-magical influence 1619
  place in Moroccan Jewish life 1857
  printing of 1772
  on proselytes 1740 n. 38
  status of rules in 1951 n. 32
Zolnay, L. 1396 n. 13
Zoroastrian scholars 301
Zoroastrianism 200, 1823
Zuckerman 506
Zunz, Leopold 100, 297, 300, 2228

INDEX OF TEXTUAL REFERENCES
(Volumes I-V)

1. Jewish Bible

Amos

1:1	1445
1:2	526
2:4	1869
3:2	1730, 484, 1296
3:12	2051
4:4	526
5:5	526
5:8	2037, 2039, 2040
5:20	611
5:25-27	145
5:26	2037
6:5	906
7:10ff.	1445
7:17	529
8:2	1445
8:10	807
9:11-12	65

1 Chronicles

1:19-20	2200
1:23	2200
4:10	1713
8:33-34	606
9:1	1440
9:39-40	606
11:1-9	525
12:32	2036
12:33	2038
13:8	906
15:16-28	906
16:13	1730
16:39-42	597
17:10-15	599
17:11-13	599
17:14	1443
21:29-30	526
22:1	526
22:10	599
23:28	596
23:32	596
28:5	1443
28:5-7	599
28:8	1440
28:19	1950 n. 11
29:23	1443

2 Chronicles

3:1	526
3:15	2240
6	525, 530
6:16-17	599
6:40-42	1443
6:42	1519
7:15	611
7:18	599
9:8	1443
13:8	1443
15:8	1789
16:12	1713
17:6	1789
18:16	1440
21:7	599
21:14-18	1709
26:17-19	597
30:25	2243
32:25	1778
35:11	2261
35:13	266
35:18	2240, 2243
35:25	906
36:6-10	600
36:9	1789
36:17-21	600

Daniel

1-6	606
2:27	2031
2:27-30	837
2:44-45	1788
2:48	536
4:6	536
4:29-34	1714
4:30	1714
4-5	1446
5:6	1710
5:10	2031
5:11	536
6:11	530, 611
6:15	2050
7:7-25	551
7:25	550
7-8	603

7-12	606
9:7	2228
9:24	2228
9:25	181, 550, 878
10-12	198
11:14	550
11:32-35	199
11:45	199
12	200
12:1-3	198
12:2	199, 202, 206
12:2-3	613
12:3	200
12:11	550
12:12	198, 199

Deuteronomy

1:1	1440, 2055, 2099
1:3	16
1:19-33	595
1:34-40	595
3:11	1712
4:1-40	1440
4:4	1107
4:9	868, 1477
4:10-20	595
4:12-13	596
4:12-18	435
4:13	596
4:15	868
4:20	1440, 1730
4:21	597
4:24	1664
4:25-40	44
4:28	1665
4:29	595
4:35	589
4:37	1519, 1730
4:44-45	1439
4-29	595
5:2-32	595
5:6-10	606
5:6-21	596, 1439
5:7	153
5:11	2172
5:16	197, 2191, 2192
5:19-16:17	42
5:31-6:9	595
5-7	198
6:4	589, 1440, 1909
6:4-5	152, 153
6:4-9	825, 1063
6:5	1505, 1652, 1750
6:5-9	817
6:9	529
6:10-19	1440
6:18	253
6:20	1056, 1057
6:20-25	42, 152, 153
6:21	1055
7	176

7:1-4	610
7:1-5	607
7:6	1440, 1730
7:7-8	1438, 1730
7:14	1708, 1709
8:1	596
8:6-8	1720
9:4-6	1438
9:5	527
9:6-29	595
9:12-16	595
9:22-24	595
9:26	1440
10:8	596
10:8-9	596
10:15	1730
10:20	2192
11:6	1440
11:8-9	596
11:8-15	1719
11:13-17	197
11:13-21	817, 825, 1063
11:18	1343
11:19	1941
11:21	2193
11:28	438
11:28-29	1479
11-26	1760
12	526, 530
12:1-26:15	596
12:3-4	2198
12:5	1443
12:7	529
12:10-18	596
12:12	529
12:15	429
12:21	1946
12:26-27	596
12:30	438
12:26	2096, 2231
13:7	1950 n. 19
14	526, 1723
14:1	807, 1708
14:2	1440, 1730
14:21	1440
14:22-16:17	47
14:22-26	529
14:28-29	51
14-15	597
15	526
15:7	2193
15:7-11	51, 53
15:9	56
15:10	2193
15:10-11	52
15:15	1439
16	526
16:1	33
16:1-8	359, 595
16:1-17	596
16:3	1054

16:4	1894
16:7	266
16:8	529
16:10-12	42
16:11	1697
16:14-16	47
16:16	1697
17	526
17:2	529
17:8	531
17:10-11	1949
17:20	253
18	961
18:10-11	832
18:11	197, 1913
18:15	1445
18:15-18	461
18:18	1445, 2258
19:9-14	612
19:21	1707
20:5-7	1944
21:1-9	1700
21:12	1708
21:18-21	288, 1700
21:23	872
22:5	1947
22:7	2128, 2192
22:9	1727
22:28	1479
23	526, 597
23:4-9	603
23:10-15	527
23:16	1942
23:18	2140
24:1	802
24:13	2192
24:15	1514
24:16	200
24:19	51
24:21	51
25:4	1514
25:5-10	207, 1479
25:12	1707
25:15	2192
25:17-19	49
26:1-10	1057
26:1-11	1440
26:3	467
26:5	591
26:5-8	1057
26:5-9	152, 153
26:8	1057
26:17-18	1439
26:19	1440, 1730
27:11-26	137
28	138, 554
28:1	1730
28:1-68	197
28:9	1440
28:15	261
28:22	1711

28:25-26	261
28:27	1708, 1714
28:28	1714
28:34	1714
29	1440
29:14	595
29:19	1899
30	90
30:6	90, 1764
30:11	1900
30:15-19	713
30:15-20	140
30:16-20	314, 321
30:19	357, 430
31:1-10	595
31:7-8	597
31:9	1444
31:10	1535
31:12	1942
31:16	475
31:26	1444
32	138, 582, 1746
32:35	2258
32:36	2216
32:39	198
33:2-3	461
33:8	1444
33:10	1444
33:14	2034
33:18	1101, 1102
34:5-6	597
34:7	2202
34:9	597, 2205
34:10	722
34:10-12	597
48	596

Ecclesiastes

2:8	906
3:1-15	323
3:17-19	321
7:2	46
7:20	1105, 1321
12:7	201
12:8	2052
12:11	251
44-50	604
49:10	604

Esther

2:19	1779
4:16	810, 1748
9	2232
9:6	2226
9:22	1861

Exodus

1	594
1:7	594
1-2	2233
2:1-10	594

2:11-15	594	13:3-10	595
2:12	1778, 1782	13:4	33
2:13	2202	13:8	1056
2:16-22	114	13:9	2048
2:21	1782	13:11-13	595
3	324	13:11-16	287
3:1	1782	13:14	1056
3:1-4:17	594	13:14-16	595
3:5	46	13:17-15:21	42
3:8	1440	13:17-15:26	1316
3:11	1782	13-17	1061
3:13-15	591, 1438	14	2202
3:14	521	14:15	2202
4	947	14:21	2202
4:6	1782	14:24	2202
4:10	1782	14:26-28	2203
4:10-11	1701, 1702	15	1480
4:18-31	594	15:1-18	906
4:24	1782	15:1-21	1061
4:24-26	90, 114	15:2	1191
6:2-3	521	15:8	2202
6:2-8	595	15:11	1307, 1308
6:3	591, 1438	15:17	1443
6:7	1439	15:21	906, 907
6:8	1440	15:22-26	595
6:11-12	2058	15:25	2203
6:29-30	2058	15:26	595, 833
7:6	2203	16:2-3	595
7:11	595, 832	16:3-4	42
7:12	832	16:16	42
7:22	832, 889	16:32-33	2135
7-12	1058	17:1-4	595
8:7	1621	17:1-7	2055
9:8-11	1708	17:8-18:28	1061
10:10	2036	17:12	2036
10:22-23	892	18:2	1782
12:1-13:16	1061	18:8-12	1791
12:1-23:19	1161	18:13-27	1782
12:1-28	359, 595	18-20	1079
12:2	33, 40	19:1-2	596
12:7	595	19:1-20:26	1061, 1316
12:8	1055	19:2b-Num 10:11	594, 595
12:9	266	19:5-6	596
12:11-13	362	19:6	149, 607, 947, 1440,
12:13	595		1730
12:19	1894	19:8	138, 596
12:21-51	42	19:13-19	906
12:22	71	19-20	43, 140, 1748
12:22-23	93	20	138, 251
12:26	1056	20:1-17	1039
12:28-36	595	20:2	137, 1663
12:29-30	595	20:2-6	606
12:35	1782, 1855	20:2-17	596
12:38	40	20:3	607
12:43-49	603	20:4	1440
12:44	90	20:4-5	434
12:46	71	20:5	438, 1254
12:48	90	20:5-6	288
12-15	1439	20:7	2172
13:1-2	595	20:8	429
13:2	798, 799	20:8-11	2054

20:9	1504	29:38ff.	1290
20:10	233	30	596
20:11	2192	30:16	1295
20:12	197, 288, 2191	31:12-13	1061
20:13	2050	31:12-17	596, 1061
20:15	906	31:13	1343
20:16	1858	32	595, 1760, 1778
20:18-21	596	32:1	2203
20:22-23:19	1439	32:1-6	595
20:22-23:33	596	32:11-13	595, 2203
20:24	1444	32:11-14	44
20-24	1760	32:13	1519
21:1-22:23	1061	32:19-20	1782
21:6	286	32:19-24	595
21:10	855	32:26-29	596
21:15	2191	32:32-33	38, 45
21:17	1703, 2191	32-33	43
21:22	1717	32-34	437
21:22-23	859	33:4-6	44, 46
21:22-27	1702	33:12-16	2203
21:24	1309, 1707	33:12-34:36	47
21-23	2048	33:17	2203
21-24	2231	33:20-23	435, 719
22:2	286	34	44, 176, 273
22:20	438	34:1-10	44
22:24-23:19	1061	34:6	324
22-27:7	1061	34:6-7	255, 2239
23	596	34:7	200
23:4	117	34:14	438
23:8	1697	34:18	595
23:10-11	1726	34:23	595
23:11	51	34:27	595
23:14	1697	35:1-3	1061
23:14-15	595	35-40	2231
23:15	1444	35ff.	37
23:16, cf., 34:22	43	39:25-26	906
23:17	137	39f.	1444
23:19	51, 1444, 1763, 1813	40:12-15	596
23:20-33	596	40:16	2203
23:26	1708		
24:1-8	1439	Ezekiel	
24:3	138, 596	1:1	2052, 2232
24:4-8	138	1:1-28	43, 127
24:7	43, 137, 596, 1446	1:2-3	2232
24:9	1128	1:4	2051, 2058
24:9-14	138	1:26	930
24:10-11	435	1:27	2058
24:11	138	1-3	1445
24:12	2066	2:6	2228
25	1444, 2237	3:12	43
25:8-31:17	596	3:18	2199
25:10ff.	137	4:13	529
25-31	2231	4:14	64
25-32	1760	5:11	436
27:21-29:46	596	5-7	591
28:4	2050	6:13	526
28:30	1444	7:26	1444
28:33-34	906	8:14	1880 n. 14
28f.	1444	9:1-2	2059
29:2	2238	9:3a	2059
		9:3b-7	2059

9.4	2059
10:4	2058, 2059
10.6	2059
11	526
11:19	869
11:20	1730
15	526
16:6	92
16:8	137
16:8-14	141
18:2-4	200
18:6	526
18:18	2236
20:5	1730
20:6	478
20:15	478
20:23	2051
20:27	1462
20:35-37	1085
25	2056
26:1	2056
27:17	2242
28	946
29:1	2056
31:18-39:16	47
32:2	2059
32:16	2059
32:17	2060
33:23-24	1440
34:23-24	614
36:22-32	2060
36:25	2228
36:26	869
36:28	1730
37	198, 206, 2273
37:11	198
37:24-25	1442
38-39	1443, 1446
40-48	181, 2232
42:3	2051
44:23	1444
45	2238
47:1-12	1443
48	2238
51:9-13	946

Ezra

1	605
1:8-11	605
2:2	2240
2:63	1444
2:65	611
2:70	611, 1440
3	605
4:1-3	370
4:2	602, 1877
4:8-10	1877
4:8-12	1877
4:10	602
4:12	2240
5:14	605

6:4	2240
6:17	1440
6:55-59	1738 n. 8
7:12	2226
8:1-9:37	137
8-10	1747, 1748
9:3	1708
9-10	608, 610
10:7-8	369
10:8	348

Genesis

1	726, 961, 1627, 1628
1:1	712
1:1-2:3	127, 128, 939, 946, 1437, 1479, 2231, 2232
1:1-2:4a	1761
1:2	727, 1330, 1344
1:5	2048
1:14	2037
1:21	590
1:24-25	590
1:26	326, 345, 443, 591, 1419, 1466, 1757, 1760, 1762 n. 22
1:26-27	590, 591, 1437
1:26-28	1721
1:26-29	589
1:27	252, 589, 1757, 1758, 1761
1:28	13, 590, 591, 855, 1040, 1437, 1655, 1721, 1755
1:28-31	1722
1:31	263, 1266, 1722, 2054
1:31-2:3	1054
1-9	1759, 1760, 1761
1-11	1320, 1446
2:1-3	1437
2:1ff.	1072
2:4-3:24	128
2:4-25	1437
2:4b-4:24	946
2:4ff.	1479, 1482
2:7	201, 1330, 1437
2:15	224, 589
2:15-3:24	444
2:15-23	589
2:16	353
2:16-17	197
2:17	260
2:18	851, 1093, 1893
2:18-20	589
2:21-23	589
2:24	851, 1107
2-3	946
3	260, 1321, 1437
3:1-6	589
3:1-22	1325
3:2-4	197
3:4-5	197
3:8	2046

3:9	1020
3:11	589
3:14-15	589
3:16	260, 589
3:17-19	197, 589
3:19	260, 806, 1437, 1505
3:22	197
3:22-24	589
4	590, 1437
4:1-5:32	128
4:1-8	590
4:9-12	590
4:13	1323
4:13-14	481
4:13-15	590
4:21	907
4:25-5:32	590
4:26	521, 591
4:26b	1758
5	590
5:1	253, 1757, 1758, 1759
5:1-3	1758
5:3	1762 n. 22
5:21-24	197
5:22	1437
5:24	590
6:1-11:32	128
6:2-4	260
6:3	590, 2128, 2202
6:4	590, 1712
6:5	260, 263, 1320, 1437
6:5-6	318
6:5-7	590
6:6	318, 1919
6:8-9	590, 591
6:9	1437
6:11-13	590
6:12	590
6:12-8:22	1437
6:17-20	591
6:18	591
6-7	260
7:1	590, 591
7:16	1893
7-8	2037
8:17	590, 591
8:20	523
8:21	1320, 1324
8:22	1437
9:1	590, 591, 855
9:1-17	147, 1437
9:2	591
9:4	1330, 1438
9:5	430
9:5-6	1761
9:6	590, 591, 1438, 1757, 1758, 1759
9:7	590, 591, 855
9:8	591
9:8-11	591
9:9-17	591
9:13	889
9:18-19	591
9:22	2140
9:36	591
10	591
10:25-26	2200
11	1438
11:1	591
11:1-9	1530
11:6	591
11:6-9	591
11:24	591
11:26	591
11:30	1708
11:31-32	591
12:1-7	138
12:2	592
12:2-3	592
12:2f	1730
12:3	1438
12:3b	1730
12:5	2046, 2231
12:6	266, 1440
12:7	526, 1440, 1444, 1790
12:7-8	523
12:8	526
12:11-20	577
12:12	407
12:13	592
12:17	1705
12-15	1318
13:4	1444
13:8	526
13:13	2128
13:14-16	592
13:14-17	1790
13:14-18	592
13:18	523, 1444
14:1	2115
14:19	2231
15	90, 138, 592, 1438
15:5	592, 841, 1730, 2037
15:5-6	67
15:6	156
15:7-21	67
15:8	1780
15:9f.	1444
15:12-16	315
15:13-14	585
15:17-21	592
15:18	1790
15:19-21	1440
16:6	577
17	90, 138, 592, 947, 1085, 1438
17:1	1755
17:2-22	1730
17:4-6	592
17:7	367
17:8	592, 1780
17:16	592

17:17	1780
17:19-21	1790
17:23-27	89
18	1464
18:1	1706
18:1-8	1067
18:8	1763
18:11	1706
18:16-33	1780
19:5	2140
19:18	2054
19:25	2054
19:37	2053
20:9	1780
21:4	89
21:14-21	577
21:33	526
22	74, 138, 526, 577, 1238
22:1	158, 1416
22:1-3	592
22:1-19	592
22:2	526
22:2ff.	406
22:12	1893
22:13	523
22:14	526
22:15-18	592
25:6	1910
25:8	198
25:21	1780
25:22	1781
25:25	1781
25:26	1781
25:51	1708
26:6	1780
26:7	1780
26:24	592
26:25	523
26:180	1780
27:1	1704
27:18-29	1778
27:19	1781
27:40	1781
28:3	593
28:10	2056
28:10-22	526
28:13-15	592
28:17	2237
28:18	523
28.20	2116
29:17	1703, 1711
29:22	802
29:27	802
29:31	1708
29:32-30:24	593
30:1	1708
30:37-38	1778
31:1	2046
31:27	906
31:36	1323
32:9	1439
32:14	1892
32:21	2054
32:23-33	502
32:24-29	592
32:26	1710
32:26ff.	1715
32:30	593
32:31-32	592
32:33	1715
33:16-20	279
33:18-20	526
33:20	279
34:3	1330
34:13-16	90
35:1-2	1760
35:2	475
35:7	526
35:9-10	593
35:10-12	592
35:11	593, 855
35:14	523
35:14-15	526
35:16-18	593
35:18	593, 1330, 1715
35:22-26	593
35:27	800
37:1	593
37:2	1782, 2047
37:3	593
37:18-22	593
37:18-28	1099
37:23-24	75
37:25-28	593
38	2201
38:7-10	855
38:25-26	1319
39:1	593, 2140
39:2-6	593
39:3	1782
39:6-20	593
40	593
41:1-36	593
41:8	593
41:16	593
41:25-32	593
41:32	593
41:39-45	593
41:46-49	593
41:57	593
42:1-5	593
42:2-8	594
42:6	594
42:21	1330
42:28	594
42:38	198
43:1-15	594
44	594
44:17	1099
45:1-5	594
45:16-28	594

46:2-3	594
46:3	806
46:13	2242
47:27	594
48:1	1706
48:3-4	592
48:16	1909
49:10	2205
49:13-14	1101
49:22	1907
50:1	806
50:3	806
50:20	1099

Habakkuk
| 3:9 | 591 |

Haggai
1:1	605
2:2	605
2:21	605

Hosea
1:3	1440
2:20	137
4:1	1436
4:6	1444, 1869
6:6	1436
8:1	1869
9:3-4	529
12:4	1440
13:4-11	1443
13:14	197

Isaiah
1:1-27	44
1:2	138, 1440
1:6	1718
1:10	1869
1:18	2228
1:23	2228
1:24-26	1445
2:1	1445
2:2-4	526
2:2ff.	1441
2:3	526, 1869
2:3-4	1443
2:22	1759
3:3	2229
3:17	1708
5:1ff.	1440
5:8-10	1725
5:12	2040
5:24	1869
6	824, 1443, 1445
6:3	1750, 2192
7:1	2057
7:2	2057
7:14-16	1720
7:21-25	1720
8:18	1443

8:19	2239
13:2	2050
14	946
14:1	1443, 1730
16:5	599
19:19	526
20:2	2057
21:6-9	461
24-27	199
25:8	199, 206
25:18	198
26:9	198
26:19	199, 202, 206
28:9	1424
30:29	526
33:16	2228
33:22	1080
37:38	2056
38:6	2056
38:14	2228
40	946
40:3-5	1439
40:18	1440
40:18-25	436
40:25	1440
40:26	2037
40-55	606, 1439
40-66	526, 533
41:8	1441
41:8f.	1730
41:17-20	1439
42:1, 6	1438
42:6	345
42:6-7	1703
42:18-20	1703
43:1	1440
43:7	1108
43:10	1730
43:15	1440
43:16-21	1439
43:19-25	1439
43:20f.	1730
44:1	1440
44:2	1439
44:5	1440
44:6-8	1440
44:19	436
44:23	1440
45	1009
45:1	2234
45:4	1730
45:7	262
45:14	1440
45:18	1440, 1916
45:21ff.	1440
46:9	1440
47:13	837, 2031
49:6	2208
49:12	1630
51:1-2	1108
51:2	1441

51:4	2208
52:13	200
52:13-53:5	1703-1704
52:13-53:12	261
53	408
53:11	200, 1436
54:1	530, 1709
54:13	751, 1093
55:6-56:8	44
55:10-11	2134
55:12-13	40
56:6-8	114
56:7	533, 611
57:14-58:14	46
58:1	1901, 2279
59:14	2228
60:3	345
60:4	530
60:22	1093
62:11-12	1443
63:10	2229
63:16	1442
63:17	2261
65:3-4	612
65:17	714
66:20-22	114
66:24	200

Jeremiah

1	1445
1:1-2:3	44
2:2-5	142
2:4-28	44
2:13	75, 2228
2:20	526
2:21	2228
3:1-2	142
3:1-13	526
3:4	44
3:16-18	528
3:17	1443
3:21	2228
3:22	2228
4:1-2	44
7	526
7:11	543, 550
7:17-18	1480
7:23	1730
7:24	2228
7:34	550
8:8	1869
8:13-9:23	44
8:19	141
8:22	1718
9:13	1869
9:16	1944
9:19-20	197
10:2	2031
10:2-5	436
10:15	436

11:4	130
11:10-13	437
14:17	1718
14:20	2228
15:18	1718
16:4	1470
16:18	436
17:1	1322
17:1-2	526
17:24-25	599
18:18	1444
21:3-7	600
22:3-6	599
22:16	1436
22-23	1442
23:5-6	614
24:7	1439, 1730
25:1-2	889
26	526
29:26	1714
30:8-9	614
30:13	1718
30:22	1439
31:29-30	200
31:30-33	261
31:31-33	712
31:31-34	69, 1441
31:33	1730
31:33-35	712
31:35-37	1441
32:38	1730
33:10-11	813
33:14-26	1442
33:15	2229
33:17	599
33:19-22	599
33:25	2037
36:26	2053
44:2-6	600
44:15-25	1480
44:23	1869
48:36	906
51:17	436
52:30	602

Job

1-2	261, 1446
3:3	2056
3:4-5	1318
4:16-5:4	1318
4:17	590
4:17-21	1321
5:24	801
6:15	2228
7:9-10	198
7:21	2229
9:9	2037, 2040
10:20-21	198
10:20-22	197
11:7-8	198

13:24	409
14:1-6	1322
14:1-10	197
14:12	199
14:21-22	198
15:14	590
15:14-16	1321
17:13-16	198
17:14	1318
25:4	590
26:11	2038
28	961
31:22	1710
34:14-15	201
37:10-42:11	1318
38	261
38:4-7	325
38:31	2040
38:33	2037
38-41	961
42:5-6	408
42:7	261

Joel

2	1443
2:10	2031
3	1446
3:4	120
4:21	1443

Jonah

1:9	1526
2:6-7	198
4:1	1778

Joshua

1:1	2239
1:1-6	597
1:7-9	597
1:8	2205
1:10-11	1783
1:18	348
1-11	1944
3:3-5	597
3:5	597
3-4	597
4:10	526
4:19-24	597
5:1-12	597
5:2-8	90
5:9	526
6	596
7	17, 598, 2206, 2211
7:19	2127
8:30-33	598
8:30-35	598
9	137
10	525
10:14	1440
10:28-36	1783

10:42	1440
11:11	1783
11:23	598
12	1779
13-17	1779
15:62	183
15:63	525
17:14-18	1719
18-22	598
22	1086, 2205
22:16-20	1087
23:1-5	598
23:2	1441
23:6-8	598
23:11-13	598
23:16	598
24	15, 138, 1080, 2257
24:1	1779
24:1-28	598
24:26	137
24:29-30	598
24:31	598
24:32	598
24:33	598

Judges

1:1-8	525
1:6-7	1707
1:21	525
3:9	1789
3:11	1789
3:15	1715
5	1440, 1779, 2207
5:1	1950 n. 23
5:1-31	1480
5:4	2047
5:31	2052, 2239
6:13	2275
6:24	526
6:25-32	1778, 1789
7	2206
8:23	1442
11:39-40	1480
13:2	1708
13:25	1784
14:12	803
14:14	1099
16:18	1784
16:21	1783
16:28	1784
17	1760
17:6	1442
17-18	437, 1778
18	1760
18:1	1442
19	525, 2140
19:1	1442
20:2	1440
20:16	1322, 1715
21:19	2238

21:19-23	1480
21:20-21	1480
21:25	1442

Judith
8:5	611
8:6	612
9:1	611
10:1-2	611

1 Kings
1:3-4	1950 n. 14
1:3-26	599
1:8	599
1:28-48	599
1:34	906, 2238
2:3	1869
2:3-4	599
2:13-25	599
2:33	599
2:45	599
6:1-38	1443
6:11-13	1443
6:19	1443
6:23	1443
6:31	2237, 2238
7:15	2240
7:15-51	1443
8	530
8:2	525
8:25-26	599
8:27-30	1443
8:28-53	530
8:29-34	611
8:46	1321
8:50	1323
8:51	1440, 1730
8:54-66	47
9:3-9	599
11:3-8	437
11:7-13	1442
11:32	1442
11:36	1442
12:1-24	600
12:26-33	1442
12:28-33	437
13:4	1715
13:30	906
14	1778
14:24	2140
15:11-13	437
15:23	1713
16:31	437
17	1717
17:14	1891
17:17-22	1717
17:17-24	814
18:20-39	437
18:28	1717
18:39	152, 153
19:9	1778

19:10-14	814
19:12-13	324
19:18	437
19:19-20	2132

2 Kings
1:1	1323
2:11	197, 1477, 2240
2:23	1708
2:23-24	1778
3:15	906
4:14	1708
4:17-20	1717
5:27	1778
6:26	2057
6:30	2057
7:6	1714
8:19	599, 1442
10:27	1778, 1789
10:31	1869
11:4	137
11:14	906
11:17	137
12:1-3	600
12:14	906
12:16	1322
13:11	1789
13:14	1706
14:6	1869
17	261, 600, 1877, 2242, 2243, 2261
17:7-23	526
17:13	1869
17:29	2242
18	2242
18:14	1322
18-20	600, 1442
19:34	1442
21	261
21:8	1869
22:1-23:20	600
22-23	1442
23:4	2261
23:7	2140
23:7-19	1789
23:15	2261
23:22	2240
23:22-23	2243
23:25	1869
23:26	2243
23:29	2261
24	600
24:9	1789
24:19	1789
25	600
25:25	45
25:27	1442

Lamentations
| 1:3 | 37 |
| 1-5 | 1443 |

2	600
2:15	531
2:20	550
3:8	2228
3:66	1061
5:14	906
5:21	2228
Leviticus	
1-7	2231
1-7:38	596
1-17	1760
2:4-5	359
2:13	2050
4:1-35	1444
6:7-9	359
6:27	197
7:13	359
7:15	2038
8	596, 1444
8:8	1444
9:10	236
9:11	236
9:13	236
9:14	236
9:15	236
9:16-17	236
9:18	236
10:10	1444
11	596, 961, 1109, 1723
11:1-46	947
11:26-31	1724
11:34	1109
11:37	1109
11:44f.	1440
11-15	1116, 1444
11-16	2231
12	368, 1109, 1117, 1479, 1484
12:1-8	1111
12:2	1845
12:2-3	90
12:2-5	1624
12:6-8	1480
12-16	596
13	961, 1121
13:40-41	1708
13:42	1708
13:46	529
13-14	1108, 1140, 1145, 1412
15	1108, 1120, 1140, 1477, 1484
15:1-15	1847
15:1-18	1712
15:1-33	1111, 1112
15:1ff.	1145
15:2ff.	1712
15:5	1842, 1844, 1845
15:8	1844
15:9	1842, 1846
15:10	1845
15:10a	1841, 1842, 1843, 1845, 1846
15:10b	1842, 1844, 1845, 1846
15:18	1712
15:19	1343
15:21	1845
15:25-28	1712
15:27	1845
15:31	1847
16	46, 947
16:12-15	1318
16:18-21	1318
16:30	2130
17:1-26:46	59
17:11	1343
17:14	1343
17-25	2231
17-26	947, 1439
18	1484
18:3	1440
18:15	2201
18:19	1943
18:22	2140, 2141
18-27	1760
19:1	339, 1503
19:2	235, 1880, 1886
19:3	2191
19:9	51
19:9-10	1704
19:10	51
19:13	1515
19:14	230, 1703
19:16	871, 872
19:17	2130
19:18	253, 978, 1255, 1472, 1477, 1886, 2130
19:19	1627, 1754
19:23	90
19:23-25	352, 1727
19:26	832, 843
19:28	1717
19:31	197, 832
19:35	2236
19:35-36	230
19:36	1440
20:1-6	832
20:6	197
20:9	2191
20:10	1479
20:12	2201
20:13	2140, 2141
20:24-26	1440
21:1-3	868
21:5	807, 1708, 1717
21:16-24	1701
21:17	1702
21:18	1712
21:20	1710
21:22	1701
22:20	1702
22:26-23:44	42
22:32	1662
23:4	1128
23:15	1814

23:16-21	43
23:17	359
23:22	51, 1704
23:24	906
23:40	47, 528
23:43	363
24:15	2192
24:15-22	1702
24:19	1717
25:1-7	1441, 1726
25:9	529, 906
25:20-22	1727
25:23	1441
25:35-36	232
25:36	871
26	582, 596, 947
26:9	596
26:16	1711
26:40-45	595
26:44-45	1439
27	596
27:11	291

1 Maccabees

1:11-24	261
1:52-54	261
1:54	550
3:44-54	611
4:46	613
4.52	550
5:33	611
9:55	1715

2 Maccabees

4:43	206, 605
6:2	2262
7	200
7:18	261
7:22-23	200
7:28	1437
10:26-27	611

3 Maccabees

2:22	1715

Malachi

1:1, 5	1440
2:7	1444
3:6	2228
3:17	1730
4:4-5	712
4:6	35

Micah

1:16	1708
3:4	409
3:11	1444
4:1	526
6:1-2	138
7:18-20	255
7:19	45

Nehemiah

2:19	1778
3:2	2240
5:15-18	605
6:6	1778
7	2244
7:5	1790
7:67	611
7:73	611
8:1-10	1374
8:14	1779
8-10	15
9	611
9:1	2041
9:7f.	1730
9:9-25	948
9:36-37	16
9-10	608, 610
10:39	2240
17	1779

Numbers

1	799
1-10	17
3	1444
3:5-10	596
3:9	596
3:11-13	596, 1068
3:13	595, 798
3:44	596
3:44-48	1068
4:1-4	596
5:2	1712
5:5-31	596
5:11-31	281
5:12	2129
5:12-31	1942
5:20-22	899, 1260
5:28	2129
5:31	281
5:32	2130
6:1-21	597
6:22-27	597
6:24-26	1906
7	48
7:1	2187
8	1444
8:6	798
8:17	595, 798
9:1-14	595
10	1444
10:1-10	906
10:33-36	596
10:35-36	16
11	595
11:1-34	597
11:4	40, 2135
11:11-23	1778
11:21	1782
11:29	1440
12	17

12:1	1782, 1789, 1790
12:6-8	435
12:8	722
12:10	1778
12:16	2128
13	595
13:33	1712
13-14	2204
14:1-45	595
14:7-9	2204
14:11-12	2204
14:13-19	2204
14:36	1707
15:15	603
15:37-41	817, 825, 1056, 1063
16	17
17:5	1308
17:26	2203
18	596, 597
18:8	1308
18:16	799
18:19	2050
19	197, 466, 529, 597, 1109
19:1-20	358, 359
20	597, 2204
20:1-13	445, 2055
20:8	2055
20:10-12	1778
20:11	1782
21:4-9	1778
21:5	2135
21:23-24	577
22:1	2054
22:28	597
22-23	2031
24:16	1436, 1710
24:18	2046
25:1-6	597
25:7-15	597
25:10-12	813
27:1-11	1782
27:12-15	597
27:14	597
27:15-23	597
27:21	1444
28:16-25	42
28:26	43
28:26-31	43
29:1	906
29:7-11	46
29:35-30:1	47
30	1403
31:17	2141
31:35	2141
32	1086, 1441
32:2	1086
34	16, 529, 1441, 2238
34:2	791
34:8	2036
34:11	529
36:2-12	1479

Obadiah
1:20	916

Proverbs
1:9	1713
1:29	1480
1-9	1446
2:4-5	2047
3:9	2192
4:13.22	2134
5	1481
5:4	2229
6:5	1723
7	1481
7:22	1723
8:22	712, 1480
8:22-32	732
8:23-31	2134
8:30	1480
8:35-37	1480
9:9	851
11:8	2236
11:31	1446
12:21	1446
14:14	443
15:15	1709
16:1	1446
16:9	1446
16:33	1446
19:2	1322
20:24	1446
21:1f.	1446
21:20	1819
22:28	1464
24:31	2228
25:2	1446
26:11	1714
27:20	198
28:24	1323
31:2-3	1481
31:10-31	1064

Psalms
2:7	1442
2:9	1909
3	1907
4:5	2066
5	907
6	907
6:3	1907
6:6	197
7	907
8	907
8:1-2	2108
9	409
9:1-2	889
10	409
11:5	1343, 1416
11:7	1444
13	409
13:4	1907

15	1444	79:6-7	1061	
15:1	526	79:8	2229	
16:8	1907	79:13	1730	
17:15	1444	79	1443	
18:50	599	80	907	
19:2	727	81	907	
19:8	854, 2047	84:5-7	1443	
20	526	87	907	
20:1	430	87:1-3	1443	
22	907	88	409	
23	808	88:4-5	198	
24	1444	88:11-13	198	
24:3	526	89:2	332	
24:4	526	89:4	599	
24:29	1443	90:4	2043	
25:7	2228	90-100	1910	
27	1853	91	808, 1907, 1911, 1913
27:8	2228	91:16	1907	
28:5	2040	92:12-15	1443	
29	2133	94:1	430	
30	1853	94:3	429	
30:2-4	198	95:7	1730	
30:4	198, 1907	99:6	2208	
30:9-10	197	100:3	1730, 2228	
31:7	436	100:4	2228	
33:12	1730	102:17	1443	
33:13-14	2233	103:3	1707	
34:13	1907	104	961, 1853	
37:25	2239	104:1-13	946	
39:13-14	197	104:17	1724	
42:3	1444	104:24	971	
43:3	1443	104:35	872	
44	409	105:6	1730	
44:23	424	105:23-44	948	
45	907	105:43f	1730	
45:2	2239	106:7-39	948	
45:15	1945	106:20	1191	
46	907, 1443	106:28	198	
46-50	907	107	1855	
47:6-9	141	110:4	1442	
48	526, 1443	113-118	907, 1059	
48:15	204	115:1	423	
49:6-13	197	115:6	1756	
50	526	115:16-18	197	
60:6	158	118:17-18	430	
65	526	118:26	93	
66:13-14	2116	119	1910	
67	1907	119:62	1854	
68:6	1446	119:89	2228	
68:16-17	1443	119:105	1860	
69	409	120-134	907	
69:25	1061	121	1907	
72	1442	121:4	423	
74	1443	122	611	
74:2	1443	125:1-2	1443	
76	526	127:1	1530	
76:3	1443	128:3	1907	
77	907	132:12	1442	
78:38-39	1321	132:13-14	1443	
78:66	1714	134:3	2231	
78:71	1730	135:4	1730	
79	1862	135:10-12	1730	

136:4-9	1059
136:10-24	1059
136	1059
137	534, 1862
140:8	1717
143:2	1321
145-150	826
146	202
146:2-4	197
146:4	201
146:5-9	200
146-150	907
147:4	2037
147:17	331
147:20	1730
148:5	2134
150:6	201
473f.	1730

Ruth

1:16	1526
1:16-17	603
2:14	394, 395
3:13	377

1 Samuel

1:2	1708
1:11	598
1:17-18	2047
1:19	1480
1:22	598
1:28	598
2	906, 1779
2:1-10	1480
2:6-7	198
2:11	598
2:11-17	598
2:18	598
2:21	598
2:22-34	598
2:25	1322
2:26	598
2:35	598
2:35-36	598
3	598
3:14	430
3:15	2208, 2209
3:17	2209
3:18	2208
4:20	1715
5:6-12	1714
7	598
7:9	423
8:1-3	598
8:4-5	598
8:4-9	599
8:6-9	599
8:11-18	1442
8:22	599
8-12	1442
9:9	2053
9:15-17	599

10:1	599
10:5	906
10:16	1199
10:17-19	599
10:20-24	599
10:24	1442
11:14-15	599
12:6-15	599
12:13-14	1442
12:15	1442
12:16-17	599
12:25	1442
13:8-15	599
15:1-34	49
15:10-31	599
15:32	577
16	599
16:2	1784
16:8-13	1442
16:14	1714
16:14-23	906
16:16	1714
17:4	1712
18:3	137
18:6-7	906, 907, 1480
18:10	1714
18:10-11	1785
19:23	1714
19:24	1710
20:6	1778
21:4-7	1778
21:14	1714
22:5-6	197
23:9	1444
25:38	1715
26:19	1778
28	198

2 Samuel

1:19-27	906
2:1-4	599
2:23	1717
3:9	599
3:27	1717
4:4	1710
4:12	1707
5:1-5	599
5:2	1440
5:4-10	525
5:5	599
6:1-15	1443
6:5	906
6:21	1442
6:23	1715
7	876
7:1	526
7:7	1440
7:12-16	599
7:13	599
7:18-29	1442
7:22	1440
11	599

11:3-4	1097		Tobit	
11:26-12:19	599		2:1-5	611
12:9	1098		3:1-6	611
12:30	2047		10-17	611
13	1937			
13:19	1943		Wisdom	
13-19:4	599		2:22-3:8	201
19:36	906, 1714		2:24	201
20	432		9:15	201
21:20	1708		11:17	1437
22:51	599			
23:10	1715, 2206		Zechariah	
24	526		1:17	1443
24:16ff.	1444		2:16	1443
			3	605, 876
Song of Songs			3:2	1443, 1530
1:1-3	908, 909		4	605
1:2	845		6:9-15	605
1:12	2239		7:5	538
1:13	1760		8:19	40, 1747
1:14	1760, 1818		8:22	1443
1:15	1760		9:14-15	906
2:1	846, 1760		12	1443, 1446
2:14	1944		12:4	1714
3:9	1811		12:11	1319
4:12	1760		13:2	2228
6:13	850		14	1443, 1446
7:5	2036		14:16-19	38, 40
7:10	845		14:16-21	1443
7:12	1515		14:19	1322
8:6	1107		14:20-21	64

2. *Anonymous and Pseudepigraphical Jewish and Christian works closely related to the Jewish Bible*

Apocalypse of Baruch			6:59	316
4:3	527		7:28ff.	878
			7:32	200
2 Baruch	603, 616, 878		8:52-53	527
			10:44-50	527
Enoch			13	614
1-36	878			
26:1	527		*Jubilees*	
91:10	200		6:32-38	2037
91-104	878		8:19	527
92:2	200		11:8	2032
			12:16	2031
1 Enoch				
6-9	606		*3 Macc.*	
20	606		1:3	609
37-71	878			
72-82	612, 2037		*Psalms of Solomon*	
			2:31	613
2 Enoch			3:12	613
6:21-26	2038		17-18	614
4 Ezra	603, 616		*Sibylline Oracles*	
3:32-34	316		4:180	200
5:20	613			

Targum Neophiti
  Numbers
    21:6   2135

Targum Pseudo-Jonathan
  Numbers
    11:7   2135
    21:6   2135

Testament of Benjamin
  10:6-8   200

Testament of Joseph
  2:6   2257

Testament of Solomon   612
  ch. 18   2032

3. *Qumran Writings, except lemmata Dead Sea Writings and Dead Sea Writings, the Judaisms of*

1Q Temple Scroll 527
1QS   15
1QS 9:11   614
1Qsa 2:11   614
4Q Exod-Lev   2253
4Q Num   2253
4Q Paleo ExM   2247
4Q Paleo Exod   2253, 2263
4Q158   2253
4Q186   612, 2032
4Q318   2032
4Q364   2253
4Q510-511   612
4Q534   2032
4Q560   612

4Q561   2032
4Qbrontologion   612
4QMMT   2124, 2264
4Qsam a,b,c   607
11Q Paleo Lev   2247
11Q PsAp a   612
11Qmelchizedek 2:4-18   314

Cairo Damascus Document
  9:2-8   2130
  12:23-13:1   614
  19:10-11   614
WD 22   2245
WD 23   2245

4. *New Testament*

Acts
  2:42-47   64
  2:44-45   64
  3:1   611
  4:32-5:11   64
  4:36   67
  4:37   67
  5:21-41   605
  6:5   603
  8:14-25   64
  8:25   2125
  9:27-30   67
  9:32-35   64
  9:36-43   64
  10:1-48   64
  10:9-16   64
  11:1-18   64
  11:19-26   67
  11:22   68
  11:24   68
  11:26   66, 67
  11:27-28   613
  12:12-17   68
  12:25   68
  13:5   68

  13:15   68
  15   66
  15:1-11   64
  15:6-11   64
  15:7-11   64
  15:13-35   65
  15:16-21   65
  15:19-20   65
  15:21   65
  15:22-29   65
  15:32   613
  15:32-33   65, 66
  15:36-41   68
  18:14-16   545
  19   1011
  21   65
  21:10-11   613
  21:17-36   66
  21:27-36   65
  23   1011
  23:6-7   203

Colossians
  3:11   493
  3:11-14   493

1 Corinthians
  8 — 65
  10:25 — 1764
  11:24-25 — 544

2 Corinthians
  11:24-25 — 1010

Galatians
  1:18-19 — 66
  2 — 66
  2:1-14 — 64
  2:11-13 — 67, 68
  2:11-14 — 64
  3:6 — 67
  3:7 — 67
  3:28 — 1875
  3:29 — 1876
  5:3 — 2126
  5:11 — 1010
  6:15 — 493

Hebrews
  1:1-2 — 70
  1:14 — 70
  2:1-4 — 70
  2:3-4 — 70
  8:8 — 70
  8:10 — 70
  8:13 — 70
  11:22 — 70
  12:29 — 70
  13:8 — 70

John
  1:1-3 — 2133
  1:4 — 2134
  1:12-13 — 69
  1:14 — 2133
  1:29 — 70, 71
  1:36 — 70, 71
  1:38 — 536
  1:49 — 536
  1:51 — 69
  2:9 — 71
  2:14-22 — 540
  2:15 — 543
  3:2 — 536
  3:9 — 71
  3:16 — 2134
  4 — 2125
  4:7-15 — 75
  4:9 — 2125
  4:13-14 — 2134
  4:24-25 — 2246
  4:31 — 536
  4:46-53 — 536
  6 — 2135
  6:25 — 536
  6:30-58 — 71
  6:33 — 2135

  6:35 — 2135
  6:41 — 2135
  6:43 — 2135
  6:48-51 — 2135
  6:61 — 71, 2135
  6:63 — 2134
  7:4 — 539
  7:19 — 2126
  7:22 — 2131
  7:23 — 2131
  7:37-38 — 2134
  7:38 — 2136
  7:41-42 — 1786
  8:37-44 — 1876
  8:47 — 1866
  8:48 — 2126
  9:2 — 536
  9:24 — 2127
  11:8 — 536
  11:47-48 — 544
  18:3-11 — 544
  18:19-23 — 1876
  19:14 — 71
  19:29 — 71
  19:31 — 71
  19:36 — 71

Luke
  2:41 — 612
  3:8 — 63
  3:23-38 — 879, 1786
  4:1-13 — 63
  5:12-14 — 543
  5:37-39 — 2129, 2133
  6:1-5 — 2130
  6:20b-21 — 63
  6:27-35 — 63
  6:38 — 2127
  7:1-10 — 536
  7:22 — 539
  7:24b-26 — 63
  7:28a — 63
  7:33-34 — 63
  7:34 — 539
  8:52 — 2125
  9:1-6 — 538
  9:3 — 538
  9:10a — 68
  9:10b-17 — 68
  9:14-15 — 68
  9:16 — 68
  9:17 — 68
  9:48 — 2133
  9:52-53 — 2125
  9:59-62 — 2132
  10:1 — 538
  10:1-12 — 537, 538
  10:2 — 538, 2127
  10:3-6 — 63
  10:4 — 538
  10:5-8 — 538, 539

10:7, 8	538
10:9	539
10:9-11	63
10:10-12	539
10:11	539
10:11-12	539
10:12	545
10:16	63
10:25-26	536
10:25-37	2125
11:2-4	63
11:20-22	539
11:39-48	63
11:49-51	64
11:52	63
13:18-21	63
14:16-20	1379
14:17	2127
14:26-27	2132
14-20	63
15:1	2125
15:7	2127
16:12	2128
17:3	2129, 2130
17:11-19	2125
17:24-27	541
17:26-27	2128
18:1	611
18:12	613
19:38	93
19:45-46	541
19:45-48	540
19:46	543
20:9-19	1876
22:2	544
22:15	63
22:18	544
22:19-20	544
22:47-53	544
23	1876
23:45	1303
24:13-27	879
24:13-35, 36-43	545

Mark

1:14	2131
1:40-44	543
2:22	2129, 2133
2:23-28	2130
2:28	2132
3:27	539
4:24	2127
5:38-39	2125
6:7	538
6:8-9	538
6:9	538
6:30-31	68
6:32-44	68
6:34	68
6:39	69
6:39-40	68

6:41	68
6:43	68
6:45-8:26	69
7	614
7:15	543, 545
7:24-31	69
8:1-10	68
8:6	69
8:14-21	69
9:2-8	64
9:5	536
9:37	2133
10:51	536
11:9	93
11:15-18	540
11:17	543
11:21	536
12:1-9	1866
12:1-12	1876
12:18-27	203
12:28-34	536
12:39	1380
13:12	2128
13:15	2126
13:35-51	1786
14:2	544
14:22	69, 544
14:25	544
14:43-52	544
14:45	536
15:8	1303
16:14-18	545
16:15	2127

Matthew

1:1-7	1786
1-17	879
5	2132
5:17-18	2129
5:19	2128
5:23-24	2130
5:46	2125
5:47	2130
5-7	2129
6:16-17	613
6:24-34	2129
7:2	2127
7:24-27	2132
8:2-4	543
8:5-13	536
9:10-13	2125
9:14-15	613
9:17	2129, 2133
9:23	2125
9:37-38	2127
10:5	538, 2125
10:7-8	539
10:8	539
10:9-10	538
10:15	2128
10:29	1723

10:29-31	2129	Philippians	
10:37-38	2132	3	493
10:40	2133		
11:5	539	Revelation	
11:19	538	4:10	72
11:29-30	2133	5:1-5	71
12:1-8	2130	5:6	71
12:5	2131	5:7	71
12:27	612	5:8	71
14:12b-13	68	5:12	71
14:13-21	68	5:13	71
14:18	68	6:1f.	71
14:19	68, 69	6:6	71
14:20	68	7:1	71
15:11	543, 545	7:2-8	71
15:21-29	69	7:4-8	71
15:32-39	68	7:9	72
15:36	69	7:9-12	71
16:5-12	69	7:14	71
17:24-27	541	7:17	71
18:5	2133	8:1-2	72
18:14-17	2125	13:1	551
18:15-17	2129	14:9-10	71
18:20	1786	17:12-14	71
19:8	2132		
19:21	56	Romans	
21:9	93	1:3	1786
21:12-19	540	2:13	2126
21:13	543	2:14	2126
21:33-46	1876	4:1-5	156
22:4	2127	4:9-12	493
22:23-33	203	4:10-12	90
22:34-40	536	4:11	91
22:41-45	1786	4:13	493
23:15	114	4:24-25	493
23:34-36	64	8:3-9	1875
24:18	2126	8:32	74
24:37-39	2128	9:3-4	493
24:41	2126	9:8	1875
25:35	2133	9:30	494
26:5	544	9:31	494
26:25	536	11	1866
26:26	68, 544	11:5-6	494
26:28	544	11:11	1876
26:29	544	11:17	494
26:47-56	544	11:17-20	1876
26:49	536	11:28	1876
26:69-70	2126	11:28-29	494
27:24-25	1876	16	85
27:25	1866		
27:51	1303		

5. Ancient Writings (a. Jewish, b. Christian, c. non-Jewish, non-Christian)

a. Jewish		1-6-56	558
Josephus		1-6-218	559
Against Apion (Contra Apionem)		1-11-12	555
1-2	558	1-14	555
1-3	558	1-20	555

1-21	555
1-22	605
1-28	560
1-29	560
1-36	560
1-37-41	560
1-41	613
1-42	1379
1-42-43	560
1-47-56	554, 558
1-59	544, 559
1-60-218	558
1-72	559
1-73-91	1027, 1039
1-93-105	1039
1-100-27	1787
1-154-55	555
1-161	555
1-162	560
1-166-67	555, 560
1-175	560
1-182	560
1-183	1026
1-183-204	1027
1-190	560
1-192ff.	17
1-205-211	1044
1-219-2.144	558
1-223	544
1-225	559
1-228-252	1027, 1039
1-279	544
1-304-311	1032
1-309	1785
2-15-17	1033
2-20	1032
2-20-21	1033
2-25	1033
2-28	1033
2-65	1033
2-68	1033
2-73	1033
2-78	1033
2-79-80	1028, 1033
2-83-84	1030
2-89	1034
2-91-96	1028, 1034
2-112-114	1033
2-115	559
2-121	1034
2-125	1033
2-127	560
2-132	1787
2-137	1033
2-143	545
2-144	559
2-145	560, 1032
2-145-295	558, 559
2-146-47	560
2-148	1779, 1780, 1788
2-165	560, 1785

2-168	560
2-179-81	560
2-209-10	560
2-211-17	560
2-220-31	560
2-232-33	560
2-236	1032
2-257-61	560
2-258	1785
2-271-75	560
2-276-78	560
2-279-86	560
2-318	559

Jewish Antiquities

1-1-6	554
1-2	558
1-8-9	556
1-11	554
1-12	556
1-14	554, 1791
1-15	554
1-17	1778
1-20	554
1-21	554
1-22	554
1-24	278
1-37	1779
1-94	1791
1-108	1791, 1792
1-148	1779
1-156	1779
1-158	1780, 1791
1-159	1026
1-159-60	1791
1-160	1791
1-161	1779
1-162	1780
1-170	1779
1-172	1779, 1780
1-175	1779
1-185	1780
1-186	1779
1-187	1779
1-192	1780, 1790
1-200	1780
1-200-201	1779
1-207	1780
1-222	1780
1-222-36	1792
1-224	1780
1-229	1779, 1780
1-232	1780
1-234	1780
1-235	1780
1-240-41	1778, 1780
1-243	1779
1-250	1779
1-252-53	1779
1-257	1781
1-259	1780

1-260-61	1780	
1-261	1780	
1-264	1780	
1-266	1780, 1781	
1-269	1781	
1-273	1781	
1-274	1780	
1-275	1780, 1781	
1-279	1791	
1-282	1781	
1-288-90	1781	
1-301	1781	
1-305	1781	
1-325-26	1781	
1-329	1781	
1-340	1781	
2-2	1781	
2-7	1781	
2-9	1781, 1782	
2-9-38	1789	
2-10	1781	
2-11-39	1781	
2-15	1781	
2-17	178	
2-17-33	1781	
2-39	1781, 1782	
2-41-59	1789	
2-42	1782	
2-43	1782	
2-46	1782	
2-60	1782	
2-63-90	1781	
2-65	1782	
2-72	1782	
2-80	1782	
2-86	1782	
2-87	1782	
2-94	1782	
2-95-166	1781	
2-98	1781	
2-122	1782	
2-124-59	1789	
2-133	1792	
2-142	1782	
2-145	1782	
2-149	1781	
2-191-93	1782	
2-196	1781	
2-210	1782	
2-224	1782	
2-230	1782	
2-232	1782	
2-238	1778	
2-238-253	1782	
2-239-53	1789	
2-258-64	1789	
2-270-71	1782	
2-277	1789	
2-348	1782, 1791	
3-5-9	1791	
3-13-32	1791	
3-33-38	1791	
3-63-74	1789	
3-66-67	1782	
3-81	1791	
3-90	1779	
3-205-11	1789	
3-268	1791	
3-302	1782	
3-307	545	
3-308	1783	
3-322	1791	
4-11-56	1789, 1792, 1793	
4-12-36	1782	
4-26-34	1789	
4-47	1782	
4-54-58	1789	
4-64-66	1789	
4-83-85	1789	
4-102-58	1789	
4-108-11	1791	
4-115-116	556	
4-125	1792	
4-129-40	1789	
4-131-55	1790	
4-158	1791	
4-165	1783	
4-223	555	
4-304	554	
4-311	1783	
4-326	1791	
4-328	1782	
4-328-29	1782	
4-328-31	1789	
4-329	1782	
5-1	1783	
5-2:3	1712	
5-15	555	
5-16	1783	
5-22	1783	
5-23-27	1783	
5-30	1783	
5-43	555	
5-45	1783	
5-48	1783	
5-55	555	
5-60	1783	
5-75-76	1783	
5-78	1783	
5-103	1783	
5-114	1783, 1792	
5-115-16	1779	
5-116	1783	
5-118	1783	
5-135	555	
5-182-24	1789	
5-185	1790	
5-185-97	1789	
5-200-10	1789	
5-213	1791	
5-231	1792	
5-276	1783	

5-277	1783, 1791
5-285	1783
5-286	1784
5-286-87	1784
5-286-88	1790
5-287	1783
5-290	1783
5-292-94	1790
5-294	1783
5-306	1784
5-306-13	1790
5-310	1784
5-310-11	1791
5-312	1783, 1792
5-337	1791
5-345	1784
5-348	2209
5-349	1784
6-19	1784
6-22	1784
6-24	1784
6-28	1784
6-32	1784
6-34	1784, 1785
6-36	555
6-37-40	1792
6-45	1785
6-45-7.6	1789
6-48	1784
6-52	1785
6-57	1785
6-63	1785
6-64	1784
6-67	1785
6-79	1785
6-98	1785
6-102	1784
6-136	1785
6-137	1785
6-143-45	1784
6-157	1784
6-157-7-394	1789
6-164	1786
6-166	1785
6-179-80	1785
6-194	1789
6-196	1785
6-199-200	1785
6-208	1785
6-210	1785
6-216	1785
6-250	1785
6-268	1785
6-290	1785
6-292-94	1784
6-312	1785
6-317	1785
6-323	1785
6-326	1785
6-343-50	1785, 1789
7-11-19	1789
7-122-26	1789
7-130-53	1792
7-135-41	1789
7-173	1792
7-181-87	1789
7-184	1785
7-191-93	1789
7-194-244	1792
7-196	1792
7-236-42	1789
7-245-47	1789
7-253-57	1789
7-272	1785
7-281-92	1789
7-318-20	1789
7-322-33	1785
7-335-42	1789
7-338	1786
7-348-62	1789
7-356	1786
7-361	1786
7-362	1787
7-370-88	1789
7-372-73	1785
7-374	1786
7-381	1786
7-384	1786
7-390-91	1785, 1789
7-391	1785
7-392	1787
8-2	1786
8-2-211	1789
8-2.5	612
8-8	1787
8-13-16	1789
8-20	1787
8-21	1787
8-23	1786
8-24	1786
8-26	1787
8-26-34	1787
8-30	1787
8-38	1787
8-40	1786
8-42	555
8-44	1787
8-45-49	1787
8-52	1787
8-55-56	1786
8-63-64	1787
8-88	1787
8-97	1787
8-106	1787
8-111-12	1787
8-116-17	1788
8-124	1786
8-125	1787
8-129	1786
8-131	1787
8-133	1787
8-141	1787

8-143	1787	10-190-92	1788
8-144-49	1786, 1791	10-194	557, 1788
8-146	1787	10-195	550
8-163	1787	10-200	1788
8-166-67	1787	10-202	1788
8-190	1788	10-203	1788
8-190-94	1790	10-207	558
8-194	1788	10-210	550, 1788, 1792
8-196	1787	10-214	1788, 1791
8-205-45	1789, 1792	10-241	1788
8-211	1786, 1789	10-246	1788
8-212	1792	10-249	1788
8-228	1793	10-250	558
8-262	1791	10-251	1788
8-265-87	1789, 1792	10-255	1788
8-316-92	1789	10-255-56	1788
8-319	1791	10-259	1788, 1791
8-324	1791	10-260	1792
8-342	1791	10-263	1788
8-349	1791	10-266	557
8-358	1792	10-269	1788
8-398-420	1789	10-277	555
8-409	1792	10-277-81	557, 1788
8-412	1792	10-281	1791
8-419	1792	11-111	555
9-28	1791	11-152	1790
9-29	2242	11-159-83	1789
9-166	1789	11-169	1781
9-177-78	1789	11-183	1789
9-178	1789	11-253	1792
9-184-86	1789	11-261	1792
9-196-202	1789	12-3.3,142	605
9-207-14	1789	12-4.2	605
9-213	1791	12-8-10	2245
9-260	1789	12-12-118	1311
9-342	2245	12-256-260	2262
10-2:1	1714	13-54	2245
10-39	1790	13-171	315
10-76	1792	13-171-73	555
10-79	557	13-173	554
10-79-80	557	13-257	114
10-89	557	13-288	557
10-90	557	13-297	1459
10-97-102	1789	13-298	554
10-100	1789	13-300-301	555
10-102-50	1789	13-319	114, 1030
10-103	1789	13-345-347	1030
10-114	557	13-372-373	541
10-119	557	13-397	114
10-120	1789	13-401	557
10-126	557	13-431-32	557
10-129-30	557	14-10.1-26	610
10-139	557	14-66-68	1030
10-149-153	555	14-111-113	1030
10-154	1789	14-403	555
10-186	557, 1788	15-25-30	2141
10-186-89	1788	15-371	555
10-187	1788	15-371-79	558
10-188	1788	15-417	544
10-189-90	557	17-2.4-3.1, 41-47	614
10-190	1788	17-41-45	557

17-149-167	542
18-1	203
18-1.5.20	614
18-12	316
18-12-21	555
18-17	547
18-20	558
18-312	540
18.1.2, 11	614
19-6.3	611
20-2.3-4	602, 603
20-2.3-5	603
20-2.41-43	602, 603
20-2.41-53	603
20-5.2,100	609
20-9	65
20-9.6,216-218	611
20-17-96	556
20-224-251	555

Jewish War

1-	550
1-1-3	548
1-3	547
1-6	547
1-6-9	548
1-10	548
1-12	550
1-17	550
1-20	550
1-32	550
1-34-35	548
1-36	551
1-53	551
1-68	551
1-70	551
1-97	1459
1-152-153	551
1-170	551
1-648-655	542
2-4.4-5	611
2-8.12.159	613
2-18	203
2-21	550
2-30	550
2-34	550
2-45	550
2-47	550
2-48	550
2-73	548
2-91	549
2-92	548
2-111-113	550
2-117-119	549
2-139	549
2-140	549
2-155-156	553
2-158	550
2-160-161	553
2-237-244	552
2-256	552
2-272	549
2-277	549
2-301-308	552
2-302	548
2-308	549
2-324	548
2-332	552
2-336	552
2-339	549
2-352	549
2-358-59	560
2-365	549
2-393-394	549
2-398-99	557
2-400	550
2-407	552
2-409	545
2-414	552
2-417	552
2-426-427	549
2-426-429	552
2-441	552
2-455	550
2-457-93	549
2-562	549
2-595-607	557
3-8.9, 403-7	613
3-30	550
3-108	547
3-108-109	548
3-136-37	557
3-193-202	557
3-263	550
3-329	549
3-333	548
3-336	549
3-350-408	551
3-352	551, 552
3-361-378	552
3-368	549
3-371-374	553
3-389	557
3-396	549
3-397-399	549
3-400-402	1788
3-501	50
4-7	1379
4-14	550
4-22	550
4-29	550
4-128	550
4-147-150	552
4-236-325	552
4-318-325	552
4-412	550
4-462-464	1791
5-2	549, 557
5-5	1381
5-11-12	550
5-19	549
5-20	550

5-391	550
5-391-393	550
5-394	550
5-402	550
5-411	550
5-418	550
5-515	550
6-7	550
6-29	550
6-96-111	550
6-103-105	1792
6-104	550
6-110	549
6-127	549
6-193-213	550
6-249	549
6-250	262
6-267	550
6-267-268	262
6-268	550
6-271-274	550
6-285	552
6-300	549
6-301	550
6-310	552
6-312	551
6-344	548
6-409-413	549
6-423-425	552
6-437	550
6-439	550
7-3	1379
7-5	1379
7-218	540
7-267	552
7-328-332	549
7-341-357	552
8-14	550
8-25	550
11-33	550
11-33-35	550
13-171	1459

Life

2	1793
8	1781
10	555
10-12	556
11-12a	558
12	547, 555, 556
54	611
113	556
189-98	556, 557
208-10	1781
336-67	556
416	1781
417-429	547
422	1781
423	1781
430	556

Wars

1.2-1:7	2141

Philo

De vita contemplativa

8:7	613

Legation to Gaius (Legatio ad Gaium)

199-202	610
356	1038

Migration of Abraham

89-93	602

On the Confusion of Tongues

183-190	278

On Providence

2.64	612

Probus

75	614

Special Laws (Specialibus Legibus)

1.195-203	613
2.62	1379

Vita Mosis

2:25-44	1311

Who is the Heir

76-85	1104

Ps-Iustinus

Cohoratio ad Gen. 9	1048

Ps-Philo

Liber Antiquitatum Biblicarum

3:2	2202
6:6	2201
6:9	2201
6:11	2206
7:4	2201
9:2	2201
9:3-4	2201
9:5	2201
9:7-8	2201
9:10	2202
9:16	2202
10:1	2202
10:2	2202
11:1-3	2203
11:15	2203
12:1	2203
12:2	2205
12:3	2205
12:8-9	2203
12:9	2204
15:5-6	2204
16	2204
19:3	2204
19:7	2204
19:8-9	2204
19:15	2204
20:1	2205
25:6	2211
25:7	2206
25:13	2203

27	2206
27:7	2206
27:12	2206
27:13-14	2206
28:10	2207
31:1	2207
32:21-24	2205
33:6	2207
49:1	2208
50:3	2210
50:4	2208
50:5	2210
50:8	2208
51:2	2208
51:6	2208
51:7	2208
52:1	2208
53:2	2209
53:7	2208
53:11	2209
53:12	2208
55:1	2209
56:5	2209
57:1-3	2209
57:4	2209
57:5	2209
59:2	2210
59:4	2210
59:5	2210
61:3	2211
62:2	2210
64:1	2210
64:9	2210

Thucydides
1.2   548

b. Christian
Ambrose
Joseph
3.16   75
3.8   75

Augustine
City of God (De Civitate Dei)
4.31   1030
6.31   1041
Concerning the Agreement of the Gospels
1.22   1030
1.30   1030
Confessions
10.13   396
Clement of Alexandria, *Miscellanies*
1.21.130.3   1028

Eusebius
Pedagogue
1.6.34   74
Preparation for the Gospel
9.1739   1028
9.18:1, 2   1048

Jerome
Comm. in Osee
12   1048

Justin
Apology
1.66.3   544

Origen
Against Celsus
1.15   1026
1.28   1046
1.32   1046
1.41   1046
1.9   1046
2.1   1046
2.11   1046
2.28   1046
2.4   1046
2.55   1046
3.17   1046
3.55   1046
4.10   1046
4.51   1046
5.14   1046
5.61-66   1046
7.18   1046
8.68   1046
Praef. 4   1046

Sulpicius Severus
Chronicle
2.30.3, 6, 7   1037

Tertullian
Apologetic
16.1-4   1037

Thomas
saying 64   541

c. non-Jewish, non-Christian
Ammianus Marcellinus
Res Gestae
23.1:2-3   1050

Apion, *apud* Josephus   1033, 1034

Aristotle
Metaphysics
1.980a   1038

Arrian
Dissertationes
1.11:12-13   1043
1.22:4   1043
2.9:19-21   1043

Celsus
apud Origen   1046

Damascius
Vita Isodori apud Photius   1050

Diodorus Siculus
apud Lydus   1030
apud Photius   1028
Historical Library
    1.28.1-3   1028
    1,94.1-2   1028
    34-35,1-5   1033
    40.3   1027
    40.3.4   1031

Galen
Anat. Hipp.
    3.4   1046
On the Pulse
    2.4   1046
    3.3   1046
On the Usefulness of
Parts of the Body
(De usu partium)
    11.2.3,11.5   1046

Hegesippus
History apud Eusebius   65

Hierocles
Philalethes apud Lactantius   1049

Homer
Iliad
    6.184   1038
Odyssey
    5.283   1038

Julian
Con. Gal.
    42e-43b   1049
    52b   1049
    96c   1049
    99e   1049
    100c   1049
    141c   1049
    155c   1049
    160d   1049
    176ab-210a   1049
    218a-224e   1049
    238ac   1049
    238d-351d   1049
    354ab-356c   1049
Fragmentum Epistulae
    89b   1049
    289c-301b   1049

Justin-Trogus
Epitome
    36.1.9-3.9   1031

Lactantius
Commentarii in Statii Thebaida
    4.516   1051
Divinae Institutiones
    5.3:4   1049

Libanius
Epistulae
    914   1050
    917   1050
    974   1050
    1084   1050
    1097   1050
    1105   1050
    1251   1050

Lucian
Hermotimus
    16.27   1046
Viatrum Auctio
    2.449-511   1046
Wisdom of Nigrinus   555

Lydus
Concerning the Months (De Mensibus)
    4.53   1030, 1047

Macarius Magnes
Apoc.
    4.2, 4.24   1046

Nicarchus
De Iudaeis apud Photius   1040

Numensis
De Bono apud Origen   1047

Ocellus Lucanus
De Universi Natura
    45-46   1040

Persius
Satires
    5.179-184   1035

Philostratus
Life of Appolonius of Tyana (Vita Apollonii)
    5.27   1043
    5.33-34   1043
    6.34   1043

Photius
Library (Bibliotheca)
    35.1.1-5   1028
    242   1050
    339a   1050
    345b   1050

Plato
Eutyphro   1068

Timaeus
22-25	1038
28a-32c	1046

Pliny
Ep.
4.30	1041
25.1	1041
39.16.8	1041
Natural History
5.71-73	183

Plutarch
On/Concerning Isis and Osiris (De Is.)
31, p. 363 C-D	1035
351d, 382b	1043
360dff., 361b	1044
361ae	1044
373	1043
Lives, Life of Cicero
7.6, p. 864 C	1035
De E.
387f.	1043
392eff.	1043
De Fac.
944e	1043
945b	1044
Def. Or.
416cff.	1043
417b	1044
944cd, cf. 415c	1044
Co.Apol
109ad	1043, 1044
De Superstitione
166a, c	1444
169c	1444
De Sera
550dff.	1444
Questiones Conviviales
V,1-2	1444
V,10:1	1444
VIII,8	1444

Porphyry
apud Macarius Magnes	1046
Epistula ad Marcell	1048

De Abstinentia
4.11-14	1049

Sallust
Catalinarian Conflict
37.3	551

Simplicius
Commentaria in Aristotelem Graeca
7.141f.	1051
7.90	1051

Strabo of Amaseia
Geography (Geographica)
14.21	1031
14.4	1031
16.2.34-46	1030
16.760-765	1040

Suetonius
Lives; Sib.Or.
512-15	551

Suida, s.v. *Gesios* — 1050

Tacitus
Histories (Historiae)
4.1-13	1035
5.1-13	553, 559
5.2:3	1038
5.5	558
5.5.4	1379
Annals
2.85.4	1037
apud Sulpicius Severus	1037

Theodoret of Cyrus
Affect.
7.36	1048

Valens
Anthologiae
1.10	1047
2.28-29	1047

Varro, *apud* Augustine — 1041

6. *Rabbinic Literature*

a. Mishnah
Ab.
1:1	2124
1:1-3	2221
1:1-9	1452
1:1-18	1200-1201
1:2	252
1:5	1942
1:6	536

1:12	1515, 2127
1:14	1515
1:16	536
2:1	1327
2:2	1507, 2067, 2286
2:4	244, 1426, 1427, 1525
2:6	1411

2:7	1483, 2134
2:8	1505, 2286
2:8-9	1453, 1471
2:11	2127
2:15	538, 2127
2:16	2285
3:1	1468
3:2	1507, 2286
3:3	2133
3.5	2133
3:10	244, 1426, 1427
3:11	2134
3:13	1462, 2124
3:13-14	340
3:14	2134
3:15	317, 444, 1411, 1508, 2287
3:16	2125, 2127
3:17	1507, 2132, 2286
4:1	1103
4:5	1507, 2287
4:6	2127
4:9-10	2287
4:10	1508
4:17	2127
4:17-19	1426
4:20	2128, 2133
4.2	1325
5:6	318, 892
5:7	1477
5:17	452
5:18	1519
Ar.	
2:3	907
2:3-6	906, 907
2:6	907
9:6	529
A.Z.	
1:1	1014
2:3	442
3:8	354
4:7	892, 1905
B.B.	
1:5	235
3:2	2125
Bek.	
6:2	1711
6:3	1711
7	1701
7:5	1711
Ber.	
1:1	1460, 1462
1:5	1056
2:1	2130
2:1A-C	448
2:2	2130
4:4A	448
4:5A-C	448
5:1A-E	448
8:1-5	1835
8:6	1628
8a	1457

9:1	442
9:5	538, 2130
Bes.	
2:4	542
4:2	2130
Bik.	
1:2	467
B.M.	
1:1-2	1691
2:11	294, 2284
4:3	230
4:4	230
6:1	1513, 2125
6:2	1513
7:1	1514
7:2	1514
9:11	1515
B.Q.	
1:1-2	229
4:4	1696
7:7	1728
Dem.	
2:2	538, 2128
2:3	538
Ed.	
1:5	1949
1:6	528
2:2	1946
2:4-6	2124
2:6	2130
3:8	2038
6:2	1843
Erub.	
10:3	2126
10:11-15	2130
Git.	
1:5	2125
1:7	2286
2:6	872
5:9	2130
7:1	1710
7:5	1710
8:3	2126
8:5	292
8:8	292
Hag.	
1:1	1697
1:8	1302, 1154
Hal.	
1:1	467
Hor.	
3:6-8	295
3:7	871, 1942
3:8	1450, 2284, 2285
Hul.	
1:1	1946
3:6	1725
12:5	2128
24a	907
Kel.	
1:3	1841

1:5	469
1:6	529
1:6-8	469
1:7	529
1:8	529, 530
15-6	1304
16:7	1842
16:8	1717
23:5	1842
23:9	1905
26:5	1717
Ker.	
1:2	451
1:3	859
Ket.	
1:1	801
3:1-2	2247
4:4	1944, 2125
5:5	283, 1504, 2126
5:9	284
7:1	284
7:2	285
7:3	285
7:4	285
7:5	285
7:6	283
13:1-2	1127
13:10	2125
111b-113a	468
Kil.	
1:1	1626
1:2	1627
1:4	1627
1:5	1627
4:1	1727
Ma.	
1:5	449
3:6	2126
4:5	2130
Mak.	
1:4	1403
3:6	2126
4:5	243
Meg.	
1:3	1503
1:8	785, 787, 788, 795
2:1	788
2:2	785
3:1	1304
3:3	2126
4:4	788, 1306
4:4-6	1319
4:6	1700
4:8	372
Men.	
1:1	451
5:1	359
Mid.	
2:2	2129
2:5	1701
5:4	1701

Miq.	
6:4	1905
7:6	2128
M.Q.	
1:5	242
1:7	242
3:7-9	242
3:8	1951 n. 28, 2125
3:9	2125
M.S.	
1:5	449
Naz.	
4:6	286
Ned.	
1:3	528
3:10	528
3;11	2130
4:4 1.16-18/22b	1470
9:9	1471
Neg.	
9:1	1905
13:12	1942
Nid.	
3:7	1624
4:1	2126
6:3	1115
7:5	2126
Oh.	
3:6-16:2	1847
7:6	859, 871
Par.	
10:1-2	1842, 1843
Pe.	
8:9	1704
Pes.	
5:1-9:11	358
9:9	360
10:4	1054, 1057
10:5	1059
10:6-7	1060
10:7	1061
Qid.	
1:7	286
1:10	2127
1:19	529
2:1	286
4:1	2262
4:3	2125
4:14	262, 1506, 2126, 2129, 2285
R.H.	
1:1-2	2040
1:2	43, 45
1:4	2130
1:5-6	2038
1:7	2037, 2039
1-6	1127
2:8	2039
2:8-9	1126
2:9	2040
3:7D-J	448

3:8	446, 1947
4:1	382, 528
4:1-3	530
4:1-4	382
4:2	530
4:3	528

San.

1:5	1944
2:1	1929
2:1-5	1835-1836
2:2	1929-1930
2:3	1930, 1936
2:4	234, 1304, 1937
4:2	1944
4:5	646
6:2	805, 2127, 2151
6:3-4	286
6:4	833
6:6	242
7:7	833
8:4	1700
8:5	288
10:1	202, 204, 372, 833
10:3	2128
11:2	543

Shab.

2:6	262, 1263
6:1	1400
6:2	1905
6:6	1713
6:10	833
7:2	2130
9:3	1910
11:6J-K	450
16:1	377, 1304
18:3	2130
19:2.3.5	2130
23:4	2125
31a	1457

Sheb.

1:1	467
4:3	2130
4:10	1728
5:9	2126
8:3.6	2126
8:10	2125
9:2	2125

Sheq.

1:1	540
1:3	540
1:5	2125

Sot.

1:7	262, 899, 1259, 2127
1:8	899
1:9-10	900
3:4	1483, 1942
3:4-5	1519
5:4	907
7:1	788, 790, 796
9:9	2151
9:15	278, 1110, 2128
21a	1327

Suk.

2:9	365
3:11	907
3:12	528
5:1-4	242
5:4	907

Ta.

2:1	2130
2:12	1304
3:1-2	1601, 1605
3:8A-P	1596
4:5	1597, 1598
4:6	43, 44, 384, 529
4:7	384

Tam.

5-7	907
7:4	907

Ter.

1:1	1698
1:2	1698
1:6	1699
2:3	448
3:8	449
3:9	2125
4:3	1698

Toh.

4:5	2126
5:8	2126
7:2	2125
7:4	2126
8:2	1842, 1843
9:4	1843

Yad.

3:2, 4:6	1304
3:4	1304
3:5	1304, 1305

Yeb.

16:7	789
18	1696

Yom.

3:11	907
8:6	1715, 1716, 2130
8:8	1329
8:8-9	1255
8:9	2130
8:9A	449
8:9A-C	1256

Zab.

2:4	1839, 1841
3:1-3	1839
4:1-7	1839
4:6	1842
5	1114
5:1	1841, 1845
5:1-3	1840
5:1-9	1839
5:2	1114, 1837, 1842, 1845, 1846
5:6	1840, 1843
5:6-9	1845
5:7	1840, 1844
5:8	1840, 1845

5:9	1845
5:10	1845
5:11	1113, 1845
5:12	1845
Zeb.	
1:1	360, 451
2:3	451
4:6	451
5:8	1054
9:14	358
b. Tosefta	
Ar.	
1:8	2039
A.Z.	
4:5	470
Bek.	
3:17	1713
Ber.	
2:12	1942, 1947, 1949 n. 5
2:21	452
3:3	1426
3:15	530
3:21	1951 n. 49
4:18	452
6:3	1702
6:24-25	1063
7:3	1712
45b	1951 n. 48
Bik.	
2:15	445
B.M.	
6:6	2127
7:1	1514
10:3a-c	1515
B.Q.	
1:12	528
9:31	1325
Dem.	
3:4	2125
5:21-24	2262
Erub.	
96a	1946
Hag.	
1:2	452
2:3-4	376
2:11	542
Hor.	
1:5	372
Hul.	
1:1	372
2a	1951 n. 49
3:6	1718
3:19	1713
Ker.	
2:4	1300
Meg.	
2:6	1320
2:17	1947
3:13	1320
3:20	1304
3(4):39-40	1306

Men.	
13:23	528
13.22	145, 146
Naz.	
1:3	2039
Nid.	
2:6	1708
Par.	
10:2	1843
Pe.	
1:2	1475
1:4	446
4:8-15	53
4:14	1718
4:19	1470
Pes.	
10:9	1060
10:12	1054
113b	1708
Pis.	
4:13	2131
Qid.	
1:10-11	286
1:11	2195, 2286
1:11F-H	287
5:16	1505
R.H.	
1:12	38
1:15	2040
San.	
2:2-3	2038
2:6	2041
2:7	2038, 2041
2:13	2044
8:7	372
11:1	2130
13:2	204, 1732
13:5	372
Shab.	
2:17-18	448
4:5	1906
4:9	1711
5:3-4	1718
7	1905
7:14	2034
8	1905
8:9	1905
12:11	1713
13:2,6	1304
13:2-3	1320
13:5	372, 2032
15:16	2131
Sheb.	
2:9	2041
2:12	2041
Sheq.	
1:6	1717
Sot.	
4:1-6	1260
5:9	1944
6:9	463
7:8	1701

7:16	1701
Suk.	
2:5-6	838
2:6	838, 2033
2:10	528
4:1	1480, 1951 n. 49
Ta.	
2:12-13	1596, 1597
3:5-3:9	1598, 1599
3:7 1.10	1476
Neg., 4:9	1708
Ter.	
1:1-4	1698, 1699
1:3	1699
Toh.	
9:4	1843
Yad.	
2:10	1305
2:11	1304
2:12	1304
Yeb.	
14:4	1718
Y.K.	
4:8	262
Zab.	
2:4	1713
3:3	1114, 1843
5:1	1115, 1842, 1843
5:1a	1838
5:2b	1844
5:3	1843
5:5a	1845
5:10-12	1845
Zeb.	
6:18	2038

c. Palestinian Talmud

A.Z.	
1:1	2041
1:2	386
2:2, 10b	1716
3:1	2038
3:1.II.AA	331
5:3.III	1134
39b	2041
42c	2038
B.B.	
5:5	2192
Ber.	
1:1	1908, 2039
1:4.VIII.D	332
2:2	2039
2:4	1713
8:5	1715
9:1.VII.E	332
9:2	2033, 2040
9:13	1712
13c	2033, 2040
Hag.	
1:1 76a	1697
1:7.V	1454, 1475

2:1	373
2:1.IIff.	331
2:3	542
15c	1906
Hor.	
3:5	1454
3:5.III.PP	331
Ket.	
1:5	1943
Kil.	
1:4	1627
2:1	1626
9:3 VI	463
Meg.	
1:9	785, 787
1:9 71c	1313, 1315
1:11 71b	1304
3:3.V	2290
4:1 7d	1306
4:1 12a	1304
4:1 74d	1319
4:1.IV	2288
M.Q.	
3:1.XI.	1134
3:7	833
3:7 83B	1304
3:7 87b	1306
3:7.X.	1134
M.S.	
2:53	1713
4:9	1915
Naz.	
9:58	1707
Ned.	
6:9.III.CCCC	332
11:42	1716
Pe.	
1:1	2192, 2193, 2194, 2195
1:1.VIII	1509
8:9	1715
Pes.	
10:3	92
Qid.	
1:7.IX.B	332
1:9.II.S	332
4,66b	1483
San.	
1:1IV.Q	331
1:2	2038, 2044
1:4.V.FF-GG	331
2:1.III.O	331
5:1.IV.E	322
6:6	2141
8:5 26b	1700, 1701
8:26	1707
10:1.IX	331
19:1	2044
Shab.	
1:3 V.3	471
6:8	1712, 1713
14:4	1711

14:14	1707	75a	2227
15c	442	B.B.	
16:1 [15c]	1302	1:5 IV.28-29/9b	1470
16:9	442	1:5 IV.37-38/10a	1470
20:17	1708	7b	235
Sheq.		8b	2193
5:4.II	2290	10a	52
Sot.		10b	1732
3:1	1943	11a	55
7:4.IV	2290	12a	1656
9:13.VI	2290	14b-15a	2052
Suk.		16a	263
4:1	2040	16b	2032
54b	2040	51b	1953 n. 73
55b	1480	57b	1950 n. 17
Ta.		58b	1713
1:1	881	97b	1709
1:1 II:5	466	119b	1941
1:1X.Eff.	331	123a	1711
1:1X.U	331	146a	1707
1:4.1	1477, 1517	147a	1720
1:6,64c	1484	154b	869
3:9	1599, 1600	Bek.	
3:11.IV	630, 833, 1524	3b	1712
4:5.Xff.	332	5b	1714
4:5.XIV.Q	332	6:10	1710
4:8	1707	7:2	1708
Ter.		7:6	1712
8:12	432	13a	798
Yeb.		19a	798
14:7	1944	24b	1708
15:2	1717	38a	1711, 1712
Yom.		38b	1711
8:5	1715	41a	1708
		43b	1708, 1710
d. Babylonian Talmud		44a	1711
Ar.		44b	1710, 1713
2b-3a	1947	45b	1710, 1712, 1715
3a	1951 n. 47	46a	798
7a	869	47a	798
9b	2039, 2043	49a	787, 798
15a-b	337	Ber.	
A.Z.		3a	1905
3a	1722, 1732	4a	891, 2034
3b	335, 1423	4b	1950 n. 14
5a	1343, 1708	4b, 23	2066
6a-6b	1703	5a	146, 320, 322, 1908
8b	543	5a-b	263
12b	1714	5b, 31-33	2067
13:11 I.2/110a	446	6a-7a	336
18a,b	1483	6a-b, 39	336, 1425
18b	2235	6b, 41-48	2071
27a	1708, 1952 n. 52	6b/1:1, 41	2071
27b	432	7a	337, 339
28a	1712, 1716, 1718	7a, 49	336, 1425
28b	1710, 1711, 1712	7a, 50	1425
29a	1706, 1715	7a, 56	334, 1419
29b	1015	7b, 59-65	2068
36b	1015, 1943	8:6 52b-53a	1629
40b	1709	8a	1657, 1707, 1854
58b	788	8a-b	1319

9:1 17.6,8/61b	284
10a	1096, 1714
14a	1946, 1952 n. 55
17a	204, 1482
18a	1913
18b	1713
20a	891
20a-b	1483
20b	1945, 1946,
	1951 n. 44
22a	1942
24a	910, 1484, 1944
26a	1712
28a	1732
28b	2048
31a	1480
32a	2198
32b	532, 868, 2033,
	2043
33a	1947
33b	321, 323
34b	536, 1330, 1898
40a	1707, 1708, 1709
43b	1913
45a	1464
45b	1942, 1948,
	1951 n. 47
51a	1914
51b	1914
54a	1909
54b	1707
55a	1714
55b	1707
57b	1706, 1710
58b	1712, 1731, 2040
59a	1711, 1913, 2033,
	2040
60a	1343
60b	1913
62a	908, 1306
62b	1710
63a-b	2040
64	1093
81a	1950 n. 17
Bes.	
4b	1463
20a-b	542
22a	1707, 1711
25b	1731
36b-37a	801
B.M.	
5a	1400
5b-6a	1691
32a	2196
33a	1302, 2048
38b	1718
59A-B	1420
59b	894, 1786, 1949
62a	871
75b	1703
78b	1711

83b	1707
83b-84a	1717
84b	1908
86b	1464
87a	1706
96a	799
107b	1706, 1951 n. 46
114b	1950 n. 24
B.Q.	
25a	1712
38b	1732
58b	1728
60b	1708, 1910
80a	1728
83b	1707
83b-84a	1309
84a	1718
85a	1707, 1718
89b	1715
92a	1100
117a	1664
Erub.	
2:1-2 5.16/ 21B-22A	1516
10:10:8 11.9/ 100b	284
13a	1304, 1305
18b	1907, 1950 n. 17
28b	1622
29b	1707
41b	1709, 1710, 1715
53b-54a	1483
54a	1713
56a	2034, 2039,
	2041
96a	1952 n. 53
100b	346, 1708
102b	1718
103b	1718
104a	909
Git.	
2b	1946
3b	1404
7:1	1711, 1714
12a	1951 n. 43
28a	805
36b	2239
45a	872
45B	1304
52a	1915
56a	1707
56a-b	1786
56b	1713
56b-57b	1913
57B	1254
67b	1712
68b	1713
69a	1906
69b	1714, 1716
70a	1709, 1710
70b	1714
86b	1404
89a	1711

96b	1710
Hag.	
2:7 2.3-2/18b	451
2b	1714
2b-3a	1697-1698
3b	1714, 2149
4a	1945, 2149
4b-5a	263
5b	1099
12a	2038
12b	1344
14b	857
Hor.	
3:3 I./11a	1417
10a	2040
11b	368
13a	868, 871, 1942
13b	1915
13b	868
14a	868
Hul.	
4b	368
7b	320, 1715
8a	1708
10a-b	2193
11b	869
12:4	2194
12:5	2194
13b	1009
17a	1946
19a	2050
28a	1946
43a	1717
44a	1717
45b	1716, 1717, 1718
51a	1716
57a	1710
58b	1728
59a	1716
63b	1462
84a	1946
89b	1715
95b	2041
105b	1713
109b	1942
110b	2192, 2199
113a	1715
115b	1763, 2050
137b	788
140a	2050
141b	2194
142a	2192
Kallah Rabbati	
2:7	2034
Kel.	
17:12	1712
Ker.	
6a	1859
9a	804
9b	1712
15b	1707

Ket.	
3a	803
3b-4a	801
10b	1710, 1714, 1716
11a	1714
13b	1943
17a	1943
19b	1304
20a	1711
20b	1707
23:1-2 1.19/17a	1476
23a	1483
25a	807
28b	1701
37a	856
50a	56
51b	2149
60a-b	1715
60b	1710, 1714
60b-61a	1711
61a	1943
61b	892
65a	1483
67b	55, 56, 59
72a	1951 n. 29
77a	1708, 1710
77b	1711
103a	1718
103b	1709
104a	1483, 1709
105a	1728
105a-b	1704
111b	204
Kid.	
16b	799
36a	1731
Mak.	
1	2151
6:1	1714
7a	1093
22b	1304
23b-24a	159, 1474
Meg.	
3a	787, 789, 908, 1306, 1311, 1315
3b	1951 n. 28
4a	1945, 1947
9a	1313, 1951 n. 49
11a	1713
12b	1714
13a	438, 1715
14b	1483
18a	278, 279
18b	1304
19a	1304
19b	1947
24b	1711
25b	442, 1304, 1306
26b	1304, 1714
28b	1951 n. 49
29b	1304

32a	4, 1304, 1306
Men.	
3:7 2.5/29b	1418
29b	278, 322, 338, 1304, 1305
37a	798, 1708
43a	1952 n. 55
53b	338, 1423
M.K.	
8b	801
20	807
22b	807
25b	807
27b	807
34b	807
M.Q.	
9:2	1711
18a	1914
26a	1304
26b	1707
27b	1709, 1710
28b	1319
Naz.	
39a	1320
Ned.	
8:3-4 II.8/62a	447
9:8	1709
20a-b	1704-1705
22a	1714
36b	1712
37b	1709
37b-38a	1306
39b	1329
41a	894, 1707, 1710, 1712, 1713
43b	1712
49b	1713
50b	1707
51a	2142
62b	1655, 1664
64b	1708
68a	1403
69b	1404
91a	1709
Neg.	
1:5ff.	1708
6:8	1711
7P4	1718
10:10	1708
19:10	1708
Nid.	
9a	1715
10:1	1718
13a	1712
16b	1908
17a	1714, 1913
21b	1715
23b	1708
24a	1707, 1708
24b	1708, 1710, 1712
25b	1708
26a	1708
30b	859, 1624, 1714
31a	1625, 1702
36b	1707
38a	1908
67a	1711
108a	1624
Pes.	
4:1-2 I.6-10/50b	1511
6b	1098
11b	1711
25b	432, 871, 1712
26a	543
36a-b	1054
42a	1709
42b	1709
43b	1951 n. 45
50A 3:7-8 II:4	1476
54a	1756
62b	1483
82b	1942
87b	532, 1732
94a	2038
106a-107a	1951 n. 44
108a	1945
108b	1946
109b	1914
110a	1708
110b-111a	1914
111a	1914
112a	1711, 1906, 1910, 1911
112b	1710, 1908
113b	2034
115b	1054
116b	1054
118a	894, 1060
119a	1330
Qid.	
1:7 II.2/30B-31A	289
1:49	1952 n. 56
2b	1712
4:13/II.13/81b	452
4:14	870, 2141
29b	1941
30b	1328, 1702
31a	2195, 2196
31a-b	2194
31b-32b	2195
32a	1703, 2192, 2194, 2195, 2196
33a	1952 n. 55
33b	1304
39b	1708
41a	2199
49a	789, 1319
49b	531
54a	1329
66a	368, 789, 1808
70a	1943, 1944
70a-b	910, 1130

70b	1732	68a, 2	2066
71b	1943, 1944	72b	871
73b	1905	73a	871, 2143
76b	2262	74a	432, 438
80b	2235	74b	1662
82a	1943, 2141	77b	1718
R.H.		84b	1717
4:4A-E I.2/31A	1291	90a	1913
6b	2039	90b-92a	204
7a	2041	91a	204
11a	45	91a-91b	203
11b	2040	94b	891, 1320
16b	1893, 1910	99b	368
18a	2233	100b	2032
19b	2040	101a	1709, 1913
20a	2040	101b	2034
20b	2041	103b	1944
22a	2230	107b	1706, 1711
25a	2039	108b	1712
28a	1710, 1714	111a-b, 6	333
29a	1947	113a	1709
31a	1462	Sem.	
San.		1:1ff.	862
2:3	1936-1937	Shab.	
2:4	1937-1938	2:6	1715
3b-4b	1306	2:6 I.2ff./32B	1263
7:5 I.2/56a	357	5:3 12.12/55a-b	1266
8:7	2143	5a	1710
11:2 10.4/103a	1475	6a	1907
11b	2041	8:1	1718
12a	2041	11a	1709, 1713
13b	2041	13a	1943, 1952 n. 56
19a	2235	13b	1713
21a	1715, 1943	14:4	1716
21b	785, 1304, 1717	14a	1304
21b-22a	1304	15a	543
24b	2140	16:2 2.42/119b	1263
27b	1092	19:2	1718
29a	1707	21b	1661
30a	1915	23a	1945, 1947
38b	2236	29b	1945
39a	1483	30b	158, 159, 1756
41a	543, 2151	31a	253, 536, 542, 1711
43b	1329	32a	54, 1330, 1707, 1713
44a	368, 1679	33a	1708, 1710
45b	1707	33b	1483
46a	1464	39a	1905
46b-47a	807	40b	1709
47b	1712	42a	1709
48b	1713	50a	1718
52a	2151	53b	1713
56a	1732	55a-b	263
58a	2141	56a	1097, 1098
59a	1739 n. 17	61a	1711
60b	1015	61b	1905
63b	1015	62a	1482
65b	1653, 1714, 1913, 1914	63a	2048
		65a	1713, 2141
66a	1703	66b	1707
67b	835	67a	1708, 1711, 1712, 1904
67b-68a	834		

67a-b	1905
75a	2040
77b	1718
78a	1711
81a	1714
82a	1714
84b	1944
85b	2227
88a	893, 1722
88b	2239
89a	336, 1421, 1424
94b	1708
104a	1043
106a	1717
107b	1622
108a	1622, 1709
109a	1718
109b-110a	856
109b-110b	1716
110a	856, 1709
111a	1718
115b	1305
116a	1666
118b	1709
121b	1715
125b	1943
128a	1718
129b	1909, 2034
130a	1095
133b	339, 1860
134a	1709
134b	1718
137b	91
140a	1714
145b-146a	1325, 1731
146a	1733
151a	882, 1910
151b	61, 862
152a	1708, 1713
152b	1346, 1714
153a-b	1699, 1700
154a	1718
156a	1911, 2032, 2033
156a-b	839, 840
156b	2034
Shav.	
39a	1100
Sheq.	
5:2	1709
Shev.	
36a	1703
Sot.	
1:1-2 5.12ff./5a	1466
2a	321
3:4	1942
3a	1323, 1714, 2149
5:1 I:1D/28A	281
5b. 16	1422
9:12 5.3	1477
10a	1713
10b	1319, 1462
13b	2140
16a	2048
17b	1949
21a	1327, 1328, 1329, 1943
22a	1489
27a	1707
30b	907
35a	1707
36a	1716
42b	1709, 1712
44b	1951 n. 37
46b	1708
47a	1711
47b	2151
48a	909
49a	909
Suk.	
26a	1713
28a	2039
28b	1945
29a	2033
29b	2230
36b	1860
37b	47
38a	1952 n. 61
38b	907
41a	1943
49b	61, 62
51a	1951 n. 49
51a-b	907
52a-52b	1325, 1326
52b	1324
55b	1480
Ta.	
2:12 XII.1, 3 17b-18a	1600, 1601, 1605
2a	1709
3:1-2 III.1-6	1601, 1603, 1605
3:11 XVI.1-4 25b-26a	1604, 1605
11a	1709
16a	910
20b	892
21a	1707, 1708
23a	950
24a	1711
27b	1707
Tam.	
27b	1710
Tem.	
4a	1703
16a	1713
Yeb.	
4a	1708
6:6 2.19-21	286
12b	1708
16:3	1718
22a	804
25a	319
31a	1714
46b-47a	804
47a	804

47b	1732
53b	2149
60b	1710
60b-61a	1731
62b	801, 1707
63	801
63b	855
64a	1709, 1710, 1716
64b	1654, 1709, 1713, 1716
65b	856, 1716
69b	859
70a	1712
71a	1708
72a	2033
75b	1716, 1717
76a	1716, 2141
79a	1304
105a	1707
109b	1732
113a	1714
114b	1717, 1718
116b	1707
120b	1717, 1718

Yom.

6b	1712
9a	2142
18a	1712
21b	2033
29a	1710
47a	1712, 1951 n. 30
49a	1715
66b	1710, 1942
69a-b	1943
78a	1712
83b	1715
84a	1715, 1716, 1906
86b	1898
88a	1712

Yom(a)

26a	1407
29a	1098
69b	1326
81b	45
82a	432
86b	1097, 1257
87a	1257

Zab.

2:3	1712

Zeb.

31a	1946
103b	1946

f. Midrashim (in alphabetical order)

Abot deRabbi Nathan

1:13	2218
4:5.2	1302
15:5.1	1457
18:2.1	287
21	1512
25.4	1380
26:3.1	471

26:6.1	470
28:1.1-2.1	470
29:8.1	1256
31:3.1	902, 1469
41:1	1709

Deuteronomy Rabbah

3:6	1709
7:6	1709
8.6	842
10:3	1709

Ecclesiastes Rabbah

1:8	1708
2:21	2034
3:3	91
8:1	1713
10:11	320

Esther Rabbah

1-2	1196-1199
1:3	1713
7:11	2034

Exodus Rabbah

1:1	1731
5:1	1708
21:6	319, 892
24:4	1708
26:2	1717

Genesis Rabbah

1:1	278, 1881, 2292
1:2.1	463
1:4	317, 841, 1731
1:14	2043
1:19	2231
3:4	950
6.9	1783
7:7	1907
8:10	333
8:10:1	1759
8:10.1	1419
9	263
9:7	1108, 1326
9.7.1	1475
10:1	2040
10:6	2034
13:6	204
14:9	1344, 1346
16:4	1710
17:3	1093
17:8	1483, 1484
18:2	1483
19:19	464
24:6	1907
31:6.1	1474
33:8	2039
34:11	1713
36	1306
39:11	1709
39:14	2046
42:2	399
42:4.1	2115
42:4.4	2115
43:8.2,3	1522

44:12	840
45:5	1483
46:2	1755
47:4	391
48:10	390
49:6	2033
55:2.1f.	1415
56.2.5	1523
61:7	489
62:2	1709
63:7	399
63:10	800
64:10	1786
65:9	1706
65:9.1	1414
65:11	1710
65:15	1708
70:1.1	2116
70:1.2	2117
70:2.1	2117
70:3.1	2117
70:4.1	2117
70:5.1	2118
70:6.1	2119
70:8	397
70:8.1-2	2119
70:8.3-6	2120
70:8.7	2121
70:9.1	2121
70:10.1	2121
70:11.1-3	2122
70:12.1-2	2122
70:12.2-4	2123
70:19.1-2	2123
71:1	1709
71:6	1708
72	2038
74:3.2	1521
74:5	1521
74:12.1	1520
76:2	1523
77:3.3	1520
77:8.1	1522
82	1655
94	2242
97:1	1706
Lamentations Rabbah	1193-1196
1:17	531
2:5	1707
2:15	1709
15:1.3	465
41:1	1709
87.1	1411
Leviticus Rabbah	
11:7.3	1476
11:9	204
13:2.1	463
15:2	1710, 1713
15:4	1718
15:5	1708
16:1	1710, 1716
16:8	1707

16:9	1714
18:4	1707, 1712
18:13	2140
20:1	1710
22:8	532
26:5	1710, 1711
27:5	1731
27:14	1709
30:1	2289
30:1.4-5	1509
34:16	616, 1508, 2288
36.4	842
37:2	1709
41:1.1	1469
Behuqotai	
1, 260:1	2162
3, 263:1	2164
8, 269:1	2165
8, 269:2	2165
Vayyiqra	
4, 7:5	2160
11, 22:1	2161
Mekhilta deRabbi Ishmael	
7:1	288
13:3	2134
13.17	2135
14:7	1731
15:22	2134
15:26	2134
15.1.26	447
16.33	2135
20:3	2131
20:24	2133
22:20	1732
22:30	1731
31:13	2131
53.2.9-10	1505
53.2.17	1504
Bo	
Pisha	
1	2033
17	1942
Kaspa	
5	1763
Shirata	
ch.1, 26.1.1-17	2105
ch.2, 27.1.1-17	2108
Tractate Shirta	
8	1307
Mekhilta deRashbi	
12	2038
Mekhilta Kaspa	
3	1704
Mekhilta Nezikin	
5	1703
Mekhilta to Exodus *see* Mekhilta deRabbi Ishmael	
Midrash Psalms	
8:2	1707
137:4	1707
Numbers Rabbah	
3:2	1731

7	2294
10:5	1709, 1716
14:1	1709
14:10	1731
16:9	1714
23:3	1713
Pesiqta deRab Kahana	
Pisqa 1,6	1184
Pisqa 4	1186
Pisqa 23	1186
Pisqa 25	1186
5:6.2	1424
5:6.3	1424
6:3.3.b	1509, 2289
7:11.3	400
15:5	2291
15:5.1	1510
16:11.1	1261
16:11.2-12	1261
21:5	399
Pesiqta Rabbati	
5	1905
14	2034
Pirke d'Rabbi Eliezer, 26	800
Ruth Rabbah	1191-1193
2.24	1791
7:13	1709
Parashah 5	392
Seder Olam	
4	2039
Sefer Hahinnuch, Mitzva	
232	230
Sifra	
7:4	253
9:8	2141
155.1.8	1412
200:3	1472, 1473
Sifra Ahare	
13:12	2126
Sifra Behuqotai	
8:10	1304
Sifra Mesora Zabim	
1:7-8	1844
1:9-13	1844
2:7	1841
2:8-13	1845
3:1-3	1841
3:3-7	1842
3:8	1844
4:1	1845
4:2-3	1845
11:1-2	1841
Sifra Qedoshim	
3:13-14	1703
195:2.2	289
Sifra to Leviticus	
18:5	1732
Sifre	
46	1941, 1942
157	1945
Sifre to Deuteronomy	
1	2135

1:1.1-5	2096
1:2.1-2	2097
1:3.1-2	2098
1:4.1	2098
1:5.1-3	2098
1:6.1	2099
1:7.1-4	2099
1:8.1-3	2099
1:9.1-2	2100
1:10.1-4	2100
1:11.1	2100
1:12.1	2101
14:1-2	1731
25:1-6	2220
32	262, 1413
32:5-6	1731
32:5.1-12	1416
32:5.5ff.	1413
32:7-9	1738 n. 9
33:2-6	1731
37	2126
40	2126
43	2111
48	2134
54.54:3	438
61	442
144	1704
152	531
161	1319
166:1-2	2224
166:4	2224
219	1700
226:2	2216, 2217
301	1058
306:22.1.1	447
306:30.2ff.	903
319	2126
323	197
333:6	464
343	2134
Sifre to Numbers	
7	2129
19	2129
22	789
44:1-3	2187
45:1-2	2189
46:1-2	2190
47:1-2	2190
78:1	212
88	2135
99:2.1-2	445
113	2130
117	1308
161:3.2	466
Soferim	
14:18	1464
18:7	799
Song of Songs Rabbah	
I:5.3	1472
1:4:2	1709
1:15	848

2:7	881
2:15:2	1710
2:16	1710
2:21	1709
3:4	1709
4:5	848
4:12	847
5:3	849
5:10	850
6.2	845
8:6	846
8:11	1707
8:12	1093
96:1.1	1475
Tanhuma Bereshit	
2.91-92	1788
29	1325
Tanhuma Exodus	
19:8	1707
Piqudei 3	1344
Tanhuma Hukkat	
39	1325
Tanhuma Mishpatim	
19	1907
Tanhuma Shoftim	
10	2034
Tanhuma Terumah	
7	1788
Tanhuma Toledot	
19	204
Tannaim to Deuteronomy	
15:9	2133
Teshuvot Mabit II	
62	1918
Yalk. Ruth	
600	800
Yalk. Shimoni, Psalms	
137	1707

g. Medieval Renaissance Rabbinic literature
Asher ben Yehiel, Baba Qamma,

10:11	1664

Halevi

Sefer Kuzari	
1:27	1733
1:47	1733
1:95	1733
1:103	1733
1:115	1733
2:30	1733, 1734
2:35	1733
2:64f	1733
2:66	1733
2:67-81	1733
3:8	1733
4:29	1733
5:20	1733
Iggarot Moshe	
Even ha-Ezer	
1:58	1951 n. 34
2:12	1951 n. 35,
	1951 n. 36

Orach Hayyim	
1:39	1950 n. 11
1:45	1951 n. 49
4:49	1947, 1952
	n. 57
Yoreh Deah	
2:44	1951 n. 41
3:87	1952 n. 54
Maimonides	
Book of Agriculture, IX	1627
Guide of the Perplexed	
1:1	722
1:61	1906
2:8	2039
3:45	910
III,33	1614
III,37	1615
Mishne Torah	
Ahava 8:11	910
B. Shab., 11:4	1715
Biyat Mikdash, 8:6	1711
Edut, 9:9	1711
Hilkhot Abodah Zarah,	
1:1-2	1952 n. 54
Hilkhot Avel, 4:5	863
Hilkhot Berachot, 5:1	1945
Hilkhot Deot, 7:4	1951 n. 49
Hilkhot Hamets u-Matsa,	
7:8	1946
Hilkhot Issurei Bi'ah,	
21:1-2	1943
Hilkhot Issurei Biyah,	
21:18	855
Hilkhot Lulav, 6:3	1952 n. 54
Hilkhot Megilla	
ve-Hanukkah, 3:7	1947
Hilkhot Megillah, 1:1	1952 n. 60
Hilkhot Melakhim	
1:5	1945
9:5.6	2141
Hilkhot Milah, 2:1	1952 n. 52
Hilkhot Rotzeach	
1:9	860
1:14	871
11:4	868
Hilkhot Tefillah, 1:1-2	1951 n. 46
Hilkhot Tsitsit, 3:9	1947
Hilkhot Yesodei ha-Torah	
2:2	1652
4:12	1652
5:1	1662
5:4	1662
Ishut, 10:1	803
Issurei Mizbach, 2:7	1711
Kings and Laws, 12:2	760
Kol Bo, 41	1913
Laws of Doctrines, 6:2	1661
Laws of Hanukkah, 3:1	1661
Laws of the Temple	
7:11	528
7:14	530
Mamrim, 2:2	1949

Milah, 1:18   1714
Nizqe Mamon, 10:3   1402
Sefer ha-Mitsvot
    Neg. commands, 353   1943
Yad
    Hilkhot Akum, 11:4   1913
    Hilkhot Tefillah, 5:6   1905
    Issurei Bi'ah, 22:2   2141
    San. 20:3   2149
    Tefillin, 5:4   1906
Moses Isserles
    Darkhe Moshe,
        Orah Hayyim, 225:1   800
        Eben ha'Ezer, 212   1951 n. 36
Rashi
    Leipzig Stadtbibliothek,
        Ms. Wagenseil,
        B.H. fol. 1   2228
    National Library St. Petersburg,
        Ms. Evr., I C 6   2238
    Oxford Bodleian Library,
        Ms. Pococke, 74   2236
Sefer Hasidim
    §23   1915
    §302   911
    §817   912
    §1141   1908
    §1146   1910
    §1154   1906
Shulchan Aruch
    53:5   910
    53:25   910
    75:3   910
    128:21   910
    197:5   806
    281:1   910
    337:2   805
    338:1   805
    338:10   909
    339   863
    339:4   801
    374   868
    493:1   801
    546   801
    551:2   801
    560:3   909

    619:1   910
Choshen Mishpat
    425:2   860
EH
    55:1   803
Even ha-Ezer
    21:1   1950 n. 27
    82:5   1918
    82:6   1918
    82:8   1918
Orach Hayyim
    1:17   1947
    53:4   910
    103:3   1913
    155:1   1854
    285   2230
    296:8   1951 n. 44
    301:24ff.   1906
    316:10   1715
    429:1   1854
    472:4   1946, 1952
                                                n. 52
    683:1   1859
    689:1   1952 n. 60
Yoreh Deah
    1:10   1950 n. 24
    2:44   1945
    157   1665
    157:2, 3   1666
    179:2   844
    179:12   1906
    263:2   1714
    264:1   1952 n. 52
Zohar
    1:17b   1908
    3:70a   1907
    3:77b   1908
    Ber.
        20b   1734
        117a   1652
    Emor, 104b   1734
    Jethro, 86a   1734
    Mishpatim, 95b   1735
    Vayikra, 14a-b   1735
Zohar (Midrash Ha-Neelam),
    83a   278